HOUSE
OF FUN
THE STORY OF
MADNESS

HOUSE
OF FUN
THE STORY OF
MADNESS

JOHN REED

OMNIBUS PRESS

London / New York / Paris / Sydney / Copenhagen / Berlin / Madrid / Tokyo

First published © 2010 Omnibus Press
This edition copyright © 2014 Omnibus Press
(A Division of Music Sales Limited)

Cover designed by Fresh Lemon

ISBN: 978.1.78305.555.5
Order No: OP55858

Exclusive Distributors
Music Sales Limited,
14/15 Berners Street,
London, W1T 3LJ.

Music Sales Corporation
180 Madison Avenue, 24th Floor,
New York,
NY 10016,
USA.

Macmillan Distribution Services
56 Parkwest Drive
Derrimut, Vic 3030,
Australia.

Printed in the EU

A catalogue record for this book is available from the British Library.

Visit Omnibus Press on the web at www.omnibuspress.com

Contents

For JoJo and Delilah xxx

This book is dedicated to the memories of
Matthew Sztumpf and Charlie Gillett

Introduction

A LOT of people became Madness fans that night in September 1979 when the lads first tumbled onto a *Top Of The Pops* stage. 2 Tone felt like the next big bang after punk – but the Nutty Boys, as they came to be nicknamed, were different. The seven gangly teenagers (though one or two were a bit older, true) felt like a gang, the Bash Street Kids of the ska revival. Back then, cool bands usually looked serious. Madness kept smirking. They might have shared the black-and-white 'rude boy' imagery of The Specials et al but these impish lads from north London felt like the polar opposite of 2 Tone's earnest diatribes.

At first, few predicted that Madness were more than mere novelty. After all, they were named after and covering a song by ska pioneer Prince Buster on the B-side of their tribute to the man ('The Prince'). Yet they endured, shunning the pantomime ska leanings of contemporaries Bad Manners for qualities more akin to that of a folk band, painting vivid caricatures of life around them in north London with a songbook crafted from childhoods exposed to The Beatles and The Kinks, ska and Motown, sax-driven rock'n'roll and early seventies glam.

Madness did seem to live in their own comic strip, throwing shapes in photo sessions, perfecting the "nutty walk" and forever namedropping their manor of Camden and Kentish Town. They even adopted their own nicknames. On piano was Barzo, Chrissy Boy played guitar, Bedders was on bass, the drum sticks were held by Woody, the bonkers saxophonist was known as either Kix or El Thommo and the singer . . . well, he was simply Suggs. They even had their own dancer, Chas Smash. Who needed *The Beano*?

Having flown the 2 Tone nest, they swiftly evolved into a hit factory under the watchful eye of Stiff Records' maverick boss Dave Robinson. Between 1979 and 1986, they notched up 23 singles on the Top 40. In fact, they spent more weeks on the chart than any other act of the Eighties bar contemporaries UB40. But Madness weren't about statistics. Their wacky image disguised a motley crew of individuals yearning for a sense of belonging – six of them came from single-parent families, often with faintly bohemian leanings towards the arts – and they found such an identity in their songs.

To a generation too young to have engaged with punk, Madness offered a soundtrack as they progressed from the playground to the park and the pub. Lyrics were – to paraphrase Suggs – "simple but not stupid", tackling those first murmurings of adulthood which kids of all ages understood. 'House Of Fun', surprisingly their only chart-topper, worked as a piece of musical slapstick which harked back to music hall; equally, its mischievous double entendres about that awkward first purchase of condoms left a twinkle in the eye of many a male teenager. They even cracked America for five minutes with the Ivor Novello-winning 'Our House'.

Behind the scenes, Madness' dysfunctional democracy was quite something. Perhaps unique in pop history, they boasted at least five talented songwriters. Decisions were made en masse. Their inventive videos – quite rightly hailed as groundbreaking at the dawn of the MTV age – were as much their creations as the songs themselves. Lee Thompson's desire to fly through the air during the video for 'Baggy Trousers', the only true soundtrack song for the *Grange Hill* generation, created one of the pop video's most iconic images. Madness even got their own *A Hard Day's Night* in 1981 with the movie *Take It Or Leave It*.

Madness were technically born on the eve of the election of Margaret Thatcher's Conservative government in May 1979 – and as time wore on, they slowly shifted from good-time music to more cerebral material railing against the injustices they saw. Around them, pop just got more escapist, from the New Romantics onwards, and that took its toll. By early 1984, Madness had been dealt two fatal body blows. Pianist and founder member Mike Barson – unquestionably their lynchpin – left the band and they fell out with Stiff Records, for so long their spiritual home.

As six, they persevered for two more years. As four, they had a brief dalliance as The Madness. But by 1989, they were history. Then in 1992, after hits compilation *Divine Madness* sold a million copies, the band reconvened to play the farewell show that never was, Madstock. Faced with 75,000 adoring fans and swelling bank balances, they felt somehow vindicated – and, in various shapes and sizes, Madness has been a living, breathing entity ever since.

While the Nineties was primarily a nostalgia exercise as Suggs flirted with a solo career, they finally staked their claim as a fully-functioning new band with 1999's *Wonderful*, uniting Madness with their musical hero Ian Dury for his last-ever recording. For a while, they were distracted by a musical, *Our House*. While their legacy appeared to have influenced everyone from Blur to the Ordinary Boys and Lily Allen, their career appeared to falter with a disappointing covers album under the muddled guise of The Dangermen. But in 2009, Madness finally unveiled their magnum opus, *The Liberty Of Norton Folgate*, a double album rich in musical textures, awash with incisive lyrics and steeped in the history of the capital city they called home. What a way to celebrate their thirtieth anniversary.

House Of Fun is also a celebration. This is the first major biography of Madness, which in itself is surprising. But for too long, these colourful characters have somehow been misunderstood, sometimes dismissed as the consummate Eighties singles act and little else. Others have had nagging doubts about their skinhead origins. Maybe they were too parochial. How could a band dressed up like extras from *It Ain't Half Hot Mum* be taken seriously? Well, *House Of Fun* sets out to reappraise an outfit who've never quite been accorded the respect they deserve. Altogether now: "Don't watch that, watch this. This is the heavy, heavy monster sound . . ."

John Reed, June 2010.

Chapter 1

HUMBLE BEGINNINGS IN NW5

ALTHOUGH Madness will forever be synonymous with Camden Town, their roots more strictly lay a half a mile up the road in Kentish Town and its environs, a fact reflected by the title of their 2009 single 'NW5' – chosen instead of Camden's postcode of NW1.

Before the development of north London, Kentish Town existed as a relatively rural, self-contained suburb on the River Fleet, and a popular daytrip location for Londoners. In the early 19th century, huge tracts of land in the area were purchased to build a railway for trains travelling northwards from the new stations at King's Cross (opened in 1852) and St Pancras (opened 1868). It was a logical location because the Kentish Town Road was a major arterial route heading north from the city – and a sizeable railway depot was built at nearby Gospel Oak.

Forgive a momentary lapse into the London A-Z in order to get our geographical bearings. To the north of Kentish Town lies Tufnell Park, then a major road junction, Archway, then beyond to Highgate Hill to the north west and Crouch End to the north east. To the east of Kentish Town lies Belsize Park and north of that, Hampstead and Hampstead Heath. Swiss Cottage and Primrose Hill are situated a few miles south west of Kentish Town. Camden is directly south; heading east from Camden leads to Holloway, Highbury and Islington.

From a historical perspective, Kentish Town's most famous resident was Karl Marx, who lived at 9 Grafton Terrace from the 1850s. During the 19th and early 20th centuries, Kentish Town played host to many famous piano and organ manufacturers. In fact, it was described by *The Piano Journal* in 1901 as "that healthful suburb dear to the heart of the piano maker". Kentish Town was to see further modernisation in the post-World War II period. However, many of the locale's residential areas date back to the mid-1800s and are much admired architecturally.

Since 1965, Kentish Town has lain within the London Borough of Camden – and it has played second fiddle to nearby Camden in terms of its nightlife and music venues. However, the roots of the Pub Rock scene of the early 1970s can be traced back to the Tally Ho, a former jazz pub in Kentish Town opposite a converted cinema which subsequently became a major rock venue as The Town & Country Club and latterly The Forum. The Tally Ho provided residencies for pub rock acts like Eggs Over Easy, Brinsley Schwarz and Kilburn & The High Roads.

"There is a big divide between Camden Town and Kentish Town," suggests the broadcaster and writer Robert Elms. "Kentish Town is simultaneously both more middle class than Camden Town – there's an old middle-class side to Kentish Town that used to be the wealthier bit – and an area in west Kentish Town, Queens Crescent, which is villainy central. There's a historical reason. It's where families who lived in the Agar, a famous 19th century slum that was cleared when they built King's Cross and St Pancras stations, were shipped up to. It's an area of market traders, old school white working-class London – very Irish in its origins. That's the kind of Kentish Town that Madness might be talking about. This whole bit of London is a fantastic interface because, on the one hand, it's dodgy market dealers and then, 300 yards away, it's two or three million pound houses on Highgate."

Camden Town itself has only existed since the late 18th century. Before that, only a few scattered farms and two coaching inns, The Mother Red Cap (established 1676; now The World's End) and the Southampton (now Edwards), marked a dangerous landscape frequented by highwaymen. Suggs later recalled his memories of the Mother Red Cap back in the 1970s as "the biggest pub I've ever been in and there was never more than four people in it – the same four!" The venue was name-checked in the Madness song 'Bingo' on *The Liberty Of Norton Folgate* (2009).

Camden stands on land which was once the manor of Cantelowes, acquired through marriage by Sir Charles Pratt (later the First Earl of Camden), a radical 18th century lawyer and politician. In 1791, he granted leases for 1,400 houses to be built and is widely credited with the establishment of Camden Town. As the first of a number of wealthy individuals involved in the development and urbanisation of this part of London, his initial building programme focused on land on the east side of Camden High Street. Pratt's role in shaping the area is marked by a street and mews that bear his name in the heart of modern Camden. Mary Shelley, the original author of the gothic horror story *Frankenstein* and the wife of the poet Percy Bysshe Shelley, was born in Camden during this period (1797).

The arrival of canals and then railways transformed the whole region; the Regent's Canal was completed in 1820, requiring the construction of Camden Lock and a flurry of nearby buildings to support the resulting local industry; the first line to the Euston terminus opened in 1837; Camden Road railway station opened in 1850. The opening of an underground station in 1907 marked the final integration of once rural Camden into the wider city. "The heart of Camden Town is surrounded by canals and railways," Suggs later observed. "All the digging of these canals and railway sidings was done by hand by Irishmen. Apparently, there were 70,000 Irishmen in Camden at one point." In his book *Suggs And The City*, he writes: "Camden was, as I always instinctively knew, pretty much the epicentre of London's comings and goings."

Railway and canal construction had brought the first Irish settlers to Camden, a process accelerated after 1840 by terrible famine in Ireland. By the end of the 19th century, soot and grime from major railway terminals to the south covered a Camden High Street busy with shops, trams and horse-drawn buses. Charles Dickens referred to Camden Town; in *A Christmas Carol*, Bob Cratchit and his family lived there, for example. Indeed, as a child, Dickens lived at 141 Bayham Street in Camden in 1823. Another renowned literary figure, poet Arthur Rimbaud (1854–91), also lived in the area for a period.

By and large, though, Camden Town was considered an unfashionable locale but that gradually changed throughout the 20th century. George Orwell lived in Camden during the 1930s, as did the poet Dylan Thomas. Around that time, live music started to become a vital part of Camden life, perhaps because of the many Irish immigrants who continued to flock to the region. Irish flute and fiddle musicians played in pubs and dance halls to enthusiastic local audiences. Two cavernous music halls attracted stars of the day. The Bedford was eventually demolished in 1969 but the Camden Theatre (which hosted the famous Goon Show in the 1950s) eventually changed its name to The Music Machine in 1977, then to the Camden Palace in 1982 and more recently to Koko. Another Irish dance hall was the Buffalo Club, which opened around 1940, before eventually being re-born as The Electric Ballroom. During the Second World War, the area around Mornington Crescent was badly damaged by bombing. Post-war, the gradual restoration of Camden Town coincided with its emergence as a centre of Greek-Cypriot settlement in London, a reflection of its cosmopolitan nature.

The first major rock'n'roll concert in Camden took place on October 15, 1966 at the Roundhouse, a converted former railway engine shed constructed in 1847 at the top of Chalk Farm Road by the Midland Railway Company for the London and Birmingham Railway. In an event which marked both the launch of *International Times* and the dawning of the psychedelic era, Pink Floyd and Soft Machine performed in front of a star-studded audience, the first of numerous musical and theatrical happenings. In the coming years, the venue would host concerts by many of rock's illuminati, including the Jimi Hendrix Experience, The Doors, Marc Bolan, The Move, The Who and The Rolling Stones.

Camden's famous street markets started in 1973 and grew steadily in popularity and size to attract thousands of visitors to the region. Other important music venues opened in Camden, from Dingwalls (1973) up by Camden Lock to the aforementioned Electric Ballroom (1978). At the same time, several local pubs introduced live music: The Carnarvon Castle (now The Fusilier & Firkin), The Royal Exchange, The Monarch, The Devonshire Arms, The Falcon, The Good Mixer and, last but not least, The Dublin Castle on Parkway.

As the 1970s wore on, Camden also became a nerve centre for second-hand and specialist record shops. Most famous was Rock On, an outlet for old rock'n'roll and R&B, which opened just around the corner from Camden tube station on the Kentish Town Road in 1975. The shop was actually the third Rock On outlet to be opened by ex-Thin Lizzy manager Ted Carroll, complementing successful open-air stalls in Portobello and Soho. (Carroll and ex-Rock On employees Roger Armstrong and Trevor Churchill would eventually form Chiswick Records, the only major rival to Stiff Records in the late 1970s to have evolved out of the pub rock scene.) It was no coincidence that the fictitious record shop Championship Vinyl in Nick Hornby's best-selling book *High Fidelity* was set in Camden.

Today, vast swathes of north London have, to a greater or lesser extent, been gentrified by a gradual influx of money and of middle-class professionals keen to live within sight of the city centre. But the Kentish Town in which members of Madness grew up was very different. "In the Seventies, it wasn't in any way middle class," says Kerstin Rodgers, who knew the band during that time. "It was pretty rough. Camden was still Irish. You still had Irish boozers, lonely Irish men sitting there with their Guinnesses. There were still collections for the IRA, although it had the hippie side, with the market, and some posher houses and streets. North London has always been cheek by jowl, poverty with money."

★ ★ ★

Madness' story actually began a couple of miles north of Kentish Town in the more middle-class environs of Crouch End – or Park Avenue South, to be precise, the home of schoolboy Michael Wilson Barson. The youngest of three brothers, Mike was born on April 21, 1958 in the Newington district of Edinburgh, Scotland, where the family lived for a period before returning to their roots in north London. He came from a family with a strong creative strain. His father Anthony had married his mother Patricia J. Gott in early 1953 in the borough of Hammersmith, west London. Born in 1926 in Rochford, Essex, Patricia was a painter (she eventually worked as an art teacher at a comprehensive in nearby Highbury). She shared this passion with Anthony, who was also an art teacher – but the couple split up when Mike was still a baby. "They were brought up by their mother," explains Barson's ex-girlfriend Kerstin Rodgers. "The dad came to visit once a year for ten minutes. Mike was a really good artist as well."

The piano occupied a central part of family life for the Barsons – and Mike's interest in playing was soon awakened by the efforts of his brothers Ben (who was some five years his senior) and Dan (who was two years older than Mike). While Ben and his hippie-ish friends were enamoured of jazz ("He had a five-album box set by Keith Jarrett, which had one good song on it!" Mike later commented), the more extrovert Dan was smitten by rock'n'roll.

From childhood, Mike was acquainted with two future members of Madness: an older boy, Chris Foreman, nicknamed "Chrissy Boy", whom Mike had met via another friend, Lee Thompson. The trio attended Brookfield Primary School in Chester Road, London N19 (in the

Dartmouth Park area, between Kentish Town and Highgate). "My favourite subject was science because we had a good teacher," Barson later remarked. Lee had even lived opposite Chris in Kentish Town for a period. "I've known Mr Barson since we were about three or four," remembered Thompson. "I think we went to see *Bridge On The River Kwai* together."

Years later, Chris recalled the start of his lifelong friendship with Mike in Madness' fan club magazine *Nutty Boys*: "At the time, I was really talking to his older brother Danny as Mike himself was only about eight. The reason they were at my house was that Mike's mum knew my parents. I must have been about 10. Mike used to live near me, and over the next few years, we would occasionally nod at each other in passing. Around 1971, kids from the Highgate Road (in Kentish Town) area amalgamated into groups. In my particular group were John Jones, Paul Catlin, Lee Thompson, Michael Barson and myself."

Lee's father, Frederick W. Thompson, was born at the tail end of the First World War in 1918 in Walsingham, Norfolk. His family eventually settled in Great Yarmouth, which is where, in spring 1950, he married Lilian F. Scannell (born in late 1925).[*] Lilian's family came from Islington – indeed, her father was a local street planner – which eventually drew Lil and Fred back to north London.

The future Madness saxophonist was born Lee Jay Thompson – named after his mother's admiration for American actor Lee J. Cobb – on October 5, 1957 in St Pancras. Thompson's father has been described as one of the top safe-breakers in Soho and seems to have spent more time in prison than at home. As such, Lee and his younger sister Tracy (born in 1961) had an unsettled childhood. By his own admission, Lee was a bit of a tearaway, getting up to mischief with school friend Robert Townshend.

"My dad was doing time and my mum couldn't handle me," Lee later confessed. "I was a bit of a Tasmanian devil, all over the place, no concentration span." In 1969, the family moved from the Highgate Road area to the Holly Lodge Estate, a set of early 20th century mock-Tudor mansion blocks which enjoyed a prominent view of the surrounding area – Highgate Cemetery to the east and Hampstead Heath to the west - but which had fallen into disrepair. "It's actually rather nice, leafy and green, in

---

[*] Lee's family in Great Yarmouth owned the fun fair which was used as a location for Madness' 'House Of Fun' video.

Dartmouth Park Hill," adds Kerstin Rodgers. "It's always been a place for single mothers . . . still is."

As a child, Thompson attended Acland Burghley School in Burghley Road, Kentish Town before moving to Haverstock Secondary School in Chalk Farm. "I was never bullied, which was a problem for some kids," Thompson commented to *Later* in 1999. "I use to turn up, get marked in and go straight down the arcade. I remember putting a magnet on a tape recorder. It erased all the information. Miss Durham made me sit in a bin all lesson! I went in for a few exams but I was really only interested in English and Art."

In his formative years, Lee proved to be a wayward character who flirted with petty crime, prompting a string of court appearances (Thompson once suggested as many as 20). One particular scam involved inserting a piece of cardboard into GPO phone boxes to extract money – but occasional house-breaking and shoplifting weren't off limits. According to George Marshall in *Total Madness*, 'Young Thommo' (as his friends called him) bunked off school on his fourteenth birthday and stole a bag containing £130 from a hospital locker. The would-be Artful Dodger then passed some of the proceeds to friends but somehow the police were informed of the crime and Lee was sent to Chafford Approved School in Harwich, Essex, from November 1971 to January 1973 – an experience later immortalised by Thompson in the Madness song 'Land Of Hope And Glory'. Thompson later admitted that he also spent time in Stamford House in Shepherds Bush – one of the most notorious secure institutions for young offenders in the country.

Having reacquainted himself with Barson in his immediately pre-teen years, Thompson felt lucky to have friends likely to keep him on the straight and narrow. "It was a fortunate privilege to have met Chris and Mike," Lee later confessed. "Prior to meeting them, I was knocking around with a chap called Bobby [Townshend] and we used to get into some pretty serious trouble. I was sent away for a year and a day, and when I was sent back into the smoke, that's when I started hanging around with Mike and Chris. I think that if I hadn't have met them, I would've gone down the pan!" Foreman later recalled that period: "[Lee] used to come home at weekends – he'd get out on Fridays and we'd spend the weekend with him and see he got back on the train OK!"

"Lee was quite well-known amongst all the parents," Barson admitted to *Later* magazine. "They knew he was a bit of a rascal. He would always have to wait around the corner because our mums and dads didn't want us to hang around with him. He was heading towards a heavyweight life of crime because he was mixing with the wrong kind of people, then he started mixing with us and we got involved in a lightweight life of crime!"

★　★　★

A couple of years older than Barson, Christopher John Foreman was born on August 8, 1956 in University College Hospital, Euston Road, London. He was the son of a folk singer (as were brothers Ali and Robin Campbell from UB40, whose father was Ian Campbell). Born in 1931 near Euston Station as the son of a postman, John G. Foreman described his childhood within the war torn city streets as happy. He married Chris' mother, a dancer named Rita M. Alden (who was born in Malton, Yorkshire, also in 1931) in 1952. The couple had two children (Chris was joined by younger brother Peter N. Foreman in 1960) but they split up when the kids were still quite young.

As a young man, John worked as a doorman at The Metropolitan in the Edgware Road, and as a "bottler" (money collector) with a Punch-and-Judy man, Professor Alexander. John regarded himself as a true cockney and held an abiding fascination for music hall. There was theatrical talent in his family: his father's mother, Elsie Naish, danced with and under-studied Adeline Genee, and through his mother, formerly a Miss Harper, he was related to Victoria Lytton, who "worked the halls" and teamed up with Arthur Cunningham, a noted singer and whistler. His mother's Uncle Charlie worked as a clown and her grandfather was a circus ring-master.

Fuelled by a lifetime's research, Foreman regularly performed these traditional songs at pubs and clubs from the 1950s onwards. His repertoire was learned both from his parents and from hearing songs via post-war music hall revival singers, particularly at London's Unity Theatre, established between Camden Town and King's Cross for working men and where Foreman would perform. He was more specifically a "broadsheet balladeer" than a folk singer*. And he would have been well acquainted

---

* Broadsheet (or broadside) ballads were the printed sheets of verses that were sold in the streets from as early as the 16th to the late 19th century.

with folk songwriter/performer Ewan MacColl, the father of future Madness labelmate Kirsty MacColl.

In 1966, Foreman recorded an album, *The 'Ouses In Between*, for Reality Records (the sleeve-notes for which provided much of the biographical information here). Some of its songs later graced a Folktrax album, *The Londoners* (1975). In 1977, Foreman contributed the song 'London's Ordinary' to a double album compilation *The Tale Of Ale*, issued by folk label Free Reed. Onstage, John was known to play steel guitar, a 'squeeze box', harmonica and 'the Spoons'. For his finale, he performed with a miniature 'Music Hall', a shadow puppet show, juggling the varied skills of musical accompaniment, sound effects and puppeteering. He still performs at such venues as London's Musical Traditions Club to this day.

John Foreman became a noted printer by trade, known as 'The Broadsheet King' through his work publishing traditional song collections, song-sheets and Broadside collections. Frequently, John operated as a busker and sold song-sheets in open markets like Petticoat Lane and at CND/ban-the-bomb marches and meetings. He taught in many different schools in London, worked at the London College Of Printing, and was a founder member of The British Music Hall Society in the early 1960s. As well as being a budding poet, Foreman was also the author/editor of several self-published pamphlets and books, including *Jumbo*, *Just Deserts: Or Ways To Martyrdom*, *Babes And Sucklings (A Book Of Jolly Lolly Sticks)*, *Ten Greenish Bottles*, *Ap Daze*, *Little Red Riding Hood* and *Heroes Of The Guillotine And Gallows*, as well as occasional reprints of deleted titles (for example, Leslie Shepard's *The History Of The Horn Book* from 1977 or John Ashton's *Real Sailor-Songs* in 1973).

Interviewed by *The Word* magazine, Chris commented that his "working-class intellectual" father once took him to the former Yugoslavia by road – when he was only nine years old – as well as introducing him to the cinematic delights of the classic Russian epic, *Battleship Potemkin*, at the South Bank. "My old man is a singer," explained Chris in 1981. "He even does gigs every now and then, performing traditional cockney songs. He always used to try and teach me guitar when I was a kid, but I was never really interested in things like 'Bobby Shaftoe'!" By all accounts, John Foreman was diametrically opposed to his brother, who was a bit of a chancer.

At first, Chris showed little sign of inheriting his father's passion, drive or motivation. "I went to a grammar school in Islington, Dame Alice Owen's," he told *Later* magazine in 1999. "It's been knocked down since but Alan Parker and Spandau Ballet went there. It was a crap school. I bunked off and went to Haverstock, Lee's school! I went into the classroom and the teacher's going, 'Who are you?' I said, 'I've come from Birmingham', so I got expelled from Lee's school!" When he wasn't attending one or other school, Chris was kicking his heels with his mates. The lads spent their free time drinking in local pubs, spraying graffiti on walls around north London or jumping freight trains.

"There was always something about railways," Mike later recalled. "They were at the back of everything somehow, round the back of houses where nobody went. We used to build little camps over the railway, and we'd hide in them and when a freight train would come along, we'd run after it and jump on the back." One time, the gang ended up in Ramsgate, missed the ferry and had to sleep under a tarpaulin on a facsimile of a Viking longboat. On another occasion, they were atop a slow-moving train in Willesden when Barson and a mate were hit by a bridge. They staggered off the train and, bleeding heavily, were dragged by their mates into a back garden where there just happened to be a wedding in progress. The assembled throng apparently looked askance at four lads in balaclavas, covered in blood and identity-concealing boot polish, carrying two wounded and shouting for an ambulance.

In the 1984 TV documentary *South Of Watford*, Lee recalled those days fondly: "On bank holidays, we used to take off on a freight train, [up to] Leamington Spa, mainly northwards. We ended up in Leigh-On-Sea once, near Southend. Jumped out, pitched the tent, woke up to find cows nibbling at the strings." In the same programme, Foreman recalled schoolboy pranks on Kite Hill, alias Parliament Hill, next to Hampstead Heath. "We used to walk from the Lido, the swimming pool, up this hill and we used to set fire to all the rubbish bins on the way. We'd get to the top, look down and survey all these glowing rubbish bins, which was quite fun. The park keepers used to chase us in vans at night."

Graffiti was still a relatively new phenomenon in the capital. "I first remember seeing an ad in the *Sunday Times* colour supplement around '73," wrote Thompson on Madness' website, "that had a piece on graffiti carried out in the dead of night on the New York subways and trains. So to pass a little time, a few of my mates would acquire some aerosol cans and get to work. My 'tag' was 'KIX681'." Thompson had apparently attracted the nickname 'Kix' because of his growing reputation for fearless stunts and crazy escapades. Some of the lads' graffiti in and around Kentish Town dating from 1973/74 still survives to this day, including a bridge at a local train station and a nearby block of flats – both of which were wrapped in scaffolding at the time and were hence inaccessible once the scaffolding was removed. "I think most of the best ones I did have been cleaned off by now," Barson suggested.

Two examples of their handiwork (including an abandoned car on Hampstead Heath customised with "Mr B." and "Kix") were featured in photographer Roger Perry's book, *The Writing On The Wall: The Graffiti Of London*, published in February 1976 with a foreword by trad jazz star and author/writer George Melly. By coincidence, Thompson had once tagged Melly's garage door as "J4 KIX", prompting an outburst in Melly's national newspaper column. "Kix was a common graffiti around Hampstead, Gospel Oak, Camden," recalls Kerstin Rodgers. "I knew his tag before I met him but he got done for doing graffiti." Another admirer from afar was future drummer Daniel Woodgate. "Mark and I vividly remember graffiti around the Hampstead area," he told *Later* magazine. "We remember seeing 'Mr B' and 'Kix' written on railway arches, and we used to think, 'How the hell did they get up there?' Mike and Lee were quite infamous, so to find out you're in a band with them years later – Mark and I were in awe!"

"Mike was very good at drawing," school friend and graffiti accomplice Simon "Si" Birdsall later commented. "I used several names – 'Columbo' from the TV series, 'Sha Na Na', 'Sneaking Sally' from the Robert Palmer album. What brought an end to it, I think, was we went up to Woolworths in Hampstead and went crazy. We got carrier bags full of spray paint, three or four of us with two carriers each. We hid them in a cemetery, and for a week after we just overdid it . . . we just got fed up with it. Mike did a good one at Highbury Station, from the Kilburn & The High Roads album . . . it's still faintly there."

By the time Mike had moved schools to Hampstead Comprehensive in Westbere Road, Cricklewood in the early 1970s, he'd picked up the rudiments of the piano. "We learnt different set pieces, rock'n'roll on the left hand and fiddling round on the blues scale on the right hand," Mike later explained. "I did have a few classical lessons but most of what I know I taught myself."

★ ★ ★

Meanwhile, older brother Dan was playing with a rock'n'roll/pub rock band, Bazooka Joe, which had been formed by Kentish Town lads John Ellis and Danny Kleinman as early as 1970. With their madcap, theatrical show (band members adopted stage names like Danny Angel, Robin Banks, Mark Time and 'Upright' Willy Wurlitzer), Bazooka Joe built up a local following, playing at art schools and on the London pub circuit. Infected with a strong vein of humour, their set mixed original material with oldies such as Frankie Lymon & The Teenagers' doo wop classic, 'Teenager In Love', The Shadows' instrumental 'Apache' and The Chantays' surf instrumental, 'Pipeline'.

When bassist Pat Collier left, Kleinman introduced a replacement, Stuart Goddard, whom he'd met at Hornsey College Of Art. A few years later, Goddard who would reinvent himself as Adam Ant. "Thinking of the two of them," one of his teachers later opined, "one would have expected Danny more than Stuart to have ended up as Adam Ant." Instead, Dan Barson is now a doctor in Vancouver. He later recalled his days with Bazooka Joe: "It was more like a friends' band – just have a good laugh, get drunk and fall over, go wild."

Comedian Arabella Weir was among their backing singers, The Lillets, while Ellis left in 1974 to found what would become punk band The Vibrators with Collier. Speaking of the impending punk scene, Bazooka Joe's other claim to fame was headlining when the Sex Pistols played their first concert on November 6, 1975 at Central Saint Martins College of Art & Design, although the line-up that night didn't include Barson. Madness would later cover a Bazooka Joe song written by keyboard player Bill Smith (alias Upright Willy Wurlitzer), 'Rockin' In A♭' – itself borrowed from 'Beatnik Flyer' by Johnny & The Hurricanes, which Bazooka Joe used to perform – on their debut album *One Step Beyond*. The song was a mainstay of Madness' set list for several years. "Bazooka Joe was *the* local rock and roll band," Foreman told musician/author Terry Edwards. "We used to see them a lot."

"I used to see Bazooka Joe at the Haverstock Town Hall and else-where," adds Kerstin Rodgers. "Danny Barson wore a gold suit. He was a natural lead singer type: all the girls fancied him. There was a big rocka-billy presence at the gigs and fantastic dancing. Sometimes, the whole hall would break out into line dancing. I was proud when later I got to go out with Danny's younger brother Mike. It's great to remember all these con-nections: Arabella Weir is the older sister of Christina Weir, who was good friends with Miranda Joyce of the Belle Stars, who went out with Mark Bedford. Mike and I used to go see The Vibrators often."

Hornsey College Of Art was also a logical next step for Mike to attend after leaving school. (By this time, Barson had also moved to Muswell Hill, much to his friends' dismay.) The college was centred around Crouch End and had previously harboured chief Kink Ray Davies – but Barson dropped out after just one year, having spent much of the time improving his keyboard skills. "Quite often I'd go into college and spend the whole afternoon just playing the piano in the hall," he later confessed.

"I used to like advertisements," he explained in *The Face* in 1982. "I never particularly liked any great works of art, I preferred commercial art and cartoons. I didn't really like it there. Art schools don't really seem to be into art: they're more into talking about it. I didn't go in very fre-quently. I applied for another three-year course at the London School of Printing, but I turned up two hours late for the interview and they never let me in!"

Another student there was Eric Watson, who would later photograph Madness. "I was on a foundation art course in 1975," remembers Eric. "I met Mike Barson there. He only did a couple of terms, as I remember. I was a little older than him and he got into a spot of bother over 'twoc'ing' (taking without the owner's consent), or something like that, and I was asked to mediate between him and the college. Mike was largely mono-syllabic in conversation and really just wanted the time at college to draw *bande dessinée* or what are now called graphic novels. I remember telling him to check out the Sex Pistols who I had seen at the Nashville Rooms."

★ ★ ★

Chris had left Dame Alice Owen's School with just one O-level (in English). He wrote about his formative years on Friends Reunited with typically self-deprecating humour: "I left school in 1972. Well, I was asked not to come back actually. During the summer holidays, I had seen a gardening job advertised in a newsagents, which I successfully applied for. After the holidays, I eagerly returned to continue my education which was sadly not to be. So I stayed at the gardening firm for about two years. I then worked for the glorious London Borough of Camden as a gardener. We used to wear donkey jackets with LBC on the back, and if people asked what it meant, we said London Brick Company (or the more fruity London's Biggest C★★t). Having by now learnt a tremendous amount about gardening, I then applied for a job on the Camden painting and decorating department and got sacked after about six months for turfing someone's front room and wallpapering their window box." For a period, Foreman's gardening chores were shared with Thompson.

Eventually, and much to the relief of Barson's mother, the threesome switched their affections to all things musical. They shared a mutual admiration for Kilburn & The High Roads (Ian Dury's band prior to The Blockheads), as well as Fifties rock'n'roll, doo-wop and R&B (Fats Domino, The Coasters and Chuck Berry were favourites), classic Motown and Jamaican ska and rocksteady. The lads were also smitten by the glam rock-influenced acts of the period: especially Roxy Music but also The Sensational Alex Harvey Band, Mott The Hoople, Slade, The Faces, Alice Cooper, David Bowie, The Sweet, Cockney Rebel and Gary Glitter (at the height of Madness' popularity in 1982, Thompson was photographed for *The Sunday Times* dressed in Glitter's trademark stage outfit).

In the 1981 film *Take It Or Leave It*, in which Madness re-enacted their early years to such great effect, Barson and Thompson were seen stealing an old Fats Domino album from Rock On. Their love of rock'n'roll – and Americana in general – was fuelled by seeing George Lucas's 1973 film *American Graffiti*, a bittersweet tale which neatly evoked US youth culture of the late Fifties/early Sixties, from hanging out in diners to cruising in open-top cars, with a rock'n'roll soundtrack to die for, which wasn't presented merely as background music but as an integral feature of the movie – where, to quote Terry Edwards, "the music was as much a star as the cast and plot".

Additionally, Barson had developed a taste for piano-based singer-songwriters, as he later revealed: "I used to listen to Elton John's *Tumbleweed Connection* and I liked Carole King and Joni Mitchell . . . the piano playing does sort of affect you. 'Fire In The Hole' by Steely Dan had a really nice piano solo which I listened to again and again." Other favourites included later Kinks albums, Dave Brubeck's jazz hit 'Take Five' and Cat Stevens' *Tea For The Tillerman* (for 'Sad Lisa', in particular).

Barson was already adept on the family piano; he was soon accompanied by the first attempts of Foreman and Thompson to master their respective instruments. The trio would play along to their favourite rock'n'roll records (a scenario re-enacted in *Take It Or Leave It*, with Fats Domino's 'I'm Walkin'' from that half-inched LP!). "Nobody could really play anything for quite a long time," Barson told *Smash Hits* in 1979. "We just played the records that we liked: a few ska records, lots of Coasters, 'Love Potion Number Nine' and 'Poison Ivy'. We just heard all that from older brothers. I definitely had a Motown [song] book with all the chords in it but I was such a lazy bum that I never learnt how to read music so it took ages!"

"Various people used to go to Mike's house and try to play any songs we liked," Chris later wrote in *Nutty Boys*. "Mike's older brother Ben had various amplifiers which we used. Mike's mum was tremendously understanding, though at times we nearly must have driven her potty." Foreman's father had tried to teach him the 'How To Play The Guitar' a few years earlier to no avail. Now motivated by Barson's enthusiasm, Chris bought his first guitar around 1976 from a second-hand shop which Lee had spotted in Camden with £20 he received from a tax rebate.

"It was a real cheapo, semi-acoustic Woolworths type guitar," Foreman later recalled to Chris Hunt. "A Waltone. I just used to play these notes – one string at a time, I wasn't even very interested in it. Then I started playing chords and that started me off. At that time, there wasn't anyone I really emulated but I did like Wilko Johnson [of Dr. Feelgood]. As he used to play a Fender Telecaster, I eventually got one and it cost me about £130. I used to use it all the time – on the first album, I used just that."

A temporary lull in Foreman's employment prospects allowed him more time to practise. "When I got the sack as a painter and decorator, I started to play the guitar by listening to Dr. Feelgood," he explained. By coincidence, both Foreman and the Feelgood's manic guitarist Wilko Johnson were left-handed but took a leaf from Jimi Hendrix and played right-handed guitars. Chris had a definite bent towards the theatrically-minded rock acts of the day. He loved Mott The Hoople and caught the very first UK performance by Australian rock band AC/DC in May 1976. "Back then, it was Chuck Berry and Duane Eddy for me. [But] Angus

[Young] was just rolling around the floor and I thought it was great," he later admitted to *The Word*.

Thompson, meanwhile, was inspired by two saxophonists: Roxy Music's Andy Mackay and Kilburn & The High Roads' Davey Payne. "First of all, I had a clarinet but I swapped it for a battered old sax down Dingwalls Market," he wrote on Pete Frame's Madness Family Tree. "Originally, I was happy just to poodle along to records by Roxy Music, Fats Domino [and] The Coasters . . . but then I bought a brand new Selmer and began to get more serious about being in a group." That first sax had been obtained in winter 1975 with a questionable "chain of title"; one of the many highlights of the film *Take It Or Leave It* was a hilarious re-enactment of Lee's one-and-only lesson at Highbury School, during which the streetwise teacher noticed that the saxophone's serial number had been filed off.

"All the American R&B I loved had sax on it," Lee later explained. "I was always drawn to that breathy, organic sound. When Roxy Music came onboard, Andy Mackay was like a God to us. I loved his style of playing – not too busy, not too John Coltrane, not too technical either." Thompson later recounted one particular shoplifting trip, which involved his mate climbing through a side window of the Fender Soundhouse on Hampstead Road. Having passed out a couple of guitars, he was about to liberate a tenor sax when two policemen appeared nearby – and he froze. Thompson and his pals created a diversion to distract the police and the sax went on to appear on all the early Madness records.

While everyone seemed to love Roxy Music, Thompson & Co. were particularly drawn to the misfit image of Kilburn & The High Roads. "I wouldn't say that Davey Payne was an influence on Lee," Barson later opined to Terry Edwards. "What's the word? Yeah, he used to copy him a lot. In various ways!" Thompson was later quoted as describing Madness' sound as "Steptoe & Son music". "It relates to the Kilburns who were a massive influence," Madness bassist Mark Bedford told Richard Eddington. "The archetypal pub-rock band. They brought in that 'music hall', fairground, cartoon image of London life."

★   ★   ★

Although Ian Dury would become a bona fide pop star with The Block-heads, it was clearly his earlier work with Kilburn & The High Roads which had the more profound influence on Madness. "When I first joined the band," Woody told Terry Edwards, "all they ever went on about was Kilburn & The High Roads. I'd never seen them – or even heard of them!"

"When you saw them sitting round before the gig, there was a real mystique to them," Barson later enthused. "They *looked* like a band, and you wanted to be in one too. It all looked pretty exotic. They were all individuals. If you watched just one of them all night, it would be a complete show. We got a lot of inspiration from them – a band of characters where there was always something to look at."

Born on May 12, 1942 in Harrow in north-west London, Dury contracted polio as a child, leaving him partially crippled. After attending grammar school in High Wycombe, west of London, the teenager attended art college in Walthamstow, east London (which may have explained his thick cockney accent) before eventually studying at the prestigious Royal College Of Art in the late 1960s. It was there that he enjoyed the tutelage of no lesser figure than Peter Blake, whose love of what Suggs later described as "the eccentricities of the music hall" rubbed off on Dury.

Dury was old enough to have witnessed first hand the arrival of rock'n' roll in the 1950s. He was particularly struck by Gene Vincent, whose volatile mix of menace and tenderness was made all the more poignant (to Dury, at least) by the fact he suffered from chronic pain and a limp in his left leg. When Vincent died in October 1971, legend has it that Dury was inspired to found his own band, Kilburn & The High Roads, recruiting a number of students he was teaching at Canterbury College Of Art. In stark contrast to the glam rock images in vogue at the time, Dury and his cohorts adorned themselves in thrift-shop attire, purveying the same gritty, working-class demeanour conveyed to such great effect in the poetic rantings of Dury's songs.

With help from managers Charlie Gillett and Gordon Nelki, their "no frills" approach won them support on the burgeoning pub rock scene, landing them a contract with Pye's progressive rock arm Dawn, a degree of critical acclaim and a prestigious support slot on tour with The Who. The streetwise suss of songs like the single 'Rough Kids' (which Barson & Co. covered during early rehearsals and gigs), 'Billy Bentley' and 'The Upminster Kid' sounded like a breath of fresh air to those tired of the manufactured bubblegum pop of the era – teenagers like Mike Barson & Co. Dury's portrayals of an altogether less savoury London were perfectly crystallised by the sleeve design for debut album *Handsome*, which depicted six scruffy, tired-looking men against a backdrop of a bleak, barbed wire fence and, behind it, Tower Bridge.

This spoke of a London beleaguered by power cuts, strikes and unemployment instead of the futuristic escapism of Roxy and Bowie or the knock-kneed bubblegum rock'n'roll of the Chinn and Chapman stable at Rak. That's not to say the future members of Madness worshipped Kilburn & The High Roads exclusively – in fact, Roxy Music were probably their favourite band of the period. But the Kilburns were one of just a handful of acts (among them Dr. Feelgood) to pre-empt that spirit of social realism which came to the fore with punk. Indeed, John Lydon was clearly inspired by Dury's off-kilter, physically awkward stage manner – an anti-hero that was part Steptoe, part Laurence Olivier's Richard III.

"Dury was brought up in a relatively bohemian, middle-class environment," suggests writer Alan Robinson, "but his disability placed him outside of his class milieu, which he was able to exploit by creating a kind of character that was constructed from elements he found around him. I think Dury was a Beatnik more than anything else. He was at least as much of a jazz fan as a rock 'n' roller and a big fan of Rahsaan Roland Kirk. The Kilburns were as much of an art-rock concept as Roxy Music. It's just that Dury dressed it up with an anti-image. On the back cover of *Handsome*, there's a black and white photograph called 'Paul Hangs Loose' by Poundcake, a reference to William Burroughs' book, *The Naked Lunch*. Burroughs was a big influence on the Brit art world of the time." 'Paul Hangs Loose' didn't go unnoticed by the likes of Mike Barson, either, who later borrowed the idea for Madness's trademark "Nutty Train" pose, immortalised on the sleeve of debut album *One Step Beyond*.

"Part of the appeal of The Kilburns was that they looked like they were assembled entirely from spare parts, kind of human flotsam and jetsam," continues Robinson, "very tall people and very short people, a black drummer and a disabled lead singer, who proudly sported a calliper on his leg. Underneath the menacing image Dury carefully cultivated, it was studied, ironic. He told me there was a geezer who had a stall in Brixton Market, who would set aside old overcoats and suits he thought would work for the band, image-wise. So the Kilburns' 'look' was not necessarily accidental. One of their bass players, Humphrey Ocean, was a trained artist, six feet six tall, and their guitarist was almost a midget. The drummer was on crutches. Davey Payne looked like he was wearing purple tights into a pair of wellies."

Kilburn & The High Roads' sound was difficult to summarise. "They were more about musical pastiches, with an element of Music Hall," Robinson explains. "A song like 'Pam's Moods' is about pre-menstrual tension, done up in a Light Programme bit of tin pan alley song-craft; 'Crippled With Nerves' is about impotence; and they played the occasional bit of mutant ska ('The Roadette Song', 'The Call Up'). Their most obviously 'London' songs were 'The Upminster Kid', an affectionate series of recollections of East End Teds; and 'Billy Bentley (Promenades Himself Around London)', essentially a 'list' song, a litany of London phrases and place names."

Although Dury emerged through London's pub rock scene, he was also peculiarly anachronistic. Alan Robinson: "The Kilburns were the most self-consciously 'London' of Pub Rock bands. Acts like Brinsley Schwarz, Ducks Deluxe, Bees Make Honey, were 'Americana'-influenced, taking their lead from Eggs Over Easy, who were essentially a live musical jukebox. The Kilburns were not singing about Honky Tonks or yearning to be The Band; they were darker, more menacing in look and intent. Whereas it's true that their milieu was the Britain – in particular, the London – of the 1970s, they were only about social commentary in an oblique way. They were quite sophisticated musically. The Kilburns' influence on Madness is most palpable in that Dury avoided Americanisms in lyrics – and their look, of course, was all-important. Their musical line-up – as well as guitar, bass and drums, they also utilised keyboards and sax – was a template for Madness, too."

Unlike those of Dr. Feelgood, the Kilburns' records didn't sell in any quantity and they disbanded in 1975. While their musical stew of Fifties rock'n'roll and flourishes of jazz captured the taste buds of future members of Madness, and Suggs' stilted, near-robotic on-stage movements bore more than a passing resemblance to those of Dury, far more vital was that sense of rekindling the spirit of old London rooted in, say, the songs of the music hall or Ealing comedies like *Passport To Pimlico*. Also, with both the Kilburns and The Blockheads, Dury created vivid characters like Clever Trevor, Plaistow Patricia and Billericay Dickie.

Quite how many members of Madness ever got to see the Kilburns is questionable – but they certainly included that initial core of Barson, Foreman and Thompson, whose curiosity had been aroused by the band's name on a poster. Thompson admitted to seeing them at Dingwalls and The Hope & Anchor. "The only thing I'd go for, though, was the sax player Davey Payne," he later admitted. "It was going to see them that made me get a sax. I got a lot of the fun element of the group from him."

According to Will Birch in *Ian Dury – The Definitive Biography*, Foreman once spotted Dury in the Tally Ho's car park. "A guy with a bow tie came limping along, and I thought he worked at the pub," Foreman remembered. "I asked him what time the band was on and he replied, 'No idea mate.' I later realised it was Ian. We started following the Kilburns around and thought they were brilliant, visually and musically." Dury himself later recalled meeting one of them at the Tally Ho: "We had to get changed into our stage gear in the toilets and I can remember Lee Thompson bunking into the gig through the toilet window and seeing us lot with our trousers down!"

Chapter 2

MEMORIES

NOW approximating a teenage gang of sorts, the lads used to congregate around the Aldenham Boys Club in Highgate Road, which had been set up as a philanthropic venture by Aldenham School, a public school in Elstree, back in the 1920s as a refuge for under-privileged teenagers in or around Kentish Town – then considered one of the poorer areas of north London. Barson would tinker on the piano in the club's main hall.

Since meeting at Aldenham Youth Club in 1972, Chris had been going out with Susan Hegarty (born in 1958 in Bethnal Green). During the long hot summer of 1976, he not only married Susan at King's Cross Registrar Office but, soon afterwards, the couple had their first child, Matthew Christopher Foreman. The couple eventually settled in Finchley, which was more affordable than Kentish Town. "I spent some most excellent quality time looking after my young son whilst on the dole and also trying to learn how to play the guitar," Foreman later wrote on Friends Reunited. "After a while, I got a job in the UCH Hospital, allegedly helping the carpenters bodge up roller blinds and repair things. I got really sick of it and applied for what was to be my last job, working for the GPO as a cleaner/tea boy which was the best one yet, money/skiving wise."

Thompson, too, was in a long-term relationship, having met his future wife Debbie Fordham at a local dance on January 6, 1974 (Debbie had also attended Acland Burghley School). Around this time, Lee was doing a bit of work with another Aldenham Boys Club regular, whose cousin they already knew from their school.

Cathal Joseph Patrick Smyth was born on January 14, 1959, in Middlesex University Hospital, west London, into an extended Irish family which in due course included Brendan, born in 1961 in Wood Green, and twins Dermot Gerard and Bernadette Mary (known as Bernie), born in Islington in 1969. The future Madness MC shared his father's name: Cathal Patrick Smyth Senior had been born on March 26, 1929 and married Maureen McGloin in 1953 in Hampstead.

"My dad's from Kilkenny, my mum's from Mayo – they were Irish dancing champions," Smyth told RTE TV in 1993. "They met through dancing and formed the first Irish dancing school in England." Actually, it was Cathal's grandfather Charlie who set up the school during the Second World War – and one of his pupils was Sheila Clerkin. "It was 1944, wartime still, and this particular ceili was in Great Portland Street, an exhibition of figure dancing by this new school in London," remembers Sheila. "It was a big public hall. I was twelve/thirteen and people were just thrilled with it all, quite a big occasion. Mr Smyth was very important. He was from Kilkenny. His wife didn't teach but she was always there at any big occasion."

According to Suggs, the club was frequented by folk legend Ewan MacColl. A prominent figure within London's Irish community, Charlie Smyth was able to carve out a good living with his classes across London, from Kilburn to World's End near Chelsea, and son Cathal (senior) was his star pupil, one of the leading traditional Irish dancers of his day (there also existed Irish commercial dancehalls which were separate from the traditional Irish dancing class).

"When I started, the Smith School Of Dancing was in an Italian church hall in Clerkenwell," remembers Sheila. "Mr Smyth had other classes in other halls. Later on, he became the first person to teach Irish dancing in the evening classes run by the London County Council. He was very proud of that – Irish dancing on the map in an official capacity. He was professional, the first teacher in London to be registered with the Irish Dancing Commission in Dublin. There obviously had been other people teaching Irish dancing in London before but Mr Smyth was the first qualified teacher, who had taken an exam and done it the official way."

In due course, the Smyth School Of Dancing were chosen to perform at the prestigious Festival Of Britain in 1951. "It was under that aegis of the LCC classes that we danced at the Festival Of Britain – an outdoor exhibition of Irish dancing somewhere on the South Bank," says Sheila. Back when the future Madness star was not yet born, his father Cathal likely appeared at the Festival Of Britain. "When I first joined the club, Cathal was already a well-known dancer," says Sheila. "In Ireland, he'd won the Munster championship. Later on, Cathal was a very good teacher and used to coach us in the classroom."

Another of Charlie's pupils was Nancy Bowler, who arrived as a champion Irish dancer in London in 1952 and joined his classes via a mutual acquaintance involved with Smyth's performances at London's Royal Albert Hall. "The school I went to was in Percy Road, north London. We used to go to the competitions around Warren Street and watch Cathal dancing. I wanted to do teaching myself and Cathal, Charlie's son, started me in a class over at Dalston. He was the nicest person you could meet and his wife Maureen was lovely, too. They lived in Swiss Cottage. Once he made up his mind to do something, it would be perfection. There was a lot of respect for them."

"My grandparents were from Ireland," Cathal junior told *The Word*. "One grandfather was a master carpenter, the other started out in the pits in Burnley. I think London was welcoming, to an extent. My auntie worked for a company where John Lydon's dad was a driver." Smyth also talked about his background to *Zani*: "I am a cradle Catholic, ex-altar boy. My uncles were educated in Trinity College, Dublin, so when I was young they would always be asking me philosophical questions about books they recommended – books like *A Portrait of The Artist As A Young Man*."

When it came to a profession, Cathal senior pursued a career as an engineer in the petrochemical industry, working for the likes of N.A.T.O. That meant the family was constantly uprooted to all four corners of the globe during Cathal junior's childhood – and as a result, the sharp-tongued youngster had something of an itinerant upbringing. According to *Nut Inc.*, they punctuated much of the 1960s and early 1970s with spells in Ireland (Dublin, Bray, Sligo and Coleraine). "My dad travelled a lot so school was a bit erratic," Cathal later admitted. "I lived in Northern Ireland for a year in 1971, a weird time to have an English accent." There, he attended The Dominican College, a grammar school in Portstewart, County Derry – but it was far from a pleasant experience. "It was pretty horrible," Smyth would later admit. "I was beaten up every day for three weeks so I stopped going to school and missed a year's education." At the risk of sounding glib, the Smyths seemed to have an affinity for countries beginning with the letter "I". "We'd lived in Iraq when I was eight and Iran when I was 13," Cathal explained. "I remember Iran particularly because I got typhoid – they read me the last rites!" The family also lived in Africa for a short time.

For the most part, though, Cathal's folks lived in north London, and Smyth later detailed his education on Friends Reunited. Between 1967 and 1971, the youngster went to various schools in the Muswell Hill area: Coldfall Junior Mixed & Infant School in 1967, moving to Our Lady Of Muswell Catholic Primary the following year and St James' Church Of England Primary. In 1971, he went to Challoner School For Boys in North Finchley, which then merged with Finchley Catholic Grammar School. "The school in Finchley was semi-private," Cathal told *Later* magazine. "We had an alcoholic teacher who used to spend his summer holidays with a crate of whiskey, tanked up. He would put you on his knee and give you three whacks with a leather strap. And another teacher would make you get changed and then make you do handstands to check if you had pants on. It was definitely perverted!"

The teenager had chosen to shorten his name to Carl, presumably to avoid any unwarranted attention on his Irish background at school. Encouraged by his father, he planned to stay on to study in the sixth form – but his hot temper got the better of him. "My headmaster had [hauled] me over the coals in his office and said, 'Smyth, pull up your socks or you will find yourself being asked to leave the school.' I looked him in the eye and told him (as I felt I had been working harder recently) that, no problem, I would leave now, and enjoyed the look of shock on his face as I walked out of that office and the school for the last time!"

His father helped secure him a role with a petrochemical company, as he later explained. "CJB in Eastbourne Terrace, Paddington. [My dad] gave me some background on the industry and got me comfortable with six terms which would show at least enough knowledge to blag my way through my first ever job interview. He then took me to Burtons men's clothes shop [and] pulled a blue pinstripe suit off the ready-to-wear rack, got a shirt and some boring shoes. When, three days after departing school, I had secured my first interview, he sent me off by saying, 'Now son, shake his hand with a firm grip, whilst looking him in the eye, and speak clearly.' I couldn't believe I was offered a position in the company – a time analysis clerk. It transpired when I met my English teacher a week later on Tottenham Court Road that I was now earning more than my teachers."

In terms of his interest in music, Smyth was open-minded. "The first record I bought was *Bolan Boogie* [1972] by Marc Bolan. I'm a child of pop – Sweet, T. Rex, Gary Glitter, Mud and Bowie. At the same time, I was listening to Savoy Brown, Mahavishnu Orchestra and Gong. My dad brought records back from Europe. My uncles would play Dvorak, traditional Irish music, 'cod' Irish music, even *Switched On Bach*, the first popular synthesizer album." But instead of following the prevalent glam fashions of the day, Cathal became fascinated by the rock'n'roll dress code of the 1950s. Together with friend Simon Spanner, Smyth would hunt down thrift shops and second-hand boutiques specialising in Fifties and Sixties Americana.

Smyth recalled hooking up with the saxophonist in *Later* magazine: "When I first met Lee, he was so cool. We were all going against the grain – that was what was exciting. We did things like painting our boots before anyone else, wearing baseball jackets from America and mixing up different cultures. We were developing our own thing, not that we were conscious of it at the time. This was from 1975 onwards."

Eventually, he ended up with a skinhead haircut but it was more by accident than design. "One of my mates had to have his head shaved because of a nasty cut on his head," he later explained, "because of a fight with some greasers at the Hampstead Classic cinema. So he was the first. Then Lee Thompson said he'd pay for anyone who'd dare to have a crop and that was that!" Cathal later recalled Lee's notoriety among certain parents. "One of the guy's fathers was a copper," he told *Later* magazine. "He checked Lee's record and banned him from the house. There were factions. There were people who were always going to be destined for a life of crime, and there was the crowd that became Madness, which was more arty."

* * *

Having invested £4 in a second-hand instrument, Smyth was recruited by Barson, Thompson and Foreman as bass player towards the end of 1976. "My cousin was a bit of a hard nut in a school which other members of the band went to, so I was hanging around with a crowd in Hampstead when these hard nuts came around and it was really frightening," Cathal later recalled. "One of them bashed one of my friends over the head with an acoustic guitar and it was like – wow, serious villains – and they seemed like a laugh so I started hanging around with them. Through them, I met the band. There was an extremely violent side and an extremely funny side: we were the funny side; the other lot ended up doing time for armed robbery and extortion, things like that!"

Soon, the lads also found a drummer, although stories differ as to how they recruited the primitive talents of John Charles Hasler (born 1958, Islington, north London). In the film *Take It Or Leave It*, we see Hasler and Foreman "signing on", which prompts the guitarist to invite him along to a rehearsal. Another version of events suggests that Smyth had befriended Hasler in pubs around Hampstead. Indeed, it was Hasler who apparently inspired Smyth's alter ego, Chas Smash, via a holiday postcard.[*]

Cathal's skills were basic, to say the least: rumour has it that he had to place stickers on frets to pinpoint where the notes were. The five teenagers met up for rehearsal sessions maybe three times a week, playing along to their favourite records – 'The Girl From Ipanema' by Astrud Gilberto or The Temptations' 'Just My Imagination'. However, quarrels between Mike and Lee often ended with the saxophonist walking out, only to return a week or two later. Smyth later recalled that Foreman's recent marriage meant that he was absent from rehearsals on frequent occasions.

Smyth's one-time housemate Simon Birdsall instigated the band's first public performance when he threw a house party at which he invited them to play – at the Birdsall family's spacious Victorian home in Compton Terrace, Islington, behind the Hope & Anchor.[†]

The date was June 30, 1977. Alongside Barson, Foreman, Thompson, Hasler and Smyth was an aspiring American actor friend nicknamed Dikron (vocals), variously named Dickson, a budding singer who was the brother of one of Mike's girlfriends. The story goes that they were

---

[*] Other sources suggest it was Thompson who found Hasler via a shared love of joy-riding.

[†] Birdsall's father is the acclaimed graphic designer Derek Birdsall, acknowledged as a pioneer of British book design, who'd worked with such famous brands as Pirelli, designing their very first calendar in 1964, Penguin Books, Lotus cars and magazines such as *Town* and *Nova*, as well as designing one of Monty Python's books. Simon's younger brother Jesse, meanwhile, would later become a successful star of stage and screen as an actor in such TV series as *Bugs*, *The Bill* and *Footballer's Wives*.

supposed to play in the living room but when Foreman phoned Birdsall, he heard grunting in the background, which was the sound of Smyth helping to move the piano into the garden – an annoying change of plan for the band.

By all accounts, their set was a ramshackle affair. Dikron mumbled his way through the lyrics to Elvis Presley's 'Jailhouse Rock' from a songbook. "He was meant to learn the words but he came along with them written in a book," wrote Cathal on Pete Frame's Madness Family Tree. "[Because] we had to play the gig in the garden, it was too dark for him to read it – so we told him to get lost and converted our set to an instrumental session!"

The band *sans* Dikron improvised their way through 'Just My Imagination', 'I'm Walkin'', Clyde McPhatter's 'Lover Please', The Cats' 'Swan Lake', Stevie Wonder's 'For Once In My Life' (via a ska/reggae version – probably the Pama 45 by Slim Smith), Kilburn & The High Roads' 'The Roadette Song' and Carole King's 'It's Too Late'. The group were still nameless, though. Inspired by a paper pirate-style party hat hanging off the back of their ex-GPO Morris 1000 van on the way to Birdsall's house, Barson is purported to have commented to Foreman that, "if that's still there when we get there, we'll be called the Pirates". Chris pointed out a potential problem: Johnny Kidd's original Pirates had recently reformed.

Meanwhile, they set about finding a new singer. One of the few who witnessed their garden performance was a friend of Hasler's, Graham 'Suggs' McPherson, who vaguely knew Barson & Co. from "hanging around Hampstead School – which was mixed!" Eventually, Suggs met Mike and his friends in a pub in Hampstead. "They were pretty cool looking blokes, when everyone else was wearing flares and sporting Kevin Keegan haircuts," McPherson later recalled. "I remember seeing a lot of them at Hampstead Fair, these blokes who were into wearing old clothes. They seemed more interested in style than the average person. There was a real 'scene' there, parties and pub discos that they all used to go over to from Highgate and Kentish Town."

★ ★ ★

Suggs' Scottish father, the impressively named William Rutherford McPherson, was born in the borough of Hammersmith in 1935 and had married Edith (or Edwina) Gower in 1960 in Paddington, London. Born in 1939, Edith hailed from south Manchester, where she was raised with elder sisters Diana and Evelyn before the family moved to Wales. Suggs' parents moved to the coastal town of Hastings, East Sussex, where Graham was born "on a stormy evening" on January 13, 1961. However, his father left when his son Graham was very young, leaving his mother to bring up the toddler.

"I'm haunted by my lost Scots father," he admitted to *The Daily Record* in 1999. "It was a disaster for my mum and dad. They were both so young. It all went wrong because he was hooked on drugs. What happened between them was very painful and it was a difficult subject for me to bring up as a child. When Madness became successful, I was convinced my dad would try and reach me. I half expected him to turn up on my doorstep but he never did. I found out that my dad had been really ill in hospital from heroin abuse, so there is every chance that he has since died."

According to *The Independent* in 1997, Suggs later discovered that his father had been sectioned due to poor mental health. As a teenager, Suggs got close to tracking him down but thought the better of it. Later, he contacted some of his Scottish relatives, as he told *The Word* magazine in 2009: "The McPhersons were from Newtonmore, near Aviemore in the Scottish Highlands. I went there about three years ago and met three Graham McPhersons. I never knew my dad, so it's hard to relate to that side of the family."

Because Edwina (or Edie, for short) found it difficult to find sustained work as a singer, the family upped sticks to Liverpool and Manchester in a desperate bid to make ends meet. "My mother's family were the Gowers from Wales," Suggs explained. "My mum used to sing in jazz clubs and had a good voice." By all accounts, it was a desultory childhood for Suggs, spent drifting from bedsits to other people's houses – which not only disrupted his schooling but made it impossible for him to forge any long-term friendships. It was a lonely time. According to *The Independent*, his earliest memory was "of cigarette packets hanging off a piece of string and going to the toilet in some kind of pan".

What Edwina's hand-to-mouth existence did nurture was Suggs' lifelong love affair with Soho, as he enthused in his book *Suggs And The City – My Journeys Through Disappearing London*. "Mum . . . arrived here from

Liverpool, and she's been singing and working in Soho's clubs ever since. We . . . moved first to Clerkenwell and later to a flat on Tottenham Court Road . . . One of my earliest memories of the place is being taken by Mum to the Colony Room Club on Dean Street in 1968, and to this day I can clearly remember the legs of those bar-stools, at eye-level to a youngster like me."

"My early life was chaotic as we moved around a lot," Suggs told *The Guardian* in 2010. "Mum was a single parent, which was a big stigma back in those days. She made ends meet by working as a barmaid and she took me round to pubs and clubs in Soho. My earliest memory of that time is of an occasional hand reaching down through a cloud of smoke to ruffle my hair. What's important is that my childhood made me stronger." Still in short trousers, he attended Park Walk primary school, just off the Kings Road in Chelsea. His singular passion was football and after he chose to support the local team, pictures of his beloved Chelsea FC would be festooned across his bedroom walls. When he wasn't ducking out of school to watch a match, young Graham was absorbing another form of popular culture, cinema, as an ABC Minor at the Saturday morning pictures.

At the age of eight, during a period when Edie was struggling to make ends meet, Suggs went to live with his Auntie Diana and her family in south Wales (initially under the auspices of a holiday). In stark contrast to the succession of cramped, urban dwellings which had characterised McPherson's home life to date, the Walkers lived in an isolated house in the tiny village of Port Lion in Haverfordwest, Pembrokeshire, set within the picturesque rural setting of the rolling Welsh countryside and the Pembroke River estuary. Graham spent much of his time with the Walkers' son Hector, who would later work for Madness for much of the 1980s (Hector later appeared on Suggs' edition of *This Is Your Life* in April 2000). "He came to live with me and my sisters," says Hector. "We lived in a little hamlet and the house looked out on the Cleddau River. Sarah, myself and Graham went to the Burton VC village school a few miles away in Houghton, Milford Haven."

With several mouths to feed, it was an extra burden for the Walkers – and especially, because his father worked away a lot, Hector's mother Diana. "Mum left me there for three years because she felt she couldn't cope," Suggs told *The Guardian*. "It was a shock and I did feel bitter and angry about it. I actually liked being in my auntie's family with my three cousins and I got to be in the countryside for the first time. In Wales, I passed the 11-plus and went to the grammar school." At first, he liked being in the country. It gave him the freedom to scour nearby fields, "eat apples and shoot rats". He later recalled this potentially idyllic life as that of "harvests and hay bales and torchlight processions in the woods – Van Morrison stuff". When asked about that period, Suggs commented: "Well, whenever I ran away, the people who brought me straight back always seemed very nice!"

Edwina later talked about her son's upbringing as part of a BBC 1 documentary, *One Life: Rock Star Kids*, broadcast in March 2008. "I was always out at work," she explained, when comparing Suggs' childhood with lines from the Madness song, 'Our House'. "I felt that he was OK with everything and didn't take into consideration that he was missing out so much. These lyrics describe a family life that he didn't have. I just had to work for a living, had to find babysitters for him. That was our life for quite a long time. He must have missed out on a great deal of being parented. And I regret that: I think he had an awful time, really. All he felt was a sort of abandonment, in a way."

No sooner had he started at a Welsh grammar school, aged eleven, than he was sent back to London. Reunited with his mum, Suggs lived variously in a bedsit over a carpet shop on Tottenham Court Road and a one-bedroom apartment in Cavendish Mansions, a Victorian block of flats on Clerkenwell Road, Holborn. He was sent to an all-boys school, Quintin Kynaston Comprehensive, on Marlborough Hill, Swiss Cottage, "set up in the Sixties as an example of the new, easy-going comprehensives", according to Suggs. "It was a very rough school," he later admitted in *Later*. "I arrived halfway through the first term. I had a uniform from the grammar school I'd been to in Haverfordwest and my mum said, 'It doesn't look that different' – apart from the fact that it had red braiding and the one at Quintin Kynaston had green. As soon as I got off the tube, two kids started attacking me!"

It was a challenging environment. "At school, I was like an ethnic minority. I was the only Scottish person. There were lots of Irish, Greeks, Pakistanis and West Indians. I got fed up of being picked on so I decided to change my name. I just put a pin in an encyclopaedia of jazz musicians when I was thirteen and decided I was going to be called Suggs [from jazz musician Pete Suggs]." That period would also inspire one of Suggs' greatest songs, 'Baggy Trousers'. "When the register was read out, I refused to answer unless they said Suggs – which only added to the demise of my education. I used to write things on walls: 'Suggs is our leader'. I never made any assumption I was going to sing, though – it happened by accident, really."*

Social acceptance for Suggs came at the expense of his studies, though, as he told *Later*: "If you follow my school career, the further I went downhill academically, the more integrated I became. I played in the school orchestra once, the double bass. I'd only had two lessons! The school was so chaotic that no one even cared if you went in the end. I used to bunk off and hang around Hampstead School, where my best mate was going, because it had girls and it was funkier."

According to Michael Aspel's script for Suggs' *This Is Your Life*, "At first, your good education in Wales kept you ahead of your classmates in London but over-crowded classrooms and lack of discipline get in the way. Your mother wanted you to be a graphic designer but you rebel. You bunk off school . . ." At which point in the programme, Suggs felt the need to lighten the moment: "How dare you! I didn't bunk off, I took time out for other endeavours!" But perhaps his good humour disguised a sense of discomfort in recalling those days. There's a brief but perhaps telling scene in *Take It Or Leave It* when Suggs makes an offhand comment about a home visit from a social worker.

When Suggs was in his mid-teens, Edie secured her son part-time employment through contacts at Gerry's Club in Dean Street, Soho. "My mum used to work [there] in the Seventies," he wrote in *Suggs And The City*. "I managed to get a job working as a butcher's delivery boy, for which I got £3 a week with unlimited use of the company push bike thrown in." His major passion was still supporting Chelsea FC. "We used to all go to football matches," he later admitted. "I was never a real mindless vandal. I was just a lot more influenced by the bad kids than the good ones. It was never my destiny to be a real hooligan." (Thompson,

---

* Kentucky-born multi-instrumentalist Pete Suggs – who made his name in the 1930s with Fletcher Henderson as a drummer and vibraphone player but whose career endured well into the 1960s – once played with the great tenor saxophone soloist Ben Webster, later cited as an influence by Lee Thompson.

incidentally, was an avid Arsenal supporter and got into a few scrapes back in the early Seventies.)

For a while, he flirted with further education. "I stayed on to the sixth form for social security reasons, and got two O-levels and a CSE on the way," Suggs later told *No. 1* magazine. By and large, though, he shunned formal education in favour of hobbies. He was an avid cartoonist, even at an early age, and adored Marvel comics – a passion which would eventually manifest itself in the Fink Brothers project in the 1980s. Equally, making sausages and scraping lard off metal trays, or even a stint working with Barson as a gardener, wasn't likely to inspire the teenager. "I desperately wanted to belong to a family, a movement," he later admitted. "So many things were waiting for me in London, like the gangs. I had no family or roots, and thought of replacing them with a gang of skinheads."

★ ★ ★

The skinhead movement of the late 1960s was a natural evolution of mod, the youth cult/fashion which had germinated in pockets of London as early as the late 1950s to spread nationally by 1964, fuelled by the notoriety of infamous clashes with rockers at seaside resorts across various bank holiday weekends. The traditional image of a mod remains the fashionable, scooter-riding youth high on pills, testosterone and American soul music – the caricature portrayed by Phil Daniels as Jimmy in the popular 1979 movie based on The Who's 1973 album *Quadrophenia*.

In his book *Something Beginning With O,* Kevin Pearce offered an "intensely subjective description of [these] obsessives, outsiders, risk takers, explorers". "The real mod spirit," he wrote, "has nothing to do with scooter-riding, beach-fighting, lumpen mod lore. The best mods had the best record collections, the best wardrobes, the best bookshelves, the best minds. What else? The real roots of the mod uprising lie in the late Fifties modern jazz world. An extension of the beats, but sharper." It was a world, then, of competitive one-upmanship.

The mods – or Modernists, as they were first labelled – had originated more as a concept or an attitude than as a movement. The idea was rooted in a late Fifties obsession with 'cool', a nebulous term which embodied cosmopolitan sophistication, cleanliness against the grime of urban life, sharp, continental styling and living in 'the now'. To attain 'cool' was to be in control. It was something to strive for. "The mod way of life consisted of a total devotion to looking and being 'cool'," wrote Richard Barnes, an old friend of The Who's Pete Townshend, in his book, *Mods!* "Spending practically all your money on clothes and all your after-work hours in clubs and dance halls. To be part-time was really to miss the point." Legendary mod Pete Meaden, who was also involved with The Who in their early years, said simply: "Modism, mod living, is an aphorism for clean living under difficult circumstances."

Of the various factors at work, the initial impetus that sparked the mod lifestyle was the affluence of post-mid-Fifties Britain and the abolition of National Service, which had given school leavers greater disposable income and time to spend it, particularly so with the introduction of hire purchase in the Fifties. "The two essentials that a full-time Soho mod needed . . . to keep him on the go," wrote Barnes, "were money and energy." This environment contributed to the evolution of the teenager, as distinct from a 'young adult', in the mid-Fifties. Suddenly, there was a generation who could deliberately set themselves apart from their elders. *The* youth cult of the Fifties was the Teddy boy, a working-class image that was unequivocally English. Their most distinctive garment, the drape jacket, was inspired by early 20th century Edwardian dress; indeed, this was the origin of the word 'Ted'.

In its most clearly defined sense, mod couldn't have been more different. "The Teds' uniform was exactly that – a uniform," wrote Mark Paytress in *Bolan: The Rise And Fall Of A Twentieth Century Superstar*, in a chapter discussing the teenager's involvement in mod. "It consisted of little more than buying the correct outfit and adorning it with the appropriate accessories. The Modernists, meanwhile, were nothing if not eclectic. Instead of sticking to one readily recognisable style, they sought continually to adapt and evolve their dress, combining functional garments designed for the country gentleman with sportswear, ladies' fashions with suits aimed at the city gent. What lay behind this obsessive one-upmanship was the new spirit of competitive individualism that had supplanted the austerity years and, in this respect, Modernist culture in its pure form marked a sharp break with the insular, herd-like outlook of the Teds' world."

Fifties' Britain was a repressed, conservative environment for teenagers, who looked abroad for cultural inspiration in the shape of a new, exciting range of products: America was seen as the future, as teenagers took to Levi's and bomber jackets, and the Italian look, popularised by sharp

Italian-American actors like Tony Curtis, influenced more formal dress. Snug-fitting three-button suits with narrow trousers were *de rigeur*, and the Modernists developed a taste for fancy trimmings and garish colours. In Lynn Barber's 2009 autobiography, *An Education* (part of which was adapted as a film, scripted by Nick Hornby), she described the English way of life as dull and routine, and it was France – and Paris, in particular – which appeared to offer a more exciting alternative.

During the early Sixties, the mod look and lifestyle spread first through London and then across England. American R&B and its more sophisticated cousin, soul, entered a golden era – music which mods could dance to. Detroit's Tamla Motown empire forged a brand of catchy, upbeat and highly danceable music which managed to cross both geographical and racial boundaries. The Stax/Atlantic camp offered a more earthy, downhome style of soul, as counterpoint to the bluesy world of Chess and the ultra-hip Sue. A nightclub scene was born, where audiences danced to the latest US tunes until the early hours. With it, the mods developed a taste for drugs – 'uppers' that kept them keen, wide-eyed and sharp.

In 1965, two London bands aligned themselves both to the sound and the style of mod: The Who and the Small Faces. The former, relatively experienced by 1964 and desperate for lift-off, adopted the image at the urging of associate Pete Meaden, while the Small Faces, younger but no less accomplished, were the real thing. Mod was now a nationwide phenomenon. Hair was now shorter and more angular than the moppy style that had swept the country after The Beatles' arrival. Expensive mohair suits, silk shirts and fancy leather shoes gave way to more casual sports wear: Fred Perry T-shirts, Harrington sports jackets, suede desert boots, colourful striped jumpers, checked button-down shirts, fancy 'hipster' trousers and tight roll-neck sweaters. Mod was now the cutting edge of high street fashion. It mutated into the living embodiment of what was labelled 'Swinging London', as the capital led the way not only in fashion but also popular culture.

The 'look' of most youth cults tends to be assimilated into the mainstream, fragmenting into new sounds and styles in the process. To over-simplify matters, mod split in two. The high street style grew fancier, as it evolved into the Beau Brummel-esque peacock parodied by Ray Davies in The Kinks' 'Dedicated Follower Of Fashion' and 'Dandy'. An extreme caricature of this image would be Mike Myers' Nineties comedy hero, Austin Powers. Popularised by the West End fashion set and pop stars alike, this flamboyancy culminated in the brightly-coloured psychedelic images of the summer of love of '67. In start contrast, a largely working-class contingent shunned the frills and evolved into skinheads, for the most part swapping soul music (or accompanying it, at any rate) with Jamaican ska, rocksteady and early reggae.

Author Michael de Koningh, a skinhead back in the late 1960s, was too young to experience the cleaving of mod culture into these contrasting identities. "I knew the fracture started with the more working-class mods being ridiculed for not being able to afford the trendy gear," he suggests, "so they turned to the opposite and went for utility work-wear, including work boots. Originally, these guys were called 'hard mods' or 'peanuts' – presumably the latter because they had crisp short haircuts. This mixed with West Indian styles (short trousers, razor parting in their hair, etc.) that they saw in inner city clubs to emerge as the 'uniform' known as skinhead. You all wore similar clothing but not to the extent that is written of nowadays. My hair was slightly longer than a true crop – more suedehead – but it didn't matter."

★ ★ ★

Skinheads didn't just look to Caribbean immigrants for aspects of their wardrobe; the Sixties was a golden era for Jamaican music. Its first boom occurred in 1964, when the island's latest sound, ska, bubbled up to the mainstream courtesy of Millie's worldwide hit, 'My Boy Lollipop', orchestrated by Island Records founder Chris Blackwell. Initiated by pioneers like guitarist Ernest Ranglin, and the island's foremost producers such as Clement 'Coxsone' Dodd, Duke Reid and Byron Lee, ska had evolved by melding traditional Jamaican styles such as mento (a form of calypso) with elements of American jazz, 'jump blues' and R&B. In particular, the music of New Orleans (from Fats Domino to Louis Jordan) held sway, partly because it was easier to pick up radio broadcasts from the Southern States than those in the North.

Fuelled by a need to feed new music through their travelling "sound systems" (ostensibly a powerful, albeit primitive, PA on the back of a lorry), these pioneering producers developed their own production line – funding and coordinating the whole process, from the writing of songs to their performance, recording, manufacture, distribution and sale. The ska style was of bars made up of four triplets, similar to that of 'My Baby Just Cares For Me' by Nina Simone, but was characterised by a guitar chop on the off beat – known as an upstroke or skank – with horns taking the lead. Drums kept four/four time and the bass drum was accented on the third beat.

Once described by broadcaster Mark Lamarr as "inside-out rhythm-and-blues", ska was Jamaica's first 'outernational' music – in other words, its first indigenous sound to travel beyond its shores. And while Millie – perceived as a novelty by some commentators – globe-trotted around the world, the true 'King Of Ska' back in Kingston, Jamaica, was one Cecil Bustamente Campbell, better known by his alias, Prince Buster. Born on May 28, 1938, Prince Buster showed early promise as a boxer, which led to him being hired as a security man in 1961 for leading sound system owner Clement 'Coxsone' Dodd.

Subsequent battles with rival sound systems earnt him his nickname "Prince"; but Buster had aspirations within music and by 1962, he was both recording himself and producing such famous pre-ska hits as the Folkes Brothers' 'Oh Carolina' and 'Humpty Dumpty' by Eric Morris. These and many other Prince Buster productions were issued in the UK on the Blue Beat label, created in 1960 by Emil Shalit as an extension of his record company Melodisc. Although it found a rival in 1962 with Chris Blackwell's Island Records, the label was synonymous with Jamaican music to the extent that ska was often referred to as 'bluebeat'.

Over the course of the 1960s, Buster produced and recorded hundreds of records. In due course, he opened his own record shop in Kingston, Jamaica, called Buster's Record Shack. His house band took the name of Buster's All Stars, who boasted some of the finest Jamaican talent of the day – including future Specials collaborator Rico Rodriguez on trombone. Quick to capitalise on interest from UK audiences, Buster made high profile visits to Britain between 1962 and 1967 and appeared on the popular TV show *Ready Steady Go!* in 1964, following a sell-out concert at Brixton Town Hall. All this activity underscored his cult status here – especially with mods, who were also struck by his dapper dress sense. Although none of Buster's singles charted during ska's brief flirtation with the mainstream in 1964, 'Al Capone' was a British hit during Jamaican music's second wave of popularity in 1967 (in fact, it was the first Jamaican recorded song to enter the UK Top 20) although the single was actually a re-pressing from 1965. And on its B-side was a near-instrumental entitled 'One Step Beyond'.

The 'bluebeat' craze of 1964 might have been viewed as a fad – and it is true to say that few records at the time sold in sufficient quantity outside of city centres to impact nationally. By 1967, that situation was changing. As the ska sound slowed into what became known as rocksteady, the framework for the distribution of Jamaican music in the UK was slowly improving – not least with Island Records' creation of a new label dedicated to this music, Trojan Records. Records which are now seen as classics of the genre such as 'Train To Skaville' by The Ethiopians, 'Guns Of Navarone' by The Skatalites and '007 (Shanty Town)' by Desmond Dekker breached the Top 40 and Jamaican music's gradual assimilation into the mainstream began.

By 1969, Dekker was headline news as reggae's first true star, topping the charts with 'Israelites'. That year witnessed an explosion in sales of Jamaican music. The charts were awash with hits like 'Long Shot Kick De Bucket' by The Pioneers, 'Wet Dream' by Max Romeo (which enjoyed brief notoriety through being banned by the BBC), 'Return Of Django' by The Upsetters, 'Wonderful World, Beautiful People' by Jimmy Cliff and 'Red Red Wine' by Tony Tribe. Trojan Records cleverly cashed in with a string of budget-priced compilation albums, including their best-selling *Tighten Up* LPs, which were targeted at working-class teenagers with little disposal income – and proved popular with future members of Madness, for example. And reggae's slow but inexorable rise onto the dance floors of youth clubs across the country was due in no small part to the growth of skinhead.

Pauline Black, later the singer with 2 Tone act The Selecter, remembered being introduced to ska and early reggae through skinhead friends at school: "Because I was the only black kid, it was easy to be the mascot for skinheads! And I really liked their music. They used to play ska, 'Long Shot Kick De Bucket', and reggae music and they were deeply into Tamla and soul and that's where I began hearing all those records. I came to black music through white skinheads."

Between 1969 and 1971, reggae enjoyed a golden era. Spearheaded by the plethora of labels associated with Trojan Records, the release of Jamaican music in Britain was both prolific and successful. Artists like Dave & Ansell Collins found themselves on *Top Of The Pops* performing

'Double Barrel'; like the ubiquitous 'Liquidator' by Harry J. All Stars (which still echoes across football terraces to this day), 'Double Barrel' wasn't some lame attempt to dilute Jamaican music for the masses but a hardcore instrumental aimed squarely at the dance floor, initial sales of which came from the skinhead fraternity. Others continued a long-held Jamaican tradition of adapting American soul and R&B, such as Bob Andy and Marcia Griffiths with 'Young, Gifted And Black'.

"People have this middle-class myth that punks discovered reggae," suggests author/broadcaster and one-time skinhead Robert Elms, author of an insightful book about the youth culture of the period, *The Way We Wore*. "In fact, reggae had been the theme music of working-class London kids since about 1966. Pretty much all of the music I grew up listening to came from Jamaica. Trojan Records was up the road. And that music had never gone away. Wherever you went, a ska or reggae record was playing in the background."

In Horace Ove's 1970 film *Reggae*, which revolved around footage of a high profile reggae festival at the Empire Pool, Wembley, he asked the question: "To what extent has reggae invaded the consciousness of white youth in Britain? Well, the first thing that emerges is that, in accepting reggae, the skinheads have rejected the middle class, with its existential, hippie-style music, which is unable to cater to the social needs of the skinheads. Through the medium of reggae, the black youth does this extremely well."

"Most things in music, fashion, are a reaction to something else," suggested Elms. "Before glam rock, the over-riding youth, working-class look had been skinhead, which was very regimented. You could only wear a Ben Sherman, Levi Sta-prest, a Crombie coat. It was all very much dictated." The skinhead uniform might have evolved from mod but its stricter code harked back to the gangland ethos of the Teddy boy – albeit in the form of utilitarian wear such as 'monkey boots', Doctor Marten's or jeans with braces. For evening wear, the smart dress code for all of these cults doffed the cap to the British class system simultaneously corrupting it by adopting – or rather, adapting – brands previously associated with the middle-class establishment. In the case of skinheads, that might be the Crombie overcoat, brogues or smart suits; during a period which experienced rapid social change, this uniform seemed to offer a sense of conservative reassurance for dispossessed teenagers.

Skinheads' aggressively male demeanour went hand-in-fist with a reputation for violence – and their notoriety was fuelled by a minority who were guilty of racist attacks on members of immigrant families from India or Pakistan. Such behaviour has tarred the skinhead identity ever since but while a fair proportion of skinheads were prone to violent clashes, the degree to which these attacks were racially motivated is open to conjecture. "From the press perspective, it was mass gatherings – the traditional bank holiday punch-ups at the coast and at football matches – which brought the skinheads to the fore in the papers," suggests Michael de Koningh. "Whilst some skins were violent so were many other teenagers. Some original skinheads did have extreme views but the vast majority were pretty cool about any and every nationality."

Like mod before it and punk since, skinhead was in many respects just a passing fashion. "I would say late 1969 to early 1971 was the peak of the true skinhead," says de Koningh. The constraints of the original look evolved. "By 1971, the 'suedehead' and the 'smoothie' emerged. Inner cities changed quicker than the provinces. But there was no set date when the fashion changed: hard-looking skins were still around in 1973 alongside longer-haired smoothies. It was just a progression of the fashion. I went from DM boots to DM shoes and tasseled loafers. My Levi's jacket was replaced by a Harrington. The other contributing factor to the demise of skinhead was that reggae had slowed down and become more rootsy or gone ultra-commercial. Some skins moved on to the new sounds around – Glitter, Bowie, T. Rex – and adopted the glam clothing worn by the followers of that music. By 1974, I'd forgotten all about being a skinhead."

Chapter 3

MADNESS (IS ALL IN THE MIND)

"A COUPLE of us were skinheads for quite a while because we liked the whole style of it and some of us had been skins first time round," Cathal later explained. "We did get quite heavily into skinhead culture and music, the boots and braces. I loved all that. We were into collecting old Motown, reggae and R&B, stuff that people weren't really into because there were hardly any other skins then. I used to collect records but it turned into an expensive hobby. You wind up paying a couple of quid for a record just because it's on a certain label."

Foreman, too, dabbled with a skinhead/suedehead image. "I used to have an imitation mohair suit," he later commented. "We used to go to this club in Barnet where all the skinheads went!" But it was primarily Smyth, McPherson and Thompson who flirted with skinhead imagery. Their gang of friends was encouraged by Thompson to get their hair cropped short as a demonstration of solidarity for Simon Birdsall, who'd had his head shaved following injuries received in a fight at a Bazooka Joe gig at Haverstock Town Hall. Heads turned: most teenagers in the mid-1970s had long hair and wore platform shoes, tank tops and flared trousers.

Other than the odd bunch of ageing Teddy boys, tribal youth culture had receded from public view. And here was Suggs decked out in oxblood Doctor Marten's boots, a collarless grandfather shirt, khaki combat trousers and a silver bomber jacket depicting mod iconography from The Who's 1973 album *Quadrophenia* on the rear. The teenager's sartorial considerations were recalled in *Suggs And The City*. "It all began when I was fifteen or sixteen years old," he wrote. "Along with a few friends from school, I'd taken to wearing my hair short and sporting clothes from the

Fifties and Sixties, which weren't easy to come by . . . it certainly made us stand out and would sometimes engender aggro."

Named after their local youth club, these Aldenham Glamour Boys were "a peculiar mixture of suedeheads, Teds and Roxy Music freaks", according to George Marshall in *Total Madness*. Decked out in spray-painted Doctor Marten's boots and unfashionably narrow Levi's 501 jeans, the teenagers definitely made an impact on their peers – including a teenage Robert Elms: "I grew up not far from there and was aware of this group of guys in Camden Town who we called Dayglo Skins or Glam Skins, who went on to become Madness. They weren't old enough to have been skins first time around, except maybe they were because I was a skin when I was only ten! That wasn't unusual so it's perfectly feasible that they were playground skins first time around in a little brother hanging on way."

Excepting the Northern Soul scene centred around north-west England, which shared the same tribal aspects as mod and skinhead before it, mid-1970s youth culture has been viewed as somewhat rudderless in terms of underground fashions outside of the mainstream. Elms disagrees with this perspective: "For me, one of the most interesting periods is 1974/75," he counters, "a strange and fleeting meeting of skin and glam rock. It's a primordial stew which, in the end, solidifies into punk and all its offshoots like 2 Tone. Glam is seen now as very art school, quite arch, quite feminine. Whereas actually, it was blokes from building sites tottering around on platform shoes. Bands like The Sweet and Slade* were very working class: the hair's grown out into a feather cut but there's a direct lineage from skinhead to suedehead into glam. It was very much a London thing. I call it 'butch camp' – bands like Mott The Hoople, The Hammersmith Gorillas."

The future members of Madness would have soaked up these influences. "When my elder brothers had parties in 1972," recalls Elms, "they played ska and reggae, soul music, T. Rex, The Faces, The Glitter Band. 'All The Young Dudes' next to 'Young, Gifted And Black'. That was the pop music of the day and also the music of the terrace. If you were a working-class kid, it was never about rock music. Rock guitars were the aberration. It was pop music sometimes but even Bolan's got that

---

* Slade adopted a skinhead image in 1969 and were condemned by the mainstream press as a result. In reality, it was a publicity stunt which was soon forgotten as the group forged their own identity.

boogie/dancey edge. The Faces were for the rough boys, central to the culture, north London's house band for terrace boys – Rod Stewart's from Archway."

Another profound influence on youth culture of the period – including future members of Madness – was the film *A Clockwork Orange*, Stanley Kubrick's infamous adaptation of Anthony Burgess' 1962 novel. Its explicitly violent depiction of a futuristic world, wherein a teenage delinquent gang dressed in matching, skinhead-like attire (boots, tight jeans, braces, collarless shirts) wreak havoc on their environment, caused a furore within the media. The film all but broke box office records on its release in 1971 but when a manslaughter case was linked to its subject matter, the film was withdrawn by Kubrick, immediately reinforcing its iconic standing.

"*A Clockwork Orange* was a big influence," agrees Elms. "The guys who went onto become Madness wore Doctor Marten's again but they painted them in bright colours. Trousers had been wide for a period of time, with Oxford bags. Suddenly, they'd gone back to skinnier trousers again which looked radical. When I saw them at first, they didn't have short hair but it was in a feather cut – very 'cut' hair." However, it's unclear whether any future members of Madness were actually able to see the film during this period, not least because they would have been too young to pass themselves off as being 18 years old.

Another key influence was the retrogressive culture within Camden Town's music scene of the period. "Camden Town was one of those places where people go looking for dinosaurs," laughs Elms, "where you find long-dead species. Back then, there were rock'n'roll shops like Rock On next to the shoe shop Holts, which sold Doctor Marten's. It was the place where youth cults never died, a magical little island. You would see original skins and Teds. And all that stuff fed into what the Madness boys wore. But they weren't alone. You'd go to football in 1974 and see groups of boys dressing in this glam/skin revival – that was the first time I saw people with brightly coloured hair, still quite long but dyed pillbox red. There's an extraordinary book called *Tottenham Boys, We Are Here*, a photographic record of Spurs fans in 1974 – of the hooligans, basically, taken by a hooligan. They've got long hair but in that feather cut, Rod Stewart style, and half have on crombies and Doctor Marten's."

In summer 1977, Suggs experienced a fashion epiphany when he discovered the holy grail of second-hand menswear outlets, Alfred Kemp's on Camden High Street. "You could find the most marvellous treasures there," he wrote in *Suggs And The City*, "from velvet-collared camel-hair coats to spats and a truly wondrous selection of suits." Much of his meagre income of £11 working in the butcher's was split between an aquamarine suit from Kemp's and jaunts down to punk club The Roxy in a dingy Covent Garden basement. While Suggs never engaged with punk as a musical style, he was caught by its youthful excitement and vitality and the sense of change in the air. "I was hit by the intoxicating feeling that this was our time and anything and everything was possible," he wrote.

It's intriguing to note how little impact punk appears to have had on the future members of Madness, other than acting as a motivating, "anyone can do it"-type catalyst. "When I heard all those punk things coming out," Barson later wrote on Pete Frame's Madness Family Tree, "I thought, well, it can't be too difficult." Mike later recalled seeing some dodgy mid-seventies rock band at north London's premier rock venue, The Rainbow, and "seeing these three guys who were supposed to be brilliant, but they were so dull I thought at the time, we can't miss." If anything, punk felt like an unwelcome distraction to the teenager. "Then suddenly the [Sex] Pistols came along and stole our glory. Their attitude was good but I don't think any of us liked their music. Punk meant nothing to me."

The as yet unnamed band never dabbled with punk rock – quite the opposite, in fact. If anything, they wilfully spurned an attitude which they abhorred. "The original idea of our nutty sound was to keep the music fun and humorous," Lee later explained, "almost as a rebellion against the punk thing. We wanted to keep music away from politics. Music should be fun and, above all, loving. I was never a punk for that reason. I wouldn't give it an inch because of the way they looked, the aggressiveness."

★ ★ ★

In October 1977, Mike Barson started going out with Kerstin Rodgers – later the subject of one of Barson's most memorable compositions, 'My Girl' – and the two were an item for the next two years. Today, Kerstin has a popular supper club business called The Underground Restaurant. Back then, she was a teenage punk who loved hanging out with bands. With her bleached blonde hair and Mike standing 6 feet 1 inch with piercing grey-blue eyes, they made for a striking couple.

"I lived in Highgate and was going out with a friend of theirs, Tony Hilton," remembers Kerstin. "Their gang used to drink at the Duke Of Hamilton in Hampstead. That's where I met Mike. He was very ambitious, very focused. The first date I had with him, he said, 'I'm going to be a pop star.' I've heard that crap from several guys over the years and he was the only one I looked at and I thought, 'Yes you are.' Like many kids, especially boys, with only one parent, he was absolutely determined to succeed. I was eighteen, a photographer at art school. I started a photography apprenticeship officially in April 1978 and I was very into the *NME* so it made sense for me to be taking pictures. I followed them around and saw everything they did. For two years, I worked very hard and helped create their visual image."

Rodgers introduced Barson to a less conventional world outside of his usual frames of reference. "Mike and I used to see Throbbing Gristle with Genesis P. Orridge and Cosey Fanny Tutti," remembers Rodgers. Throbbing Gristle were a defiantly avant garde collective who more-or-less invented a whole sub-genre of music labelled Industrial; it's hard to think of a band further removed from Madness, although it's clear that Mike was inspired by the do-it-yourself ethos of that era. "Punk did influence them in that way," agrees Rodgers,"as well as the humour. I think one of the reasons Mike wanted to go out with me was because I was a punk: I was one of the first in north London; people literally screamed when I walked down the street with pink and blue hair. So there was a fascination with it. But punk was a bit art school, it took courage. And the guys in Madness were resolutely 'non poofter', very male in their style. In a way, they were quite straight."

Barson was already too accomplished a pianist to be totally convinced by the Sex Pistols et al. "I like it when people know what they're doing," he told *Uncut* magazine. "For that reason I never really liked punk that much. I loved the spirit of rebellion, the kicking over of statues, but I missed the musicianship. It reminded me of when I was doing my foundation course at Hornsey Art School – the way in which technical skill was frowned upon. The lecturers would be really withering about the students who were good at drawing or painting, which I thought was stupid. I suppose punk was a bit like that." In those days, Barson was as likely to listen to Steely Dan, Abba, The Beatles, 10cc or Supertramp as, say, The Clash.

Even a passing familiarity with the lyrics to Barson's song about Kerstin, 'My Girl' (or 'New Song', as it was originally known), would suggest that the couple didn't always see eye to eye. "We had quite a difficult relationship," Kerstin confesses. "Mike was quite uncommunicative, not emotionally very open. He's the talent and like many talented people, he's got some issues. He had poor social skills, emotionally stilted, but I think it was all gurgling away inside. He could be quite cruel, selfish – not totally relating to how other people might feel. He had an affair with an ex-girlfriend for the first few months of our relationship, which devastated me. That pattern of lying and deceit was very upsetting, but I was madly in love with him!"

The musical backbone of 'My Girl' was initially inspired by hearing Elvis Costello & The Attractions' single 'Watching The Detectives', issued on October 21, 1977. Exactly a week later, Barson went to see Elvis Costello alongside the likes of Nick Lowe and Ian Dury & The Blockheads on the Be Stiff tour at London's Lyceum. "When Steve Nieve did a solo on the Vox Continental, I was just blown away," he later confided to Terry Edwards.*

Barson was still living at home in Crouch End. "I eventually persuaded him to move out from his mum's in 1980. His mum was quite possessive, didn't like me, and wanted to keep her last son at home as long as possible. I'm sure I was a pain, looking like a little punk, but she was hostile to me and called me Araxi, the name of his former girlfriend, the entire time I was with him." Rodgers is adamant about one aspect, though. "That band could not exist without Mike," she states. "Mike was always playing piano, maybe twelve hours a day. He was always tinkering around. All three Barson boys were incredibly talented. Mike was clearly the musical director, the one who created the sound. Lee, for instance, would have had ideas, but Mike would have had the technical ability to make those ideas concrete."

★ ★ ★

Eventually, Suggs was invited to a rehearsal after "they heard me singing at the top of my voice on the way home from the cinema". After drinking

---

* The same opening two-chord sequence that inspired Barson was also borrowed by future Selecter founder Neol Davies for their 2 Tone hit, 'Missing Words'.

vodka with his best friend from school, Andrew 'Chalky' Chalk, Suggs stumbled along to the session and slurred his way through a ramshackle version of Bill Haley & His Comets' rock'n'roll classic, 'See You Later, Alligator', in inebriated fashion. It was enough to win him the role of vocalist. "The only reason I became the singer was because they couldn't find anybody better," he later admitted. "For some strange reason, I drummed at the audition – the shittest drumming ever." Foreman was struck by the youngster's skinhead attire: "The first time I saw Suggs, he had a crop and I thought, who is this young 'whipper snapper'? Where was he in 1969? Probably in his nappies!"

No sooner had the band acquired a new vocalist than Cathal left the band after an argument with Barson when a promised lift home one night never materialised, as detailed in the film *Take It Or Leave It*. Or was it about money? "I was feeling quite used," Barson told *Later*. "Everyone was like, 'drive me home', and I was just the mug driving them. These may be petty things but we didn't communicate very well in those days." By late 1977, Smyth had been replaced by Kerstin's brother Gavin Rodgers.

The question of a name for the group was finally raised after a late night rehearsal session, and Mike's suggestion of "The Invaders" was agreed upon (although they were sometimes billed as "the North London Invaders"). It was presumably inspired by the similarly-named American science-fiction TV series of the late 1960s, which proved popular enough with British audiences to justify endless repeats. Barson even designed a band logo with a flying saucer, in time for their second live performance, which occurred because Mike knew a girl called Evelyn who wanted them to play at her birthday party at Hampstead Town Hall, Hampstead High Street.

Their set that night included 'See You Later, Alligator', 'Feeling So Fine' (which was a cover of the Doctor Bird rock-steady tune by The Gladiators from 1969) and 'Swan Lake', taken from a ska adaptation of the principal theme from Tchaikovsky's ballet which had been a minor hit in 1969 for east London ska combo The Cats (and, under the title 'Saturday Night At The Duck Pond', a smash for UK instrumental band The Cougars in 1963). Suggs' debut performance as vocalist started off well as 'See You Later, Alligator' impressed Hampstead's Teddy boy contingent in the audience. However, the ska- and reggae-influenced numbers prompted a hail of abuse and a shower of empty beer cans – one of which hit Hasler on the head and drew blood.

Barson was undeniably the driving force within The Invaders but his determination was offset by the apparent indifference of other band members, leading to frequent tensions and line-up changes. "I didn't want to be [the leader]," he later admitted. "It was the way it developed. I was always saying, 'We've got to rehearse' and there'd be a lot of whingeing. Me and Chris were the more serious ones. Lee, Carl and Suggs came and went. 'I want to go to football, I want to go to the pub, don't fancy rehearsing.' I felt I had more understanding that you have to do a lot of rehearsing to get from A to B. And with the rest of them being carefree, someone had to push to make it happen. I was a better musician [than the others] in those days. With my brothers playing the piano, I had a head start. Chris and Lee were learning as we went along."

Matters came to a head when Suggs was kicked out of the band for popping off to see his beloved Chelsea FC on Saturday afternoons instead of rehearsing. "They sacked me," Suggs later admitted, "because I wasn't taking it seriously. I was more keen on going to football than I was into music which was difficult because the band were rehearsing on Saturdays and increasingly I would stop coming. In the end, I remember reading *Melody Maker* one day and there was an ad for a singer with Mike Barson's phone number! So I rang him up and he said, 'Yeah, we're getting a bit more professional'!"

Thompson left the band, too, reportedly after Barson criticised his sax playing; he was briefly replaced by Lucinda Garland, the sister of one of Foreman's school friends. Hasler filled in temporarily as singer but vocals patently weren't his forte and by the start of 1978, McPherson was back on the mike. The earliest known footage of The Invaders – which was shown on the *Young Guns* TV documentary – revealed Suggs in a dapper maroon suit, in stark contrast to the scruffy bunch of herberts around him. Suggs had already adopted his characteristically disjointed stage movements. A star had been born – even if no one had realised it just yet.

The Invaders' first paid engagement occurred that February at the City & East London College in Pitfield Street, Hoxton, for a set which included interpretations of The Champs' hit rock'n'roll instrumental, 'Tequila', The Coasters' classic 'Poison Ivy' (later a hit for mod revival band The Lambrettas), 'Feeling So Fine' and 'Swan Lake'. Lucinda Garland then left to attend university ("She was quite posh, I seem to remember, not really the right image for Madness," suggests Kerstin), prompting Thompson's return. Unfortunately, Lee was now living in Luton. On a positive note, this had given him time to practise his sax playing, as he later recalled: "I used to go out the back of the house into the cornfield with a blanket and make a right racket!" He even demonstrated a hitherto undetected degree of commitment by obtaining a WEM amplifier and a microphone stand (the latter a gift from his girlfriend Debbie). But because of the increased travel time from his new home to north London, Thompson was often absent.

Rehearsal sessions had by now escalated to three times a week in various local church halls. Eventually, they found a more permanent setting courtesy of a friend of Mike's called Fiona (Fi Fi) Russell whose father, a dentist, owned an empty house on the Finchley Road. The Invaders were granted regular access to a dark, dusty basement which they cleaned up. Notwithstanding the hundreds of cardboard boxes containing teeth moulds, this venue was important because The Invaders now had a base to store their equipment, where they could rehearse till late into the night – as well as during their regular sessions on Saturday afternoons.

Led by the enthusiastic scribblings of Hasler, the band were now tackling the daunting prospect of songwriting. Gavin Rodgers contributed the music to a Hasler song, 'Sunshine Voice' (which, although never released, was re-created in the film *Take It Or Leave It*). Another Hasler original was 'Rich Girls' – about "all those wealthy people we saw walking around Hampstead who had fridges the size of which you couldn't imagine," according to Suggs. Barson later recalled the moment he felt this process was attainable: "When we were rehearsing in my bedroom in Crouch End, Hasler rushed into the other room and started scribbling down lyrics for 'Mistakes', later a B-side. A couple of minutes later, he'd written these words out. I think that was the first tune we wrote. I thought, if he can do it, anyone can!"

"They were playing a two-chord vamp," explained Hasler to Terry Edwards, "and I just went into the next room and wrote the lyrics." With the initial chord sequence borrowed from Billy Swan's 1974 hit 'I Can Help', Barson duly wrote some music to accompany another example of Hasler's doggerel; the result was 'Believe Me', a Coasters-flavoured number later to appear on Madness' debut album. Hasler was prolific. "Poems, songs, the first two pages of a novel," he later commented. "I'd give lyrics to Mike for him to write the music; he'd change a couple of words, then claim he'd written the whole song!"

April 5, 1978 was the date of The Invaders' next gig – at The Nightingale Pub off Park Road, Crouch End. By all accounts, the performance was positively received – despite (or perhaps because of) complaints about the noise from nearby residents. This time, they added into their set a cover version of a 1963 ska classic, 'Madness' by Prince Buster, helped by the temporary return of Lee Thompson. This might have been the show to which Suggs referred in Terry Edwards' book *One Step Beyond*, when he recalled Dan Barson joining The Invaders onstage for a version of 'Rockin' In A♭'. "All the Bazooka Joe Teddy boy fans were there and our skinhead fans were there and it kicked off a bit. Someone threw a Party Seven [beer tin], which hit John and knocked him out!"

On April 22, the band played an impromptu show at the Rodgers' house to celebrate their father's birthday. But Thompson began to spend more time rehearsing with another band more local to him, Gilt Edge, who played covers of Bruce Springsteen and Bob Dylan. Suggs, too, kept drifting off to see Chelsea play instead of coming to rehearsals and departed the band for a second time.

Undeterred, Barson and Hasler sat in with Gilt Edge at a nearby rehearsal studio. The event was notable for Hasler's vocal rendition of The Animals' hit 'House Of The Rising Sun' – impressive enough for Barson to convince Foreman and Rodgers that John should be given another chance as singer in The Invaders. During a particularly shambolic rehearsal at Hasler's house one afternoon, the vocalist indulged himself by wiring his microphone through a WEM Copycat echo machine (which Chris had borrowed from Gilt Edge), thus giving his voice plenty of reverb for his prolonged performance of 'House Of The Rising Sun'.

It was enough to signal the departure of a frustrated Rodgers, who had aspirations to become a serious musician (he'd invested heavily in a Gibson bass guitar and Marshall amplifier). "To my brother's eternal consternation, Gavin left because he thought they were going nowhere," admits Kerstin. With Hasler now up at the mike again, he suggested as his replacement a drummer friend, Gary Dovey, who was still at school. Dovey, in turn, knew a classmate who played bass, Mark Bedford – quickly nicknamed 'Bedders' by Foreman.

* * *

Born Mark William Bedford on August 24, 1961 in Islington, the young-ster had inherited a love of music from his mother Kathleen A. Lester. She had been born in Islington in 1939 and had married Edward G. Bedford (also born in Islington, 1938) in 1960. Kathleen - or Kathy - was later interviewed for *Smash Hits*. "Mark always liked music," she remembered. "When he was five, he had loads of plastic instruments – a plastic drum-kit and a Beatles' guitar. He was whistling at one year, and when he was five, his favourite record was 'Telstar' by The Tornados. He's always been quite normal really. He never climbed any trees, never got into any fights. Well . . . only once!"

"The first music I ever got into was Motown," Bedford later explained. "That was when I was at primary school. I can remember it on the radio in the morning. Tony Blackburn was on the breakfast show and he was the champion of Motown. Then I lost interest in music until I was about fourteen when someone bought me a plastic record player for my birthday and I started buying the pop songs played on the radio. The first record I ever bought was 'I Can See Clearly Now' by Johnny Nash. About a year later, I got my first musical instrument, a bass to play in a school band. It was just a typical school group doing Beatles stuff, nothing special."

Bedford played in various outfits while still at school, such as Bros Funk. Another band, Ratz, was formed with fellow pupils Will Gosling on drums and Gideon London on guitar, who were known for playing covers such as Free's 'All Right Now'. They would play various gigs with other William Ellis school bands such as Alligator (their lead singer was Tom O'Leary, whose sister dated Suggs for a period). "I got into the blues, stuff from New Orleans, R&B and soul," Bedford told Richard Eddington in *Sent From Coventry*. "And also Steely Dan, Neil Young. Then punk came along and I was a massive Clash fan."

An audition was arranged for Bedford and the band drove him from his flat in Holloway to a plush rehearsal room they'd borrowed the use of from another local band Split Rivett – where they ploughed their way through The Miracles' old Motown classic, 'Shop Around', if the film *Take It Or Leave It* is to be believed. (Possibly the earliest known recording of the band is a rough-and-ready demo of 'Shop Around' aired during a Radio 1 documentary, *Five Years Of Madness*, broadcast in 1984.) Bedders was reportedly impressed by the smart amplifiers and their general air of professionalism, an illusion shattered when he saw the Finchley Road basement.

"I got amazing blisters on my fingers because I had to borrow a bass for the day and it was dreadful," Bedford later commented. "The strings were so far off the neck, they were almost impossible to hold down with two fingers – let alone one. I remember dressing up especially for it as well, making a real effort, and had trouble playing reggae or ska. They'd obviously learnt religiously from the records so they were very good at it. Even then, they held down [the] offbeat and musically it was pretty good. Suddenly I was in the middle of all these blokes who were older than me and acting like complete maniacs. It was really unnerving!"

Despite some initial scepticism from Barson about his tender age, Bedford was invited to join the band. "The first thing that struck me was that Mike was very determined," Mark later recalled. "He was single-minded. He said to me at that first rehearsal, we're gonna make records. And there didn't seem to be any argument about that!" Such ambition would surely have impressed Bedford, who was still enrolled at acclaimed all-boys grammar school William Ellis in Highgate Road, Kentish Town – which backed onto Parliament Hill Fields, Hampstead Heath. Despite its emphasis on practical subjects (its motto was "Rather Use Than Fame"), William Ellis reared a string of artistic alumni during the 1960s and 1970s, including The Stranglers' Hugh Cornwell, Richard Thompson and film director Julien Temple, who would work with Madness on their filmed concert *The Liberty Of Norton Folgate* in 2009.*

Bedford was immediately struck by the band's fashion sense, as he recalled in *Sent From Coventry: The Chequered Past Of Two Tone*: "Suggs wore the more traditional skinhead gear – two tone suits, etc. – but I wouldn't call him a skinhead because he mixed the styles up more. Even then, he had a flat top haircut – Cathal as well. When I knew them from afar, I thought it was great that they wore a mixture of Fifties, Sixties and Seventies clothes that made their own fashion. You couldn't really pigeonhole them. Lee, Chris and Mike's friends had quite a different style. In London at the time, there was a trend of espoused Americana, the

---

* Previous pupils had included actor Andrew Sachs and writer Len Deighton, the cine-matic versions of whose novels would later inspire the Madness hit 'Michael Caine' and accompanying video.

fashions and styles in that film *American Graffiti*. People were wearing base-ball jackets, Fifties-type jackets, then some people would mix it up with Sixties fashions."

As a member of the Common Room Committee, Bedford was able to secure the new-look Invaders' first show at his school on July 3, 1978, for an end-of-term school disco. Alongside their staple cover versions were Hasler's new compositions 'Sunshine Voice' and 'Mistakes' as well as versions of The Coasters' 'Poison Ivy' and 'Giddy Up A Ding Dong', the 1956 rock'n'roll hit by Freddie Bell & The Bellboys. "I'd organised this summer bop myself, a free concert for all the kids in the school," Bedford recalled. "We hired a PA and printed tickets to make it seem like a proper event, and it turned out really well."

Mark's friend and the band's soon-to-be-drummer Daniel 'Woody' Woodgate was in the audience, later describing the show as "dreadful but brilliant – really rough". Woodgate: "They were terrible in most respects, but there was also something really magic about them, really original. I remember being impressed with Bedders, too. In the space of a couple of months, he had gone from being awful to being a really good bassist."

Chris's brother-in-law Phil Payne organised another show at the 3C's Club in Cumberland Square near Warren Street whereby his band, Low Numbers, supported The Invaders – still a five-piece of Barson, Foreman, Dovey, Bedford and Hasler. "Gary was a bit of a punk," remembers Kerstin, "and he kept speeding up. Like The Ramones, their set got shorter and shorter!"

After a spell kicking his heels in a plastering job with Thompson (their incompetence in the role reenacted to great effect in *Take It Or Leave It*), Suggs was ready to re-join. As well as attending their two gigs with John Hasler on vocals, he had even played drums during one rehearsal. While Hasler was on holiday in France, Foreman telephoned Suggs to ask if he would deputise on vocals for a gig which Bedford, now fresh out of school and in gainful employment, had organised for his boss's birthday at his workplace at roller blind factory The Blind Alley in Camden Lock. Their set was notable for the introduction of 'New Song' ('My Girl') with Barson on lead vocals. By all accounts, Thompson was heard to heckle, "Where's the sax player?"

. Actually, Thompson soon found himself back with The Invaders, but during an abortive attempt to play the Kilburn & The High Roads' song

'Rough Kids', the saxophonist attacked Dovey, graphically re-enacted in *Take It Or Leave It*. The drummer duly quit, claiming he "can't work with this madman". Around this time, the lads auditioned a black drummer named Eddie Josephs. According to John Hasler, Josephs wasn't keen on the position: "You guys play too much reggae," was his response. Eventually, Woodgate heard of the vacancy. "So I just got on the phone to Bedders and said that I'd heard they wanted me to join," Woodgate later explained. "Of course, that was the first that he'd heard of it but he invited me along to a rehearsal!"

* * *

Born in Paddington, London on October 19, 1960, Daniel Mark Woodgate and his younger brother Nicholas Leslie (born 1962) were brought up in Maida Vale then Camden largely by his father Crispian, an upper middle-class photographer who had married Anne Clare Ogden in Oldham in 1959; both parents had attended RADA (the Royal Academy of Dramatic Art) in London. Born on April 13, 1935, Crispian Roger Woodgate captured much of the British acting elite during the Fifties and Sixties (Ralph Richardson, Roy Kinnear, Peter Cook, Albert Finney, Sir Ian McKellen). He also organised the cover shot for folk singer/guitarist Davy Graham's highly regarded 1964 album, *Folk Blues And Beyond*, as well as a famous photograph of Rolling Stones manager Andrew 'Loog' Oldham sitting with bare feet, sticking two fingers up at the camera, which was used on the covers of his autobiographies in 2001 and 2003.

Prior to that, Crispian had been an actor; he was also the photographer featured in the 1969 movie *Crossplot*, starring Roger Moore. While he enjoyed a glamorous life mixing with the cognoscenti, he wasn't always that wealthy. To celebrate the fiftieth anniversary of the Mini car, Joanna Lumley recounted this anecdote to author Christy Campbell: "A wonderful photographer called Crispian Woodgate found he couldn't pay me back £120 I had lent him," she said. "Would I accept his Mini instead? I would!"

"Both my grandfathers were musicians," Daniel explained, "both conductors, one working for the BBC in London, the other with big bands in Blackpool." Woodgate's grandfather on his mother's side, Erik Ogden, was in-house conductor at Blackpool Opera House, playing host across the 1950s and early 1960s to the likes of Gracie Fields, Marlene Dietrich,

Eartha Kitt, Shirley Bassey, Billy Eckstine, Max Bygraves, Alma Cogan and Petula Clark.

Daniel's grandfather on his father's side was Hubert Leslie Woodgate. Born in 1900 in London, Leslie studied in Westminster and at the Royal College Academy of Music. He was the first-ever conductor in 1931 of the BBC Theatre Orchestra, a precursor to the BBC Concert Orchestra; from 1934, he was BBC Chorus Master, consolidating a reputation as one of the foremost choral trainers in the country. During the 1930s, he was also Musical Director to the London and North Eastern Railway Musical Society which had several male voice choruses; and he not only wrote music but created numerous arrangements. Leslie was honoured with the OBE and made an Associate of the Royal College of Music. Having married Lena Mason in 1926, the couple reared one son, Crispian, who eventually married Anne Ogden, before settling in London. Sadly, Leslie died six months before his grandson Nicholas' birth.

Without the domestic influence of their mother, the lads lived a life of bohemian indulgence – they even went to see Chelsea FC with Monty Python star Eric Idle and noted sports writer Hugh McIlvanney – and grew up to be teenage hippies. "I moved into Camden in 1965, a little road called Stratford Villas, which is quite central," he told *Later*. "It used to be a real Greek and Irish community and the biggest shop in Camden Town was the Co-op on the High Street."

"My dad earned very good money," remembered Woodgate in *The Word*. "We lived in a huge six-bedroom house in Camden. But I still went to one of the roughest schools." Daniel attended Haverstock Secondary School in Chalk Farm. "When I first went there, a teacher had been stabbed to death with a woodwork chisel," he told *Later*. "Education was whatever lesson you decided to go to. So I chose Art and Music. I ended up doing a lot of drumming. In the latter years, my mate and I used to go to Steve Hillage concerts, take the music teacher and get him stoned. My favourite was the Spanish teacher. One day, he told us to write some poetry about childhood, so I went home and found this obscure Elton John record, copied the words and gave it in. And all he did was write 'Bernie Taupin' at the bottom!"

Daniel took up his instrument of choice at a tender age. "I got my first drum set when I was about twelve," he later explained. "An old mate sold me a really ropey kit for a fiver. It was held together with sellotape and wires and the cymbals sounded like dustbins! But I used to practise on it for hours in the bedroom with my brother helping out on guitar." Brother Nick was considered extremely gifted but was diagnosed with schizophrenia early in his teens. "I grew up with him as the great genius, the child prodigy," Woodgate told Andrew Harrison.

Between 1974 and 1976, while still at school, Dan played in a band with the dubious monikers of Steel Erection and later Alive Or Dead, alongside Nick, singer Robert Verburgt and West Hampstead-based pianist Michael McEvoy from William Ellis School. "I was born in the States but came here in '73," explains Mike (who was later in Ian Dury's backing band The Music Students, who once shared a bill with Madness, before becoming an award-winning screen composer, orchestrator and multi-instrumentalist). "Nick and Dan were involved in music from a very early age – as was I. Nick was an incredibly talented musician. Robert was a Dutch guy who lived in Surrey."

The band's style slowly evolved: "It was basically a real headbanging rock group," remembered Woodgate. "Then we progressed to classier jazz-funk stuff. It was around that time that I first met Mark Bedford, who used to come along for the odd jam session." Michael McEvoy: "We'd have a lot of fun jamming – this was when the Woodgate brothers were living with their mum in Maida Vale. I played guitar and bass – me and Nick used to switch on certain songs. We were into rock and wrote a lot of stuff as well as doing a few cover versions: 'All Right Now' by Free, 'Long Train Running' by Doobie Brothers, 'Sweet Home Alabama'. We even did some recordings of our own, amateur stuff."

Verburgt recalls compositions with such titles as 'Daydreaming' and 'Grey Buildings'. "I remember Woody was a steady, rather mature, organised character," says their singer. "A really cool guy. He was a year or two older than us." Steel Erection also performed some low-key shows. "We played at school fairs and community centre do's in Hampstead," says McEvoy. Verburgt remembers one particular performance when things turned sour: "We organised a gig ourselves in Winscombe Street [in Dartmouth Park] and it was 30p for the ticket. Halfway through the set, we were invaded by football hooligans who went on a rampage. Everybody was fighting or scrambling away, running for their lives. It was terrifying!" McEvoy also recalls the invasion: "Nick's father took photographs. But a bunch of kids just trashed the place and beat the hell out of everyone. Dan and Nick are quite middle class with an arty background. We were not like 'street' people." Although Nick wasn't able to pursue a career in music, he was later credited as co-writer of the Madness song 'No Money'.

Like many other hippies, Daniel experimented with hallucinogenics. "The drugs were better then," he explained in matter-of-fact fashion in *Later*. "I defy anyone to recreate the acid that was around in the early seventies, just for the sheer strength of it. I don't take acid any more but the last time I did it was pathetic." Smyth, too, admitted to a teenage dalliance with LSD: "Different drugs were prevalent then like blues and acid – you still got microdots then rather than blotting paper. And dope! You could get Lebanese Gold. The hippies were much more discerning."

Although he didn't know any of the band, the drummer was already aware of Thompson. "I'd heard about Lee, the way he'd leapt on Gary Dovey and didn't like drummers, so I was a bit nervous about meeting him," he admitted. "Especially as I knew him because he went to Haverstock School – or should I say, he visited Haverstock occasionally and bunked over the wall!"

Woody later described his recruitment into The Invaders, during a rehearsal in which they ran through 'Rockin' In A♭': "I was picked up by Mike Barson in his van. 'Alright mate, get ya drums, is this it?' So we bunged them in the back and it was like, what a nice fellow! Mike doesn't go, 'Hello, how are you? Nice to meet you.' He's more like, 'Alright'. Anyway, we got to rehearsals and Chrissy Boy just looked at me, nodded and never spoke to me the whole session. I think Lee turned up and just stood in the corner. It was a real weird atmosphere. I thought, what have I let myself in for? Mike kept going on that he'd put an advert in the *Melody Maker* for a drummer: 'Well, I dunno yet mate, we gotta wait and see, I've spent me money.' He definitely wanted to hear if there were other drummers first!"

Woodgate's image and musical tastes were at polar opposites to that of The Invaders, with their close crops, skinhead/rockabilly attire and love of old ska and R&B. "They were like unsociable hard nuts," he later admitted. "I knew Bedders because we both knew two [guys] Martin and Laurie [whose] house was the type of place you could set up amps and drum kits and make a right racket and they didn't have neighbours who complained. Mark came from a world I understood. We were more on the same wavelength: we weren't hardened skinheads with criminal records!"

After extensive rehearsals, Woodgate became a fully-fledged member of The Invaders, although he was instructed to get his shoulder length hair cut and also encouraged to simplify his drumming technique, which was initially influenced by the busy, improvisational style of Seventies jazz rock. "There is a misconception with me," he later complained. "My musical tastes were really diverse. I was into Gong, Steve Hillage, John McLaughlin, Mahavishnu, Jeff Beck, Herbie Hancock, but equally I was a kid of the Seventies so I loved Bowie, Bolan, T. Rex, Roxy, Alice Cooper. I wasn't into soul or reggae. But I did love the glam rock stuff – Mud, Sweet. I loved intricate jazz fusion, and who didn't like 'Whole Lotta Love'? I was a big Eno fan, too. When I joined, it was a revolution in my musical taste. I'd heard of Bob Marley but I'd never really heard much Motown or Ian Dury."

Woodgate's playing style was learnt from records unknown to the rest of the band. "If you listen to Jeff Beck's albums *Wired* or *Blow By Blow*, the drummer has a wonderful technique where he drags the left hand, soft rolls," he explained. "I loved Pierre Moerlen from Gong, Narada Michael Walden, Billy Cobham, but they filled every gap on the planet. When I first joined, I'd fill the gaps with fancy rolls and triplets on the bass drum. Pete Thomas from the Attractions said, 'Why don't you do more of what Simon Kirke does in Bad Company? Solid as a rock, hardly any fills,' . . . and that suited the band better. When someone said I sounded like Charlie Watts, I was offended. But I was young. Later, I appreciated the simpler style of drumming because it allows the music to breathe. Mike used to get frustrated, kick me off the drum kit and try to play what he thought I should play!"

Woodgate was a middle-class lad. Indeed, their myriad upbringings puts paid to the myth of Madness' blue-collar image. "Oh, they're not working class at all," agrees Kerstin. "The nearest was Lee Thompson. He was the rough side but they needed him to lend authenticity. He was very creative but he didn't have the advantages that someone like Mike had. He didn't come from a middle-class background, with the education. They were always on the outskirts, though. Chris lived on a council estate in Kentish Town. Some of them came from Gospel Oak which, in those days, was quite rough. Mark was always a bit of an outsider. His parents were quite genteel."

Kerstin Rodgers was privy to the inner workings of the band. "The big rivalry was Lee and Mike, because they knew each other the longest," she admits. "They were constantly at loggerheads – and Cathal, too – competing all the time. Suggs was the child of a single mother and that was still quite unusual – it marked you out a bit. Suggs was the leader by virtue of being the singer but not on a musical level. With all these tempers and egos, you needed calm people: Mark, Chris and Woody. Chris was a mediator, quite kind. Mark and Woody were younger, less competitive than the others; they brought a stabilising effect. They weren't constantly challenging for the top spot. It's like a family: you might get terrible sibling rivalry between the oldest then there's a gap and the younger ones have a different relationship. Even Suggs, who'd joined later, didn't quite have that problem: he was very genial and didn't have confrontations."

For a couple of months during the winter of 1978, Barson and Rodgers upped sticks to live in a squat with Si Birdsall's brother Jesse. "I was always getting kicked out of home," admits Kerstin. "I'd stayed the night with Mike and my parents were sick of me not coming home, so they put all my belongings in black bin bags – that's why I had to find this squat in Royal College Street in Camden, almost opposite Swanky Modes, the retro fashion shop on the corner. It was bloody freezing; we had to burn everything to get the fire lit. I saved my money to buy pink and black paint for the walls. We lived on porridge and kebabs bought from across the road."

Having returned from his holidays to find Suggs now on vocals, Hasler was appointed as manager. His role in the embryonic days of The Invaders should not be underestimated – in fact, it's questionable whether Madness would have evolved without him. "There were maybe three camps in the band," Bedford told Terry Edwards. "Lee, Chris and Mike all knew John Hasler, the massive link between us all. John was two years above me at school. He also knew Woody." Hasler spent much of his time out and about around London, seeing bands and making useful contacts.

By now, Thompson had overcome his flighty nature, having declined an offer – along with Mike – to work on North Sea Oil rigs, in favour of pursuing his dream with the band. Also, he had settled into a flat with Debbie on Caledonian Road, King's Cross. In due course, Hasler secured The Invaders a show at the Acklam Hall (underneath the Westway flyover just off the Portobello Road in west London) on November 10, 1978, on a shared bill with The Valves and The Tribesmen. It was their first engagement with the final line-up of six members that would become Madness.

Their set-list now boasted an early rendition of their future hit, 'Grey Day', as well as 'Swan Lake', 'Madness' and 'In The Middle Of The Night'. Despite the unwelcome distraction of some particularly vicious fighting in the audience, the band noticed that former Sex Pistol Glen Matlock was at the show. More important to their future development in the audience that night was Glen's mate Clive Langer, who had made his name as a musician in Liverpool band Deaf School (who were much admired by members of The Invaders). Legend has it that when Langer asked the ex-Sex Pistols bassist what he thought of the band, Matlock said: "I can't hear the songs, Clive."

Chapter 4

THEY CALL IT MADNESS

DESPITE his associations with Liverpool, the producer who was to take Madness under his wing actually shared a similar geographical background. Born June 19, 1954 in Hampstead, Clive Langer had lived in north London until he was 16, attending William Ellis School in Kentish Town, where he befriended fellow pupil Ben Barson. "My first memory of Mike was of this little kid who was good at art and also pretty good on the piano," Clive told *Uncut* magazine. "He used to hang around in a gang, who looked really good – kind of glam mods, spray-painted DM boots, 501s." When Langer was in his early teens, his family relocated to Liverpool, which is where he ended up attending art college.

Later, Langer was briefly a member of The Portsmouth Sinfonia (founded by composer Gavin Bryars and produced by Brian Eno); the orchestra required members who were either non-musicians or who played an instrument that was entirely new to them, an experience which inspired an important do-it-yourself/experimental ethic in Langer way before punk. By 1975, Langer was busy as a musician with Deaf School. This collection of creative misfits somehow got lost in between glam rock and punk and yet their arch mix of pub rock and art school intellect won them a loyal cult following. Signed to Warner Brothers by one-time Beatles publicist Derek Taylor in 1976 after winning the annual Rock/Folk Contest sponsored by *Melody Maker*, the band swiftly found an ally in the head of Warner Music Publishing, Rob Dickins.

Born in Amsterdam but raised in Ilford, Essex, Dickins had joined Warner Publishing as a graduate from Loughborough University in 1971. Three years later, a week before his 24th birthday, he was appointed managing director – and went on to build Warner Music into one of the UK's most profitable publishing companies. His astute acquisitions included hits like Johnny Bristol's 'Hang On In There Baby' (his first signing) and acts as diverse as the Sex Pistols and Chic to developmental, longer-term relationships with such respected names as Prince and Vangelis.

Despite such achievements, Dickins yearned to work more closely with artists. "I found publishing OK but I had a latent desire to be a producer," he confesses. "So when Warner Brothers signed Deaf School in 1976, I liked them so I signed their publishing. They went to Muff Winwood to produce them but the tracks didn't capture who the band were. I said, I think I know what to do. So as a complete novice, I went into the studio and I ended up producing Deaf School's first two albums. I got really friendly with Clive Langer and Steve [Allen] and Anne [Martin]. We weren't much different in age: I was maybe 26 and they were 21/22. Particularly with Clive, we'd go and see bands, stay up late and just talk about music."

NME journalist and author Paul Du Noyer was a noted supporter. He wrote: "In the whole history of Liverpool music, two bands matter most: one is The Beatles and the other is Deaf School. After the pop revolution of the 1960s led by The Beatles, it looked as if the city's music scene had dried up forever. But in 1975, a motley band of Liverpool art students were the catalyst for the most dramatic revival since Lazarus. Their impact on the city is with us to this day."

"We saw Deaf School regularly because they were so theatrical," Thompson told Terry Edwards. "That's what drew me to a lot of bands – Kilburn & The High Roads, Sha Na Na, Rocky Sharpe & The Replays. When we used to play the Hope & Anchor, I used to Frisbee out old ska singles and throw pork pies into the audience. I had a tie which lit up, too (unashamedly nicked from the Kilburns). Do something more than just playing music, make it a bit more visual – that was an integral part." As such, disparate acts as Alice Cooper and Split Enz also appealed.

Deaf School shared that definite sense of the theatrical with acts like Kilburn & The High Roads and Alex Harvey – fellow travellers with a touch of anarchy about them who were adrift in the meandering sea of mid-1970s pop. The sense of a bizarre, multitudinous gaggle of misfits onstage had a subliminal effect on The Invaders. For Barson & Co., The Sensational Alex Harvey Band's music perhaps veered towards rock orthodoxy but their style was eclectic and unpredictable, tackling the Jacques Brel song 'Next' (its mention of soldiers sleeping with prostitutes was a probable influence on Lee Thompson's 'Razor Blade Alley') in dramatic, near-vaudevillian fashion. And Harvey's stage costume even referenced *A Clockwork Orange*. "Alex Harvey is definitely in this mix," agrees Robert Elms. "It's aggressive and confrontational but it's also theatrical – 'Vambo' and all that. Harvey would come onstage in a bowler hat, eye make-up, and that feeds directly into what Madness became."

Deaf School recorded three albums and toured England and America before eventually disbanding in 1978. "They were lauded but when punk happened, they were part of the old scene, thrown out with pub rock," admits Dickins. "We all felt Deaf School was something special and when it didn't happen, it was quite tough. But I remember Malcolm McLaren in my office picking up a Deaf School album and going, it's just as bad being too early as being too late! Clive got obsessed with punk and wanted to be in The Clash. I think he played in The Slits for a moment and then formed his own punk band, Big In Japan, as an alter-ego for Deaf School, with a bunch of people from Liverpool."

In hindsight, Big In Japan were a supergroup in the making. Among their floating line-up were guitarist Bill Drummond, who would soon found Zoo Records and, much later, The KLF; David Balfe, co-founder of Zoo, who joined Teardrop Explodes; Ian Broudie, who became a successful producer and founder of Lightning Seeds; drummer Budgie, who subsequently made his name in Siouxsie & The Banshees; and 17-year-old bassist Holly Johnson, would later front Frankie Goes To Hollywood. "Clive did Big In Japan's first single then they came to me," adds Dickins, "so I produced them for Zoo Records. Clive said to me, 'That's what I want to do. How do I become a producer?' I said, 'You find a band you love that will let you produce them.' That's what I did with Deaf School."

"When I'd come to London with Deaf School and play the Roundhouse, I'd see Mike and his mates watching us," recalled Clive in *Uncut*. "They'd meet up backstage and tell me that they were starting a band called The North London Invaders, and asked if I wanted to check them out."

* * *

The Invaders had deliberately set themselves apart from the usual run-of-the-mill pub bands – in terms of both their sound and their wardrobes. A mix of rockabilly, mod and skinhead apparel was strongly influenced by the plethora of shops and stalls around Camden and Kentish Town specialising in old clothes and records. "I was talking to Jerry [Dammers] about that," Suggs later recalled. "It was trying to find a way of expressing ourselves that wasn't just what everyone else was doing. Now, retro is so . . . retro! Then, it was a new thing, finding a Coasters album or some old songs that nobody had heard for years. To collect Prince Buster, you really had to search them out. People would be really excited if they found a record. Now, it's an industry. But in those days, all sorts of enthusiasts started to appear out of the woodwork. Rediscovering things that had been forgotten."

Their next show – at Middlesex Polytechnic – was disappointing not least because the band were pulled off after running over time. But as each member was plucked from the stage by a Student Union steward, observers could see that the band's friends Andrew 'Chalky' Chalk and Ian 'Toks' Tokins (Madness' future roadies) helped them back onstage. By all accounts, a friend and follower all but demolished the toilets which led to the band being blamed for what was perceived to be a wanton act of vandalism.

On New Year's Day 1979, The Invaders played at the London Film Makers Co-op (or LFMC) in Gloucester Avenue, Camden, sharing the bill with The Russians, The Nips (featuring future Pogues frontman Shane McGowan) and The Millwall Chainsaws. Barson detailed the show in his diary: "We supported The Russians. Everyone went home after we played. Left The Russians owing some money to the PA. Lots of snow around."

At this point, the band might best have been described as semi-pro, earning money from odd jobs elsewhere. According to Stuart Wright in his superbly-researched fanzine *Nut Inc.*, Barson had a stint as a lorry driver (delivering bananas), Bedford still had his job as an apprentice silk screen printer, and Thompson and Foreman did the occasional spot of gardening – as did Suggs.

A support slot with the Tribesmen followed on January 7 at the Nashville Rooms in Earls Court – an important west London venue since the height of punk. According to Mike's diary: "[We] got [the] gig through their manager Steve Thomas who would like to manage us. We got cut off halfway 'cause we came on too late." They had met Thomas after the Acklam Hall show; upon hearing that The Invaders wanted to change their name, Thomas's heavily-built sidekick suggested an alternative moniker, "The Iron Bars". Barson & Co. declined both offers.

The band had attempted for some time to secure a gig at Irish boozer The Dublin Castle in Parkway, Camden, as their singer later recalled in *Suggs And The City*. "Having trudged round just about every pub in Camden Town during the winter of 1978–9 in search of a gig, it was with the echo of rejections still ringing in our ears that we entered The Dublin Castle with its red-and-cream exterior and hanging baskets. 'What's your act then, lads?' enquired the genial Irish guv'nor Alo Conlon. 'Erm, we do jazz and a bit of country and western,' I replied . . . Alo took us through the Dublin's red-lit, mock-Tudor bar to the back room, which was used for functions and the occasional bit of live Irish music . . . it was pretty damn impressive, especially the stage, which was made up of sheets of hardboard laid across stacks of beer crates."

They finally got their break at The Dublin Castle as support for ABC (not to be confused with Martin Fry's band), a group who were friendly with Bedford. The historic date was January 16; by this time, The Invaders had attracted a few supporters, a fact which didn't go unnoticed by Conlon. In due course, Madness' legend became synonymous with this pokey yet charismatic venue, summarised thus in *The Independent* in 2005: "The stage is tiny; crammed into the corner of the room, it's an obstacle course of mike stands, guitars, amps and speakers. The venue may not look much, yet to aspiring young bands, the Dublin Castle is indie heaven."

The band often went to see a popular local act, Sore Throat ("Mike and I were fans", says Kerstin). Foreman vaguely knew their keyboard player Matthew Flowers and arranged a support slot with them at Camden's Music Machine on January 22. By this time, they'd heard that Sham 69 singer Jimmy Pursey was planning to start his own record label and he mentioned that he'd already signed a band called The Invaders. Although they were now calling themselves the North London Invaders, a name change was patently necessary. Stories abound of temporary monikers such as the Soft Shoe Shufflers or the Big Dippers but Mike did eventually decide on Morris & The Minors – inspired by the ex-GPO wagon they used as transport. His diary recalled this solitary show under their new name: "Some people said we blew them off stage. We had a good support from the crowd anyway." The show was also notable for providing the first evidence of Smyth's dancing: instead of his usual profile in front of the audience or in the wings, he jumped onstage for an early performance of what became his trademark "nutty dance".

During a rehearsal in February 1979, the band agreed to change their name to Madness.* Legend has it that someone suggested naming the band after one of their songs and Foreman replied, as a joke: "Oh yeah, 'Madness'." To his horror, everyone agreed, probably because their music had taken a different direction over the past few months, more heavily accented towards Sixties ska and rocksteady.

★　★　★

The sextet played their first gig billed as Madness on May 3, 1979, the night that Margaret Thatcher was elected Prime Minister. After constant badgering of the owner John Eichler by Smyth and Birdsall, who lived opposite in Compton Terrace, they'd secured a slot at Islington's famous Hope & Anchor – a vital venue since the pub rock days. "We got the gig by taking a tape around to selected pubs," Cathal later explained. "We told John that we were a band and he didn't believe us! That's the kind of relationship we had! We used to spend a lot of time at the Hope so it seemed the obvious place to play."

Situated at 207 Upper Street, the statuesque, red-brick Victorian boozer was arguably London's most famous music pub and certainly one of the first to host regular rock gigs in the wake of The Tally Ho in Kentish Town. Prior to the mid-1970s, the venue's basement harboured jazz and folk artists but Fridays and Saturdays were eventually given over to pub rock acts. When the Tally Ho changed landlords and swapped rock for Irish showbands, the Hope adopted its mantle as north London's principal venue – coordinated by Fred Grainger and Stiff Records co-founder Dave Robinson.

"The upstairs bar was dominated by at least the most interesting juke-box in London," wrote Chas De Collis, "running a spectrum of sounds from Professor Longhair to Van Morrison to in-demand 'Pub Rock'

---

* Some sources suggest they'd actually adopted their new name in time for that previous show on January 22.

singles." Down in the black, smoke-filled cellar, a motley collection of students, rock fans and drinkers could witness The Stranglers, Graham Parker & The Rumour, Dr Feelgood, Steve Gibbons Band or The Kursaal Flyers. In January 1976, the Albion Management and Agency took over the tenancy under the auspices of landlord John Eichler, who organised events like the Front Row Festival in 1977, recorded and subsequently issued as a double album.

In *Suggs And The City*, the singer recalled their days at the Hope & Anchor. "The basement bar was smaller than the Dublin and held no more than fifty people," wrote Suggs. "We'd been going to the Hope long before we made a ripple on the local scene because the choice of music on the old Wurlitzer was the best in town . . . John allowed us to put our own selection of ska and Motown on it, and the Hope became our unofficial HQ."

A laconic character, Eichler recalled his first meeting with Madness on Suggs' *This Is Your Life*: "Like everybody, they seemed to have a demo tape and after a couple of months, I listened to it and it was quite reasonable – not brilliant. We didn't have anybody on that Sunday so we bunged them on." Suggs picked up the story: "I must admit, John was very kind. I think we got paid £40. You have monitors at the front to hear your sound and I accidentally put my foot through mine, which came to exactly £40! But John, out of the goodness of his own heart, gave us £20 between us because he couldn't see us go home starving!"

In due course, they also adopted the alter ego of "The Nutty Boys". "It came from Lee, I think," Mike recalled. "He came to rehearsals and had written 'That Nutty Sound' with bleach on a denim jacket which looked smart, cool, and everyone was impressed. He coined that idea." In the 1984 TV documentary *South Of Watford*, Smyth explained how they used the phrase when trying to secure a deal: "There's a little Xeroxed piece of paper which we used to send out to record companies and it said, six musicians have been practising in secret and have finally mastered the nutty sound – that's where it came from."

★ ★ ★

By now, Madness's live set gravitated towards ska, rocksteady and early reggae classics of old – which they chose in favour of the contemporary reggae beloved of punk bands like The Clash and The Ruts. "We used to love Linton Kwesi Johnson and Bob Marley", Suggs later admitted. "But we found the righteous, Rastafarian stuff out of our league in terms of burning down Babylon. No one else was doing ska so we found our niche. Punk bands were doing contemporary reggae but it seemed to me not as realistic as us just playing the songs that we liked. The political message of Rastafari wasn't necessarily as clear for us as it was for punk rockers – maybe they felt more of an affinity with it. I don't doubt there was an idea of rebellion but the rebellion was downtrodden black people uprising against colonial white people. So I totally understood it but it didn't resonate for us. [But] we loved the attitude of people who smoked dope and wouldn't just sit around in a huddle in their bedroom, they'd be bowling down the street."

"We grew up together so our musical tastes were aligned," Mike later explained. "That was a part of the forming of the band. Also, that was a golden period in reggae music. We were listening to Bob Marley but reggae then [in the late 1970s] wasn't as good, I didn't think, as the older stuff. It was more about the producers. There were stars, of course, in Jamaica but it was more of a team thing."

Too much has been made of Madness' debt to Jamaican music, with many rock history books (especially those written in North America) pigeonholing them as a "ska revival band". Nevertheless, they were patently huge fans of the genre and clearly indebted to it. "Lee was an avid collector of Blue Beat records," said Suggs, recalling Thompson's assortment of 45s which he kept in a biscuit tin. "But we all liked that music. There was a stall in Berwick Street market which had loads of Blue Beat singles, and that's how I started getting into it. Prince Buster's 'Madness' was one I particularly liked as it was a twelve-bar, but not quite, and it had a nice lyric which I thought would suit us as a band. More apposite was that when we played it live, it was definitely going down better [than rock'n'roll]. So, bit by bit, we played more ska."

Bedders confirmed this: "It was due to Mike's older brother and his friend buying old ska records. Mike liked some punk stuff but it wasn't a great influence." In *Suggs And The City*, the singer bemoaned the passing of Berwick Street as a central hub for old vinyl. "By the time I was seventeen, my collection of Blue Beat singles had grown to a couple of hundred and a fair proportion of these 45s were by Prince Buster."

"It's funny how street music went to the West Indies for its buzz," suggests Stiff Records boss Dave Robinson. "Punk went to reggae/ska with The Clash. All of Madness played with these tracks. They'd played 'See You Later, Alligator' or whatever but mainly ska was their total interest. Ska was the underground before it became the overground. So where drum and bass or dubstep or whatever is the underground now, to them, that was the underground – some regurgitation of mods, who were into ska and Tamla."

Lee Thompson: "All the band other than Woody were brought up on a diet of Jamaican and Motown music. Mike was more interested in the ruder side of reggae (like 'Wet Dream' and 'Wreck A Pum Pum'). It was easy to play as well. We did start off playing Coasters and Fats Domino covers but these were slowly replaced as the reggae/ska interest grew. 'Walk On By' and 'Lover Please' were suggested by Mike and tried out but later dropped for more uptempo numbers for the dance element."

Suggs later described this period as one of his happiest: "I was hanging around with a group of great guys and we were all leaders of contingents in the same area so we were all aware of each other. The idea that we could become a collective became a potent thing. I remember we were kind of stars already and that it didn't really matter whether we were successful with the band or not. In our own little universe, it was already happening. We had our own records on at the Hope & Anchor, our own scene."

A string of pub gigs followed thick and fast. On May 4, 1979 Madness were back at the Nashville Rooms. Barson's diary recorded the event as having "lots of bright light but not much else". Less well attended was their own show at The Windsor Castle, Harrow Road. The story goes that Thompson asked the largest thug in the venue, who was playing pool, to collect the money – the result being 50p. "Nearly empty lost £20 for PA," commented Barson. His May 19 entry was more telling: "Mentioned by *Melody Maker* that The Specials are one of the few bands to play ska! They haven't even seen us!"

It was a pivotal moment for Madness. While they could never be described as a ska band in its purest sense, the influence of Prince Buster's music – and Sixties and early Seventies Jamaican music generally – helped to define their identity. Here was another band which seemed to draw on those very same tunes: The Special A.K.A. The brainchild of Jerry Dammers, this Coventry collective already had a clear vision about how vintage Jamaican music could be appropriated and combined with the energy of punk to forge something new.

* * *

Born in India on May 22, 1954, Jeremy David Hounsell Dammers had an itinerant childhood before his family settled in Coventry in 1965. As a youth, he is known to have rebelled against the straitjacket of the formal, religious upbringing imposed by his father, who was a church minister. While the Reverend Dammers' teachings seem to have informed Jerry in terms of his moral and political views (not least his abhorrence of racism), the teenager got into trouble both at the prestigious King Henry VIII School which he attended and with the authorities. He despised his enrolment in the choir and abandoned piano lessons when he was 13. Legend has it that his famous gap-toothed expression stemmed from an accident which occurred while riding his bicycle; and by the time he'd left King Henry VIII with the one Art O-level later immortalised in The Specials' song 'Rat Race', Dammers had more importantly been schooled in the youth subcultures of the day (mod, hippie, skinhead).

A more stable period followed at art college in Nottingham and then Lanchester Polytechnic, where he met fellow art student Stephen 'Horace' Panter and spent his time making animated cartoons. Thereafter, Dammers played in a variety of local bands and met Coventry's answer to soul singer Geno Washington, Ray King, as well as budding musicians like Neol Davies and Charley Bembridge (later in The Selecter), Silverton Hutchinson and future Specials guitarist Lynval Golding and drummer John Bradbury. They'd congregate at the Holyhead Youth Club to develop their musical talents in bands like Pharaoh's Kingdom (a ska band fronted by Ray King), The Transposed Men and soul band Nite Trane (again with King).

These bands had fizzled out by the time punk had emerged in late 1976. Dammers began writing material under the guise of Gerald 'The General' Dankey, experimenting with musical hybrids on Neol Davies's Revox tape recorder and recruiting Panter to help with various demos in a traditional reggae style. The arrival of singer Tim Strickland and then Lynval Golding on guitar completed the band, named The Hybrids, who played a couple of shows at the tail end of 1977. This fertile period led to Davies' recording of a trombone-led instrumental track 'Kingston Affair', with help from producer Roger Lomas and Dammers' flatmate Bradbury; and it laid the groundwork for what would become 2 Tone.

By the end of 1977, Strickland had been ousted in favour of Terry Hall, and with the addition of guitarist Roddy Radiation (born Roderick James Byers) soon afterwards, The Hybrids became the Automatics – or, in due course, The Coventry Automatics to avoid confusion with a similarly-named band who'd signed to Island Records. The band met local DJ Pete Waterman, who paid for some studio time, which yielded a rough-and-ready demo session issued many years later as *Dawning Of A New Era*. Dammers knew The Clash's tour manager, which led to some dates with The Clash on their On Parole tour in summer 1978, third on the bill below Suicide. The band were variously billed as The Coventry Automatics, The Special A.K.A. The Automatics, merely The Special A.K.A. or eventually just The Specials.

Legend has it that Dammers wanted to lure John Lydon into his band now that the Sex Pistols had disintegrated – and tried to send the singer a demo tape. Instead, the cassette ended up in the hands of Clash manager Bernie Rhodes, who acted as their informal advisor for a period. Aside from the recruitment of roadie Neville Staples, the On Parole tour was disappointing for the band – both financially and in terms of the lacklustre audience response. But when Alan Vega from Suicide was attacked at a show in Bracknell by a bunch of right wing skinheads aligned to Sham 69, Dammers felt inspired to counteract such thuggery with a riot of his own, as he explained to *The Guardian*:

"That was the night The Specials' concept was born. I idealistically thought, 'We *have* to get through to these people.' It was obvious that a mod and skinhead revival was coming, and I was trying to find a way to make sure it didn't go the way of the National Front and the British Movement. I saw punk as a piss-take of rock music, as rock music committing suicide, and it was great and really funny, but I couldn't believe people took it as a serious musical genre which they then had to copy. It seemed to be more healthy to have an integrated kind of British music, rather than white people playing rock and black people playing their music. Ska was an integration of the two."

"I got the ska idea from hearing a reggae band in Birmingham called Capital Letters," Jerry commented in 2009. "They did a track called 'Smoking My Ganga', which was dub reggae but had a ska-like rhythm. I was already wearing a shiny blue mod suit and suddenly it all clicked." For much of the rest of 1978, Dammers & Co. were cooped up in Rhodes' dingy rehearsal studios, located in a warehouse in a railway yard building in Chalk Farm Road, Camden – a period which helped sharpen their skills as musicians and, via an ill-fated trip to France, motivated Dammers to write a new song, 'Gangsters'. An attack on the insalubrious, gun-toting characters they'd met after problems at their hotel in Paris, as well as ne'er do wells within the music industry, 'Gangsters' was decidedly more ska-flavoured than their existing material, prompting drummer Hutchinson to leave; he was replaced by John Bradbury.

Influenced by Rhodes' input, Dammers also developed the band's image. A fan of Clash bassist Paul Simonon's dress code, Jerry honed in on a blend of Sixties mod and skinhead, from hand-me-down three-button tonic suits (worn high off the ankle with white socks), to Dr. Marten boots, chunky loafers, Ben Sherman button-down shirts and Fred Perrys. Much of this image was simply a throwback to working-class street culture from a decade before. And many punk-era bands such as Buzzcocks, The Undertones and, with a definite eye for mod, The Jam, had donned Sixties-styled, single-breasted, three-button suits. But Dammers grew fascinated with the idea of "rude boys" (or "rude bwoys"), a term coined to describe a subculture of streetwise, unemployed youths who all but terrorised Kingston, Jamaica across the mid-1960s – their reputation was akin to, say, the Teddy boys of late Fifties Britain. "Rude" was actually another slang term for "cool", and it was the concept of these rebellious teenagers with dapper dress sense, rather than their reputation for violence, which captured Dammer's imagination, fuelled by their mention in dozens of old ska and rocksteady tunes. Dammers evolved his own "rude boy" image to help define The Special A.K.A.

Disenchanted by the abject indifference with which their demos had been treated, Dammers decided to form his own label – optimistically, he dreamed of a new Motown. Having disregarded potential names such as Satik or Underworld for his label, Jerry came up with the name 2 Tone, to define a mix of black ska and white punk. "I designed the 2 Tone label based on the black-and-white sticky tape I used to decorate my bike when I was a mini mod," Jerry recalls, "and also a tracing of Peter Tosh of The Wailers, in the early days when they were trying to imitate The Impressions (an impression of an impression of an Impression!). I named this 2 Tone man Walt Jabsco after a bowling shirt I had bought in Tunisia when I was in Nite Trane, with Neol Davies." This monochromatic silhouette depicted a "rude boy" wearing a pork-pie hat (essentially a trilby with a narrow, or "stingy", brim), sunglasses, white shirt, black suit and tie, white socks and black loafers, within a grid of stark black and white checkerboard.

Having borrowed £700 from a local owner of a second-hand shop, The Special A.K.A. recorded 'Gangsters' at the start of 1979 but there hadn't been enough studio time to complete a B-side. So Jerry asked Neol Davies to dust off his 18-month-old instrumental, which only required a few overdubs. Davies re-named 'Kingston Affair' as 'The Selecter' by The Selecter (a "selecter" being common parlance in Jamaica for a DJ) – and the record was to be presented as a double A-side in Jamaican style as The Special AKA Vs The Selecter. Having pressed an initial batch of 1,500 copies in (or around) April, Dammers turned to Geoff Travis of Rough Trade, probably the most cutting edge London-based independent label of the post-punk era, to enquire about a manufacturing and distribution deal. Travis agreed to manufacture and distribute a further 5,000 copies.

While patently indebted to Prince Buster's classic 'Al Capone', 'Gangsters' was anything but a ska revival record. Its potent mix of eerie keyboards and organ, Terry Hall's deadpan, laconic vocal delivery and the bleak, confrontational lyrics all but defined the spirit of 2 Tone, updating Sixties ska rhythms for a recession-hit Britain still reeling from industrial action and the "winter of discontent". Via a former Lanchester Polytechnic lecturer, Alan Harrison, Dammers was put in touch with Rick Rogers, who had his own management agency, Trigger (whose clients included The Damned), while also working for two of the biggest independent labels of the period, Stiff and Chiswick. After being impressed both by a Special A.K.A. demo tape, and a live show on home turf in Coventry, Rogers became their manager.

As 'Gangsters' quietly attracted radio airplay from the likes of John Peel, Rogers ushered his charges to London for a string of dates both as headliners (beginning with a poorly attended show at The Hope & Anchor) and as support to major acts of the day, from Rockpile at the Hammersmith Palais to The Damned and the UK Subs at the Lyceum that April. It wasn't long before The Special AKA were the capital's hot ticket, attracting ever growing numbers of A&R men as well as name bands/ musicians like Elvis Costello, The Pretenders and Mick Jagger (who even expressed an interest in signing them).

On May 3, the very same night as Suggs & Co. played their first show billed as Madness, The Specials hosted an historic show at Hampstead's Moonlight Club (an unofficial recording of which was released as a bootleg before finally being issued legitimately). After the gig, Dammers was approached by Chrysalis Records' Roy Eldridge. Despite subsequent counter-offers from Virgin Records, a deal was struck with Chrysalis later that month – based around 10 singles a year, each with a budget of £1,000 – which would provide 2 Tone with a proper platform to reach a much wider audience.

* * *

"I remember the moment when Madness decided to become a ska band," suggests Kerstin Rodgers. "They'd been playing a mix of ska numbers and some R&B stuff, still finding their direction. But when The Specials came out, with a massive interview in the *NME*, the penny dropped: this was the route to take, expand the ska repertoire. The Specials really helped Madness at the beginning by dropping their name in interviews. Suddenly, the A&R guys were coming to their gigs."

In hindsight, it's intriguing that Madness and The Specials hadn't crossed paths before mid-1979. Several of them were Clash fans – and yet none of them had witnessed the Coventry Automatics' mix of punk and reggae onstage a year earlier. On May 5, 1979 Thompson, Suggs and Smyth attended a Rock Against Racism concert at The Hope & Anchor for a bill which included The Special A.K.A. – and were amazed to see another band updating old ska rhythms. "We had all read about this Coventry band that was playing ska stuff," Bedford admitted to Richard Eddington. "The Specials had been steadily growing at this point and so the gig had been sold out. Knowing John, the governor of The Hope, we fortunately managed to blag our way in."

"They played in the Hope & Anchor that we all drank in," explained Suggs later that year. "We hadn't heard of them really but they were similar to us. Funnily enough, the first thing I had heard about them was a half-page article in the *Melody Maker* paper. I could see they dressed the same as us, in a way. We were using The Hope & Anchor as a focal point, meeting up there regularly, monopolising the jukebox, playing obscure ska and Blue Beat tracks. That night, though, The Specials were fantastic."

After the show, Suggs met with Jerry Dammers, who needed somewhere to stay rather than driving a hundred miles back up the M1. It was a pivotal moment. "He came to stay at my mum's flat that night, and explained he was going to start his own label," Suggs later recalled. "We talked long into the night about pop music and his vision and future that was to be 2 Tone. Pretty momentous. I didn't think at that point it would ever happen." By all accounts, Dammers told Suggs that if ever Madness were interested in making a record, he'd be interested in releasing it on 2 Tone. "They'd heard about us too," added Bedders, "and some arrangement was made to do something the next time they were in London."

"Neol Davies and I went to London for discussions with Geoff Travis at Rough Trade," Jerry explains. "We were intrigued by graffiti around Euston station: 'North London Invaders', 'Chalky', 'Toks' and 'Bird's Egg'. Some time later, I realised this was the work of Madness and their road-crew. They invited me to a gig of theirs at the infamous Hope & Anchor. They had apparently hit on the idea of doing ska themselves. They had a dance which consisted of head-butting each other! They were ropey as hell, still virtually a school band. Obviously, they had to be snapped up for our fledgling label. My idea was that, instead of competing, we should work together with like-minded bands."

On June 1, Madness' show at The Dublin Castle supporting 23 Skidoo prompted Barson to note in his diary that "it was very crowded, lots of unknown punters", suggesting that the word was spreading. Indeed, the gig attracted their very first review in the music press. "All save Barson have closely cropped barnets and look vaguely threatening," wrote Mark Williams in *Melody Maker*. "Suggs is a natural showman, a street level raconteur who keeps up a constant stream of personalised banter with his audience. Vocally reminiscent of Kevin Ayers, his original songs have a strong Blue Beat feel and he's even written one extolling Prince Buster called 'The Prince'. They defy tidy comparisons. Just when you've got familiar with Barson's fairground organ or Thompson's affable knockabout sax, the former careens into 'Tears Of A Clown' or the latter has a crack at 'Hall Of The Mountain King' as if Grieg had written it after cranking up a gram of sulphate."

Williams seemed nonplussed, variously comparing Madness to the shambolic punk rock of Johnny Moped, the pub rock shuffle of Terry Dactyl & The Dinosaurs and even the garage punk swagger of The Seeds – while also arriving at the inescapable fact that Madness had something unique. "By the third encore, half the punters were jumping on tables waving clenched fists and the other half were reeling about the glass strewn floor jolly pissed," he wrote, seemingly bemused. "Catch Madness supporting the Special A.K.A. at The Nashville next week and you may find yourself similarly disposed."

It's likely this was also the first Madness show witnessed by Dammers and Horace Panter, prior to The Specials embarking on a two-week tour. The Nutty Boys had already made their mark on the venue, as Jerry later recalled: "I remember seeing 'Chalky n Suggs ov Chelsea' scraped into toilet doors and on walls." Panter concurred: "I had originally seen their name carved on a toilet door. That was my first introduction to Madness!"

"We handed Jerry a demo of 'The Prince'," Foreman later explained, referring to Thompson's ode to Prince Buster which he'd recently penned at Smyth's house. "We thought it was awful but I guess he must have liked it . . ." Jerry shared the Madness guitarist's reservations, though: "The demo they gave me was really, really bad. There was no record company going to sign them at the time in their career except 2 Tone. I did see the potential . . ."

Suggs had agreed to Dammers' open-handed request to share the bill with The Specials, even though Madness were already booked to return to The Dublin Castle that evening for their new Friday night residency slot – which the band felt was vital. Years later, Suggs compared this period to The Beatles' time in Hamburg ("except without the girls!"). This double-booking on June 8 required a frantic drive halfway across London, prompting a reconstruction in *Take It Or Leave It*. Although their audience was growing, the Nashville show was the first occasion on which they'd witnessed the first murmurings of fans adopting the 2 Tone "look" wholesale – indeed, the show was sold-out and many fans were turned away. "It was amazing," commented Woodgate. "Everyone was in all the suits and the whole gear. A massive great room full of Mikes and Suggss and Lees!"

By 1979, Clive Langer was fronting a new act, The Boxes, who featured his old school friend Ben Barson. It seems likely that Ben convinced Langer to go see his younger brother's band – and Langer was captivated. "They were the best dressed kids from north London and they were Deaf School fans," Langer later explained to author Daniel Rachel. "I offered my services to aid their recording career." The budding producer attended a rehearsal, as he recounted to *Uncut*: "You could tell this was potentially brilliant. A lot of the elements were already there. Woody was obviously a good drummer and Mike a great rock piano player, really hitting his piano hard. The rest of the band was a bit rough around the edges, but were all nearly there. Mike was singing 'My Girl' at that first rehearsal, which didn't sound right."

Langer was still keen to pursue his ambitions behind the mixing desk and mentioned his intentions to Rob Dickins, who was by now International Vice President of Warner Music: "Clive said, 'I've found a band I want to produce.' I was thrilled. We were really close friends. He said, 'They're called Madness, they're sort of like The Specials,' who were the hot A&R thing at the time. He said they were fabulous, that they had humour and an energy that he loved and he thought he could capture it. I'd seen bits in the music papers saying they were a Specials rip-off, quite demeaning, so I said, 'Are you sure?' He said, 'Yes. He'd seen other things but Madness was special.'"

Chapter 5

BUSTER HE SOLD THE HEAT

O N June 16, 1979 Madness headed for Pathway Studios, a small eight-track facility in Highbury, north London where Elvis Costello had recorded his debut album, *My Aim Is True*. Once again, this momentous occasion was re-enacted in *Take It Or Leave It*, not least the incident when Woody – who was following the band's Morris van on his new motorbike – sped off in the wrong direction which meant the session had to be re-booked. But Langer and the band had exhausted what money they had. Dickins then agreed to fund the re-booked session, in which Langer planned to record three tracks with Madness, in return for publishing rights. Eventually, the band had their first proper demo.

"We recorded 'The Prince', 'My Girl' with Mike Barson singing, and 'Madness'," Suggs later remembered. "The Yachts had recorded their first single and Elvis had recorded 'Watching The Detectives' there. It was the beginning. Then Jerry – who'd promised me, if you ever get your band going, then you've got a chance of being on the label – stuck by his word." Langer spent some time on 'The Prince', as he later described to Terry Edwards: "We developed Mike's trademark piano sound which was derived from Thunderclap Newman via Deaf School. We put the upright piano through a chorus effect to make it more out of tune, more honky-tonk. That became part of Madness's sound for the future without anyone realising it."

Rob Dickins: "Clive comes back and said, I need another £20 to do a remix! So I gave him another £20. He comes back with 'The Prince' which Lee had written, 'My Girl', which Mike had written, and 'Madness'. And I went, Clive, 'Madness' is a Prince Buster song! What happened to three songs?!" The following day, Madness visited Dickins who "said he really liked the tape", according to Barson's diary entry. "Clive played me the songs and I thought they were really fantastic," admits Dickins. "I loved 'My Girl' except I didn't like Mike singing. Clive said, 'Well, Mike wrote it about his girlfriend and he wants to sing it.' But I thought 'The Prince' was a hit. Suggs' delivery was special."

Madness' publishing was already bookmarked for Rob Dickins – but their saxophonist still had some nagging doubts. In his book *Ska'd For Life*, Specials' bassist Horace Panter recalls a conversation with Lee Thompson at the Hope & Anchor one night. "Lee Thompson sidled up to me," he wrote, "and asked if I could give him any advice on a publishing deal he'd been offered."

The band themselves had high hopes for 'My Girl' and felt more comfortable with opting for 'The Prince' for 2 Tone. Two days later, Barson wrote in his diary: "Letter from Rob Dickins offering royalty deal. He said lots of companies are interested." Madness explained to Dickins that they'd spoken with Jerry Dammers. "They said The Specials have offered us a deal so we can get this out on 2 Tone," says Dickins. "I said, 'Oh, forget 2 Tone! You don't want to be there as second cousins to The Specials. I know everyone at the major labels. I'll get you a record deal.' So, I went to Warners and they didn't get it. I went to EMI and they didn't get it. I went to all the labels, even including Stiff, and couldn't get them a record deal. So we had a meeting in my office and I sheepishly said, 'I'm broken! This is ridiculous!' I said, 'Do you think 2 Tone would still be up for it?' So they said, 'We'll go and check – yeah, yeah, they're still up for it.' So I said, give them the tapes. And that was 'The Prince'."

"I think the first meeting we had was in The Spread Eagle in Camden Town one lunchtime," Specials manager Rick Rogers later recalled. "We talked about the idea of doing a single with them – in fact, putting out the single that they'd already recorded as a demo. Everyone was very happy with it. The A&R decisions tended to be made by a committee of hundreds and there was no dissension. I think out of all the 2 Tone groups, Madness were probably the closest as friends in the first place which I think was the main reason for their survival." A deal was duly signed in a Greek-Cypriot café in Camden for Madness to join 2 Tone for a one-off single, and manager John Hasler was able to work out of Rogers' offices above Holts Footwear at 5 Kentish Town Road, Camden.

Over the next two days, Barson and Suggs met Tony Stratton-Smith, the boss of Charisma Records, and with Chrysalis Records, to discuss a possible record contract. As Madness endured their first taste of the record company merry-go-round, Barson was more concerned that their regular Dublin Castle show on June 29 felt lacklustre (in fact, they'd play their last show there for the time being on July 6): "Same pub, same group, same price, same songs, it seemed like going through the motions. Felt we should be doing new songs. Bloke from Magnet [Records] bought a round. Lots of dancing, though. No nutty Carl tonight."

* * *

"Nutty Carl" was, of course, Cathal Smyth – alias Chas Smash. Although he hadn't been a fully fledged member of the band since his departure as bass player two years earlier, Smyth had been a loyal supporter of The Invaders and had jumped up onstage during their show at the Music Machine in April.

Later, he described his CV up until this period thus: "Mr Smash left school and worked in the petrochemical industry as a vendor print clerk then an expeditor then junior buyer. He then went on to be a concrete pump operator. Next a brief stint as a window cleaner with L. J. Thompson." By 1979, he was back working in petrochemicals in Ashford on £5.25 an hour – an impressive salary for a teenager in those days. "I used to do agency work, just bullshitting my way from job to job, trying to get a better rate," he later explained.

Subsequently, he had been asked by Thompson to introduce the band when they'd arrived back late after that momentous show with The Specials. By early summer, resplendent in his pork pie hat, Smash was a regular fixture at Madness shows and it's been recorded that his first "official" show was on June 8 at The Dublin Castle. His berserk "nutty dancing" became an integral element of their performances, updating the "skinhead moonstomp" style of the late 1960s. And it was on the train journey from Ashford to London that Cathal penned the immortal line: "Hey you! Don't watch that! Watch this! This is the heavy, heavy monster sound . . ."

"Chas was basically the Robbie Williams – a brilliant dancer, good-looking, tons of charisma," suggests Kerstin Rodgers. "Everybody would be looking at him, even when he was in the audience. In the end, it made sense to have him onstage. Chas came to all the gigs with his younger brother Brendan. They were both hotheads. They'd flare up at the drop of a hat – that Irish temper."

It would be belittling to describe Smyth's 'Chas Smash' alter ego as Madness's mascot during this period – their equivalent of the Happy Mondays' Bez. Along with Suggs' undeniable charisma as frontman, Smyth's playful yet threatening stage presence as MC/dancer/compere/host quickly became an essential ingredient in their appeal. Writers have compared his role to that of dancer Gerard Malanga in The Velvet Underground but Chas Smash was reared on the age-old traditions of British music hall and Irish hospitality rather than the experimental art rock of New York City. Madness intuitively understood the concept of entertainment in a very English/Irish way. As George Marshall writes, "This was the musical version of jumping trains to Southend, kiss-me-quick hats, Big Dippers, saucy seaside postcards and goldfish in plastic bags."

"We were influenced by Kilburn & The High Roads, Showaddywaddy, Darts and looking sharp," Cathal later recalled. "Because the pub stages were so small, and there were so many of us, we started jumping up and down, dancing, because there was no room to do anything more adventurous." Suggs later described this period as a highpoint of his entire career: "As clear as a bell, I can remember that it didn't really matter what the public perception was. For me, success had already happened, getting a residency at The Dublin Castle, then seeing queues around the block. Being in the band, and the fact that we were the best thing going, was enough."

On July 3, Madness supported The Merton Parkas at the Moonlight Club, West Hampstead. Barson's diary recorded the show thus: "Only a vocal P.A. Went down better than the Mertons. The place sold out, seemed a large part came to see us. Paid extra £10 by Mertons and manager. Garry Bushell came from *Sounds*." Now a famous journalist whose columns have regularly graced the "red top" newspapers, Bushell had already been writing for the music paper *Sounds* for a year – with particular emphasis on 'street-level' music such as punk, the mod revival and the "new wave of British heavy metal". Excepting their cover of the Miracles' 'Tears Of A Clown', Bushell was impressed with Suggs & Co.: "Hey, this is good. Catchy Specials-like reggae," he wrote, "insistent dance music of the '69 kind. But Madness ain't just a ska-ed for life outfit. As the set progresses, they emerge with a little touch of Chas & Dave in the vocals. So the bluebeat hustles with doo wop [for] a neat line in lyrics. These boys are a classy dance band!"

"I liked them as soon as I saw them," Bushell readily admits today. "They were young, they had good songs and were clearly enjoying themselves – especially Chas Smash and his nutty dance routines, which he perfected pissing about to 'Liquidator' in youth clubs. Obviously, both Madness and The Specials were influenced by the brilliant pop reggae of the late 1960s which I had grown up on. But what made Madness different was they were also influenced by Ian Dury and the music hall. Madness were skinhead reggae meets cockney humour. Whereas the Specials could be a bit po-faced, Madness fused these influences with their own anarchic teenage sense of fun, along with Mike Barson's fairground organ and Lee's farting sax that was as fat and greasy as a motorway caff waitress. Their 'Nutty Sound' was distinctive and joyful. They always made me think of circus organs and summer fairs."

The Merton Parkas were part of a clutch of London-centric bands openly indebted – in terms of their clothing, at least – to mod. Its revival had been sparked by Jam frontman Paul Weller's passion for the Sixties youth cult, and by early 1979, bands like The Chords, The Purple Hearts and Secret Affair were promoting themselves via the mod ticket.* The Merton Parkas were one of the first bands of the mod revival to be signed; and were on the cusp of achieving the scene's first hit with 'You Need Wheels'. It's arguable that the mod revival didn't deserve the derisory criticism it attracted from most quarters of the music press, but there's no doubt that the scene was swiftly overshadowed by the so-called ska revival. "2 Tone incubated on the London mod circuit and then in a matter of months overtook 'new mod' altogether," suggests Bushell. "That took all of the mod bands by surprise. Ian Page of Secret Affair had been correct: the time was right for a new dance but 2 Tone provided it. The bottom line was the 2 Tone bands had better songs."

While The Specials' 'Gangsters' had been selling steadily, the deal with

---

* Cathal had owned a 200cc Lambretta scooter since 1976. "This mod stole it one night from outside the Hope & Anchor pub," he later explained. "The next night, the mod had re-sprayed it from yellow to maroon-and-grey and parked it back outside the Hope & Anchor again, so I got that back pretty quick. When all the mods were doing up their scooters really smart, we purposefully made ours really trashy. All the mods' scooters would be parked really neatly and we'd leave ours on their sides."

Chrysalis led to the single being re-promoted. The single charted on 27 July and quickly sped to number six in the charts; suddenly, the 2 Tone idea went from being a best-kept secret in London and Coventry to become a national phenomenon. The Specials toured constantly throughout June and July, which included two shows with the Nutty Boys. On July 14, the bands travelled up to Liverpool to play at Eric's, prompting a characteristically terse entry in Barson's diary: "Didn't see much of Liverpool [and] I would have liked to. The matinee was pretty crap but the late show was really good. We came on after the Specials and joined up on 'Madness'. We made £7."

More impressive was The Specials' sell-out show at Camden Town's 2,000-capacity Electric Ballroom with support from Madness, above Neol Davies's hastily assembled band The Selecter and The Mo-dettes. "Madness were definitely the fun element," Davies later observed. At the end of what must rank as the first 2 Tone showcase, all three bands joined forces onstage for a riotous performance of The Pioneers' classic, 'Long Shot Kick De Bucket'. "Playing there was a real step up for us," Suggs later wrote. "It's not much to look at from its entrance on Camden High Street . . . but inside it's a Tardis of a place . . . you can't beat the atmosphere when the whole place bounces up and down as one."

"Woody took a shine to a Mo-dette," recorded Barson in his diary. "Too many skins: although everyone danced, it seemed a bit as if they weren't listening to the music, just dancing to the trend." That same day, Bushell's *Sounds* article on Madness – their first, other than live reviews – was published. "Madness are not Rude Boys" ran the headline. "They were bright and funny and interesting," says Bushell. "I liked Lee a lot – and Chas. I found Suggs a little cagey, as he seemed a little too keen to disown his own past. He'd said he'd never been into Sham 69, for example. The actual quote was 'when Sham came along, I grew me hair', but then *Sounds* published a picture of him up to his shaven head, in among a Sham stage invasion."

On July 29, Madness were gifted a support slot with The Pretenders at London's Lyceum by promoter and admirer John Curd – subsequently cited as Madness' best-ever gig by Woodgate. But by all accounts, various band members (or their friends) sprayed graffiti all over the dressing room walls and Curd refused to book Madness again until the mess had been painted over. Two days later, Madness were headlining at The Pied Bull,

Islington. Cathal later recounted an incident at the show in his own inimitable style: "Chas notices someone flicking ash in [his] girlfriend's hair and leaps into crowd . . . one goes down . . . two go down . . . then gets kicked in the jollies by third skin with steel DM's on who straight away apologises . . . Chas thereupon Nutty dances back to stage in 'That Nutty Sound'-inspired Trance . . . wearing a pair of national health glasses . . . black frame with mirrored lenses made by Lee's [future wife] Deb, who was working in a glasses factory at the time."

★ ★ ★

Madness' debut single, 'The Prince', was finally issued as 2 Tone's second single on August 10, 1979. (There had been a few glitches, though. "Remixed 'The Prince' and 'Madness' to get rid of hum on sax solo," wrote Barson exactly a month earlier. "Mix of 'Madness' shit." The single had eventually been cut on July 12.) At first glance, critics might have been forgiven for dismissing the single as little more than a Prince Buster tribute, especially with the cover of 'Madness' on the flip, but many music journalists weren't particularly aware of the ska pioneer at the time.

"It's a bit of a rip-off of a couple of Prince Buster songs," Foreman later admitted. "One day, Lee did this saxophone solo which we were really surprised by because it sounded so professional. But he'd pinched it off a record! Lee really liked all that stuff and there's lots of references to Buster himself, Orange Street, uptown Jamaica . . ." Upon closer scrutiny, it's clear that Thompson had listened to the Buster compilation, *Fabulous Greatest Hits*, as he'd name-checked three of its songs ('Freezing Up Orange Street', 'Earthquake' and 'Ghost Dance') in the first verse alone while the sax solo was purloined from another, 'Texas Hold Up'.

In hindsight, Buster was as ubiquitous an influence to 2 Tone as James Brown proved to be to early hip-hop acts or Chuck Berry to The Rolling Stones et al. Quite apart from 'Gangsters', The Specials also covered 'Too Hot' and drew on Buster's tune 'Judge Dread' for the song 'Stupid Marriage', later covering Buster's version of 'Enjoy Yourself' on their second album. 2 Tone's next signing, The Beat, would rework two Buster songs, 'Rough Rider' and 'Whine & Grine', on their debut album.

In its defence, 'The Prince' possessed a youthful, disjointed vigour and a sense of bonhomie which set out Madness' stall. From the opening line, "Buster, he sold the heat, with a rocksteady beat", this felt like something new – quirky, even – rather than old or revivalist. "No jukebox should be without a copy," proclaimed the *NME* – and hot on the heels of 'Gangsters', 'The Prince' climbed to number 16 in the charts.

On August 14, Madness recorded a radio session for John Peel (which was aired on August 27), consisting of their single plus three tracks which they were yet to release: 'Bed And Breakfast Man', 'Land Of Hope & Glory' and 'Stepping Into Line'. The following day, they played a sold-out show at the Rock Garden in Covent Garden, earning £60 out of support band, Swedish punk band The Rude Boys, by lending them a drum kit.

Madness may have been on the brink of pop stardom – but their lifestyle was anything but glamorous. A month before being launched on a career trajectory rivalled by very few in terms of British singles chart positions, band members were chasing across London to locate stolen proceeds amassed from live shows over the previous months. According to Barson's diary, Hasler was still living in a squat in King's Cross and had stashed the band's savings behind a brick in a wall only for it to go missing: "John had £350 nicked from his squat by a punk. John didn't turn up at [The] Hope [& Anchor]. Found address. Retrieved £121. 1st class Sherlock Holmes operation! Took him round Si's though to wait for bank on Monday. Had to go back to Milton Keynes to get his passport for bank. His Mum phoned the cops and his case comes up tomorrow. He's pleading guilty! He was fined £150 on top of paying us back."

"I remember this very well," laughs Kerstin Rodgers. "I found the Milton Keynes address in amongst a stash of papers at the squat. We drove up there, found the address and phoned from a call box to establish that he was in, then went to the door and grabbed him. Back in London, he was kept overnight. I had to go home but this is what they told me: he said he'd given the money to a black guy, a drugs dealer, with fake legs. The band threatened to take his fake legs away so he coughed up!"

An *NME* feature on Madness followed on August 18, written by Adrian Thrills, who seemed captivated by the joker up their sleeve: "Chas doesn't sing or play an instrument. He simply contributes to the general air of dizzy lunacy at Madness gigs and sums the whole thing up. For as a pure fun band, Madness take some beating – something that is largely down to what saxophonist Lee Thompson has christened 'the nutty sound'. As Lee explains: 'It's a happy fairground sound with jokey lyrics.' They developed a sound rooted in ska and R&B but with plenty of unhinged edges such as Lee's yakety sax fanaticism and Suggs' wide boy charm."

In the article, Madness were keen to distance themselves from the 2 Tone tag. "One critic called us a rude boy ska band," bemoaned Foreman, "but we don't really want to be categorised like that." Suggs agreed: "We could get labelled as just another ska revival band and get our own ten minutes of fame." Thrills concluded by looking to the future: "With two major record labels already showing a keen interest, Madness want the chance to stand on their own twelve feet."

Suggs spoke about this seminal period in Madness's development to *Uncut* in 2008: "We were upfront in realising the 2 Tone thing was going off like a packet of crackers and we were in that mode stylistically. We certainly put more ska into our set and we'd been lucky to meet Jerry. Earlier than God had intended, we were suddenly the thing. [But] we were still a gang, the road crew were our pals, joining in on the backing vocals, an ebullient time. Madness were the leaders of the little bit of north London we lived in and led colourful lives, which fed into the songs. I was the idiot savant – well, certainly an idiot. I was just happy to be there. They were older than me and I just wanted to be in their gang or be cool!"

For the past two months, Madness had been talking with various record companies about a long-term contract to follow their one-off with 2 Tone. "Went to Sire Records," wrote Barson on July 10. "Sounds good, offered a tour of America. They're very interested. Saw Virgin – sounds like just another Virgin deal. Have to consult a solicitor." Two days later, Barson did just that: "Met lawyer David Gentil, seemed like a good dude. Met EMI A&R man from Trinidad."

In a rare meeting of minds between 2 Tone and the mod revival, Madness and The Selecter shared a bill at London's Lyceum on the August 26 bank holiday with Secret Affair, Purple Hearts and Back To Zero at the tail-end of the March Of The Mods tour (singled out by Bedford as his favourite show from their early years). In due course, the latter-day mods and the 2 Tone audience (dressed as skinheads or rude boys) were known to clash – or rather, the nouveau skinheads terrorised the parka-wearing Jam fans. But such tribal demarcations were several months away and the show passed without incident – at least, in terms of the audience. "We were supposed to be second on the bill," wrote Barson. "[Promoter] John Curd knocked the March Of The Mods manager for a six for trying to put us on third. Pretty good gig – lots of cheering. Secret Affair played very pro and flash."

Secret Affair were the great white hopes for the mod revival – and Madness found themselves competing with the band's debut single, 'Time For Action', in terms of a potential *Top Of The Pops* appearance for 'The Prince'. On August 29, the band met at Holts shoe shop – or more specifically, at The Specials' management office above the shop. Chrysalis Records even went so far as to order cars to take the band to the BBC TV studios. But Secret Affair were eventually chosen instead.

After a headline show at the Nashville in Kensington, Madness played one of their first gigs north of Watford at The Factory in Manchester – but the 2 Tone craze had yet to spread nationally. Mike Barson's diary entry was suitably blunt: "Not as crowded as we expected. Everyone danced to a poxy P.A. except the aggro boys we had a fight with afterwards. Had a fight with Suggs over the van and left half the chaps in Manchester but we met on the motorway about 7.30am."

On August 17, Madness played a private party upstairs at the Clarendon Ballrooms, Hammersmith, for the wedding of Stiff Records boss Dave Robinson: "We played a good gig," wrote Barson. "We came on in a long nutty train all round the room. Lots of nutty dancing later on." It was an unusual way for a band to audition. "Several people had mentioned to me that this band might suit Stiff," remembers Robinson, "but I just couldn't get to see them. I heard that Chrysalis were interested in signing them. I was getting married and I needed a band so I thought, I'll have two birds with one stone. They agreed so they played with Elvis Costello, Ian Dury and Wreckless Eric."

Unbeknownst to Robinson, his potential ability to restrain the band's wilful streak was also being auditioned. "What I didn't know is they had an alternative agenda. They thought, we'll wind up this record executive. We'll charge him handsomely, something like £400. But it occurred to me that something like this might happen so I said, before the off, it's great you're here but, if anybody causes any aggravation whatsoever, I will personally kill them in full view of the guests. If my wife gets at all irritated by any action that you might be imagining, that won't work."

"I must admit to getting a bout of nerves that night," wrote McPherson in *Suggs And The City*, "when I spied a few familiar faces in the audience, most notably those of Elvis Costello and our great hero, Ian Dury." By all accounts, Madness' performance was exemplary. "They were really good and even got Elvis Costello dancing – not very much of a dancer, our Elvis. I remember thinking, there are two singles here. I asked them afterwards about the instrumental they did, a short thing with a rant at the front, and that was 'One Step Beyond'. I thought that was a great name for an album title. So I arranged to see them early the next week."

★ ★ ★

Dave Robinson had enjoyed the kind of life which could write itself as a Hollywood script. Born in Dublin, he quickly proved himself to be something of an opportunist, carving himself a name as a photographer at a tender age in the early 1960s, capturing The Beatles at The Cavern for *Rave* magazine and the Rolling Stones' first tour of Ireland. He opened the first Beat Club in Ireland and befriended Van Morrison, briefly managing him before he moved to England in 1967. As tour manager for the Jimi Hendrix Experience from their first tour until not long before Jimi's death, Robinson toured North America and other foreign climes extensively before stumbling across a new band, Brinsley Schwarz, in late 1969.

Robinson offered to manage them and devised a plan to generate extensive publicity by flying British music journalists over to New York City to see the Brinsleys open for Van Morrison and Quicksilver Messenger Service at the Fillmore East in April 1970. Due to a variety of problems, this ambitious undertaking backfired – but it revealed Robinson as someone unafraid of taking risks, who'd gamble with the grandest of plans for artists in whom he believed.

During the first half of the 1970s, Dave worked with such acts as Graham Parker, ex-Brinsleys singer Nick Lowe, Dave Edmunds, Ian Dury and Elvis Costello, while helping to create a network of over 30 pubs where bands could play – in essence, the pub rock circuit. Having promoted gigs at The Hope & Anchor, Robinson teamed up with Andrew Jakeman (alias Jake Riviera) in 1975 to organise the Naughty Rhythms package tour featuring Dr. Feelgood and pub rock acts Chilli Willi & The Red Hot Peppers and Kokomo. The following year, the pair created Stiff Records, considered Britain's first independent label of the punk/new wave era – with the help of £400 from Dr. Feelgood singer Lee Brilleaux. In nurturing an image which was as provocative as it was witty, Stiff reflected the maverick spirit of its founders; old enough to have the requisite experience but young enough to have a flair, ambition and creativity lacking in the corporate environment of major record companies.

Propelled by eccentric yet highly effective promotional campaigns, Stiff billed itself variously as "The World's Most Flexible Record Label", with slogans like "We came. We saw. We left", "If It Ain't Stiff, It Ain't Worth A Fuck" and "When You Kill Time, You Murder Success". Many of their early signings were acquaintances from London's pub rock scene: Nick Lowe, Elvis Costello, Wreckless Eric and Ian Dury & The Blockheads; others like The Damned and The Adverts were integral to punk. "Stiff were happening," admits Robinson. "We had a high percentage of success. I once worked out that Stiff was about 65 per cent successful whereas a major was working on 10 per cent. We were more on it generally." But the original partnership was destined to fracture. Headstrong characters both, Robinson and Riviera clashed regularly; and by early 1978, Riviera had left to set up his own imprint, Radar Records, taking Stiff's twin peaks, Elvis Costello and Nick Lowe, with him.

In fact, Stiff had already been approached twice about Madness – both by Rob Dickins and by John Eichler, publican at the Hope & Anchor, who knew Robinson from his days promoting gigs at the venue. "I rang Stiff and told [label manager] Paul Conroy to check out the band," Eichler later recalled. "We'd raved about them." Conroy was another veteran of the pub rock scene and ex-manager of The Kursaal Flyers who'd been brought into the Stiff fold in late 1976 by Riviera. "Jake knew me as a solid ex-policeman's son because they were looking for a general manager," he laughs. "They needed someone to hold the fort. There were five people in the office but no one keeping order or paperwork. I was persuaded to go in – but general manager of what?!"

To Conroy, Riviera's departure felt like a fatal body blow to Stiff. "I thought, we're totally screwed. It was like a football team losing Ronaldo *and* Rooney. Although Dave was rock solid, Jake had been pretty much the ideas person and perceived to the outside world as everything Stiff was all about. We were left with what felt like the dregs, really. To the *NME*'s of this world, it was seen as, well, give them five minutes and that will be it. We gave them all a shot but we'd built a rod for our own backs promoting everyone with gusto – posters and ads. Still, one of my proudest memories is how we all managed to pull Stiff round." And this despite Conroy's reticence to sign the Nutty Boys: "I've got a feeling I saw

Madness at the Hope & Anchor with Kosmo Vinyl," he says. "We saw them quite early on – long before Dave's wedding. And I remember thinking they were interesting but my problem was, at the back of mind, we already had Ian [Dury] and that London quirkiness."

Stiff was an attractive proposition for artists like Madness who were intensely suspicious of besuited record company executives. Their office on Alexander Street was once a shop so they were able to display eye-catching posters in the window*; next door was Blackhill Enterprises, the management home for the likes of Ian Dury. Next to that was a pub called The Durham Castle, where much of Stiff's business was transacted. While Stiff might not have encouraged the same artist-friendly, laissez-faire politics of hippie-era independents like Island or Virgin – Robinson was too headstrong for that and Riviera too aggressive – the company was known to celebrate eccentricity and artistic endeavour.

Stiff had progressed from their indie beginnings to secure manufacturing and distribution deals with Island and EMI, winning the Marketing Award in 1978 from both *Music Week* and the *NME* without actually selling many records. In 1979, the label scored sizeable hits from Dury and Lene Lovich – but Dury didn't always want to include singles on albums, which made sales of the latter more difficult. Coupled with Robinson's impulsive nature, it meant that Stiff was never far from financial meltdown. Robinson needed another "banker". He needed Madness.

* Including, at one point, a T-shirt with the famous slogan 'If it ain't Stiff it ain't worth a fuck'. It was removed following a visit from the local constabulary.

Chapter 6

IF IT AIN'T STIFF . . .

FIVE days after the wedding party, Robinson met with Madness. "Struck me as a man of mucho action and no red tape," wrote Barson – a laconic, down-to-earth character who wasn't easily impressed. "He talked a lot of sense as to what we should do. Paid us a 'oner' for the wedding." Robinson was acutely aware that he had to move quickly and decisively. "We met in the pub next to the Stiff offices in Alexandra Street," he recalls. "Record companies were queuing up to sign them. 'The Prince' was 16 in the charts. The Specials looked a bit Mafia with the suits, but Madness had the skinhead look, a bit 'jack the lad'. They'd had a few meetings and had got up to some high jinks and record company executives were a bit wary after the Sex Pistols. 'That's probably a one-hit wonder on 2 Tone, would it stretch?' – I assume that's what they were thinking."

The Stiff boss took advantage of this indecision: "I said, 'What do you want to do?' And they said, 'We want to make a record as soon as possible, we've got all the songs.' I said, 'Who do you want to produce it?' And they said, 'Clive Langer.' So in between talking to them, I was buying them pints then nipping back to the office. I booked Eden Studios for two weeks hence. I called Clive on the phone and said, 'You want to produce these boys but you need a good engineer. What about Alan Winstanley?' Clive said, 'Yeah, good idea.' I went back in and said, 'I've booked the studio and your producer, we're ready to go Monday week.' They said, 'Oh fuck, that's what we thought it might be like!'"

Meanwhile, Sire Records' boss Seymour Stein had expressed an interest in signing Madness for the US. "Seymour had already spotted them," admits Dave. "Old Seymour, always very crafty – I liked him a lot. He called me and said, 'I hear you're going to sign them, that's great, but I'm getting an arrangement with them for America.' I said, 'We'll need to be fast with the paperwork because there are a lot of people scratching around.' So we went to their lawyer's office. This guy was an old-fashioned music industry lawyer. He didn't want us meeting with the band."

Once again, Robinson demonstrated quite magnificent (if unconventional) skills to manipulate a situation to his own ends. "We went to this meeting and the lawyer was being a pain in the arse," says Robinson. "He didn't want to agree anything because he wanted to make the deal himself. He'd had several record companies call him. He said, 'I don't think we'll be getting this done today, gentlemen. Tonight is my wedding anniversary and me and the missus are going to the opera. I've got my tuxedo at the club.' I thought, this is going to be a pain."

The clock was ticking so Robinson had to do something. "The phone never stopped ringing from other record companies. Richard Branson was saying, 'I'll double anything Stiff offer' – his usual! So I got out of the room, called my assistant and said, 'Find out where the lawyer and his wife live, get in touch, get someone round there with flowers and tell her that her husband has booked a limo. She's to get dressed and the limo will take her to his office before they go to the opera.' By now, Madness were losing interest, bored with anything that had been said after 10 minutes. Lee was probably thinking of some nefarious deal that he had with scooter parts up in Camden Town. I could see their eyes glaze and thought, this isn't going to happen. So I said, 'The next guy on the phone will be Dave Dee.' Because everyone else had called. Madness said, 'How'd you know?' 'Well, he's the head of A&R at Warners,' I said, 'He's always last and thinks his money will clinch the deal. Once he calls, we get this finished.' Driiinnngg! It's Dave Dee. It was an inspired guess but I was very hyper trying to get this deal! The band cracked up: Robbo knows what's happening?"

The end was in sight. "I said to Seymour, 'If we're not careful, the lawyer will go to Branson or he will try to get a percentage of the deal.' Then the lawyer said, 'I need to be going home.' I said: 'Your wife will be here at seven o'clock in a limo with champagne and flowers, which have been sent from you.' He was pissed off but now I've got the band on my side. I said, 'They're in the studio in ten days. We all need this bit of paperwork.' He was totally gobsmacked so we got a heads of agreement signed at 7.15! But in actual fact, we never signed an agreement. It was only ever done on a 'heads'."

As an interesting aside, Terry Edwards (in his book *One Step Beyond*) was keen not to overlook John Hasler's astute negotiating skills during this period, helping to secure favourable terms for both Madness' recording and publishing contracts. By all accounts, he even played Dave Robinson at his own game, pretending to be RAK's Mickie Most for hoax phone calls through to Robinson's PA.

Madness sensed that Dave shared their no-nonsense view of the world. "They were my kind of people," Robinson readily admits. "We had a great affinity straight away. It was remarkable. The company was doing well, we were making the right noises with nebulous records which nobody else could have really delivered so my ego was soaring. But I knew them intimately. There was Irish blood there, a vibe, they were all ducking and diving, and I was stressing this as a partnership big time, that we're all in this together. And they were booked into the studio – you see, that was the other hook. They'd had lunches with other record companies and thought they were all up their arses. They thought it was all crap, really."

Despite their enthusiasm for Stiff, Madness were also wary of Robinson's reputation for a "hands on" approach. "Part of the deal was that I would not go to the studio," he laughs. "They made me agree. Because they were aware that I was prone to fiddle with people's music. They were straightforward about it." While Madness didn't have a leader as such, Dave sensed they had a driving force: "You could tell Barson was the big noise. I got close as I could to Mike very quickly – but Barson didn't want to get too close. I found out he was a Taurean like me and I know how Tauruses work. I thought, I've got to flatter here, also not have any bullshit, be direct, to get Mike on my side. The rest of them didn't quite know what was happening and were all floating around. Mike was also the suspicious one. He was asking the questions. Suggs wasn't. Funnily enough, I've found some Barsons in my family tree now. At some point, I must talk to Mike and find out if there's a family connection!"

* * *

On September 3, Madness signed to Stiff Records (and Sire Records for North America), resulting in a cheque for the agreed £10,000 advance in royalties – the final encouragement for various band members to forsake their day jobs. Bedford, for example, was halfway through a two-year typography course at the London College of Printing while Foreman still worked for a postal company. Legend has it that Barson, Foreman and Suggs visited several high street banks in Camden in order to create an account for the band. However, it's recorded that staff were unimpressed by their physical appearance and seemed reluctant to grant them interviews with the respective bank managers. Eventually, they opened an account at Williams & Glyn's Bank (later re-branded the Royal Bank Of Scotland).*

It's probably not an exaggeration to claim that Madness would not have enjoyed such a productive, successful career were it not for the vision and creative freedom afforded by Stiff. Suggs agrees: "How privileged we were to be offered a deal with 2 Tone and see that whole thing unfold before our eyes. Then to bump into Dave Robinson who had this house for misfits – Ian Dury, Elvis Costello, Wreckless Eric. It was just the perfect place for Madness. It couldn't have been anywhere else. We could stay at 2 Tone and falsely remain as a ska band, which we weren't entirely, or go to Stiff which was equally independent and maverick and free."

Two days later, Madness finally recorded their first appearance on *Top Of The Pops*, broadcast on September 6 and coinciding with a show at Dingwalls in Camden Town. Woodgate's mother worked in the BBC studios for *Top Of the Pops* at the time but was transferred to another department so that there would be no perceived bias. "It was the done thing," Woody told *The Word*. "This is a bit rich: Annie Ogden's the floor manager and here's her son on the show. People are always saying, 'I know your mum' . . . David Bowie . . . Mick Box from Uriah Heep, out in the middle of America. So mum was moved to *Play School* and *Dad's Army*. I remember having *Play School*'s Big Ted and Humpty at the house. She used to bring them home, for safe keeping!"

Rob Dickins: "*Top Of The Pops* used to be recorded on one day and shown the next. And one of the moments in my career I always think of was when the band came round my flat and were all lying on the floor

* The band later parodied this episode when filming the closing credits for their *Complete Madness* video, which showed them literally "laughing all the way to the bank". William & Glyn's also figured in the lyrics to their 1982 song, 'Calling Cards'.

watching themselves on TV. I thought, we did that, this little band of people in this room! One of those snapshot moments you have in your career – something special."

Someone else who was watching with some trepidation that night was Suggs' mum Edwina. "I remember sitting watching this boy of mine on *Top Of The Pops* with a neighbour and I'm clutching a cushion to me," she later explained. "He had a little toy trumpet in his top pocket and he's dancing about and it fell out, and I knew that he was so nervous. It's amazing. He was talking about becoming a council gardener and then the next thing I know, they've got a record leaping up the charts. It gave him a direction, a purpose, a family."

Barson's diary entry was succinct: "*TOTP* was fairly good. Dingwalls was OK. I was pretty knackered though stood still through most of the set. Good sound by Specials P.A." On September 8, Madness supported Secret Affair at Aylesbury Friars. Cathal Smythe arrived late after travelling up from his workplace down in Ashford. His belated arrival onstage was dramatic: as he strode to the stage, the crowd parted in Biblical fashion, whereupon the MC lifted the mood of what had apparently been a lacklustre performance until his arrival. It acted as another reminder of his vital role within Madness.

Having inked the record deal, the band convened to discuss John Hasler's role. Barson's diary entry confirms that internal tensions were already evident: "Outvoted to give John 1/7 of all profits." The following day, such details were forgotten when Madness commenced the recording of their debut album at Eden Studios in south Acton (which had already played host to the likes of Elvis Costello, The Sex Pistols, Dr. Feelgood, The Undertones, The Pretenders and, only days before, the Specials' debut album). "Single's at 37 and we're on the BBC A-list this week," noted Barson. "Started album. Quite good so far."

★   ★   ★

Despite Robinson's claim, this wasn't Langer's first introduction to Alan Winstanley. Born on November 2, 1952 in Fulham, west London, Winstanley was the archetypal "working-class lad made good", who went to the local grammar school while being reared on a musical diet of The Beatles and Phil Spector. "I left school at seventeen wanting to be a rock star," he later told *Sound On Sound* magazine. "But when I realised my guitar playing was never going to be as good as Eric Clapton or Jimi Hendrix, I decided to try something else. As I'd always wondered why some records sounded better than others, I figured that it must be down to the production and felt that was the direction I wanted to go in."

Keen to gain experience, he joined Decca Records in the A&R administration department. "I used to hang out at a music shop in Fulham and I persuaded the owners to build a demo studio in the basement, which was called TW Studios. They took me on to run it and it proved a very good way of learning. I was slung straight in at the deep end, as their in-house engineer, doing demos for bands. It became so successful that they made enough money to buy the building next door and open a second studio." One of the many unsigned bands who passed through TW's doors was The Stranglers. In due course, Alan engineered the first three Stranglers albums at TW, with producer Martin Rushent.

Around 1978, Winstanley left TW for pastures new. "I was doing production work for Stiff Records," he later explained. "I was also in the process of building a recording studio, Genetic in Berkshire, with Martin Rushent, who had become a close friend." Alan developed his craft honing sessions by other punk/new wave acts such as Buzzcocks, Generation X and Stiff artists such as Wreckless Eric, Lene Lovich and Rachel Sweet (hence his acquaintance with Dave Robinson), as well as Amii Stewart's 1979 disco hit, 'Knock On Wood'.

Winstanley had met Langer via Rob Dickins a couple of years earlier, whilst recording some Deaf School demos at TW. "I used to say, as a producer, you've got to get yourself an engineer that you trust and I'd worked with a couple," remembers Dickins. "TW was down the road from my flat so I could pop home and come back again. I said to Clive, 'Work with Alan – that's what I've done.' I thought he got a great sound from this crummy studio. And then Clive took Alan on from me as an engineer."

The pair proved to be the perfect complement, Langer's laissez-faire attitude acting as counterpoint to Winstanley's stricter sentiments with regard to such musical disciplines as tempo and tuning. "Clive is all ideas, very musical," describes Dickins. "Clive's similar to me in that he knew what record he wanted to make but he wasn't actually gifted enough to make that happen. Alan is quiet, Clive is intense. You can rely on Alan. So Clive would have the idea of what he wanted it to sound like and Alan would make it happen. That's why it worked. When you get into that relationship, you come to rely on each other, which was born with Madness."

No sooner had the band arrived at Eden Studios than they found some tapes from the recording sessions for the first Specials album. "You could still feel The Specials' warmth in the room," Suggs later admitted. "They'd just finished recording with Elvis Costello and we found some out-takes of tape, ten seconds of stuff which had been edited and dropped on the floor and we were trying to listen to it. But they were different from us, because they were influenced by punk as much as ska and we were influenced as much by Fifties R&B or Ian Dury. It was a lot of fun. Those songs still resonate because we recorded the atmosphere of the room. I don't think we could play that naïvely and have that much fun again!"

In essence, the sessions resembled those of the classic Sixties bands – capturing Madness' live set with very little in the way of over-dubbing or musical decoration. That said, Langer and Winstanley later admitted that some preliminary groundwork was necessary. "Lee's sax was the one wildcard," Winstanley explained in *Uncut*. "He didn't realise that the sax was a transposing instrument, so when the rest of the band were playing in C, he had to play in B-flat. So we tried to compensate by pulling his mouthpiece out, loosening the reed and over blowing wildly." The pair treated Thompson's saxophone with an Eventide Harmonizer to mask such tuning deficiencies, which gave it a thick, rasping quality akin to that of Fela Kuti. The same contraption lent Barson's piano an out-of-kilter "honky tonk" sound. "Occasionally, we even put thumb tacks on the piano hammers to make it even brighter," revealed Langer. Another devil was in the detail of the microphone set-up for the drums: "The snare was horrible to play, all papery," Woody later admitted. "But it sounded brilliant on record: really crisp and punchy."

Aside from brief interruptions when Barson was struck down with a bout of food poisoning, and they filmed a second performance for *Top Of The Pops* for 'The Prince', the sessions were straightforward. "We just whacked it out," Barson commented. "We had two weeks, completely in Clive's hands. We'd been playing the songs a lot, 1-2-3-4, no fiddling around, so the work had been done already in gigs and rehearsals." Langer helped to school Woodgate in terms of his technique, recommending he adopt a "less is more" style. "It was amazing," Woody explained. "Clive tried to get me to hit the bass drum hard, cut out the rolls. I remember that on 'In The Middle Of The Night', I played so few parts, it felt alien to me, the emptiness, the gaps – painful! But when I heard the final record, it made sense. The adrenalin and the nerves were unbearable and when that red light went on, I was just relieved to get to the end!"

"I'm fond of 'In The Middle Of The Night'," admitted Suggs, "which I remember writing around at Chrissy's house when he was re-decorating his spare bedroom. Probably one of the first songs I ever wrote. I have a clear memory of Chrissy living in these flats in Kentish Town, pre-pop stardom, getting the bus and pretending we were half fares while trying to smoke at the same time, warming your feet on the heaters at the front then being thrown off. A romanticised version of the past! I'd written half a song before that called 'Lost My Head' which I don't think ever surfaced. It might be on some demo somewhere."

"Good fun, in and out," summarised Thompson. "Alan and Clive were grateful that, although we recorded the album live, there was a glass barrier between us and them because when I had to redo a part, I would scream obscenities!" On one occasion, Winstanley heard a strange echo; it transpired that some of the band had wandered into a cupboard containing an echo chamber. The original intention had been for Barson to sing his own composition, 'My Girl', and for Foreman to provide vocals for 'Bed And Breakfast Man'. Their stage show had always been punctuated by the occasional microphone swap, as Suggs later recalled: "I think it added to the show having Mike sing something, then Lee. A nice bit of vaudeville."

"That was my final involvement with Madness outside of the business," admits Rob Dickins. "I went down to TW Studios and they were playing back the re-done version of 'My Girl'. Mike was still singing. I just said, 'Clive, you can't.' Mike sings a little like Bernard Bresslaw. It was endearing but it wasn't commercial and the song was brilliant. This is just such a hit record. You've got to have Suggs sing it. Suggs said, 'I'm not saying anything – this is Mike's song. I'll sing it but someone's got to tell Mike.' They said, 'Rob, you tell him.' And I said, 'Mike's always wary of me anyway.' So I ended up in this burger bar next to TW, trying to be as diplomatic as I could. And Mike said, 'Go on, get Suggs to sing it then,' and walked off. It was something I didn't want to do but no one else would do it!"

"Clive wanted Suggs to sing this and got me to try lots of different ways, none of which worked," complained Barson to Terry Edwards, "so that he could suggest that Suggs sang it instead. Singing's a funny thing, isn't it?

Maybe [Suggs] is not a great technical singer, maybe he is, but he's got character to his voice." Barson then played Suggs' new version to his girlfriend, Kerstin Rodgers: "Mike said, 'What do you think of this?' and played me 'My Girl'," she recalls. "I said, 'God, you sound so much better there, Mike,' not realising. His face went pale and he said, 'That's Suggs singing, actually!'" In hindsight, fate seems to have dealt Barson a cruel blow, since both Clive Langer and Suggs were struck by the similarity of Barson's voice to another British institution, Robert Wyatt.

Dickins wouldn't again work directly with members of Madness until he oversaw Suggs' solo recordings in the 1990s – but his early faith wasn't forgotten. "There was a lovely moment when a few people from Stiff walked down the stairs at TW into the basement," he recalls. "As they walked into the studio, they saw me there and it was like (*adopts sarcastic tone*), oh, the publisher's here. This is why I wanted to work for a record company. You always felt like a second-class citizen being a publisher! And I remember Lee, Suggs and everyone said, 'Hey, he believed in us when you turned us down.' It was lovely!" Within three weeks, the album was all but complete. Or was it?

"We then mixed the album at Genetic," Winstanley told *Sound On Sound*. "At that stage, Genetic was only half built, because we had run out of money. However, the equipment turned up so we stuck it in a bungalow in the grounds of the main house and mixed the album there!" A playback was eventually arranged at Genetic out in leafy Streatley near Reading for Dave Robinson to hear. "Clive said, 'We've got to do a bit of mixing but essentially we've finished. You should come up and hear it,'" remembers Dave. "They'd been dying to make the record so I listened to the whole shooting match – no 'One Step Beyond'! I got a feeling there was a joke going on, an air of expectancy, so I said, 'Where's that thing?' 'Oh, we're not going to do that.' Oh. Well, that's the single, to me. So I kept them up all night till four in the morning till they acquiesced so they could go to bed. And they went back in and recorded it."

"We'd always start our set with something instrumental and funny," Suggs explained. "Originally, it was 'Hawaii 5-0'. Then we'd start the set proper. With 'One Step Beyond', we used to play it as a 30-second intro and then it's well documented that Dave saw some potential in the song." But none of the band agreed. "I thought 'One Step Beyond' was OK," Woodgate later told Terry Edwards, "but never in a million years would we have it as a single. It didn't represent the band. Suggs wasn't on it!"

When Robinson returned to the studio to listen to the recording, the track was barely 90 seconds long. "They were at it again!" he laughs. "So I went in with Alan to cannibalise bits, stretched it out to two minutes 20 seconds – they weren't aware of editing as they'd never been in the studio before, by and large. They didn't see that as a single at all but when it was a hit, that was great, because then – as far as Madness were concerned – I knew something they didn't know. I was then, without argument, appointed to be the single picker. So I didn't have to go through battles for that."

Actually, the editing process was more complicated than that, as Terry Edwards succinctly summarised in his *One Step Beyond* book. Langer and Winstanley mocked up a demonstration tape of what the edited version might sound like, having processed the track using that Eventide Harmonizer (which adds an extra frequency or 'harmony' to artificially expand the sound). A quarter-inch tape was dropped through Stiff's letter box for Robinson's approval – only for the producers to be horrified when they learnt that the Stiff boss, satisfied with the job, had sent it off for manufacture.

★ ★ ★

While Madness were ensconced in the studios, *Sounds* published a lengthy interview with the band by journalist Robbi Millar (which was later reproduced on the back cover of Madness' second album, *Absolutely*). Millar was smitten: "This is the purest form of dance music that I've heard . . . it's totally irresistible." Foreman credited their saxophonist with concocting the more idiosyncratic aspects of their music: "The nutty sound's something that Lee Thompson thought up. It's because our music sounds like fairgrounds and organs. It just sounds nutty." Both Barson and Suggs stressed the collective strength of Madness – that while "reading and writing music isn't a strong point", they worked as a team. Foreman was also wary of being tied to the 2 Tone/ska revival flagpole: "We want people to talk about the Madness sound in years to come. We don't like to be thought of as part of any revival because after that fashion's dead, the groups that rely on the fashion aren't heard of anymore."

Having attracted a minor bidding war to secure their signatures on a record contract, Madness were back in their lawyer's office to negotiate a publishing deal – now their form was proven with 'The Prince'. Needless to say, Rob Dickins' bid for Warner Music was victorious: "I ended up signing all their publishing against all the competition. Virgin were offering some ridiculous deal – huge money and taking no percentage, desperate to establish market share. Mine wasn't the best deal on the table but they came with me. It's something you don't see very often – loyalty."

Dickins was impressed with the band's arrangement for splitting royalty income for songwriting: "Madness had the best solution which I remember thinking was genius. It may be apocryphal – that I've made it up in my own mind because I liked them as people so much – but for a bunch of 18-year-olds, they had an internal deal that was whoever wrote the songs got a 50 per cent split down the middle. The other 50 per cent was split seven ways. So the writer got another piece – a fourteenth each. You see The Beatles with Lennon/McCartney and George getting bitter about not getting his songs on. In Madness, everyone got a piece of all the songs."

Dickins retained friendships with various members of Madness long after he'd switched from Warners' publishing side to become chairman of their UK record company. "Suggs and I immediately got on," he says. "Lee and I got on, too. I still think Lee is overlooked. No one got close to Mike but after our 'My Girl' thing, it took a little longer with him. He wrote 'Bed And Breakfast Man' which really convinced me they could write. I thought it was the perfect Madness song and yet it was never a single. But if I see them now, it's all very pleasant."

Suggs fell in with the social circle of Langer, Dickins and ex-Deaf School singer Anne Martin – better known by her stage name, Bette Bright. Although she was a few years older than the Madness singer, the two soon became romantically involved after meeting at the Camden Palace. "The Palace holds a lot of happy memories for me," wrote McPherson in *Suggs And The City*, "but none better than when I saw Anne's green eyes sparkle across that dance floor." The couple eventually moved in together above Camden's influential Swanky Modes boutique, which was co-owned by Clive Langer's wife, Mel Walters.

★ ★ ★

One of Robinson's first decisions was to address the issue of Madness's management. It could be argued that the band had progressed well despite the inexperience of old friend John Hasler (although some expert guidance from Rick Rogers hadn't hurt). While Madness were rehearsing in Royal College Street for a short tour in early October, Robinson called upon the services of Stiff employee John 'Kellogs' Kalinowski (also sometimes known by his initials, J.J.). Born on May 2, 1946 in Rochford, Essex, Kalinowski was a former roadie and subsequent manager for Procol Harum and their pianist Gary Brooker. An established road manager with a wealth of experience organising tours both in the UK and North America with the likes of Joe Cocker and Leon Russell, Kellogs was brought into the Stiff fold by general manager Paul Conroy.

"Kellogs had been a tour manager for everybody," adds Robinson. "He knew his way around the tours which the Nutty Boys didn't know anything about. They didn't know about an awful lot. I was amazed how naïve they were – very streetwise but naïve about the business. Kellogs didn't gel with them. They're quite shrewd guys. They don't take bullshit from anybody, they're always thinking, what's happening? They're like me: they don't like the majors, they don't like authority. That's one of the reasons maybe I got on with them in the first place."

"I had been tour manager for the Be Stiff 'train' tour in 1978," explains Kellogs. "After that, Robinson gave me a job as in-house tour coordinator for all these various acts. The record label was fantastic: they looked after every aspect of the artist's career. I was extremely busy. I knew something about Madness and that Stiff were about to sign them. Then Robinson said, 'You can take care of these guys as well.' 'Well, wait a minute, I'm much too busy.' And I was! I can't possibly. And to be honest, I was a bit frightened of what I knew to be seven likely lads from Camden Town. Oh God, no, I can't deal with this!"

Because neither of the band's existing roadies, Chalky and Toks, could drive or had any electrical experience, Kellogs' first decision was to dispense with their services and enlist professional roadies in their place. "Chalky and Toks were sweet as anything, actually. But I was a professional guy and they weren't. Madness have got their mates as roadies and they're driving me crazy because they wanted to hang out with the band. It's demanding physically and you have to be inventive about what you do, dealing with situations as they come up. They were fantastic, as it turned out, but I found them initially quite difficult."

After playing dates in Coventry and Leeds, Madness played Retford Porterhouse Club on October 5. "Some friends of the band came along and there was an incident where an office was broken into," sighs Kellogs. "Something super-mischievous happened, anyway." During a late night drinking session, the band met the club's owner, Sammy Jackson, a larger-than-life character from north London who played a trick on Suggs and Cathal by filling a tray with water and placing it on a table. He then floated two matchsticks in the water and asked Suggs and Cathal to blow the matches towards each other. As they attempted this, a barmaid slapped a tea towel across the tray, thus soaking them both. "I remember a trick being played on me around that time," adds Kellogs. "I had been driving the van and had got out to seek some directions. Somebody got into the driving seat and drove away, leaving me in the middle of the night standing there. Antics were high, all the time!"

The following night, Madness were playing in Huddersfield but the show was sold out. Among those refused entry were some Middlesbrough fans who expressed their displeasure by starting a riot. Apparently, Madness were travelling in two Ford transit vans, one of which contained a film crew led by acclaimed American video maker, Chuck Statler. He was filming material for the forthcoming video for 'One Step Beyond' as the tour progressed but both vans ended up with smashed windows and slashed tyres. On October 7, Madness interrupted their warm-up dates to shoot part of the same video, playing on the familiar stage in the basement at The Hope & Anchor. Camden's Electric Ballroom played host to the band on October 12, with support from comedy ska combo Bad Manners and Echo & The Bunnymen, the connection between the then unknown Liverpool band and Madness being Rob Dickins.

"Echo & The Bunnymen I'd signed for publishing and couldn't get a record deal, either," explains Dickins, "so I paid for 'Pictures On My Wall' on Zoo then started Korova Records. Because if I'd had a label with Madness, we wouldn't have had to go to all that trouble. So Korova was started by Warner Brothers Music and I did a distribution deal with WEA. When they supported Madness, their fans left a little to be desired. The Electric Ballroom was packed. The Bunnymen were being moody, psychedelic, and the audience were shouting 'what a load of rubbish'. Suggs came on after the second song and said, 'Look, this band are on the bill because we like them,' and he quietened the audience down which is another one of those great moments. Give them some respect. And the rest of their set was fairly uninterrupted."

Despite having signed to Stiff, Madness agreed to participate in 2 Tone's ambitious, 40-date UK tour. On October 16, they joined The Specials and The Selecter at the Roundhouse, Chalk Farm, to begin rehearsals. Three days later, proceedings opened at Brighton's Top Rank, immortalised by a photo session with all three bands on Brighton beach for the first issue of *The Face* magazine. "I remember the photo session at a service station somewhere," adds Kellogs, "in the middle of the night with The Specials and The Selecter, to announce or advertise the tour. So I got them going on this tour, organised them and their equipment, and went out on the road with them." However, Kellogs' commitments elsewhere with Stiff meant that he felt forced to delegate his responsibilities to a deputy: "At the University Of East Anglia, I handed over the reigns of tour management to a friend of theirs, Cameron McVey, a successful photographer who was keen on Madness. OK, Cameron, you can carry on from here."

McVey had followed the band avidly for several months. "I went to see them at an early show in The Dublin Castle and was immediately hooked," he recalls. "I started going to see their gigs all over the UK, eventually travelling with them. They were quite a handful to keep in order and Kellogs just couldn't take any more of their antics. I was on the road taking photos and having a laugh so he asked if I wanted to take over." By coincidence, the young photographer had once worked as an assistant to Woodgate's father Crispian. His introduction to tour managing Madness proved to be a baptism of fire when violence erupted during The Selecter's set at the very next date at Hatfield Polytechnic on Saturday, October 27. Reports suggested that the so-called Hatfield Anti-Fascist League burst in through a fire exit and slashed people with Stanley knives who they claimed were National Front supporters. Ten people were hospitalised, 11 were arrested and the bill for damage ran to £1,000. Subsequent press reports erroneously inferred some racist tendencies within the only all-white band on the tour.

"It was a heavy night," admits Cameron. "I smashed the crew van up on the gatepost of the Hatfield House car park gate. I tried to get some order into the sound check but I don't think it worked! Later on, during the show, there was an invasion by some hostile skins who broke into the venue and a lot of kids got cut and stabbed. I saw some of the so-called toughest blokes run that night once the trouble started. But the whole

Madness crew and band held pretty firm. I think I was road manager for a few shows. That's probably an exaggeration: my job was more like that of Radar on *M*A*S*H*, trying to think ahead and outwit the group before any real trouble started! Frank Murray, The Specials' tour manager, was a tough bastard – he taught me a lot."

Garry Bushell remembers the incident: "The gig was ruined by a gang who later called themselves 'Red Action' – they broke into the hall about 30-handed and started attacking people indiscriminately with knives and coshes. The SWP [Socialist Workers' Party] kicked out the Red Action lot: that's how extreme they were! Funnily enough, some of the worst trouble Madness ever encountered involved the Left. They had problems with the Ladbroke Grove skins back when they played the Acklam Hall as the North London Invaders."

Kellogs returned to the Stiff office the following Monday, blissfully unaware of the calamity. "I went to carry on my work with the other acts on behalf of Stiff," he explains. "Robinson hauled me into his office and said, 'What exactly happened?' I said, 'I don't know Dave, because you may remember me telling you that I couldn't do this all the time. So I wasn't there.' What! He blew up and summarily fired me on the spot. Gosh, I had a house to keep warm and children to feed so it was rather difficult for me. I was down in the dumps without a job. I thought it was grossly unfair because I was flying the flag for Stiff Records and trying to do my job. One didn't realise that Madness would become the mega thing that they were. Obviously, Robinson did."

* * *

On the previous Friday, October 26, Robinson finally got his wish with the release of Madness's next single: their energetic treatment of the Prince Buster classic, 'One Step Beyond'. That week, The Specials were back in the charts with their second single, 'A Message To You, Rudy' (also a cover version, in this instance of Dandy Livingstone's rocksteady classic from 1967), joining The Selecter's 'On My Radio' in the Top 10. Meanwhile, copies of The Specials' eponymous debut album – also released that week – flew out of the racks. One week, Madness, The Specials and The Selecter all appeared on *Top Of The Pops* – it felt as if 2 Tone had taken over the charts.

Robinson's intuition was spot-on: 'One Step Beyond' proved to be an instantaneous party anthem for the 2 Tone generation. Smash's opening clarion call all but defined the era. More knowing observers might have raised an eyebrow at such brazenly derivative cover versions. After all, even Smash's spoken-word intro was borrowed from past glories: "Hey you, don't watch that, watch this" was lifted from another Prince Buster track, 'Scorcher', while the equally immortal line, "This is the heavy, heavy monster sound", was filched from Dave & Ansell Collins' hit, 'Monkey Spanner'. But then much of Madness's audience wasn't even born when Buster recorded the original. 'One Step Beyond' duly stormed into the Top 10, buoyed by universal praise from press and radio – and John Lennon, who apparently cited it as his favourite record of the period.

Madness' slapstick persona was perfectly crystallised by the promotional video for 'One Step Beyond'. Live clips were expertly interspersed with footage of the band's "nutty train" walk and shots onstage at The Hope & Anchor by director Chuck Statler. "The joy of Chuck was he was very quick," Dave explains. "I think we made two videos in one day. 'One Step Beyond' was made by that process. Madness were a complete unit. They didn't like photo sessions so they would dream up moves, so the session would be an hour rather than four hours with people prancing about trying to think of something. They were fast movers – it was great."

Chuck Statler's role was vital in capturing Madness' youthful sense of anarchic good humour. Now considered one of the true pioneers of the music video, Statler made his name working with Devo, who the Minneapolis-based director had met at Kent State University in the early 1970s. Since Devo had briefly been signed to Stiff, Statler knew Dave Robinson, which led to his directing videos for Graham Parker, Elvis Costello and Nick Lowe – and Madness.

Paul Du Noyer recalls how photographers were always struck by Madness' instinctive knack for being geometrically photogenic. "They had an uncanny physical propensity to assemble themselves into shapes as a group," he explains. "Photographers don't normally like doing large groups because they're unwieldy but Madness had this innate gift. They seemed to have some kind of telepathy amongst themselves." That physical presence was akin to an old-fashioned dance troupe – another nod back to the "good old days" of music hall and variety.

"We all loved Variety," Suggs told *Uncut*. "Max Wall, Tommy Cooper,

Benny Hill, Morecambe & Wise, plus Wilson, Keppel and Betty doing their sand-dancing routine. We were lucky to have so many extroverts in the band. Carl came from a family of Irish dancers so he was a very good mover. Lee was very visual – we'd always give him the most foolish roles! And Mike, ironically because he's such an introverted character, was absolutely brilliant at encapsulating funny shapes. None of us worried about taking the piss out of ourselves. If you're conscious about looking a bit stupid, it shows. But if you're 110 per cent absorbed in the idea where you don't give a fuck, you get something else. You get something transcendent, like Tommy Cooper."

In fact, Madness' stage act felt like a logical evolution of the long-standing British tradition of working-class comedy which, within a musical setting, had characterised theatrical entertainment for the masses in the decades prior to the arrival of rock'n'roll in the mid-1950s. Although its popularity started to ebb thereafter, the music hall traditions still cast a long shadow over popular entertainment well into the 1970s. In Max Wall, Stiff Records had a sole surviving relic from that bygone era, one side of whose one-off single for the label, 'England's Glory', was written by Ian Dury.

"Vaudeville acts were still appearing around certain halls in London [in the 1970s]," wrote Stuart Wright in *Nut Inc.* "This, no doubt, crept into the Madness psyche. Duos would sing and dance and tell jokes, there'd be a circus strongman, Egyptian sand dances . . . Madness, I suppose, were the equivalent to the old war-time music hall legends of the Forties and Fifties, the Crazy Gang, with a dash of Ealing film studios thrown in for good measure." It was evident, for example, in Barson's end-of-the-pier organ or Thompson's 'Yakety Yak'-style saxophone, which echoed that madcap 1958 hit 'Hoots Mon' by Lord Rockingham's XI or Boots Randolph's 'Yakety Sax', later immortalised on *The Benny Hill Show*.

Renowned for their novelty marketing techniques, Stiff accompanied the 7-inch for 'One Step Beyond' with a then relatively unusual second format, the 12-inch, adding the Suggs/Thompson instrumental, 'The Nutty Theme'. This light-hearted, cockney-styled sometime set opener was half Chas & Dave, half *Steptoe & Son* theme with a nod to the Kilburn & The High Roads' classic, 'Billy Bentley'. On the B-side of both formats was one of Madness' earliest compositions, 'Mistakes'. Co-credited to Barson and John Hasler, the song was a surprisingly mature, philosophical ode to life's lessons learnt; Cathal later summarised it as "such an astute observation of life at a young age, it was way ahead of its time and very poignant". Its message was encapsulated by the line, "An opportunity gone is gone forever/You never know how much you could have been." On the contrary, Madness appeared to have seized every opportunity perfectly.

Chapter 7

ONE STEP BEYOND

MADNESS had the image, the sound, the dance, the humour – and a growing youth subculture for an audience. By winter 1979/ 1980, the ska revival was reaching its peak. School playgrounds were full of teenage kids wearing the "rude boy" uniform of Harrington jackets and tonic trousers, white socks and loafers, Ben Sherman shirts and Doctor Martens, Fred Perrys and pork pie hats – and collars littered with button badges. Madness, however, had evolved their own look which was distinctively different from, say, The Specials' wardrobe. Just as their music was as indebted to American rock'n'roll as Jamaican rocksteady, so their dress code melded elements of skinhead attire with the baggy one-button suits, baseball jackets and flat top crew-cuts of Fifties Americana.

At first glance, the *One Step Beyond* LP was squarely targeted at the 2 Tone generation. Its monochromatic black-and-white design depicted the six musicians (Chas Smash was yet to be deemed a fully fledged band member) standing in line, arms poised, to create the soon-to-be-famous 'nutty train'. That image on the reverse of the first Kilburn & The High Roads album notwithstanding, this 'nutty train' pose was thought to have been created by Lee, Cathal and his brother Brendan while messing about to 'Liquidator' by Harry J. All Stars. It's also been suggested that it was inspired by an old episode of *The Dave Allen Show*. Equally, such images harked back to the days of the famous early 20th century comedy troupe, Fred Karno's Army: old postcards and drawings clearly showed them throwing similar shapes, spread out in a line and seen in profile, back to back.

Dave Robinson decided to draft in an old cohort as photographer for the album cover. Chris Gabrin had known Dave since the beginning of the Seventies, having taken pictures of Brinsley Schwarz and Help Yourself (both of whom Robinson managed). He had been first choice when Stiff was founded – and his credits appeared on the label's very first single, Nick Lowe's 'Heart Of The City', as well as several Ian Dury records. "Photography was what I'd always done," explains Chris. "I got diverted into messing about with bands after doing record covers. I'd just started a studio, renovating an old loft at the Camden and running the shows at the Roundhouse every Sunday."

Madness were different from Gabrin's usual subjects, most of whom he already knew from the pub rock circuit: "We were used to an older generation of musicians, and I know Dave was impressed by their enthusiasm and energy compared with the people we'd been dealing with." In due course, Gabrin was asked to photograph the band. "Dave sent Chas round first [although] Chas wasn't officially in the band. We decided to do a series of shots of him dancing. He worked very hard, an incredibly nice bloke, we got on very well." These shots appeared on the eventual back cover in line with a Chas Smash credit for "backing vocals, various shouts and fancy footwork".

Unfortunately, Chris's second session wasn't as productive. "The following day, I was meant to do the album front sleeve," Gabrin remarks. "But they turned up four hours late. I was just about to go home. It was an evening session, I'd hired an assistant. Chas had turned up on time and he kept apologising. There was no word of apology [from the others]: they went into a big band huddle, nattering in the office and wouldn't talk to me. I did a Polaroid of the 'nutty train' but I got so pissed off with them, I told them to fuck off and kicked them out. They were new and fresh and treated people like me, photographers, with a great deal of suspicion. That classic thing of young blokes cast into the deep end."

A cover was mocked up using Gabrin's Polaroid but this was duly rejected, as Cameron McVey recalls. "They showed me the cover Stiff had done for them and I thought it sucked," he suggests, "so I blagged Dave Robinson to let me try. He was OK with this so I got them to a rented studio where I set up a white background with a soft light and a sharper spotlight within this to sharpen the image. It was a method I'd been using for my *Vogue* brides photos at the time! They did this move, the 'nutty train', onstage. They were pretty dynamic performers and all their moves

were very graphic. All I did was force them to exaggerate it to the max."
Woodgate later recalled this final session: "It was taken in a photographic
studio in Covent Garden, near where I used to work in the summer. We
were clinging onto some sort of rail to stay in position."

This is a sore point with Barson's ex-girlfriend Kerstin Rodgers. "I did
all their photographs for the first two years but when it came to the actual
album cover and some money, I was booted off, and that was at the
behest of Lee Thompson," she complains. "In fact, about a decade later,
he rang up and apologised. They took my photograph and got a posh
photographer to do a cleaned-up version of it. I feel quite badly treated.
They have not played fair with me."

Overall design of the package fell to Stiff employee Julian 'Jules' Balme
(who would later create many iconic sleeves – including The Clash's
Combat Rock). "I oversaw Chas's first photo shoot with Chris that became
the back of the LP sleeve," he recalls. "And I designed their 'M' logo. It
was a Friday morning when they briefed me: 'We want a 2 Tone man but
not – if you know what I mean.' They went to the Durham Castle next
door and by the time they surfaced, I'd drawn it. I also did the front of the
album sleeve, the photo for which was actually the second attempt.
Chris's shot with them all in front of travel posters was judged too busy.
They were still finding their feet in front of the camera and appeared
uncomfortable, whereas their mate Cameron was more successful –
bagging the iconic shot in the process. I also co-ordinated all the photo
booth pictures on the liner bag, which included sticking 'em all
down."

The inner sleeve was littered with photo booth snapshots of "nutty
punters", like some glorified fan club scrapbook. "It was my idea to get all
the fans to send in photographs," Foreman told Edwards, which led to an
invitation being placed in the London *Evening Standard* – one of many typically inclusive gestures over the years which have earned Madness an
acutely loyal, supportive fan base. The resulting collage of 150 snaps mixed
fans' headshots with images of the band's family, friends and girlfriends, as
well as choice images of the band members past and present. These
included Cameron McVey and Keith Wainwright from the famous salon
Smile (the rock hairdresser of choice who'd styled Roxy Music). Other
friends and acquaintances graced the other side of the inner, from the
dancer in the video for 'One Step Beyond' (John, alias Prince Nutty),

Clive Langer, Chalky and Toks and McVey's model girlfriend Daisy Lawrence.

★ ★ ★

Robinson was given right of veto over the track sequence, which opened with their two singles to date. 'The Prince' was re-recorded to avoid contractual issues with 2 Tone, despite some reservations from the band about its inclusion; they admired Ian Dury's value-for-money policy of excluding singles from LPs. Dave relegated the album's tales of social realism to Side 2; patently, he preferred their madcap party antics to tales of street life in Thatcher's Britain. To an extent, *One Step Beyond* pandered to Madness' image as a 2 Tone band but even a cursory listen revealed that ska was but one of many influences on the record. Madness had clearly soaked up myriad cultural references from life around them, growing up as kids during the Sixties and Seventies, from comics like *The Beano* (and, in particular, *The Bash Street Kids*) to TV comedies like *It Ain't Half Hot Mum*.

The album's primary instrument was the piano (as opposed to the guitar). Barson wrote exclusively on the keyboard – as, in due course, did most other members of Madness – which led to well-structured compositions which relied on detailed, often heavily chromatic chord changes. "I think we all find the piano quite a logical thing to write on," Barson later commented. "Everything is laid out visually. You can see the relationship between the chord changes and the tune. Most of us worked like that. Carl and Suggs and Woody are all good enough piano players to bang out a series of chord changes and sing along."

The album contained four cover versions: 'One Step Beyond' itself; a less vital re-recording of 'Madness' (a "secret" 14th track omitted from the track listing on the sleeve); 'Swan Lake' (notable at their early gigs for prompting a head-butting routine in front of the stage by roadies Chalky and Toks); and the Fifties coffee bar stomp of Bazooka Joe's 'Rockin' In A♭'. Ian Dury's persona was evident in several respects, from lyrics which felt like glorified lists to the lack of traditional choruses and the quirky time signatures.

Despite Barson's unquestionable position as the dominant musical force, he wrote or co-wrote only five of the remaining 11 tracks: 'My Girl'; 'Believe Me', another early composition with Hasler; 'Night Boat To

Cairo'; 'Tarzan's Nuts'; and 'Bed And Breakfast Man'. Inspired by the Sixties TV series starring Ron Ely or perhaps the endless re-runs of various film versions, not least the classic black-and-white movies starring Johnny Weissmuller, 'Tarzan's Nuts' was a last-minute construct in the studio, one of two throwaway numbers co-written by Smyth.

'Bed And Breakfast Man', by contrast, was the album's best kept secret. Earmarked as a single, it was even treated to a promotional video by Chuck Statler in the Masonic room upstairs at the Clarendon Hotel in Hammersmith where Madness had auditioned for Dave Robinson. ("For the same price, we could get two videos and that was one of the few tracks they'd finished at the time," explains the Stiff boss.) 'Bed And Breakfast Man' epitomised Madness' knack for songs with a laconic charm and a beguiling melody. It transpired that the character in question was based on a nickname for John Hasler – whose penchant for enjoying the hospitality of others hadn't gone unnoticed. "He'd turn up at your house," said Foreman, "and next thing you knew he was there for breakfast, eating the kids' leftovers!"

Barson later admitted that the song was his stab at Motown. "I think this started off as 'Ain't Too Proud To Beg'," Bedford told Terry Edwards. "The bass moves more than the chord sequences. The drums are straight but the bass bubbles along, trying to kick it along." It was Foreman who sang 'Bed And Breakfast Man' at their early shows and for their John Peel session; indeed, he subsequently claimed to have written some of the lyrics.

Suggs' first foray into songwriting resulted in another album highlight, 'In The Middle Of The Night', inspired by a period working at a newsagents in Clerkenwell, whose proprietor acquired a pile of "water-damaged" underwear. Suggs' imagination hatched a character driven by a furtive love of women's knickers – only to get caught stealing them. "I just liked the idea of the newspaper seller seeing his face in the paper," Suggs admitted. "What is it about England? Rather than have normal sex lives, fine wines and dining, we have perversion, greasy macs, etc. This just fitted with the idea of eccentricity . . . some sort of reality in the darker side of the British psyche. But it's also funny: comic, black humour."

If Suggs' recent comment that Madness are now the working-class Pink Floyd was serious, then this must surely be their equivalent of Floyd's 1967 hit, 'Arnold Layne'. Some crude yet effective sound effects were added by Thompson, outside TW Studios in Fulham, pretending to sell newspapers at the top of his voice while Langer revved up his van nearby, bibbing the horn. The song's central character George belonged "to an innocent age of *Carry On* films and seaside postcard innuendo alongside 'What The Butler Saw' machines at the end of the pier," wrote Terry Edwards.

In addition to 'The Prince', Lee Thompson contributed two further compositions. With Suggs on organ and Woody adopting some jazz-style drumming, 'Razor Blade Alley' was inspired by a 1978 film *The Boys In Company C*, a coming-of-age movie in the style of *The Virgin Soldiers*, set during the Vietnam War. "The razor blade bit comes from [that] film," Thompson commented. "That's how I started the song, from the line where the GI gets a dose of the clap and says, 'I feel like I'm pissing razor blades'." Better still was 'Land Of Hope And Glory', Lee's ode to his period in incarceration back in the early 1970s, co-written with Foreman and sung by Thompson.

"Up to that time, my friends thought I was a bit . . . y'know, about sex," Lee explained in uncharacteristically bashful mood to *Smash Hits*. "So I jumped in the deep end. And it was deep! I've still got a reputation that when I meet a bird, I talk and talk instead of getting down to action. They always fall asleep on me!"

Mark Bedford contributed one song, 'Mummy's Boy', written while he was still at school about a 40-year-old man who'd yet to leave home. "It was a chance remark by one of my teachers who told me that he still lived at home with his parents," Bedford later explained. "I found it quite shocking. Because I was a hot-headed teenager and independent. I wanted my own place." The subject matter pre-empted Ronnie Corbett's popular TV series of the 1980s *Sorry* while also harking back to a comedy classic from the Sixties. "I wanted it to sound like a theme tune for a comedy sitcom. *Steptoe And Son* is so sad – that they're just stuck together. With Madness, that element of the tragic and the comic was there right from the start. Musically, the song is close to Lee's description of 'The Nutty Sound' – part fairground, part music hall."

The final track on the album was 'Chipmunks Are Go!' Despite Robinson's reluctance, Clive Langer apparently pushed through this quirky comic number written by Smyth with brother Brendan – indeed, this set-closer seemed to crystallise Cathal's nebulous relationship with the band prior to him becoming a fully fledged member. "I always felt insecure in the band, never totally safe," he later admitted. By all accounts, the Stiff boss had canvassed heavily for Smyth to be granted full membership of the band because he was such an integral aspect of their image.

"Cathal wanted to join," states Robinson. "It had never occurred to me that he wasn't in the group because I didn't know all the ins and outs. To my mind, he was a member. We'd signed the agreement – and, of course, he didn't sign it. So I said, 'What about your man, the MC?' They said, 'Oh, he's not in the band.' Mike wasn't that keen because he was the leader of the band. I said, 'There's no reason why not.' I thought it was important because he had a large part to play aside from the opening rant on 'One Step Beyond'. And he was the dancer. I didn't realise until the movie that he had been the bass player briefly and had been shoved out."

By the end of the year, Smyth had become a formal member of the band on the condition that he learnt to play the trumpet. "Really, it was lawyers and the record label saying, 'You've got to make him a member,'" Cathal later admitted. "Some of the band were a bit reluctant. I remember being in a cafe with Lee and Mike and our girlfriends. I mentioned something about being made a band member, and Lee said, 'Well, six goes further than seven.' I was devastated. I'd have done it for nothing. I loved it."

As for the song's mimicking of US marines, it felt like an update of Sgt Bilko. "My father used to sing that Marines chant because he'd been in the American corps of military engineers," Smyth told Terry Edwards. Perhaps he, too, had been influenced by *The Boys In Company C?* "Members of the band were wearing Fifties or maybe Sixties mohair suits but with brothel creepers," Bedford explained. "We'd end the set with 'Chipmunks' and it went down well. [It was at] Cathal's instigation."

Suggs reminisced on their youthful lack of self-questioning to *Uncut* in 2008: "There's a flame that burns for a few years for every band where it's not mindless but it's not intellectualised either. If we did 'One Step Beyond' today, we'd be going, 'What about the middle eight? Maybe we should have a key change?' Do that and you get into committee mode and you haven't got the single-minded approach you had when you were young."

One Step Beyond entered the chart on November 3, 1979 but while history records its platinum status, the first week's sales were initially modest (entering the charts at number 16), effectively losing out to its closest rival, *The Specials* (number four). In fact, the album was the archetypal slow burner, steadily climbing over three months to eventually peak at number two in February 1980 (held off only by The Pretenders' debut) and remaining on the listings for an impressive 78 weeks (compared to 45 for The Specials' debut). Outside the UK, the LP fared well, too: it topped the charts in France and reached the Top 10 in Switzerland, Austria and Spain. Stiff were notorious for their publicity stunts – and there was no exception for their biggest album of the year. Any customer who bought a copy of the album at the Virgin Megastore in London's Oxford Street was entitled to a free skinhead haircut – and Stiff's Paul Conroy was the first to oblige!

★ ★ ★

Meanwhile, the 2 Tone tour had rolled from town to town in celebratory style, weaving its way across the Midlands and the north of England before the all-star cast arrived in Cardiff for a show on November 7. A logistical problem now presented itself. The BBC were keen to celebrate this new phenomenon with a special episode of *Top Of The Pops* boasting all three acts – but they wanted the triumvirate to be filmed in their Maida Vale studios. Eventually, a solution was found: The Selecter travelled up to record their performance much earlier. While they returned to Cardiff to open the show, Madness and The Specials appeared on the show, which was particularly memorable for Suggs & Co.'s 'nutty train' dance through the audience. The Nutty Boys then flew back to Wales in a small chartered plane – an experience they later described as nail-biting – only to discover that their tour bus had been broken into.

The 2 Tone tour was chaotic, to say the least. Suggs later recalled that, on one occasion, The Specials' manager Rick Rogers stopped the coach to find a phone box in order to try to book a bigger venue for whatever their next date was. Having been delayed in Cardiff the following day while their tour transport was fixed and after interviews with the police, the charabanc arrived at Derby King's Hall later than scheduled. While The Selecter hurried onstage without having the opportunity to sound check, Madness went to find a nearby pub to watch themselves on *Top Of The Pops*.

But when none of the local hostelries would oblige, only Cathal's perseverance led the entourage to the tiny Eagle Taxis' HQ, where they were finally granted access to a TV. Hugely appreciative, the band showered the unsuspecting staff with autographed copies of 'One Step Beyond' and free tickets to their show, during which Smyth gave the service a free plug. All of which distracted from an abysmal show which fizzled out after just five numbers due to technical troubles.

After another half dozen dates in Newcastle upon Tyne and Scotland, Madness parted company with the 2 Tone tour on November 14 because of live commitments in the USA, bidding farewell with a 'nutty dance' across the stage while The Specials were performing 'Blank Expression'. For Madness, it was the end of a brief but productive period as part of the 2 Tone family, a symbiotic relationship which benefited both parties but which would ultimately see them taking different paths. Their place on the tour was taken by Dexys Midnight Runners.

While Madness enjoyed – in the short term, at least – the collective identity of 2 Tone, the differences between The Specials and the Nutty Boys were actually as marked as their similarities. "The Specials were quite an angry, spitting animal," suggests Paul Williams, author of their biography *You're Wondering Now*. "When they played live, they were like an explosion three feet from your face. Madness were a more laid-back, fun-loving, out-with-your-mates set-up. But that was good: the angry young men of The Specials and the friendly Madness approach seemed to be the two sides of people's personalities. Obviously, The Specials were politically edged whereas Madness didn't tackle politics till later but still commented on everyday life which meant fans could instantly relate to them. The fact that Madness were friends first and foremost meant that longevity was always their destiny. In that sense, this put them ahead of The Specials, who were picked by Dammers and contained seven feisty characters that would lock horns because they didn't have those initial bonds in place."

Madness' demeanour might have been more amicable but they still shared The Specials' ability to turn concerts into a rollercoaster ride of excitement. "They were a manic bunch, always moving, always joking," recalls Williams. "Sometimes, they would play out of tune because they were going at it so fast – just watching them careering around the stage was an interest on its own! I remember Mike Barson trying to keep it all working until he realised he had lost it and just went with the flow. Their audience participation was second to none as well. I saw one gig when Carl didn't stop dancing, even between songs!"

★ ★ ★

A few days later, Madness headlined for the second time in as many months at the Electric Ballroom in Camden – only this time, for three nights (Friday–Sunday 16–18 November), the third date added due to public demand. Once again, rogue elements in the audience heckled one of the support bands, but on this occasion their motivation proved to be more sinister. The first of two support acts onstage (the other being Bad Manners) was Welsh soul band Red Beans & Rice, fronted by a black singer named Lavern Brown. In the crowd that night was Roger Armstrong, head of Red Beans & Rice's label Chiswick Records.

"The rest of the band were white but Lavern was part of that long-established Tiger Bay black community," Roger explains. "I'm pretty sure that Madness asked for them. Red Beans & Rice played The Dublin Castle a lot so Madness would have been aware of them. As soon as Lavern hit the stage, a bunch of 'boneheads' down the front started making 'monkey' noises, shouting out racist stuff then throwing things. Maybe into the second number, Suggs came flying onto the stage, grabbed a mike stand and started cleaving the [offenders] in the front row. He really meant it, too, out to inflict some real damage, and they all jumped back out of the way, probably shocked at Suggs doing this as I'm sure he knew some of them from around the Camden scene. But poor Lavern had to go off eventually." Reports of that night's proceedings suggested that a minority of the audience started *Sieg-Heiling*.

"There had been a problem with the far-Right element among some London skins since about 1978," admits Garry Bushell. "Suggs and Chas had knocked about with right-wing gangs when they were too young to know any better but certainly, by the time of Madness, they were both genuinely pro-Labour – and they both got stuck in bashing bigots who heckled Red Beans & Rice. But they preferred to have a dialogue with right-wing skins rather than just disown them."

Stiff's 'head of international', Alan Cowderoy, had representatives from some of the label's foreign distributors over to see the band. "It was absolutely rammed," recalls Alan. "I had some foreigners over who I was vaguely shepherding but left them to their own devices, keeping a watchful eye on them. Some rowdy skinheads created an intimidating, aggressive atmosphere, lagered up. Half a dozen would go round asking, 'Give us 50p.' Of course, this Dutch journalist didn't understand. Suddenly, I could see this guy about to get kicked to death by these skinheads so I had to run over and rescue him. My life is in my hands!"

As the only all-white band within the 2 Tone movement, Madness were vulnerable to accusations from the media that they endorsed such behaviour. "There were problems from the press," Rick Rogers later observed, "particularly as Suggs and Cathal had been skinheads and were young and fairly naïve at the time and not too sure about their political persuasions. I mean, they'd been in their youth gangs, I suppose. We used to talk about things like that on the tour. They were ideologically sound but just unable to know how to deal with the press."

"They did have a high proportion of skinhead guys in their audience," admits Dave Robinson, "red Doc Martens, trousers and braces. I just thought of them as the Madness crowd. I mean, we had the Blockheads and now we had the Madness crowd. They were always a bit iffy! When it sprang up, we had a meeting with the band and they were very bright about it. They knew who their boys were, what was happening, they knew they weren't going to be involved and I think it was decided that Cathal or maybe Suggs would make a statement to the press and give interviews. Dealing with it quickly in a straightforward fashion, rather than the PR guy from the record company spouting on their behalf, it went away. They were starting to attract a lot of younger kids, a whole new audience, and the skinhead thing started getting sidelined. It might have been nasty."

Journalist Paolo Hewitt had just started at *Melody Maker*: "I had to go and review them at the Electric Ballroom. This is when the skinheads were out, masses of them, all that Nazi stuff going on. I don't know where they came from. They went berserk at Sham 69, Clash and Angelic Upstarts gigs – all that Oi business. It was a threatening atmosphere. There'd be 200 skinheads in the knee-length Doctor Martens. And once they started throwing themselves around, I'm sorry. The thing is, by 1982, they'd all gone!"

Cathal later suggested in *Melody Maker* that the Electric Ballroom show was sabotaged by the National Front. "That was the worst gig ever," he admitted. "It was like a bloody rally. They were passing out leaflets at The Lyceum the week before saying, 'We want a good turnout at this gig.' And then all the mods were saying, 'should be a good bundle, lads'. What could we do? All that right-wing stuff is just fashion. Half the kids down the squats in King's Cross where I used to live are looking for a bit of excitement, they're just bored. One week they're in the NF, the next it's the BM and now there's some bunch called the Vikings. If you try and have an intelligent conversation, they've no idea what they're talking about. Fortunately, they've had their fun with us now, they don't seem to be coming to gigs any more. It's all died off."

"I think the trouble Madness had with being all white did have its drawbacks," suggests Paul Williams. "It's well documented that the 'neo Nazis' singled them out as their band. Madness were just young lads, who enjoyed playing and listening to black and white music without a thought for anything heavy. [Specials singer] Terry Hall once said he wished Madness had taken a stronger stance with the racists but they did eventually address the problem and I saw it at firsthand when Madness stopped a show in Leeds and had the *Sieg-Heiling* racists thrown out. But they didn't come with the racial aspect that The Specials had, simply because of their location, with Coventry being a relatively small city with a heavily ethnic population."

In 1984, in the TV documentary *South Of Watford*, Smash responded to questions about the accusations of racism: "It's unfortunate because we were part of the 2 Tone thing and we were all white. There wasn't a lot we could do about it. We felt at the time that we'd written a song 'The Prince' which was a tribute to a black guy Prince Buster – we were very naïve. It was just really horrible. I don't think a lot of the kids knew what they were doing."

* * *

Madness's first exposure to this predicament came during an interview with *New Musical Express* journalist Deanne Pearson, organised around the show in Derby on November 9 and published on November 29. "Nice band, shame about the fans," ran the ominous headline. Still, the article began in optimistic fashion, detailing their pre-show search for a television set and general chit-chat about their audience before Pearson's narrative switched to her presumed focus for the feature: "National Front and

British Movement supporters are often seen at Madness gigs, particularly in London, and I ask the band why."

Wary of engaging with the journalist on this delicate matter, various band members evaded the issue, until Cathal "breaks rank": "It's got nothing to do with us," he was quoted as saying. "We don't care if people are in the NF or BM, so long as they're behaving themselves, having a good time and not fighting. What does it matter, who cares what their political views are?" Woodgate attempted to diffuse the confrontation: "Look, we are not a political band, we aren't like The Clash or Sham 69, we see our music purely as entertainment, and our only concern is that everyone enjoys themselves. We never mention the NF. We neither encourage them or discourage them."

Pearson pressed further: did Madness sympathise with the National Front? "No, we don't," the drummer responded. "I think I can speak for all of us, but we don't want to interfere with their politics. We don't want to become involved." It's arguable that Pearson was justified in interrogating the band regarding this issue. But it's also questionable whether she should have continued to grill them in the absence of any evidence (outside London, at least) of a right-wing minority at their shows. Surely, Pearson persisted, Madness had a responsibility to engage with these fans?

Barson responded: "But do you think they'll really listen to us? Look what happened to Sham 69 when Jimmy Pursey took a stand and shouted about his political ideas: it just made matters worse, encouraged more violence at gigs and destroyed the band." Smyth was next to pipe up – but the journalist was already couching him as a volatile hooligan. "If we carried on like Pursey, saying we hate all NF supporters, we don't want them at our gigs, then we'd get even more coming, and other kids who were looking for a fight," Smyth explained. "It's best to just ignore them – most of them don't know what they're talking about. They're not the real older NF supporters, who follow Tyndall and Webster. They stick an armband on – and they don't know what it means. It's like supporting a football team. They're just kids, they don't know any better."

By now, judging by Pearson's account of the exchange, the atmosphere had worsened considerably. Cathal: "Some of those kids are my mates, and they're good kids. I don't talk to them because they're in the NF. They know I don't agree with their views, and so what if they wear Union

Jacks and Nazi swastikas, I don't care about that." Suggs, previously quiet, leapt to their MC's defence: "It's easy for bands to spout off about being anti-racist, and then stand on the other side of the wall while they hurl bottles and abuse at them, but it's much more difficult to go down into the audience and actually talk to them."

As the hours passed, the *NME* scribe continued to press her point home. Somewhat understandably, given his youth and relative inexperience in dealing with the media, Smyth eventually snapped: "You just don't understand, do you? They're just a group of kids who have to take out their anger and frustration on something. NF don't really mean much to them. Why should I stop them coming to our gigs, that's all they've got. It's people like you who live in a cosy flat in London, who see a few NF armbands in a crowd and say, 'Ah yes, these rumours were right', and sensationalise it all in the press, when you don't really know what's going on at all. Well, you print a word of this and I'll deal with you personally."

As tensions subsided, band members clarified their complete lack of sympathy for any far-right faction. Thompson was the only exception, relying instead on his trademark humour to help lighten the mood: when questioned, he would only respond with phrases like "eggs and bacon and sausages, with tomato sauce please" and "how do you like your eggs?"

Only after Pearson followed the entourage up to Newcastle upon Tyne did her editorial allow for more general topics. "It was just like The Beatles, wasn't it?," Woody is quoted as saying as he fought his way backstage, flushed with excitement and exertion. "Did you see them all crushed at the front of the stage – mostly girls screaming and climbing up the sides, grabbing anything they could get hold of as souvenirs?"

Pearson then delivered something approaching a character assassination of Cathal, forever linking him with the band's adopted slogan of "Fuck Art, Let's Dance" and wrapping up the article with details of that unfortunate show with Red Beans & Rice at the Electric Ballroom, spoilt by a minority of *Sieg-Heiling* skinheads nicknamed "the Tufty Club Brigade".

Unfortunately, the *NME* feature only fuelled speculation that Madness had racist tendencies. Smyth was swift to respond by co-penning the song 'Don't Quote Me On That' with the memorable opening quip courtesy of Thompson, "Eggs, bacon, beans and a fried slice". 'Don't Quote Me On That' was duly circulated as a promotional 12-inch single in an effort to minimise any damage to Madness' public image; introduced as a set closer, the song was later chosen for the *Work, Rest & Play* EP and to open the credits for their film *Take It Or Leave It*.

The song's underlying riff was reminiscent of an old reggae classic, 'Bush Doctor' by the Music Doctors. "I was aggrieved by the interview, that my comments were misconstrued," Smyth later admitted. "I wasn't all that eloquent then. I was all tongue-tied. Until I really started songwriting, I'd just free-form over a groove. I remember the energy of delivering the track and trying to be clever in an obtuse way." Suggs recalled its motivation to Terry Edwards: "A lot of stupid stuff was said about us and racism, when we were on the road with black people, friends of ours, of Cathal in particular – and he was the one getting castigated."

Thereafter, Madness remained wary of the media. In the New Year 1983 edition of their fan club magazine, Thompson devoted the back page to the potential pitfalls of press interviews, even namechecking Deanne Pearson before concluding, "All I wanted to do was play music."

* * *

In the short term, then, Madness' departure on November 21 for their first American tour was quite timely. While John Hasler was still helping to organise their affairs, the band patently needed a more experienced individual to oversee the visit, so they turned to their ex-road manager Kellogs, who picks up the story: "I did phone them up and Lee was really sorry, saying, 'Hey, you got fired, that was our fault what happened.' I suddenly realised, God, these boys were conscious of my plight and cared about me. I was deeply touched by that. To me, they were rough boys and I thought they disliked me intensely because, even though I was only in my thirties, I represented an authority figure, which was never something I'd been before! I told them what to do so I thought we were sworn and deadly enemies. Then I saw their soft side strangely enough through Lee Thompson who would be the last person you'd imagine hearing this from!"

Kellogs was duly recruited by the band. "They were off to America to do a couple of weeks there for Sire Records, and they asked me to go with them as their tour manager to look after them. We flew out to the States at about the same time as *One Step Beyond* was released. I remember being at the airport thinking, shit, these guys have a hit! It was very exciting. I was thrilled to be back in the fold from being excommunicated. Other people in the Stiff camp were rooting for me. Madness seemed to appreciate what I was trying to do for them – showing them the ropes. There was a lot of excitement and support for the band on both coasts and key cities like Boston and Philadelphia."

Kellogs' past experience working in the States made him the perfect candidate for the role. Once the party was ensconced in their hotel in New York City, he recommended a nearby bar which had traditionally been a hub for musicians. Unfortunately, that had been a few years before and times had changed. The lads eventually found the venue but it slowly dawned on them that this was now a gay bar – and their uniform of neat Crombie coats and crewcuts didn't go unnoticed. Woody, especially, found himself the subject of some unwelcome advances.

Considering that *One Step Beyond* was released that very week, but no release date had yet been confirmed for America, the Stateside jaunt seemed illogical, until their rivalry with Jerry Dammers & Co. was factored in. "We wanted to get here before The Specials, didn't we?" Suggs told *Melody Maker* during their next US visit in spring 1980. "Sire didn't want to release the album in November when it was out in England, but we said, 'We're coming over anyway.' We had to go round plastering stickers everywhere and phoning up magazines and radio stations – but that's pioneering."

Along with three shows in New York City (their show at Hurrah was reviewed in *NME*), Madness's first proper US jaunt saw them leapfrog across nearby cities (Boston, Philadelphia) before spending a few days on the West Coast, playing the legendary Whisky a Go-Go in Los Angeles (supported by all-girl band The Go-Go's) and San Francisco's The Mabuhay (supported by punk band The Dead Kennedys). According to The Go-Go's Notebook website, Suggs started dating their vocalist Belinda Carlisle, which led to The Go-Go's being invited to support Madness in the UK in late spring 1980. That wouldn't be the only romantic link between the bands, either: Bedford dated their drummer, Gina Shock. And Go-Go's guitarist Jane Wiedlin once claimed in her blog that she had had an affair with Foreman.

Back in the UK, Madness appeared on two BBC TV shows aimed at opposite ends of the music-buying spectrum: the nation's most serious-minded rock show, *The Old Grey Whistle Test* ('Night Boat To Cairo' and a new song, 'Embarrassment') and the Saturday morning kids' favourite,

Multi-Coloured Swap Shop. Many pop acts were able to straddle both worlds – essentially, children and adults – but as their career developed, it proved to be one of Madness's greatest challenges.

The day after filming *Whistle Test*, Madness headed off to Brighton for the first of 10 dates taking in the south of England, the Midlands and Bristol. Support act were power-pop combo The VIPs, who shared the same Coventry background as The Specials. "John Curd, who promoted the tour, offered us the Madness gig," explains VIPs' drummer Paul Shurey. "We loved Madness from the first time we heard them at a pub gig up in Camden. They had a brilliant, infectious live sound. Their audience were fairly similar to ours although being exposed to the skinhead element on the tour was a bit of a culture shock for us: the shows had an electric edge and energy, a sense they could kick off at any minute, which was half the fun! We were poppier so we were worried about how the skinheads might perceive us, but we were generally well received."

The tour wound its way towards their biggest headlining show in London to date – on December 30 at the famous Lyceum Ballroom with additional support from new 2 Tone signings The Bodysnatchers and Bad Manners. What should have been a celebratory culmination of a triumphant year was instead characterised by an incendiary atmosphere. "I remember The Lyceum show being halted for a brawl in the crowd," says Shurey. "It felt like the show could descend into full-on chaos at any minute. Having played with all the other 2 Tone bands, the Madness tour definitely felt different, like something special was happening, an uncontrollable force. And it would have been impossible for anyone not to have been swept along by this energy. I remember Woody describing it as an unstoppable steam train as the momentum built through the tour. They were a great bunch of lads, genuine and supportive. They didn't play any of the normal headline band tricks and shenanigans!"

* * *

A frenetic tour should have been enough to carry Madness through the festive period – but Dave Robinson had other ideas. On December 21, only four shopping days before Christmas, Stiff plucked a new Madness single from *One Step Beyond*, 'My Girl', housed in a striking cover which retained the monochromatic Sixties feel (but tellingly still excluded Smyth from the cover photographs of the band members). By any music industry yardstick, this release date seemed rash at best – and a marketing blunder at worst. While the Nutty Boys were undeniably one of the hottest new bands of 1979, record racking within retail outlets in the period leading up to and across the Christmas period is infamously tough to secure. Furthermore, it's difficult to coordinate a promotional campaign when the whole nation is in such a state of turmoil, with changes in TV schedules, buying habits and radio programming.

Robinson defends the decision: "It was about getting plays across Christmas, keeping the band's album in the shops. 'One Step Beyond' was fine and had its selling cycle but 'My Girl' was, to my mind, a more Christmassy record. I thought Suggs was going to become the sex symbol of the era. I remember going to gigs and seeing these young girls looking at Suggs in a certain way and I thought, we've got a pop phenomenon here!" In a typical gesture of impetuous genius from Robinson, what might have proved to be a death knell for the band actually gave them their biggest hit to date, eventually peaking at number three with help from a video filmed at The Dublin Castle on a specially re-built, extended stage. Further, it fuelled sales for the *One Step Beyond* album, from which they never looked back.

The band had wanted 'My Girl' to be their first release on Stiff but they had bowed to Robinson's will. Quite apart from providing a good sing-along, the lyrics were equal parts playground and poignant, giving voice to romantically driven teenage angst in language that every school kid could understand. In later years, Barson admitted the music to 'My Girl' was influenced by Elvis Costello's 'Watching The Detectives' but the song's true legacy lay in portraying Madness in a tender, very human light. This was a group that audiences, especially females, could take to their hearts.

"Things changed with 'My Girl'," Suggs later recalled. "Up until then, I could understand what was happening, but then suddenly, it was loads of girls, young girls, screaming – which wasn't what we were after. It wasn't what we expected, maybe that's more to the point, but things changed then: we became a pop group. Suddenly, I was faced with the realisation that I was maybe becoming a teenybop idol! It was only once we'd signed to Stiff and Dave Robinson got involved that there was any notion of a public perception."

Rob Dickins had spotted its strengths back in summer 1979; so too had

Clive Langer. "The song defines the poppy Madness sound, everything they typify – the down-to-earth lyric with a funny twist," Langer later commented to Terry Edwards. "I don't know if Mike thought it was funny, but I was amused by it. God knows how you write an intro like that. It's quite mad." 'My Girl' remains one of the most fondly regarded Madness songs; it was also a Top 30 hit as 'My Guy' for fellow Stiff artist Tracey Ullman in 1984, featuring Mark Bedford on bass; and its drum pattern is thought to have inspired the backbeat for David Bowie's 1980 number one hit, 'Ashes To Ashes'.

The single was backed by the frantic knees-up, 'Stepping Into Line' (co-written by John Hasler and Lee Thompson). Relegated to the 12-inch was an overlooked gem, 'In The Rain', which shared much of the same air of pathos as the A-side with its tale of being jilted on a date, perhaps accentuated by the fact that Suggs sounded particularly sorry for himself because he was suffering from a cold. Recorded at London's Basing Street Studios shortly after their first trip to America, its spacious production – awash with studio effects – sounded like a definite step forward, which explains why it was subsequently included on Madness's second album.

No one was better placed to judge the song's merits than its subject matter, Kerstin Rodgers. "One of the reasons it was one of their best was that it was emotionally authentic," suggests Kirsten. "It's a masterpiece of repressed British male emotion. It came from the heart, quite blokey, and so many people related to it." Unfortunately, by this time their relationship was even more tempestuous than the song's lyrics implied. Eventually, matters came to a head in 1980. "I dumped him," she states. "Stupidly. I should probably just have shut my mouth like all the other girlfriends who put up with the groupies for the money. They were in the middle of a tour of Europe in 1980. Mike was behaving incredibly strangely and my every instinct said he was sleeping around. Then I found out he was sleeping with groupies. I was still young and idealistic and wasn't willing to put up with it. So I flew to France and dumped him."

★ ★ ★

2 Tone fever skanked its way into 1980. The Beat were still riding high with their 2 Tone debut, 'Tears Of A Clown'; The Specials achieved the quite remarkable feat of topping the listings with a live EP, *Too Much Too Young*, at the end of January; and The Selecter were back in the Top 20

with 'Three Minute Hero' in February, swiftly joined by The Beat with 'Hands Off . . . She's Mine', their first single on new imprint Go Feet, courtesy of a new deal with Arista.

While Madness undoubtedly used the springboard of the 2 Tone movement, their challenge – in hindsight, at least – was the degree to which they could be successful in forging their own, unique identity distinct from The Specials et al. In due course, they achieved this not so much by ditching the ska/rocksteady styles and the black-and-white imagery but by drawing on what they knew best, from rock'n'roll to their music of choice in the mid-1970s. "A style which combines ska with slightly vaudevillian English pomp rock is logical if you're growing up in that period of time," suggests Robert Elms. "They're part of the same evolutionary tree as punk but they're a different offshoot. They have the same roots, in some senses. One of the mistakes is to lump them in with 2 Tone. I don't think they were part of that, really. I think they have more in common with Alex Harvey or Kilburn & The High Roads than they have with The Specials."

Meanwhile, Madness promoted Kellogs. "It became evident that Hasler was out of his depth or couldn't do what was required and that they needed a manager," Kellogs recalls. "We got together at a rehearsal studio E-Zee Hire in Brewery Road and discussed this – that I would take over the reins. We came to some financial agreement after some bickering and off I went. At that point, I was working for Jake Riviera, working for Radar as some international manager. I remember leaving that job to go and manage Madness."

Robinson claims some involvement in Kellogs' re-recruitment: "I said, 'Why don't we get him back because we need somebody to do the running?' These boys were very time consuming. They got a habit from early on of popping into the office at some point during the day – they all used to come, not together, and they expected to walk into my office. Which was fine but I needed somebody to be handling their tax, asking where's the equipment, who's in charge, what's going on? They didn't have any of that infrastructure. I was quite happy they didn't have a manager as such because managers are a pain in the arse. Very few of them are any good. They see their job as getting between the record company and the artist and then just lying about it all!"

Presumably disenchanted that his job as manager-by-default had been usurped, John Hasler returned to his original role (that is to say, as a drummer) by hooking up with two London teenagers, singer Vaughn Toulouse and bassist Tony Lordan, who were being managed by their friend Gary Crowley. Inspired by London's live music scene, and in particular the nascent mod revival, the trio had coalesced to form Guns For Hire in late 1979. Before even picking up any instruments, they'd spread word of their band name via badges and stickers. A demo tape, recorded with the addition of guitarist Mike Herbage, was funded by music publisher Clive Banks, for whom Crowley worked.

The result, a punk/ska fusion entitled 'I'm Gonna Rough My Girlfriend's Boyfriend Up Tonight', was eventually picked up by Rob Dickins' Korova imprint (courtesy of the single's producer Clive Langer), prompting kind words from the likes of Elvis Costello and Paul Weller. Guns For Hire didn't play their first live show until August 1980 – at The Rock Garden in London's Covent Garden. Hasler departed soon afterwards. Without him, Guns For Hire evolved into Department S, best known for their hit single, 'Is Vic There?', while Hasler married his girlfriend Shanne Bradley, who had co-founded The Nipple Erectors in 1976 with future Pogues frontman Shane McGowan. As The Nips, they had shared a bill with The Invaders on New Year's Day 1979 – which might be when Hasler and Bradley met. Hasler briefly played drums with The Nips in 1981.

* * *

Now firmly in the driving seat, Kellogs hired the band a new road manager, Tony Duffield (who would also act as occasional sound engineer). "I remember him uttering an immortal line to me once," Kellogs recalls. "He wanted the job. Maybe this was when he got hired? He said, apropos of going to France, 'I'm semi-lingual, man'. And that clinched it for me!" Apparently, Duffield's second language skills were soon tested during the trip but instead of speaking in French, he attempted to ask directions in English but spoken in a faux-French, Inspector Clouseau-type accent.

Duffield duly recruited a second-in-command, John Wynne (whom Tony had known from Canvey Island). "I was a telephone engineer in Basildon but left the GPO to work for them after the release of 'My Girl'," says John. "I was maybe eight years older than them. It was all very new to them but they were making big decisions about their lives. They didn't realise the money at that point but they were enjoying the fun. They were on top of the world, I would think." Swiftly nicknamed 'The Sarge' ("I have a platinum disc to prove it!"), Wynne also oversaw electrical and other technical matters at the band's shows while managing the work of Chalky and Toks in their role as roadies. "They'd never worked with bands before," admits Wynne. "That could cause friction between the management and the band because management had no power over the crew. That did become a bit strange at times!"

France had been chosen as the launch pad on January 20, 1980 for Madness's first tour of the continent because of the huge, chart-topping success there of 'My Girl'. Having spent two days in Paris (which included appearing on a high profile TV show), Madness snaked their way through Belgium, Germany and the Netherlands.

By this point, Madness were acutely aware that a large proportion of their audience was too young to be legally permitted to many of the venues they'd been playing with alcoholic licenses. On February 16, therefore, the band hosted a matinee gig entitled Saturday Morning Madness at the Hammersmith Odeon, to which only fans who were under 16 years of age were admitted, with a ticket price of £1. The landmark event sold out immediately and its popularity led to similar shows there-after. Afterwards, Madness even retained the theme by holding a junior press conference, all the reporters being kids too.

"The matinee gig was fabulous," agrees Kellogs. "That was a fantastic affair. I bet it was one of those creative minds from Camden who came up with such a terrific, innovative idea. I was keen and championed the cause. It was like the old Saturday morning pictures. Paul Conroy from Stiff came onstage and did some introductions. There was a raffle held. My son Jacek came onstage and picked the winners out of the hat. Suggs had had a bright, checked suit made by a friend of mine, a tailor called Andy Roseman, and at the same time, he made a jacket for Jacek who was about six years old! We made this show a real event for the young kids."

Madness also opened their own shop, Nut Inc., in Calendonian Road (the 'Cally' in Islington runs from Camden Road in the north to Pentonville Road in the south, next to King's Cross). Nut Inc. was financed jointly by Madness and Dave Robinson as an outlet for the sale of T-shirts, badges, pork pie hats and other memorabilia (much of which was manufactured via their mates Tots 'n' Whets) that Cathal and brother

Brendan had previously sold at gigs. The band also created their own pub-lishing imprint, Nutty Sounds, and talked of signing up other artists, including all-girl bands Mo-dettes and The Bodysnatchers. A Top 10 album, a shop, a publishing arm; Madness' empire was growing by the minute. Next stop, America!

Chapter 8

STEPPING INTO LINE

O N February 20, Madness departed for their second US jaunt. By all accounts, the band were travelling in two cars with only the radio to pass the time – and American AM stations were not to their tastes – as they endured the drives between Philadelphia, Washington DC, Boston and New York City. The photographer Jill Furmanovsky accompanied them to the 'Big Apple' for an article in the very first issue of *The Face* magazine (published that May). Furmanovsky witnessed Madness' meeting with their US record label Sire, a part of Warner Brothers: "They shot out of the lift on the 44th floor to some sort of reception committee waiting for them. Without saying a word, they all fell to their knees and started worshipping the company logo on the carpet. It was quite spontaneous. No photographer can take credit for styling Madness's pictures. They do it themselves."

Also along for the ride was *Melody Maker* journalist Mark Williams, who caught Barson in self-effacing mood, reflecting a sense of responsibility which accompanied his pivotal if unofficial role as musical director. "I sometimes get worried about our playing," said Barson. "You can go into a studio and try something ten times, and one of them is going to be OK to put on a record. When we released our 2 Tone single, I was afraid that we weren't good enough to appear as a recording group."

There followed an equally lengthy train journey up to Montreal in Canada. Apparently, Suggs and Cathal had purchased Sony Walkman cassette players to pass the time and showed them off to the train guard. "There ain't nothing that can touch ol' Big Bertha," he responded, before fetching a huge 'ghetto blaster' which put their Walkmans to shame. Unfortunately, the Montreal show was plagued by technical problems, prompting Barson to trash the band's dressing room. By contrast, a performance in Toronto passed without incident.

By coincidence, The Specials were also touring Stateside, although the music press headline, "Will the Specials break America or will America break us?," suggested that Dammers & Co. were suffering from the fatigue commonplace among British bands playing lengthy tours of the US. For Madness, that meant travelling across the Midwest (Detroit, Chicago, Cleveland) and onto the North West (Portland, Seattle), up to Vancouver in Canada and back down to the West Coast. To promote three nights at LA's Whisky A Go-Go, a competition was held, as Foreman explained: "For a bit of fun, we tried to give a car away – an estate with 2 Tone stripes which our American label Sire had got hold of – and nobody wanted it! All the kids had got their own cars anyway."

Madness experienced a phenomenon common with British bands attempting to make some headway Stateside: that it's relatively easy to attract interest on the coasts but it's a different story across the vast tracts of land in between. "America is so big, it's like lots of different countries," Suggs told *Smash Hits*. "2 Tone goes down well in hip places like New York, Los Angeles and San Francisco but Detroit or Cleveland have no idea. When we played in Portland, Oregon, the other band – some kind of heavy rockers – got so angry about our music, they were telling us to get out of the country!"

According to Kellogs, Madness dealt with the humdrum of a hectic promotional diary by going AWOL. "A lot of rowdiness and anti-social behaviour was by various turns frightening and cringeworthy," he admits. "You can't drive around the streets of San Francisco with your naked arse hanging out of the back window of the car and shouting things, banging the doors. And when you're set up for an interview with *Time* magazine, and they've arranged to meet you at your hotel, you're there. But where were they? Not there! They were in a cinema that happened to be showing *A Clockwork Orange*. They spoke about *A Clockwork Orange* but they had been unable to see it in England because it had been banned. So en masse, including Chalky and Toks, they went to the movie house up the road, which I knew nothing about. I was there greeting the reporter from *Time*. This was a big deal. I was livid while they had another chance to have a good guffaw about it all!"

Although Sire Records had approached Madness prior to Stiff, their debut album wasn't issued Stateside until spring 1980 and a peak position of 128, while encouraging, suggested that "nutty fever" was going to be tougher to promote across the Atlantic. This wasn't hugely surprising. Quite apart from Madness' overt Britishness, which might have seemed puzzling to Americans, this vast country had no tradition of growing up with Jamaican music. "The only thing they know about reggae in America is Bob Marley," Woody complained in *Melody Maker*. "They don't know the difference between ska, bluebeat, reggae and dub, so they lump it all together. One radio station played an Augustus Pablo record and the DJ said, 'That was dub? What's, er, dub?' Black music to them is either blues or soul or disco."

* * *

Back in Britain, Dave Robinson was eager for Madness not to lose any momentum, so he suggested that the near-instrumental 'Night Boat To Cairo' be chosen as the fourth single from *One Step Beyond*. The band weren't keen. For a start, they were concerned about taking advantage (or being seen to take advantage) of their fans. And also because the track's lighthearted feel reinforced their image as a madcap party outfit in line with the likes of Bad Manners, who were about to begin a string of hits with 'Ne-Ne-Na-Na-Na-Na-Nu-Nu'. "Bad Manners were a good band but we were wary of the way they were being marketed," Barson later observed.

The band preferred the idea of releasing a newer composition, 'Pete's Beat' or 'Pete The Beat' (later changed to 'On The Beat Pete', perhaps as a nod to the Norman Wisdom film *On The Beat*); or if it had to come from *One Step Beyond*, 'Bed And Breakfast Man'. After a good deal of disagreement between band and label, a compromise was reached; like The Specials, Madness would issue an EP. *Work, Rest And Play* (the title courtesy of Woody) would lead off with 'Night Boat To Cairo' but give fans value for money with three new tracks.

In hindsight, it's tempting to suggest the seeds of resentment about Robinson's forceful, persuasive nature were sewn over this issue. It still rankled with the band a year later, when interviewed by Tony Fletcher in *Jamming!* "If you spend an hour talking to Dave when he wants you to put a track out, it's really hard to come out convinced you were right when you went in," Suggs maligned. "We do get on really well with Dave. But we wanted to remix 'Night Boat To Cairo' or put another track on it, but we were away on tour. By the time we came back, it was, 'Well, you can send it back if you want, but it's on the presses.'" As Bedford succinctly put it, "It was our one big row with Stiff."

With a bass line borrowed from The Specials' 'Gangsters', 'Night Boat To Cairo' worked perfectly within the context of their debut album but despite its Top 10 success, it's arguable whether Robinson made the right judgment call in terms of Madness's overall progress. There's no doubting its appeal, though. Opening with a rasping baritone saxophone which cleverly approximated the sound of a ship's foghorn, it painted a comical picture of old black-and-white movies depicting colonial chaps marooned in foreign climes.

On Langer's insistence, 'Night Boat To Cairo' was also Madness' first recording with a string section; it's been suggested that the arranger misheard the request for a feel that was "Egyptian" as "gypsy", which might help explain the frantic fiddle playing in the background. "I thought it was the ponciest idea I'd ever heard," Foreman later told *Uncut*, "but it turned out really good. Maybe we should have had strings on some of the other tracks too!"

Suggs admitted to first hearing it as an instrumental which the band were rehearsing while he climbed the stairs at Mike's house in Muswell Hill; suitably inspired, the singer added his lyrics later. "I always thought of that song as being an approximation of what the BBC thought that music from the Eastern world would be," he later commented. "It sparked something in my mind – *Morecambe And Wise*, sand dancers, old light entertainment. That was what informed what we did – telly, movies, old jokes, football, stories." Another obvious reference point was the TV comedy *It Ain't Half Hot Mum*, alluded to in a hurriedly assembled promotional video, which depicted the band dressed in old army attire.

Kellogs: "The great thing about Madness was they were so inventive. They'd go off and rent clothes from Berman & Nathan's, a theatrical outfitters in Camden. For this particular video, they all turned up in pith helmets and desert shorts. Except, of course, Lee Thompson. While everybody else looks like somebody from the North African desert, he'd be dressed in a fez! He was always diametrically opposed to what everybody else was doing – and, I notice, still is! The word insanity comes to my mind but in an understated way. You have to watch him to get it.

Madness's first official photo shoot in summer 1979, decked out in mod/skinhead clobber in London's Hoxton district. Chas Smash was yet to become a fully-fledged member. (KERSTIN RODGERS/REDFERNS)

Left to right: Lee 'Thommo' Thompson, Mark 'Bedders' Bedford, Graham 'Suggs' McPherson, Mike 'Barzo' Barson, Chris 'Chrissy Boy' Foreman and Daniel 'Woody' Woodgate. (KERSTIN RODGERS/REDFERNS)

Still calling themselves The Invaders, the lads unwind in front of the camera during an early rehearsal in their Finchley Road basement. This probably dates from early 1979. (KERSTIN RODGERS/REDFERNS)

Madness and friends perfecting the art of the Nutty Walk for a photo session taken for *Sounds* magazine during the Scottish arm of the 2 Tone tour in November 1979. (VIRGINIA TURBETT/GETTY IMAGES)

The Nutty Train swiftly became a signature stance for Madness, as immortalised on the sleeve for their first album *One Step Beyond.* (JILL FURMANOVSKY)

Suggs in contemplative mood, modelling the very finest in skinhead attire. (KEVIN CUMMINS)

A rare shot of Thommo on the mic. Early Madness shows were nothing if not hot, sweaty and intense. This picture was probably taken from their first US dates in November 1979. (EBET ROBERTS/REDFERNS)

The Nutty Boys endured a hectic gig schedule in 1979, culminating in the 2 Tone tour and a trip to the States.
(URBANIMAGE.TV/ADRIAN BOOT)

Chas, Woody, Suggs and Chrissy Boy relax with a couple of fans up in Liverpool around February 1980.
(KEVIN CUMMINS)

TO·THE·MEN·OF·LIVERPOOL·WHO·FELL·IN·THE·GREAT·WAR

AND·THE·VICT... THAT·DAY·WAS·TURNED·INTO·MOURNING·UNTO·ALL

Another shot from February 1980. Several members of Madness had a soft spot for Liverpool – although maybe this wasn't the most appropriate location for nuttiness! (KEVIN CUMMINS)

Chas Smash, alias Carl Smith or Cathal Smyth, was Madness' dynamic MC and dancer before developing his songwriting skills. This shot was also from that *Sounds* article around the 2 Tone tour. (KERSTIN RODGERS/REDFERNS)

Mike Barson was undeniably Madness' musical foundation, upon which their mix of ska, rock'n'roll and humour was built. (KERSTIN RODGERS/REDFERNS)

Madness performing on the US TV show *American Bandstand* in March 1980. (CHRIS WALTER)

Foreman, get yer 'air cut! For a change, the Los Palmas Seven appear to be watching the show, instead of being watched? (KERSTIN RODGERS/REDFERNS)

Whereas Chas Smash might be overtly nutty, Lee is subtle. Definitely an added ingredient."

Although the makeshift props and the band's karaoke-like antics against a 'blue screen' background (over which a supposedly Egyptian background was crudely pasted), suggested a tight budget, the director had utilised the then pioneering format of video, which meant it was ready within 24 hours. "The sand dance [in the video] owes much to the off-the-wall music-hall act Wilson, Keppel and Betty," wrote McPherson in *Suggs And The City*. "However, I seem to remember we got the inspiration from two blokes who regularly used to perform the dance outside the Odeon in Leicester Square."

Its near-slapstick mood certainly appealed to Thompson's sense of humour. "The el cheapo one!" he later enthused. "The pyramids in the background are wobbling all over the show, we're clearly not in the desert at all but we're pretending we are, and Dave Robinson's dog is in it! It's a very British thing – the sets are falling down, there's a dog on the loose but [we] carry on regardless. Don't let the side down."

The other EP tracks had all been previewed during a radio session for DJ Mike Read. Alongside 'Don't Quote Me On That' was 'Deceives The Eye', a cheeky tale of a misspent youth spent shoplifting (reminiscent of Ian Dury's 'Razzle In My Pocket'). Apparently, its subject matter was based on an incident involving Foreman and Thompson in Luton when they stole "only things we wanted, not for selling", resulting in a trip to the police station for Foreman. And last but not least was 'The Young & The Old'. "This was about getting drunk in the pub and noticing how old people acted younger as the evening went on," explained Suggs.

The compromise appeared to pay off because *Work, Rest And Play* gave Madness another Top 10 hit while the band undertook promotional work in both Spain and France. Their Paris trip wrapped up with a performance at a large indoor festival alongside Stiff labelmates Wreckless Eric, Lene Lovich and another Canvey Island resident, Lew Lewis, who was known to join the band onstage on harmonica for 'Rockin' In A♭'.

★ ★ ★

By responding to both their critics and fans within their own environment (i.e. a song), 'Don't Quote Me On That' might have helped Madness weather the storm of controversy surrounding those accusations in the press about a minority of their fans – and about how Madness should deal with them. The band's media promotion was handled internally at Stiff; but their press officer Andy Murray had recently been replaced by another label employee, Nigel Dick. Both had played in a band called Stiff All-Stars, created in makeshift fashion to play at Dave Robinson's wedding – indeed, they'd followed Madness onto the stage at the Clarendon that night.

"I was an architectural student who couldn't find work," says Nigel. "I wound up in the Stiff offices as a motorcycle messenger. By the time Madness joined the label, I was working in the production part of the company. When Andy left, I became Madness's press officer for two years." Ironically, Nigel was immediately confronted with prejudice about the band's alleged political views from the music press: "One of my first forays was to allay the accusations of a journalist who said, 'As we all know, they are big supporters of the National Front, skinheads and complete racists.' My reaction was, hold on, what are you talking about? So I then wrote this person a carefully worded letter to say that the absolute contrary was the case. This is a band whose first single was about Prince Buster, a black guy, a totally positive message that this guy was their hero."

Unfortunately, the National Front now appeared to be targeting Madness' fans in earnest. "They managed to manoeuvre that boots-and-braces image towards them," admits John Wynne. "I remember in Leicester, they were passing boxes of NF leaflets through the toilet windows, then people were grabbing handfuls and passing them out. We burnt them. The band got worried because they were being labelled – and they didn't want any part of it. At the Hammersmith Odeon, NF guys were outside handing out leaflets. John Curd the promoter and I went outside and, in no uncertain terms, they threatened us. 'We're allowed by law to give this out. If you don't like it, we'll fill you in.' Well, you're not coming inside with this stuff. But they caught everybody coming in and it's all over the floor so Madness get tagged with it."

For Nigel Dick, the exercise felt like a crash course in public relations. "I was in at the dying embers of that particular flame," adds Nigel. "There were a couple of carefully worded comments from Suggs and Chas, and pretty much after that, it went away. From then on, they were Madness, regular guys. It quickly became clear that the press wanted to speak to Suggs and the band were fairly happy with that. There'd be the occasional moment when Chas would want to chime in. The minute they'd figured out there was no drink or birds involved in talking to the press, the rest of the guys would let Suggs get on with it. We can go down the bar and have a drink while he's yakking to the journalist!"

Nigel swiftly built up a rapport with the band. "The distinctive thing about them from day one was they were seven completely different, sharply drawn characters," he observes. "If you were trying to invent a band for a cartoon or a TV show, you would have been hard-pressed to find seven more perfectly cast individuals. Quite by accident, it was this perfect collision of men and ideas which all appeared at the same time in Camden Town."

★ ★ ★

Partly to promote the *Work, Rest And Play* EP, Madness embarked on another UK tour on April 21 with support from The Go-Go's (who were now signed to Stiff) and Clive Langer & The Boxes, among them Mike Barson's older brother Ben. Although still relying heavily on their debut album, Madness had already introduced several new songs to their repertoire, including future singles 'Baggy Trousers' and 'Embarrassment' as well as 'On The Beat Pete', 'Crying Shame' and 'E.R.N.I.E.'. The 16 dates erred towards areas of the UK which Madness hadn't visited before, from northern English cities such as Blackpool, Sunderland and Carlisle to shows further afield in Scotland (Aberdeen), Northern Ireland (Belfast), The Republic Of Ireland (Dublin) and Wales (Llanelli).

The carnival continued onto the continent, with a French TV show followed by gigs across Germany. On May 24, Madness were due to play Munich's Circus Krone. Unfortunately, Mike and Suggs missed the coach and, unbeknownst to the rest of their party, the pair were instead driven to the show by the promoter and arrived much later – which caused considerable concern about their whereabouts. Meanwhile, reports of the event suggested that various offensive weapons were confiscated on the door, including a Luger gun, and that a riot broke out in the audience prior to their performance. As a result, the band's nerves were on edge so they feared the worst when an important-looking gentleman – perhaps a top-ranking policeman – appeared onstage and dramatically stopped the show before speaking into the microphone in an authoritative manner. But when Foreman asked the band's translator to explain the problem, the uniformed official was apparently saying words to the effect of: "Vould ze owner of ze brown Ford car please go in ze car park as he has left his lights on."

Madness's arrival in Lausanne, Switzerland, was more welcoming courtesy of a letter from the local record company, who came bearing gifts: "As the representatives of Stiff Records in Switzerland, we welcome you in our country . . . you will find a real Swiss Military pocket knife in the enclosed package. P.S. Remember all *Mad* Swiss boys have got knives in their pockets." Needless to say, no door number or toilet sign was safe for the duration of their stay – and when John Wynne called it a night, he found that his bed fell apart. "They managed to unscrew everything they could possibly find in the hotel," laughs John, "except on their floor, to make it a bit obvious!"

Their latest road trip continued through France, Holland, Norway and Sweden before wrapping up what had been an intensive period – when they'd barely taken a break since signing with 2 Tone the previous summer – with a spate of shows in London, Cardiff and the West Country. For their two concerts in the capital, Madness were joined by a legend of Jamaican music, Desmond Dekker, whose new album *Black And Dekker* was about to be issued on Stiff. Although Prince Buster was a cult hero among Sixties mods and skinheads, Dekker was Jamaica's first true superstar, who broke through to the pop charts with '007 (Shanty Town)' and 'Israelites'. No doubt Madness felt honoured to play host to an artist of such calibre. Unfortunately, not everyone in the audience seemed to agree. Journalist Paolo Hewitt was at the show: "Desmond Dekker got booed off after two or three songs. Cathal came onstage and said, 'Look you fuckers, if it wasn't for this guy, we wouldn't be here!'"

In mid-June, Madness finally grabbed a two-week respite to prepare for their second album, rehearsing at Nomis Studios in Sinclair Road, London W14, near Kensington Olympia (Nomis also harboured an office for The Jam). Although they described Nomis as "a depressing place with no windows", they already had plenty of songs to develop. For new ideas, they grabbed a blackboard and scribbled down possible song titles and chord sequences. Recording of their second album began in earnest at Eden Studios on July 14. In due course, Madness reconvened to Genetic Studios for final mixing.

Meanwhile, Cathal recorded new vocals for a Spanish version of 'One

Step Beyond' (entitled 'Un Paso Adelante') to help counteract a cover version in Spain by an artist named Luis Cobos. The song was also issued in Italian ('Un Passo Avanti'); these variations were prompted by Stiff's head of the international division, Alan Cowderoy. "That was a magical record but I didn't really know how it was going to be received abroad. Because it was an instrumental apart from the introduction, I sent this single out to everybody overseas and said, 'Translate this and send me a recording of someone speaking it.' Then I got Cathal to overdub it in Spanish or Italian and they rather liked that we'd made the effort. A very Stiff thing to do!"

Cowderoy would travel with the band during their frequent jaunts across the Continent. "The French, particularly, absolutely loved the whole black and white 2 Tone imagery," suggests Alan. "They ate it up and the band were huge there. We did lots of TV. I travelled with them, just being a mediator. They were a complete gang, all individual in their way. Woody was quieter and quite artistic, not as vociferous as some of the others. Mike was taciturn, not very communicative but he was musical so we respected that. Cathal was a bit pushy. But none of them were difficult. You might think Lee was mental but he wasn't, particularly. I don't remember them missing a show. Obviously, they didn't love it to death. The band found some of the countries a bit of a drag but they still did it."

Having overcome their initial differences, Kellogs had grown to respect Madness, both personally and professionally. "None of them except Mike Barson and, to some extent, Mark Bedford and Woody, were natural musicians," he suggests. "Barson was naturally endowed with talent. I thought the others had just picked it up and run with it. But they were deeply clever in the way they'd mastered their instruments and were so keen on the idea of being in the band. But I felt these guys were tearaways from Camden not 'musos'. I knew a different brand of musician, a long-haired Sixties/Seventies kind. How dare these guys call themselves musicians?! And yet they were. I grew to have tremendous respect for them as a musical entity. They were incredibly inventive. From that whirlpool of energy that surrounded them emanated this fantastic force."

John Wynne was especially struck by Barson's wilfulness within the band – although, by all accounts, he wasn't always the most cooperative member. "Mike was never an easy guy to work with," he suggests. "He's a lot nicer now! He was very clever, though. The record company wanted him to write songs at home but he had to have a keyboard so whenever we was off the road, we had to hump this electric piano, in two bits, up this staircase. He'd moved to St John's Villas just off the Archway, and it was an absolute nightmare – top floor of a townhouse! My, that was hard work. But it wasn't good enough. I can understand it: he wanted different sounds and tempos so we bought him one of these organs from Chappell's. Beautiful thing. I said, 'How the hell are we going to get this into Mike's place?' I only just fit up the stairs let alone with an organ the size of a small car! In the end, we had to hire a crane. That was a fiasco!"

When it came to the band's requirements, money appeared to be no object – but it took some time for Madness to realise that perhaps Stiff weren't as generous as they assumed. "Stiff paid for stuff – or so they thought," says Wynne. "Obviously, the record company doesn't pay anything if it doesn't get paid back! Something the lads missed for a while until it was explained to them that this was actually their money!" Although John remembers that, of all the members of Madness, Mike was especially astute with money, he also had his blind spots. "He bought a Volkswagen Microbus second-hand for him and Sandra to go touring in," explains John. "So he ramped up thousands of miles. Then he said, 'I want you to sell my Microbus.' I said, 'The best I can get for it is this.' 'But I paid more than that for it!' I said, 'Of course you did. It devalues!' But he kept thinking, if you buy a new one now, it costs more than last year. So why doesn't the second-hand value go up? No idea!"

"Once, we got a private jet to go to Sweden," continues John. "It was cheaper to fly band and crew out of Stansted on a private jet plus you could pick your time slot. We all get there on time – except Mike. The pilot's there. We're still waiting so we all had a fry-up breakfast. We've been here for an hour and a half when Mike arrives. Thank goodness you're here, Mike, we're a bit late. I've had my ear bent by the pilot. Fair enough. So let's go. Mike says, 'Oh, I see you've all had breakfast then. Well, I'm having breakfast.' So we all had to sit and wait. No one in the band dared say to him, 'Look Mike, why not just get a sandwich and eat it on the plane!'"

Maybe Barson didn't like travelling. "Mike did what he wanted," says Wynne. "There were times when you could talk to him and times when he was a prickly bear. I remember in America, someone was late one day. Kellogs and Mike got the right arsehole with us and said, 'Anyone who's late from now on will be fined $100.' The next day, who's the one person who's late? Mike! Oh how did we laugh. Another time, we were just going to Australia. We're in the office, all the band except Mike. He's late. Nobody wants to ring him up because you're going to get an earful. Anyway, Kellogs rings him up and says, 'We're all here, Mike, we're all ready.' He says, 'I can't find my passport.' So Kellogs said to him, 'We've got your passport because it had to go in to be stamped for all the visas.' And he went absolutely ballistic on the phone: 'Why didn't you tell me you had my passport?!' He was an arse at times but he was a very good writer. He calmed down a lot which was good!"

★ ★ ★

On August 11, Madness travelled up to Nottingham to play two nights at the Theatre Royal, which were being filmed for TV broadcast. Along for the ride was teenage music journalist Tony Fletcher, who was editing his own fanzine, *Jamming!*, while still at school in Croydon. "I started writing for *The Face* around the time I was doing my O-levels," says Tony, who is now an established author. "[*The Face*'s editor] Nick Logan said, 'Would you be interested in writing about Madness?'"

Fletcher wasn't their biggest fan, though. "Like a lot of people my age, I felt The Specials seemed more important," he admits. "At my school, it was the 11 to 13-year-old's who liked Madness. I did like a lot of what they had but they seemed this odd combination of trouble and being too much of a pop band. We were running this fanzine at school and saw Madness as the new Slade for younger kids. Madness were a pop band making ludicrously funny videos, elevating that art of making videos. But they were strange: pop and yet skinhead/working class. You imagined your pop band to be malleable softies and here was a bunch of quite hard people."

Even at a tender age, Fletcher was astute enough to be aware of the degree to which their persona had been tarnished by adverse press. "They had come out of that Deanne Pearson story in the *NME*," explains Tony, "so even though they were one of the biggest bands in the country, they were also incredibly defensive because the word was out that they were racists – or at least Chas was. They had been portrayed as borderline NF, which was an awful thing to have to carry around. There was a sense of them being all white, which meant the Nazi skinheads could get behind the band. So Nick Logan's idea was, rather than an *NME* journalist, which they weren't going to countenance at that point, why not send out this sixteen-year-old, who's the same age as half the Madness fans? That was smart thinking on his part."

Fresh from his exams, Fletcher was assigned to travel up from London with the band. "I was wary of meeting them because I was under the impression they were tough working-class kids," he admits. "I had the idea that Suggs and Chas were total skinheads. Nobody really welcomed me when I got on that train. You could imagine how nervous I was. I did have quite cruelly short hair, a Harrington and a Ben Sherman but no sooner had I got on and the band had all their girlfriends with them, I got Suggs and Chas mixed up! A really hard one to live down! They were wary. There was definitely a sense of, who agreed to this again?! But I think they realised, once they saw me, that they weren't being stitched up."

Once he'd broken the ice, Tony was pleasantly surprised by the reception he was given. "I got to meet this group who were incredibly down-to-earth, obviously funny and much smarter than they were being given credit for. By the end of that evening, when we were doing the interview, it was cool. We hit it off. This band were so much fun and very friendly. Madness was portrayed to me as a band straight off a council estate and I caught on quickly that they were smarter than that. You can't fake the camaraderie, the humour, how witty they were. The second night in Nottingham, Mark dedicated 'Deceives The Eye' to me because I think they'd figured they had got around this music journalist – in a nice way."

By this time, Madness were bona fide pop stars – and Fletcher sensed they had made a conscious decision not to be phased by their fame. "They really were a solid working-class band, both in the sense of how they dressed onstage and, for a band who were that big, that they were perfectly happy to walk the streets around the theatre, even though all these kids were waiting outside the stage door. They'd not allow themselves to be 'limousined' in or need security or act like pop stars. But they could get up to an awful lot of mischief in a hotel. It was good-natured but the following morning over breakfast, I was amazed at the stories about what had happened the previous night. Which maybe I shouldn't have been because we're talking about a bunch of kids who'd made good and are going to have some fun."

They still had some rough edges, though. "Prior to the first night in Nottingham, Chas had been hanging out with some friends and wanted to get backstage but didn't have his pass," remembers Tony. "Now, details are inevitably fuzzy but the bouncer was like, yeah, I'm sure you're in Madness! You see those things happen a lot but Chas was ready to have a fight about it, in no small way. It actually got really heavy and was definitely kicking off. It was almost like being at a football match. It got very rowdy very quickly. So in the midst of them being nice people, very welcoming and not this super-tough band that I was scared they might be, the reality was that, if an argument came up, Chas was prepared to fight his way out."

By this time, Suggs had become the public persona of Madness, their pin-up star – but perhaps this was something he grappled with. "After the first night in the hotel, Suggs vacated the premises," recalls Tony. "It was clear to me that he wanted to share the limelight with other members of the band. I think that was important because it was becoming very much the Suggs and Chas show and I ended up interviewing Woody, Bedders and Chrissy. It was clearly a deliberate move on Suggs' part – and a good move, because they all had plenty to say."

★ ★ ★

In some quarters, Madness were still viewed as a novelty act. By mid-1980, the 2 Tone/ska revival movement was still in full swing with albums from The Beat (*I Just Can't Stop It*) and Bad Manners (*Ska'n'B*). But the Specials' two hits which bookended the summer, 'Rat Race' (May) and 'Stereotype' (September), revealed how Jerry Dammers was evolving their sound. 'Stereotype' was an altogether more sophisticated song with shades of mood music – in other words, they'd evolved beyond the "ska revival" tag. If Madness were to avoid the common pitfall of the "difficult second album", they needed something special. And that something was their next single, 'Baggy Trousers'.

Issued on September 5, 'Baggy Trousers' was a stroke of pop genius. The lyrics were written by Suggs about his memories of a childhood blighted by poverty and insecurity – and yet this tale of playground pranks and school shenanigans was nothing less than affectionate. "I was sleeping on the floor of Lee Thompson's flat in Caledonion Road," he later explained, "and I had the idea of writing a song about being at school. I was very influenced by Ian Dury. I liked the way he wrote lists of things sometimes about a small subject. Also, I'd heard that song by Pink Floyd ['Another Brick In The Wall (Part 2)'] and they were going on about 'teacher, leave them kids alone'. At my school, I used to feel sorry for the teachers sometimes. They were so put upon by us. I thought I'd try and redress the balance and write a song that was pretty objective, neither good nor bad."

While 'My Girl' had spoken to teenagers about the pitfalls and complications of relationships, 'Baggy Trousers' boasted a universal appeal from the primary school to the pub, three minutes-plus of unbridled pop ebullience which still resides within the popular imagination to this day (not least via its continued usage as background music on TV). From the opening sound of a school bell, the song tapped into the timeless images of schooldays in a long-standing tradition from the Jennings novels to the on-screen mishaps of St Trinians and Will Hay, the Bash Street Kids' capers in *The Beano* or the BBC's latest hit TV series, *Grange Hill*. "When I wrote this song – me and Chris – I was trying to write in an Ian Dury style," Suggs added at Madstock '98.

With 'Baggy Trousers', Madness raised their game. This was due in no small part to an inspired pop video, a simple creation filmed on August 12 in Islip Street School, Kentish Town which was memorable for the footage of Lee Thompson flying through the air while playing his sax, hanging on a wire from a crane. Apparently, in order to 'fly', Thompson had to wear a harness – and ended up taking one for the team. "I put it on, they winched me up and that's when I felt a sharp . . . it made my eyes water," he later admitted. "They'd caught part of my scrotum in the strapping! We did the business, I came down, took the thing off, got home and it was black and blue. I went to the doctors just for a check-up. I asked the doctor to take away the bruising but leave the swelling!"

Although still in their infancy, promotional videos became an integral aspect of Madness' hit-making machine. True, they were nothing new. "By the 1970s, artists had started making clips (or 'pop promos') for individual songs as promotional tools themselves," writes Nigel Dick, the one-time Madness press officer and video producer/director who became an award-winning, Los Angeles-based video director. "The best example [was] Queen's 'Bohemian Rhapsody', which was totally groundbreaking in its day and instrumental in making the song a massive hit. By the time

'Bohemian Rhapsody' had been at number one for nine weeks, everyone was cashing in on the fad."

As the industry expanded, this new format provided the perfect marketing tool. "Up to this point, bands had been able to promote their latest release in three basic ways: radio-play, TV appearances and touring," writes Nigel on his website. "With record markets opening up all over the world and simultaneous trans-global releases becoming the norm, it was virtually impossible for a band to appear onstage or on TV in the same week in New York, London, Sydney and Hamburg which the simultaneous record releases required. So pop promos started filling the gap: it was cheaper to send a video tape to Australia than five musicians and a road manager. By the late Seventies, these pop promos were mostly shot on videotape and so came to be called music videos."

Robinson had been quick to seize upon the potential of video for Stiff artists. But in Madness' case, he also discovered a surprise spin-off benefit from the process. "One of the key things which made it easy for me to pick singles is, in every video – and videos became the key Madness marketing tool – there's always a piano," he explains. "Barson was always playing a new tune between takes. I'd say, what's that one? So I'd actually find the single during the video for the previous single! Because I was director of the videos, I was there all the time."

"That [video] really established us," admitted Foreman in the TV documentary *South Of Watford*. "In fact, what [Lee] wanted to do was have six dummies, which represented us, and he was going to fly through the air and kick their heads off. But we thought, no, *Top Of The Pops* would never show that, so we toned it down!" Instead, the nation's favourite pop show took the unusual step of broadcasting the video instead of insisting on a studio performance (although the band appeared on a subsequent episode). It helped make 'Baggy Trousers' the most talked-about record of the period, with a saturation of media coverage. Although it stalled at number three, the single was by far their best-selling effort to date, spending some 20 weeks on the chart.

The cover design of 'Baggy Trousers' depicted a drawing based on a photo of the band, with Thompson at the front holding out his, well, baggy trousers. What the majority of Madness fans didn't realise was that the shot was copied from an old Kilburn & The High Roads group photo wherein Humphrey Ocean was wearing similarly voluminous strides –

and it was Ocean who'd now illustrated the single sleeve, itself taken from a photo session for the new album. On the flipside was 'The Business', an instrumental reworking of the forthcoming album track, 'Take It Or Leave It'.

★ ★ ★

Madness's second album, *Absolutely*, followed on September 26 – titled after an expression commonly used by Tony Duffield. In some respects, *Absolutely* followed the same pattern as *One Step Beyond*, opening with a hit single ('Baggy Trousers') before offering a cheeky mix of songs which were equal parts humorous and poignant, ska-tinged and Ian Dury-inspired. Alan Winstanley: "By the time the second album was ready for mixing – again, it was recorded at Eden, which was very much a Stiff studio in those days – Martin [Rushent] and I had earned enough money to complete Genetic, and Clive and I were able to mix in a proper control room."

It's been suggested that the overall mood was darker; certainly, Langer and Winstanley created a tense, almost 'film noir'-like quality in places. Overall, though, their production felt brighter but also busier, such that Suggs' quick-fire lyrics sounded deeper in the mix and were often difficult to decipher. If anything, the songwriting was split more evenly than before, with Thompson, Foreman, McPherson and Barson all listed as contributing to four or five compositions each. The subject matter still seemed to revolve around the seedy, nefarious aspects of everyday life told as a series of vignettes – emphasised by the record labels which were identified as "Story One" and "Story Two".

"We'd spent five years carving our own little niche," Suggs later told *Uncut*. "2 Tone was great but *Absolutely* was more of a reflection of where we were at than *One Step Beyond* – all the influences piled up in our head let out more succinctly. We were conscious of not making a carbon copy of the debut. Like The Specials, we were always aware we needed to move on with each album."

Foreman later revealed some hitherto hidden sources of inspiration: "There was a blackboard with all the songs up in the rehearsal room. We had so many influences that get overlooked – like Pink Floyd and Genesis. One night, Lee and I had bunked in to see Genesis at Drury Lane [in 1974]. At a point in the set, there was an explosion and Peter Gabriel went flying through the air. That's why Lee went flying in the 'Baggy Trousers' video – he always vowed that when he got the chance he'd do the same thing!"

'Close Escape' picked up where 'In The Middle Of The Night' left off, depicting a pervert who got his kicks from calling women to ask about their underwear. "I wanted to keep that character alive, so he went into being a heavy-breather down the public telephone-box receiver," explained Thompson. 'Shadow Of Fear' spoke of the paranoia of life in London, real or imagined; the reggae-tinged 'Not Home Today' referred to the excuses made by people to cover up the fact that a member of their family had been sent to borstal or prison; and a life of crime was also suggested in the letter of regret that was one of the album's hidden gems, 'Overdone', with Foreman's music set to Lee's novel lyric. Thompson was also behind 'On The Beat Pete', a fast-and-furious ska effort based around a day in the life of a local "bobbie", listing various fictional ne'er-do-wells in the style of Ian Dury. Another song previewed during their summer tour, 'E.R.N.I.E.', was Suggs' tribute to premium bonds, the popular lottery system introduced in 1957; the initials stood for "Electronic Random Number Indicator Equipment" and the scheme boasted the "thousand winners every week" referred to in the lyrics.

Other songs almost felt like a collection of puzzling non-sequiturs while suggesting a sense of loss in the face of rapid change. These included Side 2's opener, 'Take It Or Leave It', set to quirky music presumably inspired by Sixties spy films; and the wonderful, Motown-styled 'Disappear', one of the album's most melodic creations which was introduced by a mellifluous piano refrain and decorated by some electric sitar reminiscent of various early Seventies soul hits.

Each side closed with what might be described as a novelty number: Side 1 with Smyth's Fifties rock'n'roll pastiche, 'Solid Gone', possibly motivated by a rock'n'roll rockabilly revival which saw the likes of Matchbox following acts such as Rocky Sharpe & The Replays into the UK charts. Within a month of the release of *Absolutely*, The Stray Cats would breathe new life into Fifties stylings with hits such as 'Runaway Boy', paving the way for The Polecats et al. And Side 2 ended with the charming two-minute instrumental, 'Return Of The Los Palmas 7', which married the Hammond groove of Booker T. & The MG's with Sixties 'muzak' – the kind of ersatz jazz associated with cocktail bars. "When Mark, Mike and I were running through it," explained Woodgate, "Mike had the chords and the notes. We finally found a rhythm that fitted, Mark had the bass line, and the more I heard it, the more I wanted to go, 'hey, cha-cha-cha', you know, *Come Dancing!* I said, we've got to do a few stops, as corny as possible!"

This tongue-in-cheek number was the first to carry an individual songwriting credit for Madness's drummer (who was also listed as playing a fire extinguisher!). That wasn't Woody's only "first" that summer. When Madness played the show at Nottingham Theatre Royal on August 11, it wasn't a coincidence that the support act was Mo-dettes. Woodgate was now engaged to their bassist Jane Crockford and the couple were duly married on August 30. Apparently, the rest of Madness were completely unaware of the ceremony and only discovered the news courtesy of coverage in *The Face!*

As part of Stiff's major promotional campaign, Madness appeared on ITV's popular Saturday morning show *Tiswas*. On paper, it was a marriage made in heaven: Madness were famous for pulling pranks, in keeping with the programme's anarchic, madcap style. But Suggs and Cathal – dressed up in clown's costumes – somehow managed to offend presenter Sally James after spraying her with whipped cream, which got stuck to her false eyelashes. Rumour has it that the entire Stiff roster was subsequently banned from the show. Dave Robinson needn't have worried, though. If reviews for *Absolutely* were a tad less enthusiastic than those for *One Step Beyond*, they didn't hurt sales as the LP soared to number two, matching the performance of its predecessor in terms of chart position if not longevity (although it still hung around for 46 weeks).

The cover design of *Absolutely* might have played on the 'Baggy Trousers' theme but the photo's backdrop of a Northern Line tube station (which many fans assumed was Camden Town but was actually Chalk Farm Station at dawn) reinforced their geographical links. Once again, the inner sleeve was put to good use with 'The Birth Of The Nutty Boys', a pictorial diary of the band's history via photos of members past and present and a back-of-a-fag-packet biography. On the other side, Humphrey Ocean offered a painting of a fictional Madness tube station, Cairo East. The overall effect was to cement Madness in the public's imagination to their particular patch of north London.

★   ★   ★

"Lee Thompson was very good with his words but it was all to do with his family in the flats around Camden, local happenings," adds Robinson. "They were all very Camden Town. They didn't like long tours because it took them away. Remarkable. I had a theory that it was folk music. To me, The Beatles were folk – I liked social music which is about the environment you're in. I never understood major record companies taking people away from their roots, giving them an altered culture or putting them in hotels, buying houses in Guildford. People who ran major record companies didn't seem to have any respect for the artists. They had a cynical attitude. With Stiff, the plan was to try and teach the artists to survive the job they'd chosen, i.e. the music business. Make some money, pay your taxes, put stuff away, buy yourself a house, do some work and treat it like a job. Making the music was 30 per cent, 70 per cent was selling it."

Robinson's emphasis – that common sense was as important as creativity – seemed to be rubbing off on the band and their management. "By the time of *Absolutely*, I was well ensconced," explains Kellogs. "We had our own office by then. First of all, Jake Riviera moved out of his Radar office in Chelsea, a mews right by the river where I used to work. I took over that office." John Wynne remembers it well: "We were in Munro Terrace which is just off Cheyne Walk, three doors down from the Rolling Stones. John Curd, the promoter, was next door. It was me, Kellogs and Spike, who was the secretary."* In due course, the operation expanded to the point where new offices were required. "The guys wanted an office in Camden or somewhere close," says Kellogs. "So I found an office at 56 Baring Street which is between Camden and Old Street, the other side of the Angel. But it was north London which seemed to please them. And it suited me: I lived in north Essex."

In late summer 1980, Kellogs had dispensed with the services of road manager Tony Duffield, who subsequently worked for Yazoo, the duo formed by ex-Depeche Mode man Vince Clarke and singer Alison Moyet; their second album *You And Me Both* (1983) was named after another of Duffield's frequent sayings. With his wife Wendy, Duffield later participated in the best-selling *The Lovers' Guide* videos in the early 1990s, describing themselves as "'lifestyle consultants specialising in sex, romance,

---

* Spike was the nickname for Welsh girl Helen Wilkins, who left in 1981 to work for Pete Townshend's Eel Pie set-up.

relationship problems, and incorporating astrology".

As replacement, Kellogs hired an old Southend mate he knew from their days touring with Procol Harum. Barry Sinclair seemed perfectly qualified, having hung around with Ian Dury and Humphrey Ocean back in the early 1970s, and socialising with the great and the good on the pub rock scene. "After Procol split in 1976, I was quite friendly with the Feelgoods, managed Wilko Johnson for a month and knew Lew Lewis. And Tony [Duffield] was around because he was originally from Canvey Island." Sinclair had also served lengthy sentences on the road Stateside with Van Morrison so he was a seasoned tour manager. But J.J. had other plans for his new recruit.

"Kellogs wheeled me into a back room where there were sacks of mail and said, 'Could you sort this out,'" explains Barry. On the inner sleeve of *Absolutely*, fans had been invited to send in an SAE to join the Madness Information Service. "But of course, nobody had actually started a fan club. The MIS didn't really exist. So I had to organise it because all these people had written into this address, care of Stiff, with postal orders for the subscription fee. The first thing I did was get a database on a computer!"

In fairness, a hotch potch of the band's mates and office staff had already created *The Nutty Boys*, a *Beano*-style fan club comic which was planned to be a quarterly publication. The editorship was credited to The Big "K", an alias for Kellogs. The first issue (dated January 1, 1981) boasted several cartoon strips depicting the band's rise to fame, as well as fact files and jokes. Apparently, Kellogs had attempted to secure its distribution for sale in newsagents but when these plans fell through, the office was left with 250,000 copies – and sales at their gigs were never going to compensate for this oversight! "We had an enthusiastic printer who I presume convinced us that it was just as cheap to print quarter of a million as 20,000," Kellogs recalls. Sinclair duly co-ordinated a second edition with a more sensible print-run, circulated in spring 1981 – but his main role was the more troublesome responsibility of overseeing the Madness roadshow.

"They used to call me Uncle Barry," laughs Sinclair. "They were lovely. They had a lot of energy. It was interesting for me, having worked with Procol then Van Morrison, they were quite a handful, there being seven of them. I was about 30 and Bedders was only 17. I carried on tour managing them for the rest of that year. A guy called Harry Wandsworth [alias Wandsworth Harry] was my assistant, taking care of the band's clothes and wardrobe. It was his job to find the nearest dry cleaners as soon as we arrived."

After a couple of warm-up gigs at the Porterhouse Retford at the start of October, the band and their entourage flew out to Italy to commence their Madness Monster Tour with support act The Lambrettas. As a special treat for local audiences, the concerts finished with an Italian language version of 'One Step Beyond' ('Un Passo Avanti'). A riot broke out at their October 11 show in Padova, caused by members of a local anarchist movement who objected to the concept of paying to see live music. As the activists muscled their way into the venue armed with machetes and baseball bats, a battle ensued with police, who unleashed tear gas.

"Italy was just phenomenal, incredible," Woody later enthused. "They had a five-year ban, or something, on live acts from foreign lands. [So] we came in to maniac crowds, just such a buzz. They went really potty in Padova: they came through the glass panels with sledgehammers and axes, and there were riot police." Sinclair remembers the incident well: "We got besieged! It was sold out and they started knocking in windows. We were playing in the round. They started grabbing the lighting truss and I had to drag one of our roadies off stage because he was trying to take on 20,000 people. It was pretty hairy!"

Next stop was the Netherlands, where Madness hooked up with members of The Specials during a press conference on a canal boat in Amsterdam – only for Suggs and Jerry Dammers to aggravate the captain by jumping off the slow-moving vehicle. More mayhem ensued when the two bands performed on adjacent stages on a Dutch TV show; during the Specials' set, the stage collapsed after being invaded by the audience. The rest of the month-long tour passed without major incident through France, Germany, Sweden and Norway before Madness returned to London to play an invite-only return show at The Hope & Anchor to raise funds for Blanket Aid, a charity which aimed to help with supplies to the homeless and elderly during the winter months. And on November 12, Madness recorded the first of several tunes over the years designed for use in specific television advertisements – in this instance, a radical reworking of 'Tarzan's Nuts' which was used to promote Martini, and which would later appear as the backing music for 'The Opium Eaters'.

★ ★ ★

Two days later, Stiff released a second single from *Absolutely*. Whereas 'Baggy Trousers' was a feel-good song, 'Embarrassment' dealt with an altogether more serious issue. Lee Thompson's 17-year-old sister Tracy had become pregnant with a mixed race child, which caused consternation among some of the family's friends, relatives and neighbours, who disapproved – seemingly not of Tracy having a baby out of wedlock but of the fact she had slept with a man of colour. Thompson had been on tour with Madness and learnt of the situation via snippets over the phone, letters and family crisis meetings. 'Embarrassment' was his deeply personal response to the unfolding turmoil but while a 'half-caste' baby still carried a social stigma in some circles, the saxophonist was shocked by the reaction he saw from those he knew.

"It was just not accepted in those days," he later explained. "She was shunned by a few people in the family. My father tried to talk her into getting it terminated. My sister dug her heels in and I was caught in the middle, wanting everyone to be happy." Once Hayley was born, though, attitudes softened and their rancour evaporated. "My mum and dad were all over her," Thompson continued. "They were forever babysitting. They loved their first granddaughter. All the bad feeling just fell away. She's gorgeous now: intelligent, attractive, you wouldn't want to change a thing." Tracy was later interviewed about what had been a major domestic dispute: "Attitudes have changed without a doubt. I've got four mixed-race kids and am now married to a white man. He accepts them without a second thought."

'Embarrassment' was a brave choice, then, for a band who had traded on their sense of fun. Thompson originally had in mind the melody from 'Ghost Dance' by Prince Buster but Mike Barson had other ideas. He created a song which sounded as if Motown's backing band 'The Funk Brothers' had recorded the theme tune for *The Sweeney*, and its irresistible melody and instrumental swagger rightly rewarded Madness with another Top Five hit single. The 7-inch was backed by an overlooked Barson song, 'Crying Shame', a Coasters-flavoured ditty which was undeniably stronger – melodically, at least – than many of the tracks on *Absolutely*. Maybe this explained its later choice for the band's encores.

'The Twelve Days of Madness' amounted to their first headline tour of major UK venues in the run-up to Christmas 1980. For all but two dates, the band performed two shows a day: a matinee performance for the under

16s as well as the traditional evening slot. With support from a magician, Simon Drake, and John Otway & Wild Willy Barrett, the tour spanned the whole of England and Scotland from the Glasgow Apollo and Newcastle upon Tyne's City Hall to the Brighton Centre and Southampton Gaumont on the south coast. It culminated in three nights at the Hammersmith Odeon across December 22–24. The Christmas Eve gig was given over to a charity event, including a collection for toys which were then distributed to children's homes.

On Christmas Day, Madness were seen on a festive edition of the *Runaround* TV show with host Mike Read, filmed ice skating. On December 27, they played the Birmingham NEC as guests at Elvis Costello's Christmas Show alongside UB40, The Selecter, Rockpile and Squeeze. And on New Year's Eve, Suggs and Cathal played a secret south London show at The Venue in New Cross billed as The Rubber Biscuits on a bill which also included Suggs' girlfriend Bette Bright. "That greatly endeared me to them," says Barry Sinclair. "Cathal was the wildest one of the lot, very lively. He was rough and ready but he was very well read. When we were doing that Christmas tour, Cathal and Suggs took time off to go to a local hospital to see the young kids."

Chapter 9

THAT'S THE WAY TO DO IT

B Y the end of 1980, Stiff could boast an annual UK turnover in excess
of £3.5 million – an impressive figure bearing in mind the label had
been founded on a £400 loan only four years earlier. Much of this success
was down to Madness, who underpinned the label's forte for novelty hits
with the more stable financial platform of album sales. That said, Madness
had clocked up more weeks on the UK charts that year than any other
artist.

"You've got a momentum but you were on a treadmill," explains Stiff's
then general manager Paul Conroy. "You were only as good as your last
hit. But if you had stopped someone on the street and asked them about
Stiff, they might have said, they're a great singles label, aren't they? We
didn't have this history of big album sales other than Ian [Dury]. So we
needed someone else. And suddenly, this young band Madness came
along. What was great was that momentum: you could see when the
singles were coming out. The other 2 Tone acts didn't have that – there
wasn't that hunger to push them in the same way."

According to Conroy, that hit rate was due in no small part to Robinson:
"Dave was like, come on, where's the next one? Dave would break them
up and make sure they went off and wrote. The greed of writing kept
them going. You'd say to Barson, you've only got two tracks on this next
album, you better write another. They all realised that if they were the
writers, they were going to make more money. So there was rivalry
within the band in terms of who was going to come up with the next
single."

Although Conroy didn't work as closely with the band as Robinson, he
was able to discern distinctly different personal traits within the band.

"Mike wouldn't trust his own granny," he laughs. "I don't think Mike trusted Dave. He certainly didn't trust us! He always gave us that 'you're out to screw me' attitude. The others didn't so much. Suggs was very much a split personality. There was Suggs the family man, quite private, and Suggs as the front singer. When he goes out with the band, he acts out the character of Suggs – all-round good bloke, a bright boy.

"Cathal and his whole family isn't even a book, it's an encyclopaedia! Cathal was quite a diplomat. Because he didn't play an instrument, he was like, I'll sort that out for you, Dave. Cathal knew songwriting was going to be important but he didn't have the instrument to lean back on. But he got very involved. If they were having meetings, Lee would always be there last. He'd turn up on his bike. Chrissy Boy was quite organised. Woody was a nice bloke. Bedders was always nice, straight into the office making teas, lovely guy, always said 'hi'. He'd be there on time."

Unfortunately, Bedford's punctuality was the exception. "Dave would say, let's meet at twelve o'clock," bemoans Conroy. "You'd get to seven and there'd still be the odd person drifting in! Very rarely did Dave have meetings when they all ran to time which was frustrating because, for me, I'm trying to run a record company and you'd have them all sitting around. We never met them all because they always came in in dribs and drabs." That meant that members of Madness were hanging around Stiff HQ – and it wasn't uncommon for the odd individual to make a nuisance of themselves.

Having been based in Alexander Street, Stiff had moved to new premises on December 3, 1979 located at 9–11 Woodfield Road in Westbourne Green, situated over a taxi firm and next to both the Harrow Road and the Westway flyover, on the banks of the Grand Union Canal. "The office was run like a cross between a record company, a film studio and a crèche," sighs Conroy. "It was all open plan. And they created mayhem – especially the likes of Lee, who'd tea-leaf half the stock. They were a lively bunch but they were so young. And they'd come from a pretty chequered background. Of course, Dave didn't want them in his office so I had them all gathering. And it's like Ali Baba's cave for them – ooh, can we have one of those? They loved Dury so they were always, oh, can I get four copies of *New Boots And Panties!!*? And it's hard to say, fuck off, when maybe we hadn't paid them their royalties!"

"It was very close-knit," agrees Nigel Dick. "Basically, we were all united against Robbo who was a difficult man to work for. Because he'd say, this is what needs to be done and often it was insane but somehow we would find a way to do it. But it was enormously exciting because you could turn up to work wearing what you liked and do all these crazy things, get to travel all over the country, go to gigs every night, get free records, it was fantastic. It was bloody hard work but certainly better than doing a real job!"

The Stiff ethos, if it could be called that, was flexibility. "I was going with them to France to do some press, PR and TV shows," explains Nigel. "It wasn't like today, oh no, that's band management business, you can't do that. It was like, 'ere Nige, the lads needs to go to France next week. Why don't you go and look after them? And you'd go, OK, fine! We'd all go down the pub and have a drink. It wasn't, oh, he's with the record company. We were all quite pally."

★ ★ ★

On January 16, 1981, a remixed and overdubbed version of 'The Return Of The Los Palmas 7' (the title now prefaced with the definite article) was issued as a third single from *Absolutely*. The B-side, 'That's The Way To Do It', was Foreman's tribute to his days as an "odd job man", set to a cockney bar-room knees-up which doffed its flat cap to the bygone era of music hall. A 12-inch edition added that early treatment of 'My Girl' with Mike Barson's vocals; the record was accompanied by a copy of the first MIS comic after Kellogs had ordered a woefully large print-run.

Ever since the success of 'One Step Beyond', Dave Robinson had encouraged Madness to record instrumentals – and after all, 'Night Boat To Cairo' had very few lyrics. Once again, the Stiff boss's intuition paid off when Radio 2 play-listed the single, introducing Madness to an older – or certainly broader – audience. Statisticians might enjoy the fact that their seventh single peaked at number seven after seven weeks.

"Mike would often bring old sheet music of show-tunes and standards into rehearsal sessions," Clive Langer later told *Uncut*. "He'd never read the music, but he'd often play the chord sequences on piano. 'The Return Of The Los Palmas 7', for instance, was basically the chords to some old Kathy Kirby song played backwards! He definitely had an affinity with the Tin Pan Alley songwriting traditions." The band later recorded a Spanish language rendition, entitled 'El Regresso De Los Palmas'.

While Madness's fortunes were holding steady, 2 Tone appeared to be in terminal decline. Although The Specials' second album *More Specials* had reached the Top Five in autumn 1980 (with Lee Thompson appearing as guest saxophonist on 'Hey Little Rich Girl'), Jerry Dammers' subsequent signings (The Bodysnatchers, The Swinging Cats and veteran Jamaican trombonist Rico) failed to match the success of their predecessors and only Rico now remained on the label beside The Specials. In fact, 2 Tone's first major project of 1981 was the live retrospective, *Dance Craze*, an album and cinematic film release directed by Joe Massot, which perfectly captured that rush of youthful excitement which characterised 2 Tone's arrival 18 months earlier. Filmed on tour in 1980, it offered a wider snapshot of the ska revival scene than a mere label showcase – for example, Bad Manners were present.

Massot's directorial credentials had included the cult 1968 film *Wonderwall*, famous for its soundtrack by George Harrison, as well as involvement with the Led Zeppelin concert film *The Song Remains The Same* (although Massot was allegedly removed from the project halfway through). The director had spotted Madness in October 1979 when both parties were staying at the Tropicana Hotel in LA, a popular haven for visiting bands. "My attention was caught by the goings on in the pool," he later explained. "They looked strange with their pale skin in the California sunshine. I was interested because they looked like they were having such fun. They were playing the Whisky on Sunset Strip, a famous showcase for musicians, so that evening I went to see Madness. They were amazing and their music was so different from anything in America at that time. By Christmas, I was back in England calling Kellogs to tell him I wanted to make a film of his group. This led me to Dave Robinson [who] gave me a lot of encouragement and even offered to supply the mobile to record the gigs."

The concept of *Dance Craze*, filming a variety of bands rather than revolving it around Madness, wasn't actually Joe's. "My son Jason [was] 15 and very much into the music scene," he wrote. "It was Jason who thought up the idea of filming all the bands. He told me about the 2 Tone movement, that ska came before reggae and all about the fashions – pork pie hats and two-tone suits. I saw right away the impact that the bands and their music were having in England. [I remember] seeing Madness at Bradford where the pounding of dancing feet made the whole building vibrate and the stage shook as if it was being blown by a strong wind! I came to love this thing called 2 Tone – the sight of seven- and nine-year-olds in their gear queuing to see their favourite bands."

Issued in mid-February, the *Dance Craze* soundtrack offered 15 of the 27 tracks which appeared in the film – and the blaze of publicity surrounding its release helped propel it to number five in the UK charts. Three of Madness's six live clips were represented on the album: 'One Step Beyond', 'Night Boat To Cairo' and 'Razor Blade Alley'. Another, 'Swan Lake', had graced the 12-inch edition of 'The Return Of The Los Palmas 7'. It's been argued that *Dance Craze* happened too late to catch the wave of excitement which surrounded the ska revival bands. It might be fairer to say that it bookended an era which had begun nearly two years earlier with 'Gangsters'.

Unfortunately, Madness had no involvement with the project. "We just didn't have any say in that film," admitted Suggs to *Jamming!* "That made us all a bit sick. Jerry Dammers did. [But] when we were watching the premiere, Jerry walked out and said he wouldn't have anything to do with it! And he'd been up to the editing every day. They should have taken one number from each band and given it to the groups to do something with. We'd have gone out and talked to a few people and had a bit about the history of the band. We could have done something a bit more varied than a live show."

★ ★ ★

Madness had joined The Specials at the music industry's annual MIDEM Festival in Cannes to launch the project. On January 31, the band also attended the UK premiere of the film at the Sundown Club, Charing Cross Road; dressed in tuxedos, the lads arrived in Alan Winstanley's vintage Bentley. On February 3, Madness were booked to appear on a French TV show *Avis de Recherche* – and Kellogs deputised responsibility for organising the trip to Chalky. Apparently, he arranged for everyone to meet in the Traveller's Cafe near King's Cross railway station prior to sharing the tube to Heathrow. Unfortunately, Woodgate couldn't find the cafe. As a result, Mark and Chris got bored waiting so they went on ahead and caught the tube only for Chris to discover that he had forgotten his passport (by all accounts, he was allowed to travel with temporary paperwork which didn't actually guarantee his return!). Eventually, the band assembled in the studio in France only to learn that Suggs was still peacefully asleep at home in bed . . .

Barely a year after meeting new girlfriend Sandra Wilson, Mike Barson married his Dutch fiancée at Finsbury Park Town Hall Registry Office on February 14. Once again, no one else in the band attended, although a Stiff photographer captured the extent of their celebrations: a romantic breakfast for two at George's Cafe on Holloway Road. All in all, Madness as a unit was beginning to feel quite domesticated.

Within a couple of days, Madness had flown out to Cologne to appear on a TV show named *The Bananas*, wherein the band mimed to 'Embarrassment' whilst surrounded by topless girls holding giant bananas. Back in the UK, Madness embarked on the Fill Your Coffers mini-tour of Poole, Nottingham, Cambridge and University Of East Anglia. Having toured with a variety of sound engineers, the band now settled with veteran Ian Horne, chosen because of his work with Ian Dury; and Horne continues to work with Madness to this day.

Unfortunately, relations within the management team had soured. "Kellogs and me weren't hitting it off," admits Barry Sinclair, "so I left because I didn't want to get into big arguments. That must have been February 1981. I went out to America in the spring to work on the Stones' stage sets." In stepped Madness' live agent Matthew Sztumpf, who'd grown up in Henley-On-Thames.

"I had been a social secretary at Cheltenham Tech," Matthew explains. "I got into agency work straight from college in '74, ending up at the Bron Agency. Someone else within the agency had seen The Specials and said, 'You should check these guys out and take them on' – which I did. That naturally became the 2 Tone tour, so I picked up Madness and The Selecter, who both stayed on with me afterwards. That was my 'in' to Madness. They were great fun. It was an excellent tour, marred by a certain amount of violence!"

Sensing that the manager wasn't able to handle every aspect of the Nutty Boys' frenetic schedule, Sztumpf offered his services as Sinclair's replacement. "There came a point where it seemed more attractive to go and work for management – it seemed more exciting than being an agent," he admits. "An agent only earns from one section of an artist's earnings whereas manager earns from all sections! I called Kellogs because I could see he was far too busy to do it all on his own. Why don't you hire me? The idea being that we would then manage other acts together. He would always have Madness and we could expand the company between us."

The pair complemented each other perfectly. "I brought Matthew in as my assistant and we got on well," adds Kellogs. "I needed some help because I was stretched. He went out on the road with the band a lot." By this time, the Madness machine was properly bedded in with their own company, Sterling Holdings.

★ ★ ★

For their next single, Barson dusted off an old song dating from their earliest days of performing as The Invaders. 'Grey Day' was initially inspired by the nine-minute-plus Roxy Music song 'The Bogus Man' (from their second album, 1973's *For Your Pleasure*), in particular its laconic, mumbled vocal style. "When we first did it, the song had a really steady bassline and loads of echo on the saxophone," Barson explained. "But Bedders didn't like it because he thought the bassline was too simple. So we dropped the old version and completely re-did the song." Foreman also remembered that early prototype: "We had first done 'Grey Day' three years before, a Sixties psychedelic thing with no structure and only a few lyrics."

In both its title and its downbeat musical and lyrical nature, 'Grey Day' was the first major indication that Madness had a melancholy aspect to their music at polar opposites to their zany, fun-loving public image. Several reviewers slated the record – but they completely missed its quiet strengths. While 'My Girl' was quite pensive – introspective, even – 'Grey Day' went a stage further, offering a bleak and frankly quite unsettling portrayal of the drudgery of everyday life in Britain. Lines like "I wish I could sink without a trace", "I'm black and bloody from my life" and "I can't stand this agony" suggested an inner torment bordering on depression – an unusual sentiment to hear in a pop song. And yet 'Grey Day' was a stroke of genius, perfectly counterpointing their light-hearted persona in dramatic fashion, aided by some decorative tubular bells from Barson.

Not everyone appreciated it, though. "'Grey Day' was a definite step on for Madness," Suggs later told *Uncut*. "[But] I remember going to a club with a copy of it and Joe Strummer was DJ'ing. I asked him to put this on, because I thought I'd finally done something that he could dig, not just jumping up and down – but he wouldn't play it!"

A variation on the familiar 'Nutty Train' theme, the distinctive sleeve characterisation for 'Grey Day' was drawn by Ian Wright. "I'd studied graphic design and left college in 1978," Ian explains. "I became aware of 2 Tone and got interested in Madness as a band. It was to do with grass roots. You read about this little band and I just thought they were really interesting. That's why I drew them. I had sent in my picture for the *One Step Beyond* album and I was in there." It must have helped that he was friends with an old college associate, Jules Balme, who was an in-house designer at Stiff and had designed the artwork for the album.

"I liked the shape of Madness, the way they looked," Wright continues. "They seemed to be ideal drawing material for me so the sleeve was something I drew for myself after 'The Prince' was out, when they were getting a lot of pop attention so I could get photos of them from *Smash Hits*. I suppose 'Grey Day' was about shapes, about clothing, just to enjoy trying to portray what Madness were about. Anyway, this picture was in an exhibition so it was framed."

Wright had already designed some early single sleeves for The Undertones. "Jules knew I had this picture so he invited me to Stiff. I saw Dave Robinson for a few minutes and he said, 'Do you want to sell it?' He bought the picture off me there and then and had it on his wall. Later on, the band went round to his office to talk about sleeves with him. They were like, why don't we use that? So that was how I connected with them. I thought 'Grey Day' was a good launch, quite a credible move for my career, an important, well-respected, printed piece of work. A very happy piece to show!"

Robinson delegated the single's video direction to photographer Chris Gabrin, who'd already diversified into making pop promos for The Stranglers but who hadn't exactly parted company with Madness on good terms during the aborted photo session for *One Step Beyond*. "By this time, they'd got used to seeing me around," Chris remembers. "When I first started, there was a wonderful creative anarchy about doing music videos. Stiff business-wise was taking off. Dave didn't have as much time to devote to videos as he would have liked so he asked me to step in. 'Grey Day' was one of my favourites. I put them in a shop called Bowman's in Camden High Street on a Saturday morning which obviously drew a lot of attention. We also went down Oxford Street in an open-top bus, with Suggs leaning over the front. It was pretty loose but partly to do with the lyrics – that they were being examined, like being in a goldfish bowl. Most of the Madness videos were an idea then we'd go out with the band plus lots of cameras and film."

Gabrin had drafted in a friend, John Mills, as his co-producer. Mills had attended the Royal College of Art Film School in the early Seventies before working as an assistant editor. Mills had also worked with The Stranglers. "I had the film editing experience and once we had the bug, we teamed up," says John. "We both loved music and there were no rules in video, so there was a lot of creative freedom. We did videos for Ian Dury, Tenpole Tudor, Jona Lewie – and Madness." The clip of Suggs 'flying' down a high street like Superman was an idea also mooted for *Take It Or Leave It* (when the culprit would have been Thompson) while the idea of legs being tied up in knots came from Marty Feldman.

Video-making for Madness definitely benefited from some vital team spirit within the Stiff employees and other hired guns. "It is hard to pin down who was the driving force," suggests John Mills, who ended up working on 11 of their promos. "I was talking to Chris Morphet, a great film cameraman, who worked on Madness' videos, and we agreed that it was very much a group effort – a coming together of a bunch of creative people who, out of seeming chaos, produced some great stuff. I can't overestimate how brilliantly creative the band were, and in that respect, they were the driving force, but Dave had good ideas and a knack of knowing what the public wanted."

The "seeming chaos" wasn't always helped by the stars of the show, either. "The band were unreliable when it came to turning up at a location on time," admits Mills. "Dave was pretty good at keeping them in line – they did have some respect for him. Dave had incredible enthusiasm and drive and a knack of communicating it to others, so he was an integral part of the equation. Dave and the band did not always see eye to eye, though, and this became more obvious as time went on. I think it would be fair to say it was a love-hate relationship!"

'Grey Day' peaked at number four in the charts, following its release on April 17. This was nothing short of a reinvention. While many of Madness's subsequent hits were decidedly upbeat, not to say comical, it's fair to say that much of their musical legacy also resides in compositions of a more cerebral nature – and that more serious approach began here. In hindsight, 'Grey Day' shared much in terms of its mood and musical stylings with The Specials' classic, 'Ghost Town', issued just two months later. As Stuart Wright observed in *Nut Inc.*, both records seemed to encapsulate the hopelessness which many school-leavers (and adults) felt in the face of rising unemployment and social unrest. Its message certainly provided a counterpoint to Adam & The Ants' 'Antmania' sweeping through playgrounds at the time.

That month, Madness embarked on what was titled the 'Absolutely Madness One Step Beyond Far East Tour'. By all accounts, Robinson accompanied them to the airport and filmed the take-off in case the plane crashed! In addition to Japan, the trip also encompassed Australia, New Zealand and the USA. "When I was still at the Bron agency, I had booked what could loosely be described as a world tour over a six-week period," explains Sztumpf. "Kellogs said, you can tour manage them because you've booked it, you know the promoters, the dates. It was interesting! A baptism by fire when you've got seven guys and, as soon as you've got six in one place and go off looking for the seventh, the other six disappear. It was fun winding Matthew up! They probably didn't mean it, they were young lads. Kellogs came on that tour – I just managed it." John Wynne agrees: "Trying to get all seven in one room was pretty hard work! We called it the spider effect. They all kind of run away!"

Robinson was kept abreast of any developments, which began with their very first show in Australia. "First Aussie concerts last night in Perth were great," read the fax. "Reaction to band terrific. Unfortunately, skin-heads caused $10,000 damage to concert hall. They got a bit carried away and broke 80 seats and smashed three large glass doors. Result – government minister wants an inquiry into banning pop concerts in the concert hall. Madness made the papers front and page two. And were the first item on radio news . . . Also, a national plane strike is on. Band just got out of Perth on last plane but had to go to Melbourne and then bus it back 500 miles to Adelaide." Having endured the discomfort of traversing vast tracts of the Australian outback in an old Greyhound bus, the entourage eventually hired two small private planes instead.

After dates in Adelaide, Melbourne, Sydney and Brisbane, Madness flew to Auckland and Wellington in New Zealand in early May before a stop-over at the legendary Raffles Hotel in Singapore. Shows in Tokyo followed. While in Japan, they recorded a new song, 'In The City', for the Honda Motor Company on May 12. Three variations were taped before the advert itself was filmed. Four days later, Madness were playing in San Francisco before travelling to Los Angeles and New York for a string of sold-out shows.

On June 8, the band performed at Holland's popular Pinkpop Festival in Geleen Sportpark, alongside such disparate acts as UB40, U2, Fischer Z, the Michael Schenker Group and, by coincidence, Ian Dury & The Blockheads. Despite Dury's over-riding influence on Madness, and the fact they shared a record label, their paths hadn't yet crossed. "We never really met him until that day," Foreman told Will Birch in *Ian Dury – The Definitive Biography*. "Lee Thompson and I had decided not to fly, so we got the ferry and Ian was on the coach. I was sitting next to him, he was my hero but he was threatening me all the way. 'You young pups are trying to steal my thunder!' When we got to know him better, he became 'Uncle Ian', like a relative of us all."

On arrival at their hotel, Thompson and Foreman were greeted by the sight of a drunken, beermat-throwing contest in the expansive dining room between members of UB40 and Madness while their respective managers tried to rein them in. Madness's set boasted some new songs in 'Pac-A-Mac' and 'When Dawn Arrives', and Barson joined Dury onstage to sing along with 'Sex & Drugs & Rock & Roll'. Madness joined another multi-faceted bill for their appearance at the Crystal Palace Garden Party on June 13 – remarkably, the show was their first in the UK that year. This time, they shared an open-air stage with Ultravox, Peter Tosh, Teardrop Explodes, Tenpole Tudor and The Polecats.

In the audience was journalist Tony Fletcher. "When Madness came on, a couple of skinheads went wading into the lake," he remembers. "I thought, we're a long distance from the group. What the hell, I'm going to swim over this filthy lake to the stage – I had to throw out whatever I was wearing that day! I immediately got a song dedicated to me and afterwards, for the next year or two, they were like, we've never in our life seen a music journalist do that – they're usually too busy hobnobbing around the back. They thought that was hilarious. I'd earnt my stripes!"

★ ★ ★

On March 9, 1981, work had begun on an ambitious feature film starring Madness entitled *Take It Or Leave It,* named after the song on *Absolutely*. Funding was drawn from both Stiff (£250,000) and the band members

(£140,000 in total). "The money came from the first big royalty cheque we ever received," Suggs admitted. "We thought that the best thing would be to invest it in something like a film, rather than just blow it all. It's a great long-term investment – an opportunity to show the way we were in the early days!" John Wynne also recalls some form of outside funding: "I remember Dave Robinson saying to me that the British Film Institute had authorised some scheme where, if you put up so much for a small film, they would equal it."

"We'd talked about a film a couple of times in the past," explained Robinson, "but the band's schedule had always been so tight that it had seemed out of the question. Then, March turned out to be much looser. We sat down and discussed it in mid-February. We were going to try something fancy but eventually decided on something realistic. I'm against the one-sided thinking that is generally the rule when a director makes a film. It should be a mutual undertaking with me latching myself onto the band and helping them to make it happen."

Pop bands, of course, had a long if not illustrious tradition of starring in their own cinematic ventures. In terms of British acts whom Madness might have admired, The Beatles had set the bar high with Richard Lester's mock documentary *A Hard Day's Night* in 1964 – although subsequent attempts (*Help!*, *Magical Mystery Tour*) were rather less successful. Members of Madness probably went to see on its release in 1975 *Slade In Flame*, which attempted to portray the gritty underbelly of the music business through the eyes of a struggling young band – Noddy Holder & Co. starring as the band Flame. Only the year before, Malcolm McLaren had turned the Sex Pistols' story into parody with *The Great Rock & Roll Swindle*. Other film projects like *Quadrophenia* and *That'll Be The Day* were based around bands/musicians but ultimately stood as fictional feature films rather than glorified documentaries.

Dave Robinson's vision for *Take It Or Leave It* was more straightforward even than *A Hard Day's Night*: it aimed to recount the early history of Madness starring themselves and their friends. No blurred boundaries between fact and fiction, no aliases to protect the innocent, it was just a no-holds-barred if affectionate account of their nefarious rise, succinct and to the point. Robinson adopted a hands-on approach, extracting the various accounts of their trials and tribulations, as Bedford later explained. "The whole group sat down one day and recorded a six-hour tape, talking about our personal memories. From this, we chose the thirty favourite episodes from the past five years. That's more or less what the film is – these real-life scenes linked together."

"I came up with the idea, they really liked the idea and we very quickly got it together," quips Robinson today. With help from editor Philip McDonald, the Stiff boss then concocted a script which was both believable to the viewer and also, more pertinently, to the band themselves. "They had this folk story, I thought, to tell about groups generally and them in particular. I interviewed everybody and used predominantly their stories, welded into one thing. We had the rough parameters of what we were trying to film then we improvised on the spot." To ensure that the footage looked totally realistic, band members spent many hours poring over scrapbooks and family snapshots, checking details such as the clothes they wore and the length of their hair (or lack of it!) at the time. The film's message, according to Robinson, wasn't dissimilar to that of punk: that any young band could be successful on their own terms, if they put their minds to it. "Madness are just a group of ordinary lads," he explained at the time. "If they hadn't become pop stars, they would probably have been unemployed."

Based in a disused warehouse behind King's Cross, Robinson had ambitious plans, with 36 locations identified within relatively easy reach of their HQ – including the actual homes of messrs Barson, Foreman and McPherson. "We had a limited budget but I'd decided to film the first half of it, the old bit, on black-and-white film and then in colour when we got more into the story," he explains. "Most people would have done it on video and converted it [to black and white] but we shot it on Super 16 film, a format they didn't use often. The first few days were to be the black-and-white bit because, in order for Madness to understand the story, it was important to do it in sequence. And the filming went fantastically, all around Camden Town."

According to the film's spin-off magazine/brochure, London Transport allowed the unit to film in Aldwych Underground Station. It was closed on Sundays but on the particular Sunday when filming took place, the city was unusually busy with crowds watching the London Marathon. A member of the public somehow appeared on the platform and, after watching the filming for 10 minutes, enquired when the next train was due!

Unfortunately, the project was blighted by misfortune from the outset. "Usually, with film, you get to look the following morning at what you've done. We were doing two days of black and white shooting so they said, well, we'll do the two together because the laboratory were doing a special bath of developer. So we all sat down in the cinema to see this black and white footage. They put the film on and it was like a snowstorm with little black dots moving around occasionally. They had overcooked the bath, heated it up like a colour developer. Totally useless. They'd burnt the negative to a crisp and so we had to shoot it all again. But you can't re-shoot stuff with Madness, you have to catch it! They didn't enjoy doing the same thing again but eventually we shot the beginning again at the end. I got the insurance money but that was nothing, it was the time and the effort – I was also running a record company!"

No sooner had they gone back to the drawing board than disaster struck again, as Dave explains: "As I was directing a particularly tricky shot, I slipped and fell off a camera support on a gantry in a tube station and broke my ankle. What's worse, I didn't even get the shot I wanted! So I spent the last few days of the movie (a) in extreme pain and (b) with a cast on, in a wheelchair, trying to control Madness. Not easy at the best of times. You really had to have two feet! They were always good, they always worked. But you had to get them in a frame of mind and then you had to really sheep-dog them through it because they'd lose interest. They had a poor attention span, in the nicest possible way. Part of my talents and abilities were keeping Madness in line because they'd run off and disappear. Lee would be off selling some dodgy scooter in the middle of an important day!"

Although Robinson may disagree, the band have since claimed that the dry run was actually a blessing in disguise – an accidental rehearsal. And even after the setback, filming still only took a week or so. Having been shot on 16mm film, the footage was then blown up to 35mm at the Stockholm Film Institute in Sweden.

Certainly, most of Madness seemed quite natural in front of the camera, as did friends and acquaintances like Clive Langer, John Hasler, Gary Dovey, Andrew "Chalky" Chalk, Ian "Toks" Tokins and Si Birdsall, alongside a supporting cast of established actors playing peripheral characters. The crowds depicted at their early shows were actually Madness fans, most with freshly shaven heads. The only role played by an actor was that of the publisher (i.e. Rob Dickins), who was played by Zoot Money, who actually sat behind Dickins' desk in the Warner Brothers' offices, which spoke volumes about Robinson's (low) opinion of Dickins.

Take It Or Leave It appeared remarkably authentic, from the intra-band squabbles (memorably, Barson's barbed comments to Thompson about the ability or otherwise of his saxophone playing) to a variety of hilarious mishaps (for example, Thompson's accident involving a delivery van and a low bridge). While its theatrical success was limited, the film stands as testimony to both the ferocious, unquestioning belief of Dave Robinson in the Madness idea; and to the band's ability to rise to the occasion with their trademark mix of good humour, streetwise suss and an uncanny ability to entertain. "They're naturals and I think Lee and Mike really showed some considerable talent," Robinson enthused to *Look In* magazine. "I'll be surprised if they don't get any offers from other film producers. It was just hilarious from start to finish. We were using a 29-man film crew and it was difficult to find the boys amongst them when we wanted to shoot – though Chas could usually be found near the catering bus!"

"This film had no script, its stars had never acted and its producer/ director had never masterminded a film before," laughed Bedford. "It sounds like the makings of a complete disaster but it's turned out as we'd all hoped it would – just a down-to-earth story of how some honest guys from north London got out of a rut and made the big time. There's a scene off the Portobello Road where a big gang fight broke out during one of our gigs. It was quite eerie going through that again, in the same places they originally happened."

Thompson, meanwhile, was particularly fond of the clip in which he and Suggs worked briefly as plasterers. "Boy, did we make a mess of that," he commented, "plaster and cement everywhere and the look on the face of the boss was like something out of a horror movie! We soon got the sack! Making the film was hard work but we enjoyed every moment, though it got quite tedious. For example, one particular scene we had to take eight times – we must have spent an hour at it – but in the film, it only lasts two minutes." Lee's summary of its depiction of Madness as individuals was unerringly perceptive: "The film shows the innocence and naïvety of Mark and Woody when they first joined the group; the frustrations of Carl when he wasn't a full member; the 'humpiness' of me; the paranoia of Mike; the kindness and thoughtfulness of Suggsy; and the wit and sharpness of Chris!"

Suggs later reflected on its lack of overt humour: "The great thing I remember was that we were trying to make a serious record of starting the band but it was only about two years after we'd started! The only regret I have is there was none of the humour and the kind of theatrical elements we like. We shot it straight and then we were going to have foam rubber sheets with the lampposts bending like when we're drunk. But it never happened."

For the many re-enactments of early gigs, they relied heavily on their enthusiastic fanbase, one of whom was their future press officer, Jamie Spencer. "I first met them when I was a young skinhead fan," says Jamie. "I used to travel the country to see Madness and The Specials. I got to know Cathal and he got me into a couple of scenes for *Take It Or Leave It*. I was the little trouble-maker in the audience at The Dublin Castle. We were asked to make it real like a gig so when John Hasler got up onstage and said something about sorry for being late, I threw a pint over him! I got in trouble but we were told to enjoy ourselves and have fun and Madness concerts were known for a bit of trouble. I lived in Cambridge. By pure coincidence, I moved to London and got the nod that there was a job at Stiff. And suddenly there I was in the press office, they came in and it was like, what are you doing here?!"

Although the respective wives of Barson and Foreman made cameo appearances, one aspect which was conspicuous by its absence from *Take It Or Leave It* was a proper sense of the band's personal lives. "We didn't want all that stuff about girlfriends in," explained Foreman. "It wasn't important, and the unions wouldn't let us have our mums and dads in!" Madness' guitarist was the first to be married – and when the band's commitments increased, it put a strain on their relationship. "I was out working three nights a week and she used to get lonely," he admitted. "I missed seeing my boy growing up."

The project was edited by noted American film editor Michael Ellis, who trimmed the footage back to a breezy 87 minutes. Robinson still feels the cuts were not enough, though. "I'd like to cut twenty minutes out of it, quite honestly, and I think it would be really quite good," he concludes. "It's too turgid in places." Because the film was never supported by a soundtrack album, it's an essential document for any Madness fan, offering clips of exclusive performances from the embryonic band, including such covers as 'Jailhouse Rock', 'See You Later, Alligator' and 'Rough Kids' and exclusive compositions like 'Don't Look Back' and 'Sunshine Voice'.

Robinson was shrewd enough to recruit an outside agency Rogers & Cowan, who specialised in handling the launch of feature films. The band attended the premiere for *Take It Or Leave It* at the Gate 3 Cinema, Camden Parkway, on October 14 (opening at the venue the following day and at selected cinemas across the capital on October 18). Sadly, Mike was absent so the band grabbed nearby journalist Paolo Hewitt to take his place in front of waiting photographers. "I was coming down the stairs when Suggsy grabbed me and said, 'Come and be Barson,'" says Paolo. "All these photographers were there! But that's how they were. They didn't take anything too seriously – or didn't seem to. It was just a good craic."

The film was accompanied by a magazine-cum-book, which came with the bonus of a free flexidisc sampler of dialogue from the film – and the principal photographer for the publication was Barson's erstwhile peer at Hornsey College Of Art, Eric Watson. "One morning, I rang on the doorbell of a flat off Holloway Road where he was living," recalls Watson. "I was there to photograph each member of Madness at home for this booklet *Take It Or Leave It*, published by ITV Books for which Neil Tennant was the editor. The book was designed by Steve Bush, the original designer of *The Face* magazine and house art director of *Smash Hits*."

Watson hadn't seen Barson since their college days. "Mike came to the door, looked me up and down and asked, 'What do you want?' Barson was always direct to the point of a seeming rudeness. Over the next year and a bit, I learnt to put up with it. The flat featured a retro bar fitting from the Fifties and an enormous dog [Mike's golden retriever Chappie]. Madness also did a studio session with me where they posed for the cover of the book holding large film cans. At this point, they were in lengthy, seemingly acrimonious discussion and the session stretched out over hours as it was impossible to dislodge them from my office! Woody was the whipping boy of the band and his more obvious middle-class background was the seeming source for the bullying, which appeared commonplace. The print run sold out and was a success, which secured both Neil Tennant and myself jobs with *Smash Hits* until Neil left to form Pet Shop Boys and I left to direct music videos and TV commercials."

Chapter 10

THE SUN AND THE RAIN

AFTER a particularly hectic first half-year touring the world, Madness were afforded the luxury of recording their third album in foreign climes, flying out to Nassau's Compass Point studios on July 20, 1981. At first glance, this felt like an uncharacteristically grandiose gesture from a band who always felt more comfortable in their local boozer than living the rock star lifestyle. But their accountants had suggested that tax on earnings from an album recorded in another country would only be liable on 80 per cent of the profits. In stark contrast to their previous surroundings, then, Madness were able to enjoy a relaxed lifestyle within the pleasant environs, alternating sessions in the studio with a life of sun, sea and sand, complete with their families in tow.

"Who wouldn't want to go there?" Foreman later commented. "But it wasn't the same gang – people brought their wives and I brought my five-year-old son along. We had our own little apartments. Carl did a lot of cooking, Robert Palmer would hang out with us, the Tom Tom Club were there recording 'Wordy Rappinghood'. The surroundings didn't really affect the album – it wasn't like 'let's go to India and put some sitars down, man'. [For example,] 'Shut Up' was a kitchen sink production."

Compass Point Studios were located 10 miles west of the City of Nassau on the island of New Providence in the Bahamas. It was created by Island Records' head Chris Blackwell, who envisaged the project as a Caribbean equivalent of, say, the Muscle Shoals Studios in terms of potentially creating a unique sound which would become synonymous with a style of music (i.e. reggae). But, its most famous projects were totally unconnected with the music of the Caribbean: for example, AC/DC's huge-selling *Back In Black* album was recorded there in 1980. However, the label's core musicians, The Compass Point Allstars, forged a particular hybrid of soul, funk and reggae, led by the legendary rhythm section of Sly Dunbar (drums) and Robbie Shakespeare (bass) – most famously heard in the period prior to Madness's arrival via albums by Grace Jones.

The band's Nassau stay wasn't without incident, as Bedford recounted in *The Nutty Boys*. Thompson, Woodgate and John Wynne had problems with their visas so they had to follow a day behind the rest of the entourage. "The night was very hot and humid and was alive with the sound of hundreds of insects and birds," wrote Bedford. "The air smelt of damp earth and plants. Our houses were built on a small beach so everyone went to sleep with the sound of the sea in our ears."

At the last moment, Robinson sent out John Wynne to keep an eye on proceedings. "I used to have the money and I'd give people per diems [a daily allowance]," says John. "I think everyone got $40 a day. I'd go to the bank every third day as it wasn't the safest of places to walk around with a thousand dollars in your pocket. Anyway, Mike says to me, 'I need $200 to hire this car.' So I said, 'I've only got $40 a day for everyone.' In the end, luckily enough, some people didn't want their money that day so I gave him a hundred and he'd saved some money. So he hired this car and had some money left over. That night, he came back, really pissed off. Him and Sandra had gone on the beach, taken their clothes off and gone swimming. When they came back – money's gone, camera's gone. High as a judge, I said, 'Lucky I didn't advance you another hundred dollars, Mike, otherwise you'd have to pay that back, too.' Well, that went down like a sack of shit!"

The Stiff boss made a surprise visit to the island to check on his biggest stars. "Dave was staying in Grace Jones' house," remembers Wynne. "I remember him borrowing the hire car without asking me. Where's the car gone? Oh, Dave's borrowed it. That's clever. There wasn't much petrol left in it and the petrol station was shut so I was waiting till the next morning to fill it up. So he ran out of petrol! Communications [with the UK] were hard work. It all had to be done by telex. Everyone had to come up with various names for the album and I had to type them out every night while they were recording and send a letter back to Stiff. They spent so much time on it."

After acclimatising to the pace of the island, cut off from the outside world with only the picture postcard-quality beaches for company, the rhythm section spent a couple of weeks creating the backing tracks with help from Barson while the others perfected their snorkelling techniques to swim with the manta rays and blowfish. Barson was arguably the driving force during the recording process, which would usually start around 5pm. Around 2am, Barson would often retire to bed, leaving the others to continue. Or so he thought!

"From that control room, we could see him walk past the window, so we knew he'd passed us," says Wynne. "Then by craning your neck round the corner of the cafeteria area, we could see him walk up towards his house, at the top of the hill. And as soon as his door was shut, we'd be off down nightclubs till six in the morning! There used to be this bar up this steep hill behind the studio. Evidently, there used to be a small aerodrome there, which was why the bar was built. There was a guy there who'd lost his arm by starting planes – you flick the propeller round. So he said, 'Do you want a game of pool?' And he beat absolutely everybody!"

There were no shortage of distractions away from the studio. "It was sunny and people were doing other things," adds Wynne. "We used to play a machine that had just come out, Pacman, in the breaks. After two weeks, everybody was starting to have painful wrists and elbows like tennis elbow – repetitive strain injury! It was hard work, though. We were there for six weeks. To a certain extent, they'd had years to get material for their first and second albums. Once they got to the third, I think they were getting tired. Once they got out there, there weren't enough songs so they had to make songs from nothing and they were falling behind. Everyone was getting stressed towards the end."

Thompson had reservations about their drift towards a smoother sound rooted in jazz and funk. "Clive Langer got me to do overdubs and harmonies which I don't really like because you don't get the real true sound of the saxophone," he admitted. "I like to keep things basic, even if it means that I'm out of tune. I don't like tarting things up. I prefer a Sixties' reggae feel, more straightforward." Bedford, by contrast, seemed more comfortable with this evolution, especially the more prominent use of brass: "Carl is getting a lot better on the trumpet, Lee's still there on sax and now me and Mike have started playing horns too. With a bit of luck, there'll soon be a four-piece horn section in Madness. There is talk of an extra percussionist and maybe some girl back-up singers. That would be really exciting."

Meanwhile, the whole of Britain were captivated by the Royal Wedding – and Madness stayed up until 4am to watch the spectacle on TV. Soon the entourage were flying back to Blighty. "I remember Alan Winstanley and I brought the album tapes back through customs," Foreman later recalled. "I couldn't help laughing at the sticker, 'These Tapes Have Absolutely No Commercial Value'!"

In hindsight, the degree to which Madness downplayed their Caribbean trip is interesting – no mention was made of Compass Point, for example, within the resultant packaging of their third album. Had the band been tempted to work with the likes of Sly and Robbie? Certainly, the involvement of the Compass Point Allstars might have steered Madness's sound in an altogether different direction. It's thought the band wanted to affect a calypso feel, only to discover that all you heard on the radio in Nassau was US soul, funk and R&B!

★   ★   ★

While still in Nassau, Foreman received a telegram from manager Kellogs to wish him a happy birthday – before the message added that, after three verbal warnings, roadies Chalky and Toks had finally been sacked (John Wynne replaced them with Rob Forrest, who had worked with The Selecter). Hot on their heels, Kellogs offered his resignation via another letter to Madness's guitarist following their brief return to Japan to record another advert for Honda:

"It is with some regret that I tender my resignation as the Manager of Madness," he wrote. "Obviously, I will fulfil my contractual obligations until the end of the year. Further to this, I am prepared – should you feel the need of it – to offer my services during the understandable period of transition that will occur with the change of management. I would like to thank you personally for the enjoyment and satisfaction that our two-year relationship has brought me and wish you and yours every success and happiness in the future."

"Why did I resign? It was too difficult," admits Kellogs. "I was at the end of my tether. Individually, each one of those guys was lovely. But en masse, as seven of them, it was difficult to handle. The number one and cardinal rule, that they wanted and I totally agreed with, was for them to be a democracy, if you like. No decision – and there were a lot of decisions to make, concerning everything – was allowed without everyone agreeing to it. I would call regular meetings to discuss hopefully a variety of issues. Inevitably, one or two people wouldn't arrive on time. The four or five that were there, after an hour or so, would get pissed off and probably go away. But we needed everyone to carry the vote so we could never really have a proper meeting. After a while, it became very wearing. I was trying to keep this democratic principle alive – but nobody was really in charge."

Kellogs admits that his decision may have been rash. "Naturally, as manager, I would put in my two pence worth. But if they really didn't like the idea, we wouldn't do it. In hindsight, it was the wrong thing to do – very silly – but by that time, the balance of my mind was disturbed! It was not an astute career move. In the heat of the moment, I was an emotionally charged person. Looking back on it, God, that was dumb!"

Matthew Sztumpf: "We were in Japan at the time. Kellogs called me up and said, 'Have the band been bitching about me?' I said, 'No – no more than normal.' Because bands always bitch about the manager, I suppose! We got back about a week later and he'd written them all a letter resigning because he wanted to pip them to the post. One of them, namely Lee, had spoken to their previous tour manager and said, 'Do you fancy managing the band, we're pissed off with Kellogs.' But none of the rest of the band knew he'd had this conversation! Somehow, Kellogs got wind of it and thought he was going to get fired. So he resigned. At which point, Lee – again – said to me, 'We think it might be a good idea if you manage us', without talking to the rest of the band. Eventually, the conversation happened with everybody!"

By this time, Matthew had formed a clear perspective of the different personalities in Madness: "Mike was the musical brains behind it, the engine room. Lee was always a wheeler dealer. He was also the court jester and Chrissy Boy came up with the gags: they were a little team, the pranksters. Woody went along with the flow. Mark was the quiet, artistic one. Chas's role had already increased. He was always a handful, in your face. He had a million ideas and wanted you to act on them all at once! Suggs and Mike were the two driving forces. The difference was with Mike, everything was black and white, whereas you could persuade Suggs that, for business reasons, this might be a better thing to do than that. Mike was certainly the most difficult. Mike probably and quite rightly thought everyone was in it for their own personal gain and he wouldn't necessarily believe Dave Robinson at face value. He'd think there was some ulterior motive."

"They weren't really management material," suggests Robinson. "They needed a good tour manager, I thought, rather than someone who was going to take them over, because they didn't get on with that many people. They had their own attitude, a bit punky – very cheery, nice guys but whenever they were out of your sights, they were off doing something else. Kellogs did it under a reduced percentage. It was an opportunity which he blew. He was a bit old school for them. He was used to the older rock'n'roller, really, which they were iffy about. They needed somebody who would pick up the nuts and bolts, though. I was the only one who seemed able to control them somewhat. They were never unpleasant, just a bit boisterous and never turned up on time. They had a very relaxed attitude about the fame and fortune game!"

To an extent, Sztumpf agrees with Robinson's view. "You were never really their manager (like you aren't with a lot of acts, though)," he says. "I was the eighth member of the band. In other words, all income was split equally. I represented them to the outside world. Some managers mould their artist, put them with this producer and that stylist. Whereas I didn't need to be that kind of manager because they already had their own style. You just had to hold the thing together. It would take quite some time to get decisions out of them. Kellogs had these pads printed up with seven copies. He'd write a question on this pad with an answer section below them and give them all their copies to fill in!"

A new recruit arrived in Madness' office the day after Madness' return from Japan: Suggs' cousin Hector Walker, with whom the band's singer had spent a significant part of his childhood. "I was sixteen and I'd lost interest in school and had no great plans apart from wanting to get out of Pembrokeshire," he remembers. "I had this fascination with city life and London so my mum arranged for me to be Auntie Edie's lodger because Suggs had moved out. My mum also phoned Suggs and said, 'Are there any jobs going with the band?' I found out later that Harry Wandsworth, who looked after the band's wardrobes, had an altercation with Kellogs and left. By lucky coincidence, there was a vacancy. I went up to London and Suggs, Cathal and Chalky picked me up. They were distracted because they'd received their letters of resignation from Kellogs. Oh God, what are we going to do?! Kellogs was still around. He was upfront, friendly and welcoming."

Kellogs' bombshell had dropped on September 17, just a week after the release of Madness's next single. Introduced by a single chord reminiscent of The Beatles 'A Hard Day's Night' and followed by some evocative piano from Barson, 'Shut Up' was inspired by the subject of petty crime. Apparently, the song was originally 10 minutes long before being trimmed back to a single-friendly length. Its lyrical theme in turn informed the video (with the band dressed as 'bobbies' on the beat, an idea previously adopted by The Small Faces).

"Keystone Kops was the idea for that," says Chris Gabrin. "I think that was my idea – that and the dropping of the piano. Ever since 'Baggy Trousers', we'd always tried to do something spectacular. So I dropped the piano on Mike! That was done in Freston Road – Frestonia, as it used to be called, round the back of Shepherds Bush where the scrapyards used to be. I was renting space in a warehouse around there for my film editing. It was only down the road from the old Stiff offices. And it was where you could get away with just about anything you wanted, including turning up with a huge crane, parking it and dropping a grand piano!"

Having borrowed from Slade's style for his guitar part, Chris now acquired the distinctive "Super Yob" guitar for the accompanying video. Originally owned by Slade guitarist Dave Hill, the artefact had recently been purchased by ex-Adam & The Ants guitarist Marco Perroni. The exact chain-of-title for the item has been a subject of conjecture, though, with conflicting accounts from the respective parties. "My story was that I saw a guitar shaped like a gun in a shop (possibly in the Midlands) and asked for someone to hire it for the 'Shut Up' video," wrote Foreman on Madness Central's website. "So I was a bit pissed off when the 'Super Yob' guitar turned up instead. Someone had got it from a guitar shop."

Although the chorus of 'Shut Up' might have been less catchy than those of Madness' most memorable singles (apparently, its title had once formed part of the lyric but was later dropped), this McPherson/Foreman composition had a youthful swagger befitting its subject matter, suggestive of classic TV theme tunes (not least, Harry South's memorable music for *The Sweeney*) and even dipped into an old western TV theme momentarily. Contrast the good-humoured mischief of 'Shut Up' with the self-conscious outlaw portrayed in 'Bankrobber' by The Clash. (According to Cathal on the *Divine Madness* DVD commentary, The Clash were in a nearby recording studio when Madness rolled up in their police uniforms, fresh from filming the video. Illegal substances were duly flushed down the nearest toilet, based on the false impression that it was a bust!)

The sense of lawlessness described in 'Shut Up' continued with Foreman's splendid instrumental B-side, 'A Town With No Name', which was brazenly indebted to the Spaghetti Western film themes of Ennio Morricone; the 12-inch added 'Never Ask Twice', a charming tale of worldly exploits which replaced 'Day On The Town' on some foreign editions of *7*.

Madness and their management had nurtured a close relationship with their fan base via the MIS, the matinee shows and in their personable, approachable demeanour – always willing to sign an autograph or answer questions, for example. As a natural evolution of that process, the sleeve design for 'Shut Up' came from a fan of the group, a Birmingham-based skinhead named Paul Clewley, after he entered a 'Draw To Win' competition in issue two of *The Nutty Boys*. The design for 'Shut Up' offered a variation on Andy Warhol's famous pop-art style, with a nod to The Beatles' *A Hard Day's Night* idea of numerous head-and-shoulders portraits, by suggesting a collection of mug shots to fit the song's criminally inclined theme. Clewley would occasionally work with the band thereafter.

Although much of the forthcoming album had been recorded at Compass Point, Langer and Winstanley were still at the helm. "They were dependent somewhat on Clive and Alan," admits Dave Robinson. "Clive was a really good songwriter but he wasn't very good with the sounds. And Alan, who'd tried to be a producer, was a very good engineer. So the idea was [to have] one guy for the art, the song doctor, and the other guy to get the sound sorted. And with Madness, you needed a couple of people to do that. It's those chemical teams which really made up the music business."

Madness's third album, simply entitled *7*, was issued on October 2, 1981. The LP was housed in a typically eye-catching sleeve design – although, according to John Wynne, they were embarrassed by their sun tans! *7* attracted very positive reviews. While *Absolutely* had felt like business as usual (even if the business was good), the songs on *7* seemed less reliant on those twin pillars of ska and Ian Dury. Langer and

Winstanley's production was balanced to perfection, while Suggs' vocal style sounded more confident, more charismatic. The only hint of Compass Point's geographical location was heard on 'Mrs Hutchinson', its faint Soca/calypso vibe (steel drums, breezy melody) contrasting the serious subject matter of a terminally ill woman suffering at the hands of an indifferent National Health Service. (The lyrics were based on Barson's own experiences with his mother Pat, who had been told, after a routine check-up, that she had a terminal condition, only for the hospital to realise their mistake several weeks later.)

Equally thought-provoking in terms of its subject matter was 'Tomorrow's Dream', Thompson's vehement attack on animal testing. Its reggae beat (reminiscent of contemporaries UB40) was shared by 'Day On The Town', an affectionate ode to youthful daytrips into the West End, dodging bus fares and eating chips, before the rose-tinted spectacles were removed to describe a capital now blighted by inner city riots. Lyrically, other songs continued to portray the less salubrious aspects of life described on earlier LPs, from the ribald humour of 'Pac-A-Mac', offering a not-so-subtle metaphor for safe sex (macintosh = condom) to 'When Dawn Arrives', a quite sensitive tale of a youth caught up in male prostitution set to a melody with shades of The Kinks' 'Sunny Afternoon'.

It spoke volumes about the growing confidence of Cathal Smyth's songwriting skills that his collaboration with Foreman, 'Cardiac Arrest', opened the album. The lyrics were inspired by an incident which Smyth had witnessed as a teenager. "Every morning, I joined the rush hour tube commotion, and journeyed for an hour from Muswell Hill to Paddington Station, everyone avoiding eye contact," he later explained. "One morning, a guy in a suit like mine – I guess he was in his early fifties – had obviously had a heart attack. He was lying on the platform and two staff members of the underground station endeavoured to give him mouth to mouth. I stayed watching, saying some prayers, till it was apparent that he was dead. Most [people] were walking past him and avoided looking at the situation." The event had a particular poignancy for Cathal: "At this time in my life, and I think I was 16, I had seen my father have a mild heart attack. It first occurred when I was 13 and his job had taken us to Iran. Pretty frightening for a teenager."

Elsewhere on the album, only 'Promises Promises' fell back on the ska of early Madness, albeit underneath a veiled attack on Thatcherite policies.

The cockney comedy of 'Benny Bullfrog' was perhaps closer to Chas & Dave (or the theme to *Only Fools & Horses*!) than its presumed inspiration, Ian Dury. But its over-the-top mix of vocal slang, burping noises, bar-room piano and honking sax made this a true highlight – and Thompson's first lead vocal since 'Razor Blade Alley' (Lee considered it the best of all his songs for Madness). Another gem was the sitar-laden 'Sign Of The Times', a critique of a tabloid-driven modern society set to a brisk, Motown/Charleston beat (think of 'Heatwave' by Martha & The Vandellas). 'The Opium Eaters', meanwhile, updated that old Martini TV commercial, capturing some Caribbean ambience outside the studio to add atmosphere.

It's been said that Madness shifted towards more contemporary pop on *7* – but there's no evidence here that, say, the prevailing New Romantic/ Blitz Kid trend for synthesizers or drum machines had made any impact. Only the more sophisticated feel of the Beatlesque love song 'Missing You', with its percussive funk groove, hinted at a new approach for Madness. Perhaps they'd been influenced by Spandau Ballet's partnership with funk band Beggar & Co. on 'Chant No. 1', a style they also explored on the largely instrumental 'Don't Look Back' (first heard in *Take It Or Leave It* before being reworked as a B-side).

The packaging expanded on the album's title, with lists and pictures of famous septets (days of the week, the oceans, the wonders of the world, the dwarves, the deadly sins, virtues, etc.). Of course, no one was suggesting that the number had any true significance – although it should be noted that both the album and the single 'Shut Up' peaked at number seven in the UK charts.

Around this time, Madness were interviewed by Tony Fletcher for *Jamming!* "One of the things which came across was how this really popular band were dealing with the pressures of fame," he explains. "When I first met them in Nottingham, they were defensive against the media. By the time I interviewed them again, Suggs in particular was like, wow, we're household names and we are recognised on the streets. It was around the time the whole Blitz Kid culture happened, with Duran Duran and Spandau Ballet. We were in the middle of a sea-change where people wanted to be pop stars, larger than life, colourful, and wear ridiculous clothes and be on the cover of magazines, living this nightclub life. Suggs was like, I'm not going to allow myself to be changed by this. I am still going to the pub, the chip shop, to gigs. And if somebody talks to me, I'm going to have to handle it. I'm going to fight this all the way."

Now overseen by "Vicky and Barbara" (Barbara being the daughter of actor Peter Jeffrey), the autumn edition of *The Nutty Boys* celebrated what had been a frenetic year for the band. A striking cover design of the fan club mag depicted the band in a variation on the familiar *Snow White & The Seven Dwarves* scenario with Dispenser (Lady Diana Spencer) in place of Snow White and cameos from "The Prince" (Prince Charles), "The Hag" (Margaret Thatcher) and "The Bill" (William Whitelaw) and, of course, "the seven little elves". This "Riot Ink" cartoon was created by Tony Riot, alias Tony Wright, whose caricatures had regularly appeared in the likes of *NME* and *Melody Maker*.

★ ★ ★

Hector Walker's first role was to help out during the band's tour rehearsals – and the 16-year-old found his first meeting with the magnificent seven a little daunting. "It was agreed that I'd start working for the forthcoming tour and for my first week's work with them, they were doing a production rehearsal at a theatre in Kilburn," says Hector. "Cathal was funny, witty and charming. Lee was friendly – 'Oh, is this the geezer you were talking about?' Dave Robinson appeared, a bit abrupt and abrasive with a pencil behind his ear, his pointy shoes and tight jeans, barking orders at people!"

The teenager also caught the rough end of Barson's tongue. "I was volunteered to make tea for everybody, my first task, and I managed to unplug Mike's equipment to plug the kettle in," bemoans Walker. "That was when I first encountered Mike: 'Who's turned my piano off?!' That was terribly embarrassing. Mike appeared, on the surface, quite gruff at times. I think it was a defence mechanism, though. I remember Mike once saying, 'Where are my sunglasses? Why didn't you check my suit?' We had to go down to the dry cleaners to check if they were there. We're halfway through having this argument with the dry cleaners and he puts his hand in his jacket pocket and there they are!"

Sztumpf took over the reigns on the eve of the *7* tour, on which they were supported by fellow Stiff act The Belle Stars, an all-girl band who'd evolved out of 2 Tone act The Bodysnatchers. Their singer, Jennie Matthias, wonders if the record company saw them as a female Madness –

a theory reinforced by the fact that their debut single 'Hiawatha' was a 'Clanger/Winstanley' production. "Stiff approached the Bellies at a gig [at] Dingwalls in Camden Town," explains Jennie. "Dave Robinson was aware that the girls had come from a predominantly ska scene so maybe he thought that we could possibly be the female version: there were seven of them and seven of us. Madness were such a laugh. Most members of the band were approachable and just normal away from the camera."

Just as Suggs and Bedford had dated members of The Go-Go's, so there was romantic involvement between Madness and The Belle Stars. Saxophonist Miranda Joyce went out with Bedford while Jennie herself fell for Foreman, who'd split up with his wife Sue earlier that year. The couple stayed together for seven years. "I remember first meeting Chrissy Boy," she explains. "I threw up in his bathroom – yuk, not a fond memory! I remember being late for a gig and only just making it. The Bellies were furious and Suggs dedicated a song for me called 'Disappear', cheeky old devil. Chrissy is the most down-to-earth of them all: he has a kind heart and is very considerate. Chris is still a good friend and will always have a place in my heart."

Initially, the tour dates concentrated on four Scottish cities (Edinburgh, Glasgow, Aberdeen, Dundee); to celebrate, some mock-cabers were cut out of polystyrene and painted brown, then thrown into the audience in pure pantomime style. After the shows, various chunks were presented to the band on which to sign autographs. Madness welcomed a surprise guest onstage in Edinburgh. "Humphrey Ocean appeared," says Hector. "Everybody knew him and he was made to feel very welcome. This tall, gangly bloke in a 2 Tone suit. They were saying, 'Come on for the encore.' I had no idea who he was and I assumed he was a musician. But he launched himself across the stage doing roly poly's and gyrating, throwing himself across the floor. I'm like, what on earth is this?!"

The tour then wound its way across England and Wales. One particular show was in Gloucester on October 16. "A part of my job involved me carrying a float of money," remembers Hector. "Lee came to me and said, 'Oh, 'Ect, you got any float? I need a jumper for stage.' OK, of course. 'Right, come on then!' And we went to the nearest Marks & Spencers. It was about closing time. Loads of Madness fans were lurking around in the streets – I don't think they recognised him. Then Lee suddenly said, 'Here, 'Ect, stand behind me.' And he just whipped this jumper off the peg, stuffed it down the front of his jacket and we trotted out of the store! I don't think he really wanted it. It was like a rite of passage for me, to see how I reacted, but I was pretty cool about it. Everybody else found out about it and just laughed and didn't bat an eyelid!"

The dates culminated in three nights at the London Dominion in mid-November. For Walker, who'd led a relatively sheltered life, life on the road was totally exhilarating – even if his day-to-day tasks were less so. "That entailed making sure all their suits, shirts and clothes they wore onstage were clean and dry every day," says Hector. "First thing in the morning, you'd be up and out to find a dry cleaners and laundry. Imagine being in Tokyo on a Tuesday afternoon and you have seven dirty suits and smelly shirts and you have to get them cleaned and pressed and ready for the night's show. I was the go-fer, the runner. If they wanted a packet of fags, I'd nip out. Make sure all their drinks were onstage, the towels were ready, the dressing room was tidy."

The teenager was struck by the continuing level of violence which broke out sporadically at Madness' shows. "The skinhead thing was still there, which wasn't nice," he admits. "They were scary, actually. They appeared mostly in the provincial towns and cities. You'd get factions from surrounding towns and villages and the gig was a centralised point for those local rivalries to be played out. If groups of skinheads were fighting, the band couldn't carry on because the majority of the crowd were younger fans there for the music. They would stop if a fight erupted, get the spotlight put on the people in the middle of the fight and have them ushered out. Once, the crowd spontaneously started slow-clapping this skinhead and practically shamed him out of the building. I think the band were fed up with it. It didn't fit anymore. They were fairly passive. Why would they want people fighting in front of them?"

* * *

For their encore, Madness had chosen to perform the old Labi Siffre hit from 1971, 'It Must Be Love'. During a brief respite in Durham on October 25, Madness recorded a demo of the song. Dave Robinson was so impressed with the idea that he proclaimed that if they released it as a single, it would top the charts or, if it didn't, the band could have the Stiff label. Or did he? "There's a debate about whether he said, if it doesn't get to number one, I'll give you Stiff Records, or whether he said, if it doesn't get in the Top Five," Suggs quipped. Encouraged, the band duly re-recorded the song properly on November 9 – although the original backing vocals were retained. "Mike always liked 'It Must Be Love'," Bedford later told Terry Edwards. "Woody and I did most of the arrangement, though. Clive sorted the pizzicato strings. Our style was so well developed by then that it just fell into place."

The Madness bassist had earlier recounted the song's pedigree in more detail: "On a cold October Sunday, the Madness Touring Party – fresh from a gig in Bridlington – pulled up outside a small terraced house in the back streets of Durham. We met Clive Langer and Alan Winstanley standing outside and, expecting the unexpected, we ventured in. We found a tiny living room with some microphones scattered around the floor. My God! It was a recording studio. Nine hours later, the backing tracks for 'It Must Be Love' were finished. Originally, the band were going to record the song for a Richard Skinner Show session but we didn't have time to work it out. So we decided to play the song on the tour and it became a firm favourite. We finally finished 'It Must Be Love' in London on odd days off." Hector remembers the song being rehearsed prior to the tour: "I remember a sense of excitement because everybody was buzzing. When the crew starts whistling a tune, it's a good indicator."

Suitably enthusiastic, Robinson had rush-released 'It Must Be Love' on November 25, presumably hopeful of a Christmas number one for Stiff. His intuition was sound: the song was a huge hit for Madness, reaching an audience far beyond that for, say, 'Shut Up' or even 'Grey Day'. The promotional video adopted a funereal theme to counterpoint the happy lyrics, with a cameo appearance from Labi Siffre himself.* Not for the first time, the video's theme was prompted by Thompson. "Whenever there was a black comedy movie on at your independent cinema, I was along to see it," he later explained. "*Arsenic And Old Lace, Entertaining Mr. Sloane* and *The Anniversary* – films like that. Maybe that's why I came up with the idea of a funeral setting for 'It Must Be Love'."

The difficult job of producing the video again fell to Gabrin and Mills. "That was a collection of various people's ideas," Gabrin suggests. "The band came up with the undertakers' scene which Dave ended up doing

---

* Siffre stated at the time that he would like to return the favour by recording a Madness song but the idea never came to fruition.

because they turned up so late. They were called for seven in the morning at Highgate Ponds and by twelve, they still hadn't turned up. We had a large film crew and a studio booked for the afternoon for the 'white wall' stuff. And it all started getting behind. So we'd arranged for someone to dig the grave in a back garden in Wimbledon. I said, 'Dave, you stay and do this undertaking scene with Chas running in front of the car and then go down to Wimbledon to shoot them in the grave and I'll get the studio set up and split my crew in half.'"

Gabrin's woes didn't end there, though: "I'd booked this swimming pool at a hotel by the airport for some further shooting, the famous underwater guitar solo. One of my cameramen was a keen diver and I'd hired him an underwater housing for his camera. I suddenly came up with the idea of the guitar solo and destroyed a brand new rented Fender Strat in the process. I said to Dave, 'We'll dry it off with a towel and run a hairdryer over it, it'll be fine.' The following morning, it was all warped and cracked! Everybody thought [the video] was fantastic but when it went out on *Top Of The Pops* the following week, Jimmy Savile nearly had a heart attack and put out this announcement saying it was dangerous to play an electric guitar under water!"

John Mills: "When Chrissy's playing his underwater guitar solo, somebody dives in and swims in the background – which is me! The BBC banned it and wouldn't show the video again. Labi Siffre seemed to really enjoy himself, though!" Thompson later highlighted this video as a personal favourite. The single even gave Madness their first Top 40 hit in the United States. But in peaking at number four in the British charts, it still fell short of Robinson's bold prediction. However, any question of Stiff's ownership was quietly forgotten. "I still love that song – it's great," Suggs later enthused. "Live, it's remarkable what effect it has on people. It's a stupidly simple sentiment as are lots of great songs. It still resonates."

From John Wynne's perspective, the song also acted as a peace anthem which helped diffuse violence at gigs – even if this was an unwitting benefit. So instead of their shows culminating with a fast and furious ska-styled hit, they'd end instead with this more gentle, downbeat offering. As Hector says, "I think 'It Must Be Love' was representative of where they were as people. You get older and you're falling in love, getting married and settling down." On December 8, the band flew to Holland to perform their new single – only to find that the Dutch arm of

Stiff had chosen 'Mrs Hutchinson' instead of their new cover version!

In the wake of the tour, Sztumpf began to re-organise Madness' management team. "Matthew was instigating change," remembers Hector. "He brought with him his secretary Tamsin Blight (her boyfriend Bob Black was manager of The Mo-dettes). He invited me to carry on working full-time with the band, in the same role as well as helping out with the fan club. The band were becoming increasingly popular and the fan club was very busy. Also, Matthew had this idea of saving money by buying a printing machine so that I could then learn how to use it and print all the stationery. So he paid me seventy quid a week and that was it for the next five years!"

Meanwhile, the media focused on Suggs' marriage to Anne Martin in St Luke's Church, Kentish Town, with a reception thereafter at Lauderdale House in Highgate (during which the happy couple sang a ramshackle version of 'See You Later, Alligator', with best man Smyth in tow). This time, other members of Madness and their families attended the ceremony on December 21 to cap a magnificent year for the band. "It snowed and we had the whitest of weddings," wrote the groom in *Suggs And The City*. "After which, Anne and I were whisked off to spend our two-day honeymoon in The Ritz in Piccadilly before I was off on the road again."

As a wedding present, Suggs had managed to track down her favourite car, a Karmann Ghia. Because the car was located in Luton, he enlisted the services of Lee Thompson, who was fluent in the language of both second-hand automobile purchase and Luton-ese. Having left Anne behind at the Ritz, the pair endured treacherous weather before eventually returning safely to the couple's mews pad in Camden with the prize.

Born Catherine Anne Martin in Whitstable, Kent, Suggs' wife came from a family steeped in music and theatre. As he described in *Suggs And The City*, Anne's mother Christina shared a dance act with her two sisters and graced the stages of such illustrious London venues as the Hippodrome off Leicester Square during the 1940s and 50s. The Martin Sisters would often share the bill with The Crazy Gang.

Martin – under her stage name of Bette Bright – had embarked on a solo career following her time with Deaf School, based around updating Sixties girl group classics with her backing band, The Illuminations. Having signed to Rob Dickins' Korova imprint in 1978, she recorded covers of The Angels' 'My Boyfriend's Back' and Reparata & The

Delrons' 'Captain Of Your Ship' before skirting the charts with her third single, 'Hello, I Am Your Heart' (with help from Lee Thompson on sax). She was well-connected: musicians on those early records included Henry Priestman (of Stiff/Radar act The Yachts), Rusty Egan (Visage) and his ex-Rich Kids partner, one-time Sex Pistol Glen Matlock (who'd witnessed Madness alongside friend Clive Langer back in 1979, of course).

Bright also performed with Dutch band Gruppo Sportivo before finally committing to a solo album, *Rhythm Breaks The Ice*, in 1981. By this time, the whole set-up felt like part of the Madness family. Not only was the album produced by Langer/Winstanley but the backing band was a variation on Langer's band The Boxes, with Ian Broudie on guitar and Ben Barson on keyboards. However, Martin's musical career took a back seat following her marriage to Suggs.

★ ★ ★

With Matthew now firmly in the driving seat as manager, a "good cop, bad cop" dynamic evolved within the Madness family, Robinson acting as the bullying elder sibling and Sztumpf as the comforting parent. Although unfamiliar with the machinations of bands or record companies, young Hector Walker could see that Stiff and Madness were made for each other. "They were similar organisations in as much as they were always on a wing and a prayer," he suggests. "Robbo had that kind of attitude. Things would be made up on the spur of the moment on video shoots. We'll organise it to a degree but there was that faith that it would come together on the day – and it did, of course. Considering it was so chaotic, it's quite incredible how good their videos were."

Stiff's impetuous spirit might have explained why they'd jump through hoops to organise a new Madness single which wasn't included on an album that was barely two months old. Other labels might have ring-fenced it for future release and concentrated instead in plucking another single from the album. Alternatively, 'It Must Be Love' could have been added onto *7*, which might have propelled the album back up the charts. But Stiff Records was anything but the streamlined, well-oiled marketing machine – and common sense or pragmatism weren't always to the fore.

As if to prove this, Stiff followed 'It Must Be Love' with another selection from *7* as Madness's next single. This time, it proved to be a mistake. Issued in early February 1982, 'Cardiac Arrest' clearly wasn't single fare – although speaking of single fares, Stiff concocted a video set on a double decker bus, which stopped intermittently to pick up passengers (including several bewildered old ladies), while the band portrayed commuting businessmen. "The vibraphone solo being played on the skeleton in 'Cardiac Arrest' was nicked from *The Goodies*," Woodgate later commented.

Behind the scenes, press officer Nigel Dick had switched roles to video producer. "Robbo said, 'Why don't you start producing videos for me? I'm tired of paying these people out-of-house. Work for me as a film producer.' That was Friday and Monday morning I'm producing videos! I did quite a lot of photography and I never planned out a career path but I sensed that there weren't many old men working in the music business. So I thought, what the heck."

Nigel's first project was the video for 'Cardiac Arrest' – hopefully not a descriptive title for his baptism of fire. "When I showed up on set, the cameraman Jeff Baynes said, 'Where's the film stock?' And my response was, 'What's that?' I'd organised the bus and the driver but I assumed the cameraman showed up with his own film! Luckily, Jeff happened to have a roll of film stock in the trunk of his car. So while they were filming, I drove down to the film stock centre in Wardour Street to buy this film. So I have to open an account in the days before having a credit card! By 11 o'clock in the morning, I'd learnt as much as some film students learn in their first term at school! It was a fantastic but ridiculous way to learn. I was literally the only person on production. I had all the petty cash in my back pocket!"

In his new role, Nigel detected another facet of Madness's abilities. "Each one was a distinctive personality which came across well on film," he says. "I loved working with them. We never had any bad days. Tremendous fun. They were absolutely unique in the history of music video. The drummer, the saxophone player, the guitarist – they could all do a funny walk or dress up as an old lady. They were extraordinary, like a musical troupe. People would say, 'Oh, they're a flashback to Vaudeville.' Well, they'd not gone off to play Skegness or pantomime so it was without knowing it. But by drinking the right water, they had somehow assimilated that kind of experience. So give them a fez hat or a funny suit, they would instantly – the minute you rolled the cameras – turn into these living cartoon characters."

Robinson prided himself on their ability to deliver innovative videos with minimum overheads. "Quite simply we were a two-man crew from a production point of view," says Nigel. "Dave yelled out where the camera was going to go and I did pretty much everything else: wardrobe, art department, making sure there was a camera there and a guy with lights, food on the set. The producer worries about the budget, gets schedules together, hires people in the crew, facilitates liaison between the record label and the band's management, ensuring people turn up on set on time."

'Cardiac Arrest' became the first Madness single since 'The Prince' not to reach the UK Top 10. This plight was due in no small part to the BBC, who apparently omitted the record from their daytime playlist after deciding that a song about a heart attack victim was unsuitable, following the death of a relative of Radio 1 DJ Peter Powell. "Maybe if we'd stuck to the original song title, which was '7 Letters', the single would have gone Top 10," suggested Woodgate.

By now, the 2 Tone movement had run out of steam, not least because The Specials had finally splintered in the face of internal acrimony in the wake of 'Ghost Town'. This landmark single somehow crystallised a sense among many in Britain that society was becoming more divided, more combative. An incendiary atmosphere seemed to pervade the news, whether that referred to failed assassination attempts of Ronald Reagan and the Pope, clashes on the streets of Belfast following the death of Bobby Sands or riots in Brixton and elsewhere due to tensions between ethnic minorities and the police force.

In late January 1982, Madness were the main attraction at the MIDEM Festival in Cannes, as part of a brief jaunt around Europe which included TV shows and performances in Paris, as well as in Germany, Spain, Holland and Belgium. In Italy, Madness recorded a 45-minute special in a circus in which Foreman fell off an elephant. These trips were interspersed with appearances on such British TV programmes as *Top Of The Pops*, *Mike Read's Pop Quiz*, *Cheggers Plays Pop* and *The Kenny Everett Show*, on which Madness performed 'Cardiac Arrest' with Thompson dressed as Gary Glitter. In the midst of such activity, the band had also flown to Los Angeles to appear in two new Honda commercials – bizarrely, the Japanese ad company CM Land had picked a suburban part of the city because it looked like England instead of actually filming it in Madness' home country.

For the B-side of 'Cardiac Arrest', the band had adapted their theme from an earlier Honda commercial, 'In The City' (which had already topped the charts as a single in its own right in Japan). Set to a tried-and-tested ska beat, this charmingly frenetic song might well have borrowed its title from The Jam's debut single. But where Paul Weller's tale about the capital was from the romantic perspective of a home counties outsider, this band composition focused instead on the high-flying executive commuter.

'Cardiac Arrest' might have been a minor hiccup but Robinson was shrewd enough to take stock. Madness had enjoyed an unprecedented chart run over the past quarter decade but now was the time to capitalise on their progress. Never afraid to spend money, the Stiff boss hatched a simple yet insightful plan: a "greatest hits" album heavily advertised on TV with the bonus of a brand new single. Not only that but Robinson took a closer than usual interest in Madness' next 45. The label might have rush-released 'It Must Be Love' to great effect but more was at stake here. Even Robinson – ever the rash, compulsive individual – understood that a degree of forward planning was required.

Chapter 11

HOUSE OF FUN

"I ALWAYS thought bands should put out a 'greatest hits' several times in their career," Dave Robinson opined. "I thought, we'll add a new single to the album as well as the oldies, because their fans would buy everything, and you wanted to give them value for money. When 'House Of Fun' came up, I thought, that's really good for this greatest hits package." Behind the scenes, Barson and Thompson had written the bare bones of a song, which had been recorded in early February 1982 at Trevor Horn's Sarm West Studios in Notting Hill, west London, with a view to it being Madness's next single. "We'd finished it in the studio, it was called 'The Chemist's Façade'," Suggs later recalled. "I've still got a good demo somewhere."

John Wynne remembers the scenario well. "We sat in AIR Studios – Clive, Alan and myself and a tape op called Renate Blauel. (She was in on Thursday. She wasn't there on Friday. I looked in the paper on Monday morning and she'd married Elton John!) We were in the studio about ten o'clock at night. Alan and Clive were always a bit wary of Dave Robinson because, when he came in, they had to jump. They've done 'House Of Fun' but there was no chorus: 'Welcome to the house of fun/ Welcome to the lion's den'. Dave listened to the song, got up and said, 'There's no fucking chorus, put a fucking chorus on it, I'll be back in two hours.' And he went. Alan and Clive just shat themselves."

Suggs: "Me and Chris went into a back room and wrote the chorus which we never got credited for, I hasten to add, then Clive and Alan just cut the tape and edited in the chorus, like they did on The Beatles' 'Strawberry Fields Forever'. You can hear it changes sonically from the verses to the choruses. It just becomes brighter." The producers had to rush across town to organise the insertion. "They'd rented another studio in St John's Wood," explains Wynne. "Whizzed over there, snatched it off the tape, made it into a loop, dropped it onto the tape, brought it back then played it to Dave two hours later and he said, 'That's what we'll have.' Bang!"

With its bawdy innuendo, it was no surprise that the punning lyric was written by the saxophonist, from roots which dated back to 1980. "That was going round in Lee's head for years," explains Wynne. "I remember him telling me, 'I've got an idea for this song, all about buying condoms!' He was working it out in his head. We were sitting in a pub called The Palmerstone opposite where Toks used to live. Lee used to live at the bottom end of the road there in Cathcart Hill."

On April 7, Madness were filmed for the promotional video for 'House Of Fun' at a deserted funfair in Great Yarmouth, owned and run by relatives of Lee Thompson. The whole scene was captured in one take and, during the 'loop-de-loop' at the end, Dave Robinson promptly lost all the money he had in his pockets. Extra footage was then captured back in London in an off-licence, Brown's Chemist in Kilburn, and in a theatrical costumes/props outlet, Escapade, located in Camden High Street (with Madness photographer Clare Muller as shop assistant). The band excelled, from Lee & Co. as the dancing 'washer women' to Suggs as the impetuous teenager asking for his first 'packet of three'.

The video's producer was Nigel Dick. "I organised the chemist's shop/joke shop and rented all those costumes," remembers Nigel. "It was done on a piece of paper which Dave had in his back pocket, with no writing, no script or pre-production meetings! I have to ring the bloke who owned the joke shop and do the deal so he'd close the store for two hours while we lit the set and shot it." The results subsequently won Best Video Of The Year at the *Music Week* Awards.

★　★　★

Not content with a brand new chorus and one of the most distinctive videos of their career, Robinson also put a call into Ferret Plugging, arguably the strongest TV/radio promotions company then operating in the music industry. Ferret Plugging's modus operandi was to catch an act before their first record and offer a 360 degree advisory role for their development, a model which had worked for the likes of UB40 and

Depeche Mode. Co-run by Neil Ferris, Ferret had also helped develop hit acts such as The Human League, Heaven 17 and Spandau Ballet.

"Robbo called me from Stiff and said, 'Would you be interested in working with the Maddy Boys?'" says Ferris. "He said, 'We need somebody to take the band to another level.' I'd worked with UB40 who were also a huge bunch of people. The Ube's like Madness, Madness like the Ube's, so that worked for me. Like the Maddy's, the Ube's were democratic to the point, at times, when it was frustrating because you had to get everyone to agree."

With the component parts completed for 'House Of Fun', Robinson could now concentrate on the main prize. Issued on April 23, *Complete Madness* was a masterstroke of pop marketing. The Stiff boss had insisted that the banner "16 Hit Tracks" be emblazoned across the cover, even though the LP boasted only a dozen singles (the others being the re-recording of 'Madness', 'Bed And Breakfast Man', 'Take It Or Leave It' and 'In The City'). And the tracks were segued together, with some crude editing to top and tail certain recordings (which meant no reverb echo at the end of 'The Prince', the opening crowd noises and closing 'Goodnight' were absent on 'The Return Of The Los Palmas 7' and Cathal's introduction to 'One Step Beyond' was significantly shortened.

It didn't matter: Robinson understood the true power of their songs. Fuelled by an ambitious TV marketing campaign, centring on an advert with a voiceover from actor George Cole (most famous for playing the character Arthur Daley in *Minder*), the album spent three weeks at number one and 88 weeks on the charts in all, outstripping sales for any previous Madness record. It's even been argued that it cast a shadow over the sales of the band's subsequent album, especially in the fecund sales period prior to Christmas. The sleeve design was based on a colourful studio shot taken by *Smash Hits* photographer Eric Watson, which emphasised Madness' jocular image, a vital consideration for such a mainstream project. Indeed, two earlier photo sessions – a shoot with acclaimed photographer Anton Corbijn on top of the Scala Cinema, King's Cross and another with Eric Watson at Alexandra Palace – were deemed unsuitable.

In hindsight, Watson's first choice of location brief now has an all-too-familiar ring about it. "I was asked to do a session on Primrose Hill involving Lee being suspended from a crane and hovering above the band," he remembers. "[But] we couldn't get permission to take the crane onto Primrose Hill and were forced to relocate to Alexandra Palace. It was midwinter, the light was awful and I had to run my lights from a noisy, smoky petrol generator which backfired constantly. The pictures were poor and we all got wet and muddy. Mike's verdict was coruscating: 'We could have done that in the studio. It looks like London's just a painted backdrop behind us.'"

Watson reconvened to a studio to create the more conventional band portrait eventually chosen for the front cover. "I arrived with the transparencies of the session at the Stiff offices and went into a meeting with Robinson and Paul Conroy," Eric explains. "We were joined by another employee, who said he didn't like the pictures at all – why didn't they get the guy who did the 'Take It Or Leave It' sessions?! This was said in front of my face! I remember Anton Corbijn being quoted in the *NME* saying he had shot something but Stiff had got some advertising type after being told that 'Greatest Hits' albums sold better if the band were shot against a white background, like a toilet roll or a bar of soap. Funnily enough, the white background was my idea and was not prompted by any agenda other than I had a white background up in the studio when they arrived."

Although Madness often looked dapper, Suggs made a special effort for this photo shoot, donning a bowler hat. While other members had worn this classic English headwear (most notably, Thompson in the video for 'Baggy Trousers'), this was their singer's first dalliance with 'the coke'. Rather than a tribute to such iconic screen favourites as *A Clockwork Orange* or *The Avengers*, it was actually a twist on the "hordes of bowler-hatted gents streaming out of Liverpool Street station swinging their rolled-up brollies, like a pinstriped army".

Despite Eric's assertion, Stiff very definitely sought some outside marketing advice. "They paid out an awful lot of money for an advertising profile," says John Wynne. "They got a load of whizz-kid boys in suits in to explain to them what they should have on a sleeve. So they have a private meeting in the sound studio at AIR Studios, which ain't cheap. The idea was the record company, advertising people and the band can talk amongst themselves and we can't hear because we're outside. We're in the control room, 11.30 in the morning. Then Alan Winstanley says, this is how private it is – you have a microphone into the sound room so by pressing a button, we could hear every word they said in the studio. How stupid is that! The snatches we heard were that market forces dictate that the band are close up to the camera, smiling, big colours, and if you look at the front cover, that's exactly what it is."

The meeting dragged on for a couple of hours. "By half past one, the band had all had enough," continues John. "So I'm standing with Chrissy in a pub and he's telling me about the meeting. I said, 'Chris, you could have gone anywhere for that. Why did you have to sit in a recording studio?' He said, 'Oh, we're not paying for it, the record company are.' 'No, you're paying for it! Because the record company will take it off your next advance.' You could see the penny drop: 'Oh, I'll look into that.' He did take those things on board."

Mindful of the impact achieved by their string of pop videos, Robinson also concocted a companion collection on VHS and Betamax, which proved to be one of the most popular "sell-through" pop titles of its day, perhaps helped by bespoke links filmed with the band especially for the release. "I edited those little sequences together," adds Nigel Dick. "I'd never even been in an editing room. It was like, here's the footage. So I had to sit down at a Steenbeck, which fascinated me because all the wheels went round, and found myself cutting it together, which was amazing fun. It was one of the first video compilations." The *Complete Madness* video duly won a *Music Week* award later that year.

Although TV advertising subsequently became a commonplace marketing tool, it was rarely adopted for a contemporary pop band back in the early 1980s. Rather, the medium was most commonly associated with cheesy Seventies pop collections on labels like K-Tel and Ronco – it definitely lacked credibility. With some notable exceptions, 'greatest hits' albums were usually saved for artists who were perhaps half a decade into their careers – or who had disbanded. Few active artists who had emerged during or since punk had had their catalogue re-packaged in this manner. But there was one notable exception: it's likely that Robinson had spotted the success in autumn 1981 of *The Best Of Blondie*.

'House Of Fun' was deliberately scheduled to follow *Complete Madness* by a few weeks. As Robinson explained, their fanbase had been lured into buying the compilation with the carrot of an exclusive track, which had duly been aired on the radio. Furthermore, Madness's music had bought its way into every living room in the land courtesy of Stiff's TV advertising plan. As a result, 'House Of Fun' gave Madness their first UK number one single – despite the fact that this magnificently surreal tale of coming-of-age was pregnant (if you'll pardon the pun) with double entendres about the first fumbled attempts to purchase contraception at the chemists. In a nutshell, 'House Of Fun' crystallised Madness's skill at appealing to pre-pubescent kids who couldn't help but be smitten by the band's madcap melodies and playful antics, while also offering more poignant, substantial lyrics.

"At that point, we weren't conscious about having a message, we were just writing about things that we'd experienced," Suggs later explained. "We were young and naïve [but] we were probably aware it was risque, so we probably were trying to cover it up. But it seems funny now that you should worry about telling kids to wear condoms!" By coincidence, 1982 was the year when links were being made between sexual activity and a growing number of cases of people whose autoimmune systems were being attacked. The condition carried several different names and it was only later that year that AIDS (Acquired Immune Deficiency Syndrome) became an accepted acronym. In creating a comedic hit, Madness had accidentally offered some very sound medical advice to their audience.

★ ★ ★

On the very day when 'House Of Fun' reached number one, the band were touching down in Japan for half a dozen shows from May 24 to 31 (supported by Bow Wow Wow) so the BBC organised satellite link-up with the band for *Top Of The Pops*, to introduce a screening of the video for the single. During their two-week visit, Madness travelled to Osaka on the Super Express bullet train prior to recording a new 'Turbo City' version of 'In The City' for a second Honda TV commercial, as well as filming two variations. The first of these was themed around kung fu while the second was a humorous scenario based around a petrol station, with Madness dressed in Arab garments – though this was never screened due to concerns that it might cause offence.

By this time, Toks was back on board as roadie. "The backline crew were fairly down-to-earth, ordinary blokes, without any pretensions," recalls Hector Walker. "They were part of the gang, really. Everybody was up for a good laugh and had a great sense of humour. We were flat out, pretty much non-stop, from either recording, promoting, touring – it was just relentless. John Wynne was loyal and hard working: he knew a bit about electrics and could drive so, in that context, he was very professional. John would primarily be stage manager and look after the keyboards, Rob Forrest would look after the guitars and Toks would look after Woody and the drums. Toks lived up Tufnell Park. He had a long history with the band and was particularly old buddies with Lee, I think. Toks was really nice and would help ground everybody – 'don't talk bollocks!' Funny, witty, got on with it. Chalky and Toks had a reputation as a comedic double-act."

No sooner were the Nutty Boys back in the UK than they set about preparing to make their fourth album. What's fascinating about the Madness machine, though, is the degree to which they were able to balance promotional activities – both collectively and individually – with their personal lives and other commitments. Barely a week seemed to have passed before one or other member was sighted in the press. On May 16, for example, they had taken part in The Capital Goaldiggers, a five-a-side football tournament organised by Capital Radio at Queens Park Rangers' stadium, alongside The Beat and post-Specials trio The Fun Boy Three.

At the time, fans would have been more interested in hearing Madness's new radio session for David Jensen, which offered a sneak preview for new songs 'Tomorrow's (Just Another Day)', 'Are You Coming (With Me)', 'Tiptoes' and 'Calling Cards'. On July 10, Madness finally unveiled their next single, 'Driving In My Car' on the TV show *Saturday Live* – minus Suggs, because wife Anne was preparing to give birth (the singer's place was taken by a ventriloquist's dummy which was sat in Smyth's lap).

As the follow-up to the chart-topping 'House Of Fun', 'Driving In My Car' was an ode to that British institution, the Morris Minor 1000. In her 1995 book, *The Secret Life Of The Morris Minor*, author Karen Pender stated that the vehicle has frequently been described by writers as a design classic typifying "Englishness". While that description might not immediately evoke the spirit of Barson's ex-G.P.O van, which had been used to ferry the band around from rehearsal to gig in their formative years (or two vans, if *Take It Or Leave It* was to be believed), let's not forget that the band even toyed with the name Morris & The Minors. In due course, they wheeled out a Morris 1000 into the BBC studios for a memorable performance on *Top Of The Pops* on August 5 ("which was a real nightmare because we had to get the petrol out the car because the BBC wouldn't allow it," remembers plugger Neil Ferris).

The video was memorable for a cameo appearance by The Fun Boy Three and its novel use of a Morris Minor, hired from one Charlie Ware. "Charlie had a whole story," explains Nigel. "He was a wealthy man who'd lost his millions so he'd moved to Bath and opened up a garage renovating Morris Minors. At the time, there was that Volkswagen commercial where a VW dropped from the ceiling and crashed to the floor beside a Japanese businessman. Robbo said, 'We'll do the same thing.' So I contacted Charlie and said we needed two Morris Minors. I need to be able to drop one without an engine in it so I had them weld pieces of steel across the inside. Because I was so naïve, we had a crane outside the studio and its arms went in through the door up to the ceiling and lifted the car. I had a Stanley knife, shimmied up the boom of the crane and said, 'Roll the camera.' Everybody ran out the studio and I just cut the cable. It worked perfectly! Completely insane but that was the solution!"

The accompanying sleeve design revolved around another photo session by Eric Watson. "Working for Stiff was nerve-racking as Dave Robinson believed in a logistically stretching spontaneity which had me tearing out hair on occasion," admits Eric. "Dave also had some odd ideas about billing which meant often enough laying siege to his office until he signed a cheque! He always had a pen behind each ear and used his hands and wrists as a diary. This session was shot at South Bank Studios in a vast white 'infinity' cove. The challenge was to show Madness sitting in the convertible Morris Minor at the same time as pushing themselves pushing the car. This meant stripping them together three times mechanically – Photoshop did not exist then! Madness largely arrived on bicycles for this session."

Despite this pedigree, 'Driving In My Car' was viewed in some quarters as a disappointment. While it may have shared the same delightfully quirky, disjointed feel of its predecessor, it lacked the same *joie de vivre*. Its robotic melody might have been a clever metaphor for the mechanical subject matter (with or without the horn effects) but this over-simplistic lyrical tribute to the wonders of the automobile found few friends outside of the band's loyal fanbase, who could at least seek solace in Barson's worthy piano work. Nevertheless, the song's inane chorus and the eye-catching video rewarded the band with a number four hit. (As an aside, the B-side 'Riding On My Bike' reflected a genuine passion for cycling within the band – indeed, Lee, Chris and Mark participated in a

Radio 1 Roadshow cycling benefit, riding from Wolverhampton to Birmingham, on June 30.)

From the band's perspective, 'Driving In My Car' reinforced their 'nutty' image at a time when they wanted to develop their image – if not to be taken seriously, exactly, then at least to broaden their appeal beyond slapstick stunts and novelty antics. Instead, it felt like they'd been put in reverse (if you'll pardon the pun), a fact made all the more frustrating because it flew in the face of the song's more ambitious embryo. "Mike's original [idea] was that, during the song, he'd switch on the radio and hear another song," according to Bedford. "Then he'd re-tune and there'd be another one – and so on. I often wonder what would have happened if we'd been a bit more courageous."

To compound matters, Madness offered a dub reworking of the 7 track 'Tomorrow's Dream', on the B-side. 'Animal Farm' was named after the famous George Orwell novel, of course, but without any decipherable lyrics, its message was drowned in studio effects – which rather missed the point. Madness weren't alone in grappling with the seemingly juxtaposed ambitions of artistic credibility and commercial considerations: contemporaries like The Specials, Soft Cell and Paul Weller shared this problem. The Special AKA's brave attempt with singer Rhoda Dakar to tackle the taboo subject of rape with 'The Boiler' was foiled only by its modest sales. If Madness wanted to follow suit, they would have to confront the disparities between their fun-loving image, the commercial demands for radio-friendly hit singles and this new desire to tackle more emotive, political issues.

* * *

Despite such misgivings, Madness were at their commercial peak, enjoying widespread support courtesy of *Complete Madness*. As a reflection of their profile, they topped the bill at the Prince's Trust Gala on July 21 at the London Dominion alongside Phil Collins, Pete Townshend and Robert Plant. Apparently, Madness were asked to play the National Anthem and agreed to do so – but on kazoos. At the end, the band bowed respectfully to the audience, including Prince Charles (who set up the Prince's Trust), to reveal the letters M-A-D-N-E-S-S on their hats. Afterwards, Prince Charles was photographed meeting the band, who were dressed in white shirts and "dicky" bows – all except Thompson, who wore a shiny lamé jumpsuit!

The night before, Madness had celebrated the arrival of Suggs' first child (after his wife Anne gave birth to a daughter, Scarlett Miranda McPherson on July 20) with a private show at the Bull & Gate pub, Kentish Town, for 200 family and friends, with support from R&B band Diz & The Doormen. A few weeks later, on August 30, Lee became the proud father of daughter Tuesday Rae Thompson. By their standards, though, the diary that summer was relatively free – other than a few one-off shows. Across the bank holiday weekend, for example, Madness appeared as 'special guests' at 'The 2 Occasion At The Castle', otherwise known as the Castlebar Festival Of Music in County Mayo, Ireland (the original home of Smyth's mother). Madness headlined on the second day of the event (July 31) on a bill otherwise dominated by Irish bands such as Thin Lizzy and The Boomtown Rats. And on September 2, Madness headlined a Radio 1 Beach Party at the famous St Austell Coliseum in Cornwall.

On August 19, Madness recorded a performance for BBC2's forthcoming TV series, *The Young Ones*. Starring Rik Mayall, Adrian Edmondson, Nigel Planer, Christopher Ryan and Alexei Sayle, the sitcom spun off London's "alternative comedy" hub The Comic Strip. Written by members of the cast with help from university friend Ben Elton and Mayall's then wife Lise Mayer, *The Young Ones* proved immensely popular with teenagers – even though it only ran to two series of six episodes apiece.

Madness's appearance in the third episode (entitled 'Boring') was a definite highlight of the first series. The scenario had them performing 'House Of Fun' in the Kebab & Calculator pub but with Woodgate and Bedford swapping instruments. After they'd finished, the house mates arrived (Rik, Neil, Vivian and Mike) only to ask if there was a live band today. Madness said there wasn't, blaming a power failure. "Do you know 'Summer Holiday'?" asked Mike. "You hum it and I'll smash your face in!" threatened Suggs before the band wandered off. The episode was eventually broadcast on November 23. In January 1984, Madness filmed a second appearance for *The Young Ones* in Brighton, miming to 'Our House', aired as episode five (entitled 'Sick') of the second series on June 12.

The Young Ones was essentially a madcap update of *The Monkees* but its creators envisaged a companion series which might have been closer still to its Sixties counterpart. "As a result of our appearance [on the show], Ben Elton and Richard Curtis came up with a pilot TV show starring Madness," Foreman later explained. "It was about how we were left to run the country after Maggie Thatcher was exposed as being an alien and had to return to Mars. We'd do all these mad things and right at the end of the show, the Queen would call us and say the miners were about to go on strike. We'd ring them up and say, 'Come on boys, leave it out', and that would be our way of running Britain. The scripts were really funny, but unfortunately the show never got off the ground."

"We had a script meeting at the office one day," remembers Matthew Sztumpf. "Ben and Richard came in, kicking some ideas around. And Cathal brought this mate of his along, Harry Enfield, who nobody had heard of. We thought he was another one of Cathal's dodgy mates! Harry came up with a couple of gags, one of which was about a song being in the oven: they open the door, pull this song out and it's only half-baked so they put it back in. The next time we saw the script, Ben and Richard had nicked it!"

At the time, Bedford commented that they might do "a fortnightly TV show, as it would be the right move for the band to make". Thompson was more concerned about the content itself: "If we ever get a series, it would be a bit like Benny Hill (without tits), mixed with *Monty Python* and *Minder* – but it will be on cable knowing us!" In *Smash Hits* in February 1984, Suggs revealed that the project was still active: "A few episodes have been written and now it's got to be sold commercially as a package." Cathal was optimistic, too: "It's going to be filmed, a bit of a sit-com/satire about the state of the nation, sort of like the Monkees!"

Later still, John Hasler reported in the M.I.S. fan magazine that "negotiations were in progress with the BBC", suggesting that the earliest possible screening date would be spring 1985. Eventually, two 10-minute pilot episodes were shot but when none of the TV networks showed any interest, plans were quietly shelved. Hector Walker: "I remember Ben Elton explaining that they'd borrowed the film crew and they were saying, God, this has been the best day's work we've ever had, because it's not boring old news reports!"

The Young Ones' creators weren't the only people chasing the idea, though. "Adam Faith wanted to do a series with them using the film director Alan Parker," reveals Matthew (Parker had attended the same Islington grammar school as Foreman). "I had a meeting with them in Fortnum & Masons where Adam used to have a telephone socket and use it as his office. He'd called up and said, 'It's Adam Faith, can I talk to Madness's manager?', and you could hear all this noise and crockery in the background. I went, 'Piss off, who's that mucking about?' It sounded like somebody in a pub, the sort of thing the band would do!"

★ ★ ★

Complete Madness was still high in the charts back in the UK – and it could have been argued that Madness should have waited until the following year before committing to a brand new album. But perhaps bowing to pressure from Stiff, the band set about honing new songs for their next LP. They stood at an interesting crossroads. Their recent conquests of both charts gave them some much-needed creative freedom to develop Madness as they saw fit. And yet 'Driving In My Car' had suggested that might not be an easy task.

On August 24, Madness finally began recording their fourth album at AIR Studios, set up by Beatles producer George Martin in 1969 on the fourth floor of 214 Oxford Street. Sessions went well and mixing of the album was finally completed on October 8, on the eve of a visit to the Antipodes. They arrived in Sydney on October 12 to begin a two-week tour which interspersed all of Australia's major cities with occasional TV appearances. In Brisbane, they were greeted at the airport not only by the press but by the Brisbane Morris Minor Society. "It was Madness' second tour of Australia," explains Hector Walker. "They were the cream of the crop, really. They had a number one album and single. It was just very easy: two weeks, great venues, good transportation, nice hotels. An excellent fan reaction everywhere they went. Fans would crowd the bus and you wouldn't be able to get through – which was pretty Beatle-esque."

When *The Rise And Fall* finally arrived on November 5, both critics and fans were divided, not so much regarding the innate quality of the songs but because the album couched Madness in a more sophisticated light than they were used to. For a start, the album cover – shot on September 23 on Primrose Hill, a location first considered for *Complete Madness* – depicted each member of the band dressed in a manner befitting one of the songs contained therein. So Foreman's flat cap, slippers and armchair spoke of 'Our House'; Thompson was a 'Blue Skinned Beast' dressed in Military

Police attire; 'Sunday Morning' was reflected by Woodgate's Leslie Phillips-styled vicar; Mark Bedford played the "naughty boy" of 'Calling Cards'; 'That Face' was represented by Smyth gazing into the mirror; Barson 'blacked up' with a turban to describe 'New Delhi'; and Suggs adopted the demeanour of a street-corner orator for 'Mr Speaker (Gets The Word)'.

The whole package seemed to be wrapped in the concept of a theatrical production – not a traditional musical as such but an assortment of vignettes set to music. The theme was reinforced by the labelling of the sides ("stage one", "stage two") and the photograph inside the gatefold sleeve of the band, still in their respective outfits, on a stage watched in the gloom by a handful of rather sinister-looking old men. Was this inspired by the "comedy of menace" of playwrights like Harold Pinter ("the weasel under the cocktail cabinet", etc.)? Certainly, Madness had talked about creating a stage play around the album. And their songs – like the work of Pinter – dwelt on the underbelly of society, lingering on those who have lost their way with observations which could be both poignant and brutal, twitching open that proverbial net curtain on (London) life.

"They did those internal shots down in a lovely old theatre just off Charing Cross Road," adds Hector Walker. "In that photo, there's a picture of a World War One soldier on the back of the stage. I had to go down to an antique shop at the other end of Charing Cross Road and borrow it. But then they were talking about having people in the audience, three or four old blokes. Somebody came up with this idea, let's have some tramps. I remember clocking this conversation and ignoring it. Usually, it was seven clowns' noses or six coffees and one tea! The next thing, 'Hector, can you go and get some tramps for us?' How do you get homeless people to do that?! I went wandering off around Soho. The first guy I came across was rummaging through the bins in Berwick Street Market. He went mental and chased me down Old Compton Street. Eventually, we went to a homeless hostel and gave them tea and toast and twenty quid. Of all the things I'd been asked to organise, that was the champion one!"

The Rise And Fall was the equal of such ambitious designs, their most accomplished album to date by a country mile. Aided by some deft mixing at Genetic Studios (credited to Martin Rushent although he has no memory of it!), Langer and Winstanley outdid themselves, helping to create a new template for a Madness "sound". The string arrangements were flawless; instrumentally, the band gelled like never before, more intricate and syncopated; and the songwriting was more consistent. Melodies flowed so much more comfortably. Where before, albums might have felt disjointed or patchy, *The Rise And Fall* finally pulled all those dysfunctional elements into a holistic whole. Its success might have been due in part to Foreman stepping up to the songwriting plate, contributing at least as much as Barson.

It's tempting to describe the album as Madness' *Sgt. Pepper*; certainly, a psychedelic miasma hung over the project. "[Some] of us had psychedelic experiences in our teens," Suggs later admitted to *Uncut*. "We used to go to Dingwalls with our green bomber jackets turned inside out with the orange lining! Early Syd Barrett had a big effect on us; the videos were all psychedelically inspired. It wasn't consciously thought out but we were definitely reflecting a change in our environment. Musically, we just wanted to go deeper. Clive was very prominent in this – he was a psychedelic child, too. The other big influence was Robert Wyatt. One of the greatest days in my life was going to Elvis Costello's Meltdown and Robert made a beeline for me and said, 'You are the most important pop band in Britain – since me'!"

It was a period when "the morale of the British people was at its worst since the Depression of the 1930s," suggested *Nut Inc.* editor Stuart Wright. "Unemployment was still rising and the spectre of the previous year's riots was looming larger than ever." The most talked about TV show was Alan Bleasdale's bittersweet tale of life in early 80s Liverpool, *Boys From The Blackstuff* (immortalised by the catchphrase "Gi's a job"). The charts weren't immune to the sombre mood, from The Jam's 'Just Who Is The Five O'Clock Hero' to 'Mad World' by Tears For Fears – and themes of social realism were creeping into Madness's songwriting, too.

The band were able to witness such hardships first-hand. "At one gig in Glasgow, kids were queuing up for autographs outside the venues in the rain wearing just T-shirts," Suggs observed, "because they couldn't afford coats. You can't ignore that – and the general mood of the country was one of apathy. The last tour was quite depressing. It was hard to be wacky." With this in mind, *The Rise And Fall* had originally been conceived as a concept album with each song linked by the narration of a central character who was slowly being driven insane by sheer desperation.

The spirit of mid-Sixties Kinks was evident on the opening title track, 'Rise And Fall'. Suggs' tale of nostalgia had a gravitas of someone twice his age (and remember, he was barely into his twenties). The song was provoked by the decline of Liverpool as a major European port, but its lyrics seem merely to recall an old childhood stomping ground. "We were conscious of a change," Foreman later explained, "I started writing about places I used to play when I was a kid. Then Suggs went up to Liverpool after the riots – it looked like friggin' Beirut – and he finished the tune off." A similarly observational sense seemed to pervade 'Primrose Hill', with pithy observations of the humdrum. Fuelled by a moody musical break with an old-fashioned brass band, the song painted a bleak picture of a solitary, seemingly agoraphobic old man, peering out at the world from his window. If that provoked comparisons with The Beatles' 'Nowhere Man', then the music might have been closer to 'Penny Lane'.

The Rise And Fall sounded different rhythmically, too, from Bedford's increasingly funk-styled bass to the sense that Woodgate had significantly loosened the self-imposed straitjacket on his drumming. From the self-explanatory ode to that lazy weekend mood, 'Sunday Morning' (Woodgate's first composition), to the crisp, spartan tones of 'That Face' (their 'Yesterday', to continue the Beatles comparisons), Madness toyed with a style of disjointed funk driven by Barson's piano. It's likely they'd been influenced by Ian Dury's work with the Blockheads – but this still felt like something all of their own.

A slow, spiky funk groove also underpinned 'Mr Speaker (Gets The Word)', which built from the sound of soap box rants and Barson's rising piano into a tale seemingly about Hyde Park Corner ranters – but lyrics about wriggling from a captor's arms, running from alarms and Colney Hatch Lane (Colney Hatch being an infamous lunatic asylum in north London) suggested a darker theme. Cathal's inspiration had come from witnessing a particularly deranged man he'd seen reading from a book in the middle of the street. "This bloke had completely lost it," Smyth explained. "It was sad, really. It just seemed like a sign of the times."

Elsewhere, the sublime atmosphere of Sixties jazz infused proceedings. The punning album closer, 'Madness (Is All In The Mind)', was brazenly indebted to Little Willie John's jazzy R&B classic, 'Fever' (as popularised by Peggy Lee), its finger-clicking ska/jazz vibe in keeping with a live-for-today message. By contrast, the Bacharach & David mood of 'Tiptoes', from its mellow Hammond organ to the echo-laden backing vocals, yet again hid a genuinely unsettling lyric – this time about a man woken in the dead of night who eventually jumped to his death from a tall building. (This song had been originally mooted for inclusion on *7* but actually felt more at home here.) Geraldo D'Arbilly, the Brazilian-born drummer with Blue Rondo A La Turk, fleshed out the percussion.

'Calling Cards' was more traditional Madness fare – the album's cockney sing-a-long – with Suggs' fast-and-furious vocal about a "wide boy", a "spiv", mixing up reggae and funk with a good old bar-room knees-up. The album's grittiest acknowledgment of the modern world was Thompson's 'Blue Skinned Beast' – which, as Cathal succinctly put it, was "was about the cadaver bags from the Falklands", evoking comparisons with Robert Wyatt's version of Elvis Costello and Clive Langer's song 'Shipbuilding'. More adventurous was 'New Delhi' but its shrill, Arabic strings, vaguely psychedelic/Eastern arrangements and other-worldly atmosphere were undermined somewhat by an appalling attempt at an Indian accent towards the end (but then again, listeners surely knew that they took Madness too seriously at their peril!). It's been suggested that 'New Delhi' was inspired by Barson's new-found fascination with Buddhism.

* * *

Although Madness had used string arrangements before (most notably on 'It Must Be Love'), their use was integral to the overall vibe of *The Rise And Fall*. With this in mind, they drafted in noted string arranger, avant garde classical composer, solo artist and one-time member of Kevin Ayers' band, David Bedford – albeit by accident. "It was a mistake," laughs Bedford. "They had a track called 'Primrose Hill' for which they wanted a brass band, because I think they were imagining someone walking along hearing the song. They asked around who was the best brass band arranger and my name came up. But I'd only ever done one brass band arrangement – for Roy Harper's song 'When An Old Cricketer Leaves The Crease'. Obviously, somebody liked it when Clive Langer asked around. We used the Hendon Band – my local band at the time!"

Langer was still blissfully unaware of Bedford's pedigree. "Clive Langer said, 'Do you happen to be able to do strings?'" recalls David. "I said,

'Well actually, that's my main thing!' So then they got me in for 'Our House'. My instructions from Clive Langer were: 'I want an English Tamla Motown feel.' I wasn't given any ideas by means of musical notation. It would be onomatopoeic. Clive might say, let's have a 'daga daga' here, which I took to mean four semi-quavers! The discussions centred around where the string lines should start to help the song best – say, in the first or second chorus. The usual format is to have strings build up but 'Our House' was different in that the strings only come in the verses."

AIR Studios boasted superb acoustics, which were ideal for recording strings. "It was always a small compact group – six to ten people – to get a more intimate feel instead of a grand, sweeping string sound," explains David. "So you use a union fixer/booker/contractor who leads the session. I used two: Trevor Ford and Gavyn Wright, who was a well-known name. They were vital. English players are incredibly good at sight-reading – in other words, getting round the music quickly – so I could write difficult parts and they'd pick them up. I generally found that, for a three-minute song, you needed one three-hour session to get it absolutely right. Rhythmically, they have to be playing spot-on. It has to be very tight. Mostly, I used violins, cellos as well. Adrian Levine often led the sessions."

Although Bedford didn't often work directly with the band, he was highly impressed with their producers. "Clive was great, intensely musical," he says. "He knew exactly what he wanted and was able to explain it to me. They were all very kind. Clive and Alan swapped roles occasionally and certainly Alan had some creative input as well. He was superb at the engineering itself: the string sounds were very good. They'd decide from the feel of the song what they wanted. We got into a groove where they liked the lines I wrote for strings. They would give me a rough mix with a guide vocal. I didn't want to write the same notes as the singing, or even in the same ranges, because it would clash. So the string lines are generally fairly high compared to the voices."

"The strangest one I ever did was 'New Delhi'," admits David. "It wasn't my best string arrangement. I wanted to give it an Indian feel and there were six players so I instructed two of them to tune themselves a quarter-tone flat, two of them to be a quarter-tone sharp and the other two were in tune, so I could get that 'market' feel. But they couldn't do it. They ended up playing in tune all the time! They automatically adjusted. They felt it was wrong!"

The album's layered arrangements, exemplified on the atmospheric 'Are You Coming (With Me)', vivid imagery and nostalgic, yearning themes evoked comparisons with late Sixties Beatles and Kinks (in particular, the latter's *Village Green Preservation Society* album). While the collection was their most musically accomplished assemblage to date, most songs were arguably too subtle to work as singles – with one very notable exception, 'Our House'. While Cathal was a fully fledged band member, he must still have felt like a spare part on occasion, with no core instrumental role nor a major share of the songwriting, his contributions restricted to novelty value. That all changed with 'Our House', a stamp of authority for their one-time MC (albeit with musical help from Foreman).

The song epitomised Madness's strengths, from its affectionate, non-judgmental celebration of home and hearth to its affable, tub thumping chorus. It boasted the boy-next-door charm of 'My Girl' but with a far more commercial hook, a proper little middle eight and, granted, a perhaps unnecessary key change. Dave Robinson must have heard cash registers ringing the first time he heard it. Sharing a similarly nostalgic theme of childhood memories as 'Rise And Fall', the single came in a sleeve which depicted a painting of a house by six-year-old Karen Allen – the winner of a competition. The whole package felt perfect.

Smyth had originally envisaged *The Rise And Fall* as having stronger links between the songs. "I suggested to the others that we do a concept album around the theme of our families," he later explained. "There were a lot of things that were similar and lots of things different. But no one bothered." 'Our House' was patently themed in this way. "On the aero-plane back from the States, on a napkin, I wrote this song. Around the time of [The Jam's] *All Mod Cons*, I used to listen to 'English Rose'. When we started rehearsing again, Chrissy Boy was showing the others the chords and these lyrics came to mind and that was it. It's all about letting your subconscious do the work!"

In hindsight, it's puzzling as to why 'Our House' didn't reward Madness with their second number one single of 1982. Issued on November 19, the song did spend 11 weeks on the chart (their equal longest run) but somehow stalled at number five. And this despite a superb promotional campaign. Although the BBC were happy to show Madness's promotional videos on *Top Of The Pops* (partly because it often proved so difficult to assemble the band – and keep them there!), a special set was built in their studios for 'Our House' to resemble a front room, with the band decked out in cardigans and cloth caps. "Dave said, ''Our House' is going to be a number one record,'" recalls plugger Neil Ferris. "We need to do something really special. I want a house in the middle of the *Top Of The Pops* studio. I remember saying to the BBC, 'Would you ever?' And they said, 'Yeah.' I said, 'I want three flying ducks in a row!'"

Equally strong was the promotional video, set in a small terraced house, with extra clips filmed by way of contrast at Playboy Casino senior VP Victor Lownes' mansion Stocks, located outside Aldbury in Hertfordshire. "That was stressful because, by this time, I'm starting to realise what I needed to be doing, so I remember not sleeping the night before," remembers the video's producer Nigel Dick. "The knocking on the door was pure Fred Flintstone, the running around the garden was pure Benny Hill, us dressing as washerwomen was pure Monty Python," Woodgate later quipped.

"The row of houses was close to where I lived on Station Road, just off Harlesden High Street," adds Nigel. "They were used a lot by the BBC. The band was just about to go on tour and their gear was on the way to somewhere so two of the guitars were mine – Bedders had my bass. Victor's big swanky house with the pool was later where Oasis shot the album sleeve for *Be Here Now* with the Rolls-Royce. Of course, Robbo – moving in elevated circles – had hung out at his house. It was completely deserted. A housekeeper let us in. We shot in the kitchen and the main dining room and then the grotto."

* * *

By this time, John Mills was back on the video-making team – helping out with 'Our House' – and Nigel Dick was under no illusions as to the pecking order. "John really was a producer and had been to film school, knew about film stock," he admits. "He knew his onions and I knew jack! So I'd actually become concerned that Robbo was going to fire me. I'd met John, a lovely guy. Robbo's like, John's here to help you out so I could see things were changing."

"Dave Robinson approached me about working for Stiff full-time, looking after all the in-house video production," Mills recalls. "For the next couple of years, I worked for all the Stiff artists. I looked after the complete production process. The first stage was for the band, myself and

Dave to thrash out ideas in Dave's office. The single would be played at various volumes. The band would have an idea of the general feel they wanted and we would brainstorm scenarios. Dave was adamant that every video needed a hook that would make the video memorable (Lee flying around on the wire in 'Baggy Trousers' was a classic moment that everyone remembered), so we would come up with a strong visual idea, around which we would weave other scenarios. Some examples are the grand piano dropping in 'Shut Up' or the underwater guitar solo in 'It Must Be Love'."

Wacky concepts were fine in theory – but someone had to actually make them happen in practice. "Once an idea was agreed, I'd find and organise locations, get a selection of costumes and plenty of props, then book the crew," continues Mills. "On the day of the shoot, the band would improvise around the scenarios. There was always an air of experimentation – let's try this and if it works, develop it. The band were extremely democratic and rarely argued about how to proceed. The process of shooting was interesting: once the band were enthused, there was no stopping them, but if they felt it wasn't working, proceedings would grind to a halt while they figured out how to get things back on track. This could be frustrating but was worth putting up with when they came up with something special. The band gave the impression that everything was off-the-cuff and casual, but they had high standards and each of them put a lot of thought into what they were doing."

Robinson was still at the helm – but most of the day-to-day work was delegated. "Many of the videos were directed by Dave," adds Mills. "He would hand me all the footage and I would edit them on a 16mm Steenbeck. It was extremely hard work, especially as I was busy all day on production, leaving evenings and nights for the editing. I regularly worked 16 hour days. I had an assistant to help with production, two of whom were Sarah Wills and Nigel Dick."

Despite its disappointing chart position, 'Our House' sold solidly across the festive season. The single did top the charts in Sweden (their breakthrough hit in Scandinavia) and was an instant favourite onstage. "I remember the first time we played it live we were at some funfair in Australia," Suggs told *Uncut*, "and it was like a bomb had gone off in the crowd. It's still the same, years later. I wasn't aware that I was singing with pathos, I was just singing to the best of my ability!" Eventually, 'Our

House' got its just desserts by winning an Ivor Novello Award for Best Song. Although none of the band turned up to collect the trophy at the ceremony on May 5, 1983 (reputedly, they were too busy rehearsing), manager Matthew Sztumpf accepted the award on their behalf, declaring they were busy "writing next year's winner".

More troubling was the relatively tepid response to *The Rise And Fall*, which peaked at number 10 and dropped out of the UK charts after just 22 weeks (as compared to previous album *7* which reached number five and spent a further seven weeks in the listings). Had *Complete Madness* overpowered their latest endeavour? At the time, the band were too embroiled in the European leg of the Complete Madness tour to worry about such matters. On November 26, they travelled to Brussels to perform 'One Step Beyond', 'Embarrassment', 'House Of Fun' and 'Our House' for TV show *Pop Elektron*. Dates followed not only in Belgium but the Netherlands (including Amsterdam, where Barson had recently purchased a flat) and Germany. A show in Berlin prompted a visit to the Berlin Wall and a jaunt into East Germany – excepting Smyth, who was excluded because he was using an Irish passport (perhaps because his newly bearded appearance didn't match his photo).

This incident is fascinating because it's the first real acknowledgement that Cathal was the first generation offspring of Irish parentage. It was commonplace for the children of Irish nationals to carry two different passports so it would be wrong to read too much into this anecdote. The degree to which Smyth has acknowledged his Irish roots has varied drastically over the years. While none of Madness cared to dwell on their familial backgrounds in the early days, preferring the comfort blanket of a collective Camden Town identity, Smyth's pedigree was further disguised by his stage moniker of Chas Smash. It wasn't until *The Rise And Fall*, in fact, that Cathal adopted his true surname on songwriting credits. Here was someone who was only begrudgingly accepted into the band after the release of their debut album – and now he wanted to dignify his role as more than a sidekick, a mascot. In issue 8 of *Nutty Boys* (published in autumn 1983), when asked "Are you Irish or English?" Smyth answered: "Irish".

Smyth's prominence within Madness was further reinforced when his other songwriting contribution to *The Rise And Fall*, the sublime 'Tomorrow's (Just Another Day)' was chosen as their next single, released on February 11, 1983. The song opened with what sounded like harpsichord, with shades of John Barry's famous incidental music for *The Ipcress File*. Elsewhere, the music hinted at the theme to the TV series *Shoestring* (or the recent Jam song, 'Pity Poor Alfie', for that matter). But that didn't stop this contemplative ode of personal regret from being their bravest choice yet, Suggs sounding like some old scholar ruminating on his past – their 'Waterloo Sunset', perhaps?

"It represented how I felt, some friendships I was in," Cathal later admitted. "How your actions were misinterpreted. I whistled the idea to Mike and he put it down on piano. At the time, I wasn't very good on guitar – not good enough to write songs then." Technically, the single was a double-A-side with 'Madness (Is All In The Mind)'; more interesting was a reworking of the lead track with help from Elvis Costello, which graced the 12-inch edition. 'Tomorrow's (Just Another Day)' only reached No. 11 – but even more than, say, 'Grey Day', it offered a framework within which Madness could develop their music far beyond their Nutty Boy image.

The video was co-produced by Mills and Dick. "He and I stayed up all night building this prison cell from scratch," explains Nigel, "down in the parking garage underneath the Stiff offices. I had to borrow a spade to dig a hole for the scene with the flowers so I went round to a friend's house at seven in the morning and his girlfriend came to the door looking bleary-eyed, wearing a nightie. And as she's handing me the spade, a car draws up and it's her boyfriend, my squash-playing buddy, who's been out all night on a job. He sees me on the doorstep with his girlfriend: what the fuck is going on here?"

Unfortunately, Nigel's intuition regarding his future prospects with Stiff had proved uncannily accurate. "With two weeks of that video, I made the mistake of challenging Dave. He kept telling everybody, we make these videos so cheaply because we do them ourselves. Dave would say, the budget for this video is £5,000. Then he would keep asking for stuff and spend £15,000. We would shoot miles of film and he would then see the bill. 'Why are we spending all this?' That's how much it costs. 'Well, you've got to find another way to do this cheaper.' I told him the truth so I got fired!"

1982 probably represented the pinnacle of Madness' success. They topped *NME*'s annual table of chart singles for the second time in three years (number one in 1980, number four in 1981), way ahead of the runner-up, Adam Ant, with Duran Duran, Soft Cell and The Jam trailing behind. Meanwhile, negotiations were underway to write a book recounting their history to date – in essence, expanding upon *Take It Or Leave It*. In early 1983, the band were signed up by Barry Miles at Omnibus Press to produce an "official biography" for an advance of £5,000, £2,000 of which was paid over on signing the contract. Shortly thereafter, Miles left Omnibus and the project was inherited by his successor, former *Melody Maker* writer Chris Charlesworth.

"Under the terms of the deal, Madness could elect their own writer and they used a guy who wrote for *Sounds*," says Charlesworth. "Unfortunately, when he handed in his text, Madness decided it was boring and promptly sacked him. He wasn't pleased." Charlesworth then suggested to the band another writer who took on the project but, once again, Madness were dissatisfied. "In the end, I proposed we turn it into a picture book," says Charlesworth. "I suggested calling it *A Scrapbook Of Madness*, which they seemed to like. Trouble was, they couldn't agree which pictures to use. I had a few meetings with them to look through photos at their offices, usually after lunch – which was a mistake! One of them would like a certain picture, but another would hate it. So the book never happened. We didn't get our £2,000 back, either!"

Chapter 12

GOING BACK TO CALLY

BEHIND the scenes, Matthew Sztumpf had assembled a sizeable team of personnel including old friend John Hasler (who edited the fan club magazine *Nutty Boys* from the start of 1983) and new arrival Debbie Treloar ("a mate of Tamsin's from Cornwall," according to Hector), in place of the departing Vicky and Barbara. As a result, they had now outgrown their offices. "Especially around the time of *Complete Madness*, we were getting sacks full of fan mail," admits Walker. "The desks were swamped with letters, clipped together, people ordering merchandise – mountains of this stuff! It got worse around their birthdays, particularly Cathal and Suggs. We had to move because it was just too small at Baring Street – and it was a bit out of the way."

Eventually, Matthew purchased new premises for Madness at 167 Caledonian Road, just behind King's Cross Station, which had enough room for them to indulge their wish to build their own recording facility. "It was a wine merchants so it had a glass shop frontage," remembers Hector. "It had a wine cellar with a big extension at the back. The front of the ground floor was the fan club and I had a little back office where I sent out all the merchandise. In the basement at the front were John Wynne and Rob Forrest. We moved in while they were still constructing the studio at the back of the basement. When they were building one day, the firm were concreting the extension and the new concrete roof collapsed inwards with a mighty bloody crash. Luckily, none of the builders was seriously hurt. They had to put a chain hoist lift in the front – it was a hell of a lot of work."

"They just wanted somewhere to record their own songs," explains Matthew Sztumpf. "We bought it. They liked to own things. They weren't frivolous with money and there was a limit to what we could afford. The one real luxury was they bought themselves a Bosendorfer baby grand piano. They weren't tight, either. For example, they kept their road crew on all year long. They found jobs for them to do at the studios. The front part of the basement was under the main building. That was where we stored the gear and the back was the studio, with double doors in between and a lounge in front of that. John Wynne used to be the other side of the double doors. My office was a couple of floors up but I'd try to keep an eye on everyone because, half the time, they were doing bugger all. I went down there one day and heard this sawing and banging noises. I walked into John's bit and he's got a tape in a ghetto blaster, specifically to try and fool me!"

"We had a ridiculous table upstairs which was all cogs, seven of them, so that each band member could sit there and Matthew would sit in the middle on a stool and go round and round," remembers Wynne. "How we laughed when that arrived!"

★ ★ ★

On February 17, 1983, the band travelled up to Newcastle upon Tyne to rehearse for their appearance on *The Tube*, the new and decidedly high profile Friday night music show on Channel 4. The following day, they performed 'Our House', 'Tomorrow's Dream' and 'It Must Be Love' but because they'd transported their entire stage rig, there was only room in the studios left for a quarter of the normal studio audience! Still, it was one of the first occasions when a full stage production had been captured within a TV studio.

The visit to the north-east coincided neatly with preparations to launch their Greatest Show On Earth tour – their first in over a year. This ambitious undertaking, which involved transporting some 42 people, two coaches, two articulated lorries and a Transit van, began at Newcastle City Hall on February 21 and snaked across the country through to mid-March. As a reflection of the more intricate arrangements utilised on *The Rise And Fall*, the band were augmented onstage by a string quartet (violinists Nick Parker and Jonathan Kahan, plus Suzanne Rosenfeld on viola and cellist Caroline "Cal" Verney) plus Island/2 Tone stalwart Dick Cuthell on horns (French horn, flugel horn, cornet). Cuthell, Parker and Verney had already collaborated together with The Fun Boy Three on their version of 'Summertime', which had been a hit in July 1982.

"I did bits of session work playing with various 2 Tone people as a free-lance fiddler," Parker explains. "I'd done a track with The Specials' Jerry Dammers about the Beirut bombing ['War Crimes']. It could have been through The Specials or the Fun Boy Three that I got to know Mark [Bedford]. He recommended me to Matthew [Sztumpf] who rang me and said, 'Could you put a quartet together for a UK tour?'" For their appearance on *The Tube*, the quartet sat up on a platform, all dressed in white, behind the band. "Which was how we toured," adds Nick. "It was pretty radical – but it worked really well!"

Parker had chosen other classical musicians who he felt could adapt to the challenge of playing with a pop group. "We needed people who could play strings in a reasonably funky way, not too clean," he explains. "Cal was at university with me and Jonathan was a freelance colleague. It was a complete eye-opener. We assumed it might have been disorganised but we were surprised at the sheer professionalism: the organisation and complexity. We had a ball – it was great! Cathal, Woody and Mark were the easiest to get along with – friendly, affable, open. Mike was quite cerebral and put a lot of thought into everything he said and did. We'd have intense conversations. They were all friendly, though, and we had a lot of laughs. There weren't any loners. You didn't get the feeling anyone was peeling off or not joining in. The only down side was the fruitless waiting around in the bus. There seemed to be a competition in the band of seeing who could keep the others waiting the longest!"

Rehearsals for the tour introduced the string section to the band. "It was in a big warehouse somewhere in Finsbury Park," remembers Verney. "Our parts were brilliant, interesting and well-written. For 'House Of Fun', Mark suddenly said, 'I think the cello should be on the bass-line.' He was so sweet. He came over and taught it to me. I was really slow and pathetic but he taught me how to write it down. We did it together, from totally different spectrums. Suggs was a brilliant frontman, charismatic. Chris was good, too, working with us trying to understand how we would fit in and how our parts would be heard. There was an extraordinary alchemy about these individuals who made an amazing whole out of very disparate talents. Without one of them, they wouldn't have worked. Barson was just an amazing musician: really innovatory, fabulous. There were a lot of tensions with Mike, though. He was a shy, distant figure but a genius."

Madness were poles apart from the quartet, in terms of formal training. "Their intrinsic instrumental ability, even in terms of improvising, was relatively modest," admits Parker. "We're poncey classical musicians thinking we know about music and yet we completely got off on their extraordinary drive and energy. That was enduringly fascinating. Lee's not a great sax player – we know that. But if you listen to some of those sax riffs, they're so adept, so funky." Although the band were a tight-knit unit, the new string section travelled on the same tour bus. "They were blokey but it was nice that we travelled on the coach with the band so we were definitely included," says Cal Verney. "The coach was like a kindergarten because they all had young kids and babies with lots of buggies and bottles and nappies. They were all in relationships – actually, Bedders wasn't – and their wives and girlfriends were very much in evidence."

The band's lofty ambitions for the tour extended beyond a string quartet, too. Many songs were accompanied by vivid background footage. 'Blue Skinned Beast' was set to war documentary footage combined with sketches of a fake Margaret Thatcher; a hospital bed was wheeled onstage for 'Mrs Hutchinson'; 'Tomorrow's Dream' was illustrated with vivisection footage; and 'Mr Speaker' seemed to be performed at a mock-court. The Brighton Centre show was taped for release as a concert video but the project never materialised.

Support came from rising stars JoBoxers, whose debut single 'Boxer Beat' was simultaneously climbing the charts. "We had a great time on the tour," bassist Chris Bostock later recalled. Of the tour's finale on March 3, the second of two nights at the London Dominion, he said: "Not to be left out, we waited for 'Night Boat To Cairo' and made an impromptu appearance dressed as sphinxes by draping towels over our heads and tucking them behind our ears. Then, stripped to the waist, we crawled, looking straight ahead, across the stage to take up a formation along the front as if guarding the Pyramids. Madness were a little startled but pleasantly surprised by the extra props for their show and acted as if it had all been planned. On the radio, you [could] hear Suggs' reference to 'those naughty JoBoxers'!"

For the Dominion shows, which were recorded for broadcast by the BBC, Elvis Costello joined Madness onstage for 'Tomorrow's (Just Another Day)'. And for 'Primrose Hill', they were joined by the Washington Welfare Brass Band. Nick Parker's birthday had fallen on the previous day, when they were due to play The Lyceum in The Strand: "I went down to breakfast and thought, nothing's happening. I spent the whole day getting grumpier with no one even saying 'happy birthday!' By the evening, I was pretty pissed off! But as we came offstage, the band picked me up, pulled me right to the front of the stage and gave me 25 'bumps', with the whole audience screaming, 'One! Two! Three!' It got higher and higher. I was extremely shocked and very moved!"

By this time, Madness mania was its peak, to the extent that it occasionally put a strain on the band. "It was a bit too much like The Beatles," admits Hector Walker. "It was too hysterical. You couldn't let fans backstage. The bus would be crowded with people trying to get in. For one gig, we put the band in the crew's bus and let the band's bus go first so they could escape all that. It was too chaotic. Part of my role was trying to manage who went in the dressing room. They weren't being elitist. There were some serious practicalities. And they never travelled with security."

On March 17, Madness flew to Germany to perform 'Tomorrow's (Just Another Day)' on the *Musikladen* TV show. However, Barson failed to appear – and despite their notoriety for tardiness, this was actually the first time that any member had actually missed an important promotional performance. In the event, Hector deputised for him. The rest of the band excused Barson's absence by suggesting he was heavily involved in his relocation to Amsterdam. At the time, the incident was quickly forgotten as Madness tackled their usual array of activities. One such commitment was their involvement with the last in their series of TV commercials for Honda. However, the band was concerned that their profile in Japan might have been damaged there by the public's perception of them as a pretend, Monkees-type band created purely for the adverts. As a result, they made certain conditions: that the final commercial utilise 'Driving In My Car' (which fitted the product, after all) and that it be filmed in London.

* * *

Previously, Madness had endorsed a variety of admirable causes. On November 27, 1981, for example, they had appeared at Jobs Express, a benefit gig for the unemployed at the Rainbow Theatre, Finsbury Park, alongside reggae stars Clint Eastwood & General Saint and comedian Alexei Sayle. Monies raised helped to fund a publicity exercise whereby unemployed teenagers caught the 'Jobs Express' train from Waverley station in Edinburgh to London in search of work. The following April, Thompson and Foreman had participated in a Capital Radio fund-raising auction for Help A London Child.

Now, the band seemed prepared to lend their support to more overtly political themes. Perhaps this was due to broadening their horizons, both geographically and philosophically? "Working-class bands often start off conservative with a small 'c'," suggests Tony Fletcher. "Paul Weller was painted as a Tory for years. When you're young and come from a limited background financially, the world doesn't exist much further than your immediate neighbourhood, so you become attached to it – like football fans and their team. All you know is what surrounds you, your home turf, your manor. And you think it's the greatest place in the world because it's all you know. It's not until you travel that you realise that, actually, the world is much bigger and more colourful."

"I think Madness were a great example of this," continues Fletcher, "because they started out so entrenched: Madness is Camden Town, Camden Town is Madness. As they see the world, their music expands, and a political perspective comes into their lyrics. You see a softening from this hard stance. They still hold onto their Camden roots but what could have led to being parochial became a great example of a group who outgrew all of that. As they travelled, they dropped some of the working-class nuttiness and opened up musically. You see the band mature."

On April 30, 1983, Madness partnered UB40 at a concert at the London Victoria Apollo, a fund-raising event aimed at campaigning against the building of the Sizewell B nuclear power station on the coast of Suffolk*. UB40's Ali Campbell, Norman Hassan, Astro and Brian Travers joined Madness for a rendition of their Prince Buster namesake while all seven Nutty Boys returned the favour when UB40 played their classic hit, 'One In Ten', with Suggs and Cathal on backing vocals. Clips of both performances were aired as part of a wider programme about the campaign, entitled *Too Hot To Handle*. Despite the gravitas of the occasion, Suggs

---

* Part of a wider anti-nuclear sentiment, the anti-Sizewell B movement attracted a groundswell reaction. A public inquiry into the construction was held between 1982 and 1985, receiving a record 16 million-plus words of evidence, but the ensuing report in early 1987 stated that no substantive evidence had been found against the project, which began later that year.

quipped: "Why have the police enforced the new safety belt law? So you won't fall out of the car when you get shot."

On a desultory afternoon on May 7, in front of a 10,000-strong crowd, Madness headlined London's Brockwell Park 'CND Rock Rally', alongside punk stalwarts The Damned, Clint Eastwood & General Saint, Hazel O'Connor and Paul Weller's new venture, The Style Council. In mid-1982, Madness had been photographed alongside The Jam to publicise their bands' involvement with the anti-nuclear benefit album *Life In The European Theatre*, Madness contributing 'Grey Day' alongside such like-minded acts as Ian Dury & The Blockheads, The Specials, Bad Manners, The Clash and The Undertones.

CND – the Campaign For Nuclear Disarmament – had been formed in 1957 and had enjoyed widespread, high profile support, especially among Labour supporters, for its objections to the Atomic Weapons Establishment near Aldermaston and the development of nuclear weapons in general, up until the Cuban Missile Crisis in 1962. Thereafter, CND's popularity ebbed as anti-war campaigners focused instead on the likes of the Vietnam War. During Madness's time, though, CND's membership surged from a paltry 4,000 in 1979 to around 100,000 in 1984 – driven by concerns over the mounting tensions between the 'super powers' of the USA and the USSR. In particular, a growing army of campaigners rallied against the deployment of American Pershing missiles in Western Europe and Britain's introduction of Trident missiles in 1982.

The most famous demonstration of the period was that of the Greenham Common Women's Peace Camp, sited at RAF's Greenham Common airbase in Berkshire, which began in September 1981 to protest against the decision to allow cruise missiles to be based there. It hit the headlines in April 1983 when around 70,000 protesters formed a 14-mile human chain from Greenham to Aldermaston and the ordnance factory at Burghfield. In October 1981, 250,000 people joined an anti-nuclear demonstration in London; two years later, some three million people took part in simultaneous demonstrations across Europe, 300,000 of them in London. In the New Year 1983 edition of *The Nutty Boys* fan club magazine, Suggs expressed his support for CND: "On Greenham Common, Anne, Scarlett and me went up there because we're firm believers in nuclear disarmament. It was a magnificent sight and a great success for the women involved!"

Suggs felt acutely aware that the media appeared to be distorting the facts, as he told *No. 1* magazine: "We did the charity gigs for CND and Greenpeace because there is so much hypocrisy in the press, all the lies and slander that make people believe that Greenham Common is wrong. When we were younger we didn't have much idea, but you learn. People like Elvis Costello and Paul Weller want to be seen in a lighter context because they're supposed to be serious. With us we don't want to be regarded as a joke."

On July 7, 1984, Madness expressed their solidarity for the striking miners with a benefit concert at Liverpool University's Mountford Hall, alongside Bronski Beat and The Style Council. The rousing encore saw The Style Council and Madness team up for a performance of Smokey Robinson's 'It's Time To Stop Shoppin' Around' (the Motown star's politically-minded sequel to his first hit with The Miracles, 'Shop Around', which the lads had covered during their days as The Invaders).

Where before, Madness had restricted their affiliations with arguably apolitical campaigns, here was a social issue which was all but defined by party politics. "A dispute about pit closures and the future of mining communities was seen by much of the media and the public in more simple terms," wrote Robin Denselow, "as a show of strength between a hard-line left-winger, Arthur Scargill, the miners' leader, and an apostle of market forces, Margaret Thatcher. The media, for the most part, reflected public opinion in their hostility to the miners, particularly as the bitterness and the violence grew."

In January 1985, Madness and The Style Council joined 5,000 protestors who signed a petition against the Youth Training Scheme before marching on Downing Street. The hand-over of the petition was broadcast on *The Nine O'Clock News*. The Youth Training Scheme (YTS) was the name given to an on-the-job training course for school leavers, managed by the Manpower Services Commission, which the government introduced in 1983 to replace the Youth Opportunities Programme (YOPS). The idea behind YTS promised to draw on different training locales such as businesses, colleges of further education and training workshops run by voluntary organisations (and since trainees were to be paid whilst on the course, eligibility for unemployment benefit was withdrawn). But the scheme soon attracted widespread criticism from those who felt it enabled employers to exploit school leavers for cheap labour, and provided little substance in the way of genuine education.

Soon, Madness also expressed their public support for the efforts of Greenpeace, the organisation which had been campaigning against environmental damage and pollution since 1971. Greenpeace's most famous campaign was their direct action to disrupt the hunt of the Icelandic whaling fleet using their former fishing trawler the Rainbow Warrior. While Greenpeace's contact details would be listed on Madness's next album, their international symbol – the dove of peace – would inspire a new song which was destined to be the next Madness single.

★ ★ ★

'Wings Of A Dove' was written by Cathal, with some help from Suggs. "I was watching a documentary on this church in Islington, with The Inspirational Choir Of The Pentecostal First Born Church Of The Living God," Smyth later explained. "I'd been experimenting with the Buddy Holly idea of only using three chords. I said to Clive Langer that I wanted a Pentecostal choir and a steel band involved. The lyrics were so cool and positive." Their uplifting contribution to 'Wings Of A Dove' was remarkable while the Creighton Steel Sounds steel band (who were pupils from nearby Creighton Comprehensive School in Muswell Hill) complemented the Caribbean mood perfectly. The song's bubbly, percussive carnival mood seemed in keeping with the contemporaneous pop of Kid Creole & The Coconuts, Eddy Grant or post-2 Tone act The Belle Stars. As a nod to older influences, the whispered closing line, "Blue train taking me from you", was borrowed from the Lord Rockingham XI's 'Blue Train' (the B-side to their 1958 hit, 'Hoots Mon').

The choir's mentor, John Francis, later recalled to *Cross Rhythms'* James Attlee how they were catapulted into the limelight: "There was a competition on the programme *Black On Black* on Channel 4 for the best gospel choir – we entered and won the competition. We sang two numbers and one of the members of Madness saw us. When they heard we were based in Islington, they asked us to sing on their record. They gave us a lot of freedom over how to do it. It was brilliant but then we got a lot of stick from the church people. Then again, it paved the way because we approached Madness's record label, Stiff, and got a deal ourselves. We also picked up some of Madness's audience so we started to do concerts to people we would never have reached." The result was a sadly overlooked single, 'Do Not Pass Me By', issued as a single later that year, although The Inspirational Choir did enjoy subsequent success after signing with CBS in 1984.

The promotional video for 'Wings Of A Dove' depicted the band (complete with steel band and choir) enjoying a party on board an aeroplane piloted by Cathal Smyth. "That was done at Blackbushe Airfield [in Camberley, Surrey], where they'd had rock concerts," says John Mills. "They had all these old planes down there. We filmed all the stuff inside an old airliner. It was a fun video – they enjoyed it." When the pilot appeared to lose control, the assembled throng were seen to bail out in a white van, the final sequence showing the van parachuting gently back down to earth. This was taken from existing footage from a French TV advert which Dave Robinson had purchased the rights to some months before. The Stiff boss had apparently wanted to use it for the 'Tomorrow's (Just Another Day)' video.

At least, that's the accepted version of events but John Wynne remembers it differently. "We went for this meeting with the record company and the video people to get ideas for 'Wings Of A Dove'," says John. "Lee was saying to me, on the way there, 'I've got an idea. We're all in the back of a van which gets pushed out the back of a plane and parachutes down to the ground.' Because he'd just done a parachute drop in America – that's where the idea came from. And the looks that went between our management, the record company and everybody else – are you mad, Lee?! There's no way possible they are ever going to insure seven members in a vehicle dropped from 20,000 feet! 'Oh, I think we could.' Shut up Lee!"

"I remember making all the phone calls to the van people Iveco who had the TV ad," adds Mills. "We got everyone in the back of a Transit van and did a load of handheld stuff, turning the camera all over the place, then intercut it with the shot. It's all in the editing. I won the Design & Art Direction Silver Award in 1984 for 'the most outstanding editing of a video promo'!"

Released in early August, 'Wings Of A Dove (A Celebratory Song)' – to give it its full title – proved to be an instant favourite and was only held off the top of the charts by UB40's cover of 'Red, Red Wine'. In commercial terms, Madness were adapting to the changing pop climate with what appeared to be canny intuition. By contrast in terms of its musical style, flipside 'Behind The Eight Ball' was a near-instrumental soundscape awash with synthesized drum patterns with echoes of Seventies TV themes – here was a band stretching their musical horizons, too. Equally rooted in modern synth pop was the bonus 12-inch track 'One Second's Thoughtlessness'; Thompson's ode to his misspent youth was saved by his murmured, near-spoken delivery and the song's endearingly downbeat mood.

★   ★   ★

While 'Wings Of A Dove' underscored Madness's chart dominance in the UK, their fortunes across the pond could not have been more different. When their second album, *Absolutely*, had only reached number 146 on the US charts in late 1980, the band had promptly been dropped by Sire, leaving them without an American record contract for over two years. By chance, high-powered American executive John Kalodner (who was second-in-command at US label Geffen Records and famous for his key role with Aerosmith, among others) chanced upon Madness's latest hit. "In the fall of 1982, I was over here working with Asia," Kalodner later explained. "We were in the car and 'Our House' came on the radio and we turned to each other and said, 'That's a hit for anybody. For Madness, that'll be a hit in America.' Madness had never sold any records in America but I just knew that they could."

While Madness had an enviable reputation for creating quirky, imaginative promos which had by now become an integral aspect of their appeal across Europe, America had been closed to them after the Sire deal had expired. What made this doubly painful was the dramatic rise in the power of the pop video Stateside with the launch of MTV at midnight on August 1, 1981. "Why did MTV start?" writes Nigel Dick. "The early Eighties were the heyday of the cable boom. Everyone in the US was starting to get a cable box fitted to their TV, there were many new channels appearing and someone saw a way to make cash out of all those music videos. Even better, the record labels gave MTV the vids to use for free so the channel had to pay nothing for its programming. All it needed was three VJ's, one camera, a small studio and some editing equipment and voila: a TV channel was born."

Many of Madness' contemporaries were able to capitalise on this opportunity. "In Britain, where the pop music charts moved much faster than in the US, videos became an essential promotional tool and every band had to have one," writes Nigel, "so that when MTV started, many more British acts had videos than American ones. Consequently Duran Duran, The Thompson Twins, Culture Club and many other British bands, with stacks of videos in the vault, suddenly had huge success in the States and filled the charts while the US acts and labels busily tried to catch up. John Taylor (bassist for Duran Duran) went so far as to observe that the band would watch their success in various markets explode within weeks of MTV opening in that market."

Kalodner was friendly with Dave Robinson, who helped Madness to agree a deal with Geffen in January 1983. The label's first tactic was to offer a Stateside-only compilation simply entitled *Madness*, containing six tracks from *The Rise And Fall* and six singles – two of which, 'Night Boat To Cairo' and 'It Must Be Love', were remixed. Kalodner patently had a nose for a hit because 'Our House' gave them their biggest international hit, reaching number seven in the US charts that summer. The song benefited from consistent airplay on MTV, which had previously aired 'House Of Fun', 'It Must Be Love' and 'Cardiac Arrest' – despite the records' lack of availability in America. It helped drive sales of *Madness* to a respectable number 41; later that year, 'It Must Be Love' gave them a second US hit, peaking at number 33.

An American tour was hurriedly organised for the band, who were thrilled to be making headway in the States finally; it was their first visit there since May 1981. With the same coterie of musicians in tow as for their earlier UK tour, they spent a full calendar month traversing the country. Beginning on August 17 in Boston, Madness punctuated their own shows at smaller venues with prestigious support slots at major stadia, opening for The Police (at Philadelphia's famous JFK Stadium, third on the bill above R.E.M., San Diego's Aztec Stadium, the Phoenix Stadium in Arizona and the Oakland Coliseum, San Francisco) and David Bowie (Los Angeles' Anaheim Stadium).

"British music was hot back then," suggests cellist Cal Verney. "My abiding memory of that tour is that gig with Bowie. We were plonked in what looked like the middle of the desert, this camp of tents – marquees. I remember this cortège of huge cars driving across the desert. The cars pulled up and out got this tiny bloke who walked straight into our tent because he wanted to speak to Suggs. His son was crazy about Madness. It was like God had come in. Suggs was a bit like, oh my God! Amazing!"

Madness' somewhat fearsome tour manager was John Martin (whom they'd met when he was working with Bow Wow Wow in Japan) but they also hired old hand Barry Sinclair as production manager because of his experience working in the States (by this time, Barry was based in San Francisco). The two went way back. "John used to work for the agency who handled Procol," says Barry. "He was all right but we did not get on during that American tour. Madness had obviously been very big in England, so they came with this huge lighting rig, trying to put it in small clubs – a real pain! They must have lost lots of money on that tour because they were trying to do too much. 'Our House' was getting a hell of a lot of airplay on the radio, though, that's for sure."

John Martin wasn't particularly sympathetic to the added complication of a touring string section. "He was scary," admits Cal Verney. "Tough, no-nonsense, no shit. He was a big bruiser of a bloke. He certainly made me cry on several occasions – he was horrid! He hated us ghastly, stuck-up people! I think he thought we were Martians! But he had a hell of a job on his hands to get us all herded up and onto the coach in time." Nick Parker was also struck by Martin's attitude: "He didn't really like these poncey, snotty string players around with their white suits. We weren't his favourite people. It was hard enough for him to get all of Madness on the bus . . . which was bloody hard!"

For the most part, though, the trip felt like one big adventure. "It was a riot from start to finish," enthuses Parker. "The mood was generally pretty good. Their only tensions were to do with time keeping. Oh, I can stay in my room longer! Somewhere in upstate New York, I went to sleep on the coach with a full head of hair and woke up with no hair!" In New York City, before playing an outdoor, 8,000-capacity show at The Pier, the band were served with an affidavit by an individual who claimed he had overseen the Geffen deal; as a result, the band had to be smuggled into their show at The Pier. "There was a problem with the police," recalls Parker. "We had to keep a low profile, not wear our badges. But it was a fantastic place to play – very atmospheric." Another show was at Pittsburgh Fulton Theater on August 25. "The front-of-house sound went down so we did the gig on the stage monitors alone," adds Parker, "and it was louder than we could bear!"

During a 344-mile trip from Chicago to Cleveland, their coach driver was pulled over by state troopers for speeding and since Foreman appeared to be the only person on the bus with a credit card, he had to pay the fine of $45. "The guy in front of us pulled a gun on the copper!" adds Nick. "I remember seeing this bloke on the hard shoulder just ahead of us. Our coach driver was an extraordinary character – knew everything about everything! This huge guy with a beard who was up on the side of the road with his arms in the air and the police were searching him!"

On September 3, they were due to play at the Plaza Hotel Ballroom, Daytona Beach, with in situ accommodation. Parker picks up the story: "We arrived there, quite tired. It looked like a pretty smeggy place, but the bags were unloaded, everybody took their keys and went up to their rooms. Then everybody seemed to come straight down to the lobby again! It was so obvious the rooms were ghastly. It was a knocking shop, disgusting. We're not bloody staying here! So we all got back on the bus and went to a hotel in Orlando then travelled back for the gig in the evening!" Cal Verney grimaces: "I remember Nick and I getting in the lift and there was this guy wearing a T-shirt which said, 'Eat shit and die'. It was really scary!"

Hector Walker remembers the incident all too well. "It was a summer holiday weekend and this hotel was full of student-age American kids who were all absolutely pissed," he groans. "It was mid-afternoon when we got there and they were falling all over the place. I stayed in reception to sort out the luggage and check-in. I turn around and a guy in a wheelchair was so drunk, he fell out! When he tried to lever himself back in, his drunk buddies pulled it from behind him and he collapsed again on the floor as they rolled about laughing, thinking it was hysterical. I'm watching this chaos and then, slowly but surely, the band started appearing. Suggs said there were people pressing their faces against his bedroom window. Bedders was like, 'get me out of here'! I just phoned the tour manager and said, 'We've practically got a mutiny on our hands!'"

For the second of two shows by The Police at San Diego's Aztec Stadium on September 6, Madness played to a much smaller audience on a hastily-erected stage in the car park as temperatures soared. "We covered all the instruments in [hypothermia] foil," adds Parker, "because it was so hot the varnish was coming off! There was no shade. It was promotional, I think, for a radio station."

The band were able to squeeze in other promotional activities, such as playing (and winning) a charity baseball match with the famous KROQ radio station and playing on the famous President steamboat on the Mississippi in New Orleans. Madness also appeared on the *Solid Gold* TV show (performing 'It Must Be Love'). "That's the most I've ever got paid for not playing anything," laughs Nick. "$500 for miming! It was a big, flashy Hollywood set. We were picked up in a massive stretch-Cadillac with the number plate MUS1C!" Suggs might have described the USA as a land where "money talks, music mumbles". But Madness finally seemed able to enjoy the trappings of the rock star lifestyle, having fun while also steering their music away from their 'Nutty Boy' image towards a more mature, intelligent style. It seemed they had everything. What could possibly go wrong?

* * *

Back in Blighty, Stiff Records were approaching what music industry suits call 'Q4' (i.e. the fourth quarter of the year) with no new Madness album, for the first time since they signed them in 1979. That said, the band were in high spirits, preparing instead to launch their next single, 'The Sun And The Rain'. Many fans were already familiar with the song as the only new composition to have been heard during their previous tour. Part of the promotional video was shot in Stiff Records' car park underneath their new 'Stiff City' offices at 115–123 Bayham Street, Camden Town (where the company had moved, much to Madness's approval, in September 1982).

"It's one of my favourites," says John Mills of the video. "We had a big silver parachute canopy and a guy built a big polystyrene ear and the band were all like little creatures inside the head. I love that sequence, where I got the window of Browns in South Molton Street with a tableau, then we had a rain machine and Lee running down the street with a rocket on his back, which was hilarious to do. I mean, that rocket was bloody powerful! Lee was a great guy. He'd always do something really wacky. I think it's a lovely song, too: Chrissy does a really good guitar solo."

Released at the tail-end of October, 'The Sun And The Rain' returned to the piano-driven, four-on-the-floor Motown beat of 'Shut Up', with this bleak tale of loneliness and depression acting as counterpoint to the usual flurry of happy-go-lucky fare in the run-up to Christmas. 'The Sun And The Rain' shared more than a meteorological connection with earlier hit 'Grey Day', too: it continued Madness' strain of observational story-telling which took a peek behind the bright lights and perceived the glamour of the capital. It's questionable how apparent this was to the multitude of fans who propelled the single to number five, though, aided by the now-familiar merry-go-round of TV and radio activity. "That was done at AIR," adds arranger David Bedford. "It was very literal in that, for the rain, I did pizzicato strings going down scales which sounded like the rain falling and a long string line in the chorus."

The single's B-side, 'Fireball XL5', was Thompson's offbeat rockabilly tribute to his nefarious childhood, named after the early Sixties TV series devised by Gerry Anderson. "We never had a flip side so I had to kick arse and get people down Pathway Studios where we recorded 'The Prince'," Thompson later explained. "It was half-baked but there was an idea there." Apparently, Dave Robinson thought this novelty track should have been a fully-fledged Madness single.

On October 4, the band started rehearsing material for their next album in Halligans Heap, Holloway Road. At that point, there was still considerable excitement surrounding the concept of Madness' own TV series, which had spun off their appearances on *The Young Ones* (but which was eventually shelved). Behind the scenes, the band had finished building their own recording studio, which Foreman named The Liquidator. And then the bomb dropped . . .

Chapter 13

AND THEN THERE WERE SIX

"WE were doing *Keep Moving* and we'd been offered a TV series by the writers of *Blackadder* [Ben Elton and Richard Curtis]," Foreman later explained. "We were talking about it and Mike said, 'Look I can't do it, 'cos I'm gonna leave the band.' He'd already told our manager sometime before, but the minute he said it, I knew what he was going to say. He was on the wane in the writing side. Some of his songs were ending up on B-sides, which was unthinkable because that's where mine used to end up! Cathal spun around and hit the deck like a sack of spuds. I remember him jumping up and saying, 'Oh my good God no, Mike boy, reconsider.' And I ran up to Mike and said: 'Right, let's have him now!' It was a very sad affair but it was what he needed to do. I just thought, good on you, if that's what you want, then do it."

The first whiff of trouble had emerged after the last show of their recent US tour on September 12, prompted by some paperwork which still needed to be completed before their return home. Matthew Sztumpf: "I went to his hotel room with the Geffen contract, and asked him to sign it. He said, 'I can't, I'm leaving the band.' Having spent God knows how long it took finding an American deal, and he's walking out on the eve of signing the contract. I can't remember how we got round it with Geffen. We may have made him sign it just to get the deal closed. The Buddhism was part of it. He didn't want everybody else controlling his life, telling him what to do." John Wynne vividly recalls seeing the manager immediately after that conversation. "Matthew came out and looked like death," admits John. "I thought, God, we're on a roll. The band were never that interested in America but we were doing quite well. But Matthew wasn't happy at all and it wasn't until a week later that he called me in and said, 'Mike's leaving.' A bit of bickering started!"

It's difficult to ascertain whether Barson's decision was due to creative exhaustion after four years as the band's musical crutch and a principal songwriter; or the pressure of pop stardom and resultant public scrutiny; or because he had relocated to Amsterdam to settle down with his Dutch wife Sandra; or the logical development of his new-found Buddhist beliefs; or a combination of the above.

"I was writing songs like a crazy man, 24 hours a day," Barson later admitted, "which got a bit much for me. I was listening to the radio, ooh that sounds good, I could use that. You used to get the feeling you were being watched. If they're all saying 'great', then it's wonderful, who would complain at that? But then you've got the other side of the coin as well, when people start saying, 'Crap, no good.' Just being in the limelight all the time is not something I am particularly mad about. It's a strain. That's one of the reasons why I left the band: going into obscurity I found quite attractive."

The first concrete evidence of Barson's disillusionment might have been that 'no-show' for their performance on German TV a few months earlier. "I did that stand-in for him in Germany somewhere," remembers Hector Walker. "He'd moved from London to Amsterdam and seemed less involved in promotion and we were thinking, oh well, Mike can't be arsed to do it, little realising it was a prelude to him leaving!"

On December 21 1983, the band continued their endorsement of political campaigns by hosting a 'Madness Christmas Party' in aid of Greenpeace at London's Lyceum Ballroom, with help from Ian Dury (with new backing band The Music Students), The Skiff Skats (formed by old friend Tony 'Tone' Hilton) and Nigel Planer's Hippy Neil character from *The Young Ones*.* Instead of being a celebratory end-of-year event in aid of a good cause, the concert was overshadowed by the fact it was Mike Barson's last appearance with Madness (for nearly a decade, at least). In an

---

* Another act on the bill were Motown-styled Hackney band Bonsai Forest, whose publishing was signed to Nutty Sounds. Their song, 'The Great Escape', was produced by Mark Bedford, featured Fun Boy Three musicians Nicky Holland and Ingrid Schroeder and appeared on *NME*'s *Mad Mix II* cassette, credited to the band's new philanthropic venture, the Camden Music Company.

ensuing edition of *Nutty Boys*, childhood friend Foreman paid tribute to
"My Mate Mike – Goodbye 007".

"Mike was getting into some kind of religion," Dave Robinson recalls.
"He was studying his life in terms of some kind of Buddhist teaching. And
I think he'd quite a lot of money because he was the writer of pretty much
every tune because he did the music so he got a share of everyone's publishing. The wife had a few quid and he was going to move to Holland, a
big love story."

The Stiff boss was gloomy about Madness's fate. "When I heard he was
leaving, I thought we were really in trouble," he admits. "Barson was the
most important ingredient to me. Not to knock anybody else's lyrics and
other bits but Barson's melodies were what made everything work.
Everything was fed through Barson to make records. It worried me
that there wasn't going to be a lynchpin, a leader and, of course, they
were not going to have this melody censorship which he performed.
They relied more on Barson than anybody realised and, to me, it was
terrible."

* * *

Still in a state of shock, the remaining sextet were offered the chance to
appear on a Polish TV show and, perhaps thankful of the change of backdrop in the wake of Barson's departure, they arrived at Warsaw's Victoria
Intercontinental Hotel Banquet Room on January 3, 1984, with *NME*
journalist Paolo Hewitt in tow. "I spent a Monday to Friday with them
[for] an *NME* front cover," Hewitt recalls. "It was really tiring because
Poland was still under communist rule, of course. It was winter and we'd
taken all this stuff out there – books, records – to give to the kids. But
when we got there, we went to clubs and nobody would talk to us,
because the communist party had arranged the gig. If you imagine
Margaret Thatcher had put a show on in England in 1984, no one would
want to go. So their show was full of 50-year-old communist party
members looking like Brezhnev, all clapping politely. It was cold, we had
this translator and stayed in the best hotel in Warsaw. But we were going
to shops where there were literally two cans of baked beans on the shelf. In
supermarkets, we'd say, why are they all queuing? Oh, the socks have
arrived so they can all get one pair each. So we hit the vodka because it
was the only way through!"

A staunch supporter of the band, Hewitt had met them several times before but was struck by the challenges they now faced. "Madness cut right across the board, everyone warmed to them," he explains. "Everyone bonded together – this was their first interview after Barson leaving. It's always been thought that there were underlying tensions within the group. Look at *Take It Or Leave It*, one of the bravest pop films ever! It basically says, just because you're in a band, it doesn't mean you're going to like each other. The problem was what they thought themselves: that for them to connect with people, they had to show themselves as six/seven people who really like each other, get on and have a really good laugh. In the meantime, there's all this other stuff going on. And the trouble with Madness was they didn't have a leader. And that breeds frustration. But maybe it kept them going, funnily enough. There's a weird energy: I'm going to show you! Can you imagine working with them?! I never got a sense of those tensions, though. Perhaps it was, oh we've got a journalist with us, come on boys."

Much of their shared time in Poland was spent partying. "We actually got into a fight with two Middle Eastern guys. We've had a few drinks and we're going back to Suggsy's room to carry on. Two guys were up the other end of the corridor fiddling with their key. Cathal being Cathal was like, 'Hi, how's it going?' 'Yeah, we're OK.' Then Cathal walks up to them and says, 'Pleased to see you, welcome to Poland.' Then suddenly, he adopted a kung fu pose. The two guys look at each other and knocked him spark out! So we ran down the corridor and one guy just picks the rim off those big dustbin ashtrays: bang on my head, bang on Suggsy's head. Suddenly, we're back in Suggsy's room battered by these two guys – 39 of us and two of them. What happened there?!"

Hewitt agrees that, without a strong managerial figure, Madness might have self-destructed: "They needed a Dave Robinson-type figure in there – it really would have fallen apart otherwise – that strong someone they could respect who made them buckle down. They'd started off with this happy-go-lucky image then it got serious. But the strength of it was that Barson leaving actually brought them together. Suddenly, Cathal came through. If there was a leader, it looked like Suggs. Chrissy Boy was the joker. Bedders was interesting: he'd be talking about art or books, a more literary side. He was quite shy, maybe held back a bit. Woody was pleasant, straightforward. I was pushing them on the politics because

Thatcherism was at its height and they were wary of that – they saw it was something which wasn't quite them.'''*

★ ★ ★

On January 30, a professional-looking video was filmed for Madness' next single, 'Michael Caine'. It took the form of a mini-movie, loosely based around the 1965 film adaptation of Len Deighton's classic tale of spy-related intrigue and espionage, *The Ipcress File*, starring Caine as central figure, the downbeat, reluctant spy Harry Palmer. In order to effect a cinematic quality, the video was shot on 35mm film, which took longer to set up than the usual 16mm.

As a result, the footage of Barson – who was still a fully fledged member as far as the public was concerned – playing the piano introduction before walking off, seemed quite apt because, by all accounts, filming had taken so long that he had to catch a plane back home to Holland. But the resulting clip of him leaving the piano to play on its own seemed especially symbolic given his departure from the band. "He came back to do the video and we had to do a photo session for Fleet Street," Foreman told *Record Mirror*, "and he hung around on the edge, as he didn't know whether he should be in the line-up or not."

"We had a guy called Harvey Harrison, who was a features DOP [director of photography]," explains the video's creator John Mills. "He was fantastic. You can tell the difference with 35mm because it has that shallower depth of field. Harvey would light things with one light but it would look fantastic. And all the stuff with the projector was great. That's the most different of all Madness's videos. A lot of these were pretty much the same crew. Roger Deakins is now the top Hollywood cinematographer – he does the Coen Brothers' movies. Chris Morphet was a fantastic handheld cameraman. Madness liked him a lot and trusted him. A lot of those shots were down to Chris, really, and a lot was in the editing. These videos had to be constructed after they were shot. They weren't shot with a storyboard. It was like doing a jigsaw puzzle without any pictures!"

"We shot it down in Docklands on 35mm because we wanted to give it

---

* On leaving Poland, Madness donated their fee of a million zlotys (about £400) to Solidarity, the trade union federation founded in 1980 and led by the charismatic Lech Walesa. Because Solidarity was the first union outside the control of the communist party, the government attempted to destroy it using draconian techniques such as martial law.

that spy film feel, to be serious – like a feature film," Suggs told *Record Mirror*. "The only problem being that we all start laughing. Usually we can't laugh when we do something stupid, but this time four of the band were supposed to be coppers grabbing Chris and we kept breaking up with laughter even though it was a straight piece!" The vintage Jaguar was Thompson's own. "A Mk II," he commented. "They wouldn't hire one . . . the wheel alignment went out as it pulled up to the pavement. I did in the shock absorbers and a cameraman nearly got hit as well!"

First impressions suggested this laconic song was an offbeat tribute to a very British institution, from lines like, "All I wanted was a word or photograph to keep at home," to the opening soundbite, "I am Michael Caine" – captured by sending a sound engineer down to a private members club frequented by the actor, whose daughter was a huge fan of the group. "He did it about five times and at the end goes, 'I think we got it there, don't you?', so we used that at the end of a different song," Suggs later quipped.

Cathal revealed an altogether more serious subtext behind the lyrics. "[It] is about the informers in Ireland and the way the government were using them to put people in internment camps, in prison – but I didn't want to make it that [too] obvious. I wanted that atmosphere of distrust and I threw Michael Caine in as a red herring to confuse people. His name seemed right. I had a general admiration for Michael Caine and *Get Carter*, and *The Ipcress File* had the sort of atmosphere I wanted to create – we even used some of his phrases. Looking back to 'Give Ireland Back To The Irish' by Paul McCartney, that never got played. You've got to be careful what you say."

In this instance, Smyth had collaborated with the band's drummer, who'd by now developed his own DIY set-up. "I got into home recording, a little 8-track, ¼ inch tape, a mixing desk and an effects unit," Woodgate later explained. "That's where my abilities came out – in engineering and music technology." Smyth would circulate backing tracks to the rest of the band – "basic chords which moved in progressions, a 12-bar set-up", according to Cathal. "One particularly grabbed me and made me think of Northern Ireland living there in 1971, a feeling of unease and propaganda, a weird time to have an English accent. That was the inspiration behind it. I lived there for a year but only went to school for a couple of weeks."

It's tempting to view 'Michael Caine' as a crystallisation of the challenges which now faced Madness. Patently, their underlying lyrical themes were becoming more serious. By the same token, pressure continued for them to deliver pop hits – a situation made all the more difficult by Barson's decision. Cathal's attempt to veil such a potent message beneath a seemingly unrelated subject risked falling between two stools. Luckily, such double meanings were accompanied by a gentle, uplifting melody and a charmingly conversational vocal style which perfectly complemented the John Barry-styled backing (Barry having scored *The Ipcress File*). Despite benefiting from the muscle of Stiff's marketing prowess, though, 'Michael Caine' stalled at number 11 in the singles chart – the first evidence, perhaps, that Madness' hit factory wasn't invincible. Maybe it lacked Suggs' charismatic vocals?

The fact that Smyth replaced Suggs on lead vocals spoke volumes about his ascent within the Madness ranks from dancer/MC to a primary songwriter and now singer. "Chas started to become more vocal and powerful," recalls John Wynne. "He was on a ladder going up. It's like a slow process. Now he's writing songs, playing the trumpet or the bongos. Cathal pushed himself to the forefront so he was noticed. Fair play to him: that's what you've got to do. But he did start taking more control of everything – money matters, song lists – always trying to drive the band. Massive get-up-and-go. A whirlwind."

If Madness had a polar opposite to Smyth, a character who – for all his impish sense of humour – was calm and collected, then it was Foreman. "Chrissy was quite astute," suggests Wynne. "He kept his eye on what his management and record company were doing. Chrissy had been in the outside world. He'd been to work, had a wife, lived in a flat and had a kid. All the rest hadn't played at real life. Prior to Madness, Lee was ducking and diving as opposed to living in the real world! The rest had been looked after at that point by their mothers. Chrissy never sweated. That's what we called him: 'The man who never sweats.' Onstage, everyone else would be pouring in perspiration but Chris used to walk off and there wouldn't be a bead on him! They'd all be in bits and he looked exactly as he went onstage, shirt and tie!"

Foreman, then, had quietly adopted the mantle of (gulp) responsible adult within the band. "I remember picking Chrissy up before we started one tour early on," says John, "and his flat used to be just around the corner from where my wife lived in Kentish Town. I went in and he's cleaning the windows with newspaper. Chris, we've got to get going. He said he'd promised his wife that he'd clean the windows before he went. So I had to sit there. Chris, you're going on a huge European tour! 'But I've got to do this!' Chrissy would do what he said he would do. He was never nasty to people. There's no side to him."

Wynne was privy to the very occasional bouts of teasing within the band's inner sanctum. "Woody and, to a certain extent, Mark would get that," admits Wynne. "I remember once there was a row and Cathal said something about, oh, you're just a pair of middle-class grammar school boys, having a poke at that, in the belief that they were all street-cred working class. If they hadn't been Madness, there's a good chance that a few of them would have been on her majesty's pleasure. Lee would have definitely been there. Suggs and Cathal. The others were more sensible."

At first glance, it might have been assumed that Suggs was a driving force within the band – but not so. "To my mind, he floated along with it," Wynne suggests. "Obviously, he's the front man and has to get out there and do it. But he wasn't too bothered about, say, the money side of it. He was more interested in enjoying himself. If you met him in the pub, smoking his roll-ups and drinking his pint, he's a funny bloke, interesting to sit and talk to. He was going with the flow. I mean, the flow couldn't go unless he was going with it. But rarely was he a stumbling block."

* * *

Chart positions might have been ebbing but it wasn't due to their fading popularity within the media – although Madness' anarchic sense of humour had caused some headaches for their promotional team. "Radio was never a problem because they made great records which were a dream to get on the airwaves," says plugger Neil Ferris. "The videos were always superbly made by Robbo and TV people loved them. All of that was fine. The problems we had with them stemmed from them misbehaving. We had issues." Despite the popularity of shows like *The Tube*, only one TV programme really mattered in terms of exposure for pop bands performing their latest single.

"*Top Of The Pops* was a heavily regulated show," explains Ferris. "And the bands had to behave so everything happened exactly on time." Dropping Madness into such a stiff-upper-lip environment was bound to provoke their penchant for pranks. It's not as if Madness had a reputation for being unprofessional, though. Perhaps it was their reaction to an environment in which pop stars appeared to be taking themselves too seriously. "Spandau Ballet and Duran Duran and all those bands would turn up in limos and Madness would go there on a bike or on the bus," says Stiff (and later Madness) press officer Jamie Spencer. "And I'd be taking them down to *Top Of The Pops* either in a battered old 2CV or an old Volvo estate. Madness thought it was a waste of money. They didn't need to get a limo!"

Needless to say, Thompson was the principal source of disruption at the BBC. "If it was a dress rehearsal, Lee would do his sax solo to camera," says Spencer, "but then in the proper filming, the camera turned towards Lee and he turned away from the camera! Stop recording! He thought it was funny but it was always a headache for the director. Another time, they did a dress rehearsal and went down in the clothes they were going to be in. They'd check all the cameras and the lights. Then it came to the show: Lee turned up and he'd painted himself green! What the . . .! You can hear it in the control box. Look, he's got a green face! Lee would keep everyone on their toes but they were seven strong characters."

Neil Ferris: "At one show, every time the camera came in for a close-up of Lee, he'd take the sax out of his mouth and his gold teeth would show. Cut! Let's do it again!" For one particular episode, a stunning female singer in a chiffon dress was delivering a power ballad with a subtly lit silkscreen backdrop – that is, until such intimacies were interrupted. "Suddenly, behind the screen on this beautifully lit set, you see them doing the Madness walk across the stage," sighs Ferris. "The director Michael Hurll went absolutely ballistic. It was like the third attempt. The floor manager put an earphone to his ear and said, 'Neil, you're required in the gallery.' It was like going to the headmaster! I had to go up this long staircase, the whole wall of the studio, into the gallery where Michael sat there. He took his glasses off and said, 'Neil, this is ridiculous. This is the final warning I will give you with this band.'"

The recriminations didn't end there. "I was then called at the end of the show," continues Neil. "The floor manager said, 'Michael is really furious, it's the last straw with Madness.' So I told the band it was going to be quite serious. The studio emptied and Michael said, 'Look Neil, this is just insane. We have a show to turn around. Madness just do not understand.

This kind of behaviour is costing the BBC a huge amount of money.' At that point, Chas – who had been listening quietly at the side – came up and said, 'Michael, it's not Neil's fault. We are Madness. You tell us something's black and we'll tell you it's white. We don't do it deliberately. It's just the way we are!' He put his hand out to Michael and they shook and Chas said, 'Come on, let's come and have a drink.' So we all went upstairs and all was forgiven. Until the next time!"

In an edition of *Nutty Boys*, Thompson alluded to one particular incident at *Top Of The Pops*: "The lads are up in the canteen . . . I attempt to make myself some toast on the in-house toaster and . . . you know how it is when your mind's on other thingamajigs? You misplace, forget. As I sat back at the table with my tea and Club biscuit, I heard a scream and someone shout 'Fire!' I'd never seen so many part-time acts move so fast . . . there was uproar and all because I'd forgotten to collect me two slices. I never did admit it was me."

Unfortunately for the powers-that-be, Madness' disruptive influence showed no signs of abating. "At one point, Michael Hurll said, 'That's it, I'm not having them back again.' He couldn't actually ban them because that would have been a press story and the BBC didn't do stuff like that. But effectively, they were banned. In a meeting on the Monday morning, he said, 'Neil, they have to behave. This is your last chance.' OK, OK. So we get there: rehearsal's fine. We go up to the bar before the show. And at 10 past seven, the band's called down into make-up ready to go. Half past seven, you record the show."

Acutely aware that these cats had used up all but one of their seven lives with the Beeb, Jamie Spencer had come prepared: "Right, we've got roadies, crew, everybody down there keeping an eye so no one's going wandering. Because they had been known to lock themselves in the toilet when they're supposed to be onstage. Yes, OK, they're coming down, they're getting in the lift now." So far so good? "Just as the band got in the lift, some girls turned up from the canteen. Oh, come in, come in – and the lift got stuck because it was too heavy. So the one time when they were really on time and organised . . .!"

Ferris laughs: "Twenty past seven, the floor manager finds me and said, 'We've got a problem with Madness. They were last seen getting in a lift. It's stuck and we've called the fire brigade.' Standing by the lift door is Michael Hurll, myself, the floor manager – and Michael, by this point, has given up knowing what to say. Finally, the fire brigade got the lift down and *Top Of The Pops* is half an hour late, which costs the BBC a fortune in overtime. This isn't the main lift which came down from the bar – this only holds six or eight max. And out come about twenty people: the band, Jamie or Matthew the manager, some girls, a roadie. Michael just looked at me, shook his head and said, 'Let's get on and do the show!' "

The plugger himself would occasionally be the target of the band's mirth, as Hector Walker remembers: "We were on an overnight train back to London. Neil was getting really stressed because the train was delayed. He was the first person we knew with a mobile phone and one of the band phoned him up, putting on this accent and cancelling the appointment he had with Bowie or someone. He got really stressed! It was all so important. I think they probably realised his usefulness but any kind of pomposity would not wash with them."

On February 19, the band flew to Los Angeles to appear on various TV shows. The issue of a replacement for Barson had still not been fully addressed. "Mike was a sort of coordinator, which is something we haven't got any more," Suggs admitted to *Record Mirror*. "But Clive Langer plays keyboards now and he's like another member of the band. He's the only person we'll take criticism from, other than ourselves." That was fine for studio work but the producer wasn't about to jet off around the world with Madness on a whim. For the US jaunt, they instead chose ex-Ace, Roxy Music and Squeeze pianist/singer Paul Carrack, who received the call while working with ex-Stiff artist Nick Lowe (alongside Barson's brother Ben) after a recommendation from Madness's sound man Ian Horne.

Although he originated from Sheffield, Carrack had lived in north London for some years and fitted in well. Having admitted that he didn't own any Madness tunes, a complete set was dispatched to his door and he was ready for the American trip after an intensive two-week crash course in all things Madness. As a mark of respect, the band asked Carrack to sing Squeeze's 'Tempted' solo as an encore, which was well received. The trip included shows in LA, San Francisco and San Diego, as well as a string of TV appearances, from a return to *Solid Gold* TV to the high profile *American Bandstand* on March 3, presented by broadcasting legend Dick Clark. Apparently, Thompson pinched Clark's backside, prompting the response "Have you no respect?" from the shocked TV presenter.

During the visit, Thompson married long-term girlfriend Debbie Fordham on February 29. As detailed in *Nutty Boys*, the ceremony was held in the Hard Rock Cafe, Los Angeles (immortalised in Carole King's song 'At The Hard Rock Cafe'), with the band decked out in white tuxedos and training shoes and Woodgate's wife Jane as bridesmaid. A larger, more lavish wedding party was later held for family and friends back in London.

Unfortunately, every silver lining had a cloud, as John Wynne explains. "My wife was at home and rang me out there and said, 'Did you get *The Sun* newspaper?' There was an article which said that one person who won't be at Lee's wedding will be his dad because he was in prison. But Lee's dad was actually dead. It was a big furore. The lawyers basically said they had so much power – and at that time, they really did in the Thatcher years – that you had to go along with them. It was upsetting for Lee."

★ ★ ★

Madness' next album, *Keep Moving*, was issued in late February 1984. In some respects, it felt like business as usual since it was recorded with Langer and Winstanley at AIR Studios with arranger David Bedford, and they appeared to have retained a sense of humour courtesy of a tongue-in-cheek multiple-choice competition on the rear of the sleeve (above shots of all seven members, including Barson, wearing grins in photos of them running). The front cover also seemed faintly comical: Madness on the running track at Crystal Palace Athletics Stadium, complete with jogging bottoms and trainers (apparently prompted by some sponsorship deal with Nike). By way of contrast, this was Madness' first album to openly endorse a political campaign or organisation – namely, Greenpeace – detailing the organisation's address with the phrase 'Oh for the Wings Of A Dove'.

"We had run out of ideas at that point," Suggs glumly admitted to *Uncut* in 2008. "I wrote [the song] 'Keep Moving' inspired by Spike Milligan in *The Bed-Sitting Room*. It's a post-holocaust setting and he's in a hot air balloon with a loud hailer going, 'Keep moving, keep moving.' I identified with that – the ridiculousness of where we were going. Dave Robinson thought we should have an album cover to reflect the forthcoming Olympics – bonkers – although we all got a free pair of Nikes. You see photos of Mike at that point and he's always covering his face, he's just had enough of fame. Because of Dave, we had the success we did, but we were also burnt out. Stiff survived on a shoestring that required Madness hits to keep them going. And we were tired."

While it could be argued that *Keep Moving* probably needed some catchy, radio-friendly fare (an 'Our House' or 'It Must Be Love'), the songwriting wasn't as mediocre as has been suggested in some quarters. In fact, the album was positively received not only in the UK but in the States, in no lesser publication than *Rolling Stone*, which granted it four out of five stars (although the album only peaked at number 109). It's just that *Keep Moving* didn't seem like a particularly apt title. *The Rise And Fall* had felt like a step-change, but here Madness seemed to tread water, even if it sold respectably enough (reaching number six in the UK listings).

"It was made under a cloud," Foreman later recalled. "When we were rehearsing, Mike told us he was leaving the band. I think he'd found it hard being the main songwriter all those years. The album was a bit of a mess. It doesn't seem complete to me. Suggs and Cathal had both become more musical, which was obviously a bonus. But I had some songs that wasted away in the cupboard because there was nobody to write lyrics for them. That was part of the problem after Mike left, I think: not [so much] a balance of power but of who does what."

The album opened strongly with the title track, built upon that distinctive chord pattern from the Brill Building classic 'On Broadway' (written by Mann & Weil then tailored for The Drifters by Leiber & Stoller in 1963). At first glance, the lyrics seemed a straightforward message of positive thinking, but lines such as "Say goodbye/Don't let words stay too long/If you're leaving" seemed to echo the band's sentiments in the wake of Barson's departure. 'Keep Moving' was set to a soulful groove reminiscent of early Dexys Midnight Runners. Indeed, it featured The TKO Horns, who'd been formed in 1982 by ex-Dexys trombonist Big Jim Paterson, who had worked closely with Elvis Costello on his 1983 album *Punch The Clock*. (That album, in turn, had boasted the classic 'Shipbuilding', co-written by Costello and Clive Langer and featuring Mark Bedford on the earlier hit version by Robert Wyatt.)

"It came about through our association with Clive Langer and Alan Winstanley," says TKO Horns' tenor saxophonist Paul Speare. "Jim Paterson and I first worked with them when they produced Dexys' *Too-*

Rye-Ay album. After we left the band, we continued to work together as a brass section, bringing in Geoff Blythe and Dave Plews, under the TKO Horns name. Langer and Winstanley introduced us to Elvis Costello, who needed brass on *Punch The Clock*, which they were producing, and later called us in for the session with Madness. The track was already laid down when we came in to play the brass parts. We were only there for a couple of hours. The only band member there was Lee Thompson: he said something about not being confident enough to do the parts himself and needing 'proper' players to do them, which was quite flattering."

Also fresh from the *Punch The Clock* sessions were black vocal outfit Afrodiziak (alias Caron Wheeler and Claudia Fontaine, now with a third member Naomi Thompson), who sang on 'Michael Caine'. It's probable that the retro soul flavour of *Punch The Clock* (and maybe Costello's earlier album *Get Happy*) influenced Madness during this period. The concept of incorporating classic soul stylings into contemporary music was definitely fashionable, from the endeavours of Costello and Paul Weller (from late period Jam onwards – indeed, Afrodiziak played with them live) to Squeeze with the likes of 'Tempted', as well as more mainstream pop names like Culture Club.

A Sixties soul vibe also characterised other songs on *Keep Moving*, such as 'Turning Blue' (which seemed to speak of sinister international politics) and one of the album's undoubted highlights, 'March Of The Gherkins', a Northern Soul-styled stomper reminiscent of late Sixties 'bubblegum soul' act The Foundations. The principal lyric, "Catch me, I'm falling into my past", reflected the mix of nostalgia and middle-aged angst evident in this bizarrely named song penned by Barson and Thompson. Taking the role on *Keep Moving* which Geraldo filled on *The Rise And Fall* was Luis Jardim (full name Luis Alberto Figueira Goncalves Jardim), a Portuguese percussionist who worked extensively with producer Trevor Horn on such acclaimed albums as ABC's *Lexicon Of Love* (1982).

Another guest was General Public, the band formed by 'Ranking' Roger Charlery and Dave Wakeling after the demise of The Beat. Their vocals were prominently heard on 'Waltz Into Mischief', a superb homage to the songs of Kurt Weill, from its music hall-era audience participation to the wonky Bierkeller piano. Rarely discussed even within the most hardcore Madness forums, 'Waltz Into Mischief' is actually a missing link between the more theatrical extremes of Kilburn & The High Roads and the Sensational Alex Harvey Band and *The Liberty Of Norton Folgate*, recorded a quarter century after *Keep Moving*.

General Public were also clearly audible on 'Victoria Gardens', a deft mix of busy keyboards, funky bass and a driving beat which didn't actually sound like Madness at all on first listen ("I remember that being very Beatle-ish, slightly like 'I Am The Walrus'," suggests David Bedford). By contrast, 'Time For Tea' felt disjointed, with vaguely threatening undertones emanating from Bedford's string arrangements, while 'Brand New Beat' seemed too desperate to sound contemporary. 'Samantha', meanwhile, was more obviously guitar-based – perhaps the first indication that Madness were listening to The Smiths. 'Prospects' owed more to UB40, offering a welcome change in tempo with some downbeat reggae backing to accompany a fragile melody faintly reminiscent of The Beatles song, 'For No One'.

The album closed on a genuine high. Overbrimming with cheeky swagger, all horns and strings and Suggs' impish wit, 'Give Me The Reason' felt like a welcome return to the Madness of old, overflowing with charm and personality. As such, it emphasised that, elsewhere on the record, *Keep Moving* could feel antiseptic – cold even – and lacked that sense of naïve fun which was Madness' calling card. At its worst, the album sounded indifferent.

★　★　★

Not so 'One Better Day', the most mature, contemplative song on *Keep Moving*. Opening with shades of the jazz-pop in vogue at the time (Sade et al), this bittersweet ode to the homeless hostel Arlington House felt like an 'Underneath The Arches' for the Thatcher years. This heartfelt ballad couldn't help but evoke a reaction as, aided by some soaring strings, its bossa nova beat grew to a sublime chorus. "My favourite Madness track!" admits arranger David Bedford. "That was very moving because it was in a strange minor key for the verses and then swept into a major key for the choruses. There was a BBC radio programme last year called *The Producers* and they featured Langer and Winstanley and Suggs saying how much he liked the strings on that track."

According to the Aisling 'Return To Ireland' project (dedicated to helping vulnerable Irish people living in London), Arlington House in Arlington Road, Camden Town, was the biggest homeless hostel in

Europe, having housed more Irish men than any other building outside Ireland. Opened in 1905, it was the last in a chain of hostels built by the Victorian philanthropist Lord Rowton, to provide a clean and decent roof over the heads of working men. The 'Rowton Houses' enjoyed a reputation for providing the best value accommodation in London. In *Down And Out In Paris And London*, George Orwell wrote about staying in the Rowton Hostels in 1932; another renowned resident was Irish poet Patrick Kavanagh.

A near-Victorian disciplinary regime was maintained for over 1,000 residents at Arlington House, from a complete ban on alcohol to a strict, militaristic system of fines and punishments. Sadly, the hostel had long been in a state of decline by the time of 'One Better Day'. Conditions had fallen into a state of disrepair, but perhaps more importantly, the public's perception of the hostel had changed. In more prosperous times, the idea of a lodging house for single, working men, now seemed archaic to the Thatcherite generation. Soon afterwards, the hostel was taken over by Camden Council and extensively refurbished, with tenant numbers being halved and room sizes doubled.

"The street theatre in Camden in those days wasn't Mediterranean goths juggling and fire-eating," Suggs told *Uncut*. "It was the fellas out of Arlington House. They'd all have to leave the building between nine in the morning and four in the afternoon. Among the huge gangs of geezers drinking cans outside the supermarket in Inverness Street, I remember very poignant images. You'd see fellas in their jackets, washing their only shirt in the launderette; you'd see this old guy we called 'The Shroud' wearing full Edwardian undertakers' gear; or another fella sitting on a bench dressed as a naval captain. Or you'd see the woman I wrote about in 'One Better Day', who would go up and down Parkway with about 200 carrier bags full of, well, fuck knows what!"

'One Better Day' was unquestionably *Keep Moving*'s masterpiece – but a dispute swiftly erupted as to its suitability as a single. Dave Robinson had originally voted for a remixed version of 'Victoria Gardens' but changed his mind at the last minute, in favour of 'One Better Day' (which was why the sleeve depicted a back garden because there wasn't time to change the design). Further, Robinson was apparently reluctant to finance a promotional video, suggesting the band dip into their own pockets instead. In the short-term, a 'Mexican stand-off' ensued, which upset Madness to the extent that a rift between band and label opened. It would prove to be irreparable.

After several weeks' prevarication, 'One Better Day' was eventually issued in late May, roughly three months after *Keep Moving*. The worthwhile video was duly filmed outside Arlington House (with Suggs seen on its footsteps, accompanying the lyric "Arlington House, address no fixed abode") and at nearby Camden Lock, with the welcome involvement of a visiting Mike Barson and Suggs' wife Anne. While most of the ideas emanated from Thompson, the video was directed by ex-Stiff employee Nigel Dick. "Dave had such a thumb over them and now they were like, maybe we don't want to do that," he suggests. "They rang me up and said, 'We'd really love you to direct the next video.' But it was the first video where they did not want to be funny! Oh, great, I'm going to be the architect of their doom, killing the Nutty Boys! Everything else was in colour, this was in black-and-white. Everything else was funny, this was maudlin, about homeless people!"

The bad blood between artist and label sucked the life out of the surrounding publicity campaign and the single stalled at number 17, making it the lowliest hit of their career to date. The B-side, 'Guns', was notable for being the first song for which Suggs had written both words and music; it was recorded at the newly inaugurated Liquidator with Foreman taking Barson's role on keyboards. And on the 12-inch, Thompson offered 'Sarah', dedicated to the plight of Sarah Tisdall, a Foreign Office clerk who had been sentenced to six months in prison for passing two documents written by the Defence Secretary Michael Heseltine, relating to Cruise missiles and the Greenham Common Airbase, to *The Guardian* newspaper.

* * *

By this time, Robinson's attentions (and maybe his affections, too) were elsewhere. Towards the end of 1983, Island Records had bought 50 per cent of Stiff in an arrangement which allowed Robinson to run both labels. It's recorded that, while Island was the purchaser, the company was actually starved of liquidity and, in an ironic turn of events, borrowed £1,000,000 from Robinson to fund the share purchase and pay the payroll. Needless to say, with his new responsibilities, the Stiff boss could no longer work "hands on" with the band to the same extent as before. On a more practical level, the Stiff offices were vacated and Robinson was given a much smaller office at Island HQ – which conflicted with his traditional 'open door' policy. "It seems to have soured when I went to Island," admits Dave. "They didn't like Island. They thought my time was being spent on other things. They didn't feel they had the access but I made sure that they had. Going to Island probably was a mistake for me generally – but that's another story!"

Perhaps there was another consideration, too, according to John Wynne. "Dave Robinson told me that they demanded a record deal which had him as a 'key man clause' in it so that, if he left Stiff Records, the whole contract was null and void. He stalled and stalled and, in the end, he went, I'm not giving you a contract – you're not holding me! Then they all looked at each other and went, what do we do now?!"

In the short term, Madness had been distracted by the rigmarole of their promotional schedule. They played a benefit concert on a bill with Amazulu and Darts at Camden Dingwalls for The Hope & Anchor, which was in financial trouble (it eventually had to close). "A lot of good groups started down there and without it, we may not have been where we are today," commented Suggs. "Playing there drew a lot of attention from the press and suchlike because of its notoriety. Also, I spent (or rather misspent) many a happy hour down there in my youth. It's a great pub."

Around this time, the band also appeared on *The Tube* and on *UKTV*. However, they needed a replacement keyboard player for a forthcoming American jaunt – so their road manager Rob Forrest suggested his friend James Mackie, who he knew from his days working with The Selecter. Hailing from Lancaster, Mackie had earned his stripes in local ska band The Pharaohs before joining Pauline Black & Co. in 1980, in time to work on their second album, *Celebrate The Bullet*. When The Selecter disbanded in 1982, Mackie worked briefly with their ex-guitarist Compton Amanor before eventually bumping into Forrest again.

"Rob arranged for me to go down to Camden and meet the guys," says Mackie. "They had a live performance coming up and decided to give me a chance to prove myself. Their headquarters was an anonymous frontage in a line of nondescript shops. It was quite daunting to visit. I suddenly felt very Northern. Their constant banter, shared humour and culture were wonderfully compelling but virtually impenetrable. They had been through so much as a group of mates. They knew each other almost too well. No one could replace Mike, obviously, but I was determined to give it a bash."

With Mackie in tow, Madness flew to Paris on April 9 to perform their intended next single, 'Victoria Gardens', on the *Isabelle Adjani Show*. "Lee went completely AWOL and even the band were talking about it," says Mackie. "Some of us found a central restaurant and had lunch, then the fire water was brought to the table. After an hour of shots, we left. The guys were singing and I was zig zagging, on and off the boulevard. The piss was taken but we did the show (Lee must have turned up) and then recommenced drinking at the hotel."

From France, the band flew directly to New York City for the big prize: an appearance on the prestigious comedy show *Saturday Night Live* at New York's famous Rockefeller Plaza on Saturday April 14. "There was a shambolic, 'smoky' rehearsal one day where the fabulous Dick Cuthell, who was in charge of the brass, got frustrated and started shouting," Mackie recalls. "We all met up one evening to go and watch George Clinton and Parliament at The Apollo. On the Saturday, we ended up in the TV studio half-way up some enormous skyscraper waiting to soundcheck. Lee had disappeared to the concern of everyone except the band, who seemed used to it. He did turn up just in time and a few hours later, with a dry mouth and shaking hands, I stabbed away at the opening piano riff of 'Our House', feeling a bit sick and overwhelmed by the tens of millions of live viewers that we knew were tuning in! New York loved the guys – and so did I."

Mackie also served time with Madness for various TV performances and concerts once the band were back from the States. "Like so many of their fans, I desperately wanted to be part of their gang," he admits. "It was great being with them but always frustrating that I would never actually be 'in' Madness. Mark was a good player and always struck me as serious about his music. When Woody and he got going properly, it was good stuff. Chrissy was a great bloke – they all were. There was a TV gig in west London when Gary Glitter was in the next dressing room. He was hoisting his gargantuan silver costume on to his shoulders and looking solemnly into the mirror. I remember Suggs saying something like, 'Fuck me, Gary Glitter's in there!' We all seemed a tiny bit impressed: Gazza was a 'star'!"

On April 30, Madness were back in London filming six songs for an

Italian TV programme with noted Italian actress, film director and screen-writer Eleonora Giorgi, during a five-day shoot across London. Each tune – 'Victoria Gardens', 'Keep Moving', 'Waltz Into Mischief', 'One Better Day', 'Michael Caine', 'House Of Fun' and 'The Sun And The Rain' – was represented as a scripted short film. And on 21-22 May, Madness appeared on New Brighton Rock at the Merseyside resort's open air swimming pool, alongside Frankie Goes to Hollywood, Nik Kershaw and Spandau Ballet, highlights of which were transmitted by ITV.

For short trips to both France and Germany, Irish keyboard player Seamus Beaghan filled Barson's shoes for TV appearances. A few weeks later, they performed 'One Better Day' on various TV shows such as *Earsay*, *Razzamatazz* (with ex-Tenpole Tudor guitarist Bob Kingston deputising for Foreman, who had injured his back falling off a car boot while inebriated in Liverpool) and *The Oxford Road Show*.

On May 11, the band had travelled to Montreux for the Golden Rose Festival, co-financed by the BBC, which opened the following day with stars such as Adam Ant, Status Quo and Queen. "It was Switzerland so I bought an expensive pipe and some fragrant tobacco and puffed away on it through the entire trip and our gig," says Mackie. "One night in the hotel, Suggs leant over and pushed a brownish lump into the smoking bowl of my new briar and told me to go play the piano at the bar – which we did until the early hours when we were politely asked to go to bed!"

Meanwhile, Foreman and Thompson had travelled directly to Montreux from Germany (instead of heading home for a day). After a night of merri-ment, the pair bumped into members of UB40 and headed for the nearest nightclub. In due course, the entourage attended a party held by CBS Records, who had heard that Madness might be looking for a new record deal in the wake of deteriorating relations with Stiff. Unfortunately for the organisers, it seemed as if the band's frustrations needed to be vented. A chair and an amplifier were duly thrown from the seventh floor suite while the carpet was riddled with cigarette burns and a glass coffee table was broken ("It was my fault, I suppose," wrote Thompson in *Nutty Boys*, "because recently I have put on a considerable amount of weight"!).

By all accounts, the apartment was due to be occupied by Rod Stewart the following day. While hotel officials blamed the damage on general hooliganism, a CBS executive promised to cover the costs of cleaning and repairs and to have a word with the culprits, but Suggs tried to excuse the band's behaviour. The story, such as it was, made headlines in various tabloids, from "Rod's suite wrecked – chaos at pop party" to "Madness in hotel rampage" and "£10,000 bill as Madness and UB40 go wild at showbiz party". It must have been a quiet week for news. "We only did it for a laugh," Suggs explained. "None of the band were involved in the furniture destruction." The following day, the band's performance went without a hitch – although controversy returned with them to Gatwick Airport, where Woody was forced to convince customs officials that his giant bar of Toblerone wasn't a gun!

"A nice but poignant thing happened at their Camden studio," adds Mackie. "I had been quite affected by the recent death of the actress Diana Dors. I wrote a song about her. The chorus ended in her husband's words, 'Diana, you're just a whisper away.' I had come in early one morning to use the grand piano to work on the last verse. Cathal was first in and we ended up singing together, working out the harmonies and discussing how the verses could be developed. It was great. When the rest of the band turned up, Cathal said: 'Listen to this, I think there's something in it.' But they didn't want to listen – the time for that kind of thing was over."

Mackie had already sensed a different, altogether more sombre mood within the band: "They were well off [but] Mike had left and they had some issues with Stiff and each other. There was a fight. I got involved, I believe. Apparently, it was quite ugly. I actually have no memory whatsoever about the whole episode. I treasure my memories of being with them as a band and as individuals but I suspect that that particular brief period is not one that they relish."

Chapter 14

YESTERDAY'S MEN

M ADNESS's contract with Stiff Records expired on May 21, 1984 – and the band refused to sign a new document, ending a relationship which had benefited both parties for nearly half a decade. "The start of 1984 has been turmoil for us losing Mike," commented Bedford, "and now leaving Stiff – the two most major changes a band can go through. But we're riding the storm. The studio has been a great leveller because it lets us get in and write when we want. I think they'll be a rainbow at the end of the road!"

It's likely that Madness had grown to resent the continued expectations placed upon them by Stiff – a set-up which had proved highly lucrative but also felt like an unsustainable treadmill. "I did have an attitude which eventually they disliked," admits Dave Robinson. "I would preach to them: you're now seen as a pop band. You may not like it but that is the essence of it. You're making quality albums but the singles are the vehicle that we are getting the mileage from. And key for a pop band is to bring out material regularly. So in between the albums, you make singles. Every three months, there's Madness on *Top Of The Pops*. Eventually, they said, 'Dave, you're just trying to make money out of it.' Well, I didn't mind selling a lot of records but the bottom line is that Madness were always there. There might be a lull but the new record then came. Eventually, Madness found this onerous."

Furthermore, Robinson didn't see eye-to-eye with Madness' creative ambitions. "They said to me, 'We want to make more serious music.' Inevitably, when a group says that, you dive into your filing cabinet and read your contract! That's when we realised we only had a Heads Of Agreement. Also, we'd upped the amount of the royalty with them because originally we only had a three-album deal (Stiff's way of not getting involved in long, drawn-out negotiations [was] three-album deals). At some point, they wanted more money or more points so we agreed to add two records and they got a retrospective push on all their records. And that was a letter to the Heads Of Agreement."

The Stiff boss also saw problems in the changing dynamics within the band. "What I hadn't realised was that Madness needed a strong, tough leader. So when Barson left, Cathal took his place, which was different, because Cathal – although he wrote some key hit songs which were very good – wasn't a musician or player. And Mike was very grounded compared to Chas: when Mike was running things, there was a logic and reality to aspects of it. When Chas was running it, it got a bit flighty, shall we say, because he's a more flighty character. Chas was a bit more hippie in his music tastes. He felt the music was more serious whereas Mike had a really pragmatic attitude where he knew it had to be successful to keep such a large band [together]. That became difficult. I think the reason why Stiff and Madness split up was somewhat due to Chas's attitude – his wish to control. OK, so Chas is to become the leader and there's going to be trouble because he hasn't got his feet on the ground like Mike had. That's why they formed, what I tried to get across in the movie. Mike was, 'What are you doing, can't you do it right?' At the same time, he was the anchor."

Robinson could have tried to buy Madness' loyalty – but that was never his strategy and, in any case, his heart was no longer in it. "In hindsight, their day was passing," he admits. "Suddenly, they were having wishy washy music, slow tempos, what they thought was 'serious music', more about the underbelly of life without hit choruses. But the public had got used to the Nutty Boys and wanted 'up' music from them. That became a problem. So things changed. They had fancier video ideas; they wanted to make movies. Also, they wanted more money, more sales, but the sales were starting to dip when Barson left. Plus they weren't writing a lot and they didn't want to tour Europe – and we'd sold zillions of the first album so they were huge there. But you could only hit major cities then they'd want to go home. They'd all got married, pretty much, or had girlfriends. Not that it would have lasted five minutes if I'd have given them Maserati catalogues and houses in Guildford, especially as I'd sneered about that concept to them over the years!"

From Robinson's perspective, then, Madness were trying to make that tricky transition from a singles-oriented pop band to a more cerebral album-based act (something which they finally achieved with *The Liberty Of Norton Folgate*). "The basis of the Nutty Boys was the stuff that all those kids growing up remembered," says Dave, "and serious music it was not! But *all* their stuff was serious in a 'folk' way. They were writing about stuff they were culturally linked to, in this area of London. The problem was, musically, they moved off ska and didn't really replace it. Suggs had that music hall thing he liked and you had that carnival swirling organ vibe and also the two producers got stuck with adding strings. And the social comment didn't quite have the hooks that Mike would put into the tunes. Also, you can't swap markets. Once you've got a market, it's difficult to say, they're too young, we'll go after these older people. Today, their audience – having grown up with them – are still with them."

Matthew Sztumpf's recollection of the dispute is more succinct: "I remember why it happened. Dave Robinson didn't pay us. It was as simple as that. The statement came through, he owed us a quarter of a million pounds in record royalties. The ninety days passed and he hadn't done anything about it so we put him on notice. I remember going into his office and saying, 'Are you going to give us a cheque, Dave?' And he said, 'No.' And I said, 'Right, we'll see you in court' – which we never did. Stiff didn't have the money." In due course, matters fell to lawyers for both parties – rarely a pleasant exercise.

Meanwhile, Madness' manager had approached various major record labels. After all, here was a band with one of the most impressive string of hit singles in Britain over the past five years. At first, it seemed likely that Madness would sign with CBS Records. "I was shopping them around," says Sztumpf. "I had meetings with Paul Russell, the Head of CBS, and Muff Winwood, their Head of A&R. And we almost did the deal with them except they changed the terms dramatically when it came to the final contract. So I went to Virgin and got an advance of quarter of a million pounds from the MD, Simon Draper. Then I went back to Stiff and said, 'OK, I'll give you quarter of a million pounds if you give us the back catalogue' – which they did to settle out of court. At that point, Madness owned their back catalogue and we licensed it to Virgin for twelve years. So I was the one who got the catalogue back from Stiff Records."

Robinson is philosophical: "I've got nothing but great feelings about

Madness [except] the negotiations at the end when we all fell out. But that was down to their lawyer saying, 'The band don't want to give you the extra two albums now.' And I said, 'Well, I've been paying a [higher] royalty on the first few albums which was down to having two more albums, so where does that leave me?' He said, 'Take it back to the original Heads of Agreement.' So I retrospectively looked at their arrangements and deducted the amount that I had overpaid for something that I didn't ever get – and they never understood that. They thought: 'Dave's pulled some fast stunt here and cut, you know, £400,000 out of our income!' I was quite happy to go along with it. So I sold them the whole catalogue – actually, they did very well!"

* * *

"We said to Virgin, we want our own label," remembers Sztumpf. "The Virgin deal was a deal for Zarjazz. Cathal was particularly excited about it. Ian Horne became the in-house engineer and did all the recordings. They were all enthusiastic." The paperwork with Virgin was finally signed off in August 1984. To the band, it felt like a natural progression to create their own imprint. To help find a name for the new venture, they invited members of the MIS fan club to send in suggestions – but the final choice, Zarjazz, came from Cathal, taken from the "Betelgeusian" expression of "Zarjaz" meaning "really good" or "brilliant" in the comic *2000AD*, which was hugely popular with certain members of the band. Suggs especially was an avid follower and had written a short article about the comic in *Nutty Boys*.

At this point, Madness hadn't even thought about their next album. They focused instead on extra-curricular projects. While on the set of *Top Of The Pops* to perform 'The Sun And The Rain' back in autumn 1983, Foreman had got chatting with ex-Undertones singer Feargal Sharkey, who was there to sing 'Never Never' with The Assembly. The pair struck up something of a rapport. The guitarist happened to mention they'd been toying with a song written by Cathal entitled 'Listen To Your Father'. The tune had been road-tested as far back as the sessions for *7* in 1981 but somehow never gelled for Madness. Chris asked Feargal if perhaps he'd like to record the song with them instead?

Early in 1984, Cathal had invited Feargal along to Liquidator Studios to listen to the song. Liking what he heard, Sharkey agreed to record it and the track was completed in March (the day after the Hope & Anchor fundraiser), with backing from Madness, prior to their last American trip. "Feargal had an input into the B-side," remembers Matthew Sztumpf, "and there's this story about Cathal saying he'd buy him a couple of pints. But Feargal understood it to be that he'd have a couple of points. And I had to have this difficult conversation with his manager. It sounds like points but that's because he's Irish!"

In due course, Sharkey agreed to a 2 Tone-style one-off single deal and 'Listen To Your Father' became the first offering on Zarjazz. After what seemed like a considerable delay, the record was finally issued on October 1, 1984. The single sold well, peaking at a respectable number 23, helped by a performance on *Top Of The Pops* for which Sharkey was backed by Madness minus Suggs. It proved to be the perfect launch pad for both Feargal's solo career and Madness's ambitions to reach beyond the boundaries of their own recordings. Sharkey then reverted to parent company Virgin to enjoy huge success in 1985 with the chart-topping 'A Good Heart' and the Top 10 hit 'You Little Thief'. (Another early session at Liquidator was to record music for a Channel 4 programme composed by ex-Fun Boy Three musical director Nicky Holland, which was the studio's first experience working with classical instruments.)

★ ★ ★

On December 6, Madness played at a private party at London's fashionable Wag Club in Wardour Street alongside Bananarama, Orange Juice and Aztec Camera, punctuated by DJ'ing sessions from Paul Weller and Jerry Dammers. All profits were assigned to the Ethiopian Famine Appeal, prompted by the widespread famine in Ethiopia which had gripped the media in 1984, as the Ethiopian government's inability or unwillingness to deal with the crisis provoked universal condemnation from the international community. The regime's policy of withholding food shipments to supposed rebel areas meant that the combined effects of famine and internal war had put the nation's economy into a state of collapse. From a British perspective, observers were unaware of such conflicts; they were merely horrified at the sheer level of suffering they saw in their newspapers and on their TV screens.

The highest profile fund-raising activity from the pop music world, in response to the famine, was clearly the Band Aid single. Recorded by a "supergroup" coordinated by Bob Geldof and Midge Ure, 'Do They Know It's Christmas?' topped the charts at the end of 1984. That led, in turn, to the concert extravaganza, Live Aid, unquestionably a high water-mark in popular music history if only in terms of its sheer global reach. Madness, however, were conspicuous by their absence from both projects (as were UB40, the closest band in the mid-1980s to the Nutty Boys in terms of their success, background, musical style, even size).

Instead, Madness created their own equivalent of Band Aid for the 2 Tone generation – inspired by one of those random moments of inspira-tion. Sometime in December 1984, a Madness fan named Mick Tuohy strolled into the Liquidator Studios and suggested the band record the old Pioneers hit 'Starvation' in aid of the Ethiopian Famine Appeal. The idea met with universal agreement – and so the band invited a variety of musi-cian friends along to help out, including Jerry Dammers, General Public, UB40 and The Pioneers themselves. The resulting get-together not only yielded 'Starvation' but a track written by Dick Cuthell entitled 'Haunted'.

For the other side, a session in Paris was convened to capture a host of African stars, including King Sunny Ade and Manu Dibango, for the track 'Tam Tam Pour L'Ethiopie'. And a promotional video was filmed in Liquidator. Unfortunately, 'Starvation' met with apparent indifference from mainstream radio – indeed, it's been suggested that some DJs consid-ered the track "too ethnic". Perhaps as a result, and despite encouraging reviews from the music press, 'Starvation' was completely overshadowed by the all-star cast of Band Aid and stalled at number 33 following its release on February 25, 1985.

Another Zarjazz project had been unveiled on January 28, inspired by *2000AD*, the cult comic which had been launched by IPC in 1977 as Britain's answer to a science-fiction comic market dominated by the Americans. Cathal and Suggs' affectionate tribute was entitled 'Mutants In Mega City One' (Mega City One being the principle location of the comic's characters) and credited to The Fink Brothers (the enemies of the comic's hero Judge Dredd).

The pair had already decided to dabble with the electro-style rhythms and hip-hop beats they had heard during an earlier American visit – and the venture allowed them to experiment outside the confines of the band. "What prompted it was sitting in discos in New York where everything is just so brain-numbingly loud," explained Suggs in *Jamming!* magazine. "It immediately kind of threw us together with Mega-City One, that sort of uneasy street feeling when you're out late in New York."

The Madness members were disguised as Fink Angel and Mean 'Machine' Angel. *2000AD*'s storyline depicted them as part of a vicious band of mutants from the wasteland outside of Mega-City One, who swore to avenge Judge Dredd's murder of their family by sampling his voice then going back in time to make money with this record and take over the world. Unfortunately, the single only sold modestly (peaking at number 50). More exciting for two avid fans was seeing their alter egos actually appear in "prog 403" of *2000AD*, published February 2, the cover hinting at the spin-off project with messages like "I'll make those creeps sing!", "Fink Brothers beat the rap?" and "Judge gets criminal record".

"We wanted as much as possible to make it like the comic," explained Suggs, "not just a record by a couple of out-of-work pop stars, but something that (was) actually part of the comic, more for the people who read it and for other people to be able to get a vague grasp of what it is, as opposed to just writing a Madness song about Judge Dredd. We keep to the characters because it's more fun for the readers of *2000AD*. It would have spoiled it if it said the real people on the back." Cathal elucidated the comic's appeal: "For anyone who had any interest in the Marvel comics when they were young, they just didn't change over the years. Nothing really happens, it's still Fifties America. I think the very real appeal of *2000AD* is that it turns everything upside down: heroes may die and things aren't always what they seem."

'Mutants In Mega City One' was – in essence – a Judge Dredd tribute and boasted his famous catchphrase, "I am the law!" The story that most likely influenced the record was entitled *Destiny's Angels*. "Although it's not supposed to have any sort of relationship to reality," added Suggs, "I think it does, in a funny way, relate very much to America and the exaggerated consumer society. The thing with the mutants is just like with any minority group: they're not allowed into the city because they're mutants, which is hardly their fault, they were just blown up during nuclear wars!"

For the sleeve design, the pair hooked up with *2000AD* designer Brian Bolland. "One or two of the *2000AD* editorial team and I went to their office," Brian later wrote. "After I did the artwork and they'd paid me for it, I was wondering when I'd be getting my artwork back. Return of artwork was a hot issue. I went to see them and was perturbed to see they'd mounted it on the office wall. I explained that, technically, if they wanted the artwork, they had to buy it off me. We agreed on a figure – but I never saw it. Whenever I see people enjoying a Madness video on telly, I always say, 'Those guys owe me 300 quid!' "

Mike Prior had the pleasure of photographing The Fink Brothers for *No. 1* magazine. "That was a mad session," Mike recalls. "We had a Judge Dredd poster painted on my wall in the studio. It was fantastic. And they wore these industrial fire suits, big heavy-duty, half woollen, half asbestos, which were made to save your life – you could put a blow-torch on them! Cathal and Suggs put these suits on and they found it unbearable. They were totally uncomfortable and incredibly itchy. I got a couple of rolls off but they couldn't stand it. They broke out in hot sweats. Cathal came out in a rash, itching all over the place, in a real bad mood! But the pictures looked good!"

Zarjazz issued two other extra-curricular singles: 'Life's A Deceiver' by Charm School might best be described as synth-pop while 'Who Broke That Love' by ex-Scritti Politti drummer Tom Morley was inspired by the burgeoning jazz-dance scene of the period. Indeed, it wasn't surprising to see Morley's name in the credits for the second Working Week album *Companeros* the following year. However, none of the Zarjazz releases seem to have been afforded any degree of attention by parent label Virgin and both singles sank without trace.

★ ★ ★

Another band seriously considered for Zarjazz were very much a part of the wider Madness family. In autumn 1983, Cathal received a phone call from an old school friend of Thompson's named Tony 'Tone' Hilton, who was assembling a club band called The Skiff Skats. Tone would play tea chest bass, Rob Smith the banjo and 'Pigmeat' Pete Smith the guitar, creating a bastardised update of country and skiffle, embellished with skiffle's quintessential instrument, the washboard. "Tony and Rob worked together as council gardeners on Hampstead Heath," explains Hector Walker. "They had a work hut, 'the Boffy', where they started playing music together with Rob's brother Pete."

The Skiff Skats evolved out of a primarily north London movement of the period which updated and diversified the pub rock spirit by resurrecting myriad styles of roots music, from rockabilly to country, folk to skiffle, bluegrass to swing. It's the same scene which threw up The Pogues, bubbling up from the same grass roots which had nurtured The Invaders some five years earlier. Initially coalescing for a laugh at a party, The Skiff Skats were offered two shows at The Hope & Anchor and the Fulham Greyhound by Matthew Kleinman of The Nogoodniks (who also featured his brother, ex-Bazooka Joe member Danny). The offer prompted Tone to contact Smyth to see if he'd play washboard in the band.

"[Cathal] turned up one night with some beer and some smoke and he proved a good percussionist – so he was in," wrote Rob Smith on the Skiff Skats website. "Next, Lee [Thompson] wanted to play a 'zob stick' and Tone made him one by copying the design from an old picture." Also known as a 'lagerphone', this bizarre instrument was developed by a member of pub rock act Brett Marvin & The Thunderbolts as a variation of the 'monkey stick' or 'mendoza'. It was constructed from a stout pole affixed to a heavy base with beer-bottle tops fastened at intervals along the shaft. When played, it sounded like a combination of a bass drum and tambourine. "It was to prove a lethal weapon in Lee's hands, bits of plaster falling off walls and ceilings as he attacked them," wrote Smith.

The Hope & Anchor show attracted "a bunch of Cathal and Lee's friends" who witnessed The Skiff Skats tackle such classics as 'These Boots Were Made For Walking' and 'Johnny B. Goode'. When Cathal couldn't make the next gig, John Hasler took his place on washboard "and was instantly brilliant". A headline gig of their own at The Hope & Anchor followed on November 23. "We decided to make it an occasion," wrote Rob. "Lots of gimmicks – false teeth and a bottle of whiskey to loosen the vocal cords."

The band attracted significant publicity on the back of the Madness angle. "We played at the Madness Lyceum Christmas gig, but gradually Cathal and Lee dropped from sight," continued Rob Smith. "They didn't want to overshadow the band. However, it was a wrench seeing Cathal go as he was such a stage character. At one Hope & Anchor gig, he put on his suit, hat and shades and spent the whole gig with a massive joint hanging out of his mouth! Style! The last gig Cathal did with us was a very drunken Dingwalls gig with [ex-Specials guitarist] Roddy Radiation. It ended in mayhem with about twenty people onstage."

Thompson, meanwhile, handed his 'zob stick' over to Hector Walker (who was billed as 'Cousin Hector') and The Skiff Skats continued in earnest for a couple of years, eventually disbanding in 1985. They appeared on television (including *Saturday Superstore, Old Grey Whistle Test* and that Madness special, *South Of Watford*, performing in Cathal's front room) and made a video which was shown on *Max Headroom*. They also graced a variety of music magazines. At the 'Alternative Country Music Festival' at the Electric Ballroom, the band "made a dive for the loos where the acoustics were good and much fun was had". This jolly jape attracted column inches in *The Observer, The Face* and *Smash Hits*.

The Skiff Skats were definitely a curiosity – although critics occasionally lumped them in with skiffle-influenced duo Terry & Jerry. "Stiff wanted us," wrote Rob Smith, "Madness wanted us on Zarjazz". With a modest loan from Madness' management (Jamie Spencer was their informal manager for a period), they recorded a single 'Cripple Creek' at Liquidator, produced by Ian Horne. "John and I used our contacts to promote the single," adds Hector. An album, *Skiff Skat Stuff*, followed in 1985. Alongside sessions produced by Pat Collier (who'd once played in Bazooka Joe with Barson's brother Dan) were two tracks recorded for John Peel. Both records were issued on their own imprint, Doggo Records. "The term Doggo was what they affectionately referred to when they stood in a dog shit," laughs Walker.

★ ★ ★

By 1984, Virgin Records had evolved into one of the biggest independent record labels in Britain. Founded by Richard Branson, Simon Draper and Nik Powell in 1972, the label had spun off Branson's hippie vision of offering an alternative chain of retail outlets for kids reared on the late Sixties counterculture and early Seventies progressive rock. After making their mark commercially with Mike Oldfield's *Tubular Bells* in 1973, Virgin broadened its roots to encompass the burgeoning Krautrock emanating from Germany and the explosion of reggae out of Jamaica. Virgin's hippie image was shed in one fell swoop in 1977 with the signing of the Sex Pistols and other subsequent punk and new wave acts.

During the early 1980s, Virgin swiftly developed a more commercial sensibility, nurturing a string of highly successful pop acts, from OMD (on spin-off label DinDisc) and UB40 (on DEP International) to Genesis frontman Phil Collins, Culture Club, The Human League and Heaven 17. In 1983, Virgin purchased Genesis' label Charisma and continued to compete on the same footing as the major record labels of the day. "1983 was our *annus mirabilis*: we were the top singles label in the country, for the first time," remembers Jon Webster, who was then General Manager of the organisation. "10 Records had launched because it was the tenth anniversary of Virgin, and they had a number one with The Flying Pickets. We had hits coming out of our ears – remember Fat Larry's Band and 'Zoom'?"

In July 1984, a month before inking the deal with Madness, Virgin had moved to plush new premises at Kensal House on the Harrow Road (not far from the old Stiff offices, coincidentally). At that point, the label was enduring a brief but decidedly barren patch. "In 1984, we were cold as a witch's tit," exclaims Webster. "It was like turning the kettle off! Because everyone had made and delivered their records in '83, we had nothing. Our big hit in '84 was 'The Chicken Song'! The only other record we sold all year was the Eurythmics' soundtrack from the film *1984*."

"Simon Draper ran Virgin – he was MD and co-owner," adds Jeremy Lascelles, who was then Head of A&R. "Simon brought the deal in, or it was offered to him. At the A&R meeting, do we want to sign Madness? Absolutely!" Lascelles was somewhat sceptical about the concept of the Nutty Boys' own label. "As was often the case, Zarjazz was just a vanity label for them to put their own records out and to sign a couple of things," he admits. "Like all artists do at a certain stage, they think they are brilliant A&R men and undiscovered talent is coming their way. It's been done many times over the years, whether it was Apple or Swansong, and it very seldom is successful. It ends up, all too often, just doing deals for their mates instead of making sound commercial and creative judgement calls." What Virgin really wanted instead was a new Madness album.

Madness celebrated their new set-up in the Christmas 1984 edition of *Nutty Boys*, offering a supposed schematic of the Liquidator building and a profile on all relevant personnel, which had been swelled by ex-Stiff press officer Jamie Spencer, who had been working at Island in the interim, as Matthew's second-in-command; and photographer and old friend Clare Muller, whose darkroom was on the premises.

★ ★ ★

Madness had spent most of January 1985 rehearsing and writing material in Solid Light Studios in Camden Town and in Hotown Studios. On January 28, they played a 'secret' show at The Bull & Gate, Kentish Town, disguised as The Wayfinders, who were apparently premiering their new album *Lost In The Museum*. This spoof album title was a barbed reference to Dave Robinson, who was alleged to have told Madness, towards their end of their working relationship together, that "I'm running a record company not a museum". Instead, a packed audience of 200 grateful fans and friends were granted a sneak preview of material from their forthcoming record.

Lee was offered the welcome distraction of the birth of his son, Daley Jay Thompson, on January 26. On March 4, though, Madness returned to AIR Studios for roughly a month to begin recording. On April 1, the entourage then re-located to Langer and Winstanley's Westside Studios, a two-studio complex in Holland Park, west London where it's likely the band spent the day pulling April Fool's Day pranks on all and sundry while the producers attempted to focus on the job in hand. Recording and mixing continued until the end of April before the album was completed.

In terms of making records, Langer and Winstanley had been an integral part of the Madness team since their debut in 1979. But it was four years before the pair made a firm commitment to work as a production partnership when they created Westside in 1983 – a delay partly due to Langer's continuing aspirations as a solo artist. "Even then, we knew there would be occasions when we would work apart," Langer later admitted. "We never considered ourselves to be the eighth and ninth members of the band. Our roles were different and that was how it stayed. However, they certainly cemented our relationship as producers."

Unfettered by the traditional time constraints placed on them by Dave Robinson, the gestation period for their first Zarjazz album was longer than for any previous Madness record. But by early summer, the album was finally ready – with extra B-sides taped around July 8. The protracted sessions were fraught with a sense that, perhaps for the first time, Madness had to prove themselves – both in the wake of Barson's departure and as a calling card for their new label. "Everyone really did knuckle under and try desperately hard to pull out something from themselves that they'd not previously done," Woodgate later confessed. "It's like, if you lose a hand

The Nutty Boys in 1981, scaling the heights of pop stardom... and a lamppost.
No prizes for guessing who was at the top! (LFI)

The Magnificent 7 put on a united front. But wait, is that
a pineapple in the middle...?! (FIN COSTELLO/GETTY IMAGES)

Their prolific release schedule demanded a lot of the time in the recording studio, usually with Barson leading the way. (CLARE MULLER)

'Shut Up''s theme of petty crime prompted this Keystone Kops reenactment for the accompanying video.
(PAUL COX/LFI)

Sailing across the sea... Madness at the Crystal Palace Garden Party in June 1981. (FRANK GRIFFIN/LFI)

Save the whale! This memorable shot was taken at Windsor Safari Park as part of the promotional campaign for 'It Must Be Love'. That's Orca, the killer whale, in the foreground. (MICHAEL PUTLAND/RETNA PICTURES)

Part of the video for 'House Of Fun' was shot at a funfair in Great Yarmouth owned by members of Thommo's family. (CLARE MULLER)

Madness driving in their car – a Morris Minor – inspired by Mike's ex-GPO van from their days as The Invaders.
(VIRGINIA TURBETT/GETTY IMAGES)

On the set for the video of 'Our House', Thommo indulges his passion for flying ... dressed as a washerwoman. (CLARE MULLER)

Madness mime to their number one hit 'House Of Fun' on the set of *Cheggers Plays Pop* in April 1982. (KEVIN CUMMINS)

In September 1983, Madness played a baseball game against KROQ Radio – hence the matching outfits.
(CHRIS WALTER)

Lights, camera, anarchy! Suggs and Chrissy Boy "help out"
with the filming of the video for 'Our House'. (CLARE MULLER)

you've got to re-adjust to work a little harder. I suppose that's what it did for the whole band."

Unfortunately, Madness had grown accustomed to working with a short attention span – and patience wasn't a virtue shared by every member! "We spent a ridiculous amount on it," Thompson later complained. "We had all these musicians coming in, left, right and centre. I just thought, what's going on here? This isn't Madness anymore, this is a bunch of session players. String players, brass players. Then I sort of gave up: I ended up staying away from the band as much as possible." By all accounts, the recording was not a particularly happy affair. Minor niggles and irritations arose between certain members – and moments of mirth were few and far between. For the track 'Yesterday's Men', though, Jerry Dammers was drafted in to play keyboards. The former Specials founder ordered an old Hammond organ but it was too wide to fit through the studio door. Eventually, he was left to play it in a cold, draughty corridor!

String arrangements again fell to David Bedford. "I feel the budgets were slightly smaller once they'd moved [to Virgin]," he admits. "It's quite expensive having a group of string players so they became more stringent. From, 'Oh, it would be great to have strings, let's do it and if we don't like them, we won't use it', to only using me on the four or so tracks they knew they wanted strings on. Clive pointed out gently to me that they didn't have quite the budget! 'Yesterday's Men' has a soaring string line in the chorus. The string players came from a classical orchestra I was the 'Composer in Association' with – the English Sinfonia."

Bedford had always been impressed with Woodgate's drumming and called upon his services for a project he was recording himself for Virgin. "I had a science fiction solo album, *Rigel 9*, based on something by Ursula K. Le Guin, the well-known American author. I wanted those thuddy drums which Woody specialised in so he came along and did a session for me." Mark Bedford also contributed to the album, alongside contributions from such disparate talents as female vocal duo Strawberry Switchblade and rock guitarist Clem Clempson.

The issue of a permanent replacement for Barson had yet to be resolved. On July 29, auditions were held at Liquidator. From a list of four possible candidates, two were selected: Terry Disley on piano and Seamus Beaghen on organ. Disley's CV as a jazz musician was impressive. Born in London – indeed, he went to the same school as Foreman – he studied piano and theory of music from the age of eight. By the time he was 20, he'd studied classical repertoire, jazz, composition, piano accordion, saxophone, harmony and arranging at the Salterton School Of Music. He began composing aged just 11 and by 13, he was writing for his own electric/acoustic chamber group. In 1982, Terry and the Latin-jazz group Macondo won the Best Young Jazz Musicians Of The Year Award, endorsing his position as a highly acclaimed jazz pianist.

"The gig came about when I played some sessions for the Latin/salsa band Cayenne at Madness's studio," remembers Terry. "Ian Horne – 'Dad' – was engineering the sessions. He was also the sound guy for Madness' tours and was impressed with my piano playing. He put me up for the audition. I was doing lots of session work and Madness needed someone to step in. Chrissy Boy remembered me from school and that helped. [But] I only did some demos. Probably none of my stuff got on the album. Seamus was more suited as a character, looked the part. To him, it meant much more. He was a big Madness fan to begin with."

★ ★ ★

In August 1985, some 15 months on from their last Stiff 45, Madness finally unveiled details of their first Zarjazz offering with the McPherson/Foreman number 'Yesterday's Men' (previewed on the *Hold Tight* TV show in front of a fairground at Alton Towers a few weeks earlier) to be followed by the album *Mad Not Mad*. This was by far the longest sabbatical in their career to date – but the media welcomed them back with wide open arms, quashing the occasional rumour that Madness had actually disbanded.

In some respects, the single's sublime, downbeat nature picked up where 'One Better Day' left off. On 'Yesterday's Men', Suggs' intimate vocal delivery perfectly suited its beguiling melody while its smoky, atmospheric vibe shared a wine bar membership with Everything But The Girl and The Style Council, before drifting into a respectful nod to that Leiber & Stoller classic, 'Spanish Harlem', as a logical extension of its early Sixties Brill Building vibe. The lyrics seemed like a vague critique of those in positions of power who had outstayed their welcome – but perhaps the sentiment that "Yesterday's men hang on to today/To sing in any old way" might have been a subtle, or perhaps unwitting, attempt at self-effacement? In pointing the figure at outmoded institutions, were they also looking in the mirror?

From the outset, Virgin's relationship with Madness was considerably less involved than that of Stiff. *Mad Not Mad* had been recorded without any involvement from the company – but their response on hearing it was extremely positive. "We thought it was really good," recalls Jeremy Lascelles. "*Mad Not Mad* had some terrific songs. We went into that project with confidence. Lyrically, they've rarely been given credit for being as questioning and as challenging as they were. They've been underestimated on that front."

Jon Webster was more pragmatic: "We were all waiting for the new Madness album. But they made a different Madness album – more adult. 'Yesterday's Men' was a great record. We did think it was a challenge, though. With acts like that, if they don't have a big hit, selling albums is difficult. I've always believed that bands' fan bases, the real hardcore, are smaller than people think. There are an awful lot of people who are predisposed to buy them. It's so easy to assume that fans stay on top. But Madness was certainly a big deal for us."

Virgin rolled out an impressive promotional campaign, dropping Madness onto a hamster wheel of TV appearances, from the ubiquitous *Top Of The Pops* to *Wogan*, *TVam*, *Bliss*, *Saturday Picture Show*, *No Limits* and *Cheggers Plays Pop*. An edition of *Countdown* was filmed in Holland and, while the show's host asked Suggs about Barson's whereabouts, Mike was actually sitting nearby in the studio.

For the 'Yesterday's Men' video, they reunited with director Chris Gabrin, who'd been working in America in the interim. "There was some surrealism about it, with Lee on wires again," says Chris. "The zebra crossing was a studio set. We did this mock trial and they came up with the idea of a bouncing globe. More serious possibly but maybe I put that down to being longer in the tooth in the business. By then, I was with a production company Aldabra that later became Working Title."

The video shared the same subdued, ponderous air as the song, opening with a strange, Orwellian gathering of mock-judges before reintroducing the band members individually in bizarre locations and rolling out a variety of scenarios with the band, filmed at the Brixton Academy. Thompson was decked out as a devotee of the Hare Krishna mantra. This was commonly assumed to be another of the saxophonist's madcap guises – but it's thought that Thompson did, indeed, dabble with the faith during this period, shaving off his hair and donning the orange robes. He even declared his public support but either this was an elaborate wind-up or his devotion proved to be short-lived.

Mad Not Mad finally arrived on September 30. Six stark, unsmiling faces gazed out of the monochromatic sleeve (it was probably coincidental that Smyth's image was the largest and in no way reflecting his more dominant role in the band). The design was decorated by Ian Wright, who had become acquainted with Madness via his striking design for 'Grey Day'. For *Mad Not Mad*, Ian used subtle gold flecks to neatly embellish a portrait by Anton Corbijn, the renowned Dutch photographer famous for his sombre, moody images of such artists as U2 and Depeche Mode (although his earlier shoot for *Complete Madness* had lain unused, the band had been keen to work with him).

Ian Wright: "They'd invited me to do stuff for their fan club magazine that had them as potatoes, quite graphic! I did a few drawings of them inside, too. Then I did some stuff for *Complete Madness* that was only used on the label, them playing with puppets. Then I did a Zarjazz logo." The *Mad Not Mad* design itself was created by Simon Halfon, who was best known at the time for his striking, Blue Note-influenced work with The Style Council. Halfon was another ex-Stiff employee whom Wright had met at art college.

"I knew Simon from Stiff, working in the backroom," says Wright. "He was a huge music fan, enthusiastic and friendly and we became good mates. I'd shared a studio with Neville Brody and Simon became Neville's assistant." The pair collaborated well on the packaging for *Mad Not Mad*. "I was just given the pictures," adds Wright. "I thought I was quite respectful of Anton's photograph – just my gold, graphic bits on the faces. But he went bonkers! He wasn't happy and threatened to take his name off it. Lee came to my studio with this story and said maybe we should think of something else. He had these ideas about having lots of things coming out of people's heads. He did loads of drawing but we didn't hear any more."

One of the consistent observations of Madness during this period was their indecisiveness. "Simon and I sat with them," remembers Wright. "At one point, they couldn't make up their minds about anything. Simon came out with this great line. He said, 'Are you sure you want to be called Madness?' And they actually thought about it! It's funny because there were so many people to please. For seven lads suddenly thrust into that limelight, it must have been quite stressful. There's a balancing act and certainly they were an interesting collective of people. I remember with the *Complete Madness* project, Mike was always the one who would tell you yes or no. After Mike, they were too cooperative, in a way."

★ ★ ★

In terms of the music contained therein, Madness had clearly shed the 'Nutty Boys' tag completely. The inner sleeve listed a dizzying array of guests, from two Barson stand-ins (Elvis Costello regular Steve Nieve and Disley's pianist partner in Cayenne, Roy Davies) to one-time Clash, PiL and Level 42 saxophonist and ubiquitous sessioneer Gary Barnacle (co-credited with Lee for organising the horns) and Judd Lander (harmonica). And the frantic footfall at AIR and Westside had been further increased by the return of past contributors Luis Jardim (percussion), Afrodiziak (backing vocals) and string arranger David Bedford.

By the mid-1980s, a prevailing trend within the recording industry was towards the latest digital technology, which allowed artists and producers a broader scope of possibilities – including the creation of synthesized drum patterns. "That really is the beginning of the end because on that record, I didn't play on it," Woodgate later admitted. "We spent weeks programming the drums on *Mad Not Mad*, in case we'd used them instead of me. Clive, I think, was under so much pressure to come up with a hit record that he wanted a really clean-cut production and the easiest way of getting a good drum sound is not to have a drummer on it. But you lose all the character. It really got to me actually. That's when I really started getting depressed by the whole situation."

Despite his reservations, Woodgate was credited with "programmed Linn drum and keyboard sequences" and "triggered AMS's" – so at least he was able to supervise this process. Created in 1980, the Linn LM-1 drum machine grew to dominate the pop music of the early 1980s.* The Madness drummer appears to have been more actively involved than on previous albums; perhaps it provided a welcome distraction from his home life because he and Jane were divorced that year.

To indulge their love of classic soul, Madness recruited three male

---

* The first major hit to incorporate a Linn drum was the Human League's 'Don't You Want Me', produced by Alan Winstanley's friend Martin Rushent, in late 1981.

backing singers in Jimmy's Helms, Thomas and Chambers. Helms was the most famous, not least for his 1973 soul/pop hit 'Gonna Make You An Offer You Can't Refuse'. The Florida-born vocalist had worked regularly since his arrival with the US military in Britain in the early Sixties. He subsequently pursued a career as both a solo artist and as a jobbing session and backing singer for myriad artists, as well as a fruitful sideline in radio jingles. That very year, he'd performed on the soundtrack to the film, *Water* (starring Michael Caine, with an assortment of rock star cameos).

Jimmy Thomas also enjoyed an impressive pedigree. Born in Osceola, Arkansas, the budding singer made his name with Ike Turner's band the Kings Of Rhythm, which evolved into the famous Ike & Tina Turner Revue. By the mid-1960s, Thomas had branched out as a solo singer, recording some highly regarded 45s. In 1969, Jimmy settled in Britain, eventually capitalising on his popularity on the burgeoning Northern Soul scene, which was fanatical about old, obscure, uptempo soul 45s. He was also called upon for session work with such stellar names as John Lennon and The Rolling Stones. In 1982, Thomas was a third of Dexys Midnight Runners' backing vocalists The Brothers Just (most notably appearing on the song 'Let's Get This Straight (From The Start)'), which introduced him to producers Langer and Winstanley. Jimmy Chambers, meanwhile, was of Trinidadian extraction. Thomas knew Helms from the latter's Pye recordings in the late 1970s. By the time of *Mad Not Mad*, Thomas, Chambers and Helms had already been hired by Langer and Winstanley for Lloyd Cole & The Commotions' album *Easy Pieces*; Chambers and Helms would later form the band Londonbeat.

Judd Lander was a seasoned session musician famous for his harmonica playing on Culture Club's hit 'Karma Chameleon'. "Clive thought it would be a good idea," says Judd. "We'd heard of each other, being fellow Scousers. We got on well. He said he wanted something special and I tried to do a spin on Culture Club. My work was with Clive although the guys would walk in and out, and there was a pile of old musos who worked together. Luis Jardim chalked up more sessions than anyone, a real character. I think it was at Westside. I remember they had a pool table – we were playing and Suggsy cheated, blocked the pocket over! There was a sense of urgency. They were meticulously vetting each track, very focused." Judd played on three tracks on the album – although Madness' guitarist wasn't happy about the harmonica passage on 'Yesterday's Men'. "Lander was all right, but not on my song," Foreman told *Uncut* in 2008. "I fought and fought not to have him!"

★   ★   ★

Mad Not Mad only contained 10 songs (as opposed to the usual 12 or more), underscoring subsequent revelations that the sessions were fraught with difficulties. Although it boasted some genuine highpoints, it was short and inconsistent. On the inner sleeve, the sextet paired off in telling fashion – old school friends Thompson and Foreman, ex-skinheads Suggs and Smyth and the rhythm section "new boys" Woodgate and Bedford. They didn't look like a gang any more, rather a clutch of individuals suffering from an identity crisis. Within the barren wastelands of mid-1980s pop, who should Madness be?

From the first line of album opener 'I'll Compete', the "new" Madness appeared to be satirising their own position within the corporate music industry: "I'll be your promotional copy in this here number one band." Its cluttered assemblage of funk bass, stabbing horn riffs and artificial drums suggested a desperate desire on the band's part to sound contemporary – but its busy, overheated production also acted as an aural metaphor for the song's theme, as each instrument vied for domination like the high-flying "yuppies" who'd come to epitomise success in the mid-1980s. If Thompson really had embraced Hare Krishna, was this his rejection of the period's obsessions with material wealth?

Smyth also collaborated with Suggs on two songs. Named after the 1949 movie starring James Cagney (whose voice, as the film's central character Cody Jarrett, is reproduced in the song), 'White Heat' was a sophisticated, beautifully arranged homage to classy Sixties pop. Vibes, strings, horns and even banjo were stirred into this musical melting pot while Suggs sang about the realities of life on a council estate, plagued by loan sharks and debt collectors. Less satisfying was the clinical synth-funk of 'Mad Not Mad', reminiscent of that same year's Style Council single, 'Come To Milton Keynes'; both sounded as if two thoroughly old-fashioned bands were trying too hard to be fashionable. The lyrics were more intriguing, with mention of Georgie Fame and his backing band The Blue Flames in the opening lines, plus an acknowledgment of The Crazy Gang (the legendary comedy troupe active from the 1930s to the early 1960s, who must have influenced Madness, wittingly or not).

This brittle collision of components also blighted a song which has proved popular with Madness fans. McPherson/Foreman's 'Burning The Boats' was a poetically worded attack on government policy. Unfortunately, its attempt at blue-eyed soul ended up like some musical jumble sale. Suggs struggled to be heard above a melee of shrill keyboard, digitally-created chimes, forceful backing vocals, harmonica and horns – reminiscent of Culture Club's 'Church Of The Poison Mind' but lacking the same focus or melodic strength.

'Time' was probably inspired by the similarly titled David Bowie song from his 1974 album, *Aladdin Sane*. The song was first previewed during the *South Of Watford* documentary in 1984 – as a solo performance at the piano by its composer Smyth. 'Time' built from sparse, undecorated beginnings to incorporate a mock-fairground interlude and the odd Smiths-styled guitar riff, hinting at the work of Bertolt Brecht while offering a welcome return to that mischievous Madness humour when Suggs quips, "come on, time", as if it were a pet dog.

Less satisfying was Smyth's other solo songwriting contribution, 'Tears You Can't Hide', a reggae/gospel fusion with hints of Ben E. King's soul evergreen, 'Stand By Me', pleasant enough except for the fact that – with Cathal replacing Suggs on vocals – it sounded more like Paul Young than Madness. A more direct doffing of the cap to soul music history, 'Coldest Day' was Suggs' closing epitaph to the passing of soul legend Marvin Gaye, who'd died on April 1, 1984. Gaye had played a vital part in Motown's domination of the US charts in the 1960s – but he was perhaps most fondly remembered for his subsequent recordings in the early 1970s, namely the album *What's Going On*, which seamlessly blended a style of serene, funk-fused soul with socially conscious, spiritually uplifting lyrics.

Madness might have taken inspiration from such landmark recordings. Instead, 'Coldest Day' suffered from a heavy-handed, quite inappropriate mix of neo-house dance rhythms and clumsy synth patterns, swamping Suggs' sentiments in the process. A momentary nod to Gil Scott-Heron's anti-Apartheid anthem, 'Johannesburg', only served to reinforce the confusion: a reference to any of Gaye's many classics might have been more appropriate. Did Langer's addition to the McPherson/Foreman song-writing credit suggest one too many cooks?

Two tracks on *Mad Not Mad* felt like a nod and a wink to the Nutty Boys of old. Opening side two, 'The Sweetest Girl' was a faithful rendition of the Scritti Politti single, which had given Green Gartside & Co. their first, albeit minor hit back in 1981. Its faintly reggae bass line and stabbing horns suited Suggs' best attempt to replicate Gartside's serene vocal style but the recording was sullied by an unsympathetic synthesized drum pattern and shrill keyboards, at odds with the song's innate warmth. Ex-Scritti drummer Tom Morley was credited on the album with "computer supervision".

More satisfying was 'Uncle Sam'. The song opened with a ship's foghorn which echoed that of 'Night Boat To Cairo' before bouncing along on a jolly ska/reggae beat while taking a cheeky pop at the British armed forces' perceived tugging of the forelock to the American military (with the added sound effects of machine gun fire and the 'Taps' bugle call). The caricature of "Uncle Sam" had remained a potent personification of the United States' government since the early 19th century; he was usually depicted as a stern, elderly man with white hair and a goatee beard, dressed in a top hat and trousers with red and white stripes, reflecting the design of the American flag. Although the image was commonplace, it's likely that the song's creators, Thompson and Foreman, had stumbled across DC Comics' adaptation of Uncle Sam as a fictional superhero in the *Justice League Of America* spin-off, *Freedom Fighters*. In fact, an illustration of the Uncle Sam character had appeared on the front cover of issue eight of *Nutty Boys* in late 1983.

'Uncle Sam' was chosen as the second single from *Mad Not Mad* and issued in mid-October. The video, too, boasted all the hallmarks of classic Madness, not least in its role-playing. Foreman was a milkman, Bedford a postman, Thompson a Stetson-wearing Yankee and keyboard deputy Seamus Beaghen a TV newsreader, with footage shot in a suburban house. "I loved 'Uncle Sam'," enthuses the video's director John Mills. "I wanted to do a sequence before the track started, with Suggs as the narrator sitting on the postbox. The house was over Ealing way. It was quite difficult to find that little cul-de-sac location. The other great scene was going down Putney High Street on an amphibious army vehicle. That was a hoot. We went down the ramp into the river and up the Thames. They have all these weapons because they're dressed as soldiers. Lee's spinning a rifle on his arm and it dropped into the water! Then suddenly, there's some guy with this loudspeaker on the terrace at the Houses Of Parliament: 'You on that boat over there! That is illegal!' They gave us a stern warning and the river police came past. So that video went back to a bit of the wackiness they'd lost."

Beaghen graced the front cover of the single – although, by all accounts, he refused any offers of remuneration.* Despite the gravitas of its subject matter, 'Uncle Sam' felt like the Madness of old, shrugging off life's problems with good humour and the odd practical joke rather than being burdened by them. Unfortunately, the public didn't agree: despite plenty of airplay, 'Uncle Sam' stalled at number 21, their first single ever to fall outside the Top 20.

Had Virgin made a mistake? After all, 'Uncle Sam' might have been the safer choice to lead their campaign. "There was a debate between 'Yesterday's Men' and 'Uncle Sam' as the first single," admits Jeremy Lascelles. "We thought we'd go with the bolder choice. 'Uncle Sam' was more obvious, a tip of the hat to the old sound but the lyric had an edge to it. But they were trying to be taken more seriously and 'Yesterday's Men' was the more thoughtful track. We thought it was a good pointer to their new sound, with a slower tempo, etc. We were very much involved in choosing the singles as a team at Virgin. There wasn't a huge amount of tortured debate. We were always looking for the opportunity to do it differently and not to just play the obvious card from day one."

Mad Not Mad found one important ally in *NME*, who championed the album, from a glowing review to its lofty position as their fifth best album of the year. *NME* also accorded 'Yesterday's Men' seventh best single of 1985 while *Mad Not Mad* was Madness' sole entry at number 55 in their list of *NME* Writers All Time 100 Albums, which was headed by Marvin Gaye's *What's Going On*. Madness had always enjoyed the patronage of *NME*: *Keep Moving* had been voted 13th best album of 1984, *The Rise And Fall* the 24th selection of 1982, and *7* was the 32nd choice in 1980. But while *NME* might have heralded their latest album as the band's finest work, other critics considered it an all-time low. Madness may have craved the respect of the rock critics but perhaps it came at the expense of record sales? *Mad Not Mad* was Madness' first album not to reach the Top 10, peaking at number 16.

---

* The band had wanted to use a photograph by renowned American photographer Diane Arbus, which portrayed a young American man wearing a boater, bow tie and a badge saying "Bomb Hanoi", but were refused permission.

In hindsight, *Mad Not Mad* wasn't as wildly different as some critics would have believed – more likely, they hadn't registered later albums like *The Rise And Fall* and *Keep Moving* and were comparing the Madness of 1985 with the Nutty Boys of yore. But the band themselves were swift to disown it, Suggs infamously dismissing the LP as a "polished turd". More recently, his tone was more measured: "I just remember that Mike had gone and we were over-compensating arrangement-wise and musician-wise. But I think there are some great songs on that album, for sure."

In 2008, Suggs spoke to *Uncut*: "This was Madness' long-delayed 'difficult second album'. We didn't have songs [and] we'd have been better to take a year off. 'The Sweetest Girl' was my idea. 'Let's get really serious and take a song that we don't even understand!' The artwork was strange and the haircuts weird, but it wasn't all bad – 'Uncle Sam' was a watershed. Sting said he liked it!"

In that same interview with Gavin Martin, Foreman shared equally mixed feelings about the project, admitting that they "wanted for direction": "We'd gone right up our own arses. We'd parted company with Dave Robinson and Mike – both very strong people who gave the band direction. We had fun doing the songs, but recording was difficult – the technology, the drum machines and stuff swamped us. 'Burning The Boats' was a really good demo, organic sounding, but there and elsewhere, there was a failure to stay true to the original idea. Of all our albums, I think it's dated the worst."

Virgin's Jon Webster was sceptical about the sales potential of favourable reviews. "We were working on The Blue Nile," he recalls. "They had fantastic reviews but trying to get that across to people without having a hit was really difficult. When 'Yesterday's Men' was a hit of sorts, we worked really hard at it, then 'Uncle Sam' came out and we were realising how difficult it was. I remember them being on the case, sharp business-wise, compared to a lot of other artists I'd met. They asked lots of questions. They were cynical about the whole process."

Chapter 15

TEARS YOU CAN'T HIDE

WHILE Suggs was still distracted by the birth on July 5, 1985 of his second daughter, Viva Christina, rehearsals had begun on September 12 in E-Zee Hire Studios for Madness' first major UK tour for 18 months with an ambitious coterie of extra backing singers and musicians in tow. Cork's Castlebar Festival on September 23 acted as something of a warm-up. On October 19, Madness appeared on the *Saturday Superstore* TV show, on which Foreman was beaten by comedian Frankie Howerd in attempting to set a record for sticking stamps to individual envelopes. The band also filmed 'Uncle Sam' at London's Hippodrome for the BBC campaign *Children In Need*.

After a production rehearsal at Chippenham Goldiggers, Madness embarked on the five-week *Mad Not Mad* tour, beginning with a return to Cork to kickstart their biggest-ever tour around Ireland. Dick Cuthell remained from 1983 while Beaghen and Terry Disley handled keyboard duties. Disley was blissfully unaware of Madness' oeuvre. "I wasn't a fan at all before then," he admits. "I was into bebop jazz and classical music. I thought it was quirky postcard-humour pop and the chord progressions of tunes like 'Our House' made no sense to me. I had a really hard time learning the material for their tour dates as I couldn't see the logic in the writing and they had a lot of material in the show. Funny, looking back now I can see the brilliance and value of the whole thing. Their material is truly unique and that's rare in pop music, plus it is totally English."

Disley noticed a somewhat desultory mood within the Madness camp during rehearsals for the tour. "I went in totally prepared and knew every song backwards but there wasn't much enthusiasm among the Madness members," he admits. "Seems it was a low time for them. They referred to myself and the other session players as part-timers. At the start especially, they would be eating sandwiches, reading the paper. I was used to rehearsals where everyone worried about using the time effectively. Lee spent most of the time working out how they could get giant balloons ordered for the tour and how to fly on the Kirby wire above the crowd. He hardly played his sax and was mainly interested in the entertainment side. He was pissed off because he had rehearsed part of the show where he could run up to a small trampoline, do a forward somersault and land in front of the microphone, all playing the sax at the same time. They wouldn't allow him to do it in case he swallowed his mouthpiece!"

Terry eventually spent roughly a year touring with Madness. "I didn't really connect much with Suggs, he was always off somewhere," Disley continues. "I don't think we had a single conversation. Chas was my buddy. He used to talk wine and music with me and I found him the easiest one to hang with, along with Bedders, who was the one that kept everyone in check musically. He acted like the musical director and liaised between the session players and the hardcore band members. He was into jazz, too. Chrissy Boy was always being funny, and Woody was real nice and mellow, a real gentle and respectful soul."

Madness' world proved to be a culture shock for the pianist, though. "I remember the skinhead fans spitting on the tour bus windows after the show," he adds. "The guys told me this was a sign they had enjoyed the performance. We played to a lot of skinheads back then and that scared the hell out of me. Every night, they would climb up on the stage and get thrown back into the crowd. Once, in Cornwall, there were Hell's Angels and skinheads and some guy got stabbed. I'll never forget Suggs saying on the microphone, 'If anyone wants to fight, come and fight the band.' I was going to resign my keyboard position right then! The other keyboard player Seamus Beaghen fit in much better than I did. I had long hair and liked jazz, which didn't go over too well with the full-timers! [But] it was a great learning experience. I went in thinking just about the musical notes and came out understanding that the 'show' can be just as important – sometimes more so – and they did put 100 per cent into a fantastic show for the fans every night."

Madness also retained their backing singers for the tour: Jimmy's Helms and Thomas plus Lorenzo Johnson in place of Chambers. Luis Jardim's place was taken by Brazilian-born percussionist Bosco De Oliveira (who'd started the London School of Samba a year earlier, as well as recording with acclaimed 'new jazz' outfit Working Week). "We had such a ball on that tour," admits Jimmy Thomas. "That was a gas! So much fun! That's when I got to know them real good. They were lovely guys. My most intensive memory might have been Dublin. We checked into our hotel with those guys from Spandau Ballet. We hung out with them. Cathal, Suggs and both the Kemp brothers ended up in my room getting sizzled all night long. We were just drinking and talking shit, man! We rapped. It was fantastic!"

Undeterred by "health and safety" warnings, Thompson took along his a trampoline, prompting one of the road crew to spray the message "what is this – a tour or a circus?" on a dressing room wall in glitter paint. It's fair to say that the *Mad Not Mad* tour is not regarded as the band's best by many fans. Aside from a welcome return to The Miracles' Motown classic, 'Shop Around', resurrected from their days as The Invaders, the band seemed to lack that vital spark which had been such a trademark of their performances. Still, the tour wound its way inexorably through the major cities of England, Scotland and Wales. The dates were punctuated by a guest appearance from Suggs, Smyth and Thompson on the catwalk at the Rag Aid fashion show at the Royal Albert Hall (alias Fashion Aid), with all proceeds going to the Ethiopian Famine Appeal; and an appearance on *The Tube* on November 15. The tour finale consisted of two nights at the Hammersmith Odeon.

Support band on the tour were latter-day 2 Tone signings The Friday Club, a stylishly dressed seven-piece outfit from Scarborough with a penchant for updating Northern Soul. "This was the moment of a life-time, to be on the Madness tour and be on 2 Tone," singer/vibes player Adele Winter later enthused. "Suggs wore a green suit and red gloves for much of the tour and had a thing about asking the audience to look under their seats only to find nothing there – he loved it! As people, Madness were really friendly and supportive. Suggs, Cathal and Lee were always making sure things were all right for us and reminding us that they started their first tour staying in tents. They gave away tickets to kids for their concerts, especially in Ireland. After performing in Cork, I was out front watching them when Suggs announced he had been helped back to his hotel after some lads found him collapsed drunk outside a local radio station! Immediately, this lad of about ten said to me, 'That was us, miss!' It really tickled me . . . the same thing happened in Dublin!"

The Friday Club's main composer, singer and guitarist was Andy Brooks: "We got the slot on the tour because Jerry Dammers' manager (Pete Hadfield) had an office next to Madness' manager's office. He heard they were looking for a support act and suggested The Friday Club. We played a gig at the Marquee where Madness's tour manager checked us out and two weeks later, we were on the tour. I'm sure the fact we were a 2 Tone act influenced the decision: Jerry had signed us and produced our single ['Window Shopping']. Jerry turned up at a couple of gigs and it was clear to see how much respect the Madness guys still had for him. I have brilliant memories of the tour. Being down to earth, Madness treated us very well. Suggs was particularly friendly and Lee Thompson, too. They were aware we were staying in dodgy bed and breakfast places and we were invited back to their hotels for drinks many times, which always got messy. I have a particular memory of being in Lee's hotel room soaking wet after being in his shower fully dressed, stood on a table reading the fire instructions while he filmed me!"

Brooks appreciated the opportunity afforded The Friday Club by Madness. "They made sure we were given proper sound-check time and that the tour crew were supportive," he says. "We were aware that Madness had not toured for a couple of years and that this was their first album without Mike Barson, so there was a cloud over them, though if you saw them play in 1985 you wouldn't have guessed: they were brilliant live and the crowd reaction was amazing every night. The punters absolutely worshipped them! There was still quite a large skinhead following who at times were pretty hostile but for the most part the gigs were great for us. When the tour ended, I was totally gutted: I could have stayed forever!"

Following the tour, the band wrapped up the year with a handful of promotional performances. On November 26, they performed 'Burning The Boats' and 'Time' live on *Old Grey Whistle Test*. To help mark Finnish Independence Day, Madness were invited to the Finnish Embassy on December 6 followed by a show at the Helsinki Messukeskus (the capital's Exhibition and Convention Centre), promoted by the Ministry of Education. "When we played Helsinki, we had such a good time," says Jimmy Thomas. "It was snowing and cold and we had to leave about five in the morning because there was some blizzard coming, and if we didn't leave that early, we'd be snowed in."

On December 21, Madness hosted a Christmas party for the un-employed at the hastily-erected Finsbury Park Big Top, sharing the bill with the likes of Billy Bragg and Marc Almond and, as their special guest onstage, Ian Dury for performances of the old Kilburn & The High Roads' numbers 'Huffety Puff' and 'Rough Kids'. And on December 24/25, Madness returned for a further two nights at the Hammersmith Odeon, this time for a Mad Not Mad Party, wherein each member of the audience was asked to bring a toy to donate to children's charities. As an extension of their appearance on *Old Grey Whistle Test*, the recording was subsequently broadcast on TV and radio, a highlight of which was a rendi-tion of 'Listen To Your Father' with guest Feargal Sharkey.

A recording of the show was subsequently circulated as a promotional album, *Mad Not Mad Party*. "The first Hammersmith gig was remarkable," says Bosco De Oliveira, "because as we played this ballad, I could not see Lee onstage. The sax solo was imminent and still no Lee. Suddenly, I hear the sax and he comes in flying over the stage on a harness and a roadie pulling the other end of the rope to make him swing. Very funny guy!"

★ ★ ★

From the lyrics of 'One Better Day' to their latest singles 'Yesterday's Men' and 'Uncle Sam', Madness had engaged with a prevailing trend in certain quarters of pop music, whereby left-of-centre artists now openly expressed allegiance to the Labour Party – from artists with some history of supporting political causes, such as The Style Council, Billy Bragg and The Redskins, to pop acts like The Kane Gang and Bronski Beat/Communards. By late summer 1985, a loose aggregate of socialist-minded musicians including Madness had coalesced under the banner of Red Wedge, a press release for which was issued voicing the project's aims and ambitions:

"Red Wedge is the name of a whole host of musicians, actors, celebri-ties and assorted people, whose purpose is to bring left-wing ideas to other people. Set up by the Labour Party, it is a direct result of the wonderful Billy Bragg's Jobs And Industry tour of early this year. Red Wedge makes no bones of its intentions – we want the Tories OUT and a Socialist Government IN. Red Wedge is aimed at young people and hopefully carrying young people's aims. Action speaks louder, now get involved!"

Billy Bragg was fast emerging as the most potent political force British pop had ever witnessed. Fusing the aggression of punk and both the political tradition and one-man-band style of the folk movement, he sang about issues like civil rights, the right-wing press, the trade unions and the Falklands war in a plain-speaking style which won him many admirers. By 1985, he had already notched up two Top 30 albums, which were followed that year by two uncompromising hits, the *Between The Wars* EP and 'Days Like These'. On July 23, 1985, a meeting had been held at the Labour Party's South London HQ, where MPs, actors, journalists and pop stars – including Bragg and Weller – discussed how they could best promote left-wing issues. As a result, Red Wedge was born in September, with a loan of £3,000 from Labour and the National Union of Public Employees. The official media launch followed on November 21, 1985, with a dour assembly in the House Of Commons, which began with a speech from Labour leader Neil Kinnock. He announced with some satisfaction that a Red Wedge package would tour Britain early the following year.

The first Red Wedge tour of five or so concerts began on January 26, 1986 at the Manchester Apollo – although Madness didn't join until the third date of the tour at the Birmingham Odeon and only stayed for two days. Preceded by an open conversation with a variety of panellists, the concerts represented great value for money. For a small entrance fee, each show lasted well over two hours, which not only featured three core acts – The Style Council, Billy Bragg and The Communards – but a host of guest appearances. On various nights, audiences were treated to Jerry Dammers, Stephen Duffy, Junior, Lloyd Cole and Tom Robinson, plus members of Prefab Sprout, The Smiths, Working Week, the Kane Gang and Spandau Ballet.

Madness were represented by Suggs, Foreman, Bedford and Seamus Beaghen, since Thompson was away on holiday and Woodgate wasn't keen to participate. "We haven't got a drummer so we brought Ron with us," Suggs told audiences, by way of introducing a Roland drum machine. Their 20-minute set consisted of several new songs, from Smyth's solo unveiling of 'The Alligator Song' (the lyrics of which spoke of "loan sharks, drug abuse and abject poverty", according to Stuart Wright) to 'Perfect Place' and 'Winter In Wonderland', followed by the more familiar 'Yesterday's Men' and 'Madness'.

Live Aid had proved that, collectively, pop music *could* achieve a tremendously high profile. Despite Red Wedge's assurances that "we're not saying 'Vote Labour'", the party's direct involvement meant that the tours amounted to a travelling recruitment campaign – if not a fully blown party political broadcast. Leading pop musicians were, for the first time in Britain, advocating people to vote for an established political party at the next general election – or rather, vote to get rid of their rivals in power, which amounted to the same thing. But the effectiveness of the Red Wedge shows in raising their audiences' awareness of political issues was less certain. Labour politicians circulated in foyers and each punter arrived to find a brown paper bag on their seat, which contained a selection of pamphlets relating to such issues as the Anti-Apartheid Movement, unemployment among young people, CND and women's rights. A Red Wedge video was later issued; footage from the Newcastle City Hall concert was interspersed by interview clips explaining the reasons behind the project.

Red Wedge encountered considerable flack from various quarters. Conservatives were naturally dismissive. A more damaging swipe at Red Wedge came from within the ranks of the left-wing – albeit those whose hard-line views clashed with Kinnock's increasingly moderate position. Elvis Costello, for example, was sceptical about both the name and what he described as "the biggest badge you can wear", referring to Billy Bragg's lyric that "wearing badges is not enough in days like these". Discontentment about Red Wedge among the militant, hard-left was voiced by SWP (Socialist Workers Party) member and Redskins front man Chris Dean, alias *NME* writer X Moore, who described the project as a "very good but fanciful idea", before dismissing it as "a tidy way to sell out socialist principles in favour of electoral success for Kinnock".

Meanwhile, Virgin were desperate to drive sales for *Mad Not Mad*, which had not met with their expectations to date. In a disagreement which cruelly echoed earlier scenarios at Stiff, the label overturned the band's wish to opt for 'I'll Compete' as their next single, instead voting for 'The Sweetest Girl'. The video seemed quite straitlaced – although the director disagrees. "That's a bit more surreal, in some ways," suggests John Mills. "We shot it in an old pumping station near the start of the M3 somewhere. We used Jim Whiting, who did all the robots for the 'Rockit' video by Herbie Hancock. He made plaster casts of the band's faces and then made masks which we twisted so all their faces were distorted. I feel it suited the song."

After 'Rockit', 'The Sweetest Girl' was the only pop video to have benefited from the involvement of mechanical installation artist Whiting. "Madness came over to my house in Archway Road and they were great fun," he remembers. "John Mills wanted to interject the images subliminally which meant it didn't really get seen. But I made rubber heads of all the band members. It was quite interesting, at the beginning of special effects. When you squashed these heads between top and bottom, they looked as though they got older. So one band member squashed a rubber head while another would do the hands. We did them like this to the music and it was terrific because they were good puppeteers. John used my 'coat ride' which is this system of conveying bits across a space. And we had the animated woman's head, 'the sweetest girl', at the end." Despite such efforts, and band performances of the single on both *Top Of The Pops* and *Saturday Live*, the single stalled at number 35 following its release in February.

* * *

On Thursday March 6, 1986, Suggs probably wished he hadn't bothered getting out of bed. That is, after he'd read the headline of *The Sun* newspaper, which proclaimed – in big, bold letters – "Rock star's Nazi pal", alongside a sizeable photo of himself with Ian Stuart Donaldson, lead singer with fascist punk band Skrewdriver. It felt as if rumours of Suggs' nefarious past associations had returned to haunt him.

The story was accredited to Garry Bushell, previously a strong supporter of the band during his days as a journalist at *Sounds*. "*The Sun* printed a picture of Suggsy and Ian Stuart Donaldson purely to embarrass the Labour Party because Suggsy was part of the short-lived Red Wedge movement," explains Bushell. "The picture was supplied by former skins, former fans. Suggsy had been a roadie for Skrewdriver but this was back when the band had no political agenda – Janet Street-Porter featured Skrewdriver in her punk documentary for LWT. Ian didn't come out as a Nazi until 1983. Suggsy stayed in touch with him after he'd got involved with the National Front and Rock Against Communism. He didn't follow Jerry Dammers' advice about racist friends . . . I know the picture caused him huge embarrassment."

It was claimed that Suggs had given Donaldson money, helped him with Skrewdriver's recordings and sheltered him in the Madness singer's north London flat. While it was plausible that the two had been friends in the late 1970s, other claims were pure fallacy. Donaldson was serving a prison sentence at the time but later commented: "The article was just an attempt to blacken the name of Suggsy. We used to be mates, but we haven't seen each other for a few years and that's all there is to it. As far as I know, we're still on good terms. I've got nothing against the bloke."

Ironically, the Lancashire band had first recorded back in 1977 for Chiswick Records, the same label as multi-racial act Red Beans & Rice, who had been racially abused during that show at the Electric Ballroom in late 1979. Members of Skrewdriver had often dressed as skinheads (which might have been what attracted Suggs to them in the first place) but there was no inkling of the far-right political views for which Donaldson would later become infamous. The band were popular on the punk scene – and like Sham 69 and the Angelic Upstarts, they attracted a significant skin-head following.

By all accounts, one such fan was Suggsy, who had helped out at Skrewdriver gigs back in 1978 as an informal roadie. Whether Suggs, Smyth, Chalky and Toks were part of a 'North London Skinhead Elite' has never been substantiated – nor the suggestion that members of this crew appeared on the inner sleeve of *One Step Beyond*. It's also been claimed that Madness – perhaps when still The Invaders – occasionally borrowed equipment from Skrewdriver. But it should be reiterated that Skrewdriver never openly expressed any affiliation with far-right politics until Donaldson resurrected the band name in 1982.

"I went back down to London for a while and stayed at [Suggs'] mother's flat because he'd moved out and bought a house so I had his room," Donaldson claimed. "I was only there for about seven months . . . the picture was taken in his mum's front room." In due course, Donaldson landed a role as an extra in *Take It Or Leave It* (he played one of the skin-heads seen chasing Madness down an alleyway). "Because I didn't have much money at the time, they just got me on the film, that's all. I got the agency fee which was about £60 or something."

Needless to say, from Madness's perspective, such provocative tabloid coverage felt like a vindictive attack on both Suggs personally and the band politically. "That didn't go down too well," admits Jamie Spencer, by way of understatement. "We got a sniff from Virgin that there was going to be something about the band written by Bushell. It wasn't good news. If we called Bushell to ask what he was doing, it was going to make it perhaps bigger than it was. So let's see what happens and deal with it tomorrow. Then that night, just going to bed, they had tomorrow's papers. That caused a great deal of upset, especially as it was Garry Bushell, who should have known better. A nasty piece of work for doing that. He really shafted them because it was just unnecessary. It was cheap, tabloid shit and of no benefit other than they wanted to sell more papers."

Madness had been at pains to distance themselves from whatever minority had blighted some of their early shows. "They didn't want those people at their gigs," states Spencer. "It was fashionable for idiots who wanted to follow something but I was around then, as were a load of my mates, and we never wanted to encounter these goons. Pure stupidity if you want to get involved with a fascist organisation like that. No one that I knew who was around Madness ever did – nor wanted to. They weren't welcome."

★ ★ ★

On March 15, Madness performed at a televised event, Heartbeat City, a benefit concert in aid of a local children's hospital, again collaborating with UB40. But behind the scenes, rumours were spreading about dissent within the Madness camp. "I knew the writing was on the wall," suggests John Wynne. "Once they all had wives and kids and houses, they didn't want to go to work. They didn't want to tour. They weren't producing new stuff. Fair enough – they'd earned a lot of money. But you've got to stay in the public's perception. It was the wrong move, looking back on it, because they fell out of the eye-line."

John eventually confronted the issue of their declining workload. "I was talking to Chrissy one day," he remembers. "I said, 'This can't go on.' We were all on weekly wages, a company car and so on. They had loads of people in the office. Hector Walker, Debbie, Tamsin, Robbie Forrest. The cleaner was Lee's mother-in-law Pam! I said, 'You need to have a serious think about this.' They were planning to go to Australia and Matthew was going through the budget with me. I said, 'The money isn't there for three crew.' I knew it was coming to an end so I resigned. I didn't want to see the death throes."

Madness had been running their office/studio complex at 167 Caledonian Road while also paying their road crew a weekly wage despite a distinct lack of touring revenue. By mid-1986, something had to give. "The accountant advised us to close the office, the whole thing down," says Matthew Sztumpf. "You cannot afford to run it anymore, they said, because it was haemorrhaging money." That also meant laying off John Wynne, Rob Forrest and Ian "Toks" Tokins. "Jamie [Spencer] and I moved up to Liverpool Road into my own office to manage The Smiths and we also took on Swing Out Sister then Propaganda," adds Matthew.

"Quite suddenly, what seemed completely out of the blue, a load of people got laid off," recalls Hector Walker. "I remember being in the office and people were in tears. It was bloody awful. Then we went off on that tour, some gigs in Europe, then Australia then America, then festivals around Europe. And then that was it. Nothing was said. And nothing was said about work for everyone. It just fizzled out, really."

From the outside looking in, the picture still seemed rosy. Madness were busy out on the road with three dates on the Continent (Belgium, France, with Terry Disley and Seamus Beaghen sharing keyboards duties) from April 4 to 6, in preparation for that gruelling, month-long jaunt around Australia, beginning April 18. While the tour was uneventful, for the most part, it was clear to the band that their popularity had waned. In Melbourne, for example, they performed at The Palace, in the shadow of their previous venue, the considerably roomier Festival Hall. That said, Foreman's affable account of their trip 'down under' suggested that Madness really appreciated some of their shows in the outback, away from the glare of the media. "The reason is that the people are, as we say, 'out in the sticks' and therefore have no pretensions as to getting down and boogieing," he wrote in *Nutty Boys*.

The band then flew directly from Australia to the USA on May 13 for a handful of shows on the east and west coasts – San Francisco, Los Angeles, San Diego, Boston, Philadelphia and New York City, where they played two nights at The World Club. Apparently, the venue's owner was an eccentric character who had all the hallmarks of a troubled Vietnam veteran. On their first night there, the owner insisted on introducing the band but spectacularly failed to stir up any enthusiasm from their audience. As a result, Thompson was sent onstage the following evening to provoke some enthusiasm from the waiting crowd. Some months later, Foreman spotted the self-same club owner outside London's fashionable Wag Club, screaming "but I own the world"!

Ever impetuous, Thompson had created an off-shoot band The Argonauts, who recorded cover versions of The Kinks' 'Apeman' and The Rolling Stones' 'Under My Thumb' at Liquidator for a 7-inch sold exclusively through MIS. The band consisted of the ubiquitous Tom Morley (Lynn drum), veteran organist Mick Weaver (whose reputation was founded with late Sixties club band Wynder K. Frog; he'd also been thanked on *Mad Not Mad*) on piano, Good Godfrey (banjo), John Marshall (guitar) and Chrissie Stewart (bass).

On June 17, Madness played at a festival in Reykjavic. Three days later, they performed a benefit concert at London's Brixton Academy to raise funds for Artists Against Apartheid, the British wing of which had been launched that April by Jerry Dammers and Dali Tambo, the son of African National Congress president Oliver Tambo, to campaign for the cultural boycotting of South Africa until apartheid had been lifted. Also on the bill were Working Week, new ska band Potato 5 and reggae artists Tippa Irie and Pato Banton. Dammers had long supported this cause (most vocally with The Special A.K.A. anthem, 'Free Nelson Mandela', in 1984) and wrote a half-page letter in *Nutty Boys* to publicise various activities.

One such event which The Specials' leader then organised was an ambitious, eight-hour Freedom Festival on south London's Clapham Common on June 28. The show attracted an estimated quarter-of-a-million people with a stellar cast which included Hugh Masekela, Elvis Costello, Billy Bragg, Sting, Boy George, Sade, Peter Gabriel and Gil Scott-Heron – whose 'Johannesburg', earlier namedropped in Madness' song 'Coldest Day', was performed by both Scott-Heron and The Style Council.

On June 22, Madness played their first Glastonbury Festival on a bill shared with The Cure, Simply Red, The Housemartins (a band who were patently influenced by Suggs & Co.), The Waterboys and The Pogues, before travelling to Holland for Parkpop on June 29 and back to Hartlepool for their Dock Rock Festival on July 4. The following day, Madness played the Roskilde Festival in Denmark alongside such acts as The Cult and Giant Sand. Little did the thousands of spectators realise that this would be Madness' last show for six years.

Nevertheless, recent concerts had road-tested a number of new songs – not only 'Samantha' and '4BF', which had been aired during the *Mad Not Mad* tour, but 'Precious One', 'Be Good Boy' and 'Natural Act'. So far as recording these and other new songs was concerned, the plan was to prepare a Madness single for release in August with an album to follow. A lengthy period of rehearsing and writing began that summer in Liquidator but the sessions proved even more dysfunctional than those for *Mad Not Mad*. Around a dozen tracks were trialed but dissent and bad feeling swiftly spread between band members.

Eventually, out of desperation, the band decided to drop Langer and Winstanley – a huge wrench given their umbilical relationship with Madness dating back to their very first sessions in 1979. There was talk of new blood such as Stuart Levine (who'd worked with the likes of Simply Red) because "the band felt they were getting stale and needed a new direction and some fresh ideas". The summer 1986 edition of *Nutty Boys* spoke optimistically of their immediate priorities: "The pencilled in plan for the next three months is to record one single in early August for release in October and carry on to record (also in August) at least a 10-track LP."

While progress in the studio was stymied by squabbles and differences of opinion, their indecision clearly extended to the forthcoming album's packaging because a competition was held for MIS fan club members to design a cover. Set in a graveyard, the winning entry had a gothic quality, to say the least. While Madness might not have felt any affinity with the goth rock scene of the period (The Mission, the Sisters Of Mercy et al), they did seem to be nurturing a fascination with old-fashioned, Victorian-era ghost stories, a concept which would later contribute to *The Liberty Of Norton Folgate*. Madness might also have had a sneaking affection for 'Grimly Fiendish', the decidedly gothic 1985 hit from The Damned which hinted that the old punks had been sneaking a listen to the Nutty Boys' latest endeavours.

"I remember Lee coming up with a different concept," Madness sleeve designer Paul Clewley later explained, "which would have involved the band being photographed sitting in front of a blazing fire in a large, dark and gloomy room. The only illumination was to be the flames with the shot being taken from the actual fireplace, looking through the flames out at the band's faces. I think the idea was that they were telling ghost stories to each other."

Unfortunately, sessions dragged into September before the sextet finally realised that relations had completely broken down with the band – and that the album was to be stillborn. Later that month, a press release was issued announcing the end of Madness.

* * *

"Bedders, myself and Seamus were working really hard, concentrating on the songs," Woodgate later explained. "We'd get together what we thought would be the right rhythm section, or the right feel or beat. And one by one, the rest of the band would come in and go, like Harry Enfield, 'You don't wanna do it like this, you wanna do it like that'! It was just this constant battle. We found ourselves being left more alone, and eventually we got summoned upstairs and there was this meeting, and it was like the rest of them had all sat down together and, allegedly, said we've had enough, let's call it a day. Mark and I knew this was coming, because it wasn't fun anymore, it just wasn't happening. It's sad, because we knew what they needed to do. The four of them needed to go off and do their own thing."

Suggs recalled his sense of indecision – of being pulled in different directions: "We'd all just got slightly different ideas then about what we should do. Chris, I think, and Lee maybe, just wanted to get on with it in the studio – because we had a studio which we didn't use half enough. Cathal had different ideas everyday, about either getting a band and playing or doing it with machines. I wasn't sure myself what we should do. I didn't have a clear enough idea where we were going, I didn't feel strong enough to lead in any direction but I didn't feel like I wanted to go in the direction that anyone else who was still in the band wanted to go. So that was it."

One final epitaph was salvaged from those final 'Clanger/Winstanley' sessions: '(Waiting For) The Ghost-Train' was chosen as their farewell single, issued on October 27. Written by Suggs about the issue of apartheid in South Africa, the song boasted all the hallmarks of classic Madness, from its jaunty rhythm to its clever wordplay and a rousing chorus, "It's black and white/Don't try to hide it". Sensing the end of an era, they'd picked up the phone to Mike Barson, who'd flown over to play on the recording (although he was absent from the accompanying video). Tellingly, Barson stood at the front of their not-so-nutty train on the dramatic sleeve photo, which seemed to depict the band walking into the oblivion of mist and steam surrounding the 'ghost-train' in question. On the rear sleeve, seven sensible-looking young men were seen walking away down a platform. Only one of them had turned to smile and wave, holdall in hand – and there were no prizes for guessing it was Lee Thompson.

"It was difficult because I knew it was their last one," admits John Mills. "What do you do for the last Madness video? I think Mike was meant to turn up but he didn't. We thought we'd do the flying properly so we got a skydiver to jump out with a saxophone and play the sax solo. And then we had them all on a conveyer belt at Mornington Crescent Station. I remember editing that and thinking, I don't know how to end it. We just did this rough and ready bit of polystyrene with 'The End' which worked OK." Their final *Top Of The Pops* appearance (for the time being, at least) was broadcast on November 13. Replicating the message which closed the video, Foreman and Bedford finished by revealing the back of their instruments displaying "The End".

Sales might have been modest (the single peaked at number 18) but '(Waiting For) The Ghost-Train' offered Madness a dignified exit. The B-side, 'Maybe In Another Life', hinted at whatever (musical) problems they had encountered in recent months. Sung by Thompson and produced at Liquidator with engineers Ian Horne and Mark Saunders, its antiseptic atmosphere sounded gutless and artificial – a would-be middle-of-the-road soundtrack for the many wine bars springing up around the country. The world-weary lyrics were more substantial, dealing with death and the issue of a possible after-life. Bearing in mind Madness's subsequent resurrection, it's tempting to offer retrospective substance to such sentiments as "Maybe in another life/Who can say?" The 12-inch edition added a 'megamix' of Madness' hits entitled 'Seven Year Scratch'. Had anyone else noticed they'd chosen to bow out after seven years?

"They went on for such a long time and we had so much fun working on them," Langer later enthused. "We had a lot of hits together and became so comfortable working as a team that it was always really enjoyable being in the studio with them. When you work with a band for that length of time, you're bound to end up close friends. I used to hang out with them more than Alan did, because I lived near them in north London. For a while I was even living in the same house as Suggs!"

"One thing about Madness was they were always very respectful," adds Ian Wright. "They made sure you got your money. If you saw them in the street, they would be completely friendly. I always thought Madness were special and yet sometimes, in retrospect, The Specials got all the accolades, probably because of Jerry Dammers. When *Mad Not Mad* was out, I remember feeling sad that these boys don't fit into this pop world at the moment. I wonder what's going to happen to them? They want to move on and a lot of their stronger songs were melancholic and they didn't want to be nutty. Having visually embraced the video revolution, their videos still stand up and have a wonderful, homemade quality to them. They were the natural successor to everything they were influenced by. They were the perfect British pop band."

Matthew Sztumpf admits that the split might well have been inevitable: "The sum of the parts was greater than the individuals. As great as it was to have Paul Carrack come and tour with us, it was never Madness again in the way it was when they were a gang. It always seemed to me that, once they learnt their instruments, the songwriting got more complex and consequently less poppy. They were growing up and it was more adult but consequently less commercial. Sales were definitely on the decline."

"We were so young, and we couldn't go on forever," Suggs commented in 1994. "We had our own families, I had my own kids. We had to take a step back. It's difficult to keep that kind of thing going. We couldn't go on in that wacky madcap 24-hour-a-day existence."

* * *

Although the rest of Madness' 1986 sessions have never been officially released, they continue to be the subject of conjecture among their fans, fuelled by subsequent investigation. An early working version of '(Waiting For) The Ghost-Train' was given away as a flexidisc to fan club members – but what of the other songs? Many of the titles had been detailed in *Nutty Boys*. A number of the compositions were later reworked for the 1988 album *The Madness* and its accompanying B-sides: '11th Hour', 'Be Good Boy', 'Gabriel's Horn', 'Song In Red', '4BF' (alias 'For Bryan Ferry', their tribute to Roxy Music's front-man), the semi-instrumental 'Patience', 'Winter In Wonderland' (reworked as 'In Wonder') and 'Remember The Day' (which evolved into 'Nightmare, Nightmare').

The lyrics to another composition, 'Ghost Of Reverend Greene', were reproduced in *Nutty Boys*, reinforcing the proposed gothic theme of the album's packaging. It's unknown whether other songs which had occasionally been performed onstage, namely 'The Alligator Song' and 'Natural Act', were ever laid down in the studio. Foreman's 'Precious One', for example, wasn't unveiled until its inclusion on a single reissue of 'My Girl' in 1992 while the same year's 'House Of Fun' re-release boasted a demo of 'Gabriel's Horn'. 'It's For The Best' and the Kinks-like 'Perfect Place' were later made available by the band to download.

Behind the scenes, the plight of Madness's finances had sadly mirrored relationships within the band. Up until the period when Stiff had been sold to Island and the Madness's relationship with Dave Robinson had slowly but inexorably splintered, the issue of the band's coffers had never caused problems – at least, not outside of their inner sanctum. But the combination of their declining record sales and the prohibitive cost of both producing *Mad Not Mad* and funding such a large entourage on the road had swallowed the initial advance paid by Virgin.

Virgin Records were faced with a problem, too: here was their major investment vanishing into thin air. The company responded in traditional fashion by consolidating their losses with a new 'greatest hits' package, *Utter Madness*, issued in late November (and once again accompanied by a companion video with especially created links). Picking up where *Complete Madness* left off, this Zarjazz-branded album compiled all of the band's singles from 'Our House' through to '(Waiting For) The Ghost-Train' and issued on album, CD and a video. Its cover design stole the Nutty Train pose of the band in paper suits from the 'Ghost-Train' video, having scrapped the more novel idea to re-enact the pose for *One Step Beyond* some seven years on, echoing The Beatles' shots on *1962–1966* and *1967–1970*. But *Utter Madness* only scraped to number 29 in the charts and was out of the listings by Christmas, a damning indictment that the band's star was firmly in the descendent.

Jon Webster suspects the Virgin deal was never predicated purely on Madness's future recordings. "I think we did it because we always knew we had the fallback of the catalogue," he admits. "I'm not saying we didn't want to make *Mad Not Mad* a hit. But in financial terms, whatever happened to the new album didn't matter. I think that was just a business decision that was made."

Chapter 16

MADNESS – NOT MADNESS

A PECULIAR feeling of anti-climax often descends in the immediate period following the demise of a major pop act. So it was with Madness, except that attentions were focused on rumours that four members of the band were planning to reconvene. The final issue of the *Nutty Boys* fan club comic confirmed that Suggs, Smyth, Foreman and Thompson were working together. That said, their one-time dancer and MC was probably spending more time at home after the birth of his first child Cathal Caspar C. Smyth in October 1986 to long-time girlfriend Jo Brown (the couple had met back in 1978).

With *Mad Not Mad*, Virgin had left Madness to their own devices. Now Head of A&R Jeremy Lascelles was charged with supervising what was patently a much greater challenge. "They were venturing into the unknown," he admits. "When Woody and Mark had left, the rest were trying to re-group. They were going to change their name completely. We went through probably a hundred different names. None of them lasted. We went round the houses. They'd decided it was time to shake off the mantle of the Nutty Boys, which was why we all agreed a new name was a good idea. Part of me felt this is an exciting time for them to reinvent themselves and come up with a new direction and not be so fettered by their past. I relished the opportunity of working with them, trying to find that new direction. They'd had such an unblemished career up to that point when things went bumpy. It's not the most unusual thing to happen when people have been together in close proximity for a long period, starting when they were really young. People grow up and start to diversify. Cathal was the most prolific, the strongest force creatively. He was coming up with a lot of interesting ideas."

In an interview in *NME*, Cathal spoke of plans to perform under the banner of The Wasp Factory, a name taken from the title of the best-selling novel by Iain Banks which he'd read. However, when it emerged that there was another band using that name, other monikers were considered – including The One, More and The Earthmen. Radio 1 listeners were even asked for suggestions. Eventually, after much prevarication, the band settled on 'The Madness'. "Only after the album was finished, and we couldn't come up with a name, we went back," recalls Lascelles. "It was a tortuous, prolonged debate and ended up with a not very imaginative solution!"

When the quartet set to work at the Liquidator studio in 1987, several tracks were exhumed from those aborted final Madness sessions from the previous year. A collective decision was made to dispense with the production team of Langer and Winstanley – if only to mark out some differences between the new act, with the definite article, and its predecessor. Lacking a rhythm section or permanent keyboard player, the foursome called upon a variety of old friends to help out. Seamus Beaghen contributed to four tracks; UB40's Earl Falconer played bass on three. Steve Nieve also played keyboards; and he brought along his bass-playing sidekick from Elvis Costello & The Attractions, Bruce Thomas. Elvis himself also attended. Jerry Dammers tickled the ivories on a couple of numbers while the horn section from ska band Potato 5 also helped out. A drum machine was used throughout the sessions. Real drums were only played on one track, 'What's That', its jazz stylings benefiting from rock veteran Simon Phillips on the brushes. ("We only spent one day recording," says Simon. "Suggs made me laugh an awful lot and they were all really cool.")

Foreman explained their dilemma to *Madzine* in 1990: "Every year, [Virgin would] give us a colossal amount of money. Out of that, we'd have to make an album, pay ourselves wages and pay people who worked for us and it was working out that the money they gave us was less than the album was costing to make." As Thompson, put it, "we were slowly sinking under, clutching at straws, the albums were starting to cost an extortionate amount and they weren't quite capturing the mood they used to have." Only the Liquidator studio was retained. Zarjazz, too, was consigned to history so The Madness merely reverted to the parent label Virgin on re-signing with the company some time in 1987.

★   ★   ★

After protracted sessions, the new-look four-piece was unveiled to the world on February 25, 1988 with a new single, 'I Pronounce You'. Co-written by Thompson and Smyth (and the mysterious West), the song's faintly Hispanic feel was reminiscent of the Sixties pop classic 'Concrete And Clay' by Unit 4 + 2. 'I Pronounce You' built slowly to a pleasing, anthemic chorus via some electric sitar – but maybe too slowly. Either way, the single met with apparent indifference from both the media and the public, stalling at a modest number 44. This was despite an appearance on Channel 4's popular show *Friday Night Live*, on which they performed both the single and 'Beat The Bride' (bizarrely, another new song with a marriage-related theme). Old friend John Hasler sat in on drums; he was also seen in the accompanying promotional video, a desultory affair which only reinforced the contrast with their past glories.

The Madness' self-titled album followed on April 23. Reviewers were roundly dismissive, baffled by a concept which was neither one thing nor the other. Was this actually a "new" Madness? If so, why "The"? The album was produced by "The Three Eyes" (i.e. the band) while being engineered and co-produced by Steve 'Barney' Chase, with mixing courtesy of American hired gun Michael H. Brauer. Both have subsequently built up impressive CVs for their respective roles in the music industry – but it's understandable that they lacked the same chemistry as Langer and Winstanley had developed with the band.

Foreman later admitted there had been problems. "We were pretty depressed and split and then reformed as The Madness," he explained in *Madzine*. "We worked all the songs out here [at Liquidator], upstairs on the top floor and we said, 'We're gonna produce it ourselves, we're recording in our own studios, it'll be really cheap!' Then we ran into difficulties. It was like, 'I want so-and-so to mix it', and we spent a fortune in the studio because the engineer had a week mixing it at about – what – a grand a day?"

It's difficult to listen to *The Madness* with fresh ears because its production was so heavily influenced by the prevailing trend for programmed rhythm tracks and a 'digital' sound. The spectre of Trevor Horn's era-defining work at ZTT loomed over many of the songs. Too often, the project sounded as if it fell between two stools: neither did it boast any of the endearing Madness trademarks nor did it forge an altogether different musical identity. Closer inspection revealed the degree to which the project was driven by Cathal Smyth, who wrote half of the 10 songs and co-wrote a further three.

Smyth's opener, 'Nail Down The Days', was promising. Lines like "I was lost in my childhood feeling lonely" and "I was born an immigrant to this city" spoke of his Irish roots and itinerant upbringing – but such sentiments were smothered beneath a hail of aggressive drum patterns and sassy, percussive horns. Of Cathal's other compositions, 'Oh' was pure ZTT (with shades of both Art Of Noise and Grace Jones' *Slave To The Rhythm*). Ambitious finale 'Gabriel's Horn' was atmospheric but messy funk rock although Jeremy Lascelles has fond memories: "It was really experimental and avant garde, quite long and out there, groundbreaking, and I was proud of whatever involvement I had with that track." More satisfactory was 'Song In Red', a welcome return to traditional guitar/bass/drums/piano to underpin a heartfelt paean to a lost loved one, while echoing Matt Johnson's work as The The.

'I Wonder' (with its Middle Eastern hint) and 'Nightmare, Nightmare' (harking back to their past with an endearing reggae beat and some eerie, 'Ghost Town'-like keyboards) were Suggs' tentative stabs at solo songwriting. With no disrespect meant to Smyth's vocal capabilities, Suggs' vocals had the familiar appeal of an old friend amidst the somewhat alienating music; and his dulcet tones help lift 'Thunder And Lightning', his Motown-influenced co-composition with Foreman, out of the mire. Best of the bad bunch, though, was 'Beat The Bride', a Thompson/Smyth-penned reggae tune with some nice call-and-response vocals and a charming if somewhat weak melody – it felt like this album's 'Uncle Sam'.

"I was really into 'Nightmare, Nightmare' and 'Beat The Bride'," Foreman later commented. "'Nightmare' was a song we done [with] Mark and Woody but it got totally changed because it was an African type thing, sort of bubbly. I really didn't like it so I worked the chords out like a reggae song, Suggs wrote some different lyrics and so it came out different."

The geometric sleeve design for the album and accompanying singles utilised a distinctive if anonymous-looking style of bold, symmetrical shapes arranged to resemble human faces. The novel concept was created by two noted comic book illustrators: Dave Gibbons and Rian Hughes. "I'd been drawing comic books since the Seventies," says Gibbons. "In the mid-1980s, I drew a comic book called *Watchmen*, written by Alan Moore, and it was heavy on symbolism. The smiley face with the splash of blood on it was symbolic of the ultimate cartoon being besmirched by cruel reality. We used radiation and atomic symbols. *Watchmen* became quite celebrated because of that. Before that, I drew a character called Rogue Trooper for *2000AD* and came up with symbols to indicate the different sides of this war, which became an iconic part of that world."

Published across 1986 and 1987, *Watchmen* had blazed a trail through comic book circles. Alan Moore's creation inspired many rock and pop acts, most famously Pop Will Eat Itself in the song 'Def.Con.One' (and it's subsequently been adapted as a Hollywood blockbuster). Famously devotees of *2000AD*, the band were also keen on *Watchmen*. "I got a phone call from Chris Foreman," continues Gibbons, "and I'd always been a great fan of Madness. He thought that something like these symbolic faces I'd put into *Watchmen* could be part of the design of their album. I met up with Chris in Caledonian Road at their offices. Suggs was there. They talked about what they wanted – toxic warning symbols for hazardous chemicals or fire risks. Chris was quite taciturn but with a clear idea of what he wanted. Suggs struck me as friendly, just as I'd seen him on the TV. They were very open to ideas. They were completely un-rock star like, just a crowd of blokes."

Each song would be represented by a separate face-like schematic. "I did loads of sketches," Dave explains, "and I came up with this idea of a square symbol, which was the format of an album or single sleeve, that incorporated a full-face view and a profile view as well. They liked my vision. It was quite challenging but, creatively speaking, I always like a restriction – the fact they all had to be square, with representations of some kind of face, and also needed to tie in with the theme of each song, with elements like lightning bolts for eyebrows." Gibbons interpreted the lyrics of 'I Pronounce You' as relating to arranged marriages, for example, "so I did these Indian or Asian style minarets as part of the face".

In due course, The Madness presented their ideas to the record company. "I remember going over to Virgin Records with my portfolio. Before the meeting, they took me into the stock room and said, 'Have whatever you want!' They'd already warned me to bring a swag bag which I stuffed with CDs. It was generous of them to get Virgin to provide me with all this music! They seemed to know the woman in the stock room very well! When we walked into the art director's office, I remember Suggs saying, 'This is Dave, he's a new member of the band.' I felt like one of the boys! Although I hardly knew them, there was a sense of camaraderie and I was now in the team. This guy wasn't very receptive to the whole idea but I stood my corner and they backed me up and we got the go-ahead. They were absolutely supportive and weren't going to be pushed around by the record company. And I remember being quite happy with the fee we got."

Typically, Gibbons created pen-and-ink drawings whereas this project also required wider graphic design skills. "I enlisted the help of a friend of mine, Rian Hughes, because I knew this artwork had to have a lot of typographical elements, pin sharp. Rian's a wonderful typographer who helped me with the technical end. He was able to complete the mechanicals. We also played around with different colours – like warning symbols, you get bright red or yellow." On the resulting sleeves, the pair name-checked "the Veidt Method" on their artwork, a reference to the character of Adrian Veidt (Ozymandias) in *Watchmen*.

Sales of the album were dismal (it only reached number 65 in the charts), which wasn't helped by the lack of any tour. Out of desperation, Virgin opted for another single but instead of the obvious choice, 'Beat The Bride', they chose Smyth's decidedly downbeat 'What's That'. While the song's smoky, late night jazz feel, Simon Phillips' deft jazz brushes and a pleasant, Barson-like piano bridge offered some welcome solace from the album's otherwise harsh climate, it had no discernable hook or chorus. It sank without trace, although the company had hardly shown much faith because they'd even refrained from the expense of a video.

"Which was a massive insult," Foreman later bemoaned. "We were going to write them a letter. We just thought, we'll do another album, that's what they like – bounce back. They said, 'Unless you play us some new songs within a month, we're not going pick up your option!' So we thought, great! We owe all that money. They've got our back stuff which, if they had any sense, they'd be promoting and recouping some of their money. We started working on some new songs and we were arguing. Suggs and myself wanted to use technology to its fullest, Cathal wanted a live band and Lee had gone skiing! It was really bad and Suggs said, 'I've had enough, I want to try and earn some money.'"

In due course, Virgin quietly passed up the option for The Madness to record a follow-up album and the band, such as it was, had ceased to exist by the end of 1988. "Clearly, what emerged once the *Mad Not Mad* record was out, was a real schism in the ranks," observes Jeremy Lascelles. "It particularly emerged in the making of the record by The Madness. Woody and Mark had left. That's when they went into 'we're bored with being the Nutty Boys', which had clearly been bubbling under the surface." Although Madness' disintegration was disappointing for Virgin, Lascelles had been impressed by certain individuals.

"We've got some pretty serious, intelligent thinking artists here," he remembers, "particularly Cathal who, in that period, really emerged as a driving, creative force. He was coming up with the most songs and some challenging, different concepts. He had the creative vision and determination to move away from what everyone remembered and loved Madness for. The 'Nutty Boy' good-time band was the cause of their success but also the shackles around their ankles for most of their career. That period was when they were trying to be taken more seriously as thinking songwriters. And I think The Madness record was pretty damn good but overlooked at the time because it wasn't what people wanted."

Lascelles wonders if it was just the case that their time was up. "The whole music industry is cyclical, and they'd come to the end of a prolonged period where they'd ridden the wave of success and now the stars were not aligned for them," he suggests. "It's not as if people suddenly went, oh my God, you suck! They just didn't need any more [records] and didn't really want them to be the mature, thinking, thoughtful artist they were becoming. I don't know if calling them anything different, as opposed to The Madness or even just sticking with Madness, would have made any difference. They didn't feel like a complete, united, happy camp so it wasn't a huge surprise. We quite possibly didn't do a very good job at re-positioning them in an overall marketing sense. It was a little confused."

"As we decided to knock it on the head, Lee, Chris, Cathal and Suggs said that they would make another record because all the songs were there," Bedford later explained. "When we broke up, we had a whole album worth of songs demoed and a few of them went on 'The Madness' album. The Madness lost a hell of a lot of money because the album cost a hell of a lot to make. They spent ages doing it."

Thereafter, family life took over for some: Barson's first of three children to Sandra, Jamie, was born in August 1989. Suggs later admitted that the late 1980s were a troubling time for him – not only professionally but emotionally. According to an interview with *The Independent* in 1997, Suggs had a minor breakdown which he referred to somewhat bluntly as "a time when I just felt very fucked-up". It was enough to drive him, against his better nature, to a psychiatrist, who said that in order for him to come to terms with not being in Madness any more, he would have to confront other issues, too. In particular, he might want to think about his childhood when he was plain Graham McPherson. To accept himself now, he was advised, he would have to accept himself as he was then, too.

★   ★   ★

Meanwhile, Bedford and Woodgate had kept busy. In September 1986, Bedford answered a call from Blockhead Mickey Gallagher to tour Japan, alongside other members of Dury's band, as backing musicians for 'The Japanese Cliff Richard', Kiyoshiro Imawano. Bedford also played on Imawano's version of Ben E. King's 'Stand By Me', issued as a B-side in 1987.

In late 1986, Madness' ex-rhythm section were intrigued by a new band they'd seen at The Bull & Gate, Kentish Town. Voice Of The Beehive were fronted by two American sisters, Tracey Bryn and Melissa Brooke Belland. Inspired by such British institutions as The Kinks and The Beatles, as well more modern, female-fronted acts like The Pretenders and Bow Wow Wow, Bryn had travelled to London and had become embroiled in its thriving indie/band scene, eventually joining The Love Bombs. When they disbanded, Bryn invited Melissa to the UK and the pair were soon hanging out with members of My Bloody Valentine, Gaye Bykers On Acid, Zodiac Mindwarp & The Love Reaction and Bill Drummond (whose debut album *The Man* featured Bryn on backing vocals, credited as Voice Of The Beehives).

In due course, the sisters hooked up with Welsh guitarist and studio owner Mike Jones but the band struggled to settle on a particular bassist or drummer. When Bedford and Woodgate approached them via the mutual acquaintance of their manager, with a view to playing some shows with them, Voice Of The Beehive agreed. They also accepted an offer from independent label Food Records, run by Andy Ross and ex-Teardrop

Explodes keyboardist David Balfe (an old friend/colleague of both Clive Langer and Bill Drummond).

On January 28, 1987, Voice Of The Beehive played at the ICA Rock Week, a series of concerts at London's Institute of Contemporary Arts to showcase independent labels and their new acts. A condition of EMI's sponsorship was that every band had to contribute tracks to two spin-off compilation albums, *On The Dotted Line (Here)* and *On The Dotted Line (There)*. Mark Bedford then left the band, returning to the London College Of Printing to study; he was replaced by Martin Brett. Voice Of The Beehive's debut single, 'Just A City', was issued on Food in March 1987. Although the recording boasted the ex-Madness rhythm section, everyone wished to downplay the connection: the pair were merely thanked on the sleeve, absent from both the listed band line-up and the accompanying photo.

Healthy sales of the single led to a deal with PolyGram imprint London Records – with Balfe in tow as the band's manager. 'Just A City' was immediately re-released in April, pre-empting several months spent on the road, touring with such acts as Boys Wonder and The Proclaimers. In October, London released Voice Of The Beehive's next single, 'I Say Nothing', prompting complaints from the BBC over the lines "She says I get it every night" and "He'll rip you right in two." Despite re-recording these offending lyrics, the band could only watch as the single flopped.

Their third single, 'I Walk The Earth', was helped on its release in February 1988 by an imaginative, Madness-like video by Cure veteran Tim Pope, in which the girls bounced around a room filled with clothes while the boys played their instruments in what turned out to be a giant suitcase. That May, 'Don't Call Me Baby' (a sarcastic message which took its title from a line uttered by Ann-Margret to Elvis Presley in *Viva Las Vegas*) finally gave Voice Of The Beehive a Top 20 hit. A month later, their debut album *Let It Bee* sold equally well, offering a colourful palette of Sixties-tinged power pop in a style not dissimilar to that of American all-girl band The Bangles, prompting a more successful reissue of 'I Say Nothing'.

"I think Woody may have had a point to prove to the other guys in Madness," suggested Martin Brett to Madness Central. "Don't forget Woody had seven Top 20 hits with Voice Of The Beehive which, after being sacked from Madness, must have been quite satisfying." And did

Woodgate's presence help the band's cause? "It helped a lot in the UK but Voice Of The Beehive were so different it sort of cancelled itself out," Brett commented.

Tracey was dating singer Steve Mack from post-Undertones band That Petrol Emotion so the two bands arranged a double bill tour of the USA for early 1989. Although the subsequent dates were met with enthusiasm from American audiences, the band eventually returned to Britain in a state of complete exhaustion. Excepting a few sporadic appearances, nothing was heard from Voice Of The Beehive again until early 1991. At this point, relations between label and band began to sour.

After a respectable Top 20 placing for a new single, 'Monsters And Angels' in July 1991, London persuaded them to go with a remix of a Partridge Family song, 'I Think I Love You', and while the resulting album *Honey Lingers* (with its provocatively-rhyming name) also reached the Top 20, London's interference (courtesy of no less than seven producers) caused severe acrimony. By spring 1992, London and Voice Of The Beehive parted company and a support slot on tour with Crowded House didn't live up to expectations. By the end of that year, with commitments elsewhere, Woodgate left the band, who limped on for a few more years before finally disbanding in 1996.

★ ★ ★

Aside from his college course, Bedford's departure from Voice Of The Beehive had been predicated by his involvement with another new act, which he was assembling with ex-Higsons saxophonist Terry Edwards. Born in Hornchurch, Essex on August 10, 1960, Edwards was a multi-instrumentalist who had learnt both trumpet and piano at school before switching his curiosity to guitar aged 13. But he found his muse when given a saxophone for his 18th birthday. Like Lee Thompson, Edwards was a huge fan of Ian Dury's saxophonist Davey Payne. Terry joined what would become The Higsons at the University of East Anglia in Norwich, which he attended from 1979 to 1982; by the time he graduated with a degree in music, The Higsons were regularly troubling both John Peel's radio show and the indie charts via a string of singles on their own Waap label. That year, they signed to an ailing 2 Tone label for two singles – but found themselves back on Waap by 1983.

A deal with Upright Records in 1984 led to their sole album, *The Curse*

Of The Higsons, but after a couple more singles on different labels, The Higsons went their separate ways in 1986. Although he was blissfully unaware of it at the time, Madness had, according to Edwards, "seen The Higsons when our manager was trying to get us signed to Zarjazz, but wisely passed on it as they could see the writing writ large on the wall for us which we were totally oblivious to". Singer Charlie Higson later made his name as a comedy writer for the likes of Harry Enfield and Vic Reeves before writing and starring alongside Paul Whitehouse in *The Fast Show*. While The Higsons had plied an affectionately quirky style which mixed post-punk energy and funk rhythms with tongue-in-cheek lyrics, Edwards had created a spin-off act more strongly rooted in black American music and his long-held passion for the work of jazz/R&B alto saxophonist Earl Bostic.

"I had written some instrumental tunes and had created a band called New York New York as a Higsons side-project," explains Terry. "From 1983 to 1985, we released a 7-inch, a 12-inch EP and an album of guitar-based rhythm & blues, but without a guitar. By the time The Higsons had split up, I had some more tunes and a better idea of how to get them across. This hinged on having a double bass, but I knew no one who played it." Ex-Higsons guitarist Dave Cummings, who was now playing with Lloyd Cole & The Commotions, came to the rescue. "Bedders had played upright bass on Robert Wyatt's 'Shipbuilding' and Dave asked him, on my behalf, if he'd be interested in dusting the bass off, The Higsons and Madness having both split up around a year earlier. It was a suitable length of mourning for our first bands."

Actually, Edwards and Bedford had already crossed paths socially. "I met him briefly in The Eagle, Camden Town, where he was playing pool with Dave Cummings," adds Terry. "We didn't get to chat 'til much later when Dave gave me his number. Then we hooked up and started making music straight away, leading to the recording sessions." (By coincidence, Bedford had produced the debut EP by fellow University Of East Anglia band Serious Drinking, entitled *Love On The Terraces*, back in 1982.) When he wasn't playing sax with folk-tinged indie band, Yeah Jazz, Terry developed this new project, which was eventually named BUtterfield 8, after the 1935 novel by John O'Hara and its subsequent 1960 film adaptation starring Elizabeth Taylor, Laurence Harvey and Eddie Fisher.

"I was anxious about asking an excellent bass-player from a famous band to play some of my tunes for a weekly wage of absolutely nothing," Edwards told Madness Central, "but I think it was obvious from the start that we were like-minded." Bedford, too, wished to stretch himself beyond the confines of Madness. Although he never admitted it, perhaps Mark felt straitjacketed within such a large collective – after all, he was a multi-instrumentalist (having also dabbled with piano, guitar and saxophone) who could also turn his hand to songwriting.

The pair set about recruiting like-minded musicians who shared their love of R&B and jazz. Among them was boogie woogie pianist Louis Vause, an old mate of Edwards from his University Of East Anglia days (indeed, Vause had guested with The Higsons on Stylophone and as a narrator). Vause had been playing with 'cow-punk' band Hackney Five-O, who'd been part of that same campaign which Madness had supported back in 1984 to save the troubled Hope & Anchor from closure. "I did know Bedders," says Vause. "Around '84/'85, Hackney 5–0 played a pub in Hackney and one afternoon, Mark and Terry and a few friends got together a country band and I sang 'Move It On Over' with them. It was great with crowds of people on the pavement and excitement because Mark was in Madness. It was a one-off but Mark had known me vaguely from there."

Bedford had occasionally turned up unannounced to play impromptu sets in pubs ever since the early Eighties. "Mark said to me that he really likes turning up at a gig, which he used to do with Diz & The Doormen [who once supported Madness], not really knowing what he's going to play, just getting up onstage and dispensing with all the politics and rehearsals and other stuff that comes with being in a band. For him, it was just fun."

The trio decided to commit their exploratory compositions to tape. "Me, Mark and Terry got some session time at the British School Of Film way out in the country somewhere one evening," explains Louis. "We did a little demo of three or four Latin instrumentals. Then I forgot about it." After the demo reached the ears of Go! Discs (the label founded in 1983 by ex-Stiff employee Andy MacDonald, which had made its name with The Housemartins), they were offered a recording contract. "A complete surprise," adds Vause. "I remember Terry's excitement saying, 'This is unbelievable, we haven't even sent this out! They want to release an album!'"

BUtterfield 8 duly assembled a crew of musicians for sessions at Liquidator in spring 1988. Although the personnel was relatively fluid, they included ex-Roman Holliday trumpeter John Eacott, two ex-members of The Chevalier Brothers (vibraphone player Roger Beaujolais and drummer John Piper), percussionist Bosco De Oliveira (who'd played with Madness onstage) and two keyboard players who'd previously guested with Madness: Terry Disley (piano) and Seamus Beaghen (Hammond organ). "I was completely out of my depth so that stimulated me," laughs Louis. "I thought I better practise and get my chops together. I was working with Dave Graney simultaneously, an original Coral Snake."

The embers of British jazz had been burning brightly since a much-publicised adoption of jazz influences by pop performers around 1984. This groundswell of interest came to be labelled 'New Jazz' and Sade was definitely its most successful exponent. Her best-selling *Diamond Life* album offered a palatable cocktail of soul, light jazz and pop. In the same building as Sade, Everything But The Girl had recorded their debut album, *Eden*, which had helped inform The Style Council's debut, *Café Bleu*. Simon Booth's Working Week followed two groundbreaking jazz-fusion 12 inches (featuring Bosco De Oliveira) with *Working Nights*. Carmel's moody jazz-blues vibe was closer to the spirit of the torch singer while Jerry Dammers injected a variety of jazz influences into the Special A.K.A.'s three-years-in-the-making LP, *In The Studio*. Subtle wafts of 'New Jazz' could even be heard on Madness' later records – from 'One Better Today' to 'Yesterday's Men'.

The 'new jazz' scene had revolved around trendy London nightspots like The Wag and The Mudd, promoted by style magazines like *The Face*. Two bands in particular were initially championed by this cognoscenti: Latin dance act Blue Rondo A La Turk and jazz-pop collective Animal Nightlife. If the scene reached any kind of peak, at least in terms of profile, then it was Julien Temple's critically-lambasted film musical, *Absolute Beginners*, released in 1986 with an accompanying soundtrack produced by Langer and Winstanley.

Suggs wrote about his potential involvement in the film project in *Suggs And The City*. "Clive [was] in conversation with Julien Temple [and] it was suggested I might make a good lead. It was with a mixture of excitement and trepidation, never having acted before, that I approached an audition. I had to do a little scene with the main girl, and considering my inexperience, I thought it went quite well." Unfortunately, Madness' front man was less successful during a dance audition. He ended up with a broken toe in the casualty department of Middlesex Hospital – and the phone never rang!

Soon, this younger (if self-consciously hipper) audience developed a more serious appreciation of 'real' jazz, leading them to established venues like Ronnie Scott's. Alongside increased ticket sales for visiting American jazz legends, British jazz flourished, from new artists like Loose Tubes (including John Eacott) and The Jazz Warriors (and its founding members Courtney Pine and Cleveland Watkiss) to drummer Tommy Chase (who signed with Stiff) and Style Council drummer Steve White, who created The Jazz Renegades.

The period also saw renewed interest in Forties swing and 'jump blues' – popularised by Joe Jackson in 1981 on his *Jumpin' Jive* album and subsequently plied by zoot suit-wearing club acts such as The Chevalier Brothers, who were regulars in the mid-1980s at the Dublin Castle. "The Chevalier Brothers were successful on the live scene without ever selling many records," says Roger Beaujolais. "But a lot of people were aware of us (we averaged almost 200 gigs a year) and we played all over the world. Both Terry and Mark had been to our gigs and liked the idea of having vibes in their new project."

'New jazz' developed in tandem with the growth of interest in 'rare groove', a club-based, DJ-driven scene dedicated to unearthing elusive funk (and jazz) records from the Sixties and Seventies. In 1988, the rare groove scene was swiftly overtaken by acid house – but BUtterfield 8 still might have found a captive audience for their particular fusion of influences. Vause isn't convinced that they fitted into an existing scene. "We weren't in the jazz orbit at all," he suggests. "BUtterfield 8 tried to dispense with fifteeen solos and do jazz as it was done on 78 records in three minutes. The feeling then was that jazz went on and on so we were writing film soundtracks without a film. Soundscapes – but short."

Edwards has fond memories of Go! Discs. "Not bad as labels go," he says. "We knew a few people who worked there, so it was a pretty good atmosphere when we went into the offices. I guess not too many people would have signed a band like us at that time, but Bedders had a good track record, so I think that helped." The deal led to BUtterfield 8's polished rendering of Herbie Hancock's Blue Note jazz classic, 'Watermelon

Man', issued as a single, and an album *Blow!* (both 1988). "We did the album launch at Ronnie Scott's one lunchtime," says Vause. "Terrifying!" While the album reflected Edwards' fascination with old film scores and blues-tinged jazz and remains a highwater mark for him personally ("one of the few things that I've played on which I can happily play from start to finish still", he admits), the record failed to ignite significant interest.

Perhaps that was because *Blow!* revealed a distinct lack of funk influences; rather, the LP evoked the spirit of late Fifties jazz as heard across American TV and cinema during that period, avoiding improvisation or overt be-bop stylings for sassy riffs and strident horns. Bedford contributed five songs to their set, with such superbly evocative titles as 'Our Lady Of The Laundromat', 'St Lyle Drive', 'Itch' and 'Here Comes The Contortionist'. Edwards composed half a dozen tracks; Vause penned a pair. "BUtterfield 8 were trying to create cinematic themes with a nod to late 1950s jazz," agrees Beaujolais. "More Mingus and Monk than Miles or Coltrane. There were solos in all the tunes but they were quite often short and concise. I felt they wanted me to create atmospheres rather than play jazz. I really enjoy doing that — it's something the vibes are well suited to."

Beaujolais suggests that their emphasis was on performance rather than recording: "I always thought the band was formed to do gigs. But being instrumental, a lot of doors were closed. And not being out-and-out jazz, the jazz clubs weren't interested. We played jazz that people who didn't like jazz liked! I thought the band was as much Mark's as it was Terry's. The rehearsals were fun as both Terry and Mark have a great sense of humour. I would go to Mark's flat in Camden and he would play music that influenced him and I could see how the music the band played reflected his tastes. Mark had a nice 'loft'-style flat near the top of Camden Road. We'd often go for a drink in a Spanish bar called Bar Gansa in Camden. At that point, Mark was living on his own but was going out with Cress who he's still with."

Musicians who've tasted widespread fame often attempt to dominate their subsequent bands — but not so the ex-Madness bassist. "Mark is a really nice bloke and good company," states Beaujolais. "He didn't have a huge ego and if you didn't know he'd been in a really popular band, you would never have guessed. I'd say, compared to a lot of other successful people in the pop world, he was incredibly balanced and a lot less screwed up. I was surprised to find how much Mark just wasn't bothered about the music business and had made a decision to get out of it. He told me that Madness deflected him from what he really wanted to do – which was be a graphic designer. He'd joined his mates' band at school not expecting it to be a success and, a few years later, he realised he was doing something that he didn't really want to do. He loved music but I think there were limitations in the band. So he was reassessing his life and making plans to do what he'd thought he was going to do with his life before being massively sidetracked."

BUtterfield 8 have never actually broken up. A new line-up emerged around 1992 with Mike Kearsey, Dave Bryant and Tommy Barlow, the last of whom had earlier supported The Higsons with his band The Larks. "After *Blow!* had been recorded, we needed more horn players for live shows so I got in touch with Tommy," says Edwards. "Some time after that, we formed a 'rare groove' quartet, The Simon Lewis Partnership, which morphed into pub-funk band Swordfish." The band played "lots of festival hall foyer type things," according to Vause.

"Tommy and Terry had formed Swordfish together," explains Kearsey. "I was playing with Tommy in the Deptford Dance Orchestra, which was picked up by Jools Holland and became his big band. When Tommy was after a trombone player for Swordfish, he invited me along and that's how I met Terry. He invited me to play in his Terry Edwards & The Allskas project which is where I first met Bedders, Thommo and Chrissy Boy. We did a few gigs at The Dublin Castle playing ska covers and a few Edwards originals as well as recording a few numbers. I remember the gigs being amazing, in front of a packed audience with a burning band at such a historic venue in terms of the British ska scene."

Meanwhile, the London-based 'acid jazz' scene was burgeoning – and after a spell with Fairground Attraction, BUtterfield 8's ex-vibraphonist formed Acid Jazz label signings The Beaujoulais Band and, later, Vibraphonic. "As Roger Beaujolais says, BUtterfield 8 is more of a gentleman's club than a band," says Edwards. "I guess we're members for life, but there hasn't been an AGM for a while." Actually, the band did reunite onstage at the Royal Festival Hall on in November 2002 at the London Jazz Festival to coincide with a CD reissue of their album, and returned again in March 2006 for a performance at the Queen Elizabeth Hall.

Chapter 17

MADNESS – NOT MADNESS II

IT's tempting to ponder what might have been passing through Suggs' mind while he was being dressed up as a tramp for his cameo appearance in the film, *The Tall Guy*. The role demanded that he sing 'It Must Be Love' while on top of a piano, as part of a montage in which various characters sing along. Was this a sensible stepping stone for a possible career move onto the big screen? After all, Madness had been widely praised for their performance in *Take It Or Leave It*. And Suggs', most of all, possessed a natural charm in front of the camera which lent weight to this proposition. Or was this scenario a morbid prophecy of his future in showbusiness: Suggs singing old Madness songs to pay the rent?

Filmed in 1988, *The Tall Guy* was written by Richard Curtis (it was his feature film debut), who'd earlier expressed such enthusiasm for a TV series about Madness. Based loosely on director Mel Smith's role as straight man to long-time collaborator Rowan Atkinson, the film starring Jeff Goldblum was set in Camden Town, which presumably explains their wish to involve Madness. To coincide with the film, Virgin re-issued 'It Must Be Love' as a single but it failed to chart – possibly because the film itself wasn't hugely popular.

By the time *The Tall Guy* was released in April 1989, Suggs had already made his TV acting debut in an episode of the popular kids' comedy/drama *Press Gang*, set within the office of the *Junior Gazette*, a newspaper run entirely by teenagers. Suggs starred in episode 9 of the ITV show, entitled *Friends Like These*, broadcast on March 15. In the storyline, the team attempted to delay a pop star, Jason Wood (played by Suggs), at the local train station whilst the newspaper's editor Lynda persuaded one of the journalists, Sarah, to interview him. Suggs, for his part, was quite believable – even if the role hardly stretched his acting potential.

Uncertain of an appropriate career path, McPherson tried his hand as host in a variety of guises, from a weekly stand-up comedy night at the Mean Fiddler in Harlesden, to presenting two satellite TV shows (including *Music Box* and, in 1990, a chat show *Suggs On Saturday* on British Satellite Broadcasting's music channel *The Power Station*) and odds and ends for Channel 4. "I did that for about six months," he later recalled, "which was really good fun, and then the station closed down."

The singer also appeared in Film On Four's "low-art thriller" *The Final Frame*, which was shot in summer 1989 before being screened on Channel 4 in April 1990. The film followed young filmmaker Hadi, who captured vital evidence on videotape of the murder of a notorious rock star East (played by Suggs) onstage at an Animal Rights benefit gig. A dark, brooding film with at least one major plot twist, it was memorable for Suggs' performance of 'Animal' (written with Barson about the film's theme of animal cruelty and later reworked as a B-side by Suggs).

The Final Frame was produced by Liverpudlian writer Kevin Sampson, fresh from several documentaries for Channel 4. "I'd needed a group to play themselves on screen," wrote Sampson in 1997. "I had known Pete Hooton for many years and knew him to be a shameless self-publicist. The Farm were in the film." Suggs was already acquainted with The Farm, having produced and sung backing vocals on their debut single, 'Hearts And Minds', back in 1984 as one of the first extracurricular sessions at Liquidator with Madness' engineer/soundman Ian Horne (Suggs had met them on *The Oxford Roadshow* programme in February '84). They were a politically-informed "proliterian band", in Sampson's words, who'd built up a sizeable following in and around Liverpool with a string of indie releases – but hadn't attracted much interest elsewhere. With the fawning praise being heaped that year on their Manchester contemporaries The Stone Roses and The Happy Mondays, twin peaks of what the music press had labelled 'Baggy', The Farm were keen to capitalise on such fevered interest in music emanating from the north west.

"They burst into [my] office on 16 January 1990," wrote Sampson. "That afternoon, Suggs joined us in the Crown And Two Chairmen in Dean Street. By six o'clock, Suggs and I had signed for F.C. Farm. We'd manage the band jointly. Terry Farley agreed to provide club mixes, Produce Records was set up in Holmes Building, a chaotic warren of corridors in a Liverpool warehouse." This is a couple of months after The Stone Roses (with the era's defining moment, 'Fools Gold') and The Happy Mondays (with 'Hallelujah' from their equally iconic *Madchester* EP) had shared an episode of *Top Of The Pops*. Loose-fitting sportswear became de rigeur, "indie dance" became an accepted music subgenre and London was no longer perceived to be the epicentre of the musical universe.

Suggs had arrived at a crossroads. Should he persevere with some new role within the music industry or allow himself to drift into TV presenting? Unfortunately, judging by his uncomfortable performance the following month as co-presenter in Channel 4's new holiday show, *Travelog*, the latter career path didn't seem to be necessarily a safe bet. Gallivanting around Egypt was probably a welcome distraction but the critics had a field day; in reality, Suggs was able to keep his options open for the time being.

With Suggs in the producer's seat, The Farm delivered their first masterstroke, a radical overhaul of the Boyce/Hart classic, '(I'm Not Your) Steppin' Stone' (popularised by The Monkees in 1966/67), set to a backing track which borrowed from Snap's dance anthem 'The Power'. Engineered at Liquidator, the 'Steppin' Stone' 12-inch put The Farm on the map in spring 1990 but the infectious follow-up, 'Groovy Train' – recorded at Liquidator – turned them into bona fide pop stars that summer. Reworking an old lyric about opposing sides in the First World War who played football on Christmas Day, 'All Together Now' gave them a second Top 10 hit before the year was out, all of which paved the way for their chart-topping album, *Spartacus*, in spring 1991. The LP opened with a re-working of that debut single, 'Hearts And Minds'; all but one track was produced by Suggs.

The Farm's down-to-earth mix of terrace-friendly tunes, baggy beats and intelligent lyrics captured the zeitgeist perfectly. And in Pete Hooton and guitarist Steve Grimes, the band possessed a songwriting partnership of real integrity – which Suggs could no doubt relate to. A month after the release of *Spartacus*, they were back in the charts with fellow Liverpudlian Pete Wylie for a re-working of his old hit, 'Sinful!'. But unlike, say, contemporaries The Charlatans (who, like The Farm, were also able to carve their own niche in the wake of 'Madchester'), The Farm struggled to sustain their success. While later singles proved to be minor hits, it speaks volumes about their fall from grace that their second album, *Love See No*

Colour (1992), completely failed to chart and for their biggest hit of that year, they'd resorted to a cover version of the Human League's 'Don't You Want Me'.

Problems had arisen during sessions for that second album – "the first schisms in the previously impenetrable armour of The Farm," according to Sampson. Two band members wanted to take a Pet Shop Boys-styled disco-pop route. "Suggs wanted a darker album, a heavy, dubby undercurrent with lots of guitars and studio madness," remembered Sampson. "We all fell out horribly." But by 1992, Suggs had other projects to worry about . . .

★ ★ ★

At one point around 1985, Matthew Sztumpf must have smiled to himself. Having managed Madness now for nigh on five years, he'd been approached by The Smiths – undeniably the most respected band in British pop at the time – to act as their manager, too. The Smiths, and their singer Morrissey, in particular, admired Madness. After The Smiths disintegrated in summer 1987, Morrissey had swiftly set about a solo career, teaming up with producer Stephen Street for his successful debut album *Viva Hate*, issued in spring 1988. After some acrimony with Street, Morrissey opted instead to recruit Clive Langer and Alan Winstanley for sessions beginning August 1989. "I was a serious Madness fan years ago," Morrissey admitted at the time. "It was largely their sense of perverse fun I quite liked. I never considered the records to be standard pop fare. I quite liked the peculiarity. People say music hall, which I suppose is quite true."

Langer and Winstanley's CV had grown considerably since Madness' split. In 1986, the pair had produced the aforementioned Top 20 soundtrack for the film *Absolute Beginners*, in due course working with such artists as Sandie Shaw, Lloyd Cole & The Commotions, China Crisis, Eighth Wonder and The Stranglers' Hugh Cornwell. The pair enjoyed significant success with the Hothouse Flowers' debut album, *People* (1988), while much of 1989 had been spent in New York recording *Flood*, the breakthrough album for They Might Be Giants. In addition to running their Westside Studios in Notting Hill, the pair had also opened a residential studio, Outside, which was chosen as the most suitable location for Morrissey.

According to Simon Goddard in *Mozipedia: The Encyclopedia Of Morrissey And The Smiths*, the first fruits from these sessions were heard across both sides of a single, which would not only provoke critical comparisons with the producers' former charges but featured guest vocals from Suggs. By the time 'Piccadilly Palare' (and B-side 'Get Off The Stage') finally appeared in October 1990, Morrissey was busy recording his second album *Kill Uncle*. And on bass was Mark Bedford, who stayed for all of Morrissey's recordings up to and including his 'My Love Life' single, issued in 1991. (Although Bedford concentrated on his college course, he had still kept his hand in. For example, he played bass for a band called Bloomsday, formed by two ex-members of The Commotions, Neil Clark and Stephen Irvine, appearing on their 1990 album *Fortuny*. Along with Irvine, Bedford also featured on the 1992 album *Dans Le Lune . . .* by French musician Nicola Sirkis.)

One night, while taking a break from *Kill Uncle*, Langer had invited Cathal Smyth to meet Morrissey at Julie's restaurant in Notting Hill – perhaps in a bid to hire Smyth to assist Morrissey's quest to form a rockabilly band. While Cathal had obviously been aware of The Smiths, it was Morrissey's debut single 'Suedehead' which pricked his ears (not least because of its associations with the early Seventies cult which had so interested Smyth). "Being an ex-skinhead, that meant a lot to me," Cathal told Simon Goddard. Apparently, he was also a keen masseuse and, in a typically tactile and friendly gesture, offered to give Morrissey a shoulder rub that evening. "I clicked his neck, loosened him up a bit," Smyth explained. "That first massage, I think it proper shivered his timbers because I don't think many people touch him!"

With their shared ancestry, and Cathal's ebullient charm, it wasn't surprising that the pair hit it off – and he would prove to be the closest of Morrissey's Madness acquaintances. Smyth was even welcomed into the ex-Smith frontman's private circle of friends. The singer courted Smyth as a potential manager, but he had to suffice with Cathal's harmonies on his cover of The Jam's 'That's Entertainment'. It was Smyth who recommended that Morrissey recruit his friend, ex-Polecats guitarist Boz Boorer – who's been a backbone of his backing band ever since.

"Morrissey used little discretion in exhibiting his fondness for Smyth, developing what even Langer describes as 'an infatuation'," writes Goddard. A 'screen grab' of Smyth feigning a heart attack from the

'Cardiac Arrest' promo appeared in the video for Morrissey's single, 'We Hate It When Our Friends Become Successful'. And by his own admission, Smyth was the subject of the Morrissey song, 'You're The One For Me, Fatty'. Simon Goddard again: "Smyth is in possession of personal letters 'in safe-keeping', which he jokingly describes as 'a bit homoerotic', while in 1992 Morrissey duly presented him with a copy of *Your Arsenal*, signed in gold pen: 'To Cathal – Be bold, be brave, be a man. It's a great game. Love, Morrissey.'"

★ ★ ★

By 1989, Smyth had found himself in a pickle. "I had run out of money and was unsure of what course to take," he admits. At first, he explored the possibility of forming a new band. "But I found it nowhere as satisfying as my experience with my partners in Madness. Without the magical ingredient which infused Madness, I felt it was not worth pursuing. I examined returning to my previous career in petrochemicals but I had changed, and even though the money was good, the oil game was no longer an option. It had to be music!"

To clarify his thoughts, Smyth took a sabbatical. "I went on a Buddhist retreat in the south of France where Sogyal Rinpoche, who I had heard giving teachings in London, has an organisation called Rigpa," explains Cathal. "This cleared my mind of dust and confusion and I returned to London prepared to say those words we all find difficult to speak: Help me! I then went to see Dave Balfe, a good friend of mine who ran Food Records, and asked his advice as to what my experience might be suited for. He recommended a career in A&R and with his and Andy Winter's help, a letter was drafted and sent to various record labels."

Eventually, Cathal got a bite with Go! Discs, which was then riding high on the success of acts such as Billy Bragg, The La's and post-Housemartins acts The Beautiful South and Beats International. Smyth presumably impressed Go! Discs boss Andy MacDonald with his enthusiasm, intelligence and undoubted 'gift of the gab' and was given a role in the "artists and repertoire" department. "I engaged in a round of interviews and finally Go! Discs offered me a job," he continues. "I knew Andy and his wife Juliette and the label suited me down to the ground as its bias was on good songwriters and its politics were socialist. I was given the job after being approved by Jona Cox and Simon Dine, who were the A&R department. I believe that I was mainly hired to assist with getting The La's album released as, being an artist myself, it was useful in a trouble-shooting capacity when communicating with artists and getting to a realistic outcome. I mainly worked with The La's and took them to America to promote what I believe was an exceptional album and great body of work."

Although the band had signed to Go! Discs back in 1987, The La's' eponymous debut album wasn't released until late 1990, its Top 30 sales helped by a hit reissue of the ubiquitous jangly pop anthem 'There She Goes'. While Cathal grappled with the challenges of dealing with the most exciting band out of Liverpool since the days of one-time Madness support band Echo & The Bunnymen, he was also involved in discovering new Merseyside talent, The Stairs, who were heavily indebted to Sixties garage punk and rhythm & blues.

"We were his baby," says The Stairs' Edgar Jones. "Cathal was up in Liverpool seeing another band, Magic Clock, who were popping up to see us in the studio recording our first EP, *Weed Bus*. We were a bit awe-struck but he seemed like a decent enough bloke. Within a few days, he'd put his cards on the table that he fancied signing us. We just thought he was a straight-up cockney geezer." The four-piece were about to sign with Imaginary Records – but Smyth poached them for Go! Discs. "The Stairs were one of five bands that I went to check out in Liverpool," adds Smyth, "and their energy and Edgar Jones' charisma had me sold."

In due course, they issued a string of acclaimed EPs and a 1992 album, *Mexican R'n'B*. "Cathal was our defender and champion, really," admits Jones. "He helped us get away with a lot, like recording our LP in mono and producing it ourselves. He helped us fight that corner. Andy MacDonald had had The La's for a couple of years and there'd been a lot of trouble so to get him to sign another Scouse band took some energy." Although The Stairs were popular with the critics, Cathal seems understandably disappointed by their lack of commercial clout. "It didn't really grab people but I like to think that they were, although seemingly retro, actually ahead of their time as Primal Scream released a record similar in vibe soon after. It was an honest sound. Mark Lamarr's favourite record!" Smyth shared the label's enthusiasm for signing Paul Weller – but contrary to what's been suggested on Wikipedia, his involvement was peripheral. "All I did was encourage Andy to sign him," he admits. "This was not a difficult process as Paul is an exceptional writer."

At the time, Cathal contrasted his new role with his life in Madness. "I don't know if I'm a good A&R man," he admitted. "I think that attitude always beats technique. So I look for energy and conviction and belief. When I finished with the band, I worked with a couple of programmers and got a band together, but I stopped because it didn't have the same feeling. You come out of a relationship with people, it's really intense, you know each other inside out, you live in each other's pockets. The good thing about Madness is when you were weak, you had six other people to help you and when you were strong, you had six other people to magnify your strength. And not having that, it's like coming out of a marriage, where you realise how much you're going to have to learn for yourself."

★ ★ ★

In 1989, just as Madness' profile had ebbed to its lowest-ever level, a strange thing happened. For a brief moment, the UK live scene enjoyed another ska revival, bubbling up from an underground phenomenon into the mainstream columns of the 'red tops' and the music press. Leading this new ska vanguard were a handful of acts such as Potato 5 (who'd played with Madness), The Trojans (fronted by Gaz Mayall, DJ mainstay at London club night Gaz's Rockin' Blues), all-girl act The Deltones, The Forest Hill Billies and younger bands like The Loafers, The Hotknives and Maroon Town. Having earnt their stripes during a desultory period in the mid-1980s, these acts were playing to packed-out clubs across the capital, issuing their own records independently.

"We ended up in 1988 supporting Potato 5," remembers The Loafers' keyboard player Sean Flowerdew. "There was really quite a big ska movement then. It was all focused around London pub shows. Places like the Dublin Castle would have ska nights on." Eventually, Flowerdew hooked up with Lee Thompson. "I wrote to him and said, 'Would you like to come and play with us?'" says Sean. "I sent him some tickets and he came down to the Dublin Castle. He was great and we stayed mates. The Loafers ended up headlining The Astoria. There was definitely a new movement."

The scene didn't boil over until early 1989. "It was huge by then because you also had Laurel Aitken and Desmond Dekker gigging from the old guard," suggests Sean. "All around the country, there were decent shows. Steve Lamacq did a three-page feature for the *NME*. At the end of

1988, *The Sun* were saying, the next big thing to watch in '89 is ska." Unfortunately, this flurry of popularity proved to be all too brief. "It was really short," admits Sean. "We did one show at The Astoria in March '89 and then we headlined it in May but then by the end of that summer, it was all done. I think the reason it ended was there weren't quite the songs to translate to radio."

By this time, Thompson and Foreman were toying with creating a new band which went back to their ska roots. Unfortunately, any tentative approaches to their contacts in the music industry were met with abject indifference. "Lee and myself started writing songs together at the end of 1988," Foreman commented. Initially, three tracks were laid down at Liquidator. "We recorded them, went around the big record companies and got spun a right load of fanny like, '[are] you sure Lee can be the front man?' Some things they used to say were really stupid, 'you need to have a package', [which] meant me and him with blond hair and leather jackets! They want you to turn up with little drawings: this is our image. It was insulting to me and Lee." While major labels were dubious about this new Madness spin-off, Thompson and Foreman were still reticent about that whole process.

The pair still used Liquidator as their base – and a snapshot of their day-to-day working life was evident from an interview with Terry Hawton published in April 1990 in *Madzine*. One minute, Foreman was taking a call from Steve Nieve, whose band The Playboys were recording at Liquidator, the next he's pointing out John Hasler (who was sanding the building's exterior) or greeting Cathal, who'd happened to pop by. Thompson even alluded to other potential Madness-related collaborations: "Suggs, in his heart, wants to write music and he is doing bits and bobs with Mike Barson, who's been frequenting Caledonian Road and they've been knocking out some songs."

"When I met Lee and Chris, they had written the majority of an album," explains Flowerdew, "and I could not believe, being a big fan, that no one cared. The Madness had killed it. I don't think they had really settled on a name. They didn't want to be called The Nutty Boys. I'd run a little label, Staccato, which went through Link Records. I said, 'I can set you up a deal.' We had a meeting with Mark [Brennan] and Lol [Laurie Pryor] from Link, who came down to meet Lee and Chris at Liquidator, which was still functioning as a studio." Once the meeting had adjourned to the pub, the creative juices had started flowing. "We were sitting with the boys from Link and they suggested The Nutty Boys, probably as a joke," Foreman later told George Marshall. "I said, 'Yeah!', but Lee had his head in his hands going, 'Oh no.'"

"We played them some right dodgy old tapes which we'd recorded in the kitchen," admitted Thompson. "It was rough old stuff but they gave us the opportunity to up the money to go in the studio. Chris came up with some blinding old tunes, we done a bit of sampling here and there from old reggae songs and [Link] were over the moon. We recorded it in near enough half the time of 'One Step Beyond' and for half the price!"

Foreman explained the recording process in more detail: "I don't play the guitar much anymore. I write everything on keyboards and a few songs I just worked out on the spot. By using machines, we could do everything at home more or less exactly as it would be in a studio except it's on 8-track instead of 24. You could change the key of things. If Lee wanted something shuffled around, it's quite easy. It's what they call these days 'pre-production'! Within about two days, we'd done all the backing tracks – the drums, bass, keyboards, just the real structure of the songs. We were able to record it easily within ten days."

The Nutty Boys bagged an album's worth of material at Liquidator (with extra sessions recorded at Pavilion Studios and E-Zee Hire Studio, a rather grim, dank facility in the shadow of Pentonville Prison). The engineer was Foreman's ex-brother-in-law, Phil Payne, whose band Low Numbers had shared a bill with The Invaders several times back in the late Seventies. A 10-track album, *Crunch!*, was issued on the Street Link label in April 1990. "Lee wanted it to be released on April 1," Foreman told George Marshall, "but then we found out it was a Sunday!"

Crunch! opened with arguably its strongest track, 'Magic Carpet', which dealt with the "freedom of drugs in the city with the Channel Tunnel". The song was co-written by the pair with Suggs – a hangover of those last sessions in 1988. "Suggs did quite a bit of the music. It was one of the last songs The Madness were writing and we finished it off," explained Foreman on Radio 1 in 1992.* "Some of the songs on *Crunch!* were

---

* A demo exists with roughly the same backing track as the Nutty Boys album track 'Whistle' but with vocals by Cathal Smyth, which points to his involvement in some small way with the embryonic Foreman/Thompson band – perhaps Foreman forwarded Smyth a demo to create some lyrics?

brilliant," enthuses Flowerdew. "It's a great album. There was a ska influence although it's programmed so has that Eighties feel to it. Their second lot of recordings became more eclectic – influenced by Dury and glam." Sadly, the band were too late to capitalise on that briefest of ska revivals which had swept through the capital. "The Nutty Boys didn't start till it had all petered out," admits Flowerdew. "That album did OK but there wasn't really the marketplace for it at that time."

"The album was put together so differently to how things were 'supposed to be done' at the time," explains Laurie Pryor. "It was raw but very real and back-to-basics. We couldn't believe how good it was – so much better than The Madness album. We took it to several PR and radio plugging companies who seemed to be turning their noses up at anything to do with Madness. It seemed incredible. One top plugger was more honest and told us bluntly that he could take our money but there was no way any Nutty Boys single would get serious daytime airplay. To be honest, we were stunned!"

★ ★ ★

Brennan and Pryor suggested that The Nutty Boys assemble a band to tour, which would help promote the album. "They assembled a bunch of misfits when they became a live working outfit," reckons Flowerdew. "Looking back, they were just trying to put together their own Kilburn & The High Roads, playing out their influences. I was going to play keyboards but then I got asked to join Special Beat so I had a choice – but Special Beat was going to America! I was away in the States touring with Special Beat from October '90 and missed it." Meanwhile, the worldwide economic recession was biting. "There were ups and downs, especially in the early Nineties," suggests Sean. "Lee and Debbie his wife opened a bike shop in Notting Hill, I think. Lee did all sorts – flyposting, working on the bins, whatever he needed to bring the money in."

At various times, The Nutty Boys included 'Diamond Legs' Louis Vause on piano, fresh from BUtterfield 8. On bass was Paul 'Tad' Tadman while 'Spider' Johnson played drums; organ was handled first by ex-Madness regular Seamus Beaghen and then by 'Hong Kong' Dave Lazaro; and 'Sexy' Steve Annan shared Thompson's duties on saxophone. "I brought Tad and Spider into The Nutty Boys," explains Flowerdew. "Tad had been in The Riffs, Spider had sung as frontman in the latter days of

Potato 5 and had drummed with a few people." Paul Tadman was a relative novice, having played his first gig with The Riffs on March 26, 1989, supporting The Loafers. "My mate Sean Flowerdew introduced me to Lee briefly at a gig I was playing in December 1989," explained Tadman. "I'd met Spider a few months previously, as The Riffs supported the Potato 5." Both The Riffs and The Loafers had also signed with Link.

"Chris phoned me [and] I turned up to the 'audition' expecting to see a street filled with a long queue of bass players, and I was the only one," explained Tadman. "Had a chat with Chris and Lee about bass playing, Chris put on 'Burn Rubber On Me' by The Gap Band and I did some slap bass all over it. He handed me a copy of the album and said, 'Learn that, we'll be rehearsing in a couple of weeks.'"

Louis Vause' recruitment was similarly matter-of-fact. "I was recording with Dave Graney and got a message to ring Chrissy Boy who I'd never met," he remembers. "I was on my way back from the studio at nine in the morning and rang from a callbox in Putney Bridge Station. I only had 10p so I said, 'Can you ring me back?' Oh, another 'sheen'! He used to call everyone a 'sheen' – flaky, untogether, broke. He rang me back and said, 'Mark tells me you've got pretty quick ears.' 'Yes.' Then he said, 'How tall are you?' 'Five foot eight.' 'You're hired!' I said, 'Why?' 'Well, we're five foot eight and we don't want anyone taller than us!'" Vause was particularly impressed with their sticksman: "Spider was fantastic because he was a 'high life' reggae-type drummer, which added a completely different swing to it all."

Their first gig was at The Fleece & Firkin in Bristol on November 10, followed by the newly reopened Moonlight Club in Hampstead on November 15. Their third show saw them support Serious Drinking at Subterania in Portobello (in essence, a revamped version of the Acklam Halls that they'd played as The Invaders) on December 12. Both Suggs and Cathal were in attendance – while Barson surfaced two gigs later at The Sir George Robey on January 12, 1991. Later still, their tenth show at The Underworld, Camden Town on March 21 attracted Mark Bedford.

"Chris is hilarious," thinks Louis. "He'd drive himself mad doing accounts. I don't think it's his strong point but he'd do us little tour booklets, where we were going to play, a cast list. Lovely. He does feel the real responsibility and I think it gets on top of him sometimes. After a sound-check in Islington, he put his arm around me. 'Come on Lou, I'm going to show you where I went to school.' It had been knocked down but he'd say, 'Look, you can still see that goalpost on the wall. That's where we used to play football.' When he moved to Brighton, he said, 'You know what I've been doing today, Lou? I've been walking all over Camden and it's not my home anymore.' But he really felt moving was a big decision so he made a point of walking to all the places he loved, most of which had been altered, a whole day wandering around."

Although *Crunch!* sold modestly, The Nutty Boys were kept busy throughout the early Nineties with tours of France, Ireland, Germany and elsewhere on the Continent. On April 22, 1991, for example, they appeared on French TV billed as 'The Naughty Boys' at the premiere in Paris of Oliver Stone's movie *The Doors*, as Foreman later recalled. "I didn't realise this was going out live, me belching ferociously down the lens of a horrified cameraman's lens whilst playing 'Magic Carpet' with a borrowed 'Beatle' bass!" Tadman later recalled the shenanigans to Madness Central: "We'd just done some press after our L'Olympia gig and had a few shandies each. Lee didn't have anything to wear as all our gear was being packed away. So I suggested Lee go on as a coffee table, pointing to a table in the corner with some gingham material on it. As the curtain went up, I was playing 'Day Tripper' and we blasted through 'Magic Carpet' and 'Daydreamers' with Lee singing 'Wetdreamers'. It was hilarious!"

Inevitably, The Nutty Boys relied on old Madness fans – but sometimes, the ubiquitous heckles grew wearing. "I guess people really didn't know what to expect," suggested Tadman. "We used to do 'Razor Blade Alley' and 'Take It or Leave It' [but] we soon dropped them as new material came along. Eventually, the die-hard fans drifted away leaving a much more mixed crowd, prepared to give us a go."

In early 1993, The Nutty Boys issued a follow-up EP, *It's OK, I'm A Policeman*. "Chris would write all the tunes on his sequencer and post them out for the rest of us to learn," Tadman later explained to Madness Central. "Sometimes, Lee would put a scat vocal over or some sax, known as the 'Egg and Bacon' sessions. As we rehearsed them, the tunes would grow. One example is 'It's OK, I'm A Policeman'. We didn't really have a bass line. Ian Horne was producing and Phil Payne, our soundman, suggested I play the line similar to 'Hit Me With Your Rhythm Stick'. It is difficult to learn. We actually slowed the track down slightly so I could fit the notes in! Ian Horne put his arm around me and said, 'Don't worry about it – we've done that before!'"

'It's OK, I'm A Policeman' was a superb if eccentric development of Madness at their most experimental. "Chris's soundscapes and use of samples, I thought, were really different, fantastic," suggests Louis. "I was impressed by that. They were going in a different direction. It wasn't a Madness clone." But The Nutty Boys were predominantly a live band, troubling our European neighbours during sporadic tours. Bearing in mind that, of all the members of Madness, Thompson and Foreman boasted the most anarchic strains of humour, it's no surprise to learn that life on the road with The Nutty Boys was . . . well, nutty.

Paul Tadman later listed some of their on-the-road antics: "Forming a road block in white 'fall out' jump suits at 4am along the main north–south route in Eire . . . Spider drinking too much whisky, leaving most of it on a motorway hard shoulder . . . Louis taking a shower fully clothed in Utrecht . . . Lee jumping in the hotel swimming pool fully lathered up from a shower." Of their trip around France in 1993, Tadman wrote: "Paynie taking the tour bus for a midnight spin – he couldn't drive. Ended up in an Oyster field with the tide coming in, after we'd been thrown out of our hotel in Lille when Lee was arrested for scaling an 800-year-old cathedral."

Louis Vause remembers this last incident vividly. "I woke up in this hotel in Normandy to be told to leave," he laughs. "The French owner said, 'Either your promoter or your lead singer is in prison and either your promoter or your lead singer is in hospital.' There's a cathedral in this town that had survived two world wars and Lee had climbed up the front and these little gargoyles had fallen off in his hands, which he'd stuffed in his pockets. He'd been in a drinking competition with the promoter, who ended up in hospital with alcohol poisoning. Lee's taken down to the police station. So they said, 'Empty your pockets.' And he's pulling out these 800-year-old gargoyles. Lee loves climbing!"

Occasionally, troublesome elements within their audience would repeat themselves like a bad case of indigestion. "When we were in Germany, we were billed as Madness by an unscrupulous promoter and nearly killed by 800 skinheads," admits Louis. "It was a massive gig. We were playing with The Selecter and Pauline Black afterwards said, 'I have to take my hat off to you guys,' because people were baying for 'One Step Beyond' and we refused to play it. Lee was climbing up and someone in the front row tried to pull him down – he'd have fallen thirty feet. Tad kicked the guy who was doing it in the teeth. It was really frightening but then Chris turned to me and said, 'Lou, we'd tour every new album as Madness and everyone asked for the last album. It really pisses you off.' Then they get to hear the new album but then we're touring with the next and they're asking for the one before. It's no different."

Two years later, The Nutty Boys travelled back across the channel – but again, the visit was not without incident. Paul Tadman remembered: "Hiring a local villain to hotwire our mini-bus after the keys were lost – we had to drive to Switzerland for a gig – missed the gig. Then drove all the way back through France with hardly any headlamps, almost non-stop 27 hours. The guys making sure I stayed in the bridal suite with Louis . . . filled my bed with lots of copies of the Yellow Pages [in] Montpellier." Another escapade read like a litany of mini-disasters, according to Vause: "We were thrown out in the hotel and had to find one on the beach, then the van got stuck in the sand because Lee was mucking around driving, then the tide was coming in and we were getting coats under the tyres to try and save all the equipment in the van from being washed away in the sea!"

Foreman and Thompson were like brothers – which meant they were close but also provoked inevitable squabbles. "When they fall out, they fall out badly," admits Vause. "I've seen Chris hit Lee over the head at a Paris gig with his guitar, quite hard. Chris got pissed off with Lee trying to climb a microphone stand and he just stormed across and smashed it. Lee . . . dear oh dear. Lee does wind people up a bit, he's a mischief maker! Once, I caught him crawling on the floor out of my hotel room in Munich with his backpack rattling with my entire mini-bar which I would have been charged for! Was he trying to do it without me seeing? Yes!"

Photographer Gavin Watson joined them for some dates in Germany – but once again, this wasn't without incident. "Some friendly Germans had repaired our bald flat tyre on a routine petrol stop," explained Tadman. "They gave us food and drink and wished us on our way." Louis Vause: "We gave the proprietors signed albums and they gave us a great big pack of bacon!" Paul Tadman: "All was looking bright for Anglo-German relations when Gavin drove our tour bus into a garage awning, smashing it into a thousand pieces, crashing down around our ears." Louis Vause:

"Because they'd pumped the tyres up, when we drove away, we took the roof of the garage with us. They're all going, stop! Chris said, 'Of course we'll pay,' and that was the entire profit of the tour gone!"

Uncomfortable with a monicker which clearly traded on past associations with Madness, Foreman finally changed their name to Crunch! in 1996. Because they were without a recording contract, Foreman and Thompson started their own label, Magic Carpet Records, as an outlet for their second single, a reworked version of 'Magic Carpet'. Crunch played their last show at the Dublin Castle for three years, although they have been an intermittent entity ever since.

Chapter 18

DON'T WATCH THAT . . .
WATCH THIS

1992 wasn't a great year for British pop music. Any self-respecting teenager was either immersed in the grunge scene out of Seattle or dropping Es in a field somewhere outside the M25. The Stone Roses and The Happy Mondays had run out of steam, and although Primal Scream's *Screamadelica* won the first Mercury Music Prize that year, it felt like a pearl amongst the swine. The album charts were dominated by established acts. With the occasional exception of an indie band who'd broken through (Carter The Unstoppable Sex Machine, for example), the era of corporate pop and rock was in full swing. And for the first time, the *Grange Hill* generation who had been weaned on Madness and 2 Tone felt nostalgic.

Meanwhile, the CD age had led to vast swathes of back catalogue being regurgitated by the music industry. By the early 1990s, record labels were becoming more sophisticated at marketing their wares – and TV advertising became a more commonplace technique for reaching fair-weather music fans who rarely frequented record shops. Fuelled by the arrival of CDs in supermarkets, not previously a traditional venue for selling music, TV advertised back catalogue concepts had become big business. Now, record companies could aim squarely at older generations who no longer identified with the Top 40.

Virgin Records' new Head Of Catalogue was Steve Pritchard, who cast an eye over the company's wares and was surprised to see that Madness' music appeared relatively unexploited. "It was a catalogue lying fallow and it seemed there'd been enough water under the bridge for it to be worth a look," says Steve. "We did some market research on Madness and it was one of the most positive responses we'd ever seen! Because every generation – mums, dads, kids – thought Madness were their own personal property and loved their hits." Behind the scenes, Pritchard and his team realised that a TV-advertised Madness compilation could potentially repeat the success that Stiff had enjoyed nearly a decade earlier with *Complete Madness*.

"So we made contact with them," continues Pritchard. "Our initial contact was with Cathal because he was working at Go! Discs, over in Hammersmith. He was really up for it. His long-term plan was to get them back together again. Cathal took it upon himself to help us make it happen. So I went around with him for a couple of months while he got the band back together. I remember the first meeting we had at Virgin. I wasn't that young, about thirty, but you could see they thought, who is this whippersnapper telling us we have to get involved?! I know they've had their fallings out but I have to say it was Cathal's energy who drove that. He did have a vision."

Perhaps the first glimmer that a reunion was in the offing came in *The Daily Star* on December 3, 1991. "Nutty Eighties band Madness are planning a comeback after a campaign by their skinhead-and-braces fans," ran the article. "Chas Smash says: 'All these rumours have been flying around because Suggs and I have been negotiating a new publishing deal. Morrissey did ask us to perform at a special Aids benefit gig in December, but he was jumping the gun a little. We definitely don't want to just play the old hits; we want to perform the new material too.'"

Slowly but surely, other members became more involved but – needless to say – tacit approval from one particular individual proved to be pivotal. "The turning point was when Mike Barson came back from Holland," admits Pritchard. "It really was like the return of the magnificent seven! The gang was complete again – it did feel like a Western! They'd had their sales decline and a critical knocking for the first time and, to start off with, I think they were reluctant to get involved with anything as cheesy as a 'Best Of Madness'."

Among Virgin's promotional team was radio plugger Mick Garbutt, who'd joined the company in 1990. "The biggest acts on the label globally were Enigma and UB40; Phil Collins and Genesis were only signed to UK and Ireland. What are we doing in between? The most important department became Catalogue. They had the *Best Album In The World Ever* and *Now* series but they were constantly plundering the vaults. It kept us going through some dark years at Virgin. Their value to the company rose drastically."

In due course, Virgin devised an ambitious plan for a new compilation, *Divine Madness*, pre-empted by a reissue of 'It Must Be Love' in time for Valentine's Day 1992. Usually, a straight re-release of an old hit would have vanished without a trace, unless the song had enjoyed a new lease of life courtesy of its usage in a film or TV advert. Despite a complete lack of such activity, 'It Must Be Love' shot to number six – perhaps driven by Virgin's counter box campaign offering this small token of affection as an impulse buy for February 14.

"Radio 1 wouldn't playlist but we got an awful lot of support," explains Garbutt. "Good supporters were people like Simon Mayo on the breakfast show. We squeezed enough individual plays. There couldn't have been anything but good will: I can't imagine anyone who likes British pop music who doesn't somehow like Madness." Garbutt was a huge fan of Madness but he learnt a valuable lesson about expressing this to the band. "I was 26 years old and had grown up with Madness and collected all their singles," he explains. "As we came out of Radio 1 in the car for the first of our BBC meetings, I mentioned I had the 'Los Palmas 7' 12-inch with the comic and Suggs turns to Cathal and says, 'Oh no, we've got a fucking anorak!' I learnt something. Artists in general want you to be enthusiastic but there's a line between fan and someone who works for you!"

The band were still cautious about aligning themselves too closely with the marketing campaign – all except their one-time MC, who became actively involved in the concept of the TV advertisement. "During my tenure at Go!, I was made aware that Virgin planned to release a 'greatest hits' and I became involved in its release," says Cathal. "I made the TV advert at The Mill and designed the cover."

"Cathal came up with the idea of a play device for the *Divine Madness* ad," explains Pritchard. "They used morphing, which was actually quite cutting edge technology. There was an expensive car ad out at the time where a frog turned into the car – it was the editor's trick of choice that month! So Cathal came up with almost Fisher-Price-type bobbing heads at the bottom where their heads morphed into one another. So Cathal changed into Suggs and it cycled through. Then there were amusing captions on the ad – that was them in full, sarcastic flow. They were so hung up about their credibility. They were sitting in there coming up with the lines for the ad like, 'This album will be available in the shops. It's really quite good.' It has Chrissy Boy's sarky comments, sending up TV albums, but the public just wanted it."

It was Pritchard's first exposure to Madness' dysfunctional democracy. "They'd all turn up for the edits – and there were seven ideas about how everything should go," he laughs. "But what I think came out of it was really amusing. I mean, it took weeks of suggesting titles to stick on the name *Divine Madness*. The whole idea of playing on their strong promo video catalogue probably came from Cathal. So the sleeve had a still from 'Grey Day'. There was a gatefold double album and inside, it had a still from each video. We sold nearly 900,000 *Divine Madness*'s in a short space of time. Also, there was a VHS compilation, which did really well – over 100,000."

* * *

Issued in early March 1992, *Divine Madness* spent three weeks at number one and a total of 96 weeks on the album charts – an incredible feat which outstripped even the longevity of *Complete Madness*. "I remember seeing the posters for *Divine Madness* on every train station into London, every tube station," remembers Sean Flowerdew. "They were plastered everywhere. I didn't think it warranted being that big because I'd seen it all die off!"

At first, the band kept their distance. "They didn't really promote *Divine Madness* to start with," admits Pritchard. "Great involvement from them eventually, taking the piss but enjoying it and a classic, TV-driven album. But certainly, they weren't announcing that they were getting back together, it was a record company cash-in that they were happy to endorse. Then the reviews came in and they started to feel the warmth, the almost unequivocal worship from the press."

It's fair to say that some of Madness probably needed the money and such unmitigated success would have been most welcome. Garbutt perceived some internal conflict, however: "From the outside, you might have assumed that they all wanted the money. But it didn't seem that was always the case. Mike had family in Holland and Chrissy had a young wife*

---

* Foreman married Laurence Heinrich (born April 16, 1972) in Islington in April 1992. The couple had a son Felix Fairfax Foreman, born in 1993, before they eventually got divorced in September 1995. Cathal's second son Milo was also born during this period on December 12, 1991.

and at times he wasn't sure and would have his moments when he wasn't around. I do wonder if any of this stuff would have come together without Cathal. Ultimately, the realisation that there was a lot of financial gain helped."

Garbutt was most struck by the relentless ambition of Madness' one-time MC. "You had a band and then, in Cathal, you had an industry professional within the band," he suggests. "In that period of time when they were hugely successful, other acts seemed to take the accolades. You heard about Duran Duran, Spandau Ballet and Adam & The Ants; Madness were equally successful but somehow didn't get that kudos. I found it odd. Paul Conroy and I were arguing on the Brits panel in the Nineties about why they weren't getting 'best contribution'. There seemed to be some incredible industry resistance and yet Cathal cottoned on early to the legacy of Madness and would constantly be trying to promote it. He was passionate to the point of emotional. He seemed to understand the importance of Madness in their time, in pop music, histori-cally what they represented, way more than anyone else. I think Suggs did but he wasn't the one to articulate it."

By contrast, their singer seemed less committed to the project at first. "Suggs was slightly aloof to start with," admits Garbutt. "You have to earn his trust and respect. I remember once, I was waiting for him outside his house near the Holloway Road (Holloway Prison was right behind it) to do Simon Bates' show on Radio 1. He left me stranded. Not the first or the last time it happened! I was talking to Simon Bates who's calling me off-air. He had a rebellious nature but he started mellowing out and becoming more 'industry' – where Cathal had already got to. And Suggs did fulfil his engagement with Simon Bates a week later! We also did a major BBC documentary voiced by Steve Wright over a series of days with them all separately in Broadcasting House in spring '92." Some of them were still wary about talk of a reunion. "Can you imagine us at thirty leaping around onstage," Suggs was heard to comment.

Garbutt also got to know the rest of the band. "Lee was just wrecklessly Lee!," he laughs. "He was epitomised by his onstage persona – he wasn't much different off it. I had a great relationship with Lee in the sense that he was raving mad. The man who never grew up! Absolutely crazy but for all the tough exterior, he was one of the sweetest, loveliest guys you'd want to meet. I immediately bonded and felt comfortable with him in a way which took longer with Chrissy Boy. Woody and Bedders were always friendly. Mike wasn't around much because he was still coming from Holland."

"As a result of the album – the reviews, the first week sales – it started to gain a genuine, organic life of its own," says Steve Pritchard. In the summer of 1992, Virgin was sold to Thorn-EMI by Richard Branson for a reported $1 billion, apparently to help fund his Virgin Atlantic Airways operation. As such, the company was thrown into a state of flux, with a new managing director found in ex-Stiff general manager Paul Conroy (who, in the interim, had worked in the upper echelons of both Warner Brothers with Rob Dickins and then Chrysalis).

"The biggest album of 1992 by one place above Genesis' *We Can't Dance* was *Divine Madness*," states Garbutt. "That said everything about what was going wrong post-Branson at Virgin." Steve Pritchard: "It was one of the reissues of the year. We re-released other singles and they were minor hits again – 'House Of Fun', 'My Girl'. And then talk of a reformation started up. They got their confidence back because I think they thought nobody loved them. That's where Madstock came from."

★ ★ ★

Realising the need for a new manager, Cathal organised for the band to meet Steve Finan, the son of Merseyside comedian Tom O'Connor. For many years, Finan had co-organised gigs at Kentish Town's Bull & Gate – indeed, he would have promoted that early Voice Of The Beehive show witnessed by Woodgate and Bedford. Keen to make the leap into artist management, Finan had switched his attentions to the burgeoning British hip-hop and R&B scene, eventually masterminding the career of teenage rapper Monie Love, via his management company BAMN (By All Means Necessary). When Monie Love broke big in 1989 and made some headway in the States, Finan also got to work with US hip-hop giants like The Jungle Brothers and Ice-T, as well as home-grown artists such as Neneh Cherry, Caron Wheeler and the Young Disciples. Eventually, he stumbled across singer and fellow boxer Kenny Thomas – and a subsequent contract was structured such that Finan oversaw the production of Thomas's recordings from scratch. As a result, Finan needed to find a cost-effective facility.

"I rented the studio in Caledonian Road off Madness," says Steve. "I ended up having that building for four or five years. They were my land-lords. They owned that building and the one next door. Dave Stewart's brother John rented the other building. He had a successful video produc-tion company. Halfway through that process, Cathal came to ask if I could manage the band. They'd done *Divine Madness* and they were going to put this gig together. But I had reservations. The first two albums I remember buying as a youngster were by Ian Dury and Madness. Nah, I can't be responsible for messing up anything to do with a band I was brought up on!"

Finan is in no doubt who was driving the band's reunion. "Cathal was the petrol in the Madness engine," he states. "He asked me if I could meet the band in a pub in Camden for Suggs' birthday at The Crown & Goose in Arlington Street." This was mid-January 1992. "Lee was like, 'I hear you're a boxer, you're tough, come outside.' As we get to the door, he says to me, 'Oh, I'm only joking.' And I thought, OK, let's twist it on its head here. So I said, 'Too bad, because I'm not anymore.' So I dragged him outside the pub. Then I said, 'It's OK, I'm only joking!' So he ran inside going, 'He's all right, he is, a good bloke!' A funny start to it." Although Steve was tacitly Madness' new manager, nothing was ever signed and the relationship was quite informal. "I agreed to help but not to commit to doing everything because I wasn't sure what I could add. I was quite happy to suck it and see. I wasn't expecting it to carry on. Also, I didn't really know what I was getting into."

Having grown up in a family where his father was a celebrity, Steve was used to being around famous people – and he was struck by Madness' down-to-earth nature. "What was weird was they were all still in the same space they'd always been in. Suggs, for example, was completely progres-sive. He was always working with other bands, the latest music. Lee and Chrissy Boy were just so socially minded, from the fans' point of view always. Everything about them was grounded in social responsibility and that working-class 'rightness', almost like the John Prescott of the band! Mike was a Buddhist, Bedders a designer, so they were from a soft, creative, more easy-going end of things being aesthetically right. Madness were unique because everyone in the band contributed every time you were stuck for an idea. You had seven guys who were all switched on and clued up, giving you top drawer ideas. You've only got to look at their videos."

Buoyed by the spectacular success of *Divine Madness*, and the growing realisation that some reunion shows might prove extremely lucrative, the band reconvened in a rehearsal studio, dusting off any musical or relational cobwebs in the process. In April, all seven members of Madness reunited onstage for the first time since December 21, 1983 for a 'secret' show for the benefit of an invited audience. Although the band only performed four songs, it was an historic occasion – and a film crew from Go! Discs captured it for posterity, with a view to creating the pilot for a music TV show as part of a planned spin-off arm of the company, Go! TV. The show's working title was *Spunk*, which might be one reason why it remained in the archives!

Smyth saw it as a means to an end. "I had, in a slightly underhand way, got the band to reform and play for that pilot," he admits, "which included Dennis Pennis and Norm from *Cheers*. Once in rehearsal, the music did its magic and I loaded the audience during the pilot's making at the Notre Dame Church Hall off Leicester Square. It was a small step in getting the band to perform [again] as they enjoyed the performance and got brilliant feedback from friends at the gig. By the way, we each received £500 for the pilot!"

Interviewed at the time, Mark Bedford expressed a reluctance to reform the band, emphasising his other activities. "I went to Paris a couple of weeks ago to record on a French album for a guy named Nicola," he explained. "He's with this really big band called Andosheen and he's made this solo record. So myself and the drummer out of Lloyd Cole & The Commotions, Stephen Irvine, went over. I also go to college as well. I do design at the London College Of Printing."

Perhaps through his connections in north London's Irish community, or through dealings on behalf of Go! Discs, Cathal spoke with promoter Vince Power, who was then head of The Mean Fiddler Organisation, about ideas for a reunion show. "A gig was already in the background, building up, but it wasn't fully negotiated," says Finan. "It was still a figment of Vince Power and Cathal's imaginations. They all knew each other but I remember steering Cathal. If he's the petrol, then he's the super super unleaded and doesn't always know when to stop. He'd be turning over every stone so it was a matter of trying to get a stable line of contact throughout, an agent who was big enough. I didn't know Vince Power very well so I got Barry Dickins involved. Barry was doing all the big bands."

Barry Dickins was one of the most prominent agents and concert promoters in the country via his company International Talent Booking (ITB); he was also the brother of Madness's old friend Rob. Although Barry hadn't worked with Madness before, he was acquainted with Suggs' wife Anne from his days working with Deaf School back in the mid-1970s. "Cathal was in the lead role," recalls Barry. "He was always the one who was out and about. He's very streetwise. I take my hat off to him. He got them all back together."

"For about a year and a half, I made every effort to coax the band to reform," Smyth admits. "This met with some resistance from some band members but on St Patrick's Day at the Irish Club dinner in 1992, Vince Power of The Mean Fiddler proposed a deal which I think went a long way to making the reformation happen." Dickins and Power had already collaborated on several shows. Since 1990, Power had hosted the Fleadh in Finsbury Park, north London, a festival celebrating Celtic and Irish music – and he had exclusive rights to the location for music shows. Only a couple of miles from Camden, the 115-acre site seemed like the perfect stage for Madness' homecoming.

★ ★ ★

Eventually, the band announced details of "An Audience With Madness", alias Madstock, which was to be held outdoors on Sunday, August 9. Although the show had been prompted by the success of *Divine Madness*, Cathal's A&R role at Go! Discs led to the label securing the rights to record the concert (Steve Pritchard recalls that Virgin weren't even offered the chance to make a rival bid). The deal involved a handsome advance which allowed Go! Discs to release a live album, an accompanying video and also to license footage for a proposed documentary on Channel 4. Go! Discs boss Andy MacDonald was "very generous", according to Finan.

They were keen for Madstock to avoid any connotation of some 2 Tone revival. Instead, the opening slots went to modern bands Gallon Drunk and Flowered Up, friend and admirer Morrissey and their greatest inspiration, Ian Dury, now reunited with The Blockheads. When the 36,000 tickets for the Sunday show swiftly sold out, a second date was added the day before on Saturday 8 – Foreman's 36th birthday. With around 72,000 fans due to attend across the weekend, Madness' comeback looked set to be the biggest live event they'd ever hosted in the UK.

To coincide with the advance publicity for the event and for Virgin's reissue of 'My Girl', the band played their first *Top Of The Pops* together since 'One Better Day' in 1984. In a bid to get down to fighting weight, Madness spent a week beginning July 21 rehearsing in England before travelling to Holland on August 1 for a similar regime. As their set-list took shape, more downbeat tunes such as 'Yesterday's Men', 'Michael Caine' and 'Uncle Sam' were substituted for 'Razor Blade Alley', 'Driving In My Car' and 'Wings Of A Dove'.

The Dutch trip culminated in a dry-run at Paard Von Troje, a small club in The Hague. All went to plan – until the celebrations which followed the rapturous reception at their warm-up gig. According to the sleeve-notes for the ensuing *Madstock!* album, Thompson went AWOL, ending up on a beach "with a couple of puffs of skunk" in his lungs, "on a trampoline, with a lot of kids bouncing higher than me". Fuelled by, among other substances, the competitive spirit, Lee responded with "a midnight bounce, stark naked on a starlit night and, coming down, I missed the canvas completely and broke me toe on one of the springs".

Also in The Hague was plugger Mick Garbutt: "It was a jolly-up, bringing out people from media – we did competitions with Capital Radio and MTV did some filming. It was a hot, sweaty summer's night. One of those oddities was this neo-Nazi presence there, this hangover from a different generation. Cathal said that he peered outside the curtains and thought, oh my word! An aggressive male thing but there was no trouble, it just felt intimidating. All this history with Madness which was so contradictory to their left-wing principles, all family men."

Come Friday morning, the Madness entourage limped back to Blighty with sore heads and an array of minor physical ailments. This was hardly a picture postcard image of a band who should have been match fit. To make matters worse, Thompson was arrested at Heathrow Airport for travelling on an expired passport, but was released an hour later without charge. The rest of the day was spent getting haircuts, buying shirts, collecting new suits and – in Mike Barson's case – worrying about the impending birth of their second child back home in Holland (Timothy was eventually born on August 20). Thompson had previously swiped his white suit from the BBC wardrobe, incurring a £200 bill. Only Bedders seemed to have nagging doubts. "I can't believe all these people are going to turn up," he said. "Why would we appeal?"

Other than the band's topsy turvy behaviour, preparations for the weekend ran smoothly. Sure, some pre-show butterflies were evident when they convened that morning, as Finan recalls: "Everyone came into this room and Suggs was like, OK, who's had the dream when you're naked and you can't run very fast or you can't get to the top! It was quite funny!" They needn't have worried, though. The band had recruited two capable individuals to organise proceedings in Andy Franks and Lee Charteris. The doors opened promptly at noon and Madness were set to arrive in style inside a fleet of sleek limousines. Celebrities in attendance included Jimmy Nail, Suede's Brett Anderson, members of Depeche Mode and original choice of support The Farm. With a capacity audience, a mixed but moderate weather forecast and the collective experience of those involved, what could possibly go wrong?

Steve Finan: "What happened was the big drama. Vince comes up to me and says, 'We've got a problem with the bank drafts for the advance,' which they'd gotten from the bank on the Friday. Someone had followed Maureen, his accountant, home from the club and robbed her. Let's say the advance was maybe £600,000. A lot of money. Vince is like, 'I haven't got any money to pay you but it'll be OK, I'll give it you on Monday.' This was my worst fears come true. Every time you do a pro-motion, you start a new limited company. The worst thing that could happen would be that Monday morning, the company's folded, all the cash that has been generated from that day goes to something else, Madness can't sue. So I'm absolutely thinking, 'Great, here we go.' The last thing I wanted to be involved in was Madness coming back and it's a disaster and I'm right in the middle of it!"

His heart racing, Finan ignored the escalating feelings of panic in his gut and racked his brain to think of a possible solution. "I knew that if the band realised there was no money there, they wouldn't go on," he admits. "This is midday on Saturday. So I made Vince give me his bank manager's phone number. I managed to find him in Ireland. He was fishing. He agreed that the funds had been taken out but that the bank drafts weren't cashable by anybody else. So I said to Vince, 'I know it's a problem but if I don't have the £300,000, half of the advance, before they go on, I know they won't perform.' So between us, we start to get together every single penny we can get our hands on. Vince is going to his venues, getting money from the bars, from everywhere. Bit by bit, it was coming in. We were in the hut where Maureen was, who was getting upset because she thought we didn't believe she had been robbed."

Around lunchtime, Finan had agreed to meet with the band. "I go to the pub, The Crown & Goose, where they're now filming," Steve continues. "As I walk in, the first question they asked me is, 'Have we got the money?' I've got a camera in my face, which I know is going on Channel 4, and I'm like, 'Yes!' Fuck, what have I done? I've just lied my tits off on camera! We hadn't got any of the money at that point. I was just checking they were all right. But if I'd have said 'No', that would have been it. They're all high-fiving, great, wicked. Now I'm in psycho mode. No matter what, I'm going to make sure this happens!"

Steve was acutely aware that the clock was ticking. "What I also had in the back of my mind was that, if they didn't go on, we'd lose this massive advance from Go! Discs. So it was a catch 22. If I'd have known Vince the way I know him now, I would have said fine. But I just couldn't take any chances. Anyway, someone went to Heathrow to get the maximum off his credit card. Barry Dickins and me are in this little cabin with all this money and a counting machine! Bear in mind it was really hot so we're sweating, Maureen's still crying and Barry Dickins and Vince are having words with each other which got heated!"

Meanwhile, a vague threat of a downpour had certainly not dampened the spirits of the thousands of fans who arrived at Finsbury Park from noon onwards. What swiftly became apparent was the greater than average proportion of tattooed, shaven-headed blokes at the event than might ordinarily be seen at an outdoor festival of this kind. By mid-afternoon, the beer was flowing freely - but even if the presence en masse of thousands of grown-up skinheads was a shade intimidating to the un-initiated, for the most part the atmosphere was convivial.

Blues/swamp rock band Gallon Drunk opened the proceedings, followed by Flowered Up with their self-styled 'cockney' answer to Manchester's Happy Mondays: they owed more than a little of their impish humour to Madness. Unfortunately, both bands endured a barrage of heckling and small missiles, presumably due to a minority of fans who were impatient to see their heroes. Next onstage was Ian Dury & The Blockheads. Dury, who had recently celebrated his 50th birthday, had much to celebrate with a new album *The Bus Driver's Prayer & Other Stories*, although his set appropriately relied more heavily on past classics. For Madness, it must have felt like an honour to have Dury on the bill; but his set came and went, largely unnoticed by the increasingly ebullient audience, as the revelry continued apace.

Back in the hut, the crisis appeared to be reaching some sort of conclusion. "Giving Vince his due, he got the £300,000 together by a quarter to eight," continues Finan. "Now, this pile of fivers and tenners is on the table. Vince said, 'Can you sign off for the money?' I said, 'You've got to be kidding, there's no way I am walking out of here with three hundred grand in a bin liner. You're out of your mind. Phone a Securicor van!' We're all still sitting there. The next thing, over the radio, the Securicor van's burst a tyre over the other side of Finsbury Park. My mind is all over the place. I'm thinking to myself, I sign off on a bit of paper, walk out, somebody hits me over the head, takes the bag and everything's down to me. So I say to Vince, 'I'm not signing anything until the money goes in the back of the van!' Anyway, six bouncers, me, Vince and Barry now walk across Finsbury Park. All the crowd are there. We get to the Securicor van, the guy lifts the hatch up, I throw the money in, kiss everybody, sign the bit of paper, then off we go! Now we're going to do the gig!"

★ ★ ★

Both Madness and the audience were blissfully unaware of the unfolding drama. By this time, they were too busy watching the next performer, Morrissey. Despite the fact that this was his first British date in over eighteen months and that his new album, *Your Arsenal*, had been issued the previous week, the crowd at Finsbury Park seemed conspicuous by its absence of Smiths fans. According to author Simon Goddard in his book *Mozipedia*, a small but irascible faction within the crowd didn't take kindly to Morrissey's camp theatrics. This adverse reaction has been the source of much conjecture among both Morrissey and Madness fans due to *NME*'s ensuing – and, some might say, inflammatory – coverage. What provoked such hostility? Was it his chanted lyric "London is dead"? Could some die-hard skinheads have been aggravated by the singer's flirtation with skinhead imagery (the stage backdrop depicted two huge photos of skinhead girls) or even his waving of the Union flag (during his second song,

'Glamorous Glue', at the end of which he threw the flag into the audience)?

"As Morrissey's set progressed, they began throwing coins and beer at irregular intervals," writes Simon Goddard. "Upset by this, he made the impromptu decision to cut his set-list, leading his band off stage after nine songs. It's a common mistake to believe Morrissey was bottled off stage as a direct consequence of parading the national flag around. Neither the flag, nor his backdrop, nor even his set-list including 'The National Front Disco', had anything to do with their hostile reaction." Steve Finan was distracted by the calamity over the band's fee and missed the furore: "I asked Chrissy Boy what happened and he said, 'Somebody threw a Rizla at Morrissey and it hit him and he went off'!"

Clive Langer explained to Goddard that the reason for such antipathy was actually more prosaic. "The main problem was there weren't that many Morrissey fans there. Morrissey was only advertised for the Sunday, but he agreed to do both dates. The irony was that Morrissey refused to do the second night, which was stupid of him because his fans turned up and he would have had a great time. Looking back, I'd say that out of 30,000 Madness fans who were there, 29,000 of them were soft skinheads with their girlfriends and it was the other 1,000 hard skins who decided to let him have it. They just didn't want him." As Goddard explained, Langer, Suggs and Smyth all tried in vain to talk Morrissey back for the second night – but to no avail. Thompson later bemoaned their choice of support. "As much as he is a respected and highly rated lyricist with good musicians, Morrissey should not have been supporting us at Madstock," he admitted. "We have a certain type of audience and I wish to cater to them."

Eventually, it was time for Madness' triumphant return. Call it pre-show nerves but in the immediate minutes before walking out onstage, there'd been some momentary indecision about what to say to introduce themselves. "We had a discussion," remembers Finan. "And someone said, 'Why don't you just walk out and stand there. Don't do anything. It's been so long since you've been away.'" At around 8.45pm, that's exactly what the seven original members of Madness did, to rapturous applause from an admittedly intoxicated crowd. "They stood there and it was unbelievable," says Finan. "People just screamed forever. That idea was deliberate but was only thought of two minutes before they went onstage!

Everyone went mental then Cathal eventually came out with 'Hey You, Don't Watch That, Watch This!' Indescribable!"

As Madness broke into 'One Step Beyond', the audience erupted into a frenzy. Patently, the band had lost none of their verve – indeed, they appeared comfortable and had clearly rehearsed intensively. Physically, they looked both dapper and fit – although Cathal had maybe enjoyed a few too many business lunches. Alongside the expected barrage of hits, performed with gusto, they also chose to revisit early favourites such as 'Swan Lake', 'Razor Blade Alley' and 'Close Escape'. Aside from a glitch with the backing tape for 'Wings Of A Dove', the show was an unmitigated success.

After concerns about the crowd's safety were expressed by the local constabulary, with threats that the plug might be pulled if the crush at the front of the stage didn't ease, Suggs made repeated requests for the audience to shift back – which seemed to do the trick. Lee, seemingly, had no such health and safety worries as he sailed through the air on wires during 'Baggy Trousers' (what else?). As one of their encores, they tackled the Jimmy Cliff classic, 'The Harder They Come', which they had performed during their twilight days in 1986, before ending with a surprise guest appearance from none other than Prince Buster for a version of his song which inspired their name. "Last one out turns off the light," joked Cathal.

When Suggs had uttered the line "An earthquake is erupting" from 'The Prince' that night, he couldn't have known how right he was. During the opening bars of 'One Step Beyond' at the start of their performance, the enthusiastic 'moonstomping' from large swathes of the audience led to vibrations which registered at 4.5 on the Richter Scale (defined as "noticeable shaking of indoor items, rattling noises, significant damage unlikely"). Reports ensued of complaints from neighbouring tower blocks, which were reverberating. By all accounts, some residents had to be evacuated, prompting some perhaps exaggerated reports in the media. According to those *Madstock!* sleeve-notes, "windows broke, balconies cracked, furniture moved and panic calls were made to the emergency services"!

Aside from Morrissey's absence, the second day of Madstock passed without incident. This time, Prince Buster guested not only on 'Madness' but also his other famously covered classic, 'One Step Beyond'. The band could now divide their focus between future plans and their decidedly healthier bank balances. Unfortunately, they might have forgotten to take care of some business. Steve Finan: "I knew that their net would have been over a million pounds for the shows – not just from the gate but the Go! Discs deal. Did I have a formal agreement? No! Did anyone offer to pay me for it? No! I suppose I was just helping out, really. The person who paid me was Barry Dickins. I said to him, 'Listen, I didn't get anything,' but before we finished the conversation, he wrote a cheque for £20,000. I couldn't believe it. It was quite an eye-opener that somebody would invest in a relationship to keep it going forward."

It's been suggested that certain members of Madness were struggling to make ends meet in that period immediately prior to Madstock. If that was true, Finan certainly wasn't aware of any financial hardships. "I didn't get the feeling that anyone was ever fretting about money because they [seemed to have] managed their existence relative to whatever they had," he suggests. During his brief tenure as manager, Finan was approached by all and sundry to offer Madness any number of deals – and most propositions were rejected, regardless of how lucrative they were. "If they didn't think it was the right thing to do, they didn't do it," states Steve. "That was right across the board."

* * *

In the fall-out from Madstock, one major task was to mould the recordings from the weekend into two releasable products. The audio had been captured across both days using the Fleetwood Mobile then produced and mixed at their Westside Studios by Clive Langer and Alan Winstanley – who chose seven tracks from day one and eleven from day two. *Madstock!*, the album, was released in early November and charted at number 22 – a perfectly respectable performance for a live reunion record. A companion video, *Madstock – The Movie*, also performed well.

The *Madstock!* album boasted a suitably animated photo of the band, seemingly in mid-air throwing shapes, taken by Jill Furmanovsky, who later recollected the period in her book *The Moment*. "It was with great joy that I took on the job of photographing their comeback concert," she wrote. "I joined the band in The Hague, where they were playing a warm-up gig. The usual image is a live shot from the gig but this time I wanted to create an action shot that wasn't them in concert. Hoping to inspire the band, I brought along some pictures of dancers jumping in the air. Lee, who is an exceptional athlete, was nursing a swollen ankle, an injury sustained in the early hours by falling off a beach trampoline somewhere on the seafront while drunk."

A light bulb in the photographer's mind switched on. "'Can you find this place again?' I asked, sensing a possible solution. Lee nodded hopefully but looked doubtful. We took a chance. Seven band members were despatched in three different cars to the beach but, needless to say, became separated. To add to the confusion, Lee's estimation of the location was far from accurate. Eventually, my party found the right place and started photographing those present. In dribs and drabs, the missing musicians appeared down the beach, sweltering in their nutty-boy suits. Each took a turn on the trampoline. The final image – Madness dropping out of the sky to surprise their fans – was collaged together on a computer. The RAC sign saying 'Madness concert' with an arrow pointing to the sky was a lucky sighting on the day of the concert."

'The Harder They Come' was plucked from the album as a single to help promote the album. Unfortunately, Madness had already appeared on *Top Of The Pops* with 'My Girl' and the show's producers were reluctant to grant them another visit. Steve Finan was part of the negotiating team. "We're all sat around the table and had the BBC on speakerphone. They were saying, 'Give us a good reason why we should put you on *Top Of The Pops* again.' We're all trying – what if we did this or that? And they're literally going, no, no, no. Then Cathal says, 'I know, we'll fly to Moscow and play live from Red Square. No one's ever done that before.' And it was off the top of his head! Of course, *Top Of The Pops* were like, booked in, done. Organising that was just weird because they could only have one outside broadcast satellite in the whole of Russia. But again, Cathal knew where the guy was. He's quite incredible."

Once again, Jill Furmanovsky was along for the ride, as she recalled in *The Moment*. "Five of Madness (Lee missed the plane, Bedders had exams at college) and a small film crew went to Russia. I was invited along to shoot for *You* magazine." Apparently, the band were impressed when an old-fashioned limo, complete with peak-hatted chauffeur, met them outside Moscow Airport. "Unfortunately, it broke down at the first set of traffic lights. We met at a colossal building known as the Hotel Russia, which took up an entire block and slept 6,000."

As Sod's law would have it, the only members of their party who had a room fit for purpose were two production people from the band's office. While their pad was a "proper hotel suite – big towels, a mini-bar, a cheerful décor", Madness themselves were cooped up in rooms which were "small and stiflingly hot, the windows didn't open, there was a dish-cloth for a towel, no soap and noisy neighbours". Eventually, Jill, Cathal and Steve Finan all chose to bed down in the suite. "Suggs joined us for a midnight feast of 'little snacky things' brought from home, washed down with vodka. We spent most of the night behaving like school kids. At one point, Suggs and Cathal removed the double-glazing with a screwdriver to let in some fresh air."

In due course, Madness filmed their *Top Of The Pops* performance of 'The Harder They Come' in Red Square. "I had to be bass player," adds Finan. "I was dressed up with a hat and gloves. It was freezing. When the camera's coming to me, I'm turning away!" Despite such prestigious exposure, their Jimmy Cliff cover stalled outside the Top 40 – which wasn't really surprising given that in-concert 45s rarely sold in quantity. However, the whole campaign maintained Madness' high profile on the eve of their 'Madstock On Christmas' tour of the UK – their first in seven years. Spread across half a dozen major cities (including Brighton, Cardiff, Manchester, Edinburgh and Birmingham), the dates began with two nights at Wembley Arena on December 15 and 16 (the first of which was added "due to popular demand").

For their stage set-up, the band designed a bar and a boxing-ring – and Thompson went so far as to don a boxing oufit for several dates. Unfortunately, an old spectre returned briefly to haunt them at their first Arena appearance when some idiots were spotted waving a swastika banner during a support set from Suggs' mates The Farm (the other warm-up act being 808 State). After the offending individuals were quietly ejected from the venue, Suggs felt the need to counter accusations that they were merely trading on past glories. Madness seemed faintly out-of-shape: Thompson seemingly forgot to play his solo during 'It Must Be Love' and 'Driving In My Car' endured two false starts. Despite such hiccups, though, the reunion shows were hugely welcome to fans who probably never thought they'd have another chance to see the original Madness seven in a proper venue. For their first encore, Suggs and Cathal indulged in paraphrasing *The Bible* ("And the Lord said 'Bring back Madness'"), citing a poem before the band unveiled a promising new Mike Barson song, 'Moondance', a barnstorming call-and-response-type number in the style of 'One Step Beyond' which was strangely dropped from their repertoire after the tour.

From Madness' point of view, the Wembley shows were a resounding success. "Barry Dickins told me he got the best rental deal ever from Wembley because the guys who went bought so much beer – more beer than anyone else – and the takings were so high that they gave him a break on the rent," Finan recalls. "At those gigs, people would turn up and literally do every single dance move of every routine of every song from start to finish. It was fantastic."

Unfortunately, the Glasgow date was marred by an outbreak of violence from local football hooligans. "There was a riot," admits Finan. "These Hibs casuals have come in. When The Farm came on, twelve of them started punching everybody. It was horrible. A mass brawl breaks out. The doors get kicked open. They even came across the stage. I'm trying to lock the back door to where Madness were and they're all pushing their way in there. People are scared, getting away from the crush. They robbed all the merchandise. Decision: do we carry on? The head of the Scottish Metropolitan Police turns up. I phoned Barry Dickins and said, 'Are we insured for a riot? Do we get paid?' No."

Finan had to break the news to the band. "If we don't go on, not only do you not get the money but you pay whatever it's cost to put on tonight. Reluctantly, they were like, 'OK, let's try.' I then had to negotiate with the police who said that they would only let the gig go on if they played with all the lights on. And they played with 300 policemen on a balcony looking down on a crowd, with people throwing darts up at the police. In the middle of the ruckus, by the sound stage, a guy of about 50 has a golf club swinging it around his head at people. This was the worst gig ever! No atmosphere, going through the motions. A pretty low point."

★ ★ ★

All the while, the manager was slowly getting the measure of his charges. "By now, I've got more of a handle of the dynamic and bear in mind it involves a lot of things other than the band – the wives, the children," he explains. "Let's say, for example, a simple question like: do you want to tour at Christmas? Out of that, there'd be some heavy issues that went back years, like someone had sold them a car which didn't work and owed him a thousand pounds – real twenty-year-old petty shit where they'd go, 'I'll do it but I want him to give me that £1,000 back!' "

Finan had to devise ways of circumnavigating any such dysfunctional tendencies. "I was living in Neneh Cherry's house – I was managing her for a short time," he continues. "I had five telephone lines installed. To get Madness to make a decision, I used to have Cathal on one line, Suggs on another, Chris on the third line, Lee on the fourth then one of the other three on the fifth. (There were two cliques, then Mike, Bedders and Woody.) Cathal, do you want to tour at Christmas? If Suggsy's fine with it, I'm fine with it. Are you sure because when I put this phone down, I'm going to call the promoter. Then I'd put him on hold because if I hung up on him, he'd call Suggs. So I'd say to Cathal, just wait there. Then I'd get hold of Suggs. Cathal says he's cool with it. Oh, if he's fine, I'm fine. Again, put him on hold. Then Chris would want to know what Lee said. I'd get all four of them agreed, then the last one. I'd hang up all five lines once I got the answer. Then you could literally count to twenty and the five lines would start lighting up again where they'd called each other. But I wouldn't answer the phone for two hours until the adverts had gone out!"

Totally committed to Madness' return, Cathal felt obligated to offer his resignation to Go! Discs. "Andy MacDonald offered me 10 per cent of Go! Discs Publishing as a sweetener to get me to stay as an employee with the label," Smyth recalls, "saying I could continue with Madness and remain as an A&R man. My heart was with Madness [though] and I felt that I could bring my record company experience to the band. I also felt it was somehow dishonourable to pop off and play Wembley Arena and at the same time represent those acts' careers. How could I honestly concentrate on their interests? I thoroughly enjoyed my time [there] and I learnt much, which has helped both me personally and the band. All artistes who engage in the company side of the business seem to do well and I knew I was turning my back on a career. My first love, though, was Madness."

On February 16, 1993, Madness appeared on music industry's televised awards ceremony The Brits, performing 'Night Boat To Cairo'. That March, Virgin attempted to maintain their gravy train of the previous year by reissuing 'Night Boat To Cairo' with some questionable dance remixes by Paul Gotel, who'd made his mark working with The Shamen and various house music acts. More worthwhile was a Madness 3-CD box set, a 69-track assemblage of A- and B-sides interspersed with snippets of conversation between tracks from a dizzying array of Madness' professional acquaintances.

In July, Madness graced the bill at the Gurten Festival in Bern, Switzerland. And on August 1, they appeared on the third and final day of the Féile Festival at the Semple Stadium in Thurles, Co. Tipperary, Ireland, on a bill alongside the likes of Squeeze, Aztec Camera and reggae/funk act Inner Circle. Incensed that their set had been curtailed in order for headliner Chris de Burgh to play an extended show, Suggs made several jibes (such as spelling their Prince Buster cover as 'M-I-N-D-L-E-S-S'!). Apparently, Barson's commitment to attending a lengthy Buddhist retreat precluded further shows that summer.

The summer dates pre-empted a second round of concerts, this time under the banner 'The Man In The Mad Suit Tour', taking in a handful of arenas in the week before Christmas 1993 (the G-Mex in Manchester, Cardiff International, the Birmingham NEC, the Brighton Centre and Wembley Arena) with support from Carter The Unstoppable Sex Machine. While Thompson dressed up as a genie from *Aladdin* (complete with bodypaint), their set-list included the rarely-heard yet popular 'Shut Up' B-side 'Never Ask Twice' (alias 'Airplane'), which Suggs introduced as Roxy Music's 'Virginia Plain'; and their never-before-performed swansong single, '(Waiting For) The Ghost-Train'. During the show at the Birmingham NEC, and for reasons best known to himself, Thompson climbed into a bag to hop across the stage and promptly fell off it.

In what was to become a biennial event across the Nineties, Madness reconvened for a second Madstock across the weekend of August 6 and 7, 1994, with support from dance act the Tyrell Corporation, reggae favourites Aswad, hip-hop act Credit To The Nation, punk stalwarts Buzzcocks and a return from Ian Dury & The Blockheads. Adverts echoed the Stiff quips of old: "We came, we saw, we left, we popped back in." Madness' set was notable for Suggs quoting The Rolling Stones classic '(I Can't Get No) Satisfaction' towards the end of 'Driving In My Car' and 'My Way' at the close of 'Wings Of A Dove'; some guitar histrionics from Foreman; and best of all, Thompson taking centre stage for a cover of The Kinks' 1970 hit 'Lola'. When Lee, dressed as an undertaker, brought a coffin onto the stage, rumours abounded that this was Madness' farewell show, which was aired on BBC radio.

"No major incidents," remembers Finan of Madstock '94. "Everything by now was running really smoothly, like clockwork. We had a really good team behind us with Andy Franks and Lee Charteris. The whole set-up behind Madness went on to become Robbie Williams' team. They were amazing. To be honest, when we did that second tour, I was almost redundant, walking around saying, 'Everyone OK?' 'Yeah, we're fine, thanks!'"

Although the second Madstock weekender couldn't hope to match the same sense of occasion as their 1992 comeback, demand for all things Madness-related was insatiable. "We sold out of all the merchandise we'd produced for two days on the first day, the Saturday, by two o'clock in the afternoon," admits Steve. "That's not only a lot of money but a lot of stock. You can imagine now we've got a day and a half where we could be selling ten times that amount. So we went outside and bought seven thousand shirts off the bootleggers for five quid apiece. Couldn't believe their luck! We brought them back inside and that gave us enough time to print more in East London – another thousand shirts every hour or whatever. They were just flat out printing all night long!"

The logical development of Madstock would have been a brand new studio album – but instead of following up the live LP with a studio offering, Madness faltered. "I don't think at that time the appetite was there," admits Finan, pointing out that fully fledged reunions were an unusual commodity in terms of committing to new recordings. "No one was really coming back," he suggests. "Everything was so new and fresh. The promoters were all centred around having hit records to sell a ticket and Madstock went against the grain but you weren't growing the audience much. You were re-playing to your core people. So they needed a break. You couldn't play to them every year, otherwise it would have become pantomime."

Realising that Madness no longer required his services, Finan concentrated on other pursuits – such as bailing out James Lavelle's Mo' Wax label, which he helped run for the rest of the decade from Madness' Caledonian Road offices. "That building then became Mo' Wax's headquarters," explains Finan. "I was doing Mo' Wax and running A&M's labels. I was Lavelle's partner for ten years. Mo' Wax used the studio as well. The rent was guaranteed by A&M but socially I'd see Madness out and about." While Steve would also help mastermind the career of All Saints, Madness would spend the rest of the 1990s seemingly undecided as to how they should progress – a problem exacerbated by the conflicting plans of their lead singer.

Chapter 19

MAYBE IN ANOTHER LIFE

DURING the fallout from Madstock, Suggs was perhaps the most reticent about the idea of fully committing to a Madness reunion. Instead, he bent the ear of old friend Rob Dickins, who was still chairmen of Warner Music – one of the most powerful figures, in fact, within the UK music industry at the time. Initially, Suggs seemed undecided and early conversations were exploratory rather than decisive. Remember, the singer had already dabbled with expanding his persona onto both little and big screens, while also working behind-the-scenes as part of the management team for The Farm.

"It wasn't planned," explains Rob Dickins. "Suggs and I were friends. He wasn't out looking for a record deal. It was just a guy who ran a record company and a guy who wanted to make a record coming together. There were a lot of people at Madstock, I told him. 'You've got a following. A bit like Sting, you have a name that everybody knows. You've got a brand.' With Suggs, there wasn't a manager shopping a new deal. Let's just try to reflect who he was. When you leave a band, you have a million insecurities. He said to me, 'This is a strange process, writing a song and then recording it.' Because he was used to playing it with the band and then it'd have a bass line and a drum part. 'It's so strange because we're recording what I have in my head,' he said. 'In Madness, we recorded a development of that.' I remember thinking, 'This is why bands are usually stronger than solo artists because a song becomes a different creature.'"

Suggs wasn't that comfortable about the prospect of launching himself as a solo star but Dickins offered him some encouragement. "He'd written a couple of songs and realised Madness wasn't going to be a recording thing and said, 'I don't know what to do,'" Dickins continues. "He came to the office and played me a version of James Brown's 'I Got You' – just a hotch potch of ideas, bits of songs. One early song was 'Alcohol', which I thought was autobiographical but genius. He had a basic home studio so these were just demos. The completed ones like 'Fortune Fish' I thought were really good. I said, 'Why don't we do a solo record?' We were in one of those rare periods when The Beatles weren't omnipresent and I always loved 'I'm Only Sleeping'."

Months passed as the old friends chewed over a possible approach for Suggs, the solo artiste. "There was a long gestation period because it wasn't a career move, more a slow process of songwriting and getting ideas," Rob continues. "We went down a couple of alleyways which weren't exactly gelling so we had a meeting and I said: 'A blank sheet of paper, Suggs, who would you like to produce you? Because we've got to get some kind of sound.' And he said, 'Sly and Robbie.' Their history was well known – and they were hugely successful as pop producers as well."

While their pedigree as both a rhythm section and a production team was second-to-none, Sly Dunbar and Robbie Shakespeare were riding on the crest of a particularly popular wave in 1993 with the huge hits 'Tease Me', 'She Don't Let Nobody' and 'Twist And Shout' for Chaka Demus & Pliers. And this was at a time when reggae was conspicuous by its absence from the UK charts. At some point in 1994, Dickins approached the legendary Jamaican rhythm section to establish their availability. "They were in England – they just stayed in a studio with the different acts they were producing," explains Rob. "They agreed to do a few tracks so we booked Suggs into their schedule of sessions. We had to wait for our slot. I wanted them to do 'I'm Only Sleeping', and Suggs really liked the idea and got it completely. I thought there was something about it which had that Suggs naivety to it."

Dickins left them to their own devices before checking up on their progress at a later date. "I wanted to meet Sly and Robbie," he explains. "I thought Sly was the most brilliant drummer so I just wanted to see him play. I went down to the studio but there's no drum kit. Sly went, the drums are here, man. And he had a machine. I can't believe it! He said, 'I got so fed up playing drums that I spent a week playing every fill I've ever played and this drum machine is me.' And he programmed it out of this machine!"

Sly and Robbie had an intuitive knack of choosing cover versions appropriate to a particular artist. "Of the two of them, Sly is quiet and Robbie's vociferous," continues Dickins. "Robbie said, 'We've tried a couple of ideas with 'I'm Only Sleeping' and it doesn't work.' He said, 'We want to do 'Cecilia'.' And for most people of my generation, 'Cecilia' was the one song from Simon & Garfunkel's *Bridge Over Troubled Water* you couldn't stand! So here was my dream going wrong! 'Why don't we try both?' 'Fine, OK.' Then I get a phone call from Suggs. 'We've tried 'I'm Only Sleeping' again and it doesn't work but 'Cecilia' is shaping up really well.' No!"

Once again, the Warner Music boss drew on whatever persuasive powers he could muster. "I bang the desk with this ska rhythm, singing, 'When I wake up early in the morning . . .'! I'm saying, 'I don't get why you're having a problem with this!' Suggs was just thrilled that he was working with Sly and Robbie. Then they played me 'Cecilia' and I've got to say, this was a surprise, it really was good!" The producers had also been working with London ragga/rap duo Louchie Lou and Michie One (the stage names for Louise Gold and Michelle Charles), who had broken through with their reworking of the Isley Brothers/Lulu classic, 'Shout', in May 1993. "Sly and Robbie said, 'We want to put them on the record' and everyone loved 'Shout' so I went, 'Fine – anything to pull it away from being 'Cecilia'!' Fantastic: the two of them were a great vibe."

Eventually, Sly and Robbie produced three further tracks: the self-explanatory celebration that was 'Camden Town'; a contrasting tale of the region's homeless in 'Haunted' (updating 'One Better Day'); and 'Off On Holiday'; as well as helping to produce and mix 'The Tune'. Unfortunately, Suggs' slot with Sly and Robbie expired so the rest of his projected solo album was finished elsewhere. Behind the scenes, Suggs had been collaborating with Mike Barson sporadically since 1990 (Suggs had travelled back and forth to Amsterdam). 'The Tune' was written solely by Madness' talented pianist but he collaborated with McPherson on three compositions. Alongside 'Camden Town', they co-wrote '4 am', a tribute to The Kinks with references to Terry and Julie from their hit 'Waterloo Sunset' and lyrics like "tired of waiting", while 'She's Gone' was one of their earliest ventures after The Madness.

Some of these songs were co-produced with engineer Kevin Petrie. Another was 'Green Eyes', a Barson/McPherson/Smyth composition set in Brighton which had started life as 'Empty Stairs' back around the time of *Keep Moving*. Petrie also helped with two further Suggs tunes, 'Fortune Fish' and his autobiographical bitter-sweet ode to 'Alcohol' (with a guest appearance from Ben Barson).

The sessions were littered with guest appearances from the great and the not-so-good. "Warners had ZTT and they had this girl duo called All Saints – just Shaznay and Melanie," remembers Dickins. "They were floating around and ZTT didn't know what to do with them. But we got Shaznay Lewis to do a rap on 'I Got You', which ended up as a B-side." Speaking of ZTT, ex-Art Of Noise arranger Anne Dudley added some poignant strings to 'She's Gone', joining such disparate talents on the album as bassists Jah Wobble and Phil Spalding, multi-instrumentalist John Themis and legendary ska trombonist Rico (with Jazz Jamaica). (The album credit to The Wayfinders, was presumably an in-joke: a pseudonym Madness used for a secret show in January 1985.) Additionally, Suggs admitted to being inspired by the Happy Mondays' use of sampling so the team took advantage of modern technology to borrow from soul classics like 'Clean Up Woman' by Betty Wright and 'Time Is Tight' by Booker T. & The M.G.'s, The Champs' Fifties classic 'Tequila' and 'My Jamaican Guy' by Grace Jones.

"Part of the problem was it was bitty," admits Rob Dickins. "Through different sources, we put these songs together as *The Lone Ranger*.* I think I came up with that title because he's now on his own. I thought it was lovely that he did 'Camden Town' – a theme song for that area was nice. Suggs was a friend of [designer] Ben Kelly, who I knew very well. Ben had the idea of taking Marcel Duchamp's *Nude Descending A Staircase, No. 2* as an album sleeve."

★ ★ ★

In August 1994, a month or so after Madstock II, Suggs finally announced plans for a solo career – while speaking about the early days of Madness on Radio 1's *The Story Of Pop*. On November 12, he braved his first solo appearance on the *Danny Baker After All* show, performing a refreshingly faithful rendition of 'I'm Only Sleeping' and Morrissey's 'Suedehead' (perhaps throwing out an olive branch after the Madstock fiasco), backed

---

* Suggs claimed, during an interview around the release date of 'I'm Only Sleeping', that the album had a working title of *The Greatest Pop Record Ever Made*!

by house band the Bow-Town Bottlers (including film critic Mark Kermode). Suggs also chatted with Baker.

Meanwhile, a tabloid newspaper story suggested that Suggs had "snubbed a £250,000 advert" because of his new solo deal. Apparently, he'd originally agreed to re-record the vocal for 'Our House' but eventually failed to appear and another band member had to deputise. "Madness is in the past for Suggs as he is now concentrating on his solo career," a WEA spokesman was quoted as saying. Speaking of gossip, Suggs met up with Madonna while hosting an episode of *Top Of The Pops*. Famously, the American star was reputed to have asked the singer out on a date but Suggs politely declined. Apparently, the pair had history. "It was twelve years ago and I was an up-and-coming young thing," Suggs explained on Northern Ireland's top TV chat show *Kelly* (before performing an acoustically inclined version of 'It Must Be Love'). "I met her in a club in New York and you know how Americans are forward – and boy, was she forward! She remembered that conversation."

'I'm Only Sleeping' was finally unveiled as Suggs' debut solo single in July 1995. (It was technically a double-A-side with 'Off On Holiday', which the singer had wanted as his debut single, while bonus track 'Animal', co-written with Barson, had been performed back in 1989 in the film *Final Frame*.) It comfortably reached the Top 10, helped by rotation airplay and an eye-catching video which harked back to classic Madness, with cameo appearances from Barson and Smyth. "That was satisfying because they hadn't had a new hit record as Madness for quite some years," admits Dickins.

In early October, 'Camden Town' was chosen as Suggs' second single. Melodically indebted to The Kinks' 'Apeman' (with shades of the theme to *Only Fools & Horses!*), this reggae-tinged ode coincided with the region's close associations with Britpop (Camden's pub The Good Mixer became synonymous with the scene) and the slow-but-steady rise in popularity of its weekend markets. In short, Camden was the place-to-be in 1995 (unless you were in Manchester). The song peaked at number 14.

The Lone Ranger was unleashed a couple of weeks later, selling comfortably enough to reach the Top 20 while falling short of expectations. "Top 40 in The Faroe Islands and I'll be happy," joked Suggs. It was an album which illustrated some huge potential while perhaps not gelling as an entity – presumably due in part to the fragmented nature of the sessions.

Reggae played a stronger part than on any Madness album; and its title was possibly inspired by famous reggae DJ Lone Ranger. But it failed to engage with critics: *NME*, for example, dismissed the album with a two-out-of-10 rating. "The album both benefits and suffers from being put together in an atmosphere [without] commercial pressure but thinking we can make some music and it will probably work out well," counters Dickins.

By way of a novel afterthought which harked back to Madness' *Work, Rest And Play* EP, Warners' next ploy was *The Christmas EP*, which conjoined 'The Tune' (Barson's ode to the musicals of yesteryear) with Suggs' endearing performance of the festive classic 'Sleigh Ride' and Supergrass' Britpop evergreen 'Alright'. But whereas *Work, Rest & Play* was driven by 'Night Boat To Cairo', *The Christmas EP* lost out in the music industry's December bearpit.

"Radio 1 had a thing called the Sleigh List instead of the Playlist which was December 1 to Boxing Day," explains Dickins. "They'd play lots of Christmas records. 'Sleigh Ride' was another favourite of mine which I thought would be great so Suggs went off and did it with Anne – Bette Bright – and their two daughters, who were children at the time. It's such a great song and I think it's one of the best versions, so disarmingly charming. He did 'Sleigh Ride' and 'Alright' in his little four-track studio at home. We were thinking of it as a double-A: 'Sleigh Ride' for the Sleigh List and then flip it to 'The Tune', a great song which we thought was a big hit record. But it wasn't."

Despite his faltering chart positions, Suggs was a ubiquitous presence on our TV screens, popping up on such programmes as Chris Evans' *Don't Forget Your Toothbrush*, performing 'My Girl' and Steve Harley & Cockney Rebel's 'Make Me Smile (Come Up And See Me)'; *Later . . . With Jools Holland* saw him promote the album highlights 'Green Eyes' and 'Off On Holiday'; less worthwhile was his rendition of Kylie Minogue's 'I Should Be So Lucky' on the Irish TV panel game show *Rickety Wheel Cabaret*.

In a desperate bid to breathe some longevity into flagging sales, Warners chose 'Cecilia' as the fourth single from *The Lone Ranger*. Although it wasn't issued until April 1996, half a year after the album, the Simon & Garfunkel cover was an instant hit. Despite Rob Dickins' initial reservations, the single reached the Top 5 and remained on the listings for 11 weeks (a lifetime in the world of mid-Nineties pop), shifting nearly half a million units. It's been suggested, however, that such an overt pop hit tarnished Suggs' reputation as a solo performer.

"It just wouldn't stop selling," remembers Rob. "It stayed at number four for weeks – one of those records where you think, is it ever going to get to number one? Big marketed records would come in above us then fall below. And the video we had was fantastic. The naivety that Suggs brings to a song really clicked with 'Cecilia'. By Simon & Garfunkel it was slick, which I didn't like, but Suggs' version had an honesty. Then the rap was just wonderful, so much energy. Everything came together." Suggs performed the song on *The National Lottery Show*, in addition to pushing the button to start the balls rolling. Suggs wasn't averse to having a flutter himself. "I have just bought myself two flop-eared rabbits called Otis and Basilica," he mused, "and I'm going to get them to choose my numbers for me."

Unfortunately, the overriding success of 'Cecilia' raised the bar of expectation for Suggs' career and the sales force were under manners to shift units of *The Lone Ranger*. Yet another single in September 1996 savagely edited the endearing, 'Tequila'-sampling 'Alcohol' into 'No More Alcohol' (presumably to sate any reservations about endorsing its consumption), reworking the opening bars (ouch!) from the summer hit of that year, 'Macarena'. It reached the Top 30 but wasn't about to drive sales significantly, despite its memorable lyric, " 'I come from a long line, whose only fear is closing time".

"Our dream was let's just make records, no pressure," recalls Dickins. "Suddenly, when you have a huge hit record, all the pressure comes. Following that, we didn't sell as many albums as I wanted, so there was that post mortem. It had hits but should have sold more. Looking back, it didn't play through like an album. It wasn't one piece of work. In a way, it was a compilation of ideas, some of which really clicked with the public. But it didn't as a whole." Confirmation that Suggs' appeal was flightier than they'd have liked was confirmed when a scheduled 10-date, country-wide solo tour for December 1996 was cancelled due to poor advance ticket sales.

While 'I'm Only Sleeping' originated from The Beatles' *Revolver* – which showed commendable good taste – the music industry was in the throes of its own Beatles tribute of sorts in summer 1995. Britpop had reached its commercial zenith as Blur and Oasis indulged in a 'battle of the bands'-style race to the top of the charts, fuelling a media frenzy. By embracing the past glories of classic Sixties bands, Britpop appealed across the generations – and record sales duly soared as the pub and the playground momentarily shared the same soundtrack. Indeed, it's been suggested that *Revolver* provided a template for Oasis' entire career! While the music papers were awash with excitable headlines and the broadsheets felt relieved that here, finally, was something they could relate to, the whole shebang somehow passed by Suggs, the ex-lead singer of Britpop's "missing link" between a Sixties past and a Nineties present.

Unfortunately, Suggs was marketed purely as a pop singer. The irony is that, as part of Madness, he had felt shackled by the expectations of being in a pop band, forever feeding that teenybop audience only to revert to that pop conveyer-belt when freed from those restraints. Madstock proved that his audience had stuck with him; now Suggs was in pole position to make a record for grown-ups, which might also have intersected with the prevailing mood. While Paul Weller's career was re-born with Britpop and Morrissey was able to plough his own furrow, Suggs didn't seem able to establish a proper musical identity away from his comrades.

Before, Suggs had shared the same reservations about Madness' frivolous pop image, striving instead for a public persona which was somehow more substantial. The mid-1990s might have offered that opportunity, reinforced by the fact that the singer – perhaps more than any other member of Madness – was still fascinated by contemporary music. Instead, he's on *Top Of The Pops* like a middle-of-the-road crooner singing an old Beatles number. Maybe the uphill struggle that Suggs had endured with more contemplative songs such as 'Michael Caine', 'One Better Day' and 'Yesterday's Men' still stung?

In hindsight, it's tempting to view Suggs' launch as an error of judgment on Warner's part. Madness' unique place in the hearts and minds of the British public had already been sealed. Here was a chance to capitalise on an era when British pop was joining up the dots of its glorious past. After all, Blur's return from the wilderness began, arguably, with the distinctly Madness-like tones of 'Sunday, Sunday' at the tail-end of 1993 before being immortalised by the cockney stylings of 1994's 'Parklife'.

No surprise, then, that Blur's front man Damon Albarn loved the band as a teenager. "I was fourteen and mad about Madness," he wrote. "Suggs was my hero. I did a couple of his songs at a school party." Equally,

Supergrass' chummy pop anthem 'Alright' had Madness' charm stamped all over it while 'Man-Size Rooster' opened with a drum intro disarmingly similar to 'House Of Fun'. Suggs took his two daughters to see Blur's triumphant show at Mile End Stadium in 1995 but failed to gain access backstage. "I stood there with the other losers, going, 'Excuse me, excuse me', before my shame dragged me away."

★   ★   ★

In 1995, after recording *The Lone Ranger*, Suggs had collaborated with Tricky on his collaborative project, *Nearly God*. 'I'll Pass Right Through You' was originally to have teamed the Bristolian artist with Damon Albarn, but the sessions were apparently abandoned. Tricky then asked Suggs to record some new vocals, which was described as "a demonic, voodoo love song" with Suggs sounding like a perverted nightclub owner. But that, too, remained in the can when *Nearly God* was issued in April 1996.

In September/October 1996, Suggs was involved in an annual songwriting course organised by EMI Publishing (to whom he was signed). According to *Nut Inc.*, around 15 songwriters/performers were invited to flex their muscles for a 'writers' week' in Huntsham Court, a Victorian retreat in Devon – among them Chris Difford (ex-Squeeze), Kirsty MacColl, Henry Priestman (ex-Yachts), Graham Gouldman (ex-10cc), Motown legend Lamont Dozier and Mike Barson's brother Ben. Apparently, Suggs collaborated on five songs with Gouldman and Difford and sang on three. On 'There Was A Day' and 'Sad Old Man', Gouldman took lead while McPherson stepped up to the mike for 'That's The Way We Do It', 'Me & You Against The World' and the "cockney music hall romp" of 'Two Bacon Sandwiches'.

By the time 1997 dawned, Rob Dickins was mulling over what Suggs' next move should be. "At this point, we'd had success but needed to make it into an act. So we need to think seriously about the next album." And then the phone rang. "Suggs was back on the radar screen, with TV shows ringing him up," continues Rob. "A producer Mike Connaris called and said, 'I've written this song for Chelsea,' who were doing really well in the FA Cup. Suggs is such a big Chelsea fan, he says, 'I'd love him to do a football record.' Now, along with 'Cecilia', my pet hate was football records! 'I don't think we're interested.' He said, 'Will you listen to it?' "

Dickins was dubious. "Along comes the demo for 'Blue Day' – a cross between 'Blackberry Way' and 'Penny Lane' – so I'm thinking, this is really a good song," he admits. "It pushed all the buttons those records push but with the chant of 'Chelsea, Chelsea'. I rang Suggs up and he said, 'Oh, I don't want to do a football record.' So we played it and he didn't need a lot of persuading as it was his beloved Chelsea." Connaris co-ran music production company Mcasso, which specialised in jingles and music for TV ads. A huge Chelsea fan, Connaris had sent out a demo of 'Blue Day' to various record companies and Warners had responded immediately.

"They rang me and said, 'Would you mind if Suggs sings it?' Of course, I'd love it," remembers Connaris. "I got a call from Rob Dickins. He said, 'Don't give him a beer until after the session.' Fine, OK. 'And when you record him, double track his vocal.' On the Tuesday evening, Suggs arrived at the studio and his thumb's broken – if you watch the video, his arm is in a sling. 'Hi, I'm Suggs, have you got a beer?' What could I say?! Anyway, he was unbelievable. We did it in an hour and it's not the easiest song to sing. Then we got talking about Chelsea and went out until three in the morning. Because he knows Soho so well, he showed me all these places: one place shut at twelve so he knew one around the corner! And I never double-tracked his vocal!"

The following weekend, Connaris organised for the backing music to be recorded at Langer and Winstanley's Westside Studios, together with the vocal attempts of the Chelsea team, a session which doubled as the video shoot. Sounding like a cross between Madness and The Beatles' *Sgt. Pepper*, 'Blue Day' scored 'Single Of The Week' in *NME*. Dickins probably should have trusted his underlying instincts that (a) Suggs needed to create an album as a holistic whole, and (b) football records are rubbish. But the sniff of a potential hit single got the better of the Warner boss. "The difference really was Suggs made it into a personality from a good but bland song," suggests Rob. "I thought, this could be a number one record."

Unfortunately, Rob Dickins' incredible insight into what made a pop song tick wasn't shared by an equivalent understanding of the beautiful game. "Something quite strange happened which – because I'm not a huge football fan – I should have realised. When you wear your colours, to the people who loved you in Manchester or Tottenham or Highbury or

Leeds, suddenly he was the enemy! We got letters saying, 'I can't believe you did this!' It was really quite telling and 'Blue Day' only got to number 22. It's not like an England record. Some people weren't going to buy it under any circumstances."

For the singer, though, it must have felt like a once-in-a-lifetime occasion. "When I was watching the FA Cup Final, Suggs was a guest of honour there," remembers Dickins, "and when Chelsea won, they played 'Blue Day' so they're having their picture taken with the cup with the banner on the pitch and 'Blue Day' was playing at Wembley. It was one of those moments, fantastic!" Mike Connaris: "By the time we got to Wembley, three weeks later, half the crowd were singing it! It was just incredible!"

'Blue Day' was undeniably better than many football records (and certainly better than the jungle version of 'House Of Fun' Suggs performed that year for Comic Relief!) and no doubt felt like a lifetime high for Suggs. But as Dickins is the first to admit, it distracted from the main prize: to consolidate Suggs' solo success with something substantial. "Now we had to get serious about the next record," Dickins admits. "Suggs then wrote 'I Am' and 'Our Man' with one of my A&R guys called Nick Feldman. 'Our Man' was fantastic, as the first song they wrote. And he wrote 'Invisible Man' with Mike Connaris."

"Suggs would give me lyrics and I'd come up with melodies and chords on the piano," recalls Connaris. "We made rough demos. We had one which never made the album with the most unusual title 'Venus Refusing Chips', an incredible song, so way out and Beatle-ish. They were desperately trying to find songs for him to get a direction. Suggs played me a cassette of 10 tracks and one was called 'Make-Up', this brilliant indie pop song. Suggs and I started a demo because he loved it so much. It would have been absolutely perfect. It was originally by a Swedish band Popsicle." Mike Connaris co-wrote perhaps the most Madness-like track of the period, 'Invisible Man'.

Dickins definitely felt that Suggs needed a point of focus. "I thought, we're going down this road again, which gives us hits but doesn't give us an album," admits Rob. He used work with Altered Images and knew their singer Clare Grogan.* Her husband was producer Steve Lironi, who

---

* The former Altered Images singer was close friend of Suggs'; she had conducted interviews around VH-1's broadcast of Madstock III.

was duly approached by Dickins: "Everyone was after Steve." Lironi might have been riding high on the success of Hanson's *Middle Of Nowhere* album but Suggs would surely have been more impressed by Steve's role as one half of the production team behind post-Happy Mondays band Black Grape. Either way, the Warner boss now had a potential framework for Suggs' second album.

"We had a meeting – Steve, Suggs, Nick and I," continues Dickins. "Steve said, 'I've always loved Madness, I'd love to do this but I want to do the whole album and I want to write it with Suggs.' We thought, this is a good move. He and Suggs got on really well. And it also meant I could step away. The combination of him and Steve was fantastic. They made what we wanted: from beginning to end, this really strong Suggs record and not sonically inconsistent bits and pieces. But it had that problem of the big hit single – ever the problem. We thought 'I Am' and 'Our Man' were contenders. When everything's good, nothing stands out!"

Steve got his wish, co-writing many of the songs as well as dominating a lengthy list of musicians on the album, credited with a dizzying array of different instruments and techniques. If anything, the album sounded less programmed and more "live" than *The Lone Ranger*. Some guests were retained from its predecessor, from Jah Wobble (heard to great effect on 'Sing') to Rico Rodriguez. And it showed no signs of bowing to those conservative Madness fans who had been baffled by the rap on 'Cecilia', employing some thoroughly cutting edge guests.

DJ Cutmaster Swift injected a hop-hop edge with his 'turntablist' skills. On 'Girl', which arguably shared more than just its title with the old Beatles song, Suggs recruited ragga DJ/MC General Levy, one of the UK's most accomplished dancehall acts whose crossover hit, 'Incredible', helped define ragga/jungle. Levy joined Suggs at Church Studios, an old converted church in Crouch End, to record his vocals. "He was down-to-earth, a cool guy, quite funny," remembers Levy. "I couldn't believe that he knew one of my first songs, an underground ragga version of 'You Can't Hurry Love'. You've done your homework! Quite nice to get a compliment from such a big artist as Suggs to acknowledge my underground work which didn't go further than pirate radio stations!"

By contrast, trad jazz stalwarts the Chris Barber Band lent 'Our Man' a quaint Twenties flavour. A nostalgic, old-fashioned mood also percolated the title track courtesy of that antique microphone sound also exhumed on recent hits like White Town's chart-topper, 'Your Woman' and 'Female Of The Species' by Space. 'The Greatest Show On Earth', too, displayed a sense of history. And this was reinforced by the album's endearing sleeve design depicting Suggs in a fez with colonial cream suit-and-tie, set against a backdrop of the three pyramids of Giza in Egypt – 'Night Boat To Cairo' meets *Casablanca*. (Fans hoping for a sneak preview of such new material when Suggs appeared on *The Ben Elton Show* on the eve of the fourth Madstock might have been disappointed when he chose instead to perform The Move's 'Blackberry Way'.)

From Suggs' perspective, *The Three Pyramids Club* was based around the loose concept of his childhood experiences clutching shirttails in dinghy Soho clubs where his mother used to work and/or sing – and which inspired the album's title. While Suggs admitted to "exorcising some ghosts" in the lyrics, the music was decidedly upbeat and catchy, with little of the melancholic mood prevalent on *The Lone Ranger.*

'The Invisible Man' was co-written with singer-songwriter Boo Hewerdine, who knew Dickins through being signed to Warners. "We got on incredibly well," remembers Boo of his time working with Suggs. "A funny thing happened on the first day. I went to his four-storey house in Highgate and I needed the loo. He said, 'You can use the one downstairs and I'll be in the top room.' So I locked the door and then I was trapped in this toilet! I'm shouting, 'Suggs!' He said, 'Oh, we never lock that one,' but I wasn't to know! I have happy memories of hanging out with him. We'd have these little adventures. We'd end up in some funny pub somewhere in Soho, where his mum had been, full of these old characters. He'd tell me all about when he was young. He wasn't in confessional – he wasn't weeping! – but a lot of songs came from conversations. His skill was taking real events from his life and making them universal."

Although they amassed an album's worth of acoustic demos, only two songs were issued. 'The Invisible Man' was re-worked with a definite ska feel. "I think he was talking about himself – that you can just disappear into the world," adds Hewerdine. By contrast, the B-side 'It Really Would Be Nice' – "about old friends and how you change" – was the pair's original demo. "It wasn't in the style of Madness," admits Boo. "We recorded these demos at a tiny little basement studio in EMI – he was signed to EMI Music. That's where we put a string quartet on it."

Hewerdine remembers the period fondly – but it's almost as if the sessions might have yielded an entirely separate album for Suggs. "We wrote a load of stuff which was really enjoyable – lovely songs, auto-biographical," says Boo. "Suggs is a fantastic, underrated lyricist. I remember a brilliant song we wrote, 'Father's Day', about when people get divorced and fathers get their children on the weekend. It would have been great if we'd seen that record through, and interesting to have made a record stylistically different for Suggs."

Just when Dickins might have recalled that motto "be careful what you wish for", the phone rang again – this time from Hollywood. "We got a call from Warner Brothers saying they wanted to use 'I Am' in *The Avengers* – and the build-up was to be one of the biggest of any film that year – on the condition it was released as a single. It was certainly a contender so we got the record ready for release. I went to see the first cut of the film with Una Thurman and Ralph Fiennes, both famous at the time, and I thought, 'God, this film's quite dull, pretty dire. And where's our song?'! We've built this whole single around this film. Then halfway through the credits, it comes on!"

Dickins now had the thankless task of breaking two bits of bad news to his old friend. First, *The Avengers* was likely going to be a complete flop (which it was: the film was drastically edited, its release delayed to the late-summer "dumping ground", it was universally slammed by the critics and lost a small fortune). And the song 'I Am' – their calling card for his second album – was nowhere to be heard. "I rang Suggs," sighs Dickins. "Was it exciting? Let me tell you, the most exciting thing was waiting for your song to come in! When it came out and died, it took us with it." Promoted by a video in which, fittingly, Suggs played *The Avengers'* lead character Steed, 'I Am' married a Caribbean-sounding organ to an anthemic, guitar-driven chorus. But the single barely scraped into the Top 40 on its release in September 1998.

A couple of weeks later, *The Three Pyramids Club* album failed to even register on the charts. The real tragedy is that Dickins was right: Suggs had indeed created a consistently strong and thoroughly enjoyable body of work. It's just that no one seemed to care. Also, Suggs had sensed the different dynamic in the development of his compositions: that process of running songs through Madness was very powerful. With mentor Rob Dickins' imminent departure from Warners, maybe the stars were aligned for the singer to reunite with his old cohorts? Meanwhile, Suggs' fans voted for 'So Tired', with its infectious chorus, as their favourite track while Warners pondered instead over issuing 'Girl' as a follow-up to 'I Am' – and then didn't.

"All the things we thought we'd achieved with the record didn't really come through in the reviews," remembers Rob. "At the end of '98, I then exited out of Warners so that's why there weren't more singles. I was talking with [Island Records founder] Chris Blackwell about failures. I said, 'We have noble failures and we have embarrassing failures.' We forget about the embarrassing failures but *The Three Pyramids Club* is a noble failure! It's as strong as a Madness record but maybe without the personality. They are greater than the sum of their parts."

Dickins argues that his solo period going it alone helped Suggs muster his enthusiasm for songwriting again, fuelled by the educational process of creating two albums in his own right instead of being able to rely on five or six other individuals. "Suggs may have had a couple of meetings [with Madness] and his creative juices were flowing but he missed the band," admits Rob. "The first few songs he wrote – which is why we came up with 'I'm Only Sleeping' and 'Cecilia' – weren't working. But by the time we'd done *The Three Pyramids Club*, he had confidence in his writing."

Although their friendship now spanned two decades, Dickins was struck by the performer's depth of general knowledge, a credential which might have been belied by his light-hearted public image: "He's incredibly well-read. He ain't just the front man of Madness, there are many other dimensions to him as well, in his songwriting and thought processes. He's quite deep for someone who is a Jack The Lad. When you walk down the street with him, everyone says, 'Hey Suggs, all right mate?' 'It's amazing Suggs, everybody loves you!' But as much as he's outgoing, he can be quite introspective at times, too."

Meanwhile, Suggs hadn't abandoned his onscreen potential. He made a cameo appearance (as a singer, Rex) in the romantic comedy film *Don't Go Breaking My Heart*, produced by Bill Kenwright with a screenplay by songwriter Geoff Morrow, and released in February 1999. The singer's affable demeanour also made him the ideal guest on chat shows and panel games. Examples included *Winton's Wonderland* and several editions of the pop quiz *Never Mind The Buzzcocks*. And the singer seemed to be pursuing a parallel career as a budding TV presenter – or was that being pursued?!

Channel 5 had been launched in early 1997 – and one of the first shows they developed was a chaotic panel game *Night Fever*.

"I remember Suggs saying, 'I've been offered this programme hosting a karaoke show,'" remembers Dickins. "He said, 'I don't really want to do it.' I said, 'Suggs, it's television, a possibility you should be looking at in your career. It's Channel 5, nobody's going to watch it and you'll get all the experience.' But it became the number one show on Channel 5! 'Rob, I thought you told me no one was ever gonna see it!' He had a little bit of stage fright from doing television but it was basically a party he was fronting which is in the spirit he feels comfortable. By doing those TV shows, his confidence built without the pressure of being on your own fronting a programme." The hour-long show eventually ran for five years.

Hewerdine recalls being visited by a Channel 5 executive during those EMI basement sessions: "Suggs wasn't that keen. One time in the studio, someone came down to speak to him about it and he hid in the vocal booth on all fours! This incredible moment when I'm in this little room and there's Suggs on his hands and knees hiding around the corner and I'm saying to this fella, 'No, he's not in today!'"

★ ★ ★

On April 2, 1994, East End playwright Alan Gilbey unveiled his new musical, *One Step Beyond*, at the Stratford Theatre Royal in London's East End. Based around the songs of Madness (15, to be precise), it was advertised as "a play about the homeless". The show ran for about six weeks, with leading roles from Sophie Lawrence and one-time Flying Picket Paul Kissaun, who played a skinhead called Squirrel. *One Step Beyond* received positive reviews, *The Evening Standard* describing it as "a credit to the integrity of all involved . . . [with] streetwise dialogue, offbeat humour and warmth". However, Madness' lament to the homeless, 'One Better Day', was conspicuous by its absence.

"Because there was the melancholy underneath the happiness in the Madness songs, they had that depth and that story-telling to them, which made them very good for a musical," remembers Gilbey. "Lee rang up one day. He was lovely and we had a chat, nice and buzzy. I went back to the theatre and said, 'Great, Lee wants to be in the show.' But I left it with them and later, they said, 'We decided to not go with him!' Apparently, the band came to the show one night, didn't tell anybody and I had this awful feeling they didn't like it!"

In the summer of 1995, another play inspired by the music of the ska revival opened in Ireland. *Too Much Too Young* was written by Anto Nolan and ran at Dublin's Tivoli Theatre. Cathal Smyth went to see it. "The play's about a reunion fifteen years after the first Madness gig in Dublin," he explained. "2 Tone was about working classes dressing up and being cool and not getting into violence." Suggs mentioned the show in *FHM*: "It's based on this legendary concert that Madness did at the Olympia Ballroom there where people were diving off the balcony, off their rockers on speed, and the idea is that these four blokes who were at the concert meet up after ten years . . ."

Meanwhile, Madness' songs appeared to be de rigueur for every conceivable type of TV advertisement – not least the Midland Bank, except that they chose 'It Must Be Love', which wasn't actually a Madness song but was re-recorded especially for the occasion mimicking Madness' rendition. "It's our arrangement and our images and they've used a soundalike voice," bemoaned Suggs. "It's difficult because the band's not cohesive at the moment. There are seven of us floating around, all having separate conversations with our lawyers."

While such tributes confirmed the affection with which Madness were still widely regarded, with Suggs about to launch his solo career, the rest of the band went their separate ways. In 1993, Sean Flowerdew had partnered up with fellow Special Beat member, ex-Specials guitarist Lynval Golding, to write together. "Then Lee got involved," explains Flowerdew. "Lynval ended up leaving for The Specials Mark II. I'd give Lee the music and he'd write some really good lyrics, with a clever use of melodies. His influences came pouring out. We didn't have a band name, just trying things out. We did two tracks together: 'So This Is What It's All About' and 'Wee Wee Hours', but they've never seen the light of day."

Eventually, Flowerdew caught the next ska revival wave in the mid-Nineties with his band Skanga, who signed to A&M. But this "third wave" of ska bands largely emanated from America: bands who added punk energy to ska rhythms like Less Than Jake, The Mighty Mighty Bosstones, Reel Big Fish and last but not least, No Doubt. Many of these bands cited Madness as a major influence – and yet Madness themselves weren't able to properly capitalise on this interest.

In terms of family life, Foreman endured a divorce from his second wife, Laurence, in September 1995 while Lee was gifted a more welcome distraction in the birth of his second son, Kye Clay, on October 15. Smyth, too, became a father again with the arrival of Eloise Valentine on March 3. Suggs was knee-deep in a successful solo career, of course, while Barson seemed content to enjoy family life in the Netherlands with the arrival of third child Joey. Woodgate eventually re-married in 1997: he and Siobhan already had two daughters, Iona (born in 1994) and Mary (born in 1997). Bedford, too, was settled with girlfriend Cress and their two girls Alice and Olivia.

In early 1995, Woodgate joined hard rock band FAT (an acronym for Fuck All That), who adopted the motto "sample it, loop it, stick big guitars on it, then rap all over it". The band toured throughout the summer, including a performance at the Phoenix Festival, before their debut single, 'Downtime', was issued on Dink Records that August, with Woodgate listed as co-composer of all three songs. On occasion, the band also included Woodgate's brother Nick on guitar while Cathal helped with management duties. In 1997, Fat issued a self-titled album in the same vein, mixing rap and rock, on the DV8 label.

* * *

In December 1995, Madness reconvened for their Mad Dogs tour of Christmas shows, with support from Smyth's A&R 'find' Laxton's Superb, sticking with Britain's major venues (Wembley Arena, Manchester G Mex, Birmingham NEC, Newcastle Arena, Bournemouth International) alongside shows in Ireland (Belfast International Ice Bowl, Dublin The Point). The concerts boasted the rarely-heard 'Take It Or Leave It' and 'In The Rain' and, on a less musical note, a regular drinking contest between Lee and a member of the audience.

For the time-being, Blockheads' bassist Norman Watt-Roy replaced Bedford, who'd finally returned to his screen-printing vocation, with a view to passing an apprenticeship before forging a proper career outside of the music industry. That said, he played a gig with BUtterfield 8 on exactly the same date as one of Madness' engagements!

During rehearsals for Madstock III, tensions mounted within the band. On the one hand, they were striving forward with several new songs,

'You're Wonderful', 'Culture Vulture', 'Saturday Night, Sunday Morning' and 'Soul Denying' (although they failed to road-test the last of these in time for the festival). But on the other, Suggs seemed to be preoccupied – or distracted, at least – by his solo career.

On June 22, 1996, though, they returned to Finsbury Park, supported by ska-punk newcomers King Prawn, ex-Dr. Feelgood guitarist Wilko Johnson, Mancunian rock/reggae act Audioweb, Welsh indie band Catatonia, Britpop hopefuls The Gyres, Acid Jazz combo the James Taylor Quartet, easy listening act Mike Flowers Pops, reggae artist Gregory Isaacs and Squeeze. 'The Sun And The Rain' was introduced as 'Anarchy In The DHSS', an affectionate dig at the Sex Pistols, who'd graced the Finsbury Park stage the day before. While the new material fuelled rumours that Madness were recording a new album, it was duly announced that, for the time being, the band was 'on hold'.

One new song had a particular poignancy, as Cathal later explained: "For the record, my father passed away on June 22, 1995 and a year later, I played a song 'You're Wonderful', which I dedicated to his memory and which was about being in the band and missing those who had passed from this mortal coil – in particular, Cathal Patrick Smyth my Dada. I miss him dearly. [He] gave me so much of my character and always [had] a good ear and sound advice. In his immortal words, 'There are those of us who are and those of us who aren't and those of us who are must stick together.' I often repeat these words and in me and in my son Cathal Caspar Smyth, my father lives on."

A week later, Madness participated in the Euro '96 Extravaganza at Manchester United's stadium Old Trafford – organised to celebrate England's hosting of the European Football Championship. The band performed alongside Dodgy and local stars Simply Red and M-People, excerpts of which were broadcast on BBC TV and radio. It proved to be Madness' last concert appearance for two years.

★　★　★

Although he'd left Go! Discs, Smyth was still involved in A&R and calling himself 'The Quiet Man' (named after the John Wayne film from 1952 in which an American returns to his roots in Ireland), with an office for Quiet Man Management, which he had formed with ex-Go! Discs marketing man Paul Dowling. Initially an office in Camden Town, their base of operations was later listed as being at 326 Kensal Road, London W10.

On October 23, 1987, Thompson, Foreman and Bedford were all billed to appear onstage at Terry Edwards' Ska Extravaganza 3 at Camden Dingwalls (although Thompson failed to show). According to *Nut Inc.*, the all-star cast reeled off gutsy renditions of such ska/rocksteady classics as 'Phoenix City' and 'Return Of Django'. Bedford and various others had also participated in Edwards' two earlier get-togethers.

Flying in the face of such uncertainty, various band members eventually reconvened some time in 1997 at the Sir John Henry Studios in north London to rehearse new material for a potential Madness studio album. In addition to the compositions unveiled at Madstock III were tunes such as 'The Wizard', 'Going To The Top' and 'No Money'. It seems unlikely that the entire band were present – and it's also safe to assume that Cathal was the driving force behind this initiative. Meanwhile, Madness were approached to record a track for a tribute album to the late, great play-wright/actor/wit Nöel Coward, *Twentieth Century Blues* (issued in spring 1998), but their contribution – for whatever reason – wasn't included.

In a New Year's message to *Nut Inc.* at the start of 1998, Cathal admitted to his enthusiasm for more Madness shows. "You really don't know how much I look forward to performing live onstage with the rest of Madness," he wrote. "It's something I almost need . . . the adrenaline rush is just something else and the camaraderie that we enjoy makes it special." From April 2 to May 2, 1998, Madness returned to America for their first tour there since 1984. A live album, *Universal Madness*, was recorded at the Universal Amphitheater in LA and released in spring the following year, which followed 1997's Stateside-only compilation *Total Madness*. Such activity was prompted after Madness were name-checked by the 'third wave' American ska bands such as The Mighty Mighty Bosstones who enjoyed a Top 20 hit in 1997 (Dicky Barrett from the band wrote the sleeve-notes for *Total Madness*).

Retaining its biennial fixture, Madstock IV rolled around on Sunday, June 7, quashing rumours that Madness were no more with straplines like 'They Thought It Was All Over – It Ain't Yet' and 'Pre-World Cup Friendly' doffing the cap to the impending World Cup. The event boasted a supporting cast of Jazz Jamaica, reggae legends Desmond Dekker and Toots & The Maytals, blues/dance collective Alabama 3, the returning

Catatonia, chart-troubling scousers Space and Finley Quaye, the mixed race star who was still riding high on the back of his musical melting pot of a debut album, *Maverick A Strike*. Unfortunately, Quaye decided to provoke the audience by making jibes against the St George flag and the English football team, angering the crowd by firmly questioning their survival prospects in the World Cup. This led to some hostility and down-right stupidity from certain fans.

Prompted by the presence of Toots & The Maytals, Madness chose to cover their classic skinhead reggae anthem, '54-46 That's My Number', during one of their encores – inviting not only Toots Hibbert but also Desmond Dekker onstage, who alternated on lead vocals. Madstock '98 was recorded by VH-1 for broadcast and subsequent release on DVD as *Madness At Madstock*, with some amusing preamble which depicted Thompson waking up and preparing for the big day. Although it was only six years on from *Divine Madness*, EMI-Virgin attempted to capitalise on this rejuvenation with another compilation CD, *The Heavy, Heavy Hits*, but this time were only rewarded with a more modest Top 30 placing (not helped by some wholly ill-advised promo remixes circulated as 12-inch singles).

★　★　★

For Madness to exist beyond occasional reunion concerts, they needed a new manager. Steve Finan had helped to corral them but he was relatively young and inexperienced; and besides, he'd left for pastures new back in 1995. More than anyone else, Cathal – with the benefit of his experience at Go! Discs – understood that, if his lofty ambitions for Madness were to be fulfilled, they needed help. With this in mind, he approached a seasoned professional, Peter Rudge (Maddog Management).

Rooted in the tradition of 'old school' rock managers who relied on a mix of business acumen, dogged determination and sheer charisma, Rudge was a Cambridge graduate who began his career as an assistant to Kit Lambert and Chris Stamp at Track Records. Lambert and Stamp, of course, also managed The Who but a combination of circumstances allowed Rudge to take over this role during the group's golden era between 1969 and 1976. After relocating to New York in 1972, Rudge was recommended to Mick Jagger by Pete Townshend, and for most of the 1970s Rudge ran the Stones' tours, too, becoming a powerful figure in the global music industry. He also managed Lynyrd Skynyrd and was perhaps fortunate not to have been aboard their light aeroplane which crashed in October 1977, killing two members of the band, a backing singer, a crew member and both pilots. Shaken by the tragedy, Rudge kept a low profile for a while, returning in the 1980s as a management consultant whose clients included Roger Waters (Pink Floyd), Duran Duran and Manic Street Preachers. His specialty was advising UK bands on how to break America.

Pete Rudge had not only been involved in the marketing and promotion of some of the biggest rock albums ever (with over 150 platinum and gold albums to his name), but was a pioneer in the development of the modern rock tour and the only industry figure to win 'Innovator Of The Year Award' from *Performance* magazine two years running. When Madness came calling, Rudge was working with both ex-Kink Ray Davies and Manchester band James.

Like many of rock's most accomplished managers, Rudge was known for his no-nonsense approach. As Dave Robinson once quipped, "Peter Rudge, he doesn't budge." Perhaps his experience and strength of character could muscle the disparate members of Madness into a fully functioning musical unit?

"I was on tour with James and we had a tour manager named Andy Franks, who had worked with Madness," explains Rudge. "Chas wanted to appoint the manager. When I got involved with them, Suggs wasn't in the band, and Barso and Bedders had left, so it was Chrissy Boy, Thommo, Woody and Cathal. You could tell right away that unless it was all seven of them, it wasn't going to work on any level so I brought the seven back together again and tried to re-launch them."

With Madstock '98 out of the way, Rudge attempted to consolidate their achievements to date by discussing the possibility of a new studio album with Paul Conroy and Steve Pritchard over at EMI-Virgin. Needless to say, the record company was hugely receptive to the idea, not only because of their past successes and associations with the band but because they had already negotiated an extension to their license of the back catalogue in 1996 (which involved an alleged advance of one million pounds). Even if Madness' comeback LP failed to meet sales expectations, the surrounding publicity would drive sales of their 'greatest hits'.

Now that Suggs' solo career had petered out, the seven members eventually convened in early 1999 to rehearse new material. In late spring, *Nut Inc.* revealed that, according to returning producers Langer and Winstanley, some 14 songs had been recorded. "I really don't mind if we never make a new record again," Smyth had written in *Nut Inc.* "If you want to hear new songs then come to the shows." It's tempting to suggest that Cathal was being disingenuous: he was desperate for Madness to create a contemporary work which would allow them to progress beyond purely trading on past glories. And the one-time Madness MC was about to have his undying wish come true.

Chapter 20

WONDERFUL

PERHAPS it was their impending 20th anniversary that finally convinced Madness to knuckle down and make a reunion album. Or maybe Suggs came to realise that his solo career would never quite match the magical process of making music with his old chums? For sure, manager Peter Rudge seems to have corralled and cajoled them into submission. And they had a green light and an impressive advance on the table from Virgin boss Paul Conroy.

"Recording is going very well," reported *Nut Inc.* in spring 1999, "and the twelve-track album should be fully finished by the end of May." There was even mention that Madness had continued to pen songs way beyond the quantity required – which boded well. Foreman later confirmed that, in essence, the rest of the band had had to wait until their singer felt ready to return. "We recorded a lot of songs without Suggs," Chris told *Uncut*. "But the songs aren't Madness without Suggs – it'd be like Oasis without Liam. Suggs came back and we redid them, though I think musically some of the demos are better." Cathal nicknamed those sessions 'Madness Unsugged'.

Smyth's friend Boz Boorer helped out with rehearsals, as he later told Madness Central. "I worked quite hard with Cathal and Lee with the arrangements on that record, before it ever got finished, the demos of the tracks," Boz explained. "It was early on. I did a week with them, which was a lot of fun. I was made to feel welcome. It was like a little family and I was invited in. Cathal asked me to give him a hand with some brass parts. I think they were the last sessions they did at Liquidator. We'd been there for a couple of days without Mike and when he turned up at the studio, the sound really came together, emanating from his keyboard."

It was decided that the album should feature both a horn section and string arrangements; responsibility for the brass fell to Terry Edwards. "Having played/recorded with Mark, Chris and Lee and socialised with most of the band, I'd become a reasonably natural choice to do it," explains Terry. "By that point, I'd got a track record as an arranger, too, so it helped that I could get a horn section together and be the conduit between band, producers and other musicians. I flew back mid-tour with Lydia Lunch from Basel/Mulhouse airport and as I made that crazy 36-hour round trip, being flown around to record for Madness, I decided I had finally become an international musician!"

Edwards was charged with recruiting the horn players. "Trumpet player Jason McDermid stood in for BUtterfield 8 man John Eacott and was always on call if John wasn't available," continues Terry. "He's a great player and a great guy. Fellow Australian Jason Bruer played alongside him in Jools Holland's band for a while, as did my good pal Mike Kearsey, who joined us on trombone. Mike still does most of the Madness horn-section work. [It was] exciting to be on some new Madness stuff."

For the most part, the mood during the sessions was "very much up", helped by the familial cocoon of Langer and Winstanley. "So many of the band write songs that they must have been gagging to get something out after such a long time," suggests Edwards. "It was positive all round. Clive likes to arrange things as he goes and puts small details into songs which keeps them rolling along. He'd ask me to play a single low note on baritone sax somewhere – and Alan gets the perfect mike placements. Even in the age of digital recording when you can replace bits and pieces, he prefers the 'identical' choruses to be individually played to maintain the human element. That's why their productions sound so alive."

By and large, the strings were arranged and conducted by Simon Hale, a leading name in the music industry who had previously worked with the likes of M People, Des'ree and Seal. The keyboard player had only branched into arranging around 1995 – but Langer had contacted him on the basis of his already impressive reputation. Hale teamed up with The London Session Orchestra and their leader Gavyn Wright (himself an arranger of note with a long list of accomplishments). "Gavyn and I had worked on various things since around 1992," explains Simon, "and he was responsible for introducing me to many people – Jamiroquai, Bjork, etc. Clive would give me a musical 'brief' of what he thought, we would discuss the size of the ensemble and I would then go off and do the arrangements."

On percussion was Pablo Cook, another musician with an impressive CV who'd actually joined the same Red Wedge tour as Madness back in 1986 (he'd played with the likes of Captain Sensible, Pulp, Moby, William Orbit, Joe Strummer, Catatonia and various acid jazz acts). Cook's girlfriend had been part of the Hampstead crowd whom Suggs and Cathal especially had hung around with back in the Seventies. Roughly a year earlier, he'd been introduced to Smyth before eventually getting the phone call. "They were mature musicians, sensible," remembers Cook. "It's looking after all the top end stuff – tambourines and shakers and congas and bongos. The only people in the studio were Suggs, Alan Winstanley and Chas. On one particular session, they wanted to use whistles. Another track was covered in fairground type percussion, all very jokey."

The album was all but completed by the time Madness flew to the States on April 30 to promote the release of their in-concert album *Live Madness*. A three-date East Coast tour embraced thousand-capacity venues in New York, Washington and Philadelphia. The day before the first show, Madness scored a prestigious slot on *The David Letterman Show*, performing 'Our House' and an impromptu 'One Step Beyond' (on May 4, they also appeared on *Late Night With Conan O'Brien*).

Back in the UK, Madness' promotional roadshow kicked off in style with a mini-concert at the canal-side in Camden Lock on June 23. Initially intended as an invite-only show, some 200 people flocked to the location after a local TV report leaked the news. The band arrived by boat to perform before a backdrop displaying a dramatic new Madness logo (featuring a huge 'M' wearing a crown), with Lee dressed as a one-eyed captain.

"Paul Conroy really got involved in that," says EMI-Virgin's Steve Pritchard. "We did that big launch on a canal boat from Virgin to Camden Lock. They were back to being a band then, with lots of opinions and directions. We really wanted it to work. The turning point was Mike Barson coming back from Holland. Him joining in – the gang was complete! It really was like the return of the magnificent seven, like a Western!"

★ ★ ★

Madness' first studio offering for 13 years arrived as a single in July. 'Lovestruck' was an infectious tour de force, mixing up Motown's classic beat and chopped guitar style with shades of mid-Sixties Kinks. The song encapsulated Madness' quintessential charm: bubbly and lighthearted yet surreal and witty in equal doses, inspired by Lee's love of drinking. Barson hadn't lost his ear for a winning melody while Thompson's offbeat humour still prevailed (not least in the immortal line, "I've fallen for a lamppost"!). And its impeccable string arrangement has led to it being compared with 'The Sun And The Rain'.

As ever, some healthy debate had ensued behind-the-scenes as to the appropriate choice for Madness' comeback single. After all, a lot was riding on its impact: without a substantial hit, album sales would be an uphill struggle. The band were pushing for another new song, 'Johnny The Horse', but "we all insisted on 'Lovestruck' because it was an obvious hit", states Virgin's radio plugger Mick Garbutt. In this instance, the powers-that-be proved to be right. Powered by rotation airplay and dapper TV appearances, 'Lovestruck' was propelled into the Top 10 – their first such prize since 1983. The publicity drive was a textbook example of how to market a pop single. Madness were back. It almost felt too easy?

The merry-go-round of TV studios included *Top Of The Pops* (on the first of two appearances, Thompson was dressed entirely in green as a caterpillar), *CD:UK* (with Seamus Beaghen in place of a missing Barson), VH1's *Talk Music*, *This Morning* (Bedford's turn to be absent) and Chris Evans' much-watched *TFI Friday*.

Their appearance at the high profile Party In The Park hadn't hurt, either. On July 4, Madness performed in front of 100,000 people in Hyde Park, the event staged by Capital Radio in aid of the Prince's Trust set up to benefit disadvantaged children. With Norman Watt-Roy deputising again for Bedford, the band were only able to play four songs (including a "semi-playback" rendition of 'Lovestruck') because of the sheer volume of artists on the bill (among them contemporaries such as Culture Club, Eurythmics, Elvis Costello, UB40 and Blondie).

Looking for clues as to Madness' new direction, fans were intrigued by the accompanying songs on the single. Smyth's 'We Are Love' was a tense, punky collision of drums and guitar while 'Round And Round' was its polar opposite, from its delicate opening piano motif to the haunting minor chord structure with lyrics which, as one observer put it, "retain the uncertainty and underlying despair". Apparently, this Barson composition was his first choice to appear on the forthcoming album – but it was not to be.

On July 24, the band appeared at radio station BRMB's Cash For Kids Concert at Birmingham's Cannon Hill Park, a Midlands equivalent of Party In The Park (locals UB40 headlined). A 35,000-strong crowd flooded into the sun-drenched park for the event, which was broadcast live. The following day, Madness flew out to Hungary's capital Budapest to participate in the week-long Pepsi Sziget Festival, staged on an island on the Danube and attracting around 300,000 people. And on August 20, Suggs sang 'It Must Be Love' at the celebrity wedding of Norman 'Fatboy Slim' Cook and Zoe Ball at Babington Hall in Somerset.

To celebrate their 20th anniversary, the band were back in their old Camden stomping ground, the Electric Ballroom, on September 30. Billed as 'A Slice Of Madness', they played a show in aid of the homeless charity Shelter and *The Big Issue* newspaper. The event was sponsored by Dr. Martens, who produced a special boot in honour of the band – the company was itself celebrating four decades of the classic 1460 footwear. As part of the celebrations, Mark Bedford designed a double-CD compilation. With Madness represented by 'Shut Up', *Forty: Forty (The Dr. Martens Box Set)* was issued by Virgin in July 2000.

Madness's next release, 'Johnny The Horse', had already been tipped as a single ever since being unveiled during a Radio 2 documentary some months earlier. "The idea for the song came from an incident I had with two down-and-outs who used to sit drinking on a wall at the end of my street," Smyth later told *Ska News*. "They had become a fixture for years and I had taken to talking with them as they were pleasant. One was an Irish ex-boxer who was a gentle giant and a little punch drunk; the other was Scottish and very quiet. One day, I saw Dempsey in a state of distress: he was crying and full of grief. He told me that his Scottish friend had slept in a derelict building and some thugs had killed him. I was moved to write about this to point out there are so many who disappear onto the streets, forgotten or ignored." Smyth's resulting opus documented the downfall of a family man who became a social drop-out, up to his tragic death in Regent's Park.

Its chorus was virtually wordless, relying instead on a "doodley doop doop doop, woo!" refrain. But Virgin were more concerned about the opening line: "Johnny the horse was kicked to death, he died for enter-tainment." Afraid this might alienate the likes of Radio 1, a sanitised counterpart was created for airplay, amended to: "Johnny the Horse, he passed this way . . ." In every other respect, the song boasted all the classic Madness ingredients, from its boisterous rhythm section, melodic piano and spine-tingling sax solo to its heartfelt lyrics cloaked in Irish whimsy. With Celtic strains faintly reminiscent of *Too-Rye-Ay*-era Dexys, it proved to be an instantaneous Madness classic.

By rights, then, 'Johnny The Horse' should have raced into the Top 10, hot on the heels of 'Lovestruck'. It didn't. The single stalled just outside the Top 40, a bitter disappointment particularly to its writer. So what went wrong? It certainly wasn't the poignant video, with a cameo from Cathal's son Caspar as young Johnny. Fans were quick to the point the finger of criticism at Virgin, chiefly because the release date had dribbled back several weeks to November 1. But sometimes, such a delay can build demand. Certainly, the promotional impact was softer than that for 'Lovestruck' – but then Madness could only stage the big comeback once. Also, they did perform the song on several high profile TV shows, includ-ing *This Morning* (minus a poorly Thompson), *Breakfast News* and *Later . . . With Jools Holland*, as well as *The Late Late Show* in Ireland.

"We were B-listed with 'Johnny The Horse'," remembers Mick Garbutt – which meant the song enjoyed moderate rather than constant exposure on Radio 1. "But it just wasn't going to happen. There was no doubt that was a fantastic track, though. It was Cathal's pride and joy."

Of the single's accompanying songs, 'Dreaming Man' both puzzled and delighted fans, from its 'London Calling'-like introduction to Cathal's autobiographical, poetic lyrics reeled off at breathtaking speed. It was co-written with Foreman, surprisingly the guitarist's only contribution to the album sessions. Smyth also wrote '(You're) Wonderful', first aired at Madstock in 1996 as a tribute to the passing of his father – although the lyrics also seemed to reminisce on the band's early days. A potent mix of glam rock and acoustic guitar, this strong contender for the album was apparently omitted because certain members weren't entirely happy with the recording. Barson's 'I Was The One', by comparison, harked back to the skanking ska of old, all swirling organ and bouncing bass.

★ ★ ★

Madness' new album *Wonderful* was finally unveiled on November 1, 1999, over 15 years since all seven of them had previously appeared on *Keep Moving*. The title was Foreman's idea of a compromise in the absence of the song itself; Smyth had actually preferred the name *Nice One*. In hindsight, Mark Bedford's sleeve design was uncharacteristically conventional, framing a photo of the band emerging from an underground escalator looking distracted and bedraggled. The music was, by contrast, exceedingly well assembled, from the intricate string arrangements and brass parts to the consistency of the songwriting and instrumentation. *Wonderful* was immediately hailed by fans as one of their finest achievements while Suggs quipped that the only real changes within the band related to "weight and hair loss".

Several tracks looked over Madness's impeccably besuited shoulder to the past. An affectionate throwback to the 2 Tone era, Cathal's 'The Communicator' was a barnstorming old school ska tribute reminiscent of Dave & Ansel Collins' 1971 smash, 'Double Barrel', with its skinhead reggae organ and a horn riff borrowed from The Archies' bubblegum hit 'Sugar Sugar'. '4am' harked back instead to Suggs' debut album but Madness' performance of this offbeat tribute to The Kinks (supposedly the continuing tale of characters from 'Waterloo Sunset') was more powerful and atmospheric than that on *The Lone Ranger*.

'If I Didn't Care' was the most nostalgic of all, a beautifully constructed homage to the old Ink Spots classic from 1939 which acted like a bizarre if welcome postscript on an otherwise sonically consistent album. Having sold an incredible 19 million copies, 'If I Didn't Care' was one of the best-selling singles of all time. It's likely that Madness were reminded of the song after its prominent usage over the opening credits in the 1994 film *The Shawshank Redemption* (it also featured in Woody Allen's 1987 movie *Radio Days*).

'Saturday Night, Sunday Morning' also had cinematic connections since it was presumably named after Alan Sillitoe's famous 1958 novel and its acclaimed 1960 film adaptation. Suggs' song set very personal lyrics, like a reassuring letter to his band mates about the trepidation of reforming, to an affectionate mid-Sixties Motown rhythm (think The Supremes' hit 'You Can't Hurry Love'). The song had first been aired at Madstock III in 1996. Smyth's remaining contribution to *Wonderful*, 'The Wizard', was full of ebullient horns and sassy strings, a song with a definite spring in its step.

Similarly, 'Going To The Top' allowed writer Barson to indulge in more fairground-styled organ while its breathless, monotone vocal style was reminiscent of Scott Walker's Sixties classic 'Jacky' (it's also been compared to 1981's 'Promises Promises' from *7*).

Thompson had been busy reading up on Greek mythology, judging by the title of one of his two collaborations with Woodgate. The fact that 'Elysium' was named after a section of the mythical underworld seemed to be reflected by its wistful, baroque feel, although the lyrics actually dealt with the issue of manic depression. The pair also teamed up for 'No Money' – this time, with Woodgate's younger brother Nick. This impressive finale contrasted an upbeat musical mood with its theme, which one observer accurately described as "the root of all evil, and the unfortunate financial state that leaves the protagonist unable to continue a relationship". Did this reflect those times when members of Madness had turned their hand to odd jobs to make ends meet?

Foreman's songs were conspicuous by their absence – and his subsequent explanation implied some disquiet within the ranks. "The band had recorded a lot of those songs previously (without Suggs or Bedders)," he said in 2005, "and by the time we came to make the album, the whole selection process was becoming a bit like survival of the fittest. Quite nasty at times and Clive Langer nearly quit. I didn't even bother. We had more than enough songs although I think some good ones got trampled over in the rush."

In 'Johnny The Horse', *Wonderful* yielded one true masterpiece. But in 'Drip Fed Fred', it boasted a second. For a start, 'Drip Fed Fred' was like no other previous Madness song. Its rambunctious mood evoked the spirit of Victorian London gangs and vaudevillian shows around a central roguish character whom Foreman thought might have been inspired by Lee's father. The mock-old fashioned radio announcement, Thompson's role as the "right honourable Reverend Greene" (from that old poem in *Nutty Boys*) and, above all, the vaguely threatening chant of "we want Freddie for our leader", broke new ground for Madness. But its sheer genius lay in the casting of Ian Dury as the song's worldly-wise narrator, who deftly conveyed its black humour. "The song is a twisted tale of underworld treachery," wrote Madness Information Service, "with Dury narrating in menacing manner the part of a gangland heavy calling for 'honour amongst thieves'."

Dury had been very ill for some time. Suggs' dedication to him at Madstock '98 had been prompted by learning that he had been diagnosed with cancer. Earlier in 1999, he'd been forced to cancel his appearance at Glastonbury Festival. Although he persevered with a string of concerts across the year, public appearances were, for the most part, scarce. In November, he attended Q magazine's annual shindig at London's Park Lane Hotel to accept a 'Classic Songwriters Award' into a mike hand-held by Suggs.

"He's uncompromisingly abrasive," explained Madness' frontman. "You could call him a genius, and that's one of the side effects of being a genius: fuck everybody else if they don't realise. Our sound man [Ian Horne] has always worked with him, so he's the intermediary, and our ex-manager now looks after him – strange coincidences. There are people you always remember who had an impact before you made it – so we were nervous about meeting him."

On October 2, Madness had performed Dury's 'My Old Man' as an emotional tribute to their hero, one of two songs on BBC radio as part of a week of events at Sheffield's National Centre For Popular Music. Via a live radio link-up, Dury spoke kindly about the lads covering his song and they talked about Ian's contribution to *Wonderful*, the inner sleeve for which carried a special message for their mentor: "The band would like to dedicate this album to Ian Dury for his inspiration and happiness he has brought us." According to Dury biographer Richard Balls in *Sex & Drugs & Rock'n'Roll*, Madness returned the favour by hosting a fund-raising night at Walthamstow Dog Track for Cancer BACUP, the leading cancer information service which Ian supported after he was diagnosed. The Nutty Boys headlined the event on November 30 and raised £30,000 for its 'Living With Cancer Appeal'. The band even bought themselves their own greyhound which they decided to call Nutty Boy!

Like many of the fortuitous moments in Madness' career, this marriage was the result of serendipity. Thompson later reminisced on his chance encounter in Madness Central. "I cycled through Vondelpark from Barzo's boathouse, we had finished the demo for 'Drip Fed Fred' within an afternoon and were definitely on a roll," he wrote. "On entering the hotel reception, I noticed media bods and brightly-lit umbrellas flashing so curiously I popped my head above the crowd and there, in a comfy chair, holding court, growling on about drug laws and wars and sexual freedom and liberalism, was Uncle Ian. He had to focus, then with a shocked second look shouted, 'What the fuck are you doing here?'"

Although Dury had a bottle of fluid permanently attached to him, the pair retired for dinner in the restaurant. "I'm over here working on a few ideas with Mr Barson," Lee explained. "In fact, I've just finished a song that was made for you." Thompson summarised the ditty's subject matter: "Underworld rivalry, the Krays meets the Keystone Kops, very Kilburnsy Hi Roady." "What's it called?" enquired Dury – and was understandably taken aback by the title. "Are you taking the fucking . . .?! I like the sound of that, let's go through it at my place when we get back."

Although 'Drip Fed Fred' – with its cockney narration – felt like a grown-up equivalent of Blur's 'Parklife', its origins were less certain. A demo version issued as B-side 'We Want Freddy' implied its roots lay in Eastern stylings. "I am particularly proud of being on a record with Ian Dury," states Terry Edwards, "as we're from the same part of Essex and Blockheads saxophonist Davey Payne inspired me to take up the instrument. The arrangement I wrote included the quote from the Ian Dury tune 'Razzle In My Pocket', which I slipped in, in homage to Ian." While its storytelling style clearly pre-empted the grand, theatrical ambitions of later album *The Liberty Of Norton Folgate*, 'Drip Fed Fred' would prove to be Dury's last recording.

★ ★ ★

Despite positive reviews and the resounding success of 'Lovestruck', *Wonderful* reached no higher than 17 in the charts, which hinted that the album had failed to sell far beyond Madness' core fanbase. In the short term, that meant some hard graft from all concerned to help keep the album alive in that all-important pre-Christmas rush.

Back in October, Madness had appeared on the TV special *Abbamania*, essentially a variety show on which pop acts of all persuasions performed an Abba song. Their rendition of 'Money, Money, Money' was seen by millions and fronted the ensuing tribute album issued by Polydor on November 8 (which peaked at number two and reached double-platinum status). It's questionable whether this was a prudent move: now hovering around their 40th birthdays, Madness were far from a teenybop act and ran the risk of undermining their credibility (other artists included S Club 7, Steps, Westlife and The Corrs) but the project did raise £750,000 for the National Foundation for Youth Music charity.

Unfortunately, old tensions had bubbled up during life on the promotional hamster wheel. On Saturday October 23, Madness were performing a show for Virgin Radio in the old Battersea Power Station (on the station's website, Madness were later voted 'Band of the Year'). Afterwards in the pub, a dispute ensued between Cathal and Lee, who reputedly traded insults which escalated into a fully fledged fist fight, so much so that Thompson could be seen nursing a black eye in the video for 'Johnny The Horse', which was filmed the following day. It's thought that Smyth was blamed for this incident – and was temporarily ostracised from the band. Thereafter, Thompson would often travel to Madness shows separately.

"Certainly, Lee and Cathal had a fractious relationship, ending up with them coming to blows," admits Mick Garbutt. "Cathal was the prime mover and really wanted some professionalism. Also, I'm wondering if their resentment came from the early days because Cathal wasn't originally a full-time member. I think there was some underlying feeling that Cathal, who was now 'Mr Record Company', was taking over. It was articulated at times."

"The band have always been nice to work with," adds Steve Pritchard. "They're all genuine people. It was a great honour to work with them. But the main problem is there are seven strong characters with strong opinions about everything. They're all so individual. You'll get stories of it coming to blows but they've all got their own world views which rarely fall in the same place at the same time. So there were big arguments."

As late as 2005, Lee still seemed to harbour ill-feeling towards his fellow band member. "I had a run-in with Cathal," he stated in *Q*. "A sort of grey area there, no one knows what actually happened because there was alcohol involved but things haven't been the same since. I'm not here to make friends, I'm here to do business." Whether his last pronouncement was an offhand quip or whether it reflected a deep-seated issue is unclear but the incident reflected the inevitable strains within a band of seven wilful, grown-up men.

Throughout the Nineties, Madness had complemented Madstocks with occasional pre-Christmas dates – but The Maddest Show On Earth was their first UK tour for four years, suitably dubbed 'You've Waited Long Enough'. Unfortunately, plans got off to a shaky start when the opening show scheduled for December 13 at the Dublin Point had to be cancelled because of desultory tickets sales. The remaining shows embraced the usual range of stadiums. With no official support bands, each concert began with a DJ set of ska and reggae classics. Comedian Phill Jupitus then treated the crowd to a karaoke show. As ever, an elaborate stage set had been created, involving traffic-lights, lamp posts, an Esso tank and a fence plastered with 'Vote For Fred' banners. *Wonderful* was usually represented by six songs.

The tour was notable as much for its minutiae as anything else. Mark made a habit of playing the opening riff from The Beatles' 'Day Tripper' at the end of 'Shut Up'; 'Baggy Trousers' opened with the sampled sounds of playing children; at their 13,000-capacity show at Manchester's MEN Arena, Lee introduced Reece, a band who were managed by his brother-in-law Darren; and at Wembley, Suggs' daughter Scarlett sang backing vocals on 'Night Boat To Cairo'.

Keen to extend the album's shelf-life, Virgin committed to a third single from *Wonderful* in February 2000. 'Drip Fed Fred' was the obvious choice and a promotional video was duly shot with its guest star, evoking the dark, sinister mood of the song (although rumours suggested the band funded the filming after Virgin pulled the plug). "Ian looks like a skeleton because he was dying," his widow Sophy Tilson admitted in Will Birch's book *Ian Dury – The Definitive Biography*. "Ian and Baxter [Dury] and Madness were all in a little theatre at the top of the road. It was very moving. He was yellow and skeletal but still found the energy to make the film with Madness, a great group of men." Dury played Freddy, Phill Jupitus briefly appeared as a monk with a noose and Thompson became Reverend Greene with the white face make-up and eye-patch he'd donned for the Nutty Boys video for 'It's OK, I'm A Policeman'. Smyth's menacing silhouettes pre-empted the cover artwork (and stage show) for *The Liberty Of Norton Folgate*.

The band's enthusiastic online Madness community organised their own mock-campaign to vote for Fredrick C. Threwe as London Mayor, with a manifesto written by Jupitus. On February 16, the band had organised a day out in London to promote 'Drip Fed Fred', travelling across the city on a red double decker bus. It would have involved a procession at Speakers Corner, Hyde Park before moving to Trafalgar Square, Leicester Square, Gold Square and Marylebone. Madness had even hired a tank and enlisted the help of a scooter club to accompany them. Phill Jupitus and local radio stations GLR, Capital and Virgin were all complicit while the BBC planned to film the activities as fans from far and wide descended on the capital. Sadly, 'The Vote For Fred' rally was cancelled because the police and the local councils expressed concerns about public safety.

Unfortunately, a primetime appearance on the *National Lottery* show wasn't without incident, either. First, the BBC interpreted the line, "So we'll take pity on your souls and only cap your knees", as supporting the IRA and demanded they amend it! Then the producers had a fit when Lee strolled onto the stage dressed as Reverend Greene because, needless to say, he hadn't worn the costume at the dress rehearsal. And finally, Suggs was chastised after the show for waving some cash around.

When 'Drip Fed Fred' failed to breach the Top 40, Mark Bedford reflected the band's frustrations in the MIS newsletter. "Firstly, record releases are now totally governed by appearances on TV," he stated. "None of us think that the Lottery show is great television but it does reach 17 million people! This gets record companies very excited. So the Lottery wanted us to go on, originally, on February 12. But then [they] said, we want you on Jan 28! But this doesn't coincide with the poster campaign! Slots have already been booked, with different posters going up over three weeks. So the release date gets moved to February 21, the week of half-term! Every boy and girl band will release a single that week. So that is why the single landed the release date of February 28!"

Madness performed the single on ITV's *This Morning* and on *TFI Friday* (with Lee Thompson absent, Phill Jupitus played Fred) while the new video was aired on *CD:UK*. But 'Drip Fed Fred' was never likely to set the charts alight – the song was frankly too unsettling for mass consumption. Nevertheless, its release underscored the huge debt that Madness owed to Ian Dury. Having scarcely met him during their halcyon days at Stiff, it felt right and proper that they were now able to pay their proper respects to him during what must have been a difficult and quite painful time for the performer. "That was brilliant because he'd been such an influence on us," commented Lee. "But it was sad, too: the last time he appeared on *Top Of The Pops* was with us, doing that song."

Ian Dury died on March 27, 2000. Suggs described him as "The people's poet laureate, one of the finest lyricists this country has produced, he was still giving it his all to the end." At his funeral on April 5, a traditional plumed horse and glass-sided carriage led the cortege from

Belsize Park, north London, picking up mourners from his family home in Hampstead and passing near Kilburn High Road before arriving at Golders Green crematorium. "They wanted a couple of members of Madness to carry the coffin," Foreman later explained. "I thought the front-men would be asked, but because The Blockheads were small, they asked Lee and me! So we carried Ian and I was crying – it was all very emotional."

Suggs spoke at length about Dury's overriding impact on Madness' music. "[When] I joined Madness, they were always talking about Kilburn And The High Roads," he remembered. "Lee got me the album, *Handsome*, which was a huge influence. Punk was the prevalent musical force then but here was a band who had attitude yet also used saxophone and piano – elements that later became Madness. We used to see The Blockheads. Stiff Records, which Ian Dury was on, was the obvious choice. The Blockheads had a massive influence. Ian's lyrical quirkiness was a big factor. We liked 'Razzle In My Pocket' because it was about stealing magazines from newsagents. 'Baggy Trousers' was supposed to sound like Ian. I liked all the details and the aspects of ordinary London life."

A fund-raising memorial concert for Dury's family was organised at London's Brixton Academy on June 16. Madness joined Robbie Williams, The Clash's Joe Strummer and Mick Jones, Kirsty MacColl, Kathy Burke, Tom Robinson, Keith Allen, Phill Jupitus and Mark Lamarr as part of an all-star cast paying tribute to the man and his music. Madness performed four songs, including the Kilburns' 'Crippled With Nerves' and 'It Must Be Love'. In addition, Suggs teamed up with The Blockheads for 'My Old Man' while Cathal sang 'What A Waste' and Lee took the mike on 'Plaistow Patricia'. Also, Glen Matlock performed the Ronnie Lane song 'Debris' with Thompson, Davey Payne, Terry Edwards and Mick Jones.

"The concert was an emotional event and an honour and privilege to participate in," Smyth later opined to *Ska News*. "To see fellow artists show their respect and admiration for the passing of a true genius and excellent observer of human nature was impressive to see. The whole venue swelled with emotion and love for him as his songs were echoed throughout the four thousand people there. It was a night I will ever remember."

"He was probably the biggest inspiration to me and the band," Suggs concluded. "We copied his lyrical and singing style. Ian Hunter once said you could call a song 'All The Way To Memphis' but you could hardly write a song about Walthamstow. Ian Dury was the person who proved that wrong and, for ordinary Londoners like myself, that was inspiring. I saw his last concert at The London Palladium, which was a very poignant experience." In due course, Madness recorded 'My Old Man' for a tribute album *Brand New Boots And Panties*, issued in April 2001.

* * *

In the cold light of day, *Wonderful* had failed to meet the expectations of either the band or the record company. "We've all had our periods in the wilderness and mine came around this time," Suggs later told *Uncut*, referring to his earlier solo dalliances. "But then I got back right into it. My thoughts were, we'd do this album, reconnect with each other and then really get our act together with the next one."

"There is a wonderful feeling towards them," qualifies Mick Garbutt. "You can get the front cover of glossy magazines at the weekend with a picture of Suggs but you then fail again because people want the hits. They're loved but it's nostalgia. So you have that burst and keeping that going: that's the difficulty."

"We were really pleased with *Wonderful*," recalls Steve Pritchard. "We thought it was a great album. I think we sold over 60,000 in the end, not as much as they'd wanted us to sell of it. We weren't massively unrecouped – it wasn't a financial disaster. Around that time, though, there was that wind change at commercial radio. Capital said, there are no automatic passes onto the playlist. That ageist thing kicked in. The first Madness single was the right side of that line and the other tracks weren't. On the day the album was released, HMV were describing the people buying it as the people you saw at Madstock, core fans, stubbly-looking blokes. Despite the illusion of a hit single, it came and went in a week, an older male fanbase, and it wasn't crossover family pop at all. That's difficult for those older acts to re-capture."

Virgin executives were able to accept this disappointment. After all, albums under-performed regularly and, in this instance, the company could disguise this shortfall with increased sales of the band's past wares. Not so for Madness: this was their official comeback and, for some in the band, the relatively tepid response to *Wonderful* was a bitter pill to swallow. It's been suggested that Cathal took this quite personally – and he expressed mixed feelings about the project to *Ska News* in July 2000.

"[With] the complexities involved with recording the album, the personalities, the process itself and then the marketing, the record company, etc., I honestly think, after all those years waiting, it should have been so much better and more enjoyable to be involved in," he admitted. "Saying that, I am so pleased we did it and I think it stands up next to our other work well. I cannot be more happy about the commitment [from] Virgin Records. They were extremely helpful and enthusiastic. A major factor was Radio 1's lack of support with radio play. What can you do?"

Manager Peter Rudge describes this period as difficult, in terms of managing expectations. "We had a big hit single, which surprised me a little because I wasn't sure," Rudge admits. "The boys were stunned that the album wasn't bigger. It got some momentum, some gravitas, but their fan base had moved on and the new people were discovering Madness through the catalogue, which is historically what happens. Therein lies the rub. The band all had a whipping boy to blame. They couldn't understand why Virgin or I couldn't get it to translate. I knew there was a glass ceiling on them. It's always tough. Their insecurities were fuelled by their need to be contemporary. They couldn't understand why their music was not recognised in the way it once was. They were looking back on past glories and trying to take shortcuts. They thought they were owed it rather than they still had to earn it."

Rudge was bemused by the bickering within the band, which could reach internecine proportions before a truce was somehow achieved. "I'd never seen that kind of in-fighting before – different points of view and perceptions," he ponders. "There was something quite endearing about Madness. They were so unbelievably, wonderfully dysfunctional. All seven of them were strong characters who marched to their own drum individually. Each had a slightly different perception of who and what Madness was. The in-fighting was quite dramatic but in the end they always circled the wagons and moved on as seven. It was almost tribal in the way that they dealt with life."

The clear-cut factions earlier observed by Steve Finan were now more convoluted, according to Rudge. "Suggs popped in and out of Madness as he was building a career around and inside it but hadn't left the mothership," Peter continues. "Mike was strange, one of the most complex figures I'd ever managed. Undoubtedly, he was incredibly talented, the musical anchor and creative force, but he was also dysfunctional. Mike was a strong character but he'd be sitting on a houseboat in Amsterdam in an ivory tower, completely unaware of what was going on in the world. Chrissy Foreman was adorable, one of the funniest, nicest guys. Thommo was amazing – mad, eccentric, brilliant, totally uncontrollable. He was still going around at four o'clock in the morning on a motorbike fly-posting for a living. He saw himself as the protector of Madness' street image, the boys from Camden Town. That was the role they let Thommo play."

As a strong personality himself, Rudge was always likely to clash with as forceful a personality as Smyth. "Cathal saw himself as the band's in-house organiser and recruited the managers – as he did in my case," explains Peter. "He had this vision of Madness as something which they frankly aren't. He aimed particularly high. His vision was wonderful but his expectations were just so unrealistic. He was one of the most unreliable, unpredictable, inconsistent human beings. Totally scatter-gun, he never closed anything and it was all big ambition, big money. Cathal pushed it out and the band would pull it back in a little – provide barriers. A strange chap. All of them tolerated him so it worked on a certain level. But for me, he was a nightmare. I found my relationship with him to be the most unpleasant I've had with any artist I've managed. In a way, he was harmless but he could be physically intimidating and he was constantly overreaching."

Madness' manager found other members to be less confrontational. "Woody and Bedders were lovely – the Greek chorus," he continues. "I liked Bedders a lot, very straight and took it all with a pinch of salt. He established his priorities in life, with a career that Madness had to coexist with. He had a great deal of integrity. Woody was a simple, gentle soul, a nice guy. They're the glue not the predominant personalities or talents. Chrissy Boy was somewhere in between. He was the Charlie Watts of the band, who everybody talked to, the lightning rod. Barzo and Suggs and Chas – as much as he'd listen to anybody – would listen to Chrissy Boy. Chas was slightly in awe of Suggs and what he'd accomplished and he also respected Barzo's musical ability."

Like many familial organisations, Madness felt like a topsy turvy world of Chinese whispers, petty disputes and evolving factions and loyalties. "Chrissy had the relationship with Thommo," says Rudge. "Suggs had a relationship with everybody. Barzo had a relationship with Thommo and also Barzo looked to Chas to tell him what was going on in the business. They all clucked: wasn't Barzo difficult or wasn't Thommo out of control or wasn't Chas an embarrassment or wasn't Suggs duplicitous – one minute he wanted Madness then he wanted his own TV show. But it worked for them. It really was like a family."

* * *

From the outside looking in, Madness looked set to build on the foundations of *Wonderful*. On May 25, 2000, they received a second Ivor Novello Award for an 'Outstanding Song Collection'. That summer, Virgin re-vamped *Divine Madness* with new artwork, two extra tracks from *Wonderful* and a bonus DVD, as well as issuing a box set containing their entire album output, suitably entitled *The Lot*. And plans were announced for Madstock V on June 11 and a possible US tour. But when both live events were cancelled, fans wondered if problems were stirring behind the scenes.

What's more, the new millennium found Suggs increasingly lured away by his parallel career as a TV presenter. Beginning on January 3, he was a team captain, vying with a team led by the equally jovial Noddy Holder, on the BBC's new music quiz show, *A Question Of Pop*, aired on Saturdays at 6pm (which meant that, for a period, he was on two primetime weekend TV shows because Channel 5's *Night Fever* was still running). On May 3, he hosted a three-hour late morning radio show on XFM as something of a pilot episode. As a result, Suggs was gifted the slot from Monday to Thursday.

"I was out with the guv'nor drinking absinthe one night," he explained. "And about four in the morning, he asked me if I'd like to try a spot of DJ'ing. He said, 'Do you want to start on Monday?' and I thought, why not?" Over the ensuing months, the singer shared a studio with the likes of Maxim from The Prodigy, The Charlatans, Space, Mark Thomas and David McAlmont. "It's a pretty random affair," Suggs admitted. "The best thing about it is hearing great records and inflicting my opinions, of which there are many, on an unsuspecting world." It was also announced that, from July 2000, Suggs would co-host ITV's *The Real Car Show* on

Monday evenings, a six-part series recounting real-life car stories with a twist.

Suggs' growing persona as an all-round celebrity was endorsed when he joined a long list of household names to be the subject of *This Is Your Life*, with host Michael Aspel interrupting an episode of *A Question Of Pop*. Aired on April 10, the show involved his wider family as well as band members Woodgate, Thompson, Bedford and Foreman, Hope & Anchor landlord John Eichler, Boy George, Jools Holland, Phill Jupitus, Noddy Holder, old school friend Richard Dickson, Clive Langer, two members of The Farm, *Night Fever* conspirator Tony Blackburn plus various footballers from Chelsea FC past and present. Notable by their absence were Messrs Barson and Smyth.

At short notice in July, the singer also appeared at Party In The Park, performing Ian Dury's classic 'Hit Me With Your Rhythm Stick' followed by 'It Must Be Love'. Having befriended Graham Gouldman, Suggs guested on the ex-10cc star's solo LP *And Another Thing . . .* (which included 'There Was A Day', co-written with Suggs during that Huntsham songwriters' retreat). The album was issued in September 2000 on Dome Records.

* * *

Meanwhile, Cathal Smyth struck out with his own band. In Madness' long and convoluted history, no chapter is more enigmatic than that of The Velvet Ghost. They only played one show – at the Fleadh in Finsbury Park on June 10, 2000 – but in the absence of any further performances or official product, fans continue to ponder on what might have been.

The Velvet Ghost was an eight-piece collective which fused Celtic folk, glam rock, rockabilly and that familiar London-centric barroom style. Cathal's cousin, lawyer Sean MacGloin, played violin, harmonica and bagpipes. Sean's father was Tommy MacGloin, who had been name-checked on 'The Return Of The Magnificent 7' (as "Tommy MacGloin and his Combo"). The Velvet Ghost's musical director and guitarist was Martin 'Boz' Boorer, the aforementioned friend of Smyth's who had made his name with early Eighties rockabilly revival band The Polecats.

Alongside spells with Jools Holland, Joan Armatrading and Edwyn Collins, Boorer had played with Kirsty MacColl and Adam Ant alongside David Ruffy, who became The Velvet Ghost's drummer (Ruffy's CV also boasted spells with The Ruts, Aztec Camera and Sinead O'Connor). Double bassist Jason Wilson and saxophonist Damian Hand were fellow members of the band Bap Kennedy. And trumpeter Jason McDermid was a member of Jools Holland's band who'd played on *Wonderful*. Last but not least were BUtterfield 8 and Nutty Boys/Crunch! regular Louis Vause (keyboards, accordion) and ex-Madness/Nutty Boys pianist Seamus Beaghen (who wasn't able to play with the band at the Fleadh).

"Cathal often rings up out of the blue, full of plans," says Vause. "He has an idea in the middle of the night and then forgets about it. He was going to write an opera at one point and wanted piano lessons." At first, The Velvet Ghost proved to be more than a mere fancy. "We rehearsed for a week at a studio up in Mill Hill East. That was a joy. We recorded there, too. It went really well. Sean was introduced halfway through rehearsals. The music was really organic, mainly live takes, me and Seamus alternating on organ and piano."

The spectre of his recent tangle with Thompson still loomed. "In the studio, we were talking about Lee and suddenly Cathal's face went very cold," admits Louis. "He looked at me and it was frightening. I had to say, 'Cathal, this is Louis here!' He was saying, 'Lee's been winding me up for twenty years.' The last day of recording, me and Seamus were walking away with Cathal and we said, 'Do you think there'll be any money in this?' And he pulled out a wad of money and gave us I think £200 each and said, 'There you are.'"

Cathal spoke about their Fleadh performance to *Ska News*. "At 1.25pm, with my cousin Sean playing the Scottish warpipes, we walked through the crowds to the stage," Smyth recalled. "I knew no one would be familiar with the songs and that this was the acid test. What would it be like to front the band as the singer – would I be happy? Would it feel right? We played nine songs, and seeing the reaction of the people, I knew I wanted to continue this as it felt so completely fulfilling. To say I was over the moon gets close to how ecstatic the feeling was."

As regards The Velvet Ghost's re-moulding of recent tunes, Smyth said: "Some songs recorded by Madness were altered and not completely to my satisfaction, so the Ghost performs them in their original form as I had intended. 'Johnny The Horse' I will record with the original long intro [as] it is stronger. My main focus is to complete enough material for an album. I am hoping to record in September and the album will then be available on my website. It will be interesting to release the album myself. I want it out this year. I feel confident that I know the dynamics and moods which I want."

Now that Foreman and Thompson had reactivated Crunch!, with a comeback show at Camden's Underworld on June 14, 2000, *Ska News* speculated that Madness might have disbanded. "I don't think we have but in the same breath, we are not performing this year as a few members do not want to do anything with Madness for reasons of their own," Smyth conceded. "The Velvet Ghost is a means of stimulus for me. I feel I have to be performing so if Madness don't want to work then I have an outlet." Would the Velvet Ghost album benefit from the involvement of anyone else in Madness? "Mark or Mike . . . I hold their talents as musicians in high regard, but I think it unlikely because The Velvet Ghost is for me to tell my story." When asked whether Madness would reunite again, Cathal's retort was decidedly pessimistic: "Anything's possible in this life but don't hold your breath!"

The interview concluded with talk of Velvet Ghost activities stretching well into 2001: "Perform some shows soon. Next year tour album through Europe. Hold a special event in the summer which is now being planned." The article finished with The Velvet Ghost's set-list from the Fleadh. 'The Wizard', 'We Are Love', 'Johnny The Horse', 'You're Wonderful', 'Light Of The Way' and 'The Communicator' were retained from the *Wonderful* sessions. 'The Alligator Song' (sometimes listed as 'Alligator With A Stanley Knife') had been performed as a solo piece by Cathal during Madness' ill-fated Red Wedge dates in early 1986. Other songs were fresh compositions: 'This Friend I Know', 'Hoodle La La' and 'Welcome To The Dark Side'.

In late 2004, Smyth belatedly uploaded a raft of recordings onto his website, which were extremely promising. Captured during an intensive session between 25 and 29 September 2000 at Mill Hill Studios were most of the tunes performed at the Fleadh, but there were also several others. Cream of the crop was arguably 'Why Be Brutal'. Others have since been plundered for subsequent Madness songs. 'Viva Londinium', for example, was re-fashioned as 'Mk II' on *The Liberty Of Norton Folgate* while some lyrics from 'The Weak And The Strong' were exhumed for the 2005 B-side 'Dreader Than Dread' and, later, for the film presentation of . . . *Folgate*. Other recordings included 'As Stars Above', 'My Heart Is True', 'This

Friend I Know' and 'Bewdley Street' while Cathal performed a song during this period entitled 'I'm Going Mad Again' (written for daughter Eloise).

An album title was even chosen from suggestions in an online competition: *The Father, The Son And The Velvet Ghost.* But it was not to be. "It was very short-lived," adds Vause. "I ran into Cathal after he'd dropped the idea. 'Cathal, why?! It was really good.' 'Oh, I don't know, it doesn't sound as good as I want it to sound.' Well, nothing ever does. I might have quoted Robert Graves to him, who said, 'a poem is never finished, only abandoned'. I went to his office one day and said, 'Why don't you send 'The Wizard' to the Harry Potter film producers?' He got straight on the phone but we were too late. It would have been ideal for the end credits!"

As a tantalising postscript, Cathal reconvened for an acoustic set of Velvet Ghost material in Camden's Mac Bar on September 23, 2001, as part of Louis Vause's regular Big Chill slot on Sundays. "He was really nervous," adds Louis. "There were fans at the bar who'd come especially. 'It'll be all right, Cathal.' I reminded him of a couple of Velvet Ghost tracks he'd forgotten about. 'Oh yeah, I remember that.' And he put in a really good show for half an hour."

It may say something about Smyth's impulsive nature that he was so passionate about the Velvet Ghost during summer 2000 and yet, to all intents and purposes, the project was stillborn by the autumn. "Cathal never stops writing," Boorer later explained to Madness Central. "That's how it started really. He'd written a load of songs and I said, 'I've got a studio you can use. Put them down on tape to get them out of your head so you can hear them as a collection.' They were all his ideas. There was only one song I co-wrote with him. It might've been called 'Check The Fruit'. Madness was on the backburner. He was still being creative, something he needed to get out of his system."

Within sight of The Velvet Ghost's Fleadh performance, Cathal was interviewed by *Freemasonry Today* about his life as a Freemason. By this time, he regularly attended Islington's Canonbury Masonic Research Centre. The article revealed that Smyth joined the Craft in 1994. Over time, his interest had snowballed. "In the 1980s, I read a number of 'shock-horror' books while on tour," explained Cathal. "Later on, I found myself working with a mason, who asked me if I was interested in going to

The lads appeared on *The Tube* on several occasions. Here they are performing on the TV show in March 1984. (ITV/REX FEATURES)

Sans Barzo, the serious six take stock of their future on the set for 'One Better Day'... (MIKE CAMERON/REDFERNS)

Madness spell it out to adulatory audiences in Japan, May 1982. (ANDRE CSILLAG/REX FEATURES)

By 1985, some band members had adopted a more grown-up, mature image. Lee had even grown a beard. (JILL FURMANOVSKY)

The fun four? Woody, Suggs, Chrissy Boy and Chas hamming it up when times were good in 1992, just after their triumphant first Madstock concert. (STEVE DOUBLE/RETNA UK)

In 1999, Madness launched their own range of Doctor Marten's boots to tie in with the footwear company's fortieth anniversary. (DF/LFI)

Atop the King Cross Scala, June 2002: the expanding waistlines and contracting hairlines didn't detract from the excitement surrounding the Madness musical, *Our House*. (RAY TANG/REX FEATURES)

Come the new millennium, that "leaning tower of pisa" pose wasn't much fun for the one on the end. Is that Madness ... or Squeeze?! (JILL FURMANOVSKY)

After nigh on two decades, Mike Barson returned to the studio with Madness.
His musical input has been a vital aspect of their comeback. (ED WESTMACOTT/RETNA PICTURES)

Chrissy Boy left the fold for a period in the mid-naughties.
Thankfully, he's now back in the fold. (SIMONE JOYNER/GETTY IMAGES)

Despite their impish good humour, a sense of dignity and maturity now surrounds Madness, forever a British institution. This shot was taken during rehearsals for their acclaimed performances at the Hackney Empire in June 2008. (LEON NEAL/AFP/GETTY IMAGES)

Suggs is a past master at throwing shapes on stage. Here are Madness playing at a promotional event for Ben Sherman at London's Flowerpot pub in May 2010. (ANNABEL STAFF/REDFERNS)

Madness filmed at the famous Georgian house in Folgate Street to promote their magnum opus, *The Liberty Of Norton Folgate.* (NEIL WILDER/CORBIS OUTLINE)

a 'lodge of instruction' supper one night, and I really enjoyed it, so I joined. I then joined a masonic trip to Washington DC a couple of years ago, and I became really enthused. I think it tempers the wild side of me. You've got to plan ahead to learn your work and that gives me a discipline, a good sense of succeeding as an individual. I was interested in Buddhism for a while and used to go away on retreats – introspection, I suppose."

* * *

As if to solidify the sense of unrest within the Madness camp in the wake of *Wonderful*, the due publication date for an officially endorsed biography of the band was announced for autumn 2000 but pushed back to the following spring before eventually being abandoned altogether. With a working title of *Don't Watch That, Watch This: The Official Story Of Madness*, Virgin Publishing had commissioned noted music journalist Adrian Thrills, who'd first interviewed the band back in 1979.

"They were a band with an itchy social conscience and also a dark, melancholy side," read the press release. "A group prone to internal ructions and divisions, who once spent an acrimonious Australian tour travelling to shows on separate vehicles." Perhaps such a 'warts and all' account of their trials and tribulations felt too painful because, by all accounts, the band pulled the plug on the book's publication. In fact, manager Peter Rudge says he was involved with several such biographies, all of which stalled when various band members realised the extent to which the authors might expose wounds in the relationships within the band that had still yet to heal.

"Some members have an unrealistic or warped view of Madness's place in the market," suggests Rudge. "Madness have a certain position in the history of English music. Some members believe their influence, their accomplishments, have not been recognised as much as they should. Therefore, some of them are a little in denial about exactly the gravitas the band are viewed with. And therefore, they expect publishers to react to them rather like chasing Bill Clinton's memoirs! Some of the boys were sensitive about revealing the inner workings of the band. No publisher worth his salt is going to give unconditional approval on what's written. But Chrissy Boy's tales about Cathal Smyth particularly or Barson was something which would cause such a problem. It's funny. There are seven books – an apt way of putting it!"

A 40-minute documentary about the band was screened on September 27 on BBC 2, as part of the *Young Guns* series about Eighties bands who had reunited. All seven of Madness participated in this worthwhile programme, which boasted unique archive footage of The Invaders from 1977, as well as numerous interviews with the band and such associates as Ian Dury in various locations (from A.H. Holt's shoe shop to the local washeteria and nearby pubs). But with a lingering sense of uncertainty, the show ended with a simple statement, accompanied by footage of each member peeling off separately from outside Camden tube station: "The band are currently unsure of their future."

Chapter 21

OUR HOUSE

THE history of rock musicals – whether they be onstage or screen – isn't exactly illustrious. Although there's a case for earlier examples, the genre is generally regarded to have been born in 1967 with the stage show *Hair*, which captured the hippie/counterculture zeitgeist to become a huge international phenomenon. Throughout the Seventies, rock and pop musicals enjoyed huge success both in the theatre and in the cinema, from the work of Tim Rice and Andrew Lloyd-Webber to American inventions such as *Godspell*, *The Wiz* and *Grease*.

For the most part, the rock musical's fortunes declined in the Eighties, by which time a curious sub-genre had emerged in the 'jukebox musical', which revolved around existing hits from a particular genre or artist. One of the first successful jukebox stage musicals was *Elvis*, prompted by Presley's death in 1977 while *Sgt. Pepper's Lonely Hearts Club Band* (1978) and *The Blues Brothers* (1980) translated the concept to the big screen to varying degrees of success. But again, the format was all but ignored for most of the Eighties until *Buddy – The Buddy Holly Story* and *Return To The Forbidden Planet* (both 1989) solidified the jukebox musical as a successful theatrical concept.

While most subsequent shows veered towards popular styles of music (disco, rock'n'roll, etc.), the end of the Nineties saw a flurry of productions based around the story/music of individual artists, from the ultra-successful *Mamma Mia!* (Abba) to *Love, Janis* (Janis Joplin) and *We Will Rock You* (Queen), the last of which was first staged in 2002. By that time, Madness had been approached to be involved in their own jukebox musical, *Our House*. If the band felt uncertain about the prospect of another new studio album, perhaps a theatrical production would keep the

Madness flame burning – and also help to patch up old wounds?

"The idea for *Our House* actually came from the band," Cathal explained. "Suggs and myself were working on an idea in 1999 for a musical and I went home and told my wife the idea whereupon she said, 'Why bother writing new songs, why not use the hits?'" Suggs later recalled his initial inspiration: "Writing a musical never occurred to me until Ian Dury did one called *Apples*, which I really enjoyed. It wasn't, 'Right, I'm going to be the new Andrew Lloyd-Webber!' but it did make me think that, given the right circumstances, I wouldn't mind having a go at this West End lark. We started a few ideas, on the back of cigarette packets in north London pubs. We wrote the idea for the first half-hour years ago – it was set in a pub adjoining a house."

The wheels were set in motion by producer Rupert Lord (who was involved with *Mamma Mia!*). "Rupert had approached the band with the notion of a stage musical," explains the writer of *Our House*, Tim Firth, "and having been given a papal blessing, he took the idea to [chairman] Peter Bennett-Jones at Tiger Aspect. Peter knew me from television and radio and rang to see what I thought."

A graduate from Cambridge University (where he became close friends with budding director Sam Mendes), Tim Firth had already made a name for himself as a writer, having worked with the famous playwright Alan Ayckbourn on various plays as well as penning several TV and radio programmes. In 2002, Firth's profile was in the ascendant, having co-written the script for the forthcoming films *Calendar Girls* (which became the fifth most successful British film ever) and *Blackball,* as well as numerous TV programmes. Firth had made his name with the 1992 play *Neville's Island* and the BBC's TV comedy *(All Quiet On The) Preston Front.* Tiger Aspect, meanwhile, were one of the UK's leading stage and screen production companies behind such hits as *Billy Elliot, Mr. Bean, Rescue Me* and *Teachers,* so this would clearly be a major project.

"After some networking, we were finally introduced to Tim," said Smyth. "In the early stages of the musical's creation, the band met individually and in pairs with Tim. After immersing himself with the music for a few weeks, he came back to the band with an outline of the proposed story. After reading his outline, which received rapturous applause from the band, it was obvious we had the right man for the job. An agreed draft of the book (theatrical term for script) was then workshopped with actors reading the parts. Various band members attended to stick in their valuable tuppence worth."

"I didn't want to work on a musical where people cheered when the songs started," explains Firth. "It worked well for the musicals featuring the music of Abba and Queen because there was an element of tongue-in-cheek camp endemic in their music. I was drawn to Madness by their corresponding lack of sentimentality, something I shared. This is the band who undercut their only out-and-out love song with a video implying the girl in question had just died! The madness of Madness has always been a by-product of the videos and the stage work. The songs themselves are lyrically of considerable substance. I set myself the goal that if, at any point, anyone laughed when a song started, then I would have failed!"

Firth began stitching a story together around themes from Madness' songs. "I collected every lyric and went searching for the musical they didn't realise they'd written," he continues. "There is not one single line or song that gave me the inspiration but rather a dilution of the entire Madness canon. The themes of duality, adolescence, the underclass, the importance of home and family all coalesced into their own plot. If anything, the central shaded area of that Venn diagram was the seemingly innocuous line 'Casey Street in the afternoon, once again it's over too soon' in 'Rise And Fall'. That was the trigger. It's where I got the name for the lead character and a scent of the sentiment I wanted in the story."

Firth was impressed with the songs' creators. "The band struck me as a dysfunctional family who somehow functioned brilliantly," he observes. "Sometimes you couldn't understand quite how guys of such varying temperament had ended up together but the music was the emotional glue that bound them and in turn benefited from the differences in temperament. The reason Madness have enjoyed longevity is that they have seven guys co-writing in an incalculable number of permutations. I don't know any other band that functions this way. I came to them when the script was first assembled and told them I needed two new songs. I met them in Camden a month later and they played me nine."

From this shortlist, Firth chose the sublime ballad 'Sarah's Song' and 'Simple Equation'. "It was hilarious," he explained. "I'd be getting lyrics from them, and I'd say, 'That's a strong first draft.' They'd go, 'A what draft?' No one asks a band for a second draft!" In summer 2002, newspaper reports suggested 'Sarah's Song' would become Madness's next single. "Having never written to order," Suggs told *Rolling Stone*, "that was a very enjoyable part of the process. The songs really arrived as naturally as possible out of a really good story, as opposed to the other way round."

"Funnily enough, 'Sarah's Song' was written by Lee a while ago," Suggs explained to radio DJ Gary Crowley, referring to its roots in a song which took a working title from the old Supremes classic, 'Back In My Arms Again'. "Lee is always writing. This was supposed to be a follow-on to 'Embarrassment', all about a girl trying to reclaim a kid that she had taken away from her by social services. So now, twenty years later, we adapted it for the musical and it's sung by the lead girl about her relationship. 'Simple Equation' relates to the idea of these two parallel universes going on and the point of the play really is [that] you don't always know when you've done right or wrong until afterwards."

All seven members lent their support to the project. "The band's support for the musical was unwavering but varied in tone," remembers Firth. "Cathal would give huge numbers of thoughts but never demand they be included. Lee, Mike and Woody would make quiet comments about certain points in the early stages but everyone was respectful of the need to make the songs work in their new life, as bearers of a greater story. When it was completed, they told me that in never attempting to be a biography of the band, it had unwittingly become a virtual biography of their own upbringings – not in any single detail but in overall spirit."

★ ★ ★

To launch *Our House*, a press conference was held at The Scala cinema in Kings Cross on June 14, during which the team – including the band – revealed details about the casting, design and inspiration for the £2.5 million show, which was to open at the West End's Cambridge Theatre in October. The musical was directed by Matthew Warchus of the Royal Shakespeare Company and choreographed by Peter Darling. Theatrical website What's On Stage reported that the musical comedy was going to be billed as 'A London Love Story', a modern-day morality tale set in Camden Town about central character Joe Casey and his mates.

The plotline began with Joe committing a petty crime to impress his girlfriend Sarah; thereafter, *Our House* followed the two courses that Joe's life would have taken had he a) stayed to face the music when the police arrived, or b) bunked the law and made a run for it ('Good Joe' and 'Bad Joe'). This provoked comparisons with the 1998 film *Sliding Doors* although Firth revealed that this parallel plot idea was inspired by the duality he discovered in Madness' songs, while admitting that it was "phenomenally complicated to stage". Magician and illusionist Paul Kieve was recruited to assist in realising such tricky stage directions as "Joe splits in two" – which, joked director Warchus, was the point where "you long for a flying car or a helicopter". The 26-strong cast was led by newcomer Michael Jibson as Joe.

"We were always kind of theatrical without ever really understanding theatre," added Suggs. "Now we've got some experts to lead us gently by the hand. We would never authorise a biography about the band: we never saw one which got it quite right. We didn't want our reasonably illustrious career turned into a cheesy tribute show. It would have been easier to do a slap-and-tickle, here-comes-the-circus cockney knees-up but with Tim being a Madness fan, we've got songs in the show which even I'd forgotten about." Madness were credited as assistant producers. The show boasted over 20 Madness songs incorporating all their major hits bar 'Michael Caine'. To increase the theatricality, alterations were made to include new lyrics and musical arrangements. Warchus commented that the stage show would incorporate much of "the style and energy that you find in Madness' videos . . . an almost cartoonish quality".

After previews beginning October 7, the show had opened to mixed reviews on October 28, 2002. While some favourably described it as London's answer to *Rent*, *The Evening Standard* was gushing yet accurate: "It started as a weird, wild idea, dreamed up by Madness . . . a thoroughly modern pop opera. *Our House* is a compelling, knife-sharp affair . . . Warchus keeps *Our House* speeding at a terrific state . . . *Our House* is that rare thing, an original musical." Other critics were more dismissive, but the show went on to win the 2003 Olivier Award for 'Best New Musical' (one of three nominations) on February 14 and also won the Hilton Award for 'Best Musical'. From April 7 for five weeks, Suggs himself played the part of Joe's absent father.

"My most pungent memories of the band during the show's life were not to do with script but rather Cathal giving me a kung fu massage on the floor of the stalls bar," laughs Tim Firth, "Mike giving me a lesson in playing 'Our House' on the piano, and Suggs giving me a Chinese burn on the left arm when it was announced we'd won the Olivier!" To capitalise on the media attention, Virgin issued a companion CD in October, entitled *Our House: The Original Songs*, which was notable for including the two new songs plus an exclusive remix of 'It Must Be Love'.

Unfortunately, it wasn't enough to guarantee *Our House* an extended run and the show closed after less than 10 months on August 16. Nevertheless, a special recording of the show was broadcast on BBC 3 on December 24, 2003. While talk of Steven Speilberg adapting the show as a Hollywood blockbuster was probably just tabloid tittle-tattle, a DVD *Our House – A Musical Love Story* was released on November 1, 2004. A new production toured Japan in July 2006, before *Our House* was finally revived back in the UK at Birmingham Repertory Theatre in 2008. It was also performed in Ramat Gan, Israel, by the Beit Zvi Company in May 2010.

"The show is entirely driven by young people," says Tim. "Ninety per cent of the cast were in their late teens/early twenties – and I think it speaks directly to people of that age. Those largely aren't the people who buy tickets to expensive West End musicals. It's telling that when the rights were released to amateurs, the take-up was the greatest the publishers had known – almost entirely by schools and youth theatres."

* * *

If nothing else, *Our House* reflected the enduring appeal of Madness' songs and acted as a welcoming distraction to keep the band focused while avoiding the thorny issue of what they should do next. Meanwhile, solo endeavours had continued and family lives had evolved. Woody, for example, set up a company called DRUMadness as a team building exercise which encouraged work colleagues to cooperate via their collective use of percussion. At one point, the drummer also tried his hands at a flooring firm, Woody's Floors.

As for Mike Barson, he still lived in Amsterdam but took time out to contribute piano to a No Doubt song, 'Everything In Time', produced by Langer and Winstanley. The recording was supposed to have been on their *Rock Steady* album, issued in late 2001, but was eventually excluded. Instead, it became the title track of their compilation of B-sides, rarities and remixes (available as part of a box set in late 2003, then separately a year later). Barson played on the 'London' version of the song rather than the 'Los Angeles' alternative.

In 2001, Suggs had co-written the song 'Oranges And Lemons Again' with Jools Holland as a tribute to Ian Dury. The song appeared on the *Later . . .* presenter's album *Small World Big Band*, on which each track boasted a guest vocalist, before belatedly being issued in September 2002 as a single. In 2003, the pair reconvened on the title track to the third instalment in Jools' *Small World Big Band* series, *Jack O The Green*. Suggs performed the song when he joined Holland and his Rhythm & Blues Orchestra on *Jools' Spring Hootenanny* on May 3, 2003, on which he also sang versions of 'Madness' and 'Enjoy Yourself' with none other than their creator Prince Buster. In 2002, Suggs also worked with fellow member of famous Soho private members' club the Groucho and one-time Kilburn & The High Roads' pianist Rod Melvin on John Lennon's 'Oh My Love' on the album *Anything But Summertime*, produced by the club in aid of the region's homeless.

The singer's parallel career in broadcasting showed no signs of relenting, either. Suggs was chosen as one of the principal presenters when *BBC 6 Music* was launched in March 2002. When The Blockheads performed a radio session on the station, Suggs sang on the final two tracks, 'One Love' and 'Cowboys'. And he was a guest on two BBC1 shows: the popular sports quiz *They Think It's All Over* on February 22, 2002 and *There's Only One FA Cup* that May. The Madness frontman also appeared on BBC Radio 4's institution, *Desert Island Discs*, choosing some obvious tunes (Prince Buster, Ian Dury, The Kinks, The Clash, Van Morrison) and not-so-obvious (from jazz vocal tracks by Peggy Lee and Julie London to poet Sir John Betjemen, from an album played to him by his wife Anne).

Another career path for Madness' frontman lay in voiceover work for TV advertisements. Suggs' dulcet tones have been heard on a plethora of commercials over the years, including those for Norwich Union*, MFI, Worthington's Bitter (reciting a Kipling poem), Toshiba (taking Ian Dury's place), Bird's Eye (which prompted ridicule from the rest of the band) and, perhaps most embarrassing of all, a magazine called *Full House* (on which he sang 'Our House' with new words).

In a light-hearted acting role, Suggs teamed up with the late Bob

---

* Madness fans calling Norwich (now Aviva) to renew their car insurance might have been surprised to hear Suggs answer their call and run through the usual push-button phone options.

Monkhouse on the BBC Radio 4 musical sitcom *I Think I've Got A Problem*, which also starred comedian Phil Cornwell. "Somebody I know came up with the idea of a guy who had an imaginary band in his mind," explained Suggs, "and Bob seemed the perfect person to be the psychiatrist. It's so surreal that it seemed to make sense. Actually, the same goes for the rest of my life. It's preposterous but wonderful!" First broadcast in August 2001, the series ran to four episodes, followed by a second series in spring 2003, around the same time Suggs also appeared in the second series of the TV show *Salvage Squad*, in which the team faced the challenge of restoring an item of classic machinery.

Chris Foreman married for the third time in July 2001 to Melissa Jobbins, their relationship further sealed with the arrival of a baby boy, Francis Albert Foreman on April 13, 2002. While Chris was distracted by family matters, Lee created a band with the self-explanatory name, Like Father Like Son. The six-piece included Thompson and drummer son Daley; singer/songwriter Kevin Burdett and his son Danny (both guitar); and Seventies rock stalwart Nick Judd (bass guitar) and son Alex (piano). Lee and Kevin had played one show together as Mr Wheeze before expanding the line-up in late 2001 to play a pub near Thompson's home in Barnet.

Like Father Like Son's set-list mixed classics from Thompson's major influences (Ian Dury, Beatles, Alex Harvey, Split Enz, ska, sixties, glam, etc.) with Madness songs, including the unissued Barson/Thompson compositions 'Culture Vulture', 'Soul Denying' and 'Idiot Child' (which later appeared on . . . *Norton Folgate*). They were reported to have been recording with John Hasler in spring 2002. Thompson mentioned that the band had an album's worth of material which they'd considered selling at their shows – but it never materialised.

Meanwhile, Cathal Smyth worked as an ambassador to the Prince's Trust. In terms of future plans, he appeared to have been inspired by the success of *Our House*. "I am quite a long way down the road of writing my own musical," he explained in late 2002. "I began seriously writing new songs a few years back and have now about twenty written, along with the story outline. The plot is quite dark and I am hoping to have something onstage next year. The title of my work is Welcome To The Darkside." Perhaps this was Cathal's development of The Velvet Ghost, who recorded a song with that same title?

In January 2002, Smyth announced the creation of his own record label, Rolled Gold Records (or RGR Music), run from an office at 3 Parkway in Camden Town (they later moved to 98 White Lion Street near the Angel). One of Cathal's first signings was Just Jack, the stage name for Camden-born teenager Jack Allsopp. Just Jack's debut album *The Outer Marker* was issued on RG Records in September 2002, promoted by three singles 'Paradise (Lost & Found)', 'Snowflakes' and 'Triple Tone Eyes'. "I got into the music industry after blagging a job interview with Cathal in 2002," Jack later told *The Guardian*. "I heard he was starting a record label and looking for a PA. I thought that if I played him my demo and he liked it, he'd sign me to his label. He did, two weeks later." Cathal's A&R instincts were sound but the rapper wouldn't achieve significant success until 2007 with the hit 'Starz In Their Eyes' and the Top 10 album *Overtones*. By that time, he was on another label.

For RG's second single, Cathal took a leaf from Suggs' solo career and launched his own with the World Cup football anthem 'We're Coming Over'. Credited to 'Mr Smash & Friends', the song relied on the tune from 'The Great Escape' (from the 1962 film starring Steve McQueen), while the promotional video assembled the likes of 'celebrity gangster' Dave Courtney, boxer Gary Mason and The England Supporters Brass Band. Issued on On May 27, the single peaked at number 67.

Several other artists were namedropped when RGR was launched – Fat Kidz, 3 Kings, Anonymous People, Drum Major Instinct, Sweet Spot, Quince and Seorais – but nothing materialised. In 2003, they signed hip hop act Border Crossing, leading to an album *Ominous* and three singles. The label's third and final signing were dance act Autamata (an alias for Dublin-based songwriter/producer/studio owner Ken McHugh), leading to an EP *Tales From My Sanctuary* and accompanying album *My Sanctuary*. But Cathal seems to have tired of RGR Music, or the funding dried up, and the label was quietly abandoned.

* * *

Perhaps prompted by the collective sense of purpose offered by the forth-coming musical, Madness had finally reconvened for some live shows. "Madness has a life of its own," suggested Suggs. "Just when you turn your back to walk away from it, it wolf-whistles down the street and calls you back. But it's a charmed existence. We've been through being controlled by Madness and now it's the other way round. We fluttered with the idea of giving it a proper go again, but it's a strange vehicle, Madness. The joy of playing and writing together is that we don't do it all the time. We've always been around each other and speak to each other all the time."

On April 20, 2002, they had appeared at Ahoy in Rotterdam, at an event billed as Heinekin Night Live, playing a short set for a Dutch TV broadcast. On August 11, another documentary about Madness was screened – this time on ITV as part of the *Smash TV* series (other than fresh interviews, however, the only 'new' footage came from the Rotterdam event). On the back of *Our House*, the band performed 'It Must Be Love' on *Parkinson* on October 10 with Thompson's role on sax taken by Terry Edwards. "I played on my knees dressed as Toulouse-Lautrec," remembers Terry. "I told them I wouldn't stand for it!" And on November 15, they appeared on *Children In Need* with 'Our House'.

From December 11 to 23, Madness played their first arena tour in three years, under the banner Don't Watch That, Watch This!, hopping between London Docklands, Newcastle, Cardiff, Glasgow, Bournemouth, Birmingham and Manchester. In place of a support band, shows warmed up with classic promo videos by the likes of The Jam, The Specials, Ian Dury, etc. Thompson had to fly back to the UK for the shows, having agreed to a six-month 'house-swap' with a family in Australia.

Conspicuous by their absence from the tour were Madness' new compositions from *Our House*, all the more surprising given that 'Sarah's Song' had been circulated as a promotional CD by Virgin. However, the shows were notable for the inclusion of such rarely heard gems as 'Not Home Today', 'Land Of Hope & Glory', 'In The Middle Of The Night' and 'Razor Blade Alley'. Fans were delighted that 'Johnny The Horse' was now performed with its acoustic introduction. And halfway through each show, band and audience watched the video to 'Drip Fed Fred' in tribute to Ian Dury.

Prior to the tour, Suggs spoke about their future plans to *Rolling Stone*. "It's still the very early days," he explained, "but we've been talking to people at Trojan [Records] about doing a pure ska-ish reggae album, a back-to-the-roots kind of thing." When interviewed the following February, Mike Barson seemed to share Suggs' enthusiasm for the concept of recording a whole LP's worth of ska classics. "We'd definitely be up for it," he told Joe Behan. "An album of covers [is] something we've wanted to do for years. We got a strong love of that music – as long as we pick all the songs that I like!"

Predominantly a back catalogue concern, legendary ska/reggae imprint Trojan had been purchased by Sanctuary Records in summer 2001 before being re-launched at the start of 2002 with an ambitious reissue programme. In summer 2002, Trojan had struck gold with a Top 10-charting double-CD compilation entitled *Young, Gifted & Black* – but the west London company had yet to expand the label back into contemporary recordings.

Trojan was also approached by Smyth for another of his extracurricular projects. Cathal was seeking investment and sponsorship for The Ska Bar, which would be based near Camden Lock and would be devoted to the legacy of Sixties Jamaican music. Although the plans were vague, the idea was for the venue to attract veteran ska performers and others linked to its heritage. A proportion of the profits would then somehow be passed to those ska producers/performers who made the effort to frequent the establishment. A meeting was held at a private members' club in which Cathal presented to a coterie of record label executives, journalists and investors. Alongside Cathal was his friend Terry Hall, who was keen to be involved, but to date the Ska Bar has yet to be developed.

Another project which failed to materialise was Cathal's autobiography, which he described as being "my version of being in the band. If anyone wants to know the inside track from an insider then I can assure you it will be an interesting read." Smyth also explained why Madness had vetoed the publication of Adrian Thrills' biography. "The book was generally written in a wishy washy style," he suggested, "and the band as a whole just thought it wasn't up to scratch."

In summer 2003, Trojan followed the success of their TV-advertised albums *Young, Gifted & Black* and its follow-up, *Reggae Love Songs*, with *One Step Beyond*, a double-CD joint venture with EMI which married the original Jamaican ska, rocksteady and reggae of Trojan with the best of the 2 Tone generation. Although Madness' management demanded an 'over-ride' on the royalty percentage for the title track, the Top 10 album actually boasted Prince Buster's original version. Instead, the Nutty Boys were represented by 'The Prince', 'Night Boat To Cairo' and 'My Girl'. Interest in vintage Jamaican music hadn't subsided. If anything, new generations were being turned on to the island's past treasures and its 2 Tone offspring, evinced by the acclaim afforded to up-and-coming bands such as The Ordinary Boys and the Dead 60's (both of whom later enjoyed ska-styled hits).

On March 29, 2003, Madness played a charity concert at London's Royal Albert Hall for the Teenage Cancer Trust. They also appeared on an episode of the TV series *The Kumars At No. 42* and ITV's *Ant And Dec Show*, alongside Ant (who many years earlier had written to *Jim'll Fix It* to perform with Madness!). Now permanently back from Australia, Lee turned his hand to acting when he began rehearsals for the part of Fagin in a production of *Oliver!* The fund-raising show was eventually staged at different venues in October. And in July, the band appeared at Guilfest festival in Guildford, Surrey.

Barring a couple of corporate appearances, the band were decidedly quiet for the rest of the year until their traditional end-of-year trawl around the country's arenas under the banner The Wonderful World Of Madness, with extra horn players Terry Edwards and Steve Turner (from Madness tribute band Los Palmas 6) in tow. The December shows were notable for some unusual additions to their set-list: 'Disappear', 'Victoria Gardens', 'March Of The Gherkins' and 'Prospects' (the last of which was used in *Our House*). The performances opened with the music from *Mary Poppins* (as well as Mick Jagger's spoken word diatribe from Suggs' favourite film, *Performance*, which they'd first adopted in 1999). They also performed covers of John Lennon's aforementioned 'Oh My Love', (occasionally) Dandy Livingstone's 'Big City', Desmond Dekker's 'Israelites' and Jimmy Cliff's 'Wonderful World, Beautiful People'. Support came courtesy of Aswad.

While Suggs turned up on a Christmas edition of *Eastenders* and spoke about aborted attempts to write his first novel, Cathal confirmed that while various band members were collaborating on new songs. "We are at the moment demoing an album of covers. Hopefully it will go something like this," he wrote, "covers album released next year . . . songs tribute to our youth . . . everybody happy . . . pull original material from under seven respective beds . . . record new album . . . very proud and happy with result."

In March 2004, rumours suggested that "the original seven members of Madness are set to sign a record deal for the band in the next fortnight". Suggs alluded to recent activity during a BBC Radio 2 interview with

Steve Wright. "We did a bit of recording last year," he explained. "We really enjoyed working together, and we're talking to record companies." On April 1, Suggs was a guest with Jools Holland's band at The Teenage Cancer Trust's annual shindig at the Royal Albert Hall, as part of a star-studded cast. And the Madness frontman hosted a show at Hammersmith Working Men's Club on April 14 to help raise funds for London mayor Ken Livingstone's re-election campaign. Suggs and Mike Barson turned in a brief warm-up slot with stripped down renditions of 'My Girl' and 'It Must Be Love' prior to a set from headline act Badly Drawn Boy.

★ ★ ★

During the evening of Tuesday May 11, 2004, an announcement was wired which immediately had Madness' fanbase clamouring for tickets. "You are cordially invited to witness the debut performance of London's hottest new ska combo The Dangermen, who will be appearing at the Dublin Castle on 19–22 May," read the bulletin, before listing seven famous names. "They will be ably assisted by the Monkey string section, a full brass section and various loop de loops," it concluded.

To celebrate the 25th anniversary of Madness (who, strictly speaking, had been born from The Invaders in May 1979), the Nutty Boys were returning to their roots for a series of low-key shows. This superb publicity stunt cum homecoming tallied with the inspiration behind their forthcoming covers project, which harked back to their set-list of the late Seventies. The alter ego was borrowed from the Sixties TV series *Danger Man* starring Patrick McGoohan, and its accompanying cult theme tune.

On Wednesday May 19, The Dangermen achieved the contortionist's trick of fitting seven grown men (some larger than others) plus three extra horn players onto the venue's tiny stage, filled to the rafters with fans who couldn't believe their eyes. A kilted bag-piper heralded their return onstage at the Camden Parkway venue for the first time since the making of *Take It Or Leave It* in spring 1981. The four-night stint at the Dublin Castle was a resounding success, wiping away the cobwebs of insecurity about Madness' future with sheer excitement and sweat, as they pounded their way through a short, sharp, hour-long set. "Has this place shrunk or have I grown?" quipped Suggs. "It's been 25 years since we last trod these boards but it remains a special place for us. It's all about Camden Town."

Only their famous brace of Prince Buster covers, plus 'The Prince' and

'Night Boat To Cairo', were drawn from their back catalogue. Instead of their hits, fans were treated to a smattering of ska and reggae classics. Some they'd performed before: 'Israelites', 'Big City', 'Wonderful World, Beautiful People'. Others were introduced: the calypso/ska standard 'Shame & Scandal' (a Trinidadian-themed tune popularised by Lord Melody and recorded by all and sundry, including The Wailers), Prince Buster's 'Girl (Why Don't You Answer To Your Name)', Desmond Dekker's hit 'It Mek', Roland Alphonso & The Soul Brothers' ska classic 'Phoenix City' and Honeyboy Martin & The Voices' rocksteady favourite 'Dreader Than Dread'.

Their set also boasted some Sixties soul classics but closer inspection revealed that Madness probably drew on their Jamaican covers. For example, The Supremes' Motown hit 'You Keep Me Hanging On' had been adapted by Ken Boothe while Barbara Lynn's R&B gem 'You'll Lose A Good Thing' was later intrepreted by Audrey Hall. On some nights, they also opened with a ska version of the 'Danger Man' theme, written and performed back in 1965 by Edwin Astley but also issued as 'High Wire' by The Bob Leaper Orchestra.

Once the afterglow of excitement from the shows had worn off, life appeared to return to normal. Suggs landed a Friday slot as presenter/DJ on Virgin Radio as news circulated about his potential role as a "Camden music czar" backed by Culture Minister Estelle Morris. On 8 July, Madness appeared at Lancashire County Cricket Ground for Manchester's Move Festival, headlining the opening Thursday night ahead of Ocean Colour Scene, The Stranglers and Jimmy Cliff. In September, Suggs opened the Kitsch Lounge Riot night at the newly opened Koko (refurbished from the old Camden Palace) with live performances of 'Baggy Trousers', 'It Must Be Love' and 'Our House'. On October 18, Suggs hosted Camden Borough's second Youth Question Time, which aimed to give young people a chance to question local politicians about various issues. Meanwhile, Cathal's guest appearance with Neville Staples appeared as a bonus DVD with the Specials singer's new album, *The Rude Boy Returns*. And in November, Suggs appeared on Children In Need in a re-make of the 'Our House' video, featuring various TV makeover stars.

Behind the scenes, Peter Rudge had been speaking with several different record companies about signing Madness. Their manager was already dealing with V2 in relation to ex-Kink Ray Davies so when the company responded with an acceptable offer for Madness, a "straightforward record deal" was signed in late summer/autumn 2004. "V2 liked the covers album idea," explains Rudge. "They were entirely comfortable with it but maybe it was a tacit admission that they weren't able to write new material that would resonate with the public any more. That felt a little like rolling over. We just thought the lesson of *Wonderful* was that new repertoire was not going to compete effectively. When you saw those live shows, ska hadn't gone away. Madness were looking at those songs from the Trojan era and saying, 'Why don't we just take these and turn them into Madness-sounding tunes, just as they did originally with 'It Must Be Love' or things of that nature.'"

★ ★ ★

Founded by Richard Branson in 1997 five years after his old company Virgin Records had been sold to EMI, V2 Records had carved its own niche as one of the leading independent labels in the UK. During this period, the label seemed hungry to expand their roster beyond contemporary talent, competing to sign acts who were longer in the tooth yet had that core credibility. Within sight of Madness, V2 also snatched Paul Weller and Ray Davies, artists who were also an integral part of the fabric of British popular music culture (another case in point was Morrissey, who ended up at V2's major rival Sanctuary).

"We were interested in certain established artists who we felt were still making great music," explains Tony Harlow, their company CEO who ran V2 worldwide from 2002. "If I was to put it in a nutshell, we had this idea that if all our acts, old and new, were in our bar together, they would have a mutual conversation and respect. V2 was a well-funded indie without an identity. In my tenure there, we tried to develop that identity." Harlow didn't take much persuading. "I was an original Madness fan," he admits. "I saw them at the Nashville back in the day when 2 Tone went off. We all got the short haircuts, Mr Byrite tonic trousers and a pair of Dr. Martens!"

Managing director of their UK operation was David Steele, an ex-Virgin employee (indeed, he was there during Madness' tenure in the mid-Eighties) who'd been with V2 from the start, signing the likes of The Stereophonics and Elbow. He, too, had grown up as an admirer of the Nutty Boys. "I was a huge fan of reggae and early ska, brought up on a staple diet of the originals which everyone in that 2 Tone era were doing," explains Steele. "Peter Rudge approached me and said, 'They're thinking of doing an album of classic covers.' I thought that was a great idea. They were talking to Universal but they came to us. So this was about finding the songs to cover and then finding the right people to record with."

David was directly involved in this selection process. "The band and myself made a long list because we wanted some well-known and some not so," he continues. "We didn't want to do a *Labour Of Love*, UB40. It had to have proper ska, some great tunes. I loved that idea of them going back to their roots, playing small clubs and that excitement. These are people that you're just proud to have on your label." As they dug deeper into potential selections, Steele is clear about the band's authority on Sixties Jamaican music.

"Lee was the true aficionado of all those old ska records," he remembers. "The inspiration definitely came from Lee. It was totally engrained in him. He was just infectious. The energy behind the group was Suggs and Chas but where they looked for leadership and making decisions, was Barson. He was really the captain of the ship, who said little and never seemed to smile but was focused, intelligent, knew what he wanted. Woody was a really nice guy but just a little sullen at times. When you've got all those big characters, there's not much room. But I really liked them and enjoyed working with them. A good experience."

In addition to the material aired at the Dublin Castle, the resulting shortlist of tunes included Max Romeo's 'I Chase The Devil', Lord Tanamo's 'Taller Than You Are', Rudy Mills' 'John Jones', Bruce Ruffin's hit version of Jose Feliciano's 'Rain' and 'So Much Trouble In The World' by Bob Marley & The Wailers. So far, so Jamaican so why the inclusion of The Kinks' 1970 hit 'Lola'[*], previously played at Madstock II? Well, the song had been interpreted by reggae artist Nicky Thomas on Trojan Records (though he had omitted the overt transvestite references towards the end).

By all accounts, Clive Langer wasn't keen on the covers idea so the band opted to work instead with veteran Dennis Bovell. Born in Barbados in the West Indies, Dennis had stamped his authority on the seminal British reggae scene of the mid-Seventies with his band Matumbi. By the end of

[*] Lee Thompson later remarked that 'It Mek', 'Lola' and 'Double Barrel' by Dave & Ansel Collins were probably the first singles he ever bought.

the decade, he'd branched out with myriad, often dub-based offshoot projects (sometimes under pseudonym Blackbeard), worked with reggae poet Linton Kwesi Johnson and developed a growing reputation as a producer (not least, Janet Kay's huge lovers rock hit 'Silly Games'). In the early Eighties, he shifted towards the white pop market, often at the cutting edge, working with contemporaries of Madness such as The Slits, Orange Juice, Bananarama, Dexys Midnight Runners, The Pop Group and Thompson Twins.

"I went over to see them at the premises in Shoreditch where they were rehearsing," remembers Dennis. "I forgot my earplugs and regretted it! They were so loud but they were really good. I thought, the best place to record Madness is the studio of the Mad Professor! But we couldn't get all the band in there. We wanted to record them all at once and it was too tiny." The original concept was for Bovell to produce half of the album; the rest of the material would be overseen by On-U-Sound's Adrian Sherwood. "Adrian said he was going to record in Livingston Studios in Wood Green," continues Bovell. "So we started there the next day. The rooms were sufficiently large that we could set the whole band up. I knew Woody was fantastic and I wanted to get a really good drum sound so I needed a big room. I'd worked with his ex-missus Jane when she was a bass player with Mo-dettes, who I produced in 1980."

Dennis immediately hit it off with Madness – and found a release valve for their inherently impatient nature. "They liked a brew," he admits. "When they weren't needed, they were in the pub. I had the number of the local landlord to say, can you send the lads over now?!" In the studio, however, Bovell was impressed by their focus. "As far as professionalism goes, they were a great bunch of lads. They definitely knew what they were doing. Suggs would steam into it. But I needed him to understand what I would class as good or not up-to-scratch and it's unnerving to make a singer stop every time he makes a mistake. So I came up with the idea of, you know what, do it again. 'Waddaya mean, do it again?!' I'd just let him sing it five or six times then go through and get the best of every performance. Once I'd knitted them together and he heard himself, he could go out and do it all in one." Bovell even played on a few tracks, notably 'Shame & Scandal'.

Unfortunately, the results conflicted with V2's expectations. "The problem we had with Dennis was the band would go in there, smoke lots

413

of weed and instead of being ska, it had become roots reggae," suggests David Steele. "We didn't want to just copy those old tunes, we wanted more excitement, to be contemporary, in the same way as the US punk bands loved their ska – like Smash Mouth. They all cited Madness as their inspiration so we wanted to give that back and a stoned out reggae record wasn't the way to do it. They had it in them because during those shows at the Dublin Castle, they were going mad, really sweaty – the energy of ska as opposed to chilled-out reggae."

Furthermore, the sessions hadn't been without incident. "There was some internal squabbling between them and Chrissy Boy," admits Dennis. "He was like, 'I'm not feeling this. I'm going through the motions but my heart's not in it.' Chrissy's a great guitar player. Also, I think Cathal had a medical problem looming.* He was taking a back seat, letting Suggs be upfront." In due course, Foreman left the band on the brink of the album's release. "Chrissy Boy had fallen out with them," remembers Steele. "I think Chas and Chrissy Boy just lost it. Chas was in a strange place. He was massively creative, a load of ideas and real enthusiasm but could be mad as a brush and a little destructive."

Meanwhile, their slot at Livingston Studios had expired. "In the interim, we went off to Mark Angelo's studio and to Adrian Sherwood's studio but it wasn't working," explains Bovell. "Then the record company were going, shall we get someone else to mix it? They got in Segs and Dubby, two friends of mine who work out of south-east London." The pair had previously built up a rapport together working with Alabama 3. Dubby was a nickname for Steve 'Dub' Jones, a dance music producer based at Miloco Studios. John 'Segs' Jennings, by contrast, was rooted in a similar fusion of rock and reggae as Madness, having been bassist with punk act The Ruts (whose hits had included the 2 Tone-inspired 'Staring At The Rude Boys' and who had backed ska pioneer Laurel Aitken back in 1980).

"Steve was working with Audio Bullys and this is the connection," explains Segs. In the hierarchy of British dance music, Simon Franks and Tom Dinsdale – alias Audio Bullys – were fast becoming the new Basement Jaxx. The west London duo were patently Madness fans, having opened their *Back To Mine* compilation of favourite tunes (issued November 2003) with 'My Girl'. They approached Suggs to guest on the track

---

* In late summer, Cathal had to have his appendix removed.

'Flowers' (circulated as a white label promo), as well as 'This Road' for their second album, *Generation*. "Suggs started talking to Steve and said, 'Look, we're a bit stuck with this Dangermen album. We've been doing it for ages. Dennis Bovell's done all the recording but the rough mixes weren't all that good. Can you help?'"

Segs and Dubby duly took over the project. "Steve came to my house and said, 'I've heard these Madness tracks,'" says Segs. "Being a big ska fan from the first time round, I knew all the tunes and, although I loved Madness, this was them covering some of my favourite songs. I said, 'It's either make or break.' Steve said, 'For us or them?!' Well, for everyone because if it comes out wrong, it's going to be terrible. These are great records!"

In due course, the pair were hauled in for a meeting with V2. "David Steele said, 'I think it's a great idea to do a reggae version of [Outkast's] 'Hey Ya',''' recalls Segs. "Oh great – this was without any of the band there! We did about thirty seconds and took it in for a meeting with David and Mike Barson. I like Mike but he's pretty scary when you first meet him. The 'bad Buddhist', Dubby calls him! We played it and Mike just went, 'Yeah, I like it, but what else can you do?' Anyway, they were prepared to give us the gig if we could sort the album out." Steele maintains this was a shrewd decision: "It just worked a lot better. We got some of that energy back. We were even considering using an American producer but couldn't find the right chemistry with anyone."

"I started 'producing' Suggs's vocal on 'John Jones'," says Segs. "We got on really well. It cost them a bit more money but we hired loads of old keyboards for Mike, to make the songs sound more vintage. We worked out of a little room called The Toyshop in Miloco." Without Foreman, Segs was the logical substitute for any extra guitar overdubs. "I'm not a brilliant guitarist but I'm OK at chops," admits Jennings. "The next minute, the record company wanted more tracks so we recorded 'Lola' and 'Rain' – which was always a bone of contention – at a studio called The Garden in Hoxton, which was also owned by Miloco. We set them up as a band to record and I said, 'I'm not being funny putting myself up for the job of being the guitarist on the session but I'm here anyway, instead of you training up another guitarist.' So we did it."

★ ★ ★

By way of a teaser, footage of Suggs and Woodgate in the studio with Dennis Bovell appeared in a Channel 4 documentary *Two Tone Britain* aired in December 2004. And then . . . well, nothing for several months. Cathal popped up with The Blockheads on February 8, 2005 at the Hackney Empire's Tsunami Benefit Gig to sing 'What A Waste'. And Crunch! announced some gigs. Suggs, meanwhile, had landed another acting role – this time, in a serious drama 'short' called *Talk*.

Foreman formally announced his departure on May 12, 2005 on the official Madness website: "I won't be appearing at anything else to do with Madness/Dangermen. The band have known this for some time. As for the reason for my actions, I was just sick of the petty, time-consuming bollocks that goes on in the band. Which is about as diplomatic as I can get! I have played on most of the *Dangermen Sessions* which I understand is turning out really good (despite me leaving) and is due out on V2 (who are right good geezers and I should apologise to them as well)."

Chris cited a recent corporate show from 2004 as the least favourite of his entire career. "[It] was like being in a Madness covers band who were playing at the wedding of two sprightly 60-year-olds," he wrote. "My whole life flashed before me as my honourable esteemed and illustrious career flushed down the pan. I don't ever want to do anything like that again. No bands like doing these sordid affairs. It's just for the £MONEY£ man. Which wasn't that much after tax." Peter Rudge sighs: "Chrissy Boy was agonising over whether he wanted to be in the band. He couldn't co-exist with Chas and he thought the band was losing its *raison d'être*. He'd met someone else and had been quite prudent with his money, quite sensible."

In late spring, half a dozen open-air concerts on Forestry Commission land were announced billed as 'Madness In The Forest'. Throughout weekends in June, they would play a selection of woodland locations across England – their very own Woodstock, perhaps?! Support act was the Lee Thompson-managed Jag. This three-piece had evolved out of Like Father Like Son – whose guitarist Kevin Burdett now took Foreman's place in Madness. The al fresco performances were well-received and their old favourite, The Miracles' 'Shop Around', was resurrected for one show as an encore, suggesting it might even appear on the imminent album.

Meanwhile, Suggs and Barson appeared on Johnnie Walker's show on Radio 2, during which the first fruits of the Dangermen sessions were finally aired: 'Shame & Scandal' and 'Taller Than You Are'. 'Shame & Scandal' was announced as their next single, issued on July 4 and fanfared by the band via a performance at Channel 4's *T4 Beach Party* show in Weston-Super-Mare. Although considerably slower than when it had been performed live, the song's style of tackling a taboo subject (incest) with mischievous humour perfectly suited Madness. Despite a hefty promotional campaign, though, the single stalled at number 38 in the charts – although it fared much better in France.* The B-sides comprised two out-takes from the Dangermen sessions: 'Dreader Than Dread' and a version of Horace Andy's classic, 'Skylarking'.

For obvious reasons, V2 had felt nervous about Madness using a pseudonym. "We had difficulty in just getting exactly what The Dangermen was," admits David Steele. "We were a little unsure about this concept. We thought it would be quite cool as an alter ego, almost like they were a band in the late Seventies. But that was hard to get across because everyone thought, 'Oh, that's Madness with a different name.' Anyway, we had made sure Madness was on there because we had to sell it so, in the end, it was 'Madness Presents The Dangermen'. The shows were great, there was a good vibe and the record did all right but we never had that one killer song for the radio."

The Dangermen Sessions – Volume One album followed in early August housed in a direct yellow/black design depicting the band in silhouette. "We wanted the CD sleeve to make you think of a gang," explained Woodgate. Within the packaging, the musicians extended the concept of their alter egos, concocting pseudonymous identities and bizarre professions (continued, *Oceans 11*-style, into the video for 'Shame & Scandal', which otherwise played on the song's Trinidadian origins). The credits revealed a raft of extracurricular musicians, from horn and string players (with David Bedford back as arranger) to additional production staff. At first, the album seemed to perform better than its predecessor, *Wonderful*, charting at number 11. But reviews were mixed.

Despite Steele's strenuous efforts in attempting to capture the effervescence of those Dublin Castle shows, the songs for the most part felt too

---

* 'Shame & Scandal' peaked at number 12, their first hit of note in France since 1981. On June 8, Madness travelled to Paris with Segs and a three-piece horn section in tow to record a three-song performance for TV show *Taratata*, their equivalent of *Later . . .*

relaxed, too clean. The album opened with a short, sinister collage of sounds entitled 'This Is Where' before breaking into a respectful take on Prince Buster's 'Girl Why Don't You?', built around an organ riff reminiscent of The Drifters' 'On Broadway'. 'I Chase The Devil' worked well, too, partly because the "Iron shirt" refrain from Max Romeo's original had been heavily sampled by The Prodigy – which lent the song another, altogether more contemporary frame of reference.

The most intriguing renditions veered towards the obscure, such as the skinhead reggae gem 'John Jones' or 'You'll Lose A Good Thing'. As reviewer Neil Spencer summarised, "antique Jamaican is dispatched with predictable gusto, lashings of horns and squeaky Farfisa organ". Unfortunately, other treatments were too end-of-pier in their production – or, in the case of 'Israelites' and 'Lola', the songs were just over-exposed. For reasons best-known to V2, Madness surfaced on *Top Of The Pops* performing 'Lola', which sent out exactly the wrong message about the album: 'pop reggae' was a much-maligned marriage which Madness had always avoided, perhaps purposefully.

Desperate to prolong the album's shelf-life, V2 plucked 'Girl Why Don't You' off as a single but its release date in early November felt like too little, too late and it was lost in the competitive pre-Christmas rush. Conspicuous by their absence were 'Wonderful World, Beautiful People' (a popular live track, after all), 'Shop Around', Desmond Dekker's 'It Mek' and Martha Reeves & The Vandellas' Motown gem 'I'm Ready For Love', which had appeared on salesheets for the album.

If the record missed the target, then the opposite was true of The Dangermen's live shows. At short notice, they announced performances at The Scala near Kings Cross (a stone's throw from their old Cally Road offices) on June 28 to preview the album. Three additional shows at the venue were subsequently booked. In addition, they returned to Camden's Electric Ballroom on July 18 (with support from Sean Flowerdew's band Pama International, with whom Thompson had played). "I was MC which was quite fun, bringing them onstage," says Dennis Bovell. "I tried to do my James Brown MC impression!"

The dual Madness/Dangermen identities had no doubt been confused by the recent forest shows. But they sounded vibrant and totally committed, playing with an excitement, pace and determination rarely witnessed since their heyday. Some shows added as an encore a ska version of the old

Pigbag hit, 'Papa's Got A Brand New Pigbag'. "It was a bit of a party," remembers Segs, who deputised for Foreman during the shows. "It was all about the vibe, what you're going to wear, how you're going to have a party. They were small gigs for them – the Scala was packed. Everybody was up for just doing songs they loved. Just the ska stuff. I was the new boy which was quite good for them: (a) they had a bit of sport, and (b) they had somebody new, a bit of new energy. It was good fun."

"I did one radio session with them live, the Ken Bruce Show," continues Segs. "They said, 'Do you know 'It Must Be Love'?' I said, 'No.' I had the wrong guitar and didn't have time to learn that bit in the middle. I wasn't prepared. Barson said, 'You seemed to have a problem there with the solo.' But I was brought in just to do a few chops, a few licks. They were going to start incorporating the Dangermen songs into Madness gigs and I didn't get asked to do those. They had another guitarist from a tribute band, Kevin Burdett, nice guy. They said, 'We can't have two different guitarists.' Also, he could do all the Chrissy Boy licks!"

On Saturday July 16, Suggs and Cathal joined Billy Bragg onstage at the London United Festival at Burgess Park, Camberwell (renamed from Rise in the wake of the horrific London bombings on July 7). "We learnt these last night in Billy's bedroom in ten minutes," Suggs declared, before the band ploughed through 'My Girl', the decidedly poignant 'So Much Trouble In The World', 'It Must Be Love' and, with the Madness pair on backing vocals, a reworked version of the Bob Marley classic as 'One Love (Drop The Debt)'.

Madness chose not to tour the Dangermen concept across the UK. Instead, the band headed out to the States for half a dozen dates on the West Coast across September 18–24 before returning for shows in Brussels, Paris and Amsterdam on October 16–18. Mindful that the concept of their alter ego might be lost outside of the UK, they sensibly merged their setlists, interspersing Madness classics with Dangermen covers. Nevertheless, this compromise still rankled with certain members of the band – and by the time Madness played a couple of low-key shows at the end of 2005, the Dangermen theme had all but dissipated altogether.

"The Dangermen name was a fun conceit," suggests MIS editor Jonathan Young. "It was harder to keep that up as they toured with the album, though. Hollywood's Troubadour Club had a cinema-style billboard sign hanging over its entrance, and the billing for that gig changed from 'Madness' to 'Madness The Dangermen Sessions' and later still to 'The Dangermen' at Barson's insistence. The US dates started to alternate Madness hits back in with the cover versions, so the LA ska crowd therefore got to enjoy 'Our House' but they also sang 'John Jones' as 'Steve Jones, you son of gun!' to the Sex Pistol up in the gallery, who was by now a noted LA DJ."

It's evident that *The Dangermen Sessions* wasn't a comfortable experience for at least some of the band. "Mike Barson struggled intellectually, conceptually, to understand why we were doing it," suggests Peter Rudge. "I put my hands up. It's an imprecise science. But at that time, there was no interest from anyone in a new Madness album and Madness, like any other band that's had major success, were not cheap so the return on investment was not healthy." On the one hand, Madness' legacy was taken more seriously than ever – evinced by a *Mojo* magazine 'Hall of Fame' award that year for being 'an artist's artist'. On the other, a seemingly light-hearted project which should have bound them together led to in-fighting and the departure of a founder member.

In hindsight, then, *The Dangermen Sessions* maybe missed the point. An album which was meant to capture the sheer immediacy and *joie de vivre* of a live-and-direct ska show, warts and all, actually did the opposite. Bovell might have been proud to nail a baker's dozen of songs in less than two weeks but the project might have sounded more vital had they recorded the album live at the Dublin Castle – or even live in the studio. Instead, the sessions somehow fell between two stools: neither gritty enough to properly recreate the vibe of Sixties ska and, therefore, earn some valuable credibility 'brownie points' nor slick enough to woo radio playlisters.

Cathal's original intention had been to launch his Ska Bar project in Camden by recording The Dangermen at the venue – but that wasn't possible because the venue stalled at the planning stage. Several shows were recorded with a view to a more ambitious, audio-visual release. "Thommo had the Dangermen idea and they all bought into this defence mechanism: 'we're going to do it as an alter ego'," explains Peter Rudge. "At the beginning, it was intended to be audio-visual. We were going to film a gig, this band that turned up from nowhere and played all these great ska hits. But we didn't have the resources. It was a half-cocked idea that had merit but we were unable to execute it effectively. And a lot of that came from the band: they were uncomfortable with it."

By the end of 2005, it's safe to say that relations were deteriorating between band and manager. "Everything was a soap opera," Peter admits. "They weren't functioning effectively, even on the level they used to before. It was like pulling teeth and it wasn't pleasant. For David Steele and Tony Harlow, it was a nightmare. They couldn't give them what they'd been used to with Paul Conroy: he spent a lot of money on *Wonderful*. And the writing was on the wall for V2, you could see." By this time, Rudge was busy with his new project Il Divo and when that led to further acrimony, he parted company with the band.

"The only terms of revenue you make with a band like Madness is live touring and they only toured once maybe every two years for ten days," concludes Peter. "I remember having this chat with Chas and he was saying, 'You're spending too much time with Il Divo.' 'Well, Chas, I have to pay the rent. OK, let's move on.' It was so complex. I was kind of relieved when we parted ways, even though I found them enjoyable, amusing and quite rewarding. They're a fantastic live band who've created a niche in the business for themselves. Unfortunately, it wasn't a global footprint. But they've leveraged a point when they had twenty big singles in a short period of time into quite a career and they've become an endearing part of British culture now. They're embedded as 'The Nutty Boys'. I'm really full of admiration for what they've done. They're not to be underestimated when they focus on something. God bless them!"

Chapter 22

THE LIBERTY OF MADNESS: PART 1

O N Wednesday 8 June 2005, in the midst of the build-up for *The Dangermen Sessions* album, Suggs wrote and presented a regional programme for BBC 1 entitled *A Picture Of London*. During the show, the singer was filmed in different locations across the capital, talking to locals about everyday life. Among the regions he visited were Soho (where he interviewed his mum in The French House pub in which she used to work) and Camden Town (including his first time inside Arlington House, as depicted on the Madness hit 'One Better Day'). "Those people and those streets are exactly what I'd define as the grand painting that is the landscape of London," Suggs explained by way of an introduction.

Aside from footage of 'Lola' being recorded in the studio with a string section, and mention of some five songs with Audio Bullys on which Suggs and Lee Thompson had worked, *A Picture Of London* was notable for one particular interlude. With Cathal on piano, Suggs was shown developing a poetic piano ballad about London life, namechecking Samuel Johnson. Commissioned exclusively for the episode, 'Cracks In The Pavement' felt like a poignant testament to his love of London and its people. "One of the ideas some of the band have been having is writing an album about London as a concept," Suggs revealed. "Although our guitarist said recently, 'What the **** do you think all our other songs have been about?', as if it was a brand new idea!" It may have been a light-hearted aside but the quip also hinted at the ex-Madness guitarist's disquiet.

Suggs wanted "to write in a bigger way about London as an organism, without sounding pretentious, and putting people in it, as opposed to normally just looking at their lives and blowing them up". Creating the TV show seemed to have acted as a catalyst. "It's a vast place and it's not such an easy thing to do," Suggs admitted. "Writing that song has helped because I've always been a bit scared about even trying to approach it as a whole subject. Just thinking about the lines, about the cracks in the pavements to the tops of the cranes, helped a bit. London's always changing."

Marvelling at the multi-generational audiences seen at their recent forest concerts, Suggs had suggested that "the Holy Grail for Madness" was "to be simple without being stupid". Never a truer word was said: the band's whole appeal had always lain in the balancing act between these two aspects. Madness' most cherished hits were pop nuggets of simplistic perfection. When the Nutty Boys tried to get more complex, their record sales dwindled and fans started to lose interest. Neither were the Nutty Boys that nutty anymore; in any case, some clever ideas lay behind even their zaniest moments. But with this goal in mind, how could Madness recover from the relative indifference afforded to *Wonderful* and *The Dangermen Sessions* from outside of their ever-loyal fan base?

As ever, Foreman was right: references to a London which wasn't reflected in the tourist brochures were scattered like confetti across Madness' songbook. From Muswill Hill in 'Driving In My Car' to Tottenham in 'Lovestruck', 'NW5' and Colney Hatch Lane, the Old Kent Road to Purley, 'Victoria Gardens' to 'Primrose Hill' or the two-up/two-down London terrace at 47 Stephenson Street, Willesden Junction for the video for 'Our House'. They weren't afraid to tread the tourist trail, either, namedropping Big Ben in 'Mad Not Mad' or London Bridge in 'Burning The Boats'. Elsewhere, they sang of London summers in 'Day On The Town' or Camden nights in 'Shadow Of Fear': the list felt endless.

"Many of the songs were written from images, memories and places that played a part of Madness' life," Suggs opined. "Today, London is still my main inspiration for songwriting. I'm endlessly fascinated by the people and the streets they live in. I grew up in and around Soho, a maze of tiny, narrow streets and alleys filled with some right old characters. Where better to observe this vaudeville show of street life? I was on Primrose Hill with my nephew and we were looking at the lovely London skyline and we both realised it was covered in cranes. And he turned to me and he said, 'Uncle, London's lovely but when will it be finished?'"

As the perfect riposte, the programme ended with Suggs' reply, "I hope the answer will be, never!" In hindsight, it's clear that, back in 2005, the seeds were already sewn for Madness' next album: a fascination with London and its people and an ambition which now sought to envelope its spirit within a collection of songs rather than merely namechecking it. Also, this wish to capture the "spark to London" wasn't a nostalgic journey but rather an exercise in documenting the pace of change, to portray that there's a "speed to the way things happen".

Suggs reiterated his wish when interviewed at the end of the year. "I hope to do an album of new material with Madness," he revealed. "Chris has been taking some time out but we're all hoping he'll be back to work on some new songs. My idea is to do a concept album about London, the fabulous nature of the ever-changing city and our experiences there. Madness moves very slowly. There are seven us all going round in circles and different directions. When we're working and playing music together, it just clicks. It's when we're not playing music that we start squabbling!"

★ ★ ★

The rest of 2005 was wrapped up with the fall-out from *The Dangermen Sessions*, from a performance in Amsterdam in October to two low-key Christmas shows at the London Astoria and in Nottingham, which merged their Dangermen set-list with Madness hits. They also committed to a variety of events for good causes. In late November, they travelled to a charity fundraising event in Wrexham, Wales, as part of the BBC's annual Children In Need appeal, buttoned up to the nines for a chilly, outdoor performance of five songs. In December, the band appeared at Arlington House to celebrate its one hundredth anniversary, performing 'One Better Day' and 'Wings Of A Dove' (whereupon a hundred doves were released).

While plans for a forthcoming Crunch! show were cancelled (suggesting Foreman needed a break from performing altogether), Thompson reeled in Madness' rhythm section for a one-off show billed as The Camden Cowboys (one of their old Stiff-era nicknames). Bedford and Woodgate joined Lee onstage on Saturday November 12 at Arts Depot's Pentland Theatre, Finchley, North London alongside Foreman's stand-in Kevin Burdett and Nick Judd on keyboards. This 'Make Poverty History' event was a fund-raiser for the Sudan Appeal. That month also saw Suggs and Cathal offer their services to charity. Those phoning a premium rate number might win the chance to have a song written about them by

Madness' frontmen, as well as two backstage passes to a Madness show in 2006. Money raised from the phone-in was allotted to provide safe drinking water in Northern Mozambique.

Suggs' fascination with the capital continued when he hosted a new TV series, *Disappearing London*, a regional show which began on ITV on Tuesday January 10, 2006. In essence, the programmes expanded on themes explored in *A Picture Of London* as a vehicle for him to wander round his beloved city chatting with eccentrics and poking around in the nooks and crannies of London's underbelly. From Victorian tobacconists and red telephone boxes to a night at the dogs at Romford Stadium, Suggs was able to convey London's quirkier qualities with charm and affection. *Disappearing London* was successful enough to justify a second series in 2007, which coincided with Suggs scooping the gong for Best Presenter at the Royal Television Society awards.

He also appeared as a guest of DJ Chris Evans on BBC Radio 2 on February 4. "We've the premise of writing an album of new material which we started working on this week," he revealed. "Only four of the band turned up but there are seven of us so it's like flexi work! It's great in the studio now because we haven't written together for four or five years."

On Saturday May 27, Suggs was seen at a reunion show in Liverpool by Deaf School, fronted by his wife Anne, alias Bette Bright, and Clive Langer*, to re-launch local venue The Picket. "I always loved Deaf School," he commented. "I first saw them when I was sixteen in London and it was a revelation. There was nothing like that around, it was all dinosaur rock. Our kids are all grown up now but it was the first chance they have had to see them play and they were in tears." Meanwhile, the singer's burgeoning diversion into radio was reinforced with a slot on Virgin Radio's Party Classics channel every Friday and Saturday night. By the end of 2006, his popularity as a radio host also landed him a two-hour 'Afternoon Tea' slot on Virgin.

★ ★ ★

---

* Fourteen months earlier, Suggs had guested, along with Dexys Midnight Runners' Kevin Rowland, when Deaf School played a reunion gig at the Magnet in Hardman Street, Liverpool. Suggs joined the band for a well-received rendition of 'Shipbuilding', co-written by Langer with Elvis Costello.

Having recently relocated to Hove on the south coast, Foreman unveiled his future plans to Madness Trading Ring's Steve Bringe. "You may have seen these rumours about me and the Madness boys," he wrote. "Well, truth is *they (* Mike, Suggs, Woody and sort of Chas) have been rehearsing, and I attended a meeting which drove me well away. Barso called . . . he was apologetic but I was just about to move. Clive Langer calls and asks if I will participate and I always have a lot of time for [him]. Some six new songs have been recorded with [a] stand in bass player, no Thommo. They are good songs . . . a 7 album feel."

Barson had earlier hinted about exhuming songs from his fecund period writing with Suggs at the dawn of the Nineties. Chris now confirmed they were dusting off some past prototypes. "Two, I think, I can recall from way back before *Wonderful*. I said to Clive I would play on them. So last week, I set off for merry London (ToeRag Studios) and I goddamn laid down some geeeetar on them. ToeRag is a basic 8-track studio [which is part] of the appeal for me. I did three songs in four hours. The usual stuff. Twanging and so on."

News that Madness had discovered ToeRag was greeted with enthusiasm from those in-the-know. Previously a best kept secret among bands searching to capture the analog sound of the Sixties, the Clapton-based studios – run by garage punk fan Liam Watson – had been thrust into the spotlight after playing host to the making of the White Stripes' acclaimed 2003 album *Elephant*. Suggs would interview Watson during an episode of *Disappearing London* in early 2007. The band was also reunited with their original production team. "ToeRag was kinda my idea," claimed Clive Langer in *Mojo*. "The last album was incredible live, but then they got into the studio and put loads of synthesizers on it! So I wanted to limit them. Rehearse, play, go in. Keyboards, one drum kit. It's all new material and Suggs has written his best song since 'Baggy Trousers' which is called 'Norton Folgate'. It's quite exciting."

"We wanted to go to Pathway Studios, where we recorded our early stuff, but that's gone now," Suggs explained to *Record Collector* that autumn. "We found out that a lot of the equipment from there, including the piano, is in ToeRag. We've done eight new songs that are coming along swimmingly. *The Dangermen Sessions* was music that made us want to play in the first place. With the new material, it's like we've leapt forward in time. It's a really rich album of great British pop songs. 'The

Liberty Of Norton Folgate' is fifteen minutes long, a history of Brick Lane from beginning to end, about the history of Shoreditch. It's written from the time of the great street markets of Brick Lane to today and it ends up with a tourist going 'in the beginning there is a fear of the immigrants'. It's a tremendous piece of work but it's not self-indulgent."

Foreman was now optimistic that this momentum would lure the remaining Nutty Boys back into the loop: "This will definitely make Thommo come out of the woodwork and play some sax, and I think Bedders has done something as well. The situation is similar to before we did *Wonderful* when a lot of songs were demoed without Suggs and Bedders. Chas, Mike and Woody really want a manager but Mike is apparently off to that Buddhist thing. Honourable mention to Chas who is on the by-line, as it were. I actually might send him some tunes."

★ ★ ★

For the most part, 2006 for Madness was punctuated only by occasional shows on the Continent. In January, they performed a shortened eight-song set at the Paris Rex, excerpts from which were broadcast on French and German TV. Suggs joined The Ordinary Boys onstage at London's Brixton Academy on Saturday March 25 for a cover of 'My Girl', the guest poking fun at singer Preston's newfound pin-up status via his appearance on *Celebrity Big Brother* by dedicating the tune to "everyone in the audience who has fainted".

In July, Madness committed to a tour of sorts, spread across festivals and other one-off shows in July and early August, encompassing Germany, France, Spain, Belgium, Portugal and Monaco. This included an appearance at Spain's burgeoning festival Benicàssim and was punctuated by a rare excursion to Japan for a mini-tour which included a headline slot at the Fuji Rock Festival, notable for an exhumation of their old Japanese 'advert' song, 'In The City'. During their trip east, Cathal spoke about his enthusiasm for their new opus dedicated to London. The tune, he said, would be closer to a "classical piece" with movements and strings.

Meanwhile, Foreman had a joint celebration in August. His second child with wife Melissa, a baby girl named Elfie, was born in Brighton on August 5, just three days before the guitarist's fiftieth birthday. The personal lives of some other members were less positive. While Thompson recovered from keyhole surgery for a heart problem, Cathal had endured the break-up of his 28-year relationship with Jo Brown. He was patently shaken by the experience, eventually choosing to relocate to Ibiza. "The songs he plays me on the piano – not really Madness, just his own work – are desperately sad, the sound of real grim experience," wrote Andrew Harrison in *The Word*. "But then he recites a Dickensian poem from the London musical he's been working on and we're off in The Land of Mad once more."

While at the Fuji Festival, Madness had chatted with Scottish band Franz Ferdinand, whose front man, Alex Kapranos, had previously been in Madness-styled ska band The Amphetameanies. The bands bonded and, when they returned to the UK, Woodgate guested with Franz Ferdinand on August 23 (drumming on their song 'Outsiders'). Kapranos revealed that *Absolutely* was the very first album he'd purchased as a pre-teen. Woodgate also joined them onstage at that year's Reading Festival. Meanwhile, Suggs was heard on BBC Radio 4 singing the theme tune to a new sitcom, *Not Today Thank You*. And on Saturday August 19 in the Virgin Radio tent at Chelmsford's V Festival, the singer joined comedian Al Murray (on drums) and the Ordinary Boys' Preston for an impromptu performance of 'It Must Be Love'.

On September 22, most of Madness joined fusion outfit Ska Cubano for four songs at a Cuba Solidarity gig at London's Barbican. "Hooking up with Ska Cubano is something we have been trying to do for a while," wrote Bedford. "They are quite interesting as they are part Cuban, part Jamaican and part British. It will be an exciting experiment!" The 16-piece line-up performed shambolic renditions of 'Dreader Than Dread', 'Madness' and another Prince Buster classic, 'Al Capone', with Bedford and Woodgate on bongos – and Thompson back among their ranks. Suggs was one of many alumni who paid tribute to the life and work of the late Sir John Betjeman at a Gala at the Prince Of Wales Theatre on September 11. He expressed his admiration for the Laureate's fascination with Metroland, reading the poet's comically bleak poem, *On A Portrait Of A Deaf Man*.

Beginning in October, Suggs presented yet another TV series devoted to London life, this time a regional BBC1 current affairs show entitled *Inside Out*, devoted to "surprising stories from familiar places". He continued this theme by fronting a two-part documentary *Suggs In Soho*, in which he shared his love of that unique corner of the capital, which was broadcast in May 2007 on ITV1. He also collaborated with Billy Bragg, penning a charity record for Pakistan to be sung by both Western and Asian artists, including British rapper Apache Indian. Madness travelled to Argentina to appear at Personal Fest 06 on November 17 – although Burdett remained in place of Foreman while an absent Thompson's boots were filled by Steve Turner. Suggs also participated on Ant and Dec's primetime Saturday show *Takeaway*, in which he performed 'It Only Takes A Minute' (Tavares' disco classic via Take That) with his own boy band.

★ ★ ★

In amongst such distractions, Madness announced on their new MySpace page MadSpace the impending arrival of a brand new song 'Sorry', a sassy collision of mariachi horns, a pacey ska rhythm, undenial charm – and a rap. When 'Sorry' went live in November, its rap segments immediately divided opinion among their fans. Many slammed its mix of overt pop and rap as being too reminiscent of Suggs' solo career (MIS playfully called it a "Marmite track"!). Suggs, of course, had worked with various rappers during his solo stint, in keeping with his underlying wish to remain contemporary. "We had heard that Sway liked Madness and 'Sorry' had been offered to us by the house producer Tim Deluxe," explained Cathal, "and [we] thought he could add something to it. He did it within a day – he brought [female MC] Baby Blue along."

North London hip-hop artist Sway had already been nominated for a Mercury Music Prize for his debut album *This Is My Demo* – and he'd grown up adoring 'Driving In My Car' because it name-checked his childhood stomping ground of Muswell Hill. "I remember reading an interview with Sway saying what a big fan of Madness he was," Suggs explained. "My daughters played me Sway's album, which I thought was great. I heard what he was doing with those guys who work with The Streets, The Mitchell Brothers: 'Harvey Nicks' was this hilarious song about being looked at as a thief just because they're rappers. Telly, movies, old jokes, football, stories informed what we did. People like Sway, Mike Skinner [The Streets], Jamie T or Lily Allen are still connected to that context."

'Sorry' was an ebullient aside but if it didn't feel like 'proper' Madness, that's because only a handful of the band actually appeared on the recording. Sway might potentially have offered Madness a renewed credibility, especially with a younger audience, but the opposite was true of their performance (albeit with only four of the original seven) of 'It Must Be Love' on *Strictly Come Dancing* that month. The original of 'Sorry', *sans* rap, was made available as a seven-inch during their December UK tour, To The Edge Of The Universe And Beyond, on their own Lucky Seven imprint, distressed to look like a vintage ska 45.

"Chrissy Boy is back on board too: he's back in the studio and will be with us at Christmas," enthused Suggs. "The whole band dynamic works so much better when there's seven of us onstage." The tour opened with the relatively intimate environs of the Brixton Academy, with DJ support from Jerry Dammers and an enthusiastic guest appearance on 'Night Boat To Cairo' from Smyth's daughter Eloise. Support act were Los Angeles' infectious funk/reggae band The Aggrolites, with whom Thompson had guested during their own show at Camden's Underworld earlier that month. To help promote the tour, two in-concert CDs of the Nutty Boys were given away with *The Mail On Sunday*. Not only was this a lucrative venture but, by all accounts, another 20,000 tickets for their forthcoming concerts were sold off the back of subsequent visits to MadSpace.

The tour was notable for resurrecting old songs 'On The Beat Pete' and, for their Brixton show only, a shambolic 'Rise And Fall', plus the unveiling of both 'Sorry' and a completely new song, 'NW5'. This tribute to their Kentish Town roots sounded like a lighthearted, heavily Motown-accented love song which reeled in fans with its accessible chorus, "I would give you everything". Embracing the flexibility afforded by modern technology, Madness made double-CD recordings of each performance available to buy after each of their eight arena shows nationwide (though the track 'Suggs Sings Help!' from some concerts was merely him voicing a few lines from the Beatles' classic at the beginning of 'House Of Fun').

Looking ahead to 2007, Cathal sounded upbeat: "We have five songs more or less completed. The plan is that we'd ideally have another single around April/May then release the album in June with some preview shows at the Hackney Empire. The album has numerous titles which we'll be fighting over at some length!" Suggs, meanwhile, was splashed all over the tabloids following his inebriation at that year's Brit Awards. "My wife and daughter were going on holiday and I saw them off saying I was just going to have a quiet night at the Brits with the Virgin Radio team," Suggs admitted. "Then my daughter rang me up from the ferry and said, 'Dad, have you seen *The Sun?*' There was an article saying that Amy Winehouse and Noel Gallagher were disappointments in the caning department. At number one in the Top Five caners was me. It's still 1979 and I'm 18-years-old – and I carry on like that!"

★ ★ ★

Perhaps taking heed from their fans' adverse reaction, the rap version of 'Sorry' was quietly relegated in favour of a more palatable alternative. Issued on March 3, 2007 with the help of a promo video depicting the band performing the song while Thompson paraded around in a fetching tutu and fez, 'Sorry' reached the Top 30 as well as number three as their first listing on the independent charts. On the day of its release, Suggs and Woodgate took to the sofa on TV show *Soccer AM.* "We got new managers last year, the last of a run of about fifteen with no hair or marbles left!" laughed Suggs. "Because there's seven people in Madness, it's a difficult process for sure."

In the wake of their split with Peter Rudge, Madness had hooked up with two separate management teams. One was led by Garry Blackburn, head of the successful Fulham-based music promotions company Anglo Plugging and sister company Anglo Management, the latter created in 1995 to aid the career of Norman Cook. Blackburn and his team, which included Dylan White, had also founded a publishing company, ASongs, oversaw a dance music record label, Southern Fried and, in due course, launched a music download service, Trax2Burn. From his humble days as a plugger at Island Records in the Eighties, Blackburn now oversaw what might be described as a 360 degree service for artists.

"I began my career about 20 years ago when, with an economics degree under my belt, I took a job as an office boy at a record company," he wrote in 2005. "Now, my companies work with leading world talent, managing Fatboy Slim and the Stereo MCs, promoting Oasis, U2, Franz Ferdinand and The Kaiser Chiefs and recording Armand van Helden." In autumn 2006, Blackburn took over the management of Madness as a joint venture with Hugh Gadsdon of HannaH Management, a company Gadsdon had created with Dennis Muirhead in 2004 to manage Clive Langer and Alan Winstanley.

Not only would the Anglo-HannaH relationship likely secure prestigious slots at festivals, for example, but a deal was eventually structured
with private equity investment to allow Madness the freedom and scope to
develop projects in their own time*, without being compromised by the
constraints placed upon them by a major record label. Having their own
imprint, Lucky Seven, was the first benefit from this set-up.

Towards the end of 2006, an advert appeared requesting extras for the
shoot of a Madness promo: "We are looking to cast four police officers,
four criminals and a prostitute. The video is for a track from a forthcoming
feature film. Madness will be starring alongside two comedians who
appear in the film." Thompson elucidated: "Clive Langer and Alan
Winstanley are behind the production and I can confirm the men at C&A
are doing a thoroughly good job!" However, only Suggs, Smyth, Woodgate and Kevin Burdett were present for the filming.

The film in question, *Neues Vom Wixxer*, was a sequel to German
comedy *Der Wixxer* (2004). Madness' involvement was organised by
long-time fan and popular German comedian Oliver Kalkofe, who
co-wrote, co-produced and starred in both films, which pastiched a
popular old film series, *Der Hexer (The Wizard)*. "*Der Wixxer* (which translated as *The Wanker!*) turned out to be a surprise hit with nearly two
million viewers," claimed Kalkofe. "I convinced everyone to choose 'The
Wizard' as the final song of the film. Unfortunately, due to problems with
the final production, 'The Wizard' was performed by Right Said Fred."

Second time around, Kalkofe was determined to succeed. "I met Suggs
and Chas in December 2005 and tried to convince them to work with us,"
he continued. "After more negotiations, we got a deal! 'It Must Be Love'
– newly recorded – is the final song of the film with the whole cast
miming along and a fantastic longer ending! And the brand new, absolutely fantastic 'NW5 (I Would Give You Everything)' is used in a
wonderful montage sequence in the middle of the film. The sequel
opened on March 15 and was number one in German cinemas for the last
two weeks!" In addition to a soundtrack CD for *Neues Vom Wixxer*, the
band was given their own CD single in Germany comprising various

* "I've realised there's normal time and there's Madness time," joked Suggs. "What seems
like seconds to us turns into decades for everyone else. There's a whole different
time-space continuum!"

mixes and videos for the two songs in question (although neither featured Foreman).

★ ★ ★

In a glorious prelude to their impending new album, Madness was the musical attraction as part of a theatrical night of all-round London entertainment on Wednesday March 28, 2007 under the banner Down At The Old Clapham Grand at the popular south London venue. Envisioned as a TV spectacular by independent production company Pozzitive Television, the show was billed as "a one-off night of glorious Comedy, Music, Variety, Entertainment & Kerfuffle to give you a taste of modern Music Hall". Organisers were keen to distinguish the show from some nostalgic period piece ("no stripey blazers, no Victorian parlour songs") while playing with old-fashioned proclamations: "Laugh! As comedians Milton Jones, Marcus Brigstocke, Harry Enfield, Jo Caulfield entertain you. Cheer! As Madness take to the stage once more. Gasp! As daredevil magicians Stuart and Barry play with your mind. And keep your ears scrubbed! As Bill Bailey presents a musical maelstrom of delight!" The event was subsequently broadcast as *Music Hall Meltdown* on BBC Four as part of their 'Edwardian Season'.

Meanwhile, Suggs participated in a concert organised by DJ Sean Rowley. Guilty Pleasures Comes Alive! was an extension of his BBC London radio show concept wherein he'd play hoary, decidedly unfashionable Seventies and Eighties pop/rock tunes which were actually rather good. Guilty Pleasures swiftly took off as a club night at the Hammersmith Working Mens' Club and as a CD compilation concept – and now Rowley was taking that show on the road. And the venue? At the faded Victorian glamour of the Hackney Empire in north-east London, Rowley had assembled a cast including Terry Hall and Catatonia's Cerys Matthews, to re-enact "those songs that you love but shouldn't", accompanied by the BBC Concert Orchestra. Suggs capped the night, a recording of which was broadcast on BBC London, with a cracking rendition of John Paul Young's 'Love Is In The Air'.

So by late spring 2007, when Madness were knee-deep in recording, they'd unwittingly stumbled across two crucial pointers which helped to fashion the identity of their new studio album: old-fashioned music hall and, historically, one of its finest emporiums. Crucially, Suggs & Co. had also been doing some background reading, fuelled in no small part in the singer's case by the hands-on research of his *Disappearing London* series. Suggs (and Cathal) began to namecheck writers from all ages who'd defined themselves by the capital, from the 18th century wits of London's burgeoning Georgian coffee houses like Dr. Samuel Johnson to acclaimed modern novelists such as Peter Ackroyd and Iain Sinclair. The focal point of this outpouring of enthusiasm for London's rich historical tapestry, from the band's perspective, was their magnum opus, 'The Liberty Of Norton Folgate' ("that might also be the title of the album or it may be called *We Are London*", it was suggested).

"When London was still a very small place in the 1700s, there was the City of London itself, right in the middle, just one square mile which had a wall round it," Suggs recounted. "Newcomers to the city could never get in there, so they had these places called Liberties where the first immigrants would go – the Huguenots, the Irish, Welsh and Jewish people. The law was inside the walls. On the outside, you could just do what you liked. So people on the inside on a Friday night would go to the outside and hang out with newcomers and the crazy goings on. That's a great analogy for the way London is, especially at the moment with [worries] about too many people coming into this country. That's the way it's always been, with new people bringing in ideas. There'd always be fear but London is like an enormous port and people have always come and gone. So this song starts off with a Jewish orchestra and then goes into Irish and Welsh music and then, at the end, Bhangra music."

The writings of Ackroyd, in particular, seemed to have captivated Suggs. "He talks about the tradition of 'street music' that's always existed in London," the singer explained in *Time Out*, "writing about where you live with a vaguely black humour about the trials and tribulations of everyday life. It's been there since the days of music hall. And I think the public identified with that aspect of Madness rather than perceiving us as chirpy. I also like his idea that you can catch something culturally in the air."

Madness had recently covered 'Lola' for *The Dangermen Sessions*, but now the Kinks' pithy, first-person vignettes about everyday life began to have an even more profound effect on their songwriting than before. "My earliest memory of Ray Davies is The Kinks performing 'Waterloo Sunset' on *Top Of The Pops* in ruffled shirts," wrote Suggs in *Time Out*. "They were from Muswell Hill, where we used to rehearse and got our earliest gigs. It meant a lot. I first saw them live at the Brighton Pavilion when I was sixteen. 'Waterloo Sunset' is a simple song about people meeting at an underground station and yet it has something fantastical, the magic of the street you were brought up in. It's very English to be able to write a narrative and still make it have some mystery and charm. I loved the way Davies told stories – Ian Dury was in a direct line from Ray and I'd like to think Madness were at the end of that line." Actually, the baton had currently been grabbed by the biggest new act in Britain, Arctic Monkeys.

Suggs detected further similarities between these fellow inhabitants of Muswell Hill. "I think some of what The Kinks did was chirpy [like us] although I'm sure Ray Davies would hate to have it described as that," he continued. "I saw a great old film for 'Dead End Street' just like a Madness video. They were walking down the street dressed as undertakers with a coffin on their shoulders, knocked on a door and Dave Davies comes out dressed as an old woman. Totally by accident, we replicated that in the video for 'It Must Be Love'! 'I never thought I'd miss you half as much as I do' is a corny line but when you are singing it into the mouth of an open grave, it becomes something different – so we shared some sense of that black humour."

Although The Kinks were part of the fabric of Sixties London, their songs betrayed an 'outsider' quality, too, observing rather than participating. "Even though he went to art college, Davies talks about never feeling completely part of the swinging Sixties although he bungled through it," Suggs continued. "I completely identify with that. Madness weren't fashionable but we weren't really unfashionable either. New romanticism was a big party going on, on one side of the road, and Madness were on the other with a popped balloon on a piece of string, like Eeyore and Winnie the Pooh – quite happy in our own corner of the world!"

Suggs guested on a lounge music/chill-out album by leading design/fashion house English Eccentrics. Issued that May, *How To Dress Sensibly* sported a reading from McPherson on 'Valse/Ladies How Vain', a 1922 poem by one of the Bloomsbury set, Edith Sitwell. "This album embodies a kind of whimsical nostalgia, which harks back to the last days of the empire," claimed co-producer Colin David. "[It] also expresses a genuine affection for England and London, which as a long-standing resident of the city I find very enticing." Which might equally have described Madness' work-in-progress?

"We have recorded half an album," revealed Woody in June. "The problem is we've written too many songs. For the second half, we've got 18 songs [so] we have to whittle that down a little." There was also talk of developing a film project to tie in with the subject matter of their 14-minute epic. Meanwhile, talk of updating of 'Baggy Trousers' with Sway as 'Baggy Jeans' perhaps thankfully came to nothing as Madness instead embarked on one of their busiest summers for a good while.

★ ★ ★

From the start of June until early September, the band rolled through a plethora of festivals, foreign climes and farms. They played the Peel Bay Festival in the Isle Of Man; Glastonbury Festival (their first visit there since 1986); Cream's equally muddy Knowsley Hall Music Festival in Liverpool; quick excursions to Athens, Zottegem (Belgium) and Cork; Guilfest, where they closed the proceedings on a Sunday night on a bill shared with Toots & The Maytals and The Beat; racecourse gigs at Newmarket and Ascot; the majestic surroundings of Blickling Hall stately home in Norfolk; the Sziget Festival in Budapest, Hungary (The Specials also played); and last but not least, Bestival, "the world's biggest fancy dress party" at Robin Hill Country Park on the Isle Of Wight on September 7–9.

At Athens' Ejekt Festival on Saturday June 16, a riot broke out while the members of Madness were unwinding from their performance in the dressing room. "Their high spirits were soon extinguished as raised voices, angry shouting, crashing windows, mace-wielding security guards and violent explosions signalled total mayhem in the backstage compound," reported MIS. "The Beastie Boys were forced to abandon their performance amid genuine fears for their safety. Absolute chaos ensued, as forty masked, baton-wielding assailants labelled as 'anarchists' by the authorities, carrying CS gas canisters, vandalised and robbed bars, attacked festival security workers, destroyed portacabins and petrol bombed vehicles. Fortunately, the band's experienced crew kept them barricaded in their dressing room whilst the attack went on. After thirty terrifying minutes, the group made a dash for it, stopping passing traffic to escape the scene."

"I realised when I saw the way those people were dressed (crash helmets, baseball bats, machetes) that it was some sort of anti-establishment anti-global anti-property type thing," admitted Foreman. "They petrol bombed the dressing rooms. They could have easily killed us all if they wanted to [but] just ushered us out. I knew something was up when I got on the plane at gate 13 and on seat 13 on the way there!"

By contrast, Madness' late night performance in Lost Vagueness' enormous 'big top' marquee at Glastonbury on June 24 hosted a stunt to break the Guinness World Record for the number of people kissing at the same time in the same location. The band halted their set at 1.30am for singer Suggs to instruct everyone to start smooching. Organisers hoped to entice 30,000 people to start necking, thereby shattering the current record of 12,800 people. 'The Big Kiss' was initiated by an internet dating site. Madness' set then ended on a high with a guest appearance by Specials guitarist Lynval Golding for 'Madness' and 'Night Boat To Cairo'.

In addition to hearing 'NW5', fans at their Cork show were the first to be treated to two brand new songs: 'Bingo' and 'Let's Go'. The latter was a saloon-bar rocker, in which Suggs delivered a gravelly rant *à la* Ian Dury over Foreman's deep, Duane Eddy-styled guitar twang. With lyrics courtesy of Suggs, 'Let's Go' was patently about his youth, with lines like "Painting the soul of your Dr. Martens white/Rolling on Hampstead High Street on a Saturday night" and "Bazooka Joe, Deaf School and Sha Na Na/Kilburn and the High Roads and we drive your daddy's car". Lee Thompson's collaboration with Barson, 'Bingo', also spoke of a London past – namechecking one of Camden Town's most ancient hostelries, Old Mother Redcap (later World's End).

At Bestival, their frontman appeared to have over-indulged rather. "A drunken Suggs invaded the stage during a Primal Scream gig," claimed *The Sun*. "The Madness singer ran onto the stage and took the microphone from Bobby Gillespie's hands, before shouting, 'Fuck the Rolling Stones! This is the best rock'n'roll band in the world!' The singer had to be pulled off stage by security, while a crowd of around 20,000 watched on."

Riots, kissing, drunken antics and fresh material notwithstanding, the Nutty Boys' roadshow was seen that summer by hundreds of thousands of people. Unfortunately, they had nothing new to promote. Optimistic claims that spring that just maybe their new album would be ready were quietly forgotten. Of course, festival season was now arguably Madness' major source of income. But such frenetic activity seems to have stymied their progress in the studio – temporarily, at least.

"The recording sessions are not happening lately," admitted Foreman to Steve Bringe. "Most of the new songs were recorded last year." However, he did reveal that another new song, the Thompson/Woodgate composition 'Dust Devil', was about to be tackled while both 'Bingo' and 'Let's Go' were now in the can. The guitarist also commented on his once fractured relationship with Cathal: "[We get on] really well. We have probably both changed. It's Barso who drives me mad the most these days!" Smyth was similarly optimistic about the mood within the band: "There were a couple of fallings out but Madness is seven dysfunctional men who come from dysfunctional families so the band became a surrogate family – the ties that bind us are so strong." And the new album? Due in January 2008, apparently. "It will be fantastic," gushed Suggs. "We'll incorporate a huge amount of new influences, the critics will analyse it for years. It will be *Dark Side Of The Moon* meets *Sgt. Pepper.*" Blimey.

* * *

In the short-term, Suggs might well have been distracted by writing his autobiography, announced for publication that October by Orion (but indefinitely postponed). Or by filming his cameo role as Thirties/Forties singer Al Bowlly in a forthcoming Hollywood film, *The Edge Of Love.* Or by enthusing about his Vespa collection to *Scootering* magazine. Or by visiting Pentonville Prison to present certificates to inmates in recognition of their work in creating guitar-themed art for charity. Or by hosting another geographical/historical-themed show, *Suggs' Survivors* (which was eventually broadcast in the New Year). In the autumn, having just quit his DJ job with Virgin Radio, Suggs revealed they now had maybe 50 songs to choose from. "I hope we'll have 70 by the end of the year that we will boil down to 10 and we will have an album. We've got some brilliant songs, about seven so far."

What about a release date? "March," he suggested on BBC Radio 2. "This recording is going extraordinarily well. Although it may be slow. But we made an executive decision to do it ourselves. We are not tied to any schedule. We will present it when it's duly ready." Live on air, Suggs and Barson then performed an acoustic version of 'NW5', which was announced as Madness' next single. On November 2, Madness appeared at London's Grosvenor Hall, a fund-raising event to a children's leukaemia charity. Meanwhile, details were announced for their end-of-year

Transport From London tour embracing Aberdeen, Belfast, Liverpool, Cardiff, Plymouth, Birmingham and London's Astoria and O2 Arena (with support from The Bees). This time, only recordings of the London shows were available to buy at the end of the evening.

The opening night of the tour at the Astoria on December 3 boasted another unveiling – this time, not one but two new songs. With its mellifluous melody, 'Forever Young' was another ode to childhood with its key refrain "before paradise lost and innocence gone". 'Sugar And Spice' might have shared a title with The Searchers' old Merseybeat classic but this was a charming, Motown-esque ode to the fragility of relationships. Awash with London references such as Golders Green, the Finchley Road and the Hippodrome, the song echoed Squeeze's 'Up The Junction' (it's subsequently been suggested that Barson was writing about the break-up of his marriage some years earlier). And to seal an evening dominated by nostalgia, Prince Buster strolled onto the stage to end the evening with 'Madness'. For their O2 show, the band played "in the round" and were joined on some numbers by a four-piece all-female string section The Demon Strings, evoking memories of their tours of 1983.

Publicising the shows, Cathal unveiled lyrics for yet another arrival: "Down to Chinatown for duck and rice/Along old Compton Street, the boys are nice" (taken from the as-yet-unheard 'We Are London'). Ever happy to offer impromptu performances of new compositions, Smyth – in a separate interview – was also heard playing what would come to be titled 'Fish & Chips'.

In an interview with *Sky News*, Suggs and Smyth revealed grandiose plans to unveil their new work in 2008. "We want to present our album in a more theatrical way at the Hackney Empire," announced Cathal, "with an intermission and to have fun creating the framework within which the songs are presented. Over five days, just completely new stuff. It'll be a challenge, it will be fun." Cathal also hinted at a possible biopic about Madness' long and convoluted story: "A friend of mine, involved in Pulse and a lot of English films, said he'd love to film the story which is nice because there's a *Jekyll & Hyde/West Side Story* aspect to it."

★　★　★

By now, the Madness roadshow very much involved their numerous offspring, many of whom were now teenagers or in their twenties. For the

O2's aftershow party at IndigO2, matters were formalised with 'A Family Affair', boasting appearances from Deaf School; Suggs' daughters Scarlett and Viva (helped by their parents on one number); Man Like Me (who included Clive Langer's son Johnny); a "battle of the organs" between Mike Barson and son Tim; Milo Smyth; and Ashley Beedle (whose wife, Katy Ellis, works with Madness' management team); with a DJ slot from Cathal's son Casper.

Suggs was caught finishing off a studio rendition of 'Bingo' during an interview for *Metro*. "It's about meeting somebody undesirable on a tube train," Suggs explained. Actually, 'Bingo' related to an unfortunate incident when Thompson was mugged on the tube while returning home to High Barnet one night. Somewhat the worse for wear, Lee got chatting with some lads, who responded to his benevolent nature by stealing his bag and his gold ring. The article also revealed that the forthcoming album's working title wasn't *Lucky 7*, as had been suggested, but would share its title with their epic song 'The Liberty Of Norton Folgate', after the tiny 15th-century independent district where Shoreditch now stands.

To usher in what would be a hectic 2008 for Madness, the band performed four songs, including their forthcoming single 'NW5', on Jools Holland's annual *Hootenanny* show broadcast on New Year's Eve. While Lee Thompson could be seen on TV screens, the saxophonist was actually playing in a Barnet pub with a new band, Damaged Goods, assembled from members of previous bands Like Father Like Son and the Camden Cowboys – namely, Kevin Burdett and son Dan plus bassist Nick Judd, a keyboardist named Jimmy and a drummer simply known as John. Thereafter, Damaged Goods played selected shows. Crunch! played a reunion gig that year at Brighton's Barfly on May 4 while Thompson also founded a new ska band Dance Brigade with ex-Belle Star Jenny Matthias, appearing for a one-off show at the 100 Club that September.

On January 8, 2008, Madness performed at a fund-raising event celebrating the life of Joe Strummer at The Palace Theatre in his adopted home of Bridgwater, Somerset. Organised by the Strummerville charity, the concert coincided with the sixth anniversary of the death of the former Clash front man. "Suggs and the band knew him well and are happy to give their time in his memory," commented film director and Strummerville supporter Julien Temple, a neighbour and close friend of

Strummer's in later life.* It must have been a thrill for the rest of the band to welcome Roxy Music's Andy Mackay on sax for 'One Step Beyond' in place of Thompson, who was absent. They climaxed their performance with a version of the Clash classic, 'London Calling'.

* * *

'NW5' was finally released that month to widespread praise from their fanbase. "It's about a friend of mine from NW5 who I used to hang about with as far back as the mid-Sixties, who unfortunately passed on," explained Lee. "I went on to become a pop star and he got into the dark side of life. I'm no angel, I got into alcohol but he got into the hard stuff, some pretty heavy drugs. It's about friendship and how life can change you." This new recording definitely benefited from the presence of both Foreman and Thompson, who had been absent for the German film rendition. Promoted by a video montage of recent live clips, 'NW5' matched the success of 'Sorry' by gracing the Top 30 for a solitary week (albeit it topped the indie chart).

That must have been relatively disappointing: the song boasted Madness' strongest chorus since 'Lovestruck' and had enjoyed substantial and positive pre-publicity. ("Its stomping piano hook is the beating heart around which Suggs and Carl hang their spine tingling harmonies," enthused one review. "Luxuriant string work and a classic nutty boy arrangement propels 'NW5' into its colossal chorus, combining the effortless familiarity of a football chant with the bittersweet pathos of a Madness tale.")

The three formats (7-inch, CD, DVD – each packaged like an old 45) offered a raft of extra content, including an exclusive cover of The Undertones' obscurity 'Bittersweet' (recorded back in 2005 at The Bunker during rehearsals for the Dangermen project), an acoustic session from Suggs and Barson at Bestival and a remix courtesy of Clive Langer's son Johnny. So what went wrong? Was it more difficult to promote your wares without the muscle of a major label? Rumours suggested the novel CD packaging meant that HMV couldn't rack the title in the 'New Releases' section.

---

* Temple was already talking with the band about their plans for a film project, which probably explains their involvement in the gig.

Namechecking two hitherto unheard songs 'Idiot Child' and 'This Is London', *Mojo* announced that *The Liberty Of Norton Folgate* was now due to surface in March. Chatting in *Clash* magazine that month, Suggs was optimistic: "I think the songs have come on really well. 'The Liberty of Norton Folgate' is like 'Bohemian Rhapsody' for pop kids, five pop songs stuck together rather than anything particularly indulgent. We did that all in one go with The Ukulele Orchestra of Great Britain*. I think it's a tremendous piece of work."

Suggs' TV career continued apace with an episode of *Teachers TV*, a series which depicted successful people from all walks of life returning to their schools to see if they could teach today's children. McPherson hadn't returned to Quintin Kynaston for 30 years, provoking memories of his earliest musical endeavours. "In my music classes, I was told I had to play the double-bass because I was big," Suggs remembered. "People were given instruments according to their size. I'd only played it once and that following Friday, I was in the school orchestra playing the double bass!" His mission was to teach the class to write a song. Despite some trepidation, he won over the kids with his usual self-deprecating charm by adopting a similar approach to that which he'd used to write 'Baggy Trousers' about his time at the school some 35 years earlier.

In spring 2008, Madness did a handful of shows, from a Snowbombing Festival in Mayrhofen, Austria (March 31–April 6) to playing their part at the annual Teenage Cancer Trust shows at the Royal Albert Hall (April 8), organised by The Who's Roger Daltrey. Barson had the privilege of playing the RAH's grand pipe organ, built in 1871 and only restored to its former glory in 2003, for the introduction to 'Swan Lake', bringing some class and sophistication to the proceedings.

On May 2, Suggs and Cathal joined Pet Shop Boys onstage for a dance version of 'My Girl' at London's famous gay club Heaven, a fund-raiser for the family of their minder Dainton Connell, who'd recently died in a car crash (the Madness frontmen had known Dainton since he was a young lad). Two versions of the song were issued roughly a year later on Pet Shop Boys' *Christmas* EP. McPherson made another guest appearance for a

---

* Formed in 1985, The Ukulele Orchestra was a group of seven players who had attracted widespread publicity for their willingness to play all manner of musical styles on the instrument most commonly associated with George Formby.

charitable cause – this time with rock covers band Damage Case in wife Anne's home town of Whitstable, Kent. He also surfaced as surprise vocalist on 'The Girl Who Loves Herself' by Little Massive, formed by ex-members of late Nineties Creation Records band Arnold (the connection being that Arnold had included Foreman's ex-brother-in-law Phil Payne) and produced by ex-Creation artist Edward Ball.

With talk of the new album ready for July, Foreman confirmed they'd dusted off an old song discarded during the *Wonderful* sessions, 'Hunchback Of Torriano', cited by the guitarist in 2005 as his greatest regret as "one that got away". "It's about a guy who lived in Torriano Villas, a block of council flats off of Torriano Avenue," he revealed to Steve Bringe.

★ ★ ★

In early May, Madness finally unveiled plans for three consecutive nights at the Hackney Empire from June 24–26. "Mayhem, Pandemonium and Madness," declared the Victorian style advertising. "Enthralled, Enraptured, Exhilarated . . . A stunning rendition of the forthcoming gramophone recording . . . to be followed shortly after by Classic Madness Popular hits."

As a taster, a six-minute 'Mood Board' edit of the much anticipated title track was uploaded to Madspace and to YouTube, accompanied by a film montage of "suitable skullduggery and phantasmagoria", stitching together clips from such films as *Oliver!*, *Edward Scissorhands*, *Sleepy Hollow*, *Elephant Man*, *Fear And Loathing In Las Vegas*, *Bram Stoker's Dracula*, *A Clockwork Orange*, *Jacob's Ladder* and *Brazil*. Fans were uniformly ecstatic: the musical assemblage was unquestionably Madness' most ambitious endeavour to date and yet utterly compelling, from its distinct sections to its vaguely threatening atmosphere, poignantly evoking the spirit of London's slow but inexorable evolution.

Even though 'The Liberty Of Norton Folgate' had been spliced to half of its eventual length, the song's dashing spirit of audacity and adventure – from its lyrical depth to its musical pot pourri – were a revelation. From its opening spoken line, "Old Jack Norris, the musical shrimp, and the cadging ramble" via impeccable string and horn arrangements and constant shifts in melody and tempo to the mantra, "they made their home there down by the riverside", Madness were clearly functioning as a creative, cohesive whole.

And the album's release date? That had slipped back to September, with Foreman suggesting it might take the form of a newspaper cover mount after a precedent set by Prince. A track listing even surfaced with the nine songs so far namedropped plus a new title, which was duly unveiled by the guitarist. "It is nearly ready . . . about another two . . . months. One song is called 'Africa' but a lot deal with those familiar Madness themes and are set in London." To further reinforce the links, Suggs spoke out in favour of the capital for a competition organised by the Arts Council to identify the nation's 'Most Musical City'; and details were announced for his next TV series *Suggs And The City* (geddit?), a chat show format beginning May 29 on ITV London.*

The first of several concerts at racecourses that summer began with Aintree on Friday June 13, Madness' first stage appearance of 2008. Fans hoping for a sneak preview of the forthcoming album should have noted the date: they were duly disappointed. That same day, *Sky News* broadcast an interview with Madness rehearsing at their north London studios. "It's finally seeing a bit of shape," admitted Suggs, "and I'm very pleased with it. Making a new record is announcing to the world that we're here to stay, because up to this point we've been having a great time primarily just doing greatest hits."

Those attending their intimate Dublin Tripod show four days later were luckier when 'Idiot Child' was unveiled, a poignant autobiographical gem penned by Thompson: "Always made to grow up/Always told to shut up". After the show, manager Hugh Gadsdon commented that some 22 songs were now completely finished – certainly enough for a double-album. The band had another opportunity to get fighting fit at Barcelona's Sonar Festival on June 20. Meanwhile, 'Norton Folgate' – or an excerpt from it – received its first radio broadcast when Suggs appeared on Steve Wright's show on BBC Radio 2.

★ ★ ★

Rumours floated around Hackney for most of that first day, June 24. Fans drinking in The Old Ship were a stone's throw from the Empire's

---

* A similarly punning title, *Suggs' Italian Job,* was adopted for another small screen venture on Sky Arts to be broadcast in the autumn, which saw him traverse most of Italy in a Mini. A few years earlier, having fallen in love with the Puglia region of southern Italy, Suggs and Anne had bought an ancient, fortified farmhouse near the city of Lecce.

backstage entrance. Occasionally, band members would flit through the pub while muffled sounds drifted by on the ether – was that really a polka? Violinists taking a fag break were heard complaining about the unnecessarily convoluted arrangements. Others spoke of hearing the entire album during a recent all-night drinking session with Lee – only they had been too drunk to remember much. Much speculation surrounded the grandiose plans concocted by the show's producer, Luke Cresswell, who'd made his name with the famous dance percussion show *Stomp*. Alongside Steve McNicholas, Cresswell had developed their widely acclaimed act out of the ashes of their band Pookiesnackenburger, a madcap skiffle/jazz combo who'd been signed to Stiff back in the early Eighties. That was presumably when Luke had befriended Cathal, who later made a cameo in Stomp's short film 'Brooms' in 1997.

Cresswell made sense, then – but what about Julien Temple? His name was synonymous with *The Great Rock'n'Roll Swindle*, the controversial death knell for the Sex Pistols, and the ill-fated film *Absolute Beginners*. True, he had won the plaudits for recent ventures *Glastonbury* (detailing the history of the festival) and *Joe Strummer: The Future Is Unwritten* about his late friend. What on earth did he have in mind for Madness?

Opened in 1901, The Hackney Empire had come to embody the faded glamour of London's bygone era. In its heyday, the venue had played host to all the greats: Charlie Chaplin, W. C. Fields, Stan Laurel and Marie Lloyd. Most contemporary venues of its sort had long since closed or been refurbished out of recognition whereas the Empire's modernisation in 2001 still retained much of the theatre's original character (and frontage). In fact, the theatre – situated on Mare Street – was now a grade II listed building.

As a tantalising incentive for fans (beyond the premier of the most ambitious album of Madness' entire career), recordings of each night's performance could be purchased prior to the show, then available afterwards as USB wristbands. As the audience settled nervously into their seats, a hushed expectancy fell over the auditorium, punctuated only by the occasional clatter from the front-of-house orchestra in their pit.

The Victorian-styled stage set resembled a cobbled street, complete with vintage lamp posts, behind which were projected related images to accompany each song. London landscapes past and present, some black and white Madness memories, film of Russian dancing and even some Banksy graffiti art were joined by a plethora of illustrations and graphics created by art group Le Gun, were displayed under the watchful eye of Mark Bedford.

The gallery boxes boasted people in fancy dress as part of the act as chimney sweeps or 16th-century courtesans, Dickensian urchins or Victorian gentlemen in top hats and supposed ladies of ill repute. And the whole evening was theatrically enhanced by Cresswell's performance troupe appearing as jugglers, buskers, a marching drummer and some old-fashioned dancing girls. Genuine pearly kings, queens and princesses of St Pancras and Kings' Cross rounded out the eccentric cast of extras.

"It was thrilling enough that Madness would be performing new songs," recalls MIS editor Jonathan Young, "but on being greeted by these characters wandering amongst the crowd inside such decorative surroundings, it felt like being taken on a journey. We were wished 'cockney luck' by smiling pearlys, and there was a slight feeling of menace emanating from the grimacing, gap-toothed stares of the 'old world' street characters, as they heckled or letched at the arriving audience or threw flowers and kisses at whoever took their fancy!"

The evening was divided into two sets: the new album followed by their hits. And the opening set was presented in three acts, punctuated by orchestral interludes. Musical director was trombonist Mike Kearsey, who'd previously worked with Madness on both *Wonderful* and *The Dangermen Sessions*, having been introduced by Terry Edwards. "I was charged with sorting out the 'pit band' of eight musicians who were in front of the stage during the first half," explains Mike. "I worked closely with the band, management and technical staff resolving issues such as synch-ing all the players up and re-arranging the parts to work with the musicians. Early on, I suggested that as it was a theatrical show, we should maybe have a traditional overture to the show. The band agreed and I took elements of the new *Folgate* set and pieced together an overture to give a taster of what was to follow and set the scene."

After the 'Overture', the curtains opened and Madness took to the stage to unveil the first segment, *The Liberty Of Norton Folgate*, with Cathal playing acoustic guitar. They began with the triumphant tones of 'We Are London' and, after 'Idiot Child', 'Bingo' and 'NW5', ex-2 Tone artist Rhoda Dakar joined them for another revelation, 'On The Town', a song about fractured relationships. Cue curtains.

Act 2 opened with 'Mk II', which had evolved out of an old Velvet

Ghost composition, 'Viva Londinium'. That was followed by the more familiar 'Sugar And Spice and 'Dust Devil' before that distinctive 2/4 time signature heard wafting out of their soundcheck revealed itself as 'Clerkenwell Polka'. After another interval, that left the third act to the album's 10-minute cornerstone, now performed in its glorious entirety. Madness patently felt obligated to follow such a majestic preview with 10 hit singles – but they needn't have bothered. It was merely a postscript to what already felt like a work of genius. It was that simple.

Chapter 23

THE LIBERTY OF MADNESS: PART 2

B LINK for a second and you'll miss Norton Folgate. It's the name accorded to a tiny stretch of the major artery (the A10, no less) running up from Monument on the north bank of the Thames through the City as first Gracechurch Street then Bishopsgate, passing Liverpool Street railway station to the west. For one block, the road then exists as Norton Folgate before being swallowed up heading north as Shoreditch High Street.

Its name is a historic reminder of the tiny 'liberty' of Norton Folgate situated in that area, which existed as a distinct administrative unit. Originally, the land was occupied by the Priory and Hospital of St Mary Spital while its name seems to have been coined in the 15th century (as Norton Folyot). When the region reverted to the Crown, Norton Folgate retained its status as an extra-parochial liberty (that is to say, a self-contained entity on the edge of, or outside of, the traditional parish structure), under the jurisdiction of the Dean and Chapter of St Paul's Cathedral.

The nine-acre site contained Folgate Street and Spittle Square (next to the famous Spitalfields Market) to the east and a small area of land between Primrose Street and Worship Street on the west side of the main road. Among the 1,500–2,000 inhabitants, the enclave harboured at various times such notable residents as the playwrights Christopher Marlowe and Ben Jonson (it played host to the City Of London Theatre) and the London Gas Light & Coke Company. This was the original Soho, a dissolute, bohemian district full of artists, drunks and demimondes. It's easy to see how the area's picaresque history appealed to Madness.

"I was asked to be on *Desert Island Discs* a few years back and one of the songs I chose was The Clash's 'London's Burning'," Suggs told *The Irish Times*. "The author Peter Ackroyd was listening and asked The Clash's Paul Simonon to introduce us. I was big fan of Ackroyd's book *London: The Biography*, so I went to meet him and Paul and I were just chatting about London's history. That's where the initial idea came from and I knew the area around Norton Folgate quite well – we all used to go down to Spitalfields and buy our second-hand Crombies in the market [but] I had no idea of the history of the area."

The liberty was thought to have been abolished in 1900, to be divided between the metropolitan boroughs of Stepney and Shoreditch, while the civil parish of Norton Folgate existed between 1889 and 1921 (when it was absorbed by the parish of Whitechapel). And that might have been that, had it not been for plans to demolish the fashionable Light Bar (originally built as a power station for the Great Eastern Railway) in order to build an office block. Local activists claimed that documents in the council archives showed that the abolition of 'The Liberty of Norton Folgate' in 1900 was technically invalid and that it still existed.

"Its parliament last convened a hundred years ago," Suggs told Zoe Ball. "It had its own laws, its own pubs, a place for outsiders, crazy writers and musicians. It struck a chord with me and 'The Liberty of Norton Folgate' I just thought was a great title. So we wrote this song about this little part of London and the joy of having no laws, and it just fitted with an idea: the whole album is about the more obscure parts of London that we have inhabited."

With wonderful synchronicity (and such delightful quirks of fate have characterised many of the best moments in Madness' story), Cathal had already delved into the subject. "I was reading the books of Patrick O'Brian," Smyth told *Mojo*, "and he mentions Captain Jack Aubrey going into 'The Liberties' where he couldn't get nicked. This whole concept's been a moment of magic realism – like *One Hundred Years Of Solitude* or *The Master And Margarita*." The spirit of magic realism – of blending fantastical or even absurd elements within a vividly real, perhaps gritty environment – might have unintentionally been present in Madness' music already. 'Drip Fed Fred' married images of guttersnipe cockney life with otherworldly themes. But now Cathal was consciously informing his songs with this aesthetic.

"Residents intend to declare 'independence' to prevent it being built in their small parish of Norton Folgate," ran a piece in *The Observer*. "Like the fictional residents in the Ealing comedy, *Passport To Pimlico*, opponents claim they could have an ancient right to self-determination which they will use to stop Bishop's Place, a £700m scheme. They say maps uncovered in the City of London's Guildhall Library show that Norton Folgate still has the status of a distinct district and that its historic boundary gives them the right to resist central planning law in the capital."

The campaign to preserve the district – or the Light Bar, in particular – gained significant momentum, drawing support from English Heritage, Cabe (Commission for Architecture and the Built Environment), the Georgian Group and the Spitalfields Trust, resulting in a petition with 5,000 names. The effort was worthwhile: the bulldozers were stopped after a heated three-hour debate by Hackney Council's planning committee on July 24, 2008 and proposals for the tower block next to Liverpool Street station were declined.

What appealed to Madness wasn't so much the historical detail or even the campaign, although its similarities to the plot in *Passport To Pimlico* won't have gone unnoticed. Suggs and Smyth especially were smitten with the idea of Norton Folgate as a magnet for society's revellers and outsiders – those of an artistic bent. But equally, the story of Norton Folgate (such as it existed at all) acted like a neat microcosm for London's turbulent, ever-changing history as a whole. When Suggs spoke of his trepidation about how they might embody the spirit of the city, here was the perfect vehicle. Imagine if the very building blocks of London carried memories of past events?

The song itself was riddled with references to both the region and its nefarious past. "Brick Lane connects nearly all the names mentioned in the song," MIS astutely observed, with regard to the geographical references in this epic composition. For example, Banglatown is a modern nickname for the Brick Lane district, which had earlier played host to several breweries, the first being the "Mr Truman's beer factory" name-checked in the song. Arnold Circus, Petticoat Lane, the Shadwell Basin and the Thames itself: using that name-dropping, list-making style popularised by Ian Dury, McPherson and Smyth painted a vibrant picture of London's ever-changing face, drawing on Old Jack Norris, a character from the 1824 book *The Cabinet Of Curiosities*; "Battling Levinsky versus Jackie

Berg", who were two noted Jewish boxers; and "Dan Leno and the Limehouse Golem", from the title of a 1995 novel by Peter Ackroyd, a gothic comedy tale about a serial killer in 19th century London.

★ ★ ★

Before their shows at the Hackney Empire, Cathal had admitted to suffering some pre-performance butterflies. They shouldn't have worried. Universally applauded by the pundits, the concerts were an unmitigated success. But while *Heat* et al were excited about the plethora of celebrities in attendance, from actors Martin Freeman and Matthew Horne to Terry Edwards' old bandmate Charlie Higson and Londoners Bobby Davro and Shane Ritchie, their lasting impact lay far beyond mere column inches. This triumvirate of performances felt like a vitamin jab to boost what some saw as Madness' ailing credibility (having not issued a collection of new songs for nigh on a decade, for example).

The band might have been basking in the afterglow from those concerts but there was still the little matter of the album to deliver. "It veers between a Ridley Scott film and an Ealing comedy," suggested Cathal in the August 2008 edition of *Mojo*, which listed one hitherto unheard song, 'Suicide Bridge'. "I'm hoping Madness are going into a darker phase, plumbing the depths of the 'madder' side." On reflection, the Hackney Empire had been notable for excluding such songs as 'Let's Go' (because it didn't fit the theme, apparently), 'Africa', 'Hunchback Of Torriano' and yet another new tune namedropped by Lee and Woody to fans before the shows: 'One Fine Day'.

Proceedings were now, for the most part, at the mixing stage with some 23 songs on the shortlist – according to Foreman, at least. Rumours suggested that indecision continued unabated about an appropriate format for the album. As for their next single, the prime candidate appeared to be 'Forever Young'. Meanwhile, news arrived that broadcasting rights to Julien Temple's filmed concerts had been sold to ITV.

Madness had fulfilled their usual litany of live obligations that summer, with little hint to audiences who hadn't been privy to the Hackney Empire shows that something special was happening. Along with a trio of racecourses (Doncaster, Newmarket and a disappointing show at Sandown Park, with Barson arriving late), they travelled to Spain for the Bilbao Festival on July 6 followed by the 42nd Montreux Jazz Festival in Switzerland two days later. Thompson even found time to fashion a new line-up of the Camden Cowboys (in essence, a variation on Damaged Goods) to perform at Bermondsey Fair.

In early September, Suggs lent his support to two good causes. The first was Busking Cancer, a week-long, nationwide event to raise funds for Cancer Research UK which saw artists perform on the streets. The second was *NME*'s Instigate Debate, a well-meaning initiative designed to "dumb up" celebrity interviews. Lending his support, Suggs subjected himself to questions on camera such as "should we bomb Iran?" and "do you feel like a subject or a citizen?"

Speaking of September, wasn't the album now imminent? Not according to Foreman on the official Madness website. "We have been mixing it and have taken a break," he admitted. "Between 10 and 23 songs will be released one way or another." In fact, news surrounding Madness was distinctly quiet as summer gave way to autumn 2008. Chris namechecked yet another new composition, 'That Close', which had been recorded but which "was a bit messed up in terms of the arrangement". Otherwise, you could hear a pin drop. "It may appear as if not much is going on," ran a message on Madness' website on October 6. "Beware of appearances, they can be deceptive! Your wait is almost over. There will be a storm of activity spanning 2009 . . . anniversary year!"

While fans waited with bated breath for news about their future recordings, the license for Madness' back catalogue passed from EMI-Virgin to Union Square Music, the successful and widely acclaimed Shepherds Bush-based back catalogue company who'd made a splash in recent years after re-presenting the music of Slade, as well as re-packaging the old Stiff catalogue in handsome fashion. "USM and Madness will re-issue the entire catalogue, physically and digitally," ran a press release issued that December, "with initial marketing activity centred around the 2009 30th Anniversary of the classic single and album *One Step Beyond . . .*" If Madness didn't get their skates on, mightn't this distract from their new project? Apparently not: "With the band concentrating on their new album for the first half of next year we're still formulating our release plans . . ."

As a stopgap, Foreman would upload the odd snippet of work-in-progress to YouTube, including a snatch from another new song, 'Rainbows'. "I was mixing the songs this week and I filmed a bit," revealed

Foreman. "When I say mixing I mean getting the guitar up louder!" Another clip, 'Madness – The Kiss Mix', showed Foreman and Alan Winstanley mixing a song (the tune in question being another discovery, 'The Kiss'). As the band rehearsed for their imminent shows at Manchester Central, Brussells' Forest National and London's 02 (supported by the Stereo MC's) between December 15–18, their official website was mysteriously revamped with a new circular M stamp, red velvet and a wooden pegboard. Something was afoot. The festive shows interspersed familiar classics with a reasonable proportion of new material, including that elongated title track which, shorn from the bespoke environment of the album showcase, caused some of the natives to get restless. For one of their encores, a bagpiper played solo renditions of 'When The Saints Go Marching In' and 'You Are My Sunshine'.

To coincide with the concerts, plans were finally unveiled for a deluxe 3-CD box set of *The Liberty Of Norton Folgate*, due for March 2009 to coincide exactly with Madness' 30th anniversary. Available only through their website, the lavish affair would boast a 22-track double-CD album plus an expurgated version on vinyl and a third disc of demos and live tracks (including a pass granting access to exclusive content on their website). One incentive for those dedicated enough to fork out the princely sum of £40 three months early was a downloadable 12-track edition just in time for Christmas. A single-CD would then be released for general consumption in May. Not only that but Madstock V was announced for summer 2009. What's that phrase about being like London buses?

Such ambitious plans would never have been possible within the straightjacket of a major label deal. But in the absence of the hefty advance usually coughed up by a record company, band and management had negotiated a partnership with a third party, prompting yet more announcements. This "investment agreement" with Power Amp Music was described as a "groundbreaking long-term deal". Founded as recently as early 2008 by a combination of music industry personnel and city bankers, the company claimed to specialise in "facilitating music industry funding for established artists through Enterprise Initiative Scheme (EIS) investments".

Traditionally, a record company would pay an advance for the delivery of a new album. They would then recoup that advance against royalties accrued as a percentage of sales revenue (i.e. the band wouldn't get any more money until the label had got their advance back) but then the act was free to earn from other sources of revenue like concerts, merchandising and publishing. Power Amp's arrangement was different because it encompassed all of Madness' potential income streams – as a result, the initial investment would no doubt have been more substantial.

Here's the technical breakdown from Power Amp's press release: "Employing an 'artist-centric' model, the company takes a holistic view of the growth of an artist's overall career as a business and brand and participates in all revenue streams generated including record sales, music publishing, touring income, merchandising, branding and sponsorship among others." That's a major commitment on both sides because that relationship has to work – and no doubt the collective experience of Anglo-HannaH was brought to bear. It's likely that the pregnant delay of roughly six months after the Hackney Empire shows allowed the devilish detail of this groundbreaking structure to be ironed out. Garry Blackburn summed it up thus: "Through this agreement, the band feel they have much more control over their commercial activities than they have ever had before and stand to receive a much fairer share of the revenue they generate."

* * *

After nearly four years of conversation, rumour, speculation and a slow, unsteady drip-feeding of new material, Madness had finally unleashed their masterpiece. Sort of. Although the pre-release download felt like an affectionate gesture to their fans, it did rather fly in the face of the album's lofty, even ostentatious ambitions. Not that Madness fans were complaining. First impressions of this vanilla edition of *The Liberty Of Norton Folgate* were of universal adulation.

Cathal's opening proclamation, 'We Are London', arrived with a jovial swagger and a twinkle in its eye, vaguely reminiscent of early Roxy Music, setting the scene with its opening lyrics: "From Regent's Park mosque onto Baker Street/Down to the Cross, where all the pipes smoke neat". We are London? Madness staked their claim with the bravura of well-connected scoundrels-about-town. Suggs' lilting reggae ode 'Forever Young', by contrast, evoked a more innocent spirit of teenage naivete. And the 10-minute 'The Liberty Of Norton Folgate' – essentially four songs stitched together – felt like a quixotic carousel of a journey through time.

'Dust Devil' grooved on an infectious funky reggae backbeat, built around a chanting chorus, "Come down I'm missing you/If these little fingers could paint you into my picture". Madness Central eloquently described it as just the latest Lee Thompson song to be "lyrically birthed from below the beltline", with lines like "she keeps a gizmo under her pillow". "It may have something to do with my sex drive," he admitted, "which has always been extremely active. Writing about another broken heart/hard luck story has never been that inspiring to me. Check out Ian Dury's 'You're More Than Fair' or 'I Made Mary Cry', Roxy Music's 'In Every Dream Home A Heartache', The Sensational Alex Harvey Band's 'Next' or 'I Love The Dead' from Alice Cooper's *Billion Dollar Babies*. It's all their fault!"

'Clerkenwell Polka' felt altogether darker and more threatening, with faintly revolutionary overtones*, Cathal's poetically florid language about man's tendency to conform, set to music which Kurt Weill would have been proud of. The opening message of 'Bingo', "This train is for all stations to High Barnet," introduced the saxophonist's tale of woe neatly. Lee also penned 'Rainbows' (with Woodgate), its gorgeous late Sixties pop arrangements lifting a delightful paean to the miracle of childbirth with a piano riff spookily echoing Foreigner's AOR hit 'Cold As Ice'. For 'That Close', the saxophonist had instead collaborated with Foreman to recall, seemingly, their nefarious teenage past (had the pair nearly had a car crash or was that too literal an interpretation?). 'Idiot Child' was less open to speculation: this was nothing less than Lee's autobiography, its naked vulnerability making it quite possibly the album's highlight.

One of the more subdued moments of the download version was Cathal's quite beautiful ballad 'Mk II', named after the vintage Jaguar of the opening line. If it hadn't been written before the film was released, listeners would be forgiven for thinking the song was inspired by the love affair, set in the early Sixties, depicted in the movie *An Education*. Quite why Smyth dispensed with the original Velvet Ghost lyrics of 'Viva

---

* Although Clerkenwell had been nicknamed Little Italy, Smyth in his writing more likely drew on the district's associations both with the printing industry and as a hotbed for communism – indeed, Vladimir Lenin even lived nearby at one point.

Londinium' is intriguing, since its theme would surely have fitted the album like a glove.

Built on the style of ornate arrangements which had defined the Sixties Brill Building sound, Mike Barson's 'On The Town' twisted a well-worn boy/girl formula with zest, with shades of Del Shannon's 'Runaway' (Suggs described it as a "dysfunctional Sonny & Cher"). On closer inspection, the tune had evolved out of a demo which Mike had created during 1983 sessions for *Keep Moving*. In fact, traces of the chorus dated back even further to an improvised rehearsal circa *The Rise And Fall*, listed simply as 'Mike On Piano'. "We were going through everyone's songs old and new for the album," explained Mike. "I came across that and thought it was a good song. Some tunes are just darn timeless."

Rhoda Dakar had guested on 'On The Town' at the first two Hackney shows and the more recent concert at the 02. But intriguingly, the download instead featured a singer named Amber Jolene. "I was asked to sing a guide vocal back in 2007 just for a demo," she told Madness Central. "Then I got a phone call asking if I was free to record that track for the album and could I perform it at the Hackney Empire three days later." Because Rhoda had a prior commitment with her band Skaville, Amber had taken her place for the third show.

★ ★ ★

After this stampede of activity, the Madness herd were once again strangely quiet for the next quarter (aside from Suggs' involvement in BBC 1's Saturday night celebrity competition *Let's Dance For Comic Relief*), leading up to their first Australian dates since 1986. Bedders was absent. His place taken by Graham 'Bushers' Bush, who had first played with Madness at the charity gig in Wrexham in November 2005, having been introduced by Madness' previous stand-in, Norman Watt-Roy (the Blockheads bassist having taught Bush how to play).*

From March 26 to April 5, they joined a quartet of shows 'down under' in different locations with the touring V Festival; a handful of new songs punctuated their 'golden oldies' set which boasted the rarely heard 'Tarzan's Nuts'. The only UK sighting of the band of late was being

---

* Graham Bush also played on some tracks on *The Liberty Of Norton Folgate*.

spotted filming on Southwold Pier on March 11 – presumably for their forthcoming film? "Julien Temple has been working with us," revealed Suggs. "We did some acting for that as well – down by the river – and some shows with Luke Cresswell. So it will be a combination of all three: a live concert, a documentary and some theatrical pieces. It's going to be done in the next couple of weeks."

Once back in the UK, the build-up to the formal launch of *The Liberty Of Norton Folgate* began in earnest. As fans waited patiently for their box sets to arrive, the official Madness website unveiled accompanying content – including a chance to hear 'Hunchback Of Torriano'. To accompany this premier, Foreman revealed some background to its origins, claiming (as he done all those years earlier for 'Bed And Breakfast Man') that his contribution to this Thompson/Woodgate song had once again gone uncredited. "I was riding my bike along the canal and the guitar part just came to me," he claimed, admitting he'd been inspired by Duran Duran's Andy Taylor. The tune had first been slated for *Wonderful* (a demo of which existed with Lee on vocals).

Mike Kearsey oversaw the album's brass arrangements. "As ever, it was the result of a late-night conversation in a hotel bar with the band's management," explains Mike. "I had done a few arranging/MD jobs before, orchestrating and conducting *Out Of Nowhere* by Jimi Tenor and for recordings and film scores for Barry Adamson. I met Clive to discuss what was needed for the brass on the album. We went through track by track and Clive gave great guidance about the effect they were after. By this point, the band had spent a long time rehearsing and recording so the demos I was given to work with were, as a whole, pretty close to the versions which appear on the album. With such a rich melodic content, it was a joy to write the horn arrangements. A lot of ideas came from Mike's keyboard parts which contained so much character. Simon Hale worked his magic once again on the string arrangements and orchestrations. My remit was much narrower than my MD role for the shows."

Kearsey was struck by the camaderie within the camp. "They have been together for so long and have such strongly established inter-relationships that when I first began working with them, it felt almost like stepping into someone's marriage," he suggests. "The guys are still so passionate about what they do, still have such a blast onstage and they are all very supportive and go out of their way to make additional musicians feel comfortable and part of the team. Working with other bands, there tends to be significant individuals who make the calls but Madness works, more than any other band I have experienced, as a collective. I guess that with seven such strong and creative personalities, this is the only way the band could have survived."

The Violin Monkeys had originally been created for the *Wonderful* tour – but it seemed like a contrary name for a horn section. "We were (briefly) called the Brass Monkeys until Woody came up with the 'Violin' bit," laughs Mike. "Steve [Turner] had been working as Thommo's sax tech so he played baritone sax. Terry Edwards had been busy when the shows happened so asked if I could recommend a trumpet player to take his role. I had worked with Joe [Auckland] previously so put him up for the gig. He initially turned it down as his beloved Millwall were playing in their first FA Cup final. I remember him calling me back, slightly panicked: 'It was a Madness tribute you were asking about, wasn't it?', since Madness had always been one of his favourite bands!"

The trombonist was struck by the contrast in the working methods from his previous involvement with the covers album. "The tunes which appeared on *The Dangermen Sessions* were honed during the live shows at The Dublin Castle," he explains. "The raw material was there already so the rehearsals had more of a workshop feel with all the band in one room throwing ideas about and trying things out. When you are creating a new number from scratch, its components will always be subjected to more scrutiny than when covering someone else's material. That's how it felt working on the *Folgate* album – hours in the studio picking out elements of a layered guitar or keyboard track for inspiration for a horn line. It was great to work so closely with Clive. For *The Dangermen Sessions*, my role had been as the trombone player so I didn't have any involvement with the producers beyond seeing them through the glass of the recording booth!"

Without the infrastructure of a record company behind them, and the inherent momentum which that brings, the band were feeling the pressure. "We're still wrangling," admitted Suggs while down under. "We would argue about what trousers we should wear, now we're arguing about what should be the first single. We have to get the pieces of the jigsaw – I mean, we're doing this all by ourselves so it's hard to work out what comes first and how we promote the album. Simple things like whether we should even make a single for radio and how do we get this film shown!"

* * *

The box set edition of *The Liberty Of Norton Folgate* had postmen ringing doorbells across the country in late March. For sheer creative ambition alone, Madness deserved a medal. Was this really the same outfit who delivered such a desultory covers album only a few years earlier? The box itself mimicked a battered old book embossed simply with a Masonic-like M in a circle on the front. This vibe was reinforced inside via a humorous letter from Foreman on headed paper, a metal badge and a 'Membership In Perpetuity' to the 'M' section of their website. Throw in a replica of their mock-Edwardian poster for their Hackney Empire shows and bijou hardback 'M' rulebook and it all felt rather like joining an exclusive, private members' club.

The handsome vinyl album was a superb bonus. More intriguing, though, was the impeccably packaged 2-CD edition. So what of the remaining 10 tracks? Well, 'Overture' was simply an orchestral fanfare. As with the LP, the remaining 10 songs on Disc 1 drew from the download edition. Disc 2 opened with the sleazy rock'n'roll of 'Let's Go', its 'Peter Gunn' feel now all the more apparent. Another Thompson/Barson partnership, 'Mission From Hell' was pure mid-Sixties Motown (complete with a splendid Hammond organ solo), as counterpoint to Thompson's scathing attack on the British government's tackling of gun crime.

A surrogate offspring of The Kinks' 'Sunny Afternoon' and The Animals' 'We've Gotta Get Out Of This Place', 'Seven Dials' was named after the famous convergence of roads in London's Covent Garden, infamous in the 19th century for housing some of the city's worst slums (or rookeries). Suggs' colourful, evocative lyrics seemed to echo a description of the junction by no lesser scribe than Charles Dickens, who wrote: "The stranger who finds himself in the Dials for the first time . . . will see enough around him to keep his curiosity awake for no inconsiderable time."

Fans were already familiar with 'NW5' and, to an extent, the baroque pop of 'Hunchback Of Torriano' (named after the Torriano area in Kentish Town). 'Fish & Chips' was Cathal's lighthearted nod to music hall, awash with cockney rhyming slang and accompanied by cornet and euphonium, continuing the noble tradition of The Kinks ('Holiday Romance', 'Have A Cuppa Tea'), Small Faces ('The Universal'), The Beatles ('For The Benefit Of Mr Kite') and much of Dury's work.

One of only two compositions on the album carrying a credit for Chris Foreman (both with Suggs, the other being 'That Close'), 'One Fine Day' stole its title from the old Chiffons nugget. The song just might have been the album's slow burning fuse. Melodically slight, it skewed Madness' staple reggae backing with a Germanic Bierkeller flavour (copyright Kurt Weill), lyrically pondering on Madness' long, strange trip with such lines as "We had our ups/We sure had our downs". "I had been such a big fan of 'House Of Fun', so perfect in its mixture of comedy and youthful vigour against a backdrop of the fairground," writes Jonathan Young. "From its midlife perspective of 'one more time, before the light fades', 'One Fine Day' returns to that theme of a travelling entertainment troupe as it packs to leave town."

Another McPherson/Barson marriage, 'The Kiss' possessed a breezy, filmic quality befitting the *Brief Encounter*/school playground crush themes of the lyrics. Along with 'Rainbows', it dated from the earliest album sessions at ToeRag. Which only left Mike Barson's jazz/dub fusion 'Africa'. Summarised by Foreman as "an evocative, atmospheric number, quite slow – I did some moody Edge-like tune plus some wah-wah," 'Africa' wrapped up a double album's worth of tributes dedicated to the capital by dreaming of an escape from its clutches (echoing his own departure for Amsterdam years earlier).

If that wasn't enough, the box set also boasted a bonus CD conjoining a handful of Norton Folgate demos with a live recording from the Hackney Empire under the banner *Practice Makes Perfect/Hackney Live + Correct*. The only song conspicuous by its absence was 'Suicide Bridge', name-checked by Cathal in *Mojo*. The double-CD case carried a colourful poem written in florid, Victorian English by Cathal, while the accompanying booklet opened with an extract from *Dan Leno And The Limehouse Golem* by Peter Ackroyd before an outline of the album's pedigree, penned in fine style by M. Barzo Esq. From the "burnout that was the Dangerman Fiasco" to "Liam Watson and his strange assemblage of recording equipment and techiques from time long since past" to the "final leg of the journey" on April 9, 2008, "Your Captain on the good ship, Madness" stamped his claim on the masterpiece.

The small print revealed that sessions had shifted from ToeRag to Miloco's studios The Garden and The Yard, sucking up a variety of extra-curricular musicians in the process. 'On The Town' now boasted Rhoda Dakar in place of Amber Jolene, who was instead heard singing backing vocals on 'Mission From Hell', 'Dust Devil' and 'Forever Young'.

For so long seemingly stymied by disparate forces (conflicting band members, personal strife and other outside pressures), *The Liberty Of Norton Folgate* finally caught the stars of the seven members in alignment. Positively overbrimming with musical panache and lyrical substance, the album was surely the crowning glory of their entire career. Even the cover design was a revelation, shunning the predictable approach of seven middle-aged men for a dramatic silhouette of a man with top hat and cane, bowing to the audience from his stage on the cobbled street*. Without wishing to overstate their achievements, it felt as if Madness had married the colour and vibrancy of *Sgt. Pepper* with the sheer breadth of *The Beatles*.

"Something is happening recently to do with our legacy in terms of what people feel about us," thought Suggs. "The way I describe our sound is to say we are continuing the folk music tradition of the real London. Tommy Cooper was a big factor. Benny Hill – those speeded-up bits – used to tickle us. You knew it was naff but it was also deliberately anti-intellectual. Then in later life you get interested in Samuel Beckett and get this innate feeling that there's a parallel. Beckett was really interested in music hall and Tommy Cooper and Max Wall – that thin line between abstraction and just being an idiot. Pathos was a word I learnt from Neil Tennant . . . it sums up what we were doing unconsciously all those years, a mixture of happiness and sadness. Sometimes it's jolly music with sad words and other times it's sad words with jolly music but the most interesting work is mixing the two."

★ ★ ★

On April 17, Julien Temple's 75-minute film of *The Liberty Of Norton Folgate* was premiered at the London Independent Film Festival at the Coronet in Notting Hill, west London. Footage of both band and

---

* It's intriguing to note that the last three Madness albums – *Our House*, *The Dangermen Sessions* and this – all carried front cover designs depicting silhouettes.

audience from their Hackney Empire shows was interspersed with clips of Suggs and Smyth as 19th Century ne'er-do-wells, "marauders of the night", recounting stories and poems of mischief and wrong doing while wandering through the smog-filled cobbled streets and graveyards of a gas-lit London of yore. Afterwards, Temple hosted a question and answer session. "The audience are characters themselves, shown in the best chosen moments of their joy, while the city of London plays a part too," explained Temple.

Snippets could also be heard of music hall star Marie Lloyd, who sang at the Hackney Empire in its early years, reinforcing the project's sepia-tinted glow. "When I was a kid, there was that funny old programme *The Good Old Days*," remembered Suggs, "with mustachioed blokes pushing ladies in big dresses on flower-festooned swings, singing: 'Daisy, Daisy give me your answer do, I'm half crazy all for the love of you.' The Kinks and Ian Dury picked up on this thread of street music. And now our album praises working people but not in a patronising way."

A week later, on Friday April 24, Madness launched *The Liberty Of Norton Folgate* with their 'World Tour Of Camden', a series of free shows as part of the annual Camden Crawl. Details were revealed on BBC 6 Music, who then broadcast highlights of their performances. Between 3pm and 9pm, Suggs, Bedford, Thompson and a competition winner on kazoo busked in three different locations around Camden before the whole band performed atop a double-decker bus parked up in Camden High Street (just outside The Electric Ballroom) to an excited audience in nearby Inverness Street Market which included Mike Barson's mum. Madness were greeted like rock royalty – and to the people of Camden, that's exactly what they were.

'Dust Devil' had been announced as "our new single" while Madness were in Australia. Issued on May 11, Lee's mischievous ode was accompanied by various remixes of the A-side and a version of Kilburn & The High Roads' 'The Roadette Song', which they'd performed back in the late Seventies as The Invaders and had slated for possible inclusion on *The Dangermen Sessions*. The single was promoted by a thoroughly contemporary-looking video starring Jaime Winstone (daughter of actor Ray) and her boyfriend Alfie Allen (brother of Lily, son of Keith), which depicted Jaime as a 'dust devil' enjoying a riotous night out on the tiles. *Skins* director Adam Smith's first-person *cinéma vérité* style borrowed from the controversial video for 'Smack My Bitch Up' by The Prodigy, mimicking Amy Winehouse's real-life antics. While it boasted only cameo roles from three members of the band and divided opinion among fans, the video attracted significant exposure.

While Suggs fronted another documentary – this time, hosting an episode of *Brilliant Britain*, entitled 'Seaside Out Of Season' for the Blighty channel – Madness busied themselves on the promotional merry-go-round, drifting through the studios of *Later . . . With Jools Holland*, *The Paul O'Grady Show*, *The One Show* and many more. They also hosted a CD signing session at HMV's Oxford Street branch. In *The Times*, Suggs talked about the pot pourri of British/London influences on Madness from all walks of entertainment, namechecking author Phil Larkin alongside comedian Peter Cook and reggae artist Linton Kwesi Johnson.

On the Thursday of release week, Madness hosted a lavish launch party for . . .*Norton Folgate*. Early rumours had suggested a secret gig at the Water Poet pub, namechecked by Suggs in the album's sleeve-notes. Instead, they opted for the more fitting environs of The Light Bar. During the afternoon, a BBC film crew descended to see Norton Folgate's parliament reconvened for the first time in a century. Proceedings were opened by a town cryer against the backdrop of a huge billboard poster which read, "Welcome to the Liberty of Norton Folgate", with the slogan "In the City of London, you are never far from Madness."

In a novel twist on the free bar at album launches, Suggs claimed that prices for alcoholic beverages were fixed at those charged in 1901, including bottles of 'Madness' beer – and a lucky few were able to secure a mock-passport for the liberty. Outside the venue, the contrast in architecture in the surrounding area was remarkable, from the untouched charm of Georgian-era buildings in Folgate Street to the daunting, ultra-modern panorama of towering glass skyscrapers such as the famous London 'Gherkin'. Inside, an ebullient crowd of fans, friends, famous faces and industry types witnessed a shortened set mixing up highlights from the new album with past classics. Meanwhile, a photo shoot for *The Observer* was conducted at the nearby Folgate Street house of artist Dennis Severs, whose 'still-life drama' reconstructed an early 18th century Huguenot home.

'Dust Devil' only reached number 64 but it topped the independent chart and attracted welcome airplay. This exposure helped fanfare the commercial editions of . . . *Norton Folgate* (a 15-song CD, with two bonus tracks on the download edition), issued a week later to a tumultuous reception from the critics. *The Word* summarised it thus: "Peter Ackroyd writing for The Kinks, it's Sherlock Holmes in Albert Square, it's a Mike Leigh movie of *Parklife*, it's *Passport To Pimlico* meets Brick Lane, and it is Madness's masterpiece." In a five-star review, *The Financial Times* stated that they had "ripped up the form book and delivered a knockout album" while the BBC thought that this "magnificent magnum opus" was "the most sophisticated and satisfying album of their career".

The band had never been treated to such gushing and widespread acclaim – not even for their debut album back in 1979. Its reception helped tilt the axis on which Madness resided, in terms of their public image. Suddenly, they were quite fashionable, not only re-engaging with elements of their old fanbase but attracting new fans beguiled by hearty recommendations in the pages of the broadsheets and music monthlies. Word swiftly spread. *The Liberty Of Norton Folgate* peaked at number five, an amazing achievement in the absence of a major hit single – their best placing for a new studio album since *7* in 1981.* Equally, significant sales proved harder to attain abroad – excepting Russia, where the album topped the listings.

* * *

Meanwhile, older strains of the music press had worked themselves into a frenzy over The Specials' reunion and the resulting spat played out in the media between ostracised founder Jerry Dammers and the rest of the band. The contrast between the 2 Tone flagship's revival roadshow and Madness' renewed contemporary vigour couldn't have been greater.

Their confidence reaffirmed by the adulation surrounding *The Liberty Of Norton Folgate*, Madness embarked on a hectic summer schedule. Starting in late May, they played Newbury Racecourse, Norfolk Showground and Stroud's Gatcombe Park, popping across the Channel for festivals in Holland (the famous Pinkpop event), Germany, Portugal, Spain and France. On June 20, Suggs, Thompson and Bedford busked a short acoustic set (including The Kinks' 'Waterloo Sunset') on the HMS

---

* The album was reissued as a 'silver edition' in the autumn with the added incentive of Julien Temple's documentary as a bonus DVD.

Belfast on the Thames, as part of a campaign launch party organised by charity Busking For Cancer.

All of which led to Madness' triumphant return to the Pyramid Stage at Glastonbury Festival on the final night, Sunday June 28, for a magnificent set sandwiched between Tom Jones and Nick Cave & The Bad Seeds (with Blur then closing the festival). At the end of the performance in front of an estimated 75,000 people, a large number of their children flooded the stage to huge applause from the audience – which seemed an incredibly touching celebration of their 30th anniversary and recent good fortune. The only glitch was that Thompson had cracked a rib while falling off a human pyramid at Dizzee Rascal's show – and then had to fly around the stage with Madness in a harness. Ouch.

The band spent early July accepting a prestigious Silver Clef 'Icon' Award before traversing the Continent, from Poland and Serbia to a jaunt in Scandinavia, at festivals in Sweden and Denmark. But the big prize for Madness fans that month was the long-awaited return of Madstock on July 17 – relocating east to Victoria Park, Hackney, with support slots from their extended family (Suggs' daughters, Man Like Me), ska band The Aggrolites, reggae star Gregory Isaacs, The Blockheads, Jerry Dammers & Spatial AKA, Abba covers band Bjorn Again and The Pogues. In terms of the music, Madstock V was an unmitigated success, the magnificent seven seemingly playing with more gusto than ever.

During a suitably long set, Madness performed 'That Close' for the first time, revisited 'Take It Or Leave It' and presented a 2 Tone all-star finish for the last few songs joined by Rhoda Dakar, Terry Edwards and Jerry Dammers. During 'Night Boat To Cairo', Jerry was heard to shout, "What key is it in?" Suggs' reply was succinct: "It's in fucking C, Jerry!" A recording of this momentous show was available as a USB stick and also as a download from their website. Unfortunately, Victoria Park was a less salubrious location than its north London counterpart and many fans suffered at the hands of pickpockets while sporadic outbursts of violence clouded an otherwise celebratory day – a slur on the festival's good character worsened by inclement weather.

On August 2, 'Sugar And Spice' had been plucked from . . . *Norton Folgate* (with slightly different lyrics and intro) as their first-ever download-only single to help sustain sales of the album. After a couple more festival appearances (Romsey Broadlands, Nottingham Splendour), the band had two weeks off before travelling to Moscow to play the Afisha Picnic on the back of the chart-topping success of *The Liberty Of Norton Folgate* there. More flights followed: to Norway's Oya Festival then Paris' Rock En Seine, Ireland's Electric Picnic on September 4 (sharing the bill with the likes of Billy Bragg and their one-time support band Echo & The Bunnymen).

At the Rock En Seine Festival on August 28, Madness took centre stage with a rapturously received, unscheduled second set after Oasis cancelled their performance. "I loved that gig," Cathal told *The Big Issue*. "For a couple of months beforehand, Oasis didn't want to follow us on the main stage, so we just said, 'We don't care, we'll play the second stage.' Then Oasis split up, on the day of the show. The promoter came up to us and said: 'Will you play? We've got no one!' We said, 'Of course we'll play.'"

Later that month, McPherson's first foray into the world of authorship arrived with *Suggs And The City*, which merged his scotched autobiography with themes from his TV series via the strapline 'My journeys through disappearing London'. Its mix of pithy, humorous anecdotes and more substantial historical material proved to be a highly entertaining companion to both the show and to Madness' latest album. The singer returned as a DJ to BBC 6 Music to host *A Month Of Sundays*. And Suggs also kept his toe in the acting waters with a cameo role as himself (filmed in Soho) in the independent film *Billy And Lilly Go To New York*.

Unfortunately, the festival season ended with a damp squib when their Summer Madness event on the Isle Of Wight had to be cancelled due to licensing issues. However, the band played a free open-air concert to a quarter of a million fans as part of the tenth annual Regent Street Festival in London to coincide with the first birthday party of Absolute Radio (having been re-branded from Virgin Radio) on September 27, while raising money for Cancer Research. "We live in a world full of clipboards and folk who don't want people to have fun," laughed Suggs, "but we've burnt the clipboards and got permission to close off the street." Thereafter, Mark Bedford announced he'd be returning to his parallel career in printing for the indefinite future.

Meanwhile, Union Square unleashed a comprehensive marketing campaign for yet another compilation, *Total Madness*, opting for a similar CD/DVD coupling as had previously been issued by Virgin. Issued September 21, the compilation sold well – following a 'soft launch' for a reissue of *Complete Madness* earlier that year. In due course, Union Square – on their Salvo label – re-packaged all of Madness' Stiff albums as deluxe 2-CD editions with a raft of bonus material and celebrity sleeve-notes, followed by collector's double-vinyl 10-inch sets. While *Total Madness* peaked at an impressive number 11, *The Liberty Of Norton Folgate* flew past the 70,000 sales mark – making this their most successful year in terms of album sales since 1992.

As BBC 4 announced a special 'Madness night' of programming, the band unveiled details of their latest Christmas tour – with 12 shows around England and Scotland, culminating in a concert at London's O2 Arena. The tour was a resounding success, the . . . *Norton Folgate* material now firmly integrated into their canon as a whole. As an affectionate nod to their past, a few of the gigs (Southend, Newcastle) were also accompanied by matinee shows for younger members of their audience. Madness concerts have a strong sense of tradition – for example, audiences will always chant "ole ole, ole ole" before the band arrives onstage. A relatively new feature of their performances came courtesy of Chris Foreman, who would announce, in excitable fashion, "Showtime!" towards the end of each show before their home straight of hits.

"We did a gig last year and I was a bit 'refreshed'," Chris admitted. "I looked at the set list and something occurred to me related to *The Matrix* film. We saw the first one in New York in 1999 and this guy was sitting in front of Suggs, Chas, Thommo and me, quite excited and animated. During the scene when they ask for 'guns, lots of guns', this bloke was rubbing his hands with anticipation. He turned to his date and said quite calmly, with no shouting, 'Showtime' – meaning some arse was about to be quite righteously kicked. Back to the gig, I thought this is the last part of the set here, all killer, no filler, all thriller, in other words . . . 'Showtime'! I think the gig where I had this epiphany was the O2 in 2008. [Now] Suggs always makes me do it!"

Meanwhile, Madness performed 'It Must Be Love' on *Children In Need*. And as a spirited P.S. to the tour, the band played their part in the New Year's Eve celebration that was Edinburgh Hogmanay. "We've heard it's one of the world's best New Year bashes so we are expecting mayhem," declared the band. "Edinburgh's laid down the gauntlet, we're there to take up the challenge!"

After rumours that Madness might try their hand in the pre-Christmas singles bearpit, common sense prevailed and 'Forever Young' was finally scheduled for January 2010. A firm favourite, the song was this time issued not only as a download but also on physical formats, accompanied by another Dangermen-era cover version – this time, Billy Ocean's Motown-styled mid-Seventies hit, 'Love Really Hurts (Without You)' – alongside various remixes of the A-side. Unfortunately, it failed to chart.

While Union Square's reissue programme continued in earnest, the Madness diary slowly became less frenetic. As ever, plans were announced for a plethora of festival fixtures (Camp Bestival at Lulworth Castle, Devon, for example, as well as V Festival on its twin sites of Chelmsford and Leeds).

Although it was too early to consider how Madness might follow their magnum opus, Cathal was already discussing future plans during an interview with *Zani*, mentioning that he was developing two possible concepts – a dub step project and a "relationship album" – as well as writing a play entitled *HMS Misery*, which he described as "*Cape Fear* meets *Oliver Twist*".

Now that his daughters had bought a pad of their own, Suggs had returned to mulling over penning his autobiography, with specific reference to the father he never knew. "I've got the chance to do [BBC genealogy show] *Who Do You Think You Are?* but I want to write my memoirs," he recently admitted to *The Scotsman*. "It's going to be a quest, to learn about my dad's story, and I don't want to say it's going to be some big therapeutic bollocks but that's exactly what it'll be. It would have been great to talk to him about all the stuff I've found difficult, like the journey from boy to man. That's still a struggle for me, to be honest."

★   ★   ★

After such a hectic 2009, it was perhaps inevitable that Madness would take their foot off the accelerator. They deserved it. Few other acts could boast such a career renaissance as had been achieved by *The Liberty Of Norton Folgate*. Critically acclaimed with sales approaching those of their heyday at the dawn of the Eighties, it was a vindication of their self-belief. Back in the mid-Eighties, they struggled to make such a transition from a zany pop production line to cerebral album-based artistes. Now they'd finally made that quantum leap. Quite what the future might hold for this mismatched yet synergistic bunch of fifty-somethings is anyone's guess but the chances are that they have a few more surprises up those elegantly turned shirt-sleeves.

As a splendid postscript to what must have felt like a tremendous year for the band, with their new album nestling among the critics' annual choices, Catherine Tate (as her character 'nan') presented Madness with a gold disc for *The Liberty Of Norton Folgate* on December 1. "What a fucking liberty" indeed! The guys then returned the favour by appearing, somewhat bemused, on the comedian's TV special *Nan's Christmas Carol* later that month, posing as carol singers before performing at the end of the show.

What next? Well, in an interview with RTÉ 2fm radio on May 24, 2010 ahead of the band's show in Cork, Ireland, Woodgate stated that Madness were currently finalising songs for the follow-up to *The Liberty Of Norton Folgate*. They hoped to be able to start recording their next album later in the year. News also percolated out about lavish forthcoming box sets and Ben Sherman clothing ranges while Suggs and Cathal lent their support to Chris Difford's admirable Songs In The Key Of London project at The Barbican.

The sense of seven distinct personalities is now stronger than ever. Suggs as the dashing all-rounder, forever holding court; Cathal as their book-ish 'renaissance man'; Woodgate as a ball of energy, the noted marathon runner; Foreman always mindful of their fans, forever online via his 'Chris's Cupboard' question-and-answer sessions and 'Axecam' clips on YouTube; Lee as perhaps their most talented yet least understood songsmith, totally unpredictable; Bedford the 'quiet one', content to take a back seat from Madness for the time being; and Barson as their vital musical rudder. "Madness is a surrogate family," Cathal has suggested. "All our families of origin are dysfunctional, so we came together looking for some sort of family substitute."

The internal disputes which threatened to open fatal fissures within their ranks for much of the Nineties and beyond now seem to be under control. "We hit each other fully on the nose in the wee small hours – occasionally," Suggs explained. "Mad late night things standing outside a hotel. That's how we get our therapy – going absolutely barmy at each other, for each other, against other people." Their guitarist now understands the value of restraint. "I've tried to stay calm", Chris recently commented. "I still argue and get annoyed but it's quite levelling, what the people in the band tell you about yourself. I try to learn from it."

Beyond any mortal need to pay the bills, the love that Madness engender in their audience appears to be their spiritual lifeblood. "At Glastonbury, there was a guy being lifted across a whole wave of the crowd," Suggs told *The Big Issue*, "on a sofa, smoking a fag. And there was a child on someone's shoulders at Regent Street. Lee jumps off stage and gives the kid his saxophone mid-song. The kid's face lights up in amazement and Lee proceeds to climb up this lighting rig. Moments like that are extraordinary."

How long can Madness continue? Let's leave the last word to Suggs: "I remember seeing the Buena Vista Social Club a few years ago. They were all about eighty – the singer came on with two walking sticks and then the music started and he threw them into the air! And I thought there is a way to still be dignified and have fun [and] I hope we'll still be doing it at that age. I don't know if I'd be able to sing 'Sixteen today and up for fun' but I hope I will!"

UK Discography

SINGLES

All vinyl singles were issued in picture sleeves unless otherwise stated. Chart positions are in parenthesis.

8/79	The Prince/Madness (7, 2 Tone label sleeve)	2 Tone CHSTT 3	(16)

Notes: Originally with paper labels, later plastic (silver or blue).

10/79	One Step Beyond.../Mistakes	Stiff BUY 56	(7)
	One Step Beyond.../Mistakes/Nutty Theme (12″)	BUYIT 56	

12/79	My Girl/Stepping Into Line (7″)	BUY 62	(3)
	My Girl/In The Rain/Stepping Into Line (12″)	BUYIT 62	

3/80	WORK, REST AND PLAY EP (7″)	BUY 71	(6)
	Night Boat To Cairo/Deceives The Eye/The Young And The Old/Don't Quote Me On That		

9/80	Baggy Trousers/The Business (7″)	BUY 84	(3)

11/80	Embarrassment/Crying Shame (7″)	BUY 102	(4)

1/81	The Return Of The Los Palmas 7/That's The Way To Do It (7″, canteen or title p/s)	BUY 108	(7)
	The Return Of The Los Palmas 7/My Girl (Demo)/That's The Way To Do It Swan Lake (Live From 'Dance Craze') (12″, with *Nutty Boys* comic issue 1)	BUYIT 108	

4/81	Grey Day/Memories (7″)	BUY 112	(4)
	Grey Day/Memories (cassette in box)	ZBUY 112	
	One Step Beyond (Spanish)/Baggy Trousers/Grey Day/Take It Or Leave It (12″)	BUYIT 112	

Notes: Although a companion release to Grey Day 7″, this led off with One Step Beyond (Spanish).

9/81	Shut Up/A Town With No Name (7″)	BUY 126	(7)
	Shut Up/Never Ask Twice/A Town With No Name (12″)	BUYIT 126	

Notes: Never Ask Twice included on non-UK editions of the 7 album as Aeroplane.

11/81	It Must Be Love/Shadow On The House (7″)	BUY 134	(4)
	It Must Be Love/Shadow On The House (12″)	SBUY 134	

2/82	Cardiac Arrest/In The City (7″)	BUY 140	(14)
	Cardiac Arrest (Extended Version)/In The City (12″)	BUYIT 140	

5/82	House Of Fun/Don't Look Back (7″)	BUY 146	(1)
	House Of Fun/Don't Look Back (7″, picture disc)	PBUY 146	
7/82	Driving In My Car/Animal Farm (Tomorrow's Dream Warp Mix) (7″, some in foldout poster p/s)	BUY 153	(4)
	Driving In My Car/Animal Farm (Tomorrow's Dream Warp Mix) (7″, picture disc)	PBUY 153	
	Driving In My Car/Animal Farm (Tomorrow's Dream Warp Mix)/Riding On My Bike (12″)	SBUY 153	
11/82	Our House/Walking With Mr Wheeze (7″)	BUY 163	(5)
	Our House/Walking With Mr Wheeze (7″, picture disc)	PBUY 163	
	Our House (Special Stretch Mix)/Walking With Mr Wheeze (7″, "jukebox issue", numbered die-cut Stiff company sleeve)	BUY JB 163	
	Our House (Extended Version)/Our House/Walking With Mr Wheeze (12″)	BUYIT 163	

Notes: 12″ artwork/labels list same tracks as 7″.

2/83	Tomorrow's (Just Another Day)/Madness (Is All In The Mind) (7″, double-A-side)	BUY 169	(8)
	Tomorrow's (Just Another Day)/Madness (Is All In The Mind) (7″, picture disc)	PBUY 169	
	Tomorrow's (Just Another Day) (Warped 12″ Version)/Blue Beast (Warp Mix)/Tomorrow's (Just Another Day) (guest vocal Elvis Costello)/Madness (Is All In The Mind) (12″)	BUYIT 169	

Notes: 12″ stock reissued in 1986 stickered as Virgin VS 78712.

8/83	Wings Of A Dove/Behind The 8 Ball (7″, white embossed card p/s; later in coloured paper p/s)	BUY 181	(2)
	Wings Of A Dove/Behind The 8 Ball (7″, picture disc)	PBUY 181	
	Wings Of A Dove (Blue Train Mix)/Behind The 8 Ball/One's Second Thoughtlessness (12″, sleeve lists 'Extended 12″ Version')	BUYIT 181	
10/83	The Sun And The Rain/Fireball XL5 (7″)	BUY 192	(5)
	The Sun And The Rain/Fireball XL5 (7″, picture disc)	PBUY 192	
	The Sun And The Rain (Extended 12″)/Fireball XL5/My Girl (Live Version) (12″)	BUYIT 192	

Notes: My Girl recorded at Brighton Centre, 5th March 1983.

2/84	Michael Caine/If You Think There's Something (7″)	BUY 196	(11)
	Michael Caine/If You Think There's Something (7″, picture disc)	PBUY 196	
	Michael Caine (Extended Version)/Michael Caine/If You Think There's Something (12″)	BUYIT 196	
5/84	One Better Day/Guns (7″, some in poster p/s)	BUY 201	(17)

One Better Day/Guns (7″, picture disc)	PBUY 201	
One Better Day/Guns/Victoria Gardens/Sarah (12″)	BUYIT 201	

8/85 Yesterday's Men/All I Knew (7″, initially without artist/
title text on front cover) — Zarjazz JAZZ 5 — (18)

Yesterday's Men/All I Knew//Yesterday's Men
(Harmonica Mix)/It Must Be Love (Live at Brighton
Centre 5th March 1983) (7″, double pack: square
picture disc + bonus disc, PVC wallet) — JAZZ SD5

Yesterday's Men (12″ Version)/All I Knew/
Yesterday's Men (Demo Version) (12″) — JAZZ 5-12

10/85 Uncle Sam/Please Don't Go (7″) — JAZZ 7 — (21)

Uncle Sam/Please Don't Go (7″, "flag bag" edition) — JAZZ F7

Uncle Sam/Please Don't Go/Inanity Over Christmas
(7″, picture disc, stickered PVC sleeve, B-side 33rpm) — JAZZY 7

Uncle Sam (Ray Gun Mix)/Please Don't Go/Uncle
Sam (Demo Version) (12″) — JAZZ 7-12

1/86 Sweetest Girl/Jennie (A Portrait Of) (7″) — JAZZ 8 — (35)

Sweetest Girl/Jennie (A Portrait Of) (7″, picture
disc, 1-sided, plays 33rpm, stickered PVC sleeve) — JAZZY-8

Sweetest Girl/Jennie (A Portrait Of)//Tears You Can't
Hide/Call Me (7″, double pack, gatefold p/s with bonus
Valentine single) — JAZZD-8

Sweetest Girl (Dub Mix)/Sweetest Girl (Extended Mix)/
Jennie (A Portrait Of) (12″) — JAZZ 8-12

11/86 (Waiting For) The Ghost-Train/Maybe In Another
Life (7″) — JAZZ 9 — (18)

(Waiting For) The Ghost-Train/Maybe In Another
Life (square picture disc) — JAZZS 9

(Waiting For) The Ghost-Train/Maybe In Another
Life/Seven Year Scratch (12″) — JAZZ 9-12

(Waiting For) The Ghost-Train/Maybe In Another
Life/Seven Year Scratch (12″, gatefold p/s with
8-page booklet) — JAZZ B 9-12

11/92 The Harder They Come (live)/Tomorrow's Just
Another Day (live)/ Take It Or Leave It (live) (7″) — Go! Discs GOD 93 — (44)

The Harder They Come(live)/Land Of Hope & Glory
(live)/Tomorrow's Just Another Day (live)/Take It Or
Leave It (live) (CD) — GODCD 93

The Harder They Come (live)/Embarrassment (live)/
Grey Day (live)/Baggy Trousers (live) (CD) — GOLCD 93

The Harder They Come (live)/Tomorrow's Just
Another Day (live)/Take It Or Leave It (live) (cassette) — GODMC 93

Notes: recorded live at Finsbury Park, London, 8–9 August 1992.

7/99 Lovestruck/Round And Round/Maddley (CD) — Virgin VSCDT 1737 — (10)

	Lovestruck/We Are Love/Lovestruck (video) (enhanced CD, gatefold Digipak)	VSCDG 1737	
	Lovestruck/Round And Round/Maddley (cassette)	VSC 1737	
	Lovestruck/We Are Love (7″, jukebox issue, black label, large centre, no p/s)	VSLH 1737	
11/99	Johnny The Horse/You're Wonderful (Remix)/Johnny The Horse (video) (enhanced CD)	VSCDT 1740	(44)
	Johnny The Horse/I Was The One/Dreaming Man (CD)	VSCDX 1740	
	Johnny The Horse/I Was The One/Dreaming Man (cassette)	VSC 1740	
	Johnny The Horse/You're Wonderful (Remix) (CD, Euro release, wallet p/s)	VSCDE 1740	
	Johnny The Horse/I Was The One (7″, jukebox issue, large centre, no p/s)	VSLH 1740	
3/00	Drip Fed Fred (The Conspiracy Mix)/Elysium/We Want Freddie (enhanced CD)	VSCDT 1768	(55)
	Drip Fed Fred (The Conspiracy Mix)/Elysium/Light Of The Way (CD)	VSCDX 1768	
	Drip Fed Fred (The Conspiracy Mix)/Elysium/We Want Freddie (cassette)	VSC 1768	
7/05	Shame & Scandal/Skylarking/Dreader Than Dread (CD)	Live & Intensified/ V2 VVR 5033243	(38)
	Shame & Scandal/Shame & Scandal (Dub) (7″, 2,500 only)	VVR 5033247	
11/05	Girl Why Don't You?/I Chase The Devil AKA Ironshirt (BBC Radio 2 Session)/Girl Why Don't You? (Dub) (CD)	V2 VVR 5035013	
12/06	Sorry (featuring Sway & Baby Blue)/Sorry (7″, no p/s, large centre hole with adaptor; initially available at Christmas 2006 shows)	Lucky Seven LUCKY701	
3/07	Sorry (Radio Edit)/Sorry (Featuring Sway & Baby Blue)/ Sorry (Original)/Sorry (Live In Manchester 13.12.06) (CD)	LUCKY701CDS	(23)

Notes: Downloadable version of Sorry (Tim Deluxe Mix) available during Xmas 2006 tour.

Also available in March 2007 as downloads: 'Madness Is All In The Mind' (Live @ Hudson River NYC 1983) and 'Sorry' (featuring Sway & Baby Blue – Dr Rubberfunk Apologetic Dub).

1/08	NW5 (Radio Edit)/NW5 (Full Length Version)/ Bittersweet/Man Like Me (Remix) (CD)	LUCKY7002CDS	(24)
	NW5 (Full Length Version)/Bittersweet (7″, die-cut sleeve, stickered PVC outer)	LUCKY7002S	
	NW5/Night Boat To Cairo (Live)/My Girl (Live)/It Must Be Love (Live) (DVD, plain brown sleeve, stickered PVC outer)	LUCKY7002DVD	

Notes: DVD live tracks are acoustic session by Barson & Suggs at Bestival, 7–9 September 2007.

05/09	Dust Devil (Radio Edit)/Dust Devil (Warbox Remix)/ The Roadette Song/Dust Devil (Practice Makes Perfect Reggae Style) (CD)	LUCKY7 004CDS	(64)
	Dust Devil (7″ Mix)/The Roadette Song (7″)	LUCKY7 004S	
	Dust Devil (Original Version)/(Extended Dubplate Special) (10″)	LUCKY7 004T	
08/09	Sugar And Spice (Radio Edit)/Sugar And Spice (Mike Barson Demo Version)/Africa (Ashley Beedle's Going Home Edit) (download-only)	N/A	
1/10	Forever Young (Music Melt Edit)/(Future Cat Remix)/ (J Star Mr Wallace Dub)/(Live From *Later With Jools Holland*)/Love Really Hurts (CD)	LUCKY 006CDS	(199)
	Forever Young (Original Version)/(J Star Mr Wallace Dub) (7″, gatefold p/s)	LUCKY7 006S	

THE MADNESS SINGLES

3/88	I Pronounce You/Patience (7″)	Virgin VS 1054	(44)
	I Pronounce You/4BF/Patience/11th Hour (7″, stickered box set:		
	contains 33rpm EP, no p/s, plus badge & 2 postcards)	VSX 1054	
	I Pronounce You/4BF/Patience/11th Hour (12″)	VST 1054	
	I Pronounce You/4BF/Patience/11th Hour (CD)	VSCD 1054	
5/88	What's That/Be Good Boy (7″)	VS 1078	(96)
	What's That/Be Good Boy (interlocking shaped picture disc, 'Saw' disc)	VSS 1078	
	What's That/Flashings (interlocking shaped picture disc, 'Jig' disc)	VSJ 1078	
	What's That/Be Good Boy/Flashings (12″)	VST 1078	

SINGLE REISSUES/RETROSPECTIVES

3/81   MADNESS ('The Grab Pack', 6 × 7″ in clear plastic folder) Stiff GRAB1
Notes: the first six 7″ singles on Stiff in a pack designed for hanging on a wall.

6/85	Our House/Walking With Mr Wheeze (7″)	Virgin VS 786
4/86	PEEL SESSIONS (14/08/79) EP (12″)	Strange Fruit SFPS 007
4/86	PEEL SESSIONS (14/08/79) EP (cassette)	SFPSC 007
7/88	PEEL SESSIONS (14/08/79) EP (CD) The Prince/Bed And Breakfast Man/Land Of Hope & Glory/Stepping Into Line	SFPSCD 007
2/87	The Prince/Madness (7″, no p/s)	Old Gold OG 9685
11/88	Baggy Trousers/Embarrassment (7″, no p/s)	OG 9821
11/88	It Must Be Love/ My Girl (7″, no p/s)	OG 9826

5/89	It Must Be Love/The Return Of The Los Palmas 7 (7",
'Tall Guy' reissue)	Virgin VS 1197	

Notes: Reissued to tie in with film The Tall Guy, in which Suggs made a cameo singing the song.

2/92	It Must Be Love/Bed And Breakfast Man (7")	VS 1405	(6)
	It Must Be Love/Bed And Breakfast Man/Airplane/Don't
Quote Me On That (CD)	VSCDT 1405	
	It Must Be Love/Bed And Breakfast Man/Airplane/Don't
Quote Me On That (CD, Valentine's Day edition, die-cut
sleeve, picture disc)	VSCDP 1405	
	It Must Be Love/Bed And Breakfast Man (cassette)	VSC 1405	
4/92	House Of Fun/Un Paso Adelante! (One Step Beyond –
Spanish Version) (7")	VS 1413	(40)
	House Of Fun/Un Paso Adelante!/Yesterday's Men/
Gabriel's Horn (Demo) (12")	VST 1413	
	House Of Fun/Un Paso Adelante!/Yesterday's Men/
Gabriel's Horn (Demo) (CD)	VSCDT 1413	
	House Of Fun/Un Paso Adelante! (cassette)	VSC 1413	
8/92	My Girl/Madness (live) (7")	VS 1425	(27)
	My Girl/E.R.N.I.E. (live)/Embarrassment (live)/
Tomorrow's Dream (live) (CD1, gatefold Digipak with
room for CD2)	VSCDG 1425	
	My Girl/Precious One (live)/My Girl (live)/Disappear
(live) (CD2)	VSCDT 1425	
	My Girl/Madness (live) (cassette)	VSC 1425	

*Notes: Madness, Hammersmith Odeon, 12/80; E.R.N.I.E. & Embarrassment, Cambrai, France, 1/6/80;
Tomorrow's Dream, Aylesbury, 9/11/81; Precious One, Bombay Rock, Australia, 7/5/86; My Girl
Chicago, USA, 27/8/83.*

2/93	Night Boat To Cairo/Night Boat To Cairo (Paul Gotel
Rude Edit) (7")	VS 1447	(56)
	Night Boat To Cairo (Paul Gotel Rude Mix)/(Paul Gotel
Rude Edit)/(Well Hung Parliament Dub Edit)/(Paul Gotel
Rude Instrumental) (12")	VST 1447	
	Night Boat To Cairo (Paul Gotel Rude Mix)/(Paul Gotel
Rude Edit)/(Well Hung Parliament Dub Edit)/(Paul Gotel
Rude Instrumental) (CD)	VSCDT 1447	
	Night Boat To Cairo/Night Boat To Cairo (Paul Gotel
Rude Edit) (cassette)	VSC 1447	

ALBUMS

Notes: All titles were also issued originally on cassette, up to and including The Dangermen Sessions.

10/79   ONE STEP BEYOND (LP, with picture inner sleeve)   Stiff SEEZ 17   (2)
One Step Beyond/My Girl/Night Boat To Cairo/Believe Me/Land Of Hope & Glory/The
Prince/Tarzan's Nuts/In The Middle Of The Night/Bed And Breakfast Man/Razor Blade
Alley/Swan Lake/Rockin' In A♭/Mummy's Boy/Madness/Chipmunks Are Go!

Notes: Madness and The Prince are re-recorded versions of 2 Tone single.

9/80   ABSOLUTELY (LP, with picture inner sleeve)   SEEZ 29   (2)
Baggy Trousers/Embarrassment/E.R.N.I.E./Close Escape/Not Home Today/On The Beat
Pete/Solid Gone/Take It Or Leave It/Shadow Of Fear/Disappear/Overdone/In The Rain/You
Said/Return Of The Los Palmas 7

Notes: Two different sleeves exist with variations on front cover photo.

10/81   7 (LP, with picture inner sleeve)   SEEZ 39   (5)
Cardiac Arrest/Shut Up/Sign Of The Times/Missing You/Mrs Hutchinson/Tomorrow's
Dream/Grey Day/Pac-a-Mac/Promises Promises/Benny Bullfrog/When Dawn Arrives/The
Opium Eaters/Day On The Town

11/82   THE RISE AND FALL (LP, gatefold sleeve)   SEEZ 46   (10)
Rise And Fall/Tomorrow's (Just Another Day)/Blue Skinned Beast/Primrose Hill/Mr Speaker
(Gets The Word)/Sunday Morning/Our House/Tiptoes/New Delhi/That Face/Calling
Cards/Are You Coming (With Me)/Madness (Is All In The Mind)

2/84   KEEP MOVING (LP)   SEEZ 53   (6)
         KEEP MOVING (LP, picture disc, U.S. running order)   PSEEZ 53
Keep Moving/Michael Caine/Turning Blue/One Better Day/March Of The Gherkins/Waltz
Into Mischief/Brand New Beat/Victoria Gardens/Samantha/Time For Tea/Prospects/Give Me A
Reason

9/85   MAD NOT MAD (LP, with picture inner sleeve)   Zarjazz JZLP 1   (16)
1986   MAD NOT MAD (CD)   JZCD 1
I'll Compete/Yesterday's Men/Uncle Sam/White Heat/Mad Not Mad/Sweetest Girl/Burning
The Boats/Tears You Can't Hide/Time/Coldest Day

Notes: A small batch of the LP sleeves were mispressed without the gold pattern.

11/99   WONDERFUL (CD)   Virgin CDV 2889   (17)
         WONDERFUL (MiniDisc)   MDV 2889
Lovestruck/Johnny The Horse/The Communicator/4am/The Wizard/Drip Fed Fred/Going To
The Top/Elysium/Saturday Night, Sunday Morning/If I Didn't Care/No Money

08/05   THE DANGERMEN SESSIONS – VOLUME ONE (CD)   Live & Intensified/
                                                                V2 VVR 1033232   (11)
This Is Where/Girl Why Don't You?/Shame & Scandal/I Chase The Devil AKA Ironshirt/
Taller Than You Are/You Keep Me Hanging On/Dangerman AKA High Wire/Israelites/
John Jones/Lola/You'll Lose A Good Thing/Rain/So Much Trouble In The World

3/09   THE LIBERTY OF NORTON FOLGATE (LP + 3-CD 12" box set includes poster,
         membership card, rule book, letter & badge)   Lucky 7 LUCKY 003SE
Disc 1: Overture/We Are London/Sugar And Spice/Forever Young/Dust Devil/Rainbows/That
Close/Mk II/On The Town/Clerkenwell Polka/The Liberty Of Norton Folgate

Disc 2: Let's Go/Idiot Child/Mission From Hell/Seven Dials/Hunchback Of Torriano/Fish & Chips/Bingo/NW5/One Fine Day/The Kiss/Africa

Disc 3 (Practice Makes Perfect): Dust Devil I/Let's Go/Clerkenwell Polka/Forever Young/ 7 Dials/On The Town/Fish & Chips Parade/Idiot Child/We Are London – Chas Demo/(Hackney Live + Correct): We Are London/Idiot Child/Bingo/NW5/On The Town/Mk II/Sugar + Spice/Dust Devil/Clerkenwell Polka/Forever Young/The Liberty Of Norton Folgate

5/09   THE LIBERTY OF NORTON FOLGATE (CD)   LUCKY7 003CD   (5)
Overture/We Are London/Sugar And Spice/Forever Young/Dust Devil/Rainbows/That Close/Mk II/On The Town/Bingo/Idiot Child/Africa/NW5/Clerkenwell Polka/The Liberty Of Norton Folgate

11/09   THE LIBERTY OF NORTON FOLGATE (SILVER EDITION)
        (CD/DVD set, adds DVD of Julien Temple's film)   LUCKY7003CDX

THE MADNESS ALBUM

4/88   THE MADNESS (LP)   Virgin V 2507   (65)

        THE MADNESS (CD)   CDV 2507   (65)
Nail Down The Days/What's That/I Pronounce You/Oh/In Wonder/Song In Red/Nightmare Nightmare/Thunder And Lightning/Beat The Bride/Gabriel's Horn/11th Hour ★/Be Good Boy ★/ Flashings ★/4 B.F. ★ (★ = only available on CD)

LIVE ALBUMS

11/92   MADSTOCK! (LP, with picture inner sleeve)   Go! Discs 828 367-1   (22)

        MADSTOCK! (CD)   Go! Discs 828 367-2
One Step Beyond/The Prince/Embarrassment/My Girl/The Sun And The Rain/Grey Day/It Must Be Love/Shut Up/Driving In My Car/Bed And Breakfast Man/Close Escape/Wings Of A Dove/Our House/Night Boat To Cairo/Madness/House Of Fun/Baggy Trousers/The Harder They Come

Note: recorded live at Finsbury Park, London, 8–9 August 1992.

98   UNIVERSAL MADNESS (LIVE IN LOS ANGELES)   Goldenvoice 44402-2
        (U.S.-only CD)

Notes: Recorded at the Universal Amphitheater, Los Angeles, April 26, 1998

06   ON STAGE (8 x 2-CD Digipaks from 2006 tour: London, Glasgow, Manchester,
        Newcastle, Birmingham, Bournemouth, Brighton, London)   Lucky Seven 1-8

Notes: available to purchase after each concert, 1,000 only of each.

07   LIVE AT THE O2 ARENA 14.12.07 (2-CD Digipak,
        1500 only)   Lucky Seven (no cat. no.)

07   LIVE AT THE ASTORIA 3.12.07 (2-CD Digipak,
        1,500 only)   Lucky Seven (no cat. no.)

6/08   THE LIBERTY OF NORTON FOLGATE (USB
        wristband; 3 different versions from Hackney Empire
        shows on June 24, 25 & 26 2008)   Lucky Seven

7/09   MADSTOCK IV (USB stick in presentation box)   Lucky Seven

12/09   CHRISTMAS SHOWS (emblem shaped USB sticks and
boxed MP3 players)   Lucky Seven

COMPILATION ALBUMS

4/82   COMPLETE MADNESS (LP, gatefold sleeve)   Stiff HIT-TV 1   (1)
Notes: Tracks segued, some edited.

Embarrassment/Shut Up/My Girl/Baggy Trousers/It Must Be Love/The Prince/Bed And
Breakfast Man/Night Boat To Cairo/House Of Fun/One Step Beyond/Cardiac Arrest/Grey
Day/Take It Or Leave It/In The City/ Madness/The Return Of The Los Palmas 7

1983   MADNESS (LP, US/Canadian compilation, with picture
inner sleeve)   Geffen GHS 4003   (41)

1983   MADNESS (CD; later reissued as GEFBD 4003)   GEFMD 4003
Our House/Tomorrow's (Just Another Day)/It Must Be Love/Primrose Hill/Shut Up/House Of
Fun/Night Boat To Cairo/Rise And Fall/Blue Skinned Beast/Cardiac Arrest/Grey Day/Madness
(Is All In The Mind)

Notes: 'Night Boat To Cairo' and 'It Must Be Love' were different mixes from those in the UK.

11/86   UTTER MADNESS (LP)   Zarjazz JZLP 2   (29)

UTTER MADNESS (CD, adds 'Seven Year Scratch')   Zarjazz JZCD 2
Our House/Driving In My Car/Michael Caine/Tomorrow's (Just Another Day)/Wings Of A
Dove/Uncle Sam/I'll Compete/(Waiting For) The Ghost-Train/Yesterday's Men/The Sun And
The Rain/Sweetest Girl/One Better Day/Victoria Gardens

9/90   IT'S ... MADNESS (LP)   Virgin VIP VVIP 107

IT'S ... MADNESS (CD)   Virgin VIP VVIPD 107
House Of Fun/Don't Look Back/Wings Of A Dove/The Young And The Old/My Girl/Stepping
Into Line/Baggy Trousers/The Business/Embarrassment/One's Second Thoughtlessness/Grey
Day/Memories/It Must Be Love/Deceives The Eye/Driving In My Car/Animal Farm

10/91   IT'S ... MADNESS TOO! (LP)   Virgin VIP VVIP 115

10/91   IT'S ... MADNESS TOO! (CD)   Virgin VIP VVIPD 115
The Prince/Madness/One Step Beyond/Mistakes/The Return Of The Los Palmas 7/Night Boat
To Cairo/Shut Up/A Town With No Name/Cardiac Arrest/In The City/Our House/Walking
With Mr Wheeze/Tomorrow's (Just Another Day)/Victoria Gardens/The Sun And The
Rain/Michael Caine

Notes: above albums often referred to as being on Pickwick, which was actually the distributor.

2/92   DIVINE MADNESS (2-LP, gatefold sleeve)   Virgin V 2692   (1)

DIVINE MADNESS (CD)   Virgin CDV 2692
The Prince/One Step Beyond/My Girl/Night Boat To Cairo/Baggy Trousers/Embarrassment/
The Return Of The Los Palmas 7/Grey Day/Shut Up/It Must Be Love/Cardiac Arrest/House Of
Fun/Driving In My Car/Our House/Tomorrow's (Just Another Day)/Wings Of A Dove/The
Sun And The Rain/Michael Caine/One Better Day/Yesterday's Men/Uncle Sam/(Waiting For)
The Ghost-Train

1993   THE BUSINESS (3-CD box set)   Virgin MADBOX 1
Disc 1: The Prince/Madness/One Step Beyond/Mistakes/Nutty Theme/My Girl/Stepping Into
Line/In The Rain/Night Boat To Cairo/Deceives The Eye/The Young And The Old/Don't
Quote Me On That/Baggy Trousers/The Business/Embarrassment/Crying Shame/The Return

Of The Los Palmas 7/That's The Way To Do It/My Girl (demo)/Swan Lake (live)/Grey Day/
Memories/Shut Up/A Town With No Name

Disc 2: Never Ask Twice/It Must Be Love/Shadow On The House/Cardiac Arrest/In The City/
House Of Fun/Don't Look Back/Driving In My Car/Terry Wogan jingle/Animal Farm/
Riding On My Bike/Our House (Stretch Mix)/Walking With Mr Wheeze/Tomorrow's (Just
Another Day)/Madness (Is All In The Mind)/Wings Of A Dove/Behind The 8 Ball/One Second's
Thoughtlessness/The Sun And The Rain/Fireball XL5/Visit To Dracstein Castle/ Michael Caine

Disc 3: If You Think There's Something/One Better Day/Guns/Victoria Gardens/Sarah/
Yesterday's Men (Harmonica Version)/All I Knew/It Must Be Love (live)/Uncle Sam/
David Hamilton jingle/Inanity Over Christmas/Please Don't Go/Sweetest Girl (Extended
Version)/Jennie (A Portrait Of)/Tears You Can't Hide/Call Me/(Waiting For) The
Ghost-Train/One Step Beyond (Italian Version)/Maybe In Another Life/Seven Year Scratch
(Edited Version)/Release Me/Carols On 45/The National Anthem

1997	TOTAL MADNESS: THE VERY BEST OF… (US/Canadian-only CD)		
		Geffen GEFBD-25145	

6/98   THE HEAVY HEAVY HITS (CD)   Virgin CDV 2862   (19)
Notes: Divine Madness re-titled with addition of 'Sweetest Girl'.

12/1999 THE LOT (6-CD box set of all Madness albums to date)   Virgin MADBOX 2

12/2000 ULTIMATE COLLECTION (U.S.-only CD compilation) Hip-O HIPP490699-2

10/2002 OUR HOUSE – THE ORIGINAL SONGS (CD)   Virgin CDV 2965   (45)

2003   SINGLES BOX VOL. 1 (12 × CD singles)   Virgin MADBOX 3
Notes: Volume 2 of the Singles Box was later available by download only.

2005   DIVINE MADNESS – SIGHT AND SOUND (CD/DVD set)
                                                       Virgin CDVX 3014   (80)

Notes: This combined the CD and DVD releases in one package.

5/2005   THE BEST OF MADNESS: MILLENNIUM COLLECTION (US-only CD
                                                          compilation)
                                                       Hip-O 069 490 699-2

9/2009   TOTAL MADNESS (ALL THE GREATEST HITS AND MORE!)
        (CD/DVD set, foldout Digipak)   USMTVCD 001   (11)

Disc 1 – CD: One Step Beyond.../Baggy Trousers/House Of Fun/Our
House/Embarrassment/My Girl/It Must Be Love/Wings Of A Dove/The Sun And The
Rain/Grey Day/NW5/Cardiac Arrest/Tomorrow's Just Another Day/Driving In My Car/Bed
And Breakfast Man/Lovestruck/One Better Day/Michael Caine/The Return Of The Los
Palmas 7/The Prince/Shut Up/Madness/Night Boat To Cairo

Disc 2 – DVD: One Step Beyond.../Baggy Trousers/House Of Fun/Our
House/Embarrassment/My Girl/It Must Be Love/Wings Of A Dove/The Sun And The
Rain/Grey Day/NW5/Cardiac Arrest/Tomorrow's Just Another Day/Driving In My Car/Bed
And Breakfast Man/Lovestruck/One Better Day/Michael Caine/The Return Of The Los
Palmas 7/The Prince/Shut Up/Night Boat To Cairo

10   ULTIMATE MADNESS (CD, exclusively available via Tesco's)
                                                       Union Square USMCD021 (27)

ALBUM REISSUES

7/86	COMPLETE MADNESS (LP, gatefold sleeve)	Virgin HIT–TV 1	
	COMPLETE MADNESS (CD)	Virgin HITCD 1	
8/88	ONE STEP BEYOND (LP, generic Virgin inner)	Virgin OVED 133	
8/88	ONE STEP BEYOND (CD)	CDOVD 133	
8/88	ABSOLUTELY (LP)	OVED 134	
8/88	ABSOLUTELY (CD)	CDOVD 134	
8/88	7 (LP)	OVED 135	
8/88	7 (CD)	CDOVD 135	
12/88	THE RISE AND FALL (CD)	CDOVD 190	
11/89	KEEP MOVING (CD)	CDOVD 191	
90	ONE STEP BEYOND/ABSOLUTELY/THE RISE AND FALL (3-CD set; CDs were exclusively picture discs [CDOVDP 133, 134 & 190])	Virgin TPAK 8	

Notes: it's possible that the above picture discs were also available separately.

3/90	MAD NOT MAD (LP)	OVED 232	
	MAD NOT MAD (CD)	CDOVD 232	
4/90	UTTER MADNESS (LP)	OVED 287	
4/90	UTTER MADNESS (CD)	CDOVD 287	
1992	IT'S MADNESS (CD)	Virgin CDVIP 105	
1992	IT'S MADNESS … TOO! (CD)	CDVIP 117	
1994	DIVINE MADNESS (DCC)	463 166	
1994	DIVINE MADNESS (MiniDisc)	MDV 2692	
1998	IT'S MADNESS (CD, new artwork)	CDVIP 228	
1998	IT'S MADNESS TOO (CD, new artwork)	CDVIP 229	
2000	ONE STEP BEYOND (CD, 'Digitally Remastered')	MADCD1	(100)
2000	ABSOLUTELY (CD, 'Digitally Remastered')	MADCD2	
2000	7 (CD, 'Digitally Remastered')	MADCD3	
2000	THE RISE AND FALL (CD, 'Digitally Remastered')	MADCD4	
2000	KEEP MOVING (CD, 'Digitally Remastered'; reissued again 2003)	MADCD5	
2000	MAD NOT MAD (CD, 'Digitally Remastered')	MADCD6	

Notes: The above reissues added relevant promo videos to each disc. One Step Beyond... charted in 2005.

2000	DIVINE MADNESS (CD, 'Digitally Remastered')	CDV 2905	

Notes: adds 'Lovestruck' and 'Johnny The Horse'.

2001	DIVINE MADNESS (2-LP)	Simply Vinyl SVLP 309	
2003	COMPLETE MADNESS (CD, 'Digitally Remastered')	Virgin HITCDR 1	
2003	UTTER MADNESS (CD, 'Digitally Remastered')	HITCDR 2	
2003	COMPLETE & UTTER MADNESS (2-CD box set)	EMI-Virgin VBX 30	
2004	MADSTOCK! (CD)	Universal 80100725	

House Of Fun: The Story Of Madness

2006   COLLECTION (CD, reissue of It's Madness, red artwork, withdrawn)
EMI Gold 340 7132

2009   ONE STEP BEYOND… (CD)   Salvo SALVOCD02

3/09   COMPLETE MADNESS (CD)   Union Square Music
USMCD016   (38)

4/10   ONE STEP BEYOND… (2-CD, foldout Digipak)   Salvo SALVOMDCD02 (67)
Disc 1: One Step Beyond…/My Girl/Night Boat To Cairo/Believe Me/Land Of Hope &
Glory/The Prince/Tarzan's Nuts/In The Middle Of The Night/Bed And Breakfast Man/Razor
Blade Alley/Swan Lake/Rockin' In A♭/Mummy's Boy/Madness/Chipmunks Are Go!/The Prince
(promo video)/One Step Beyond… (promo video)/Bed And Breakfast Man (promo video)/
My Girl (promo video)/Night Boat To Cairo (promo video)

Disc 2: The Prince (John Peel session)/Bed And Breakfast Man (John Peel session)/Land Of Hope
& Glory (John Peel session)/Stepping Into Line (John Peel session)/One Step Beyond… (7″
Version)/My Girl (Mike Barson Demo)/Mistakes/Un Paso Adelante (One Step Beyond… Spanish
version)/Nutty Theme/My Girl (Ballad)/Stepping Into Line/Un Passo Avanti (One Step
Beyond… Italian version)/Deceives The Eye/The Young And The Old/Don t Quote Me On
That/Razor Blade Alley (live)/Night Boat To Cairo (live)/One Step Beyond… (live)

6/10   ONE STEP BEYOND… (CD, jewel case)   Salvo SALVOVCD02
Notes: original album with no bonus tracks, initially a Tesco's exclusive.

4/10   ABSOLUTELY (2-CD, foldout Digipak)   Salvo SALVOMDCD06 (87)
Disc 1: Baggy Trousers/Embarrassment/E.R.N.I.E./Close Escape/Not Home Today/On The
Beat Pete/Solid Gone/Take It Or Leave It/Shadow Of Fear/Disappear/Overdone/In The
Rain/You Said/Return Of The Los Palmas 7/In The Rain (Single Version)/ The Business/Crying
Shame/That's The Way To Do It/El Regresso De Los Palmas 7 (Spanish version)/Swan Lake
(live)/Release Me/Close Escape/Solid Gone (Patches flexidisc)/Baggy Trousers (promo
video)/Embarrassment (promo video)/The Return Of The Los Palmas 7 (promo video)

Disc 2 (BBC Live In Concert - Hammersmith Odeon 23/12/80): One Step
Beyond…/E.R.N.I.E./Mistakes/Disappear/Bed And Breakfast Man/The Return Of The Los
Palmas 7/Close Escape/Overdone/Not Home Today/Razor Blade Alley/My Girl/Take It Or
Leave It/On The Beat Pete/Embarrassment/Shadow Of Fear/You Said/In The Middle Of The
Night/The Prince/Baggy Trousers/Rockin' In A♭/Madness

4/10   7 (2-CD, foldout Digipak)   Salvo SALVOMDCD07 (107)
Disc 1: Cardiac Arrest/Shut Up/Sign Of The Times/Missing You/Mrs Hutchinson/Tomorrow's
Dream/Grey Day/Pac-A-Mac/Promises Promises/Benny Bullfrog/When Dawn Arrives/The
Opium Eaters/Day On The Town/Grey Day (promo video)/Shut Up (promo video)/It Must Be
Love (promo video)/Cardiac Arrest (promo video)

Disc 2: Missing You (Richard Skinner session)/Sign Of The Times (Richard Skinner
session)/Tiptoes (Richard Skinner session)/Memories/A Town With No Name/Never Ask
Twice/It Must Be Love (Single Version)/Shadow On The House/In The City/Cardiac Arrest
(12″ Extended Version)/Grey Day (live)

6/10   THE RISE AND FALL (2-CD, stickered foldout Digipak) Salvo SALVOMDCD 10
Disc 1: Rise And Fall/Tomorrow's (Just Another Day)/Blue Skinned Beast/Primrose Hill/Mr
Speaker (Gets The Word)/Sunday Morning/Our House/Tiptoes/New Delhi/That Face/Calling
Cards/Are You Coming (With Me)/Madness (Is All In The Mind)/House Of Fun
(video)/Driving In My Car (video)/Our House (video)/Tomorrow's (Just Another Day) (video)

Disc 2: Rise And Fall (BBC Kid Jensen session)/Tomorrow's (Just Another Day) (BBC Kid Jensen session)/Calling Cards (BBC Kid Jensen session)/Are You Coming (With Me) (BBC Kid Jensen session)/House Of Fun (7″ Version)/Don't Look Back/Driving In My Car (7″ Version)/Animal Farm (Tomorrow's Dream Warp Mix)/Riding On My Bike/Our House (12″ Extended Version)/Walking With Mr Wheeze/Mad House (Our House Instrumental Mix)/Tomorrow's (Just Another Day) (Warp Mix)/Our House (Stretch Mix)/The National Anthem - Madness & Elvis Costello

6/10   KEEP MOVING (2-CD, stickered foldout Digipak)   Salvo SALVOMDCD 11
Disc 1: Keep Moving/Michael Caine/Turning Blue/One Better Day/March Of The Gherkins/Waltz Into Mischief/Brand New Beat/Victoria Gardens/Samantha/Time For Tea/Prospects/Give Me A Reason/Wings Of A Dove (video)/The Sun And The Rain (video)/Michael Caine (video)/One Better Day (video)

Disc 2: Wings Of A Dove (7″ Version)/Behind The 8 Ball/One Second's Thoughtlessness/Wings Of A Dove (Blue Train Mix)/The Sun And The Rain (7″ Version)/Fireball XL5/My Girl (live)/The Sun And The Rain (12″ Extended Version)/Michael Caine (12″ Extended Version)/If You Think There's Something/Guns/Sarah/Victoria Gardens (Remix)

6/10	ONE STEP BEYOND (2 x 10″, gatefold sleeve)	Size 12 SIZE 1001
6/10	ABSOLUTELY (2 x 10″, gatefold sleeve)	Size 12 SIZE 1002
6/10	7 (2 x 10″, gatefold sleeve)	Size 12 SIZE 1003
2010	WONDERFUL (2-CD)	SALVOMDCD 13
2010	THE MADNESS (2-CD	SALVOMDCD 12

SELECTED PROMOTIONAL RELEASES & FOREIGN ITEMS

Notes: Restricted to historically interesting items or those which offered recordings exclusive to that format.

1/80	Don't Quote Me On That/Swan Lake (live) (12″, 500 copies only)	Stiff MAD 1
1983	Our House (Special Remix – Extended Dance Version)/Mad House (Our House – Instrumental Dubb Version) (US/Canadian 12″)	Geffen 99 96670
11/92	The Harder They Come (live)/Land Of Hope & Glory (live)/Tomorrow's (Just Another Day) (live)/Take It Or Leave It (live) (12″, promo only)	Go! Discs GOXDJ 93
92	Divine Medley (Julian Mix)/Seven Year Scratch (Spanish 12″)	MADNESS-1
98	One Step Beyond (The Remixes) (12″, as Madness vs. R.I.P.)	Virgin MADT 98
98	The Prince (The Remixes) (12″, as Madness vs. Wubble U)	Virgin MADJ 98
98	The Prince/One Step Beyond (CD, containing remixes from both 12″s)	Virgin MADCDJ 98
11/99	GENERIC RADIO INTERVIEW (CD)	Virgin MADCDINT1

Notes: Interview with Suggs, Lee & Woody, October 1999

4/01	My Old Man/CERYS MATTHEWS: If I Was With A Woman (CD, Digipak)	NEWBOOTS2PRO2

From the Ian Dury tribute album Brand New Boots And Panties!!

02	Our House NW1: A London Love Story: Simple Equation/Baggy Trousers (CD)	Virgin (OURHOUSE01)
02	Our House – Taster: Sarah's Song/Our House/Baggy Trousers (CD, card p/s & press sheet)	Virgin CDVDJ2965
12/05	THE DANGERMEN SESSIONS – VOLUME ONE (US LP, picture disc)	Jump Up
03/07	NW5 (I Would Give You Everything) (Radio Edit)/ It Must Be Love (WiXX-MiXX 2007)/NW5 (I Would Give You Everything) (Album Version)/NW5 (I Would Give You Everything) (Live At Wembley Arena 12/06)/ It Must Be Love (2007) Video/NW5 (I Would Give You Everything) Video/Making Of NW5 (I Would Give You Everything) Video (enhanced CD, German-only)	Tone Art 92 88697089922
06/08	The Liberty Of Norton Folgate (CD, p/s, to tie in with Hackney Empire show)	Lucky Seven
08/09	Sugar And Spice (promo CD-R for download-only single)	Lucky Seven
08/09	Sugar And Spice/Sugar And Spice (Mike Barson Demo) (French promo CD, p/s)	Naive

MADNESS INFORMATION SERVICE RELEASES

1982	30 MINUTES OF CULTURE (cassette, 'Madness Presents The Radio Players')	M.I.S.

Notes: Exclusive artwork by Suggs.

12/81	Carols On 45 (flexidisc)	LYN 10719
12/84	Christmas Greetings To All Our M.I.S. Friends: Inanity Over Christmas/Visit to Dracstein Castle (flexidisc)	LYN 15280/81

Notes: free with MIS comic.

85	From Us...To You (Mad Not Mad Tour 1985) (flexidisc, free with tour programme)	LYN 16676
12/85	Merry Christmas M.I.S. Members (Enjoy This Turkey): Samantha (live)/Mad Not Mad (live) ('Live From The Mad Not Mad Tour' flexidisc)	LYN 16981
12/86	Last Christmas With Madness: Ghost Train 'The Demo'/ The Final Goodbye (flexi)	LYN 18251
86	SONGS FROM AROUND THE PLONET – LIVE TRACKS 1979–1986 (cassette)	M.I.S.

MAGAZINE 'FREEBIES'

1981	Patches Brings You A Few Minutes Of Madness (flexi with *Patches* mag)	Lyntone LYN 8680
10/81	Take It Or Leave It (clear flexidisc with *Take It Or Leave It* film magazine/book)	LYN 10208
10/81	The Madness Flexi-Disc (square or round flexi with *Event* magazine)	LYN 10353/EVENT 2
1982	My Girl (Ballad) (green or clear vinyl flexidisc, with *Flexipop* mag issue 19)	LYN 11546/Flexipop 019
1982	My Girl (Ballad) (hard vinyl test pressing, white label)	LYN 11546
11/02	Our House/Our House (Stretch Mix)/Our House (Video) (CD, free with *The Sun*)	SUNW 012
11/06	MADNESS LIVE: TO THE EDGE OF THE UNIVERSE AND BEYOND PART 1	(no cat. no.)
11/06	MADNESS LIVE: TO THE EDGE OF THE UNIVERSE AND BEYOND PART 2	(no cat. no.)

Notes: 2 CDs free with The Mail On Sunday)

VIDEOS/DVDs

Several of the early titles were also issued on Betamax.

4/82	COMPLETE MADNESS (VHS)	Stiff VH STIFF 1
1985	COMPLETE MADNESS (VHS, reissue; reissued Virgin Vision 1988)	Virgin VVD 112
1987	COMPLETE MADNESS (VHS, 2nd reissue, 2 different designs)4Front 083 786 3	

Notes: collection of promo videos as companion to album.

1982	TAKE IT OR LEAVE IT (VHS)	Stiff VH STIFF 3
1985	TAKE IT OR LEAVE IT (VHS, reissue; reissued Virgin Vision 1988)	Virgin VVD 114
1995	TAKE IT OR LEAVE IT (VHS, reissue)	Virgin VID 2794
2002	TAKE IT OR LEAVE IT (DVD)	Virgin VDVD 2794

Notes: motion picture.

11/86	UTTER MADNESS (VHS)	Virgin VVD 180
1988	UTTER MADNESS (VHS, reissue)	Virgin Vision VVD 180

Notes: collection of promo videos as companion to album, omitting I'll Compete and Victoria Gardens.

1986	COMPLETE & UTTER MADNESS (Video, box set)	Virgin VVD 112/180
2/92	DIVINE MADNESS (VHS; reissued Virgin Vision, 1994)	Virgin VVD 1003
1995	DIVINE MADNESS (VHS, reissue)	Virgin VID 2692

2002   DIVINE MADNESS (DVD)   Virgin VDVD 2905

Notes: collection of promo videos as companion to album, adding 'Bed And Breakfast Man' and 'I Pronounce You' by The Madness. 2002 version adds 'Sweetest Girl', 'Lovestruck', 'Johnny The Horse' and 'Drip Fed Fred' plus commentaries.

11/92   MADSTOCK (VHS, two different designs)   Polygram Video 086 014-3

1994   MADSTOCK (VHS, reissue)   4 Front 638 868 3

Notes: live show as companion to album, adding 'Land Of Hope & Glory', 'Razor Blade Alley', 'Tomorrow's (Just Another Day)', 'Take It Or Leave It', 'Swan Lake' and 'Rockin' In A♭'.

1998   THE HEAVY HEAVY HITS (THE BEST SOUNDS EVER) (VHS)   Virgin VID 2862

1998   AT MADSTOCK (VHS, Madstock '98)   Eagle Rock ERE 107

1999   AT MADSTOCK (DVD)   Eagle Rock EREDVD110

4/06   AT MADSTOCK (DVD, reissue)   EV Classics EVDVD 007

2003   TAKE IT OR LEAVE IT/DIVINE (2-DVD box set)   Virgin VBXD 6

11/04   OUR HOUSE – THE MADNESS MUSICAL (DVD)   Universal/BBC 8227140

11/04   OUR HOUSE – THE MADNESS MUSICAL (VHS)   Universal/BBC 8227139

IMPORTANT VARIOUS ARTISTS COMPILATIONS

2/81   DANCE CRAZE (LP, initially with poster, includes 'Razor Blade Alley',
        'One Step Beyond' & 'Night Boat To Cairo')   2 Tone CHRTT 5004   (5)

1988   DANCE CRAZE (VHS, includes 'The Prince', 'Swan Lake', 'Razor Blade Alley',
        'Madness', 'Night Boat To Cairo' and 'One Step Beyond')   Chrysalis CVHS 5022

1982   ROCK GALA (THE PRINCE'S TRUST (VHS, includes
        'Madness'; reissued 1989)   MGM/VA.

Notes: live at London's Dominion Theatre, July 21, 1982.

1993   THE GIFT OF SONG (VHS, includes Madness' performance of
        'Yesterday's Men' on *Wogan*)   Weinerworld

1994   RADIO 1 SESSIONS (cassette, free with *Vox* magazine,
        includes 'Embarrassment' from Madstock II)   Vox

11/99   ABBAMANIA (CD, includes 'Money Money Money')   Polydor 543 359-2

6/01   BRAND NEW BOOTS AND PANTIES (CD, tribute re-recording of Ian Dury
        album *New Boots And Panties!!*, includes 'My Old Man')   East Central One
                                                                 NEWBOOTS 2CD

        BRAND NEW BOOTS AND PANTIES (2-LP, some on gold vinyl)
                                                                 NEWBOOTS 2LP

NON-MADNESS ZARJAZZ RELEASES

FEARGAL SHARKEY SINGLE

10/84   Listen To Your Father/Can I Say I Love You (7")   Zarjazz JAZZ 1   (23)

        Listen To Your Father/Can I Say I Love You (7",
        picture disc, stickered PVC sleeve)   JAZZY 1

        Listen To Your Father (Extended Remix)/Can I Say I Love You
        (12", some in stickered p/s with poster)   JAZZ 1-12

THE FINK BROTHERS SINGLE

2/85	Mutants In Mega City One/Mutant Blues (7″)	JAZZ 2	(50)
	Mutants In Mega City One/Mutant Blues (shaped picture disc)	JAZZ S2	
	Mutants In Mega City One (Mutie Mix)/Mutant Blues (12″, with poster)	JAZZ 2-12	

Notes: Suggs and Chas under a pseudonym.

STARVATION SINGLE

3/85	Starvation/Tam-Tam Pour L'Éthiopie (7″, double-A-side)	JAZZ 3	(33)
	Starvation/Haunted/Tam-Tam Pour L'Éthiopie (12″)	JAZZ 3-12	

Notes: Charity record featuring Madness with numerous guests.

CHARM SCHOOL SINGLE

3/85	Life's A Deceiver/Your Passion Is My Pain (7″)	JAZZ 4
	Life's A Deceiver (Reem Mix)/Life's A Deceiver/Your Passion Is My Pain (12″)	JAZZ 4-12

TOM MORLEY SINGLE

9/85	Who Broke That Love/Who Broke That Love (Dawn Mix) (7″)	JAZZ 6
	Who Broke That Love (High Noon Mix)/(Midnight Mix) (12″)	JAZZ 6-12

THE ARGONAUTS SINGLE

?/85	Apeman/Under My Thumb (7″, 200 only)	Lyntone LYN 18249/50

Notes: Lee Thompson's solo project issued via Madness Information Service.

BUTTERFIELD 8 RELEASES

88	Watermelon Man/Rag (7″)	Go! Discs GOBUT 1
88	Watermelon Man/St Lyle Drive/ Be On It/Rag (12″)	Go! Discs GOBUT 112
88	BLOW! (LP)	Go! Discs AGOLP 12
12/02	BUTTERFIELD 8 (CD, 16 tracks, reissue with new artwork & bonus tracks)	Sartorial FIT008CD
06/08	BUTTERFIELD 8 (10″ LP, 500 only, 9 tracks)	Sartorial FIT008LP

CD track listing: Watermelon Man/St Lyle Drive/Harlem Nocturne/Be On It/Oakapple Tango/Our Lady Of The Laundromat/Here Comes The Contortionist/Miserable/It Was Nothing/The Lurch/Anita Said Goodbye/The Talented Mr Ripley/Gatemouth/Itch/Rag/ Watermelon Man (Extended Version)

THE NUTTY BOYS RELEASES

4/90	CRUNCH! (LP, gatefold sleeve, 1,000 copies only)	Street Link STRLP 001
4/90	CRUNCH! (CD)	STRCD 001
	CRUNCH! (CD reissue)	Dojo DOJO CD101
02	CRUNCH! (expanded CD reissue)	Mapps Café MAPPS 2

Magic Carpet/(Always) The Innocent/Daydreamers/Complications/Pop My Top/ Whistle/Pipedream/Fur Elise/People/You Got It!/Just Dreamin' ★/Whistling ★ (★ = only available on CD)

12/92	It's OK, I'm A Policeman (7″)	Nil Satis NIL 0037	
	It's OK, I'm A Policeman/Fight Amongst Yourselves/ Birthday Girl (12″ EP)	NIL 00312	
	It's OK, I'm A Policeman)/Fight Amongst Yourselves/ Birthday Girl/Saving For A Rainy Day (CD EP)	NIL 003CD	
	It's OK, I'm A Policeman (cassette EP)	NIL 003MC	

CRUNCH! SINGLE

| 96 | MAGIC CARPET (CD EP) | Magic Carpet MCRCS 001 | |
| 96 | MAGIC CARPET (12″ EP) | Magic Carpet MCRT 001 | |

Magic Carpet/Danger Zone/Hereditary/Magic Carpet (Live)

SUGGS SINGLES

8/95	I'm Only Sleeping/Off On Holiday/Off On Holiday (Instrumental) (CD, double-A-side)	WEA YZ 975CD	(7)
	I'm Only Sleeping/Off On Holiday/Animal/When You Came (CD + 3 photo cards)	YZ 975CDX	
	I'm Only Sleeping/Off On Holiday (cassette)	WEA YZ 975C	
	I'm Only Sleeping/Off On Holiday (7″, withdrawn/unissued)	WEA YZ 975	
	I'm Only Sleeping/Off On Holiday (7″, no p/s, jukebox edition, black label)	WEA YZ 975	
10/95	Camden Town/Bedazzled/Camden Town (Camden Chili Pepper Dub)/(Ragga In London Dub Instrumental) (CD)	WEA 019CD	(14)
	Camden Town/Bedazzled (7″)	WEA 019	
	Camden Town/Bedazzled (cassette)	WEA 019C	
12/95	Christmas EP: The Tune/Sleigh Ride/Alright (CD)	WEA 031CD	(33)
	The Tune/Alright (7″)	WEA 031	
4/96	Cecilia/I Feel Good/The Tune (Instrumental) (CD, featuring Louchie Lou & Michie One)	WEA 042CD1	(4)
	Cecilia (7″ Mix)/(Rapino's 7″ Mix)/(Rapino's 12″ Disco Instrumental)/(Rapino's 12″ Disco Mix)/(Deep Pan Mix)/ (Drumapella Mix)/(Alternative Mix) (CD)	WEA 042CD2	
	Cecilia/I Feel Good (cassette)	WEA 042C	
	Cecilia/I Feel Good (7″, jukebox edition, no p/s, black label)	WEA 042LC	
	Cecilia (Rapino's 12″ Disco Mix)/(Deep Pan Mix)/ (Drumapella Mix) (12″, promo only)	WEA SAM 1789	
	Cecilia (7″ Mix) (Speeded Up Version)/(Rapino's 7″ Mix)/ (Rapino's 12″ Disco Instrumental)/(Deep Pan Mix)/ (Rapino's 12″ Disco Mix)/(Drumapella Mix)/ (Alternative Mix) (12″, European import)	WEA 0630-14447-0	
9/96	No More Alcohol/No More Alcohol (Rapinos Dance Mix)/ Fortune Fish (CD, featuring Louchie Lou & Michie One)	WEA 065CD1	(24)

No More Alcohol-Cecilia (Segue Mix)/No More Alcohol
(100% Proof Mix)/No More Alcohol (Karaoke Mix) (CD) WEA 065CD2

5/97   Blue Day (Stamford Bridge Mix)/(Strawberry Fields Mix)/
       (Stamford Bridge Karaoke Mix)/Alright (CD, as Suggs &
       Co. featuring the Chelsea Team)   WEA 112CD   (22)

5/97   Blue Day (cassette)   WEA 112C

8/98   I Am (Radio Edit)/Same Again/It Really Would Be Nice (CD)
                                                          WEA 174CD   (38)

       I Am (Radio Edit)/Same Again/It Really Would Be Nice
       (CD, with Avengers poster)   WEA 174CDX

SUGGS ALBUMS

10/95 THE LONE RANGER (CD)   WEA 0630 12478-2 (14)

I'm Only Sleeping/Camden Town/Alcohol/4 AM/The Tune/Cecilia/Haunted/Off On
Holiday/Green Eyes/Fortune Fish/She's Gone

Reissued November 96 re-sequenced with 'No More Alcohol' and different 'white' artwork.

98   THE THREE PYRAMIDS CLUB (CD)   WEA 3984-23815-2

I Am/So Tired/Straight Banana/Invisible Man/Sing/Girl/Greatest Show On Earth/
Our Man/On Drifting Sand/Three Pyramids Club

7/07   THE PLATINUM COLLECTION (CD)   WEA 5144231402

MR SMASH & FRIENDS SINGLE

6/02   We're Coming Over (CD, featuring The England Supporters' Band)
                                                          RGR RGRCD 2   (67)

Acknowledgements

I'LL be honest. I'd forgotten how much work it takes to write biographies. My only previous experience was a tome dedicated to Paul Weller – and that was 15 years ago - but however much effort and time are required from an author, few if any such books exist without the expertise, memories, time and input from a host of other people.

Since *House Of Fun* tackles Madness' long and convoluted career in roughly chronological order, forgive me for approaching the very many acknowledgements in the same manner. First up, therefore, and a round of applause, if you please, for Chris Charlesworth, the long-serving editor at Omnibus Press. A music journalist of some renown back in the day, Chris inherited an official Madness book when he arrived at Omnibus in 1983. It never happened. So he tried and failed again. And again. And again. The Nutty Boys' story evolved into his holy grail. Meanwhile, Chris gave this humble scribe his first stab at being an author back in the mid-nineties. After a sabbatical in the music industry, I was back at Chris's door. And on uttering the magic seven-letter word, book number two was on. But bearing in mind that *House Of Fun* was delivered a year late, please do put your hands together once again for the book publishing world's most persistent and patient editor.

The Weller book was commissioned when I worked for *Record Collector* magazine, whose long-suffering editor was Peter Doggett, now an acclaimed author. Peter kindly read much of this book, offering welcome insights and amendments disguised with heavy sarcasm. I thank you. For the perfect sounding board on all things Madness-related, I needed to look no further than *Mojo* journalist and Clash biographer Pat Gilbert, whose endless fascination with the Nutty Boys helped motivate this project in the first place.

And so to Madness. This is tricky. While I prevaricated about the project, an offer arrived out of the blue to interview most of the band for a piece in *Record Collector* in late summer 2009. That got awkward when their management spotted the book, which was already listed on Amazon. Why do I mention this? Well, unofficial biographies have been known to aggravate artists, even before they're written. A polite thank you, then, to the band and their management for dealing with that thorny issue professionally.

One daunting task with any such project is the research itself. In the internet age, the potential sources of information are seemingly infinite. Trying plugging "Suggs Madness" into Google! But the Nutty Boys are very fortunate to have attracted a hardcore fanbase which just might be without equal among their peers. Names will be named but the people behind both Madness Information Service and Madness Central are as decent and helpful a . . . what is the collective pronoun for fans?! . . . as I've ever come across. I salute you all! Quite apart from individual advice, help and cooperation, the immeasurable resources of their respective websites were absolutely vital, from MIS's bulletin archive to Madness Central's ever-growing database of press interviews, live listings, YouTube clips, etc.

I must single out two particular Madness devotees for special mention. Lee Buckley, alias Looby Loo, from Madness Central has been a Godsend in spotting errors and qualifying my criticisms and comments. A true star. Equally, Jon Young boasts a unique knowledge of the Camden Cowboys' recordings and was nothing if not patient in helping me to unravel the less well-documented chapters of their career. Pork pie hats off also to the ever-charming Steve Bringe, the hard-working Kevin Tizzard, Robert Hazelby, über collector Chris Carter-Pegg and, last but definitely not least, Stuart Wright (the creator of the wonderful *Nut Inc.* fanzine).

Our story began in the backstreets of north London in the Fifties and Sixties. One resource I most definitely didn't benefit from for past projects was ancestry.co.uk. I've no idea if this is the best or most thorough for researching family histories but it proved invaluable in expanding what was already documented about the background of the magnificent seven. Apologies to those families for any unintentional errors – hopefully, we've got it about right! And thanks to Sheila Clerkin and Nancy Bowler for memories of the Irish dancing school run by Cathal Smyth's grandfather.

Madness drew influences from far and wide. But while it didn't feel necessary to outline the background to such widely documented subjects as Motown or The Kinks, this book does provide some historical context (or attempts to, any rate) to some touchstones in Madness' development. For a perspective on Ian Dury's early years with Kilburn & The High Roads, I have to doff my cap to Alan Robinson, who may be a Geordie but who, nevertheless, has a keen understanding about this most London-centric band. Also, a moment's silence, if you please, for the late Charlie Gillett who managed the Kilburns and was as charming and gracious as ever when we spoke.

For a first-hand account of life as an original skinhead, I have to thank author and reggae record dealer Michael de Koningh. Another lad who'd shaved his head at the end of Sixties was DJ/journalist Robert Elms, a north London contemporary of Madness'. His colourful ability to join the dots within the youth culture of the early-to-mid Seventies brought vividly to life the world in which Madness grew up. I can't praise his book *The Way We Wore* highly enough.

In documenting their time prior to evolving into Madness proper in 1979, the band's official website has a thorough and detailed diary of their activities. For a more personal, impressionistic account of that era, Mike Barson's ex-girlfriend Kerstin Rodgers was wonderful. Do investigate her culinary activities and blogs as the Marmite Lover and the Underground Restaurant. Acknowledgements also to journalist Paul Du Noyer for his perspectives, especially on Liverpool band Deaf School, who were such a vital influence on Madness' life and work.

The 2 Tone era has been dissected many times – but I would like to raise a glass to Paul Williams, author of the Specials biography, *You're Wondering Now*. Also, I had the pleasure to interview Jerry Dammers for an unrelated project and I make no apologies for absorbing some of the resulting material. Although 2 Tone helped launch Madness, the band got their first real break by bumping into ex-Deaf School performer and budding producer Clive Langer. While I wasn't able to interview Clive or his long-time partner Alan Winstanley, I did speak at length with the man who helped bankroll Madness' first proper demo. Rob Dickins was a colossus of the music industry who ran Warner Music for many years. He gave up hours of his time to recount his key roles during Madness' formative months and, latterly, with Suggs' solo career.

Once we arrived at Madness' golden era with Stiff Records, one man stands head and shoulders above the pack: Stiff boss Dave Robinson. Having spent a considerable time in Dave's company during past exploits working at a record company, I was extremely pleased to cajole from him some of the many memories and perspectives he has from those halcyon days. Subsequently, Dave voiced some concern that perhaps he has been over-represented. Poppycock. Robinson was more vital to Madness' success than George Martin ever was with The Beatles. "The eighth member of Madness" sounds too clumsy. Crudely put, he was a vital cog in their wheel of fortune. Thanks also to other ex-Stiff personnel – Paul Conroy (who later ran Virgin), Andy Murray, Alan Cowderoy, Jamie Spencer et al – and also to gold-plated plugger Neil Ferris.

All bands can only function with a backline team and I was lucky enough to speak with their first proper manager, John 'Kellogs' Kalinowski. His role was then taken on by Matthew Sztumpf, whose pleasant company I shared for half an afternoon up in Henley-On-Thames in a pub he was managing. Tragically, Matthew subsequently passed away – so his many wry comments within *House Of Fun* now feel like a small tribute of sorts to his memory. Matthew's quiet strengths helped steer Madness through troubled waters with Virgin Records during the mid-Eighties.

Thanks also to Matthew's aide, Jamie Spencer and to the many other interviewees who spoke about Madness' heyday, especially those who worked on their unique string of videos: Chris Gabrin, John Mills, Nigel Dick and special effects man Jim Whiting. Of those who worked diligently behind the scenes, respect is particularly due to road managers John 'Dad' Wynne and Barry Sinclair and to Suggs' cousin and 'head of wardrobe', Hector Walker. I hope Hector is able to fulfil his ambition of having his own account of life with Madness published one day.

In terms of music making, thanks to arranger David Bedford and string players Nick Parker and Cal Verney, who offered some classy pearls amongst the swine. A nod also towards Terry Disley, James Mackie, veteran soul singer Jimmy Thomas, Friday Club's Andy Brooks and harmonica player Judd Lander. For Madness' original tenure with Virgin, I spoke with executives Jeremy Lascelles and Jon Webster as well as sleeve illustrators Dave Gibbons, Rian Hughes and Ian Wright. And smile please for photographers Eric Watson, Cameron McVey, Mike Prior and Clare Muller.

Journalist/authors Tony Fletcher and Paolo Hewitt had separately approached Madness in the past about the prospect of an official biography. With that in mind, I am grateful to them for sharing their thoughts, and to another revered rock writer Johnny Rogan for his index and editorial insight. Simon Goddard, author of *Mozipedia*, was also kind enough to clarify the intersection in the Morrissey/Madness Venn diagram. Sean Flowerdew helped plug some gaps between Madness' demise and their resurrection at Madstock, as did Laurie Pryor. Cathal Smyth himself gifted this book a first-hand account of his time working at Go! Discs. Thanks also to The Stairs' Edgar Jones and Simon Dine for their input about that period.

A special thanks to Steve Finan, Madness' manager in the early Nineties. His tale of woe about missing money from the first Madstock might well be worth the price of admission alone. EMI-Virgin's Steve Pritchard and radio plugger Mick Garbutt were also forthcoming. For Suggs' career, Boo Hewerdine, General Levy and Mike Connaris were very obliging. A firm but manly handshake should also go to pianist Louis Vause for his charming accounts of periods playing with The BUtterfield 8, The Nutty Boys and Velvet Ghost. It almost felt as if he'd played with certain members of Madness more often than the band themselves. Cheers also to Boz Boorer, the irrepressible Terry Edwards and Roger Beaujolais.

Writer Tim Firth kindly and thoroughly explained the background to the musical, *Our House*, while the Dangermen period was covered by V2's management (Tony Harlow, David Steele), John 'Segs' Jennings and the mighty Dennis Bovell. Many thanks also to their manager during this period, Peter Rudge, who oversaw a difficult chapter in Madness' career, and to horn player extraordinaires, Steve Turner and Mike Kearsey.

Also to be thanked in dispatches: John A., Roger Armstrong, Jules Balme, Mark Brennan, Garry Bushell, Laurence Cane-Honeysett, Vince Carden, Chas Chandler (USM), Mark Charlesworth, Gary Crowley, Andy Davis, Bosco De Oliveira, Simon Draper, John Eacott, Jill Furmanovsky, Rick Glanvill, Pippa Hall (Go! Discs), Mike Hodges (Friday Club), Chris Hunt, Dermot James, Tom Kane, Paul Kernick, John Masouri, Jennie Matthias, Tom Morley, Dennis Munday, Andy Neill, Tom O'Leary, Mark Paytress, Kevin Pearce, Simon Phillips, Eddie Piller, Nigel Reeve, Andy Roberts, Martin Rushent, Fifi Russell, Paul Shurey, Paul Speare, Nigel Tufnell, Robert Verburgt, Lois Wilson, Nicky Woodgate, Graham Yates.

A line all of his own for John O'Leary for his friendship but also for his regular stimulation of my mental synapses and occasional if unintentional damage of them in the pub.

Acknowledgements

All of the above played their part in the creation of this book. What they didn't have to contend with was putting up with me writing it. My daughter Delilah said, "Will daddy talk about his book a lot after he's finished it – like when he painted the front door?" I daren't. I would be nowhere without our precious cargo JoJo and Delilah or, above all, Angela. Thank you.

Bibliography

A FTER a 30-year career, it is unusual that Madness – one of the most successful pop bands this country has ever produced – has never been the subject of a lengthy, in-depth biography. It transpires that many journalists have attempted to document their long and convoluted story in an official capacity with the band's blessing. All have failed. In the absence of the unique opportunity to hear their tale told first-hand, I gratefully acknowledge the many writers and publishers of the myriad sources I have accessed and sometimes quoted from during the course of my research.

There have been previous attempts at Madness biographies or, in the case of Terry Edwards' illuminating tome, a particular album:

Mark Williams, *A Brief Case History Of Madness* (Proteus, 1982)

George Marshall, *Total Madness* (S.T. Publishing, 1993)

Terry Edwards, *One Step Beyond* (Continuum, 2009)

Suggs has been threatening his memoirs for some time. Hints of what we might expect from Madness' colourful frontman were contained within a thoroughly enjoyable spin-off from one of his many TV series:

Suggs And The City (My Journeys Through Disappearing London) (Headline, 2009)

The 2 Tone era, in which Madness made a fleeting but vital appearance, has been well documented via such worthwhile tomes as:

George Marshall, *The Two Tone Story* (S.T. Publishing, 1990)

Richard Eddington, *Sent From Coventry: The Chequered Past Of Two Tone* (Independent Music Press, 2004)

Dave Thompson, *Wheels Out Of Gear: 2 Tone, The Specials And A World In Flame* (Helter Skelter, 2004)

Horace Panter, *Ska'd For Life (A Personal Journey With The Specials)* (Sidgwick & Jackson, 2008)

Paul Williams, *You're Wondering Now (The Specials From Conception To Reunion)* (Cherry Red, 2009)

The following books were also useful:

Roger Perry, *The Writing On The Wall* (Elm Tree, 1976)

Richard Barnes, *Mods!* (Eel Pie, 1979)

Jill Furmanovsky, *The Moment* (Paper Tiger, 1995)

George Marshall, *Spirit Of '69: A Skinhead Bible* (S.T. Publishing, 1991)

Michael de Koningh & Marc Griffiths, *Tighten Up! (The History Of Reggae In The UK)* (Sanctuary, 2003)

Paul Du Noyer, *In The City: A Celebration Of London Music* (Virgin, 2009)

Richard Barnes, *Mods!* (Eel Pie, 1979)

Mark Paytress, *Twentieth Century Boy – The Marc Bolan Story* (Sidgwick & Jackson, 1992)

Kevin Pearce, *Something Beginning With O* (Heavenly, 1993)

Robin Denselow, *When The Music's Over – The Story Of Political Pop* (Faber & Faber, 1989)

Simon Goddard, *Mozipedia – The Encyclopedia Of Morrissey And The Smiths* (Ebury Press, 2009)

Richard Balls, *Sex & Drugs & Rock'n'Roll: The Life Of Ian Dury* (Omnibus, 2000)

Will Birch, *Ian Dury: The Definitive Biography* (Sidgwick & Jackson, 2010)

On occasion, I delved into the archives of the popular music press, including:

NME, Melody Maker, Sounds, Record Mirror, Smash Hits, Jamming!, Q, Mojo, Uncut, The Word, Record Collector and *The Face.*

More thorough in their coverage of Madness' career have been various fanzines devoted to the Nutty Boys:

M.I.S., *Nutty Boys* (their own fan club magazine which ran from late 1980 until 1986)

Stuart Wright, *Nut Inc.* (probably the best-ever Madness fanzine, which ran for most of the Nineties).

Vince Carden, *Madness Unsugged*

Jermaine, *Tour Madness*

In the internet age, Madness' official website has been a vital source of information: www.madness.co.uk

This stylishly designed portal has an exclusive 'M' area for purchasers of the deluxe edition of *The Liberty Of Norton Folgate*. The first place for breaking Nutty news. Several band members have contributed but Chris Foreman often replies personally to letters (in his Chris's Cupboard section).

The twin peaks for Madness fans in terms of unofficial websites:

Madness Information Service

www.mis-online.net

Picking up the baton from the old fan club, this venerable institution has delivered weekly bulletins of news for over a decade, while its MIS Online website is a hub of news, information and useful links. They also have a French counterpart: www.french-mis.be

Madness Central

www.madness-central.com

Spinning off the previous Madness Trading Ring, this website offers a welcome companion to MIS Online with a raft of information about Madness' past and present, all of which has been assembled in barely a year or so.

Two websites also worthy of mention:

Dangermen

www.dangermen.net

One of the most detailed online discographies, accompanied by Andy Clayden's history of the band.

Retro Madness

http://retro-madness.co.uk

A museum-cum-shop with one of the most detailed breakdowns of Madness' output worldwide by renowned collector/dealer Chris Carter-Pegg.

Index

Singles releases are in roman type and albums are in italics.

Printed in Great Britain
by Amazon

14810099R00322